P9-CMO-314

THE PAPERS OF ULYSSES S. GRANT

OVERLEAF:

Lt. Gen. Ulysses S. Grant.
Courtesy Lloyd Ostendorf, Dayton, Ohio.

THE PAPERS OF

ULYSSES S. GRANT

Volume 16: 1866

Edited by John Y. Simon

ASSOCIATE EDITOR

David L. Wilson

EDITORIAL ASSISTANT

Sue E. Dotson

Assisted by Wendy F. Hamand

SOUTHERN ILLINOIS UNIVERSITY PRESS

CARBONDALE AND EDWARDSVILLE

Library of Congress Cataloging in Publication Data (Revised)

Grant, Ulysses Simpson, Pres. U.S., 1822–1885.
The papers of Ulysses S. Grant.

Prepared under the auspices of the Ulysses S. Grant Association.
Bibliographical footnotes.
CONTENTS: v. 1. 1837–1861—v. 2. April–September 1861. —v. 3. October 1, 1861–January 7, 1862.—v. 4. January 8–March 31, 1862.—v. 5. April 1–August 31, 1862.—v. 6. September 1–December 8, 1862.—v. 7. December 9, 1862–March 31, 1863.—v. 8. April 1–July 6, 1863.—v. 9. July 7–December 31, 1863.—v. 10. January 1–May 31, 1864.—v. 11. June 1–August 15, 1864.—v. 12. August 16–November 15, 1864.—v. 13. November 16, 1864–February 20, 1865.—v. 14. February 21–April 30, 1865.—v. 15. May 1–December 31, 1865.—v. 16. 1866.
1. Grant, Ulysses Simpson, Pres. U.S., 1822–1885. 2. United States—History—Civil War, 1861–1865—Campaigns and battles —Sources. 3. United States—Politics and government—1869–1877 —Sources. 4. Presidents—United States—Biography. 5. Generals—United States—Biography. I. Simon, John Y., ed. II. Wilson, David L. 1943–. III. Ulysses S. Grant Association.
E660.G756 1967 973.8'2'0924 67–10725
ISBN 0–8093–1467–3 (v. 16)

Printed in the United States of America
Designed by Bert Clarke

To Howard C. Westwood

Ulysses S. Grant Association

Contents

Introduction

By THE BEGINNING of 1866, President Andrew Johnson and congressional Republicans had formed a battle line over Reconstruction, and both sides hoped for support from Lieutenant General Ulysses S. Grant. Through the year his sympathies remained in doubt, so far as the public and politicians knew, but private correspondence reveals Grant's growing dislike for Johnson and his policies, heightened when Grant reluctantly accompanied Johnson on the "Swing Around the Circle," ostensibly to dedicate the tomb of Stephen A. Douglas in Chicago, actually to rally popular support for presidential Reconstruction policies. Grant privately called Johnson's political speeches "a National disgrace" but maintained public silence. Grant's distaste for politics continued, with the result that Republicans and Democrats vied to honor him. In July, he received an appointment as full general, which elevated him to a rank previously held only by George Washington.

Grant believed that purely military problems required his attention; increasingly, however, politics became intertwined with military administration. Southern white intransigence toward Reconstruction created constant friction with officers charged with preserving order. Grant's support went to his officers and troops, and the latter included black veterans. The Freedmen's Bureau, in constant conflict with Southern authorities, included army officers and former officers with whom Grant had ties of loyalty. Riots in Memphis and New Orleans demonstrated the continuing need for military force in the former Confederacy to preserve order and to protect black lives and rights. A sense of obligation to the army ultimately shaped Grant's views on Reconstruction. Although his own policy had not taken clear form, by the end of the year he had already broken with Johnson.

Grant provided Secretary of War Edwin M. Stanton with the opinion that "the Gen. in Chief stands between the President and the Army in all official matters and the Secretary of War is between the Army, (through the General in Chief,) and the President." As Johnson and Stanton became bitter adversaries, Grant's formula, unclear at best, broke down. From the start, Grant, the most popular man in the nation, could hardly play the simple role of intermediary during a period regarded by all as marking his transition from Appomattox to the White House.

Affairs along the border with Mexico continued to claim Grant's attention. Although Northern victory in the Civil War doomed Maximilian's Mexican empire, it died slowly as French troops remained in Mexico. Grant's task was to maintain enough strength along the border to threaten the imperial government and maintain the semblance of neutrality while encouraging the Nationalist forces of Benito Juárez. Impatient with the slow pace of French withdrawal, Grant privately condemned Secretary of State William H. Seward as a "powerful practical ally of Louis Napoleon." Mexican affairs as well as Reconstruction issues influenced Grant's disaffection with the Johnson administration. Major General Philip H. Sheridan, commander of the Military Division of the Gulf, held responsibility for an area in which Reconstruction politics, Mexican diplomacy, and Indian policy presented complex problems. Much of Grant's correspondence through the year related to administration of Sheridan's department.

Major General William T. Sherman, commanding the Military Division of the Mississippi, supervised a vast western domain including most of the Indian frontier. His conservative views on Reconstruction appealed to Johnson, who hoped to use Sherman as a counterweight to Stanton and Grant, and in October Johnson attempted to send Grant on a mission to Mexico and to bring Sherman to Washington, possibly to replace Stanton. When Grant adamantly refused the Mexican assignment, Sherman went instead, then returned to St. Louis, which he much preferred to the superheated political atmosphere of Washington, and Grant, having bought considerable land in St. Louis County, acquiring the former estate of his father-in-law, would also have found

St. Louis more congenial. Grant, however, fearing that Johnson might seize power from Congress, believed it his duty to remain in Washington to protect officers performing their duty. In this critical year, Grant's military responsibilities actually increased.

We are indebted to Sara Dunlap Jackson for assistance in searching the National Archives; to Harriet F. Simon for proofreading; and to Jacqueline Moore, a graduate student at Southern Illinois University, for research assistance.

Financial support for the period during which this volume was prepared came from Southern Illinois University, the National Endowment for the Humanities, and the National Historical Publications and Records Commission.

JOHN Y. SIMON

August 17, 1987

Editorial Procedure

1. Editorial Insertions

A. Words or letters in roman type within brackets represent editorial reconstruction of parts of manuscripts torn, mutilated, or illegible.

B. [. . .] or [— — —] within brackets represent lost material which cannot be reconstructed. The number of dots represents the approximate number of lost letters; dashes represent lost words.

C. Words in *italic* type within brackets represent material such as dates which were not part of the original manuscript.

D. Other material crossed out is indicated by ~~cancelled type~~.

E. Material raised in manuscript, as "4th," has been brought in line, as "4th."

2. Symbols Used to Describe Manuscripts

AD	Autograph Document
ADS	Autograph Document Signed
ADf	Autograph Draft
ADfS	Autograph Draft Signed
AES	Autograph Endorsement Signed
AL	Autograph Letter
ALS	Autograph Letter Signed
ANS	Autograph Note Signed

D	Document
DS	Document Signed
Df	Draft
DfS	Draft Signed
ES	Endorsement Signed
LS	Letter Signed

3. Military Terms and Abbreviations

Act.	Acting
Adjt.	Adjutant
AG	Adjutant General
AGO	Adjutant General's Office
Art.	Artillery
Asst.	Assistant
Bvt.	Brevet
Brig.	Brigadier
Capt.	Captain
Cav.	Cavalry
Col.	Colonel
Co.	Company
C.S.A.	Confederate States of America
Dept.	Department
Div.	Division
Gen.	General
Hd. Qrs.	Headquarters
Inf.	Infantry
Lt.	Lieutenant
Maj.	Major
Q. M.	Quartermaster
Regt.	Regiment or regimental
Sgt.	Sergeant
USMA	United States Military Academy, West Point, N.Y.
Vols.	Volunteers

4. Short Titles and Abbreviations

ABPC	*American Book-Prices Current* (New York, 1895–)

CG	*Congressional Globe* Numbers following represent the Congress, session, and page.
J. G. Cramer	Jesse Grant Cramer, ed., *Letters of Ulysses S. Grant to his Father and his Youngest Sister, 1857–78* (New York and London, 1912)
DAB	*Dictionary of American Biography* (New York, 1928–36)
Garland	Hamlin Garland, *Ulysses S. Grant: His Life and Character* (New York, 1898)
HED	*House Executive Documents*
HMD	*House Miscellaneous Documents*
HRC	*House Reports of Committees* Numbers following *HED*, *HMD*, or *HRC* represent the number of the Congress, the session, and the document.
Ill. AG Report	J. N. Reece, ed., *Report of the Adjutant General of the State of Illinois* (Springfield, 1900)
Johnson, Papers	LeRoy P. Graf and Ralph W. Haskins, eds., *The Papers of Andrew Johnson* (Knoxville, 1967–)
Lewis	Lloyd Lewis, *Captain Sam Grant* (Boston, 1950)
Lincoln, Works	Roy P. Basler, Marion Dolores Pratt, and Lloyd A. Dunlap, eds., *The Collected Works of Abraham Lincoln* (New Brunswick, 1953–55)
Memoirs	*Personal Memoirs of U. S. Grant* (New York, 1885–86)
O.R.	*The War of the Rebellion: A Compilation of the Official Records of the Union and Confederate Armies* (Washington, 1880–1901)
O.R. (Navy)	*Official Records of the Union and Confederate Navies in the War of the Rebellion* (Washington, 1894–1927) Roman numerals following *O.R.* or *O.R.* (Navy) represent the series and the volume.
PUSG	John Y. Simon, ed., *The Papers of Ulysses S. Grant* (Carbondale and Edwardsville, 1967–)
Richardson	Albert D. Richardson, *A Personal History of Ulysses S. Grant* (Hartford, Conn., 1868)
SED	*Senate Executive Documents*
SMD	*Senate Miscellaneous Documents*
SRC	*Senate Reports of Committees* Numbers following

	SED, *SMD*, or *SRC* represent the number of the Congress, the session, and the document.
USGA Newsletter	*Ulysses S. Grant Association Newsletter*
Young	John Russell Young, *Around the World with General Grant* (New York, 1879)

5. *Location Symbols*

CLU	University of California at Los Angeles, Los Angeles, Calif.
CoHi	Colorado State Historical Society, Denver, Colo.
CSmH	Henry E. Huntington Library, San Marino, Calif.
CSt	Stanford University, Stanford, Calif.
CtY	Yale University, New Haven, Conn.
CU-B	Bancroft Library, University of California, Berkeley, Calif.
DLC	Library of Congress, Washington, D.C. Numbers following DLC-USG represent the series and volume of military records in the USG papers.
DNA	National Archives, Washington, D.C. Additional numbers identify record groups.
IaHA	Iowa State Department of History and Archives, Des Moines, Iowa.
I-ar	Illinois State Archives, Springfield, Ill.
IC	Chicago Public Library, Chicago, Ill.
ICarbS	Southern Illinois University, Carbondale, Ill.
ICHi	Chicago Historical Society, Chicago, Ill.
ICN	Newberry Library, Chicago, Ill.
ICU	University of Chicago, Chicago, Ill.
IHi	Illinois State Historical Library, Springfield, Ill.
In	Indiana State Library, Indianapolis, Ind.
InFtwL	Lincoln National Life Foundation, Fort Wayne, Ind.
InHi	Indiana Historical Society, Indianapolis, Ind.
InNd	University of Notre Dame, Notre Dame, Ind.
InU	Indiana University, Bloomington, Ind.
KHi	Kansas State Historical Society, Topeka, Kan.
MdAN	United States Naval Academy Museum, Annapolis, Md.

MeB	Bowdoin College, Brunswick, Me.
MH	Harvard University, Cambridge, Mass.
MHi	Massachusetts Historical Society, Boston, Mass.
MiD	Detroit Public Library, Detroit, Mich.
MiU-C	William L. Clements Library, University of Michigan, Ann Arbor, Mich.
MoSHi	Missouri Historical Society, St. Louis, Mo.
NHi	New-York Historical Society, New York, N.Y.
NIC	Cornell University, Ithaca, N.Y.
NjP	Princeton University, Princeton, N.J.
NjR	Rutgers University, New Brunswick, N.J.
NN	New York Public Library, New York, N.Y.
NNP	Pierpont Morgan Library, New York, N.Y.
NRU	University of Rochester, Rochester, N.Y.
OClWHi	Western Reserve Historical Society, Cleveland, Ohio.
OFH	Rutherford B. Hayes Library, Fremont, Ohio.
OHi	Ohio Historical Society, Columbus, Ohio.
OrHi	Oregon Historical Society, Portland, Ore.
PCarlA	U.S. Army Military History Institute, Carlisle Barracks, Pa.
PHi	Historical Society of Pennsylvania, Philadelphia, Pa.
PPRF	Rosenbach Foundation, Philadelphia, Pa.
RPB	Brown University, Providence, R.I.
TxHR	Rice University, Houston, Tex.
USG 3	Maj. Gen. Ulysses S. Grant 3rd, Clinton, N.Y.
USMA	United States Military Academy Library, West Point, N.Y.
ViHi	Virginia Historical Society, Richmond, Va.
ViU	University of Virginia, Charlottesville, Va.
WHi	State Historical Society of Wisconsin, Madison, Wis.
Wy-Ar	Wyoming State Archives and Historical Department, Cheyenne, Wyo.
WyU	University of Wyoming, Laramie, Wyo.

Chronology

1866

JAN. 2–4. USG attended the wedding of Bvt. Maj. Gen. James H. Wilson at Wilmington, Del.

JAN. 6. USG acknowledged receipt of a library presented by citizens of Boston.

JAN. 9. USG recommended that arms be sold to an agent of the Mexicans fighting against the French.

JAN. 9. USG opposed arming militia in the South.

JAN. 12. USG issued General Orders No. 3 permitting military and civil officers of the U.S. and other loyal persons in the South to transfer cases from local to federal courts.

JAN. 12. USG submitted recommendations to U.S. Senator Henry Wilson concerning reorganization of the U.S. Army.

JAN. 17. USG listened to speeches on Reconstruction in the Senate.

JAN. 25. USG instructed Maj. Gen. Philip H. Sheridan to withdraw troops from Mexico.

JAN. 29. USG informed Secretary of War Edwin M. Stanton of his concerns about their respective roles in the chain of command. He met with Stanton the following day without resolving the issue.

FEB. 1. USG consulted with Maj. Gen. George G. Meade, Maj. Gen. William T. Sherman, and Maj. Gen. George H. Thomas who had been ordered to Washington concerning reorganization of the U.S. Army.

FEB. 9. USG recommended to President Andrew Johnson that U.S. troops remain in Miss.

FEB. 13. USG ordered the suppression of the *Richmond Examiner.*

FEB. 16. USG defended army actions in crossing the Rio Grande.

FEB. 17. USG compiled a list of outrages committed against Negroes in the South; on March 14, he submitted a supplemental list.

FEB. 17. USG acknowledged a gift of $105,000 from citizens of New York City.

FEB. 21–27. USG visited New York City; on Feb. 22, he accepted a portrait of Bvt. Lt. Gen. Winfield Scott at the Union League Club.

FEB. 28. USG wanted to extend General Orders No. 3, Jan. 12, to include Ky. and Mo.

MAR. 1. USG applied to Johnson for a United States Military Academy appointment for his son Frederick Dent Grant, who became a cadet as of July 1.

MAR. 3. USG discussed the sale of arms to Mexico with Johnson, disagreeing with Secretary of State William H. Seward's view that such sales were a violation of neutrality.

MAR. 5–7. USG took Fred to board at West Point so that he could prepare for the entrance examinations.

MAR. 6. Bvt. Col. Theodore S. Bowers, USG's adjt. and friend, killed in a railroad accident at Garrison Station, N.Y. Bowers had accompanied USG and Fred to West Point.

MAR. 8. USG went to West Point to attend Bowers's funeral, and returned to Washington the following morning.

MAR. 12. USG instructed Meade to prevent Fenians from invading Canada.

MAR. 14. USG praised Maj. Gen. John Pope's report on Indian affairs and recommended that the Bureau of Indian Affairs be transferred from the Dept. of the Interior to the War Dept.

MAR. 24. USG informed Maj. Gen. John M. Schofield in Paris of his regret that the French had not been driven out of Mexico as the last act of the Civil War.

MAR. 28. USG again recommended that the U.S. furnish arms to Mexicans.

APRIL 2. Johnson issued a proclamation declaring an end to the insurrection except in Tex.

APRIL 3. USG directed Maj. Gen. Alfred H. Terry to close bars in

Richmond to prevent trouble during the Negro celebration of the fall of the city.

APRIL 6. USG held a reception with guests including Johnson, former C.S.A. Vice President Alexander H. Stephens, and U.S. Representative Thaddeus Stevens.

APRIL 9. Congress passed Civil Rights Bill over Johnson's veto.

APRIL 17. USG at Philadelphia.

APRIL 19. USG recommended the transfer of Maj. Gen. Edward R. S. Canby from New Orleans because of a quarrel with Sheridan.

APRIL 21–25. USG visited his sister-in-law in Richmond.

APRIL 27. USG approved seizure of Fenian arms and munitions.

APRIL 27. USG directed Maj. Gen. John G. Foster to protect from civil suits individuals who held title to lands in Fla. gained from U.S. tax sales.

MAY 1. USG's proposal to supply arms to Mexicans rejected at cabinet meeting.

MAY 1. Riot at Memphis with many Negroes killed.

MAY 9. USG and U.S. Representative Elihu B. Washburne at Baltimore.

MAY 14. USG directed Meade to seize arms intended for Fenian use in Canada.

MAY 16. USG recommended Maj. Gen. George A. Custer for a position with the Mexican forces fighting the French.

MAY 19. USG directed Sheridan to facilitate delivery of an arms shipment purchased privately by the Mexicans.

MAY 29. Scott died at West Point; USG attended the funeral on June 1.

MAY 31. Fenians battled Canadian militia.

JUNE 2. USG at Buffalo issued orders concerning Fenian activities.

JUNE 4. USG visited J. Russell Jones at Chicago.

JUNE 5–15. USG at St. Louis attended to legal business concerning his property.

JUNE 6. Johnson issued neutrality proclamation to prevent Fenian raids on Canada.

JUNE 16. Fourteenth Amendment submitted to the states for ratification.

JUNE 16–17. USG at Louisville consulted with Bvt. Maj. Gen. Jefferson C. Davis.

JUNE 19. USG met Sherman at Cincinnati and visited his parents at Covington.

JUNE 21. USG returned to Washington.

JULY 2. USG recommended publishing an order granting amnesty to deserters who returned to the U.S. Army by Aug. 15.

JULY 4. USG attended celebration in Philadelphia.

JULY 6. USG issued General Orders No. 44 directing U.S. Army officers in the South to arrest Southerners for crimes when local civil authorities refused to act.

JULY 7. USG endorsed the idea of building a canal across Central America.

JULY 8–17. USG at West Point to visit Fred.

JULY 16. Congress passed New Freedmen's Bureau Bill over Johnson's veto.

JULY 18. USG directed Thomas not to interfere with civil affairs in Tenn.

JULY 18. USG asked Stanton to approve Sheridan's request to sell or give arms to Mexicans; on July 20 the cabinet again rejected the proposal.

JULY 25. USG confirmed by Senate as gen.

JULY 28. USG recommended suspending an order prohibiting sale of surplus weapons to permit arms to go to Mexico.

JULY 28. Johnson signed the bill reorganizing the army.

JULY 30. USG arranged to have naval vessels patrol the Mexican Pacific Coast and the mouth of the Rio Grande.

JULY 30. Rioting erupted in New Orleans with many Negroes killed.

JULY 31. Sherman arrived in Washington to accept his promotion to lt. gen.

AUG. 3. USG began to recommend appointments to the new army, a process that consumed much of his time during the following year.

AUG. 18. Johnson directed USG to attend ceremony at White House welcoming a delegation from the Philadelphia Union Convention.

AUG. 20. Johnson issued proclamation declaring insurrection ended in Tex.

AUG. 28–SEPT. 17. USG reluctantly accompanied Johnson on the

"Swing Around the Circle," growing disgusted with Johnson's behavior at public meetings.

SEPT. 4. USG at Detroit after leaving Johnson's party the day before at Cleveland.

SEPT. 9. At St. Louis, USG wrote to his wife that Johnson's tour was a "National disgrace."

SEPT. 11. USG at Cincinnati annoyed by public demonstration in his favor.

SEPT. 22. USG ordered all surplus arms quietly removed from Southern posts in case of a renewal of rebellion.

SEPT. 24. USG ordered investigation of reports of secret military organizations in Tenn.

SEPT. 25–29. USG visited New York City and West Point.

OCT. 8. USG supported Sheridan's refusal to allow Tex. authorities to raise vols. ostensibly to fight Indians.

OCT. 12. USG revealed to Sheridan his concern that Johnson might provoke a renewal of the rebellion.

OCT. 15. USG arranged to negotiate claims against his property in St. Louis.

OCT. 17. USG privately admitted his growing estrangement from Johnson and he refused Johnson's request to accompany a diplomatic mission to Mexico.

OCT. 18. USG informed Sherman of his belief that Johnson wanted Sherman in Washington "either as Act. Sec. of War or in some other way."

OCT. 20. Johnson directed USG to order Sherman to Washington and discussed with USG his concern about possible electoral violence in Baltimore.

OCT. 21. USG again refused Johnson's request to accompany the mission to Mexico.

OCT. 23. USG decided not to go to a wedding at Galena because of the situation in Washington, and he again refused Johnson's request to go to Mexico, this time at a cabinet meeting.

OCT. 27. USG refused a request through Stanton that he go on the Mexican mission.

OCT. 30. Stanton issued orders directing Sherman to accompany the Mexican mission in place of USG.

Nov. 1. USG observed the situation at Baltimore.

Nov. 2. USG instructed Canby to prepare troops for trouble in Baltimore.

Nov. 4–5. USG returned to Baltimore and negotiated an agreement to keep the peace during the election, which occurred the following day without incident.

Nov. 21. USG submitted his annual report and again recommended that the Bureau of Indian Affairs be transferred to the War Dept.

Nov. 28–30. U.S. forces briefly occupied Matamoras, Mexico.

Dec. 1. USG agreed that Sheridan should go to the Rio Grande.

Dec. 6. USG encouraged Maj. Gen. Edward O. C. Ord to work for the passage of pending constitutional amendments by Ark.

Dec. 11–22. USG traveled to St. Louis to pursue a lawsuit concerning his St. Louis property.

Dec. 17. U.S. Supreme Court decided *ex parte* Milligan, restricting power of military to try civilians.

Dec. 20. Sherman arrived at New Orleans after an unsuccessful trip to Mexico.

Dec. 21. Sioux defeated U.S. forces under Capt. William J. Fetterman near Fort Philip Kearny, Dakota Territory. On Dec. 31, USG reinforced Sherman.

The Papers of Ulysses S. Grant

1866

To George B. Upton et al.

Washington D, C. Jan.y 6th *1866*

MESSRS UPTON, HOOPER, LITTLE DANA & AMORY;

GENTLEMEN:

Yours of the 1st of January announcing that a collection of Books had been sent to me by Gentlemen of Boston is received. Through you permit me to return my thanks to the Gentlemen of Boston who have done me this honor and to assure them that this token of their kind feelings is duly appreciated.—The kind expression of confidence conveyed in the note announcing this valuable and substantial present will be preserved by me as possessing an extrinsic value beyond that of goods which can be bought with money.

I remain Gentlemen
very respectfully
your obt. svt.
U. S. GRANT
Lt. Gn. U. S. A.

ALS, Boston Public Library, Boston, Mass.

Books from this library, displayed (1893–1915) by Ulysses S. Grant, Jr., at the U. S. Grant Hotel, San Diego, Calif., later at the California Building, Balboa Park, San Diego, were itemized and offered for sale by Dawson's Book Shop, Los Angeles, Catalogue 262 [1952].

To Hugh McCulloch

Washington D. C. Dec. [*Jan.*] 8th *1866*

HON. H. MCCULLOUGH,
SEC. OF THE TREASURY:
SIR:

Bvt. Brig. L. Kent, late of the volunteer Service, has applied to me for a letter which may aid him in securing the Collectorship of Galveston Texas. The General has served directly under me in various capacities from a company officer up to regimental commander and as Provost Marshal. I know him well and can speak in his favor for qualifications and integrity.

Very respectfully
Your obt. svt.
U. S. GRANT
Lt. Gn

ALS, DNA, RG 56, Collector of Customs Applications, Tex. On Jan. 8, 1866, Brig. Gen. John A. Rawlins wrote to Secretary of the Treasury Hugh McCulloch. "Understanding that the name of Brevet Brigadier General L. Kent will be submitted for your consideration in connection with any contemplated or probable change in the Collectorship of the port of Galveston, Texas, and being desirous that such consideration may be favorable to him, not more from personal friendship than the services he has rendered his country, and his peculiar fitness for the place, I avail myself thus early of the opportunity of placing them briefly before you. At the date of the commencement of hostilities by the South against the Government he was a resident of Alton, Illinois, and on the call of the President entered the service as a private and as such served out his three months enlistment, when he immediately re-entered it as 1st Lieutenant in the 29th Regiment Illinois Infantry Volunteers, and by his gallantry and merit alone in the battles of Fort Donelson and Shiloh, and the advance on Corinth succeeded to the Lieutenant Colonelcy of his regiment When Gen. Grant's main army had got south of the Tallahatchie in the movement against Pemberton in Dec. 1862, our railroad was seriously threatened at Jackson and as far south as Grand Junction by Forest's rebel cavalry, and forces including two companies of Col. Kent's regiment, which at his own solicitation he was put in command of, were sent back from Holly Springs, Miss. by rail to repel it, and while thus detached the remainder of his regiment, with its Colonel, was included in the surrender of Holly Springs by Col. Murphy to Van Dorn, and sent to St Louis, paroled prisoners of war, thus leaving only the two companies of his regiment with him in the field, and these owing to Admiral Porters urgent necessity for men were ordered to report to him for duty on the gunboats, and the Colonel was assigned as Assistant Provost Marshal on General Grant's staff, and served as such in the campaign and siege of Vicksburg until June 15 1863, when he succeeded Col. Hillyer as Provost Marshal General of the Department and Army of the Tennessee; and continued in that capacity on Gen Grant's staff throughout the remainder of the siege, and had sole charge of the paroling of Pemberton's army. The order and quiet with which it was done, and the regularity, neatness, and completeness of the returns and all the papers connected therewith, attest in a remarkable degree his soldierly and business qualifications. The portion of his regiment ~~having been~~ paroled at Holly Springs having been exchanged and returned to the field, and joined by that that had been on the gunboats, at his own request he was relieved from staff duty to take the command of it, and succeeded to the Colonelcy vice Col. Ferrel resigned in September following the fall of Vicksburg, and served in the field continuously from that time until the muster out of his regiment a few weeks since. He participated in the defeat and repulse of Hood, and Forrest's movement north, and in the campaign and capture of Mobile; and his muster out found him in the faithful performance of the duties of Provost Marshal General in Texas. For his gallant and meritorious services on the recommendation of his superior officers, strongly approved by the Lieutenant General, he was appointed a Brigr General of Volunteers by brevet in March 1865. As a soldier he was always brave and efficient, of great purity of character and strictest fidelity. He has a good knowledge of men, and fine business qualifications. Politically he is an original republican, and unswerving Unionist, in sympathy with and an honest supporter of the President's policy of restoration and treatment of the late rebellious States, and intends making Galveston, Texas, his home, where he is well and favorably known by all classes of citizens." LS, *ibid.* Additional papers are *ibid.* Loren Kent was confirmed as collector of customs for Tex. on March 12.

To Edwin M. Stanton

(Confidential) Washington D. C. Jan.y 9th *1866*

HON. E. M. STANTON,
SEC. OF WAR,
SIR:

I would respectfully recommend that the Ordnance Dept. be directed to deliver to Brig. Gn. P. de Baranda,[1] of Mexico, at the City of New York, Five thousand (5.000) stand of Springfield Rifles and equipments complete, and Three Million (3.000.000) rounds of fixed ammunition to serve them. I would recommend that the price of these articles be fixed either at their cost or the price Government has been receiving for them, in case there has been sales, and that General Baranda's individual note be taken for the purchase.

In case this course is entirely inadmissable then I would urgently recommend that $5000 00 in money be received as full and complete satisfaction for the whole number of Arms, Munitions &c. ~~I urgently r[eco]mmend [as o]f interest to the United States as well as the [Liberal] cause in M[exico] that Gen Baranda be allowed to get these a[rms] without delay~~

Very respectfully
your obt. svt.
U. S. GRANT
Lt. Gn.

ALS, DLC-Edwin M. Stanton.

1. Pedro Baranda, born in 1824, fought against imperialist forces in Tabasco before traveling to the U.S. to purchase arms. See Thomas D. Schoonover, ed., *Mexican Lobby: Matías Romero in Washington, 1861–1867* (Lexington, Ky., 1986), pp. 124–25, 128.

To Charles W. Ford

Washington D. C. Jan.y 11th *1866*.

DEAR FORD.

A letter just received from Judge Dent leads me to fear that his finantial affairs endangers his land adjoining the house where he lives on the Gravois Road. I think probably Benoist may have a Deed of Trust upon the land. Will you do me the favor to ascertain if this is so and if it is inform Benoist that if Lewis Dent cannot meet his engagement, at maturity, I will do so for him.—I will write to Mrs. Dent also on the same subject, and believing that you will like a ride into the country will send the letter with this to your care.

I really do not want any land but rather than to see it sacrificed will buy at its full cash value paying cash down.

This is what I want to do: rather than Lewis Dent's property should be sold under a Deed of Trust I will pay it, transfering the trust to my credit, and then pay the Judge the balance of what the property is worth and mate it a complete purchase, giving him a year if he wishes it to redeem the property in.

May I trouble you with this matter. If I could spare the time I would go out to St. Louis. I would like to see a little to my trial with White.

My family are all well and wish to be remembered.

Yours Truly
U. S. GRANT

ALS, USG 3.

General Orders No. 3

WAR DEPARTMENT,
ADJUTANT GENERAL'S OFFICE,
Washington, January 12, 1866.

GENERAL ORDERS, No. 3.

To protect loyal persons against improper civil suits and penalties in late rebellious States.

Military Division and Department Commanders, whose commands embrace, or are composed of, any of the late rebellious States, and who have not already done so, will at once issue and enforce orders protecting from prosecution or suits in the State or Municipal Courts of such States, all officers and soldiers of the armies of the United States, and all persons thereto attached, or in any wise thereto belonging, subject to military authority, charged with offenses for acts done in their military capacity, or pursuant to orders from proper military authority; and to protect from suit or prosecution all loyal citizens or persons charged with offenses done against the rebel forces, directly or indirectly, during the existence of the rebellion, and all persons, their agents or employees, charged with the occupancy of abandoned lands or plantations, or the possession or custody of any kind of property whatever, who occupied, used, possessed, or controlled the same, pursuant to the order of the President, or any of the Civil or Military Departments of the Government, and to protect them from any penalties or damages that may have been or may be pronounced or adjudged in said Courts in any of such cases; and also protecting colored persons from prosecutions in any of said States charged with offenses for which white persons are not prosecuted or punished in the same manner and degree.

BY COMMAND OF LIEUTENANT GENERAL GRANT:

E. D. TOWNSEND,
Assistant Adjutant General

Copy (printed), DNA, RG 107, Letters Received from Bureaus. See letters to Edwin M. Stanton, Feb. 28, Nov. 22, 1866.

On March 23, 1866, Mayor A. H. Van Bokkelen, Wilmington, N. C., wrote to USG. "The amount of disturbance caused in this city by the soldiers composing the garrison of this post, and also those on duty at the posts in vicinity when visiting the city is such that I have taken the liberty of trespassing on your time that you might aid in remedying the evil which is so annoying to the City Authorities and at the same time very detrimental to that good discipline and decorum which it is your desire to have prevail among the officers and soldiers of the Army which you have the honor to command. General Orders, No. 3, January 12, 1866, is so interpreted by the officer commanding at this post that he requires all officers and soldiers committing any offence against the peace and quiet of or contrary to the ordinances of this city to be immediately turned over to his Headquarters and of the many cases so turned over or reported, action in one case alone has been taken, for the reason that the military take no steps to ascertain offence and punish same. On 21st inst., two soldiers belonging to 37th Regt., U. S. C. T., reached the city from one of the neighboring posts and were arrested for creating a disturbance in the most public part of the City where they resisted the police and came very near causing a riot; they were carried to Headquarters and no person being there to receive them they were brought to the City Police Quarters there to be detained until some person would be at Head Quarters, to whom they could be reported. Two Officers of U. S. A. *not on duty*, came to city Police Quarters and abruptly demanded of a private of the Police the liberation of the two soldiers. When the City Marshal made his appearance he desired orders to be exhibited. As soon as Genl Orders No. 3 were exhibited, the Marshal turned them over, at same time not construing the order as having the meaning the U. S. Officers gave it but desiring to have no feeling in the matter. The soldiers were on the streets early next morning and no charges against them asked for. I cannot say they were immediately turned loose, but think they were. Feeling satisfied that your earnest desire is to aid and assist the citizens of the Southern States as much as in your power lies, in their work of establishing law, order and prosperity among them I have to ask at your hands some action which will cause the military not to be an element of disturbance in our city, which you can no doubt do by the following plan: If Gen'l. Orders No. 3, or any other order, takes the trial of Officers and soldiers committing offences against the State or Municipal laws, *not* done in their military capacity or pursuant to orders from proper military authority from the state and municipal authorities, I would suggest that an order be issued directing that when any offence is committed against the State or Municipal laws by an officer or soldier not acting under orders, and an arrest is made that he be carried before the State or Municipal authorities, who are *immediately* to inquire into the facts and the arrested party turned over to military Headquarters with a statement of the case and proper punishment administered to offenders after military trial. In case Genl. Order No. 3, has been misinterpreted, please inform military commanders at this post accordingly and, thereby, stay the unlimited license which is given to the soldiers by the course now pursued." ALS, DNA, RG 108, Letters Received. On April 14, Maj. Gen. George G. Meade endorsed this letter. "Respectfully returned to the Head Quarters of the Army, and attention invited to the reports of the Comd'g officer Post of Wilmington and the Comd'g officer Department of North Carolina. In view of the recent construction placed upon the Presidents Proclamation, the practice of trying by military courts, persons in the military service, in that Department, is approved. The abrogation of martial law would, however, require a change in this respect" ES, *ibid.*

To George H. Stuart

Washington D. C. Jan.y 12th *1866*

GEO. H. STUART,
CHAIRMAN U. S. C. C.
DEAR SIR:

Your letter of the 10th inst. announcing that the U. S. Christian Commission is on the eve of closing its work is received. I hope the same labor will never be imposed on any body of citizens again, in this country, as the Christian Commission have gone through in the last four years. It affords me pleasure to bear evidence to the services rendered and the manner in which they have been rendered. By the Agency of the Commission much suffering has been saved on almost every battle field and in every Hospital during the late rebellion. No doubt thousands of persons now living attribute their recovery in great part to volunteer agencies sent to the field and Hospital by free contributions of our Loyal Citizens. The U. S. Sanitary Commission and the U. S. Christian Commission have been the principal agencies in collecting and distributing these contributions. To them the Army feel the same gratitude the Loyal public feel for the services rendered by the Army.

Very respectfully
your obt. svt.
U. S. GRANT
Lt. Gn.

ALS, DLC-George H. Stuart. On Jan. 10, 1866, George H. Stuart, Philadelphia, had written to USG. "The U. S. Christian Commission is on the eve of closing its four years' work. Our distributions of Hospital Stores and Publications, to the Army and Navy during that eventful period have amounted to over *Five Millions* of *Dollars*. Our list of Delegates, employed in carrying these gifts of the people direct to the soldier, numbers nearly *Five Thousand*. From no Military Commander have we received more hearty and constant countenance than from the Lieutenant General. To your evident appreciation of our endeavours we are largely indebted for any success that has attended our efforts. Perhaps the appreciation of the aid received from your kindness is best expressed by an extract from a despatch of our Field Agent—at Chattanooga, in November 1863:—'In these difficulties, I took my brief but all-important requests direct to Gen. Grant. He received me most kindly asked a few questions, and gave me such assurance of aid, as sent me back to our quarters, singing the Long Metre Doxology, all the way down the hill. The facilities which Gen. Grant has to-day ordered, will double our work in extent and efficiency, through all this Military Division.' The Executive Committee has decided to publish *a History of the Commission*. We desire to record the confidence and facilities afforded by officers in the field, and it seems eminently fit that a testimonial as to results—how far the Commission has justified the endorsement of its early and constant supporters—should enter into that permanent record. If you can favor us in this respect, by such *statements* as your *observation* and *impressions* of the work of the *Commission* prompt you to make, we shall be under renewed obligations." LS, USG 3.

To Henry Wilson

Washington Jany. 12th *1866*.

HON. HENRY WILSON,
CHAIRMAN MIL. COMMITTEE, U. S. S.

In compliance with your request I have looked over your bill for the reorganization of the army and find that it differrs in some respects from the recommendations I have made, especially in regard to the employment of colored troops and the formation of regiments of disabled officers and men.

I have recommended that the President should be authorized to raise twenty thousand colored troops if he deemed it necessary, but I did not recommend the permanent employment of colored troops because our standing army in time of peace should have the smallest possible numbers and the highest possible efficiency—aside from the influence this consideration might have, I know of no objection to the use of colored troops and think they can be obtained more readily than white ones. I am not in favor of colored artillery regiments because I regard our artillery in time of peace merely as an artillery school for time of war—in peace, infantry can do all the duties of artillery—and in time of peace I think the efficiency of the artillery as a school will be higher if composed solely of white troops.

If colored troops be made part of the regular army I would recommend that the promotion of officers of colored troops be confined to colored troops of their arm of service, and the promotion of officers of white troops be confined to white troops, of their arm.

In reference to regular regiments for disabled officers and soldiers, I have already recommended that the President designate such regiments in the reorganization—this would avoid the organization of regiments of disabled officers and men which would gradually dwindle and become inefficient. The number of such regiments might be fixed at eight as in the bill.

I fear that officering certain new regiments exclusively from the regular army, and others from the volunteers would create jealousies, and discord, and think it would be better to fix some ratio for appointments from the two branches; say for all grades above that of 1st Lieutenant, one third to be from the regular army and two thirds from the Volunteers.

In promotions from the volunteer service, I would have the limit of time of volunteer service as two years for all appointments. If for appointments to colored regiments two years service with colored troops was required many of our best officers of colored troops who entered colored regiments from the volunteer service within the last two years, would be rejected, while if their term of service with white troops was included they would be eligible.

In reference to the Adjutant General's Department, I do not think the senior officer of a Department is always the best one for its head and therefore would not recommend that all vacancies be filled by regular promotion.

I would recommend however in the A. G. O., Qr. Mrs., Subsistence, Medical, Engineer and Ordnance Dept., that the head of the Corps shall always be taken from the Corps.

In reference to the Corps of Engineers and Ordnance I would recommend that their numbers remain as at present.

The effect of S 16 and S 21 of this bill would be to put out of service a few of the lowest lieutenants in each Corps.

The above are some of the points that occur to me. I take the liberty of enclosing a copy of a previous recommendation to the Sec. of War, for the Staff of the army.[1]

I have the honor to be
Very respectfully
Your obt. Servt.
U. S. GRANT
Lieut. Gen'l

LS, Boston Public Library, Boston, Mass. See letters to Henry Wilson, Feb. 5, 6, 1866; letter to Edwin M. Stanton, May 16, 1866.

On Dec. 18, 1865, USG wrote to U.S. Representative Robert C. Schenck of Ohio, chairman, Committee on Military Affairs. "In compliance with the request of your committee, I submit herewith, my recommendation for increase of the Line of the Regular Army. I will soon submit my recommendations for the necessary change in the different Staff Corps, to conform to the increase requested." Copies, DNA, RG 94, Letters Received, 1387A 1865; *ibid.*, RG 108, Letters Sent; DLC-USG, V, 47, 109. USG appended his suggestions. "There shall be added to the Regular Army of the United States as now authorized by law: Six regiments of cavalry having the same organization as those now existing, and that one third of the entire cavalry force of the army may, at the option of the President, be dismounted and ordered to serve as infantry. That the five artillery regiments shall have a uniform organization which shall be that of the present Fifth regiment of artillery. There shall be added to the first ten regiments of infantry fifty two regiments having the same organization. That twenty seven of these regiments be organized by adding to each battalion of each of the nine regiments authorized by the act of July 29th 1863 two companies and such number of officers and non commissioned officers as shall complete the compliment prescribed for the regimental organization. Provided the eight First Lieutenants and eight Second Lieutenants of the first eight companies of the above twenty seven regiments be transferred according to seniority from the Lieutenants of infantry of the regular army. That each company of artillery, cavalry and infantry, shall have a minimum strength of sixty four enlisted men, and a maximum strength of an hundred enlisted men; that between these limits the President shall have power so to increase or diminish the number of enlisted men per company as in his judgment the exigencies of the service may demand. That officers to fill all original vacancies hereby created shall be appointed as follows: one third of the entire number of each grade above that of Lieutenant to be selected from the regular army, all others to be selected from volunteers who have served meritoriously at least two years during the late Rebellion. That the President shall be authorized to retain in service, in addition to the above regular army, as many regiments of colored troops as he may deem necessary, and to disband the same when their services are no longer required. That the limitation to the present organization of the Corps of Engineers and Ordnance by section 12 of the act of March 3d 1865, be repealed." Copies, *ibid.* On the same day, USG wrote to Secretary of War Edwin M. Stanton. "I herewith submit a copy of recommendations for increase of the Line of the Regular Army, made in compliance with the request made of the Military Committee of the House of Representatives." LS, DNA, RG 94, Letters Received, 1387A 1865. See letters to Edwin M. Stanton, Oct. 20, Nov. 3, 1865.

1. On Jan. 5, 1866, USG wrote to Stanton. "I have the honor to submit herewith my views in relation to the reorganization of the Staff department of the army." LS, DNA, RG 94, Letters Received, 954A 1865. USG appended his plan for staff reorganization. "*Inspector Generals Department.* That the Asst. Inspectors General shall have the rank, pay and emoluments of Lieutenant Colonels of Cavalry. *Quarter Masters Department* There shall be added to the General Staff of the Quartermasters Department the officers necessary to complete the following organization: One Brigadier General and Quartermaster General, eight Colonels and Quartermasters, sixteen Lieutenant Colonels and Quartermasters, sixty four Majors and Quartermasters; and such number of Military Storekeepers as may be necessary, not exceeding sixteen: Provided, that no officer of the Department shall be discharged from the Service in the execution of this law; and that vacancies occurring hereafter in the grade of Major shall be filled by selection from the Captains of the army. Master wagoners and wagoners may be enlisted or appointed as now provided by law. In each regiment one subaltern shall be assigned to duty as regimental quartermaster who shall have, while so assigned and acting, the pay and emoluments of a First Lieutenant of cavalry. Acting quartermasters at permanent posts and stations, or with commands where no officer of the General Staff of the Department is available to perform the duty, shall be detailed from the captains and subalterns of the line, and shall receive, while so assigned and acting, the pay and emoluments of mounted officers of their respective grades. Officers of the line detailed to act as regimental quartermasters, or as quartermasters of permanent posts, or of commands of not less than two companies, shall, when the assignment is duly reported to and approved by the War Department, receive as compensation for their duties and responsibilities with respect to the money and property of the Quartermasters Department under their charge, ten dollars per month while so assigned and acting The provisions of the act for the better organization of the Quartermasters Department, approved July 4th 1864, shall continue in force so far as they do not become obsolete and unnecessary upon the disbandment of the volunteer army. The Secretary of War shall have power to assign officers of the

Quartermasters Department of skill and experience, not exceeding two at any one time, to act as chief quartermasters of armies in the field, or of great geographical military divisions, who, while so assigned and acting, shall have the rank, pay and emoluments of brigadier general, and when relieved from such duties shall return to their lineal rank in the Department. *Medical Department.* That the Medical Department of the regular army as now authorized by law shall be increased by the addition of the following officers, viz. Fifty Surgeons and eighty-six Assistant Surgeons. That eligibility to promotion as Surgeon be dependent upon satisfactory examination by a Medical Board,—convened by authority of the Secretary of War—, after not less than three years continuous service in the Medical Corps as Assistant Surgeon. That the appointment of Assistant Surgeon continue to be governed by existing laws. That upon the recommendation of the Surgeon General the Secretary of War will detail a Surgeon as Chief Medical Purveyor, who, while performing such duty shall be in charge of the principal purchasing and issuing depot of medical supplies, and have the rank, pay and emoluments of a Colonel of Cavalry; and not to exceed five medical officers as Asst Medical Purveyors, who, while on such duty in the different Military Geographical Divisions or Departments, shall have the rank, pay and emoluments of Lieutenant Colonels of Cavalry. That the Surgeon General be empowered to detail from time to time—, subject to the approval of the War Department—, not to exceed six officers of the grade of Surgeon, for duty as Medical Inspectors, who, while performing such duties, shall receive the rank, pay and emoluments of Colonels of Cavalry, and who shall receive their instructions from, and make their reports direct to, the Surgeon General. That the following grade of rank, pay and emoluments, dependent upon continuous service in the Medical Corps, be established: After (30) Thirty years as Colonels of Cavalry After (20) Twenty years as Lt Cols. of Cavalry After (10) Ten years as Majors of Cavalry Less than (10) Ten years as Captains of Cavalry Provided, that no rank already acquired by promotion as Surgeon shall be invalidated hereby. *Pay Department.* That the organization of the Pay Department of the regular army shall be constituted as follows, viz. One, Pay Master General with the rank, pay and emoluments of a Brigadier General, one Asst Pay Master General with the rank, pay and emoluments of a Colonel of Cavalry, eight Dep'ty Pay Master Generals with the rank, pay and emoluments of Lieutenant Colonels of Cavalry; and sixty five Pay Masters with the rank, pay and emoluments of Majors of Cavalry. Corps of Engineers. That section (12) of an act entitled 'an act to promote the efficiency of the Corps of Engineers, and of the Ordnance Department and for other purposes,' approved March 3 1863, be repealed There shall be appointed in the Corps of Engineers by selection from among the officers of that Corps, four Inspectors of Fortifications and other Engineer operations, who shall be Colonels of Engineers, but the number of officers of said Corps as heretofore established by law shall not be increased hereby. The five Companies of Engineersoldiers and the Sergeant Major and Quartermaster Sergeant of Engineers heretofore prescribed by law, shall constitute a Battalion of Engineers, to be officered by officers of suitable rank detailed from the Corps of Engineers. The officers of Engineers acting respectively as Adjutant and Quartermaster of this battalion shall be entitled to the pay and allowances of an Adjutant, of a regiment of cavalry. In the organization of each of the Companies of Engineer soldiers, there shall at once be a reduction of twenty enlisted men, to be apportioned equally among the two classes of privates, but in time of actual war the President may at his discretion restore the present organization of these companies. That the number of cadets at the United States military academy shall be increased to four hundred Of the additional number herein authorized two from each State shall be appointed by the President, upon the nomination of the United States Senators from their respective States. The remainder shall be appointed by the President, the selection to be made from the sons of officers of the Army and Navy and of soldiers and sailors and such other persons as have no congressional representation. *Ordnance Department.* That in order to increase the number of field officers in the Ordnance Department without increasing the total number of officers therein, the organization of the Ordnance Department shall be constituted as follows, viz. One Brigadier General, three Colonels, six Lieutenant Colonels, twelve Majors, twenty Captains, twelve First Lieutenants, ten Second Lieutenants, and fifteen Military Storekeepers. The above changes to be made by promotion according to existing laws. *Signal Corps.* That there shall be one Chief Signal officer of the Army, who shall have the rank, pay and emoluments of a Colonel of Cavalry. That the Secretary of War shall have power to detail from the Army, upon the recommendation of the Chief Signal Officer, such number of officers, non commissioned officers and privates as may be deemed necessary for the efficient performance of signal duty. Provided. That no officer or enlisted man shall be detailed to serve in the Signal Corps until he shall have been examined and approved by a military Board to be convened by the Secretary of War for that purpose That officers, while so detailed, shall receive the pay and emoluments of mounted officers of their respective grades. That enlisted men, while so detailed, shall receive the pay of engineer soldiers of similar grades, and shall, when deemed necessary, be mounted upon horses provided by the Government. *Promotion* That no officer of the regular army below the rank of a field officer shall hereafter be promoted to a higher grade, before having passed a satisfactory examination as to his fitness for promotion, before a board of three officers of his Corps or arm of service, senior to him in rank; and should the officer fail at said examination, he shall be suspended from promotion for one year, when he shall be re-examined, and, upon second failure, shall be dropped by the President from the army. Provided, That if an officer be found unfit for promotion on account of moral disqualifications, he shall not be entitled to such re-examination." DS, *ibid.* On Jan. 6, USG wrote to Schenck. "In compliance with your request I recently submitted my views in relation to the reorganization of the line of the Army. I ~~how~~ now have the honor to submit a plan for a corresponding reorganization of the Staff departments together with the views of prominent staff-officers in reference to this subject." Copies, DLC-USG, V, 47, 109; DNA, RG 108, Letters Sent.

On Dec. 15, 1865, Brig. Gen. Alexander B. Dyer, chief of ordnance, had written to USG. "I have the honor to recommend that, in the reorganization of the Army, the Ordnance Department be constituted as follows: 1. Brigadier General: 3. Colonels: 6. Lieut Colonels: 12. Majors 20. Captains 12 First Lieutenants 10 Second Lieutenants 64—Total.—The proposed reorganization will not increase the number of officers of the Ordnance Department, but is deemed proper, for the following reasons: The Engineer Department consists of 105 Officers, 35, or one third of whom are Field. officers. The proposed reorganization of the Ordnance Corps, as above will give 22 Field officers or or one third of its whole number, and place it on an equality with the Engineer Corps, in this respect. By examining the Army Register, it will be seen that the Senior Captain of Ordnance graduated in 1847, while the junior Major of Engineers, graduated in 1854, and that the more rapid promotion in the Engineer Department is due to the larger proportion of Field Officers. An examination of the proportion of field Officers, in the other Staff Corps, in the Army, will show that a larger proportion than one third of their organization are field officers, while in one of them—the Adjutant General's Department—all are field officers It may be proper, also, to observe that the enlisted force of enlisted soldiers of Ordnance is fifteen hundred—while that of Engineer Soldiers is only about one half of that number. The important and enlarged duties of Commanding Officers of Arsenals and Armories, it is thought, warrants the recommendation that the number of field officers in the Corps should be increased, so that the Commanding officer of each Arsenal, of any considerable importance shall have the rank of Major, at least, and it is believed that his authority will be beneficially increased by the possession of this rank. . . . P. S. I desire to call your attention to the 12, Section of the Act of March 3, 1863, and to recommend its repeal." LS, *ibid.*, RG 94, Letters Received, 954A 1865. On Dec. 16, Brig. Gen. Joseph K. Barnes, surgeon gen., wrote to USG. "In compliance with verbal instructions to that effect, I have the honor to submit the following projet for increase of the Medical Corps U. S. A—to correspond with an increase of the rank and file to One hundred thousand men—As at present organized the Corps consists of one Surgeon General—Fifty Surgeons, and one hundred and fourteen Assistant Surgeons—and is calculated for an Army of Twenty five thousand men only—Of these 19 (nineteen) are on duty as Medical Directors; 10 (Ten) as Medical Purveyors; (34) Thirty four on special or detached duties; leaving (101) one hundred and one, for duty with Troops—In the event of an increase of the Army to one hundred thousand troops an increase of the Medical Corps would be necessary, but not in corresponding proportion—First It is therefore respectfully recommended that for an increase to 100 000 men—Seventy five (75) Surgeons and one hundred and eighty six Assistant Surgeons—be added to the Corps—making One hundred and twenty five (125) Surgeons, and Three hundred ~~As~~ (300) Assistant Surgeons—Second That for an increase to Fifty thousand (50000) men Fifty ~~five~~ (50) Surgeons, and Eighty six (86) Assistant Surgeons, be added to the present Corps—making One hundred (100) Surgeons—and Two hundred (200) Assistant Surgeons—Third That eligibility to promotion as Surgeon U. S. A—be dependent upon satisfactory examination by a Medical Board,—convened by authority of the Hon. Secretary of War—, after not less than three years continuous service in the Medical Corps as Assistant Surgeon, U. S. A. Fourth That the appointment of Assistant Surgeon U. S. A. continue to be governed by existing laws—That the Surgeon General have the rank pay and emoluments of Major General U. S. A. Fifth That, upon the recommendation of the Su[r]geon General, the Hon. Secretary of War will detail a Surgeon U. S. A—as Chief Medical Purveyor, who while performing such duty shall be in charge of the principal purchasing and issuing depot of Medical supplies, and have the rank, pay and emoluments of a Brigadier General U. S. A.; and not to exceed Five (5) Medical officers U. S. A. as Assistant Medical Purveyors, who while on such duty in the different Military Geographical Departments shall have the rank pay and emoluments of Lieutenant Colonels of Cavalry—Sixth That the Surgeon General be empowered to detail from time to time—, subject to the approval of the War Department—, not to exceed six officers of the grade of Surgeons U. S. A—for duty as 'Medical Inspectors', who, while performing such duties, shall receive the rank, pay and emoluments of Colonels of Cavalry, and who shall receive their instructions from and make their reports direct to the Surgeon General—Seventh That the following grades of rank, pay, and emoluments, dependent upon continuous service in the Medical Corps U. S. A—be established—After (30) Thirty years—as Colonels of Cavalry After (20) Twenty years as Lieut Cols of Cavalry After (10) Ten years as Majors of Cavalry Less than (10) Ten years as Captains of Cavalry—Provided that no rank already acquired by promotion as surgeon shall be invalidated hereby—" LS, *ibid.* USG noted on this letter. "In preparing bill uniformity will be observed in assigning rank to the Chiefs of all the Staff Corps. The rank of Brig. Gn. will be adopted. In the Medical Corps therefore ~~grades~~ rank will be reduced one grade for Surg. Gn. and Med. Inspt. Gn." AN (undated), *ibid.* On Dec. 16, Bvt. Maj. Gen. Benjamin W. Brice, paymaster gen., wrote to USG. "The following suggestions were made by me to the Secretary of War October 11th in reply to his call for a plan for the permanent increase of this Department on the basis of a standing force of one hundred thousand troops The Department now consists of 1. Paymaster General with rank of Colonel 2 Deputy Paymaster Generals, Lieutenant Colonels 25 Paymasters Majors. The Paymaster General should be placed on the same footing as to rank pay and emoluments of the other Chiefs of Military Bureaux. And there should be added one Assistant Paymaster General with the rank of Colonel, six Deputy Paymaster Generals and fifty Paymasters of the same rank &c, as is now by law provided for those grades. I am now more and more confirmed in the opinion that the above would constitute for our service the simplest and very best organization of the Pay Department that can be devised Should the standing force be less or greater than one-hundred thousand troops; a corresponding increase or reduction of the number of Paymasters named would be proper. But in no event should the Assistant Paymaster General be dispensed with, nor should the corps in any event have less than eight Deputy Paymasters General—These are necessary to the proper efficiency of this Department under any supposable circumstances Should however the standing force be made to exceed one hundred thousand men, I would then suggest two instead of one Assistant Paymaster General and a further increase of the Deputies and of the Paymasters I refrain from giving reasons or argument in support of these suggestions as I suppose them unnecessary here, but I feel sure they exist in such force as will weigh convincingly upon your mature judgement or that of any officer of large military experience and observation." LS, *ibid.* On Dec. 18, Bvt. Maj. Gen. Montgomery C. Meigs, q. m. gen., wrote to USG. "As requested by you I have the honor to submit a project of law for the increase of the Quartermaster's Department in proportion to the proposed increase of the regular army and in view of the near discharge from service, by limitation of the laws under which they now serve, of the numerous officers of volunteers now attached to the Quartermaster's Department. The organization is based upon a force of 50,000 men, so organized as to admit, by filling up the companies to the maximum, of an increase to 82,600 men. The number of commissioned officers of the regular Quartermaster's Department is now by law 67. I recommend that it be increased to 89, distributed as follows: One Brigadier General, Quartermaster General, eight Colonels, and Quartermasters, sixteen Lieutenant Colonels and Quartermasters, sixty-four Majors and Quartermasters, discontinuing, as in other staff corps, the rank of Captain in the regular establishment, and giving up also the awkward titles of Assistant and Deputy Quartermaster Generals, which are relics of the days when the Corps was a civil, not a military body—attached to, rather than forming a constituent part of the Army. It appears to me to be important that the officers now in the Corps should be promoted, and that vacancies caused by their promotion should be filled by appointment from the officers of volunteers who have had at least one year's experience in the Quartermaster's Department during the war, and have gained credit therein. The magnitude and importance of the duties of the officers of the Corps will, I trust, be found to justify the changes recommended. The Regimental Quartermasters I recommend to be taken from the subalterns of the regiments. Their duties will require them to be mounted officers, and they should receive the pay and allowances of such officers. For permanent posts and for bodies of troops when no officer of the regular corps of the Department is available, which, with the number of officers herein recommended, will be frequently the case, I recommend that either captains or subalterns of the line shall be detailed. While on such duty, which will require them to be mounted, they should receive the pay and allowances of mounted officers. The names of officers of the line detailed or assigned to such duties should be promptly reported to the War Department. Upon such report and the approval and confirmation of their assignment by the War Department, they should be allowed, as regimental quartermasters and under existing laws, the additional compensation of ten dollars per month for their duties and responsibilities with respect to the money and property of the Quartermaster's Department under their charge. This allowance is, by existing laws made to regimental quartermasters, but not to acting assistant or post quartermasters, whose duties and responsibilities are frequently much greater than those of regimental quartermasters. If the allowance is paid only upon confirmation and approval of the assignment when reported to the War Department, it will prevent officers known to be inefficient being assigned to or remaining long in such positions, as is too frequently the case under the present system when the assignments are not promptly reported. The Military Storekeepers are now limited to twelve—It has been necessary to assign commissioned officers or to hire agents or clerks to perform the duties of Military Storekeepers at many posts. I recommend that the limit be extended to sixteen. The number of Master Wagoners and of Wagoners, as regulated by existing laws, requires no change. The provisions of the act of 4th July, 1864, for the better organization of the Quartermaster's Department, have been tested by the experience of the Department in the closing and most active year of a most extensive war. They have enabled it to meet, with the aid of the volunteer officers, allowed by law, every demand upon its resources or upon its officers for an army of a million of men. I recommend that the provisions of this law be continued in force, except so far as they become obsolete by the disbandment of the volunteer army. The power which this law gives the Secretary of selecting young, vigorous and zealous officers for important stations and duties, and assigning them to such duties with corresponding rank, such rank to continue only while they remain on such duty, is most valuable. It acts as a spur to exertion. The officer knows that his rank depends upon continued activity and success in the discharge of his duties, and it opens to all the younger officers the prospect of promotion, which may be early gained by distinguished ability and merit. The officers of high rank in the corps will inevitably in a few years be too old for active field duties, as was the case at the beginning of the present war. It is desirable that the organization of the permanent army should, as far as possible, be such as to enable it at any moment to take the field fully organized for vigorous and active operations. This power of selection and detail in the Quartermaster's Department will enable the corps to supply to any army taking the field hereafter officers in the vigor of life, and with experience, ability and rank, to act as chief quartermasters of the corps, division and brigades, as inspectors, or to take charge of depots and bases of operations. I trust that this power will be continued in the Secretary of War. I recommend that the right to assign to duty with temporary rank, pay and emoluments of brigadier general, not more than two officers, be conferred upon the Secretary of War, these officers to be assigned only when their services are necessary, as senior, or chief quartermaster of large armies ~~assigned~~ organized for active service, or of great military geographical divisions. Experience during the past four years has shown the necessity for conferring such rank upon the chief quartermasters of such commands. The rank has heretofore been generally conferred by appointing the chief quartermaster a brigadier general of volunteers, or, when that was not possible, by giving him a brevet of brigadier general, and assigning him to duty according to his brevet rank. For an active army about to take the field, or for a geographical division remote from Washington, in which important military movements are to originate, I am of opinion that a quartermaster with the rank and power of brigadier general, should be available. If the rank is temporary, conferred by assignment, the most capable and zealous officer of the Department can be selected and placed in the most important station, and the rank will be necessary to enable him to command others junior in the corps." LS, *ibid.*

On Dec. 20, Brig. Gen. Richard Delafield, chief of engineers, wrote to USG. "I enclose herewith the draft of an Act of Congress, embodying all the legislation now desirable for the more perfect organization of that branch of the military service confided to this Department. By it a saving on the peace establishment for the active branch of the Department, will be effected of $26,322 24. In the course of the morning, I will send you an explanatory communication on all the several subjects embraced in the 'Act'." LS, *ibid.* The enclosure is *ibid.* On Dec. 21, Delafield wrote to USG. "I enclose herewith the concluding page of Explanatory remarks accompanying the draft of an Act to promote the efficiency of the Corps of Engineers forwarded to you yesterday afternoon. Will you do me the favor of having it attached thereto" Copy, *ibid.*, RG 77, Miscellaneous Letters Sent. The enclosure is *ibid.* On Jan. 13, 1866, Delafield wrote to USG. "I notice that Senator Wilson's Bill for reorganizing the Army, presented by him a few days ago, proposes to reduce the organized strength of the Engineer Corps, by cutting off ten (10) Second Lieutenants, and nine (9) First Lieutenants I presume this was not intended by Mr Wilson, and that he supposed the Army Register of January 1st 1865, gave the full legal organized strength of the Corps, while in fact there were nineteen vacancies among the first and Second Lieutenants at that time. Nine of these vacancies have since been filled. The present organized strength of the Corps, as fixed by the Act of March 3rd 1863, should, by all means, be retained, Viz: one (1) Brig. General & Chief Engineer; four (4) Colonels, ten (10) Lieutenant Colonels, twenty (20) Majors, thirty (30) Captains thirty (30) First Lieutenants, and ten (10) Second Lieutenants The four (4) Inspectors provided for by Sec. 17 of Mr Wilson's Bill, should also be appointed but without increasing the number of officers in the Corps. I would recommend a slight change as given below, in the phraseology of Section 17. creating these Inspectors, in order to make it perfectly clear Sec. 17. That there shall be appointed in the Corps of Engineers, by selection from among the officers of that Corps, four (4) Inspectors of Fortifications and other works of Engineering, who shall have the rank, pay and emoluments of Colonels of Engineers, and the vacancies occasioned by these appointments by selections shall be filled by regular promotions, provided the number of officers in said Corps as heretofore established by law shall not be increased hereby I respectfully request that you will call Senator Wilson's attention to this matter beleiving it to have arisen from inadvertence" Copy, *ibid.* On Jan. 30, Delafield wrote to USG. "On the 20th of December ultimo, I had the honor to lay before you a recommendation for certain legislation for the Corps of Engineers, deemed necessary at that time, in order to increase its usefulness and efficiency. The only change which I recommended in the existing organization of the *officers* of the corps, was the appointment by selection of four inspectors of fortifications, with the rank of colonel, but without increasing the number of officers in the corps, which by the act of March 3rd 1863 was fixed at 105 of all grades. Circumstances that have transpired, and information that I have received since the date of my letter, have convinced me that some legislation is necessary in addition to what I then recommended, in order to prevent the efficiency of the corps from becoming seriously impaired by the resignation of many of its most valuable and experienced officers, greatly to the prejudice of the vast civil and military interests committed to its charge. As might be expected, the officers who leave the service to seek the pursuits of civil life, are generally to be found among those more or less conspicuous for talent and professional ability, their services being sought all over the country to fill positions of great trust, responsibility and profit. The grades of Major and Captain of Engineers have particularly suffered from this cause already. Within the last few weeks four officers of these grades (Turnbull, Palfrey, Merrill and Wharton) have resigned; four others (Generals Smith, Wilson, Michie and Major Casey) have requested leaves of absence preparatory to resignation, and it is reported that Generals Warren and Witzel intend to do the same thing. To prevent, in a measure, this exodus of valuable officers, whose places can be filled by graduates of the Military Academy only, by offering some additional inducements to remain in the service, I earnestly recommend that the number of officers in the grade of Lieutenant Colonel, which now contains ten, be increased to 16, retaining the present number of Majors and Captains, and diminishing the number of first and second Lieutenants from forty to thirty. This would provide regular promotion for six majors, six captains and six first Lieutenants, and it would beyond question have a most beneficial influence on the permanence and efficiency of the corps. A section in the following words will accomplish all I have in view both with regard to the four inspectors recommended in my letter of Decr. 20th, and the increase of the number of Lieutenant Colonels. It does not increase the number of officers in the corps but makes four additional Colonels and six additional Lieutenant Colonels with a corresponding reduction in the number of Lieutenants: SECTION—*And be it further enacted*; that the officers of the Corps of Engineers shall consist of one Chief Engineer with the rank, pay and emoluments of a brigadier-general, eight Colonels, sixteen Lieutenant Colonels, twenty Majors, thirty Captains, twenty first and ten second Lieutenants, who shall have the pay and emoluments now provided by law for officers of the Engineer Corps; *provided* that the four additional Colonels of Engineers authorized by this act, shall always be appointed by selection from among the officers of the Corps of Engineers, and the four officers thus appointed shall be inspectors of fortifications and other works of Engineering, *and provided further* that the President may, when the exigencies of the service require it, appoint any Colonel of Engineers an inspector of fortifications, without additional pay or emoluments. The importance of so organizing the Corps of Engineers as will fill up its numbers and retain in service experience only to be gained by prolonged service in the corps is becoming more apparent from month to month. Since the commencement of the Rebellion the corps has lost not less than *53 of its number* (eight by cecession) and but recently three field officers by death. Such a drain upon a corps of only 105 authorized by law, cannot exist without so impairing its usefulness as to make it impracticable to attend to the many duties assigned it throughout our vast and extended Country, all parts of which call incessantly for the services and talents of the officers of this corps. Being strongly impressed with the necessity of adopting some means of retaining the experienced officers, who have gained this invaluable qualification, I urge the increase of rank as a measure best calculated to effect the object without asking increased numbers." Copy, *ibid.* On Feb. 2, USG endorsed this letter. "Respy. referred to the U. S. Senate Committee on Mil Affairs. I do not look with regret on officers of the Army leaving the Army in time of peace to take responsible and important places in Civil life. If a West Point education eminently fits them for such positions, they are rendering the nation more service by pursuing them in time of peace than they could render by staying in the Army. In case of War the Country could get their services, and being found among the volunteers they would have a much larger Corps than they could do if in the Reg service, where all have more, or less military education & experience" Copy, DLC-USG, V, 58.

To George H. Stuart

Washington D. C. Jan.y 15th *1866*.

GEO. H. STUART, ESQR.
CHAIRMAN U. S. C. C.
MY DEAR SIR:

Your letter of the 12th inst. informing me that your Commission will hold their closing meeting in this City on the 11th of Feby. and asking me to preside on that occation is received. I will endeavor to be present on that occasion but beg to be excused from presiding. I never purposly presided at any public meeting and never but once, that I remember of, happened to be called on for such a purpose. That was at a meeting in Galena for the purpose of raising the first company that went from that City under the the first call of President Lincoln for Seventy-f[iv]e thousand men. Please excuse me from spending an uncumfortable evening as I should do presiding at a meeting where so many will be present that could do it so much better.

Yours Truly
U. S. GRANT
Lt. Gn.

ALS, DLC-George H. Stuart. On Jan. 19, 1866, George H. Stuart, Philadelphia, wrote to USG. "We are depending upon your acc[epting] invitation to preside at anniversary meeting of Commission, [on] February eleventh, at the Capitol. You must not disappoint us." LS, DNA, RG 94, U.S. Christian Commission, Letters Sent (Press). On Jan. 22, USG telegraphed to Stuart. "Please excuse me from presiding at annual meeting of Commission. Others can do it so much better" Telegram sent, *ibid.*, RG 107, Telegrams Collected (Bound); copy, DLC-USG, V, 109.

On Jan. 29, Bvt. Col. Adam Badeau wrote to Stuart. "Your letter of the 25th reached these hdqrs yesterday Sunday morning; I opened it, and on discovering its contents took it at once to Gen Grant's house. He sent me the same day to the Sec of the Navy, with directions to say that Gen Grant was anxious to have your request allowed; that you were a personal friend, and one to whom he was greatly indebted. But the vessel had already sailed. The General directs me to inform you in Detail of the effort he made to serve you, and of the regret he feels at its failure. Mrs. Grant desires me to enclose for yourself and Mrs Stuart, and for the young ladies cards for her Receptions, and to say that she will be very happy to have the young ladies come on to one of the parties, and remain her guests while they are in Washington. If you will apprise her in time, she will send her carriage to the Depôt to meet them." ALS, DLC-George H. Stuart.

On Feb. 4, Badeau telegraphed to Stuart. "Gen Grant suggests Generals Hancock Augur and Eaton" Telegram sent, DNA, RG 107, Telegrams Collected (Bound).

To Maj. Gen. William T. Sherman

Jan.y 16th *1866*

DEAR GENERAL:

You have no doubt noticed Washburne's Bill to *revive* the grade of General in the Army? Before the notice of the bill was published in the papers I knew nothing of it nor had I ever been consulted in any way about it. Since that however I have spoken to Washburne and told him that I thought if the bill was passed it was highly proper that it should expire (the grade) with the vacation of it by the first appointee. The reason I assigned for this was that now there are plenty of officers whose past services will warrant appointing them to any Military position but we have no assurance that when the vacancy occurs it would not be given to some one who would prove wholly incompetant in case of War. I advocated however that two or three Lieut. Generals be added if a change was made. Washburnes answer to this was that he did not like to add too much for fear of defeating the whole but would leave that for some one else to propose besides he said his bill left it discretionary with the President to fill the vacancy of Lieut. Gen. and the whole country pointed to you as the man who would get it. On that he thought there would be no division. But if another Lieut. Gen. was added he thought there would be a goodeal of division as to who would have it and that the decission would fall on one who he thinks should not be the second choice. Whilst I am ready to give all the credit I think due to the ability of each and every officer I am clear in my own mind that no officer should have the rank of Lieut. Gen. who the country would not feel perfectly safe in entrusting with the entire controll of any Army or Armies the Country might ever call into the field. I do think next to yourself Sheridan has proven himself to be entitled to that confidenc[e.] I fear he would not get the promotion unless three Lieut. Generals are added.

This letter is entirely private and is written to let you know that I would not be so entirely selfish as to see bills introduced so evidently intended for my advancement without saying a word for those who I think equally at least entitled to credit.

Yours Truly
U. S. GRANT

MAJ. GN. W. T. SHERMAN

ALS, DLC-William T. Sherman. On Jan. 22, 1866, Maj. Gen. William T. Sherman, St. Louis, wrote to USG. "I have your confidential letter, and renew the assurance I have ever felt that in your judgmt and motives I feel the most implicit reliance. The Country owes you any honor it can confer, and I hope you will receive that which seems in preparation for you. If the second exalted place falls to my lot I will attribute it to your favor. I agree with you that as the Record now stands, Sheridan ranks very high, and you will be justified by the fighting army in continuing to him your support. His fight in the Shenandoah and the intense energy with which he acted at the Five Forks, and subsequent pursuit of Lees Army, entitle him to receive any thing you can bestow. I doubt if the Armies about Richmond had any other man, who comprehended your plans as well, or who had the capacity and courage to inspire troops with the requisite intensity of action. His youth should be an element in his favor rather than the contrary. I want to keep out of that & all other controversy. I have this moment recd the despatch of Bowers, ordering me to Washington. I could start today, but suppose tomorrow will do. Therefore at 3 p m tomorrow I will start, and come East by the route that Seems best, say by Cincinati and the Baltimore & Ohio RR. I will stop with my brother John Sherman, but will be at your office within a few hours of my arrival. The Mississipi was closed—but opened, and now ~~again~~ by the intense cold is again closing, but I hope tomorrow I can cross on solid ice. Trusting to meet you in a few days in health, I am as ever your constant friend." ALS, USG 3.

To Edwin M. Stanton

Washington, January 22d *1866*.

HON. E. M. STANTON
SECRETARY OF WAR.
SIR:

I have the honor to return herewith the communication of the Honorable, The Secretary of the Interior, in reference to the erection of a military post at the north base of Black Hill, referred to me for report, and to invite your attention to the enclosed copy of a letter received from Major General W. T. Sherman, to whom was referred a memorial on the same subject from the Legislature of Dakota.

I would not recommend the establishment of a military post at Black Hill at present. It may be practicable to do so as soon as the regular force of the army is increased.

Very respectfully, Your obed't servant
U. S. GRANT
Lieutenant General.

LS, DNA, RG 108, Letters Received; copies (misdated Jan. 20, 1866), *ibid.*, Letters Sent; DLC-USG, V, 47, 109. On Jan. 1, Solomon L. Spink, secretary, Dakota Territory, had written to Secretary of War Edwin M. Stanton requesting the establishment of a military post in the Dakota Territory. LS, DNA, RG

108, Letters Received. On Jan. 5, Bvt. Col. Theodore S. Bowers endorsed this letter. "Respy. referred to Maj. Genl. W. T. Sherman, Comdg. Mil. Div: Misspi for remarks." Copy, *ibid.*, Register of Letters Received. On the same day, Secretary of the Interior James Harlan wrote to Stanton on the same subject. LS, *ibid.*, Letters Received. On Jan. 9, Maj. Thomas T. Eckert, act. asst. secretary of war, forwarded this letter to USG for report. ES, *ibid.* On Jan. 13, Maj. Gen. William T. Sherman, St. Louis, wrote to Bowers. "I have now before me the papers referred by your endorsemt of Jan 5, being a petition for the establishmt of a military Post in Dacotah near the Black Hills. I will write to Mr Spink Secretary, to the effect that at this time we cannot establish any new Post, nor make any permant change on the Frontier until Congress determines & fixes the military establishmt, and I know what specific troops I am to have. My own opinion is that we should encourage actual bona fide settlements westward as far as the the Land will yeild corn, & grasses, that we designate two or three Routes of travel to be guarded by Lines of Blockhouses, and small patrols that travel by emigrants be restricted to those Routes, and prohibited by all others. We may have to make Posts in the nature of depots of forage and provisions in the Rocky Mountains and trust to Cavalry expeditions to maintain a General condition of security on the Plains, by traversing them during the Season of Grass. Next summer I will either go myself or send some officers in whom I have confidence to make personal inspection of the new Territories after which I can be certain that military Posts built one year on interested information will not have to be broken up the next. I will give respectful attention to the representations of responsible parties such as I recognise these to be, but we must be more than usually circumspect as local parties in that section have already involved the Governmt in vast and seemingly useless expense." ALS, *ibid.* On Feb. 12, Sherman wrote to Bowers. "I have the honor to acknowledge receipt of the Petition of the Memorial of the Territorial Assembly of the Territory of Dacotah on the subject of Military Head Quarters. The subject matter hardly falls within their province but it is well to notify them that when Congress determines the Military Peace Establishmt and determines our relations to the Indians, I will make such distribution of troops, as will best fulfil the general interests of the United States." ALS, *ibid.* On April 7, Sherman endorsed another memorial requesting the establishment of a military post in Dakota Territory. "Respectfully forwarded to HdQrs of the Army. The whole subject of protection & Routes of travel north of 'Platte' is now Confided to Genl Cooke who will study the whole case and do what is right & to the interest of the US." AES, *ibid.*, RG 107, Letters Received, H81 1866. On April 11, USG endorsed these papers. "Respectfully returned to the Hon. Secretary of War, inviting attention to letter of Gen. Sully and endorsements of Gens Dodge and Sherman." ES, *ibid.*

On Jan. 17, U.S. Representative Robert C. Schenck of Ohio wrote to Stanton transmitting a memorial from the Minn. legislature requesting the establishment of military posts along the route from Minn. to Fort Walla Walla, Washington Territory. LS, *ibid.*, M82 1866. On Jan. 23, Sherman wrote a letter received at USG's hd. qrs. "Recieves Hon R. Schencks letter with memorial of Minnesota Legislature praying the establishment of Military posts to Walla Walla, Oregon. Genl Sherman expresses his views rather to the contrary, saying Route will be opened from Minn. to Montana &c." *Ibid.*, RG 108, Register of Letters Received. On Jan. 25, Christopher C. Andrews, former bvt. maj. gen.,

Washington, D. C., wrote to USG. "As my residence is in Minnesota near the frontier, and as I have had some personal observation of the settlements in that region during the past autumn I beg leave to recommend that one or more military posts be established for the better security of the settlers there. I believe that forts Abercrombie and Wordsworth are the most advanced posts for the protection of our Minnesota frontier. Last Spring a party of hostile Sioux Indians came to within a few miles of the town of Mankato and killed a family of white people. And it is the opinion of men acquainted with the Indians that such raids are liable to occur again. It is unnecessary to mention how damaging to the frontier—to the whole state indeed—it would be if more white people should be killed by the Indians. Every such calamity recalls vividly to the emigrant the unparalleld massacres of 1862. I do not feel competent to advise precisely where another post should be established; but have heard Devil's lake (Mennewauken) recommended as a suitable place. This lake is forty miles in length; its average width is fifteen miles; and it is wooded on one side. For establishing a post there it might be urged: 1st it is in the neighborhood of the British frontier. And it is known that the hostile Indians have found refuge the other side of that line, and made it a sort of base of operations. 2d a post at Devils Lake would be on the Northern emigrant route to the Pacific, or to the gold mines of Montana. I do not wish to disguise the fact that the people of Minnesota desire a protected route to the gold mines of Montana. And one or two additional posts would probably render the route safe between Fort Abercrombie and Fort Union. Reports of explorations by Nicollet in 1839, by Gov. Stevens, and by Capt. Mullan show the practicability of such a route. The protection of a route is of course incidental and subordinate. I should think another post on the Big Sioux River in Dacota would be necessary for the security of the southwestern frontier of Minnesota. Settlements in Dacota Territory have not advanced far North, and Southwestern Minnesota is a good deal exposed. The frontier people—the thin and more remote settlers—now live in dread of the Indians; and undoubtedly emigrants feel it unsafe to go as far out as they would like even in the limits of Minnesota." ALS, *ibid.*, RG 393, Military Div. of the Miss., Letters Received. On Feb. 21, Sherman wrote to Bowers. "I have the letter of Maj General C. C. Andrews refering to the Establishmt of a New Post up at Devils Lake, in Minnesota. The subject is already under advisemt, and if I had a Regimt of Infantry and one of Cavalry to spare, would most likely attempt to cover all the settlements of Minnesota, and make a thin line of Posts from the head of Minnesota River, by Fort Wadsworth, and Devils Lake to the Missouri River near the Great Bend, and so on up to Fort Benton and Montana: but with the present Regular force in the Division I would not be justified in attempting it. Nor do I think even if the Bill now before Congress passes in all april we will be able to enlist troops in time to attempt it this summer. I shall aim to make two Routes westward safe to emigrants this year, and to make such Explorations as will enable us to act understandingly for the year 1867. I have already presented my views on this and kindred subjects and expect to lay before the Lt Genl Commanding the Armies of the U. S. in great detail, a projet as large and comprehensive as it will be prudent for us to attempt with the present Army, and such as we have reason to expect this year. This projet will not embrace the Posts suggested by General Andrews, simply because we cannot attempt them with a due regard to other greater interests that demand attention." ALS, *ibid.*, RG 108, Letters Received.

To James W. Beekman

Washington Jan. 24th *1866*

HON. JAS. W. BEEKMAN,
DEAR SIR:

Our mutual friend Sr. Romero, Minister &c. from the *Republic* of *Mexico* has just shewn me a letter from Senator Morgan strongly recommending your son for a Cadetship at West Point, with the view of obtaining from me an endorsement. I shall be glad to give such and make it as favorable as I can. But there are some things not shewn in the papers before me that it will be necessary to know before the Warrant could issue. It is to provide this deficiency that I now write.

Let your son write an application for a Cadetship, addressed to the President and state in it his exact age, hight, when born and where now a resident. Let this come to me and I will make on it a favorable endorsement. The letter of Senator Morgan should also accompany the application. It is a strong recommendation, besides, if the bill passes increasing the number of Cadets it is likely each Senator will have the privilege of naming one Cadet. In that case nothing more would be wanted.

The appointment to West Point will not probably be made before March.

With great respect,
your obt. svt.
U. S. GRANT
Lt. Gn.

ALS, NHi. James W. Beekman, born in New York City in 1815 into an extremely wealthy and socially prominent family, graduated from Columbia College in 1834 and served two terms as N. Y. state senator. See letter to Hamilton Fish *et al.*, [*Feb. 22, 1866*]. On Jan. 29, 1866, Beekman, New York City, wrote to USG. "I was greatly honored by your very kind letter of 24th instant—According to your friendly suggestion, I enclose to your care, my son's application to the President—Senator Morgan's letter is also sent, for such use as may be advisable—For your kindness in this matter, I am most grateful, and should my boy succeed, I trust he will be no discredit to his friends—He is now studying with Prof L. H. Böeck, who has a mathematical & Engineering School—and will make a very good preparation for West Point—The boy stands over six feet in his shoes, can ride, swim, shoot, and speak the truth—and is a dutiful—son, of correct habits My good friend Romero has taken a very lively interest in Willy's case, and to him I owe many a kind and friendly service—The success of his country's cause is, like that of all genuine things, *slow*, but sure—" ALS, DNA, RG 94, Cadet Applications. Beekman enclosed a letter of the same day from James W. Beekman, Jr., to President Andrew Johnson requesting an appointment to USMA. ALS, *ibid.* On Feb. 3, USG endorsed these letters. "The application of J. W. Beekman Jr. for a Cadetship, at large, is respectfully recommended, and urged, if it can be given without prejudice to stronger claimants. The father has, I believe, been one of the strongest supporters of the Govt. during the rebellion and has contributed largely in supplying men and money to the support of the Army." AES, *ibid.* No apppointment followed.

On Sept. 18, 1867, Beekman wrote to USG. "Some of us propose to give our friend Romero a parting dinner—You love him as I do and I write to beg you to accept the invitation which will be sent you (not as a mere matter of course) but with sincere desire to see you present—Let me assure you that your coming here will do great good to the cause Romero has at heart" ALS, USG 3.

To Maj. Gen. Philip H. Sheridan

Washington, D. C. Jany 25 *18656* [*1:00* P.M.]

MAJ GEN SHERIDAN
NEW ORLEANS LA

Order our troops from the Mexican side of the Rio Grande if you have not already done so. Examine too if damages have been done to private property by our troops in this raid over the river. If claims are hereafter made, it is better we should Know the justice of them from the reports of Known parties

U. S. GRANT
Lieut Gen

Telegram sent, DNA, RG 107, Telegrams Collected (Bound); copies, *ibid.*, RG 108, Letters Sent; DLC-USG, V, 47, 109; USG 3.

On Jan. 8, 1866, 10:30 A.M., Maj. Gen. Philip H. Sheridan telegraphed to USG. "Unofficial information from the Rio Grande makes affairs very much mixed, It will I fear be impossible to preserve neutrality strictly without breaking up Crawford about whom I have heretofore telegraphed you I will not hesitate to do this, should it become necessary—" Telegram received (at 1:00 P.M.), DNA, RG 107, Telegrams Collected (Bound); *ibid.*, RG 108, Telegrams Received; copies (one sent by mail), *ibid.*, Letters Received; DLC-USG, V, 54; DLC-Philip H. Sheridan.

On Jan. 12, Sheridan telegraphed to USG. "There is much excitement on the

Rio Grande on account of the execution of prisoners of War by the Imperial authorities at Matamoras, but no serious trouble need be apprehended, as the most positive orders have been sent there to preserve neutrality I directed Gen Weitzel to break filibustering recruiting stations without hesitation, should he deem the neutrality of our country in any danger" Telegram received (at 10:00 P.M.), DNA, RG 107, Telegrams Collected (Bound); *ibid.*, RG 108, Telegrams Received; copies (one sent by mail), *ibid.*, Letters Received; DLC-USG, V, 54; DLC-Philip H. Sheridan.

On Jan. 16, 3:00 P.M., Sheridan telegraphed to USG. "In the New Orleans newspapers of this date it is reported that some of the colored troops crossed over the Rio Grande to assist in the capture of Bagdad—I do not believe one word of it. Weitzel has the most peremptory orders to preserve neutrality and I look on this crossing of the Rio Grande as a sensation story. I have no official information from that quarter. I have sent order to Weitzel to break up all fillibustering recruiting parties if necessary to preserve neutrality" Telegram received (on Jan. 17, 3:00 P.M.), DNA, RG 107, Letters Received from Bureaus; *ibid.*, Telegrams Collected (Bound); *ibid.*, RG 108, Telegrams Received; copies (one sent by mail), *ibid.*, Letters Received; DLC-USG, V, 54; DLC-Philip H. Sheridan.

On Jan. 17, 1:00 P.M. and 6:30 P.M., Sheridan telegraphed to USG. "The following official information has just reached me from the Rio Grande: Bagdad was captured on the morning of the fifteenth (15th) January between the hours of two and four a. m. The attacking force was about sixty men. They captured the Franco-Mexican garrison, about three hundred strong, one half of which joined the Liberalists and garrisoned the place. The attacking party had all disappeared before daylight. Neither Escabado nor any one else had any knowledge of this transaction, but both Escabado and Crawford posted to the place at once, and a quarrel ensued between them, and at the request of the Commander of the post, a garrison was sent by Gen. Weitzel to protect the private property of the place, with instructions to withdraw should any Imperialists approach the place. I do not sustain this action, but I presume there can be no objection on the part of the Imperialists, as I protect them. An investigation is now going on to ascertain if any of our troops were engaged in this transaction. It appears that they were all present at tattoo and reveille. If Gen. Weitzel has not already arrested Crawford on the order already given, I will arrest him, and send him beyond the limits of my command. His conduct and manner will not permit his sojourn on our side of the river any longer." "I have directed Gen. Wright to go at once to the Rio Grande, to examine into the condition of affairs there and break up the filibustering parties there who are giving us much annoyance. I will probably go there myself in a day or two; meantime, but little credence should be given to published exaggerations in the newspapers." Telegrams received (on Jan. 18, 10:40 P.M. and Jan. 17, 9:50 P.M.), DNA, RG 107, Letters Received from Bureaus; *ibid.*, Telegrams Collected (Bound); *ibid.*, RG 108, Telegrams Received; copies (sent by mail), *ibid.*, RG 94, Letters Received, 909A 1866; DLC-USG, V, 54; DLC-Philip H. Sheridan. Also on Jan. 17, Sheridan wrote to USG. "I have the honor to forward to you letters of direction given at various times to the Commanding Officers on the Rio Grande frontier: also miscellaneous correspondence between the commanders on the respective sides of the river, and other letters bearing on the condition of affairs in Northern Mexico. These letters I did not consider of much importance and did not forward to you, as I considered my own authority sufficient on the subject matter. Then the information which I received one day was liable to be contradicted the next or found inaccurate." LS, DNA, RG 108, Letters Received. A summary of the correspondence is *ibid.* On Jan. 18, Secretary of War Edwin M. Stanton wrote to USG. "You are respectfully requested to furnish to this Department copies of all letters received from General Sheridan or other Officers of the Department of Texas, in regard to the present condition of Affairs on the South Eastern [Western?] frontier & especially in regard to any violation of neutrality on the part of the Army on the right bank of the Rio Grande." LS (brackets in text), *ibid.* On Jan. 19, USG wrote to Stanton. "In obedience to your note of yesterday I have the honor to transmit herewith copies of all letters received from Maj. Gen- Sheridan in any manner relating to the condition of affairs and our neutrality on the Rio Grande from July 31st 1865, and of all telegrams relating thereto from September 1st 1865 to the present time. no letters or telegrams touching this subject have been received except through him." Copies, DLC-USG, V, 47, 109; DNA, RG 108, Letters Sent.

On Jan. 22, noon, Sheridan telegraphed to USG. "Order number one sixty eight (168) has just reached here. It leaves me in a pretty bad fix for good officers to command the District of Texas, particularly the Rio Grande. Our colored troops have become so excited over the villainous abuse of them by the rebel paper (the 'Ranchero') published in Matamoros, it requires the closest vigilance to prevent them from doing mischief. While we are making every effort to preserve neutrality, this villainous paper is permitted to abuse our colored troops, to call the President the assassin of Mrs. Surratt, to abuse all our officers, to publish the most villified and execrable falsehoods." Telegram received (at 9:35 P.M.), *ibid.*, RG 94, Letters Received, 745G 1866; *ibid.*, RG 107, Telegrams Collected (Bound); *ibid.*, RG 108, Telegrams Received; copies, *ibid.*, RG 393, Military Div. of the Southwest and Dept. of the Gulf, Telegrams Sent; DLC-USG, V, 54; DLC-Philip H. Sheridan. At 11:25 P.M., USG telegraphed to Sheridan. "If there are among the Generals Mustered out any whos retention you deem important to the proper management of affairs on the Rio Grande you are authorized to retain them. ~~in~~ If such report their names and the order of musterout will be revoked in their cases. Report also the names of others whos services can be dispensed with. . . . Respectfully referred to the Secretary of War for approval before being forwarded." ALS (telegram sent—without endorsement), USMA; telegram sent, DNA, RG 107, Telegrams Collected (Bound); copies, *ibid.*, RG 108, Letters Sent; DLC-USG, V, 47, 109. On Jan. 28, 11:00 A.M., Sheridan telegraphed to USG. "Your telegram came duly to hand—Wright has been directed to remain on the RioGrande until the little excitement there subsides. There is in the newspapers much ado about nothing, unless it is the intention of the French to provoke hostile acts. I respectfully request that Gen Getty be sent to me to command the District of the Rio Grande—I want some one that will mind his own business and who is a good soldier. Can you let me have him?" Telegram received (on Jan. 29, 1:00 P.M.), DNA, RG 107, Telegrams Collected (Bound); *ibid.*, RG 108, Telegrams Received; copies (one sent by mail), *ibid.*, Letters Received; DLC-USG, V, 54; DLC-Philip H. Sheridan. On Feb. 1, Sheridan wrote to Brig. Gen. John A. Rawlins. "I have the honor to report that the only General Officers now under my command are Major General J. G. Foster Commanding Department of Florida—Major General E. R. S Canby Commanding Department of Louisiana Major General H. G. Wright

Commanding Department of Texas, and Brigadier General and Brevet Major General T. W. Sherman Commanding Eastern District of Louisiana, which includes the City of New Orleans—None of these officers could at present be mustered out without detriment to the public service" LS, DNA, RG 108, Letters Received. On Feb. 6, 3:30 P.M., Sheridan telegraphed to USG. "I have had no reply to my telegram asking for Bvt. Maj Gen'l Getty to command the District of the RioGrande—I was much influenced in making this request, as an officer would thereby be put in command, who is free from the prejudice created by the abuse of the ~~New Orleans~~ Ranchero Newspaper.—I want to go to the RioGrande & would like to know the result of the application—There is now no trouble there and I wish to arrange the number of troops for that line—" Telegram received (on Feb. 7, 4:30 P.M.), *ibid.*, RG 107, Telegrams Collected (Bound); *ibid.*, RG 108, Telegrams Received; copies (one sent by mail), *ibid.*, Letters Received; DLC-USG, V, 54; DLC-Philip H. Sheridan. On Feb. 8, 10:55 A.M., Bvt. Col. Theodore S. Bowers telegraphed to Sheridan. "Gen Getty was ordered to report to you on the twenty ninth of January, and is now en route The order you desire in the case of Gen Forsythe will be made" Telegram sent, DNA, RG 107, Telegrams Collected (Bound); copies, *ibid.*, RG 108, Letters Sent; DLC-USG, V, 47, 109.

On Jan. 22, 4:30 P.M., Sheridan telegraphed to USG. "Bvt. Lieut. Col. Kip of my staff has just returned from the Rio Grande. There is a good deal of excitement there, but no danger of trouble. The investigation of the Bagdad affair to ascertain if any United States troops were engaged in it, is still going on—Weitzel has not yet withdrawn the small force in the captured town of Bagdad on account of humanity. Gen. Wright ought to be there now and has directions from me to restore the equilibrium—Weitzel without thinking is putting up some thirty pound Parrotts in old Fort Brown, to be even with Mejia who has dug a ditch on the Mexican side. There was no necessity of mounting guns. There will be no fight. The Mexicans bluster when they think they will not be taken up—" Telegram received (at 9:10 P.M.), DNA, RG 107, Telegrams Collected (Bound); *ibid.*, RG 108, Telegrams Received; copies (one sent by mail), *ibid.*, Letters Received; *ibid.*, RG 393, Military Div. of the Southwest and Dept. of the Gulf, Telegrams Sent; DLC-USG, V, 54; DLC-Philip H. Sheridan; USG 3.

On Jan. 23, 12:30 P.M., Sheridan telegraphed to USG. "R. Clay Crawford who for some time has given annoyance by his blustering and swaggering manner on the Rio Grande frontier, and who it appears was connected with the Bagdad affair, escaped from the Rio Grande to this city, and was last night arrested by me, and confined at Fort Jackson pending the Bagdad investigation" Telegram received (on Jan. 24, 11:00 P.M.), DNA, RG 107, Telegrams Collected (Bound); *ibid.*, RG 108, Telegrams Received; copies, DLC-USG, V, 54; DLC-Philip H. Sheridan. Also on Jan. 23, Sheridan wrote to Rawlins. "I have the honor to transmit the enclosed copy of Lieutenant Colonel Lawrence Kips report for the information of the Lieutenant General" Copy, DNA, RG 108, Letters Received. On Jan. 21, Bvt. Lt. Col. Lawrence Kip wrote to Sheridan. "In compliance with Special Orders No 8 from these Head Quarters dated New Orleans La January 8 1866: I sailed for Brownsville Texas on the morning of the 9th, reached General Weitzel's Head Qrs. on the afternoon of the 15th. R Clay Crawford who represented himself to be a Major General in the mexican (Liberal) Army and Commander of the 'american Div' of that army, closed his office at Brownsville on the 13th, and left for Brazos, with the avowed intention of returning to the north. After the capture of Bagdad, however, he crossed the river and assumed command of that place but was soon afterwards deposed by Col Mejia, and he was on the 16th relieved by General Cortina who now commands the troops in and about that place. It is supposed the object of this last change is to give the command to one Reed who is announced by Crawford as Colonel, on his Staff. During C's stay at Brownsville he was not recognized in any way by the U S. Authorities and but few men joined his party. Numerous applications were made by him to General Weitzel for guns, clothing ammunition &c but no assistance of any Kind was given him. He was informed that no liberal Officers on this frontier were recognized by General Escobedo, who exercises the functions of General-in-Chief—(and is so recognized by Juarez) and his subordinates. Crawford had in his possession on his arrival a large number of Mexican bonds, and it is supposed his mission was finiancial as well as a Military one. The Directors being in Wall Street as well, as on the Mexican frontier. On Crawfords trip to Texas and after his arrival he represented himself as acting under the instructions of President Johnson & General Grant.—General Grant's orders to General Weitzel referring to Crawford says—his mission 'is purely of a private nature, and need not engage your attention' At the desire and one the application of General Escobedo, General Weitzel sent a force of three hundred (300) men to Bagdad immediately after its capture to prevent pillage and to Keep the peace.—The most of the enemy on its surrender went over to the Liberals & now constitute the greater portion of the garrison. About four thousand (4000) men occupy Matamoras including most of the able bodied citizens—of these twenty seven hundred (2700) are reliable and out of these three hundred & fifty (350) are Austrians and French Marines Eight hundred (800) can be mounted in an hour's notice, and two hundred (200) are Rebels from the United States—These last go by the name of the centra-Guerrillas and are the worst men in the country. A forced loan of one hundred and twelve thousand (112,000) dollars was recently made. American citizens being included among the contributors—but three of the latter declined to acceede to this demand; these had their places of business closed, a seal placed over their doors and are prohibited hereafter from doing business in Mexico. These parties propose to bring civil suit for the damage done them.—The Liberals have an effective force of about twenty five hundred (2500) men, this is the most number of men that they can bring against Matamoras. Earthworks are being thrown up by the Imperialists along the river front, as well as in the rear of the town. The Officer holding Matamoras has been notified, that in the event of a deliberate shot being thrown into Brownsville, the guns from this side will be opened upon the town. Old Fort Brown is being put in repair and two 30 pdr parrotts and four field pieces will be mounted. Field works are also being thrown up below this point." Copy, *ibid.* See telegram to Maj. Gen. Philip H. Sheridan, Dec. 1, 1865.

On Jan. 25, 1866, 12:30 P.M., Sheridan telegraphed to USG. "When I arrested R. C. Crawford I got his baggage and also his correspondence—I will send copies for your information" Telegram received (at 5:40 P.M.), DNA, RG 107, Telegrams Collected (Bound); *ibid.*, RG 108, Telegrams Received; copies, *ibid.*, RG 393, Military Div. of the Southwest and Dept. of the Gulf, Telegrams Sent; DLC-USG, V, 54; DLC-Philip H. Sheridan. On Jan. 28, Sheridan wrote to USG. "I have the honor to transmit herewith copies of all the papers pertaining to the late 'affaire' on the Rio Grande that were found among the baggage of R Clay Crawford. As some of them are unfinished and therefore without signature, and as in others no address is given, I furnish the annexed list for your information . . ." LS, DNA, RG 94, Letters Received, 909A 1866. The enclosures are *ibid.* See letter to Edwin M. Stanton, Feb. 16, 1866.

To Maj. Gen. Daniel E. Sickles

Washington D. C. Jan. 26, 1866

MAJ. GEN. D. E. SICKLES,
COM'D'G DEPT. S. C.
GENERAL:

I have received your order restoring Governor Aiken's Plantation, and with the proofs in the case approve of it. As, however, Congress is now in session and will probably at an early day settle the status of all land covered by Gen Sherman's Order, I would say leave all land, to which Freedmen have obtained possessionery titles, until such settlement is had.[1]

Gen. Scott[2] has gone to S. C. as Agt. of the Freedmen's Bureau. I hope under his judicious management the affairs of the Bureau will work smoothly; at all events give his administration support and a fair trial.

Very respectfully
Your obt. servt.
U. S. GRANT
Lt. Gen'l

Copies, DLC-USG, V, 47, 109; DNA, RG 108, Letters Sent. On Jan. 19, 1866, Maj. Gen. Daniel E. Sickles, Charleston, had written to USG. "I avail myself of the visit of Mr Trescot, the Agent of the State of South Carolina, to Washington, to Commend him to your regard and Consideration. His Excellency Gov. Orr, is at present in Charleston, and I See no reason to apprehend any disagreement between the State and Military Authorities upon any of the matters Committed to the Governor and myself. In the interior of the State the progress made in the organization of Labor is quite satisfactory. I regret that I Cannot report Encouraginly on this Subject along the Coast. The unsettled Condition of the territory Embraced in Gen. Sherman's reservation, demoralizes the Colored population as well upon those lands as in the vicinity, and until that Matter is decided little more can be done. After a Careful investigation I have restored Gov. Aikens plantations—being satisfied they had never been 'abandoned' in the sense of that term as defined by Congress, and no freedpeople being on the premises by authority of the United States. Last year a few certificates were given by the Freedmens Bureau with permission to locate on Gov. A's lands, but the persons who received them are no longer there—Maj. Roy 6th Inf.'y, reported to me that only the former slaves of the Governor were on the premises and these had all been sent there by himself. None of the people on the place have been disturbed—the Governor having treated them with the utmost liberality. Enclosed I have the honor to transmit a Copy of my order; and also Copies of several reports from Gen. Beecher (brother of the famous Henry Ward Beecher) and of Maj. Delaney (Colored) of the 104 U. S. C. T.—that may interest you in forming your Estimate of the Situation in South Carolina. The Governor, at my request, has decided not to put the 'Code,' which was passed by the Legislature, into operation; and I have prepared a General Order, which will be issued at once, now that I have Conferred with him on the Subject, guaranteeing Equal rights and justice—to the Colored people, and providing remedies for all reasonable Complaints on the part of planters.—In regard to the Militia, the Governor will proceed no further than to Complete the Enrollment; he will not arm them until the United States Governmt is prepared to issue arms to the State, for the Militia, in accordance with the Act of Congress. I am happy to add that I have the Cordial and Energetic Cooperation of the Governor in the preservation of order, which has not been anywhere recently, seriously disturbed." ALS, *ibid.*, Letters Received.

On Jan. 22, Sickles had written to USG. "Permit me to send to you unofficially a copy of my Genl Order superseding the code passed by Legislature—the code was passed reluctantly by the Legislature and hesitatingly approved by the Governor at the close of the Session,—and contains many provisions deemed inadmissable by the soundest jurists and best men in the State. The Governor readily consents to withhold the Proclamation required by the terms of the Law, to put it into operation, and acquiesces not unwillingly, in the provisions of the Genl. Order, which did meet the approval of Genl Saxton, and Genl. Scott his successor. So far as the Press of South Carolina has given expression to public sentiment, it is also favorable indeed, as yet, without dissent. I regret that neither Genl. Scott nor Gen'l. Saxton were willing to make Post Commanders ex officio agents of the Bureau. I proposed it, and urged it but yielded in deference to their relation to the Freedmens Bureau. The efforts made to organize labor and set the land under cultivation were leading to gratifying results.—contributing to the pacification of the population and the concentration of attention upon industrial pursuits,—but the agitation of the measure proposing grants or leases of land to the negroes has suspended all further operations in the region of the lands to be ceded and the demoralization will spread. What will the Soldiers say if negroes have land given them and the Soldiers and the widows and orphans of the fallen get none? If it be not contemplated to give or lease land to all the freedpeople, will it not be difficult and unjust to discriminate among them? Tese questions suggest their own answers." Copy, *ibid.*, RG 393, Dept. of the South and S. C., Letters Sent.

1. On Feb. 16, Sickles wrote to Bvt. Col. Orville E. Babcock. "Enclosed I have the honor to forward direct to Hd Qrs Armies of the United States, reports from Bvt Brig Genl Beecher and Bvt Maj Genl Devens containing several interesting facts and suggestions in regard to the situation of matters on the Sea

Islands and Coast lands in this Department, embraced in General Sherman's Field Order No 15: Jan.'y 1865, and which have been the subject of recent legislation. It is very desirable that some regulations be adopted at an early day, on the subjects suggested in the enclosed papers, and inasmuch as the field of operations extends to three Departments (South Carolina, Georgia and Florida) the rules should, if convenient, be made general and be promulgated from Head Quarters, as these Departments are in several Military Divisions, as well.—In the main I concur in the views of Generals Devens and Beecher. I would reduce my own views to form if I did not deem it perhaps useful to forward these enclosures this evening, on the day of their receipt, inasmuch as I presume the subject is now under consideration. If the subject be remitted to me I will do the best I can: but I am not inclined unless required by the law or orders, to favor the extension of the system of free grants of lands belonging to other people, to those, whom I believe, incapable of cultivating them; and I would prefer to settle at once the grants to be made, to the extent required by good faith, or the letter of the law, or orders, so that titles, contracts for labor and the general cultivation of the soil could be speedily quieted and adjusted. At present, crowds of negroes are coming down from the interior, abandoning contracts and homes, and flocking to the Islands and the cost as to the 'Promised Land',—thus unsettling their minds and making them not only dependent upon the Government, but, in connection with the large number of Colored Troops mustered out, often defiant and disorderly. They begin to say 'We will and must have lands.' They are eager to buy any, and boast of their of their possession often in menacing language and temper. I am happy to assure the Lt. Genl Commanding that no serious disturbance of order has yet occured, although several reports to that effect, absurdly suggested, have been printed; and as a general rule, I think he will be justified in assuming all such stories to be without foundation, in absence of official reports, at least so far as my Department is concerned. I will also enclose for the information of the Lieut. Genl. Comd'g a report from Capt Corbin (of the Freedman's Bureau) a communication from Gov Magrath and another from Hon C. H. Dudley, as to matters in the interior—and a Copy of a letter from Gov Magrath to Hon Simeon Fair of Newberne; the latter refers to the disaffected temper of the population in Genl Ames District (Western), the former are more encouraging and relate to the Central and Coast region.—I trust this long letter and these long documents may not prove tedious and it is in the belief that they may contribute to an accurate appreciation of all phases of the situation, that I venture to request leave to bring them to the notice of the Lieut General Commanding.—It is so late that my clerks have all turned in, so that I cannot have my letter engrossed and made legible—You may decipher it, with patience, I trust." Copy, *ibid.*, RG 108, Letters Received. The enclosures are *ibid.* On March 3, USG endorsed these papers. "Respectfully forwarded to the Hon. Secrety of War." ES, *ibid.*, RG 94, Letters Received, 180A 1866.

2. Robert K. Scott (future governor of S. C.), born in Pa. in 1826, an Ohio physician and merchant, appointed lt. col., 68th Ohio, as of Nov. 30, 1861, brig. gen. as of Jan. 12, 1865, and bvt. maj. gen. as of Dec. 5, 1865. On Nov. 20, 1866, USG wrote to Secretary of War Edwin M. Stanton. "I have the honor to recommend that the order to Muster out of service Bvt. Maj. Gn. R. K. Scott, & Bvt. Maj. Gn. D. Tillson, be suspended until further orders." ALS, *ibid.*, ACP, G582 CB 1866.

To Charles W. Ford

Washington D, C,
Jan,y 28th 1866.

DEAR FORD:

Your letter written after having seen Benoist,[1] and one from Judge Dent in answer to the one to Mrs. Dent, are received. Dent is anxious that I should buy and I have written to him this morning that I will do so. Now I want to ask another favor from you not being able to go to St. Louis myself. I want to pay Benoist what Dent owes him and have the note and Deed of Trust transfered to my credit. Will you see *B.* and have this done for me? Either you or Benoist are at liberty to draw on me, at sight, for the money necessary to do this, includin all the expenses of recording, having the transfer made legal &c.

I suppose soon you will get to think I am making you my ~~pri~~ agt. for the transaction of all my private business! All I can say is call on me for a return of favors.

My family are all well and join in respects to you—

yours Truly
U. S. GRANT

ALS, USG 3.

1. Louis A. Benoist, born in St. Louis in 1803, studied medicine and law, then opened the first bank in St. Louis in 1832.

To Edwin M. Stanton

Washington D. C. Jan. 29th *1866*

HON. E. M. STANTON,
SEC. OF WAR,
SIR:

From the period of the difficulties between Maj. Gn. now Lt. Gn. Scott with Secretary Marcy, during the Administration of

President Polk, the Command of the Army virtually passed into the hands of the sec. of War. From that day to the breaking out of the rebellion the General in Chief never kept his Head Quarters in Washington and could not consequently, with propriety, resume his proper functions. To administer the Affairs of the Army properly Hd Qrs. and the Adjt. Gens office must be in the same place.

During the War, whilst in the field, my functions as Commander of all the Armies w~~as~~ere never impaired but were facilitated in all essential matters by the Administration and by the War Department. Now however that the War is over and I have brought my Head Quarters to this City I find my present position embarassing and, I think, out of place. I have been intending or did intend, to make the begining of the New Year the time to bring this matter before you with the view of asking to have the old condition of affairs restored but from diffidence about mentioning the matter have postponed it until now.—In a few words I will state what I conceive to be my duties and my place and ask respectfully to be restored to them and it.

The entire Adjutant General's office should be under the entire controll of the General in Chief of the Army. No orders should go to the Army, or the Adjt. General, except through the General in Chief. All official papers and Correspondence should be addressed to the Adj. Gn. to be acted upon by the General in Chief. Such as require the action of the President would be laid before the Sec. of War whose actions would be regarded as those of the President. In short in my opinion the Gen. in Chief stands between the President and the Army in all official matters and the Secretary of War is between the Army, (through the General in Chief,) and the President.

I can very well conceive that a rule so long disregarded could not, or would not, be restored without the subject being presented and I now do so, respectfully, for your concideration.

Very respectfully
your obt. svt.
U. S. GRANT
Lt. Gn.

ALS, DLC-Edwin M. Stanton.

On Jan. 29, 1866, USG again wrote to Secretary of War Edwin M. Stanton. "Several persons, Gens. Thomas and Tower among them, are now in my office and will probably detain me for some little time. If therefore it will suit your convenience just as well I will call to see you in the morning on the subject of my note of this date." ALS, *ibid.* See William T. Sherman, *Memoirs of Gen. W. T. Sherman* (4th ed., New York, 1891), II, 446–50.

To Henry B. Anthony

Washington D. C. Feb.y 1st *1866*

HON. H. B. ANTHONY
U. S. SENATOR:
DEAR SIR:

Yours of yesterday making enquiry as to the services, cause of death &c. of late Capt. & Bvt. Maj. Gore, 4th U. S. Infantry, is received.

I knew Maj. Gore and family well having served in the same regiment with the Major from 1843 to date of his death in 1852.[1] It might be well to state in passing that Mrs. Lucy Porter, the wife of Major Gore, and now a widow for the second time, has been an uncompromising Union woman from the begining of our struggle to the present time. Her only son, and the son of Maj. Gore, now a lad of less than seventeen years, has also been strongly for the Union in the midst of secessionests. He was too young to enter the service during the rebellion but he did, as I have understood, the next thing to it: that is entered the Home Guards (Union) and was frequently called out to expell Guerrillas from his section of Ky.

Maj. Gore was a man of feeble constitution from the time I first knew him. His services in the Mexican War probably tended to still further enfeeble it.

The immediate cause of Major Gores death was Cholera contracted near Panama, N. G. when enroute for the Pacific coast with his regiment. His constitution was so impaired that a hope was scarcely entertained of his recovery after the attack. How far this loss of constitution was the result of field services I am unable to say. But he was a zealous officer. He has left a widow and one orphan child in destitute circumstances. That widow and orphan have remained true to their country under circumstances which tested their loyalty. Living during the rebellion in the midst of a disloyal ~~section~~ community they have been outspoken in the expression of their opinions. On the whole I think a more deserving applicant for pennsion will not appeal to Congress for help.

Very respectfully
your obt. svt.
U. S. GRANT
Lt. Gn.

ALS, deCoppet Collection, NjP. Henry B. Anthony, born in R. I. in 1815, educated at Brown University, elected governor of R. I. in 1849 and U.S. senator in 1858.

1. See *PUSG*, 1, 252–53.

To Mathew B. Brady

HD. QRS. ARMIES OF THE U. S,
Washington, D. C., Feb. 3, '66.

M. B. BRADY, ESQ.

DEAR SIR:—I am glad to learn that you have determined to place on permanent exhibition, . . . your Collection of Photographic Views of Battle-fields, &c., taken on the spot, while the occurrences represented were taking place.

I knew when many of these representations were being taken, and have in my possession most of them, and I can say that the scenes are not only spirited and correct, but also well chosen.

The Collection will be valuable to the student and artist of the present generation; but how much more valuable it will be to future generations!

U. S. GRANT,
Lieut.-General.

Brady's National Photographic Collection of War Views, and Portraits of Representative Men (New York, 1869), p. 6.

To Francis C. Barlow

Head Quarters Armies of the United States
Washington D. C. Feb'y 5th 1866.

GEN F. C. BARLOW
SEC. OF STATE
DEAR GENERAL

Your letter of the 3d inst. asking for a testimonial in favor of Dr E. B. Dalton[1] is received. This is asked with the view of securing to him the appointment of "Sanitary Superintendent" under the proposed "Health Bill" of the State of New York.

As a rule I very much dislike to give any recommendation for place or appointment except purely Military. In this case, however, being personally cognisant of the eminent services of Dr Dalton, and conscientiously believing that he is one of the very best men in the whole country for the proposed place, I take great pleasure in departing from this rule.

Originally possessed of the right qualifications to fill the place of "Sanitary Superintendent" in a great emergency like the one anticipated, or at least intended to provide against, the great experience of Dr Dalton during the War, and especially as chief Superintendent of the immense Field Hospitals at City Point Va. during the last year of the War gives him qualifications for the position, that but few men can have—

I believe it would be difficult to make a better selection for "Sanitary Superintendent" than Dr Dalton

Very respectfully
your obt svt
U. S. GRANT—
Lt. Gen—

Copies, New York State Library, Albany, N. Y.; DLC-USG, V, 47, 109; DNA, RG 108, Letters Sent. Francis C. Barlow, former maj. gen., elected N. Y. secretary of state in 1865. See *PUSG*, 10, 495*n*.

1. Edward B. Dalton, born in Mass. in 1834, graduated from Harvard and trained in medicine in N. Y. Appointed surgeon, 36th N. Y., as of Oct. 31, 1861,

he was appointed surgeon of vols. as of March 26, 1863. In March, 1866, Dalton became sanitary superintendent of the New York City Metropolitan Board of Health. See *New York Times*, March 7, 1866.

To Henry Wilson

Washington, D. C. Feby. 5th 1866.

HON. H. WILSON
CHM. MIL. COMMITTEE
U. S. SENATE:
SIR:

Since the recommendations for changes in the "Senate Bill" for the reorganization of the Army my attention has been called to several points of some importance which did not occur to myself nor I presume to either of the Major Generals making the recommendations.[1] One of them is in fixing the number of non-commissioned officers, and musicians, for the company for each the maximum and the minimum organizations to conform to tactics. If these points were fixed I have forgotten it and have not got the ~~b~~ labor of those officers before me to refresh my memory.

In the matter of the Staff Corps the Senate Bill, as prepared, prevents the possibility of rewarding officers who have rendered the most conspicuous services. I beg leave therefore to suggest the propriety of giving to the chief of each of these the rank of Major General and making corresponding changes in the lower grades.

I have ventured to make these suggestions not wishing to dictate the course of legislation, but because you have done me the honor to submit for my views the different bills affecting the Military establishment of the country. The motive is ~~the~~ to reward eminent services and I know therefore you will excuse the liberty

Very respectfully
Your Obt. Servt.
U. S. GRANT
Lt. Gen'l

Copies, DLC-USG, V, 47, 109; DNA, RG 108, Letters Sent. See letters to Henry Wilson, Jan. 12, Feb. 6, 1866.

1. On Jan. 22, 1866, 9:50 A.M., Bvt. Col. Theodore S. Bowers had telegraphed to Maj. Gen. William T. Sherman. "Lieutenant General Grant directs that you report in person to him in this city with as little delay as practicable." ALS (telegram sent), DNA, RG 107, Telegrams Collected (Unbound); copy, *ibid.*, RG 393, Military Div. of the Miss., Telegrams Received. On the same day, Sherman, St. Louis, wrote and telegraphed to Bowers. "I have this momnt received your despatch ordering me to Washington. The Mississipi River is almost impassable, but if possible tomorrow I will cross over, and come by the most expeditious Route, reporting in person on arrival. Col Sawyer will in my absence transact all Routine business." AL (signature clipped), *ibid.*, RG 108, Letters Received. "Despatch recd. Will start tomorrow" Telegram received (at 12:50 P.M.), *ibid.*, Telegrams Received; copy, DLC-USG, V, 54. On Jan. 24, Bowers telegraphed similar instructions to Maj. Gens. George G. Meade and George H. Thomas. ALS (telegram sent to Thomas), DNA, RG 107, Telegrams Collected (Bound); telegram sent (to Thomas), *ibid.*; copies, *ibid.*, RG 108, Letters Sent; DLC-USG, V, 47, 109.

On Feb. 1, USG wrote to U.S. Senator Henry Wilson of Mass. "Enclosed herewith I have the honor of returning to you Senate Bill, No. 67, which you were kind enough to submit to me for such remarks as I might wish to make on it, with such changes as have been suggested by three Major Generals of the Regular Army, distinguished for their services in the field, Maj. Generals Sherman, Meade and Thomas, interlined; and also their reasons, briefly stated, for these changes.—I fully concur with the views given by them and respectfully submit the matter for the consideration of Congress" Copies, *ibid.* On the same day, Meade, Sherman, and Thomas wrote to Brig. Gen. John A. Rawlins. "Pursuant to the instructions of Lt General Grant, we have carefully examined Senate Bill no 67. with its Amendments, and all the papers submitted to us, and herewith return you the Amended Bill, with our suggested modifications interlined. We desire to submit some of our reasons for the proposed changes, and classify them under the headings of the Amended Bill. Section 1. We have added the Professors and Corps of Cadets as a part of the Army of the U. S. lest its mission might operate to exclude it from the Rules for the Governmt of the Army. Section 3. We judge that the same financial result will be attained, and a better Military system be reached by dismounting one Battalion (⅓) of each Regt. of Cavalry, rather than one third of the number of Regiments. This dismounted Battalion will be most useful to hold some Military Post where it could be prepared to recruit the active Battalions and at the same time could guard the Regimental stores, spare horses and equipments. Section 4. The only essential change proposed is to omit the Veteran Reserves altogether. In any army no matter what pains be taken in selecting recruits, when we come to put them in service, experience teaches that nearly 30 per cent fail by reason of the ordinary imperfections of human nature. Now if eight Regts of the 55, be taken from invalids or men of impaired strength we add 15 per cent, or in all 45 per cent of invalids which is too large a proportion. In the end it is cheaper to provide directly by way of pensions to this class of Soldiers. If officers of the Veteran

Reserves have a good record, and rank—and health they can be appointed just as other officers of the Volunteer Army. Section 7. The additions explain themselves. Section 9. Fifty privates make a small company, and when that is the lawful limit, the recruits at the General Rendezvous have to be deducted lest the Grand total should exceed the lawful limit. By giving a small margin, the companies on distant service can be full, and yet~~t~~ recruiting be continued within the 'margin' hereby proposed. Section 9. Some of the Volunteer Generals have earned a just fame, & claim to serve the Country in their new profession. This addition will enable the President to reward the most meritorious for a few years, without a serious increase of the Military establishmt. This seems only a just recognition of past services, and in after years may be an example to encourage other Citizens to aim at Military fame. Section 10. We have added a few of the lowest grade, to enable the President to reward some young assistnt Adjt Generals who have attained great proficiency in their special branch of Military business. Section 18. We have added a few to the Grades of surgeon & assistant surgeon to approximate the request of the Surgeon General, but do not deem a very large increase necessary, because the Country can at short notice, in case of War give us an unlimited number of skilled surgeons. Section 25. We omit altogether, as the Chief Engineer can accomplish the small reduction herein contemplated without a law, and we have in a subsequent clause drawn details for special duty for this Battalion. Section 27. Some of us think the Signal Corps, might be omitted altogether in time of Peace ~~devolving~~ imposing its duties on the engineer corps, but have agreed to submit the bill with the single limitation of the number of officers & men to be used for the Corps. We design to prevent details from Line officers & soldiers as much as possible as such details disturb very much the efficiency of 'Companies in the Field' *General.* All other changes suggested are merely in the distribution of Rank in the Staff Corps without any material increase of aggregate numbers. We object to increase the Rank of the Quarter Master General, and Surgeon General, unless the Rank of the Chief Engineer, Chief of Ordnance, and Commissary General are also increased which seems not to be asked for. It ~~may be~~ is a fair ~~subject~~ question for Congress to ~~determine such a question~~ act upon, but ~~as the Scale of~~ to secure the economy aimed at by this Bill we prefer to suggest no alteration in this regard in the Amended Bill herewith. . . . Sect—8 and that recruits may be collected at the General Rendezvous in ~~excess of~~ addition to the number required to fill the Regimts and Companies herein provided for, provided the number does not exceed in the aggregate three thousand men." ADf (in Sherman's hand), DLC-William T. Sherman.

Also on Feb. 1, USG wrote to Wilson. "Enclosed herewith I have the honor of returning to you Senate Bill, No. 108, with the changes suggested by Gen's Sherman, Meade & Thomas. I concur with the views expressed by them and respectfully submit them for the consideration of Congress." Copies, DLC-USG, V, 47, 109; DNA, RG 108, Letters Sent. On the same day, Meade, Sherman, and Thomas wrote to Rawlins. "In accordance with the instructions of the Lt. Genl Comdg we have carefully examined Senate Bill No 108 and have now the honor to return it, with such modifications as in our judgements it requires; and to submit herewith our reasons for the same. Enacting clause—The change proposed is for the purpose of including the sons of a large class of individuals who have not heretofore ~~not~~ had this privilege—As in a few years the class composed of the sons of those who have fallen in this war will be exhausted, the law if amended as we propose will then provide for the sons of worthy public servants, who from the nature of their duties, being without permanent domicils are without congressional representation—In Section 2d—The changes in paragraphs 1—2 & 3 of this section are predicated on our fears that a construction might be put on the terms of the bill, such as would establish too high a standard of knowledge & virtually exclude the sons of poor parents or of those so situated as to be unable to give their sons the education required Sec. 4—This addition is made on our firm conviction that opening the superintendency to the whole army ~~will add greatly to the facility for selection~~ will not only remove difficulties heretofore encountered in finding suitable superintendants, but that it will tend materially to improve the tone & spirit of the Academy & corps of cadets." ADf (incomplete—in Meade's hand), DLC-William T. Sherman.

On Feb. 2, USG wrote to Wilson. "Enclosed herewith I have the honor of returning to you 'Senate Bill' No 111 with the changes suggested by Gens. Sherman, Meade and Thomas, with their reasons, briefly stated, therefor. I think the bill, with the suggested changes, probably as good as can be devised well to start on leaving changes to be made hereafter if the system does not work well." ALS, deCoppet Collection, NjP. On Feb. 1, Meade, Sherman, and Thomas had written to Rawlins. "At the request of Lieutenant General Grant, commanding the armies of the United States, we have this day examined carefully Senate Bill No. 111—'To provide for the national defence by establishing a uniform militia and organizing an active volunteer militia force thro'out the United States,' and herewith return the same to you with such modifications as our judgment suggests. *Section 3.*—We would not leave the States to exempt any class of her citizens from enrolment or militia duty. Any State could defeat the whole object of the Bill by unreasonable exemptions, or make confusion by special legislation. We leave the whole matter where we think it belongs: the National Congress. *Section 4.*—We strike out the words 'common drunkard' and 'vagabond' lest these words might also in case of alarm or danger get too broad a meaning. *Section 5.*—We make the adjutant general's department of the militia a part of the Adjt. General's Department of the Regular Army, to ensure uniformity and to obviate special and separate bureaus, too likely to become independent, if not antagonistic. *Section 6.*—The same reasons as for Section 5 influence us to keep the active volunteer militia plainly and openly subject to the same general command as the Regular Army, and we feel certain that the militia will feel impressed with their importance by being thus classified and governed by the same general system, and by the same Commander-in-Chief as the Regular Army. *Section 8.*—An inspection herein is provided for both by the Governors of the States and an Inspector General of the Regular Army, by which alone uniformity can be secured. *Section 10.*—When a district is represented in the Congress of the United States it is inferred the inhabitants are loyal enough to be entrusted with arms, &c *Section 15.*—Having in Section 10 provided that regiments of the active volunteer militia shall alone be raised in Congressional Districts represented in the National Congress, we think retrospective oaths must be omitted, for otherwise we could not expect any militia could be raised, so large a portion, if not all subjects being cut off by the retrospective part of the oath. The oath prescribed for future loyal conduct covers the whole case. *Section 20.—New*—If the Commanding General of the Army has the lawful power to inspect the offices of the Adjutants Generals of States and of the militia provided for by this Bill he can bring his influence and authority to bear on the militia. Without this power there is danger that this system like those which have gone before will fall into disuse, if not worse. With this power of inspection and control through the Adjutant General of the Militia, he can make this volunteer army a most valuable auxiliary to the Regular Army in case of apprehended invasion, insurrection or general disturbance of the peace in any quarter of the country." LS, DNA, RG 46, Senate 39A–B2, Senate Bills Acted Upon.

To Capt. Theodore J. Eckerson

Washington D. C. Feb.y 6th *1866*

DEAR CAPT.

Although I have received the letters which you have written to me, and attended to your request, I have not heretofore answered any of them. I believe it was on my endorsement that your appointment in the regular Army was given. I now write to congratulate you and to express the wish that you and yours may prosper through life.

We have no special news at this Capital except such as is derived from the Action of Congress which is all spread before the public, daily, through the Columns of the public press. Having just imerged from a great rebellion of course all that is said and done by them is listened to with great interest by the entire public, loyal and disloyal. One or the other borrow comfort as they think the measures proposed are calculated to unite more firmly or estrange those who have supported the Government, and our Armies, during the rebellion. I am glad to say that our representatives from the far off Pacific Coast, so far as I have observed their course, have done nothing to give comfort to aiders in rebellion. Particularly is this the case with Nesmith[1] of Oregon with whom I have more personal acquaintance than the others and have therefore watched closer. He has been the particular friend of the Army, both regular and volunteer, and has, if I am not mistaken, sustained every measure intended to overthrow rebellion and sustain the

Union of all the states. Oregonians may congratulate themselves on having in the National councils such a representative.

The few of your acquaintances on the Pacific Coast who are here are all well.

Yours Truly
U. S. Grant

Capt. Theo. J. Eckerson
Asst. Q. M. U. S. A.

ALS, OrHi. See *PUSG*, 14, 208–9; letter to Brig. Gen. Rufus Ingalls, Feb. 7, 1866.

1. James W. Nesmith, born in 1820 in New Brunswick, Canada, of American parents, moved to Oregon Territory in 1843 and became a lawyer. He supported Stephen A. Douglas in 1860 and was elected to the U.S. Senate. For his friendship with USG, see Horace Porter, *Campaigning with Grant* (New York, 1897), pp. 354–59. An undated note from USG to Nesmith may date from the unsuccessful effort to assist in his reelection. "Please read the enclosed and if you think it necessary seal it up and deliver as addressed." ANS, OrHi.

To Henry Wilson

Washington, D. C. Feb.y 6th *1866*

Hon. H. Wilson,
Ch. Mil. Committee,
U. S. Senate,
Sir:

On rereading "Senate Bill" No 67 the following changes suggest themselves; towit:

Sec 2 should give each Regt. of Artillery 2 Princial Musicians & One Reg.l Hospital Stewar~~t~~d.

Sec. 3d should give each Regiment of Cavalry One Hospital Stewar~~t~~d only instead of two.

Sec. 6 Should give each Regt. of Infantry Two Principal Musicians, One Hospital Stewar~~t~~d and each Company two Artificers.

Each Regt. of Artillery, Cavalry and Infantry should have three additional 1st Lieutenants for the places of Adjt. Regl. Qr. Mr. and Regl. Com.y.

Sec. 9 Add next after 10 Brigadier Generals the words "exclusive of Chiefs of Permanent Bureaus, ~~or~~ Corps or Chief of Staff to the Gen. in Chief.

Sec. 12 to be clear might abolish the office of Judge Advocate ~~Gn~~ with the rank of Bvt. Major authorized by Sec. 4 Act approved 2d of March 1849.

If Sec. 11 becomes law the Act approved 6th of August 1862, Chapt. 58 should be repealed as the Two additional Inspector Gens were appointed under the Act approved 6th of Aug./61 Chapt. 57, Statutes at large. ~~Both Acts~~

As stated in my letter of yesterday I would be pleased if some provision could be made in the reorganization of the Staff Corps of the Army by which more rank could be given to officers of the Staff Corps of the Army who have rendered conspicuous and meritorious service during the War. I have no specific recommendations to make on the subject but would respectfully refer to the views expressed by the Chiefs, and other officers, of those Corps on the subject. Having furnished all these, so far as they have been entrusted to me, to the House Committee on Mil. Affairs I have no copy of them to submit with this.

I have the honor to be
Very respectfully
your obt. svt.
U. S. GRANT
Lt. Gn.

ALS, James S. Schoff, New York, N. Y. See letters to Henry Wilson, Jan. 12, Feb. 5, 1866.

On Feb. 7, 1866, Governor William R. Marshall of Minn. wrote to U.S. Senator Alexander Ramsey of Minn. concerning the use of Indians as scouts. ALS, DNA, RG 108, Letters Received. Enclosures are *ibid.* Ramsey endorsed these papers to USG. AES (undated), *ibid.* On Feb. 23, Maj. Gen. William T. Sherman, St. Louis, wrote to Bvt. Col. Theodore S. Bowers. "I have before me the letter of Govr Marshall of Minnesota of Feb 7, endorsed by the Hon Alex Ramsey, covering the paper of J. R. Brown, Adjt Gen Van Cleve and Genl J M Corse, all of which are herewith returned to enable the Lt Genl to suggest such Congressional action as he may deem necessary. These papers go to show that a small force of scouts, acting in connection with the fixed Military Posts, but subject only to the control of the District Commander, would contribute much to the defense of the Frontier against the Small and roving bands of hostile Indians. I concur fully in this and go further that such a system could be made to fulfil another purpose, of making one part of the Indian tribes hold in subjection the other. I think the proper checks in the expenses of such a system could easily be devised, and that all the legislation of Congress necessary, would be the insertion in the Present Army Bill of a Clause to the effect that the President might employ in the Territories and Indian Country Scouts and Indian Allies, not to exceed in number at any one time say 1000, who should mount and equip themselves, and receive in lieu of all compensation whatsoever, not to exceed the pay clothing allowance, and horse hire of a Cavalry soldier, say —— Dollars a month, with a Capt and Lieut to every 50 men. These could be raised, and be paid without attempting exact periods of enlistment, and discharged at the discretion of the District or Dept Commander. All officers who have served on the frontier know that our Common Infantry soldiers can only secure the safety of fixed Posts, and that our Regular Cavalry is ruined by being scattered in small squads, but parcels of scouts acting in concert with the Regular Posts, and with squadrons of Cavalry can be of infinite service. The system would be applicable not to Minnesota alone, but to New Mexico, Montana Colorado, and indeed where ever the Mongrel race of Indians, Mexicans and trappers abound." ALS, *ibid.* On March 2, USG endorsed this letter. "Respectfully forwarded to the Hon. Secretary of War, attention being invited to the views of Gen. Sherman respecting the insertion in the present Army Bill of a clause empowering the President at his discretion to employ in the Territories and Indian Country scouts and Indian allies to meet exigencies, said scouts and allies to be discharged whenever the necessity for their employment has abated, or at the discretion of the Department Commander." ES, *ibid.* See letter to Edwin M. Stanton, Aug. 1, 1866.

To Brig. Gen. Rufus Ingalls

Washington D C Feb. 7th *1866*

DEAR INGALLS,

My office was crowded yesterday up until I left it so that I had no chance to write the letter you requested. This morning however I have written the enclosed to Eckerson who I know instead of to Ainsworth[1] who I do not know. It would really look like taking sides in politics to write to a stranger on such a subject. That I want to avoid and would like at the same time to help Nesmith if what I can say will do it. I hope sincerely that he will be returned to the U. S. Senate for another six years because he has been a good friend to the Country without runing wild after matters that can neither benefit it or those intended to be benefited.

If the letter which I have written does not answer send it back with suggestions.

Yours &c.
U. S. GRANT

ALS (facsimile), Frank A. Burr, *Life and Deeds of General Ulysses S. Grant, . . .* (Philadelphia, 1885), pp. 849–50. See letter to Capt. Theodore J. Eckerson, Feb. 6, 1866.

1. Probably John C. Ainsworth, president, Oregon Steam Navigation Co., which monopolized all commercial shipping on the Columbia River.

To Edwin M. Stanton

Washington Feby 8th 1866.

HON. E. M. STANTON
SEC. OF WAR.
SIR:

I have the honor to request that the Ordnance Department be directed to prepare five thousand sets of Infantry Accoutrements, and that the Quartermasters Department be directed to prepare five thousand knapsacks, haversacks and canteens, according to the plan proposed by Mr. Oliver E. Woods, and that three thousand of each of the above be sent to Maj. Gen. W. T. Sherman, one thousand to Maj. Gen. G. H. Thomas, and one thousand to Maj. Gen. P. H. Sheridan in order that their merits may be thoroughly tested by actual service in the field.—Mr. Woods improvement was passed upon by a board of officers, of which Gen Rucker was President, who reported favorable upon it. It has recently received the favorable opinion of Gens. Sherman, & Thomas and Meade, after careful examination.

As Mr. Wood proposes to adapt his improvement to the accoutrements now in use, the expense will not be great, and I think the trial should be made.

U. S. GRANT
Lieut. Gen'l

Copies, DLC-USG, V, 47, 109; DNA, RG 108, Letters Sent. On May 24, 1866, Oliver E. Woods wrote a letter received at USG's hd. qrs. concerning the manufacture of his inf. accoutrements. *Ibid.*, Register of Letters Received. On Jan. 29, 1867, Woods, Philadelphia, wrote to USG. "I have the honor to report that on Nov 1st 1866, I proceeded to the Department of Tennessee, to instruct the troops in the use of my accoutrements. Through an error in the requisitions, the troops at Nashville were provided with but one half the equipment. I therefore proceeded to Louisville, and found the troops there, properly equipped. I remained there four days, instructing them. I also took in an ambulance, about a dozen sets over to Jeffersonville, to show to the Officers and Men, the operation of the accoutrement, none having been issued to those men. On my return to Louisville, I addressed a communication, to the Secretary of War, asking that the transportation furnished me, should be changed to commutation, expressing a willingness to have the whole cost to the Goverment deducted from whatever compensation, I might ultimately receive for my invention. My reason for this proposed change—was that the error in the equipment at Nashville, would add largely to my expenses, if I was expected to return there to instruct the men. I shewed the above letter to Gen. Thomas, and it was returned to me, with his endorsement to the Sect of War, for a favorable consideration. I then proceeded to the Military Division of Missouri. I found that owing to the very late period Gen. Sherman received the equipments from the Quatermaster's Department, he had determined to issue none of the equipments untill Spring. Gen. Sherman being absent from St Louis, after consultation with the Chief Officers of the Staff, it was determined to send Fifty Sets up to Fort Leavenworth. I proceeded there with the Fifty Sets, which were issued to Comp. C.—Regiment, Brev. Lieut. Col. Moale Commanding. I instructed the men, and after they were well instructed a Board of Officers was convened, before whom the troops appeared, and the Board made a report of their observation of the marching of the men, and of other matters that appeared of interest to the Board. On my return to St Louis, I addressed a note to Adj. Gen. Nichols, requesting that Searg. Frederick Theis of Comp. C. be detailed to instruct troops in the use of this accoutrement. In St Louis, I received a communication from the Quatermasters Department, to which it appears, my letter to the Secretary of War had been referred, adverse to my proposition. I thereupon requested that the Quatermasters Department would so change the Transportation Order already given me, as to enable the Quatermaster at New Orleans, to give me return transportation to Gen. Thomas' Headquarters, and the Quatermaster of Gen. Thomas' Division to give me transportation to Philadelphia. This was necessary to enable me to instruct the troops at Nashville. My letter was dated Dec. 20th, and requested that the necessary authority would be in New Orleans, no later than the first week of the present year. I proceeded to New Orleans, and instructed the troops of the 1st Regiment to whom my equipments had been issued. Before I left the City, I exhibited the operation of my accoutrements to Gen. Sheridan his Chief of Staff and some other Officers. After waiting untill the tenth of January, and no word from the Quatermasters' Department changing my transportation, being received, I started with transportation direct, by way of Chattanooga for Philadelphia. At Decatur Alabama, I left the route and paid my way to Nashville arriving Jan. 12th, and found the troops since my former visit, had received full equipments. On Saturday afternoon I went out to the Barracks, and notified the Officer Commanding Post, that on the next morning, Sunday, I would be there to drill, and desired a general attendance of Officers and men. The next morning I went to the Barracks, and explained to the Officers and men, the properties of my accoutrement. This closed my tour of instruction, and that evening I proceeded to Philadelphia. At Nashville I was very ill, but with stimulants furnished by the Officers, I was enabled to go through the drill, my state of health warning me to hurry as fast as possible to Philadelphia. This report would have been furnished earlier, but for my continued indisposition. I respectfully request, if admissable, that copies of the reports from the Departments of Generals Sherman, Thomas, and Sheridan, in relation to the operation of my accoutrements, that have been sent to the Headquarters of the Army, be furnished me" LS, *ibid.*, Letters Received. On Feb. 18, Woods wrote to USG. "I would respectfully direct your attention to the following extract from a letter addressed by me to the Actg. Assist. Scty of War in March *1866* the original of which is on file in the War Department. 'Philadelphia March 13th 1866 BG. GENL. THOS. T. ECKERT. ACTG. ASSIST. SCTY OF WAR. GENERAL, With the view to remove as far as lies in my power all obstacles to the completion of the order made by the Scty. of War to fulfill the requisition made by the Lieut. General for five thousand (5000) setts of Equipage and accoutrements adapted to the plan of Oliver E. Woods I have made the matter of compensation for my invention wholly dependent on the operation of the invention itself. I take the ground that if my accoutrement lacks merit that then its projector is undeserving of any compensation at all, and if on the other hand it proves to have merit that then its degree of merit conjointly with the royalties directly or indirectly paid by the U. S. to other inventors will serve to grade my compensation' The foregoing proposition in regard to the five thousand setts was made by me in order to satisfy the Hon. Scty. of War that I did not wish payment for my accoutrements unless they were deserving. Reports of the operation of my equipments have probably by this time reached the Head Quarters of the Army from the several Military Departments to which the accoutrements have been issued. A perusal of those reports will enable you to determine the general opinion of the equipment entertained by Officers of the Army who have seen service in the *field.* I propose when my health permits to visit Washington and request from the War Department compensation for the five thousand setts of accoutrements now in use. The Hon. Sectry of War will doubtless require the opinion of Genl. Grant, Circustances may cause your absence from Washington at the period I am able to get there, therefore I respectfully solicit that if after an examination of the reports in regard to the equipment you will feel justified in recommending that compensation be given me for those now in use, that you will make an endorsement of that nature on *this* letter, so that the letter can be produced if in your absence from Washington the Secty of War should require your opinion." ALS, *ibid.*, RG 156, Correspondence Concerning Experiments. On June 24, Woods wrote to Maj. George K. Leet concerning adverse reports on his accoutrements. ALS, *ibid.*, RG 108, Letters Received.

To Andrew Johnson

Washington, D. C. Feb. 9th *1866*

His Excellency, A. Johnson,
President of the U. States;
Sir:

I would respectfully recommend the extension of full Amnesty to P. D. Roddey, late a General in the Southern Army. Gen. Roddey has high testimonials from radically loyal men of Alabama for his humanity and kindness to the families of Union refugees whilst the War was in progress. I will also add that whilst I commanded in the West, and when Gen. Roddey was in command of troops about Decatur, I was told that his course towards Union families within his lines, the heads of many of them within our lines and some actually serving in our Army, was most kind and courteous.

Hoping that Amnesty will be granted in this case, I subscribe myself,

Very respectfully
your obt. svt.
U. S. Grant
Lt. Gn.

ALS, DNA, RG 94, Amnesty Papers, Ala. Docketing indicates that Philip D. Roddey received a pardon as of Feb. 17, 1866. AN, *ibid.*

To Andrew Johnson

Washington, D. C., Feby. 9th *1866*

To His Ex. Andrew Johnson
President of the United States

Sir: Referring to the Resolutions of the Legislature of Mississippi requesting the withdrawal of Federal troops from that State, &c., referred by yourself to me, I have the honor to remark that the condition of things in the State of Mississippi, does not warrant the belief that the civil authorities of that State "*are amply sufficient*" to execute the laws and good order. When however the civil authorities prove themselves amply sufficient to fairly and justly execute the laws among all her citizens and to perpetuate their loyalty, the troops will not be permitted to interfere in civil matters.

No action is deemed necessary upon the affidavits submitted.

Very Respectfully
Your Ob't Servant
[U. S. GRANT]
Lieutenant General.

Copy (unsigned), DNA, RG 108, Letters Received. This letter may not have been sent. On Nov. 8, 1865, the Miss. legislature addressed a resolution to President Andrew Johnson requesting withdrawal of U.S. troops from Miss. and complaining about the behavior of Negro troops; on Dec. 22, Johnson endorsed the resolution to USG. Goodspeed's Catalogue 510, April 10, 1963.

On Nov. 11, Maj. Gen. Peter J. Osterhaus, Vicksburg, wrote to Brig. Gen. John A. Rawlins. "I have the honor to enclose a letter from the Governor of Mississippi making a request for arms for the militia generally now organizing in this State and Specially for a Section of Artillery for Captain (late General) Martin at Natchez. I informed the Governor in reply that I had no authority to order the issue of any arms to him but that I would forward his communication to the Lieut General Commanding the Armies of the U S. An early decision would be very desireable as Similar demands are likely to be repeated in the immediate future. Companies of Militia are forming every where, here in Vicksburg alone three are organizing (the Sharpshooters, Cadets, and 'Jeff Davis' Guards) and from the Country I learn Similar movements. The cause of this extraordinary military Spirit coming over the people is the passage of the new Volunteer Bill by the legislature and, principally the fear of a negro insurrection General Martins letter (enclosed in Governor Humphrey communication) gives his reasons in full for apprehending an 'emeute.' True enough they are only generalities but the fear of an emeute Seems to be universal, even though the constant vigilance of all military officers under the Command of Major Generals Davidson, Force, and myself and of the Asst Commissioner of Freedmen Col Samuel Thomas have failed to find a trace of the great conspiracy, and although the Argus eyes of the very nervous civil authorities could find no cause to arrest a Single negro or gain any information as to the persons and objects Connected with the dreaded insurrection The only plausible proof of existing differences between the colored people and the citizens of Mississippi consists in the undeniable fact that a great number of murders are committed in almost every portion of the State where there are negroes, but in every case the latter class have been the victims and the Whites the aggressors, with hardly an instance in which the offender was arrested by the civil authorities. It is altogether a very mysterious affair. For information I enclose a copy of the Volunteer act; the revised code of 1857 therein referred to has no particular feature worth mentioning here except that the oath required of the militia does not bind them to Support the Constitution of the United States—Awaiting your instructions . . ." ALS, DNA, RG 108, Letters Received. See *ibid.*, RG 94, Letters Received, 770P 1865.

On Feb. 28, 1866, USG endorsed papers requesting arms for Miss. penitentiary guards. "Respectfully submitted to the Secretary of War. As a general rule I am not in favor of issuing arms to states occupied by U. S. forces. But in consideration of the small number of arms required—(25 muskets & 3. Revolvers—with 1000 cartridges for the former and 300 for the latter,) of the object for which they are required—(for the guard to the Penitentiary—) and of the recommendation of the Department commander, I recommend the issue in this case." ES, *ibid.*, 219A 1866.

On Dec. 30, 1865, Governor Robert M. Patton of Ala. wrote to Maj. Gen. George H. Thomas. "Preparatory to the withdrawal of the Federal Troops from the State of Alabama we have organized One Hundred and four Companies of local or State Malitia, Say an average of Two Companies to each County in the State, the Companies Contanig Sixty Men each in all 6440 Men In order that this organization May be effective in Mantaining order and Cival Law, I very respectfully appeal to the Federal Government to Aid the State by furnishing the Arms and Ammunition Necessary to equip Said Companies, To Wit. 6440 Stand of Arms, and Two Hundred rounds of Catrage to each Gun It gives me pleasure to pledge the Executive department and people of Alabama that these Arms and Ammunition shall be faithfully used Sustaining the laws, and Constitution of the State of Alabama and of the Federal Union" ALS, *ibid.*, RG 107, Letters Received from Bureaus. On Jan. 1, 1866, Thomas endorsed this letter. "Respectfully forwardd for the consideration and orders of Lt Genl Grant Governor Patton having pledged the Executive and people of Alabama that these arms shall be used solely for the maintenance of equal justice to all classes in the state and to sustain the authority of the United States, this Requisition meets my approval and I further recomend the withdrawal of the troops from the interior of the state as soon as there can be a perfect understanding between the Freedmans Bureau and the Civil authorities as to the civil rights and duties of the Freedman." AES, *ibid.* On Jan. 9, USG endorsed this letter. "For the present, and until there is full security for equitably maintaining the right[s] and safety of all classes of citizens in the states lately in rebellion, I would not recommend the withdrawel of United States Troops from them. The number of interior garrisons might be reduced but a movable force sufficient to insure tranquility should be retained Whilst such a force is retained in the South I doubt the propriety of putting Arms in the hands of the Militia." AES, *ibid.*

To Bvt. Maj. Gen. Montgomery C. Meigs

Washington, D. C. Feb.y 10th *1866*

I have examined Dr. Alex. Dunbars method of treating diseases of the hoof in horses, and the practical method devised by him of preventing such diseases by proper shaving, and am satisfied that the information if imparted to Army Farriers would save to the goverment thousands of dollars annually. More horses become usless from diseases of the hoof probably than from old age and all other diseases combined though in ignorance in the majority of cases the disability may be attributed by Veternary Surgeons to other Causes.

I think his information on this subject well worth procuring for the use of Govt.

U. S. GRANT
Lt. Gn.

TO MAJ. GN. M. C. MEIGS
Q. M. GN.

ALS, DNA, RG 92, Supplies and Purchases, Public Animals, Letters Received. On Feb. 23, 1866, Bvt. Maj. Gen. Montgomery C. Meigs wrote to USG. "*unofficial* . . . Mr Alexander Dunbar who seems to me to have great knowledge of the horse's foot and who long since shewed me a variety of interesting anatomical preparations of diseased feet and claimed great skill and success in treating lameness of the foot, has presented to me your letter which shows that he made upon you the same impression as to his ~~skill~~ knowledge as upon myself. Though I do not think that the Quarter Master's Department has any legal authority to purchase such a secret and found it impracticable when he came here in the year 1864 to make any arrangement with him, I directed on his again appearing that he be requested to state in writing his terms and the mode in which he proposed to make his knowledge available. He asks One Hundred Thousand ($100.000 00) Dollars for which he offers to teach a number of Officers or Veterinary Surgeons his methods—requiring from each person instructed an oath to keep the secret for Ten (10) years. I have no authority to make any such arrangement and have so informed him. If he has a greater knowledge than others and has made any valuable discovery or invention he can secure it by patents. If he prefers to keep his secret or to make sale of it he will find the only practicable method to be to advertise, as quacks do, his superior skill and teach individuals or treat diseased horses for such fees as he can collect. This Department would not be authorized to buy his teaching even for the whole country at One Hundred Thousand Dollars or at any sum and Congress will never pass a law purchasing it. His skill and knowledge are not of a kind to be thus sold. If he will print a book and copy-right it, he can, if the secret be as valuable as he thinks it, make money by sale of the copy-right. His personal skill and experience, if established by success, would give him always an advantage in the practice of his business and the sale of his book would bring him all that the book may be worth. With this he is not satisfied but asks the Government to give him One Hundred Thousand dollars on the promise to teach a few persons how to treat certain diseases. I enclose a copy of the letter of this Office to Mr Dunbar declining his proposition." LS, *ibid.*, RG 108, Letters Received.

Probably on March 15, Charles Knapp wrote to USG. "Mr. Dunbar has operated on one of my carriage horses with great success. I think Mr. Dunbar entitled to much consideration, and would be glad to have you exercise your influence in his favor." Dated March 15, 1871, but addressed to USG as lt. gen., suggesting a date of 1866, in Alexander Dunbar, *A Treatise on the Diseases Incident to the Horse*, . . . (Wilmington, Del., 1871), p. 232. On Nov. 23, 1866, USG wrote to Dunbar. "Explaination of your system of treating the feet of horses satisfies me not only that it is the best treatment yet devised but that almost all complaints, leading to lameness of the horse, though apparently in the knee, hip, shoulder or elswhere, really exists in the foot. I have had your treatment applied, with advantage to four very valuable horses of my own and have witnessed the effect of your treatment on some of the most valuable horses in the United States.—I do not hesitate to recommend your treatment to all persons having large numbers of horses, or a few very valuable, as well worthy of their attention." ALS (facsimile), *ibid.*, between pp. 124–25.

On March 11, 1867, USG wrote to an unknown addressee. "Dr. [D]un[ba]r gave me on Saturday the pedigree of John Clay's Horse [which] he told me was at your place, and also delivered the message if you will send me directions where to direct the mares to be sent. I will send a groom with the mares who can return as soon as they are delivered." ANS (damaged), Stauffer Collection, NN. On March 17, George Wilkes, New York City, wrote to USG. "Several of the friends of Mr. Dunbar who is now in Washington, in consideration of his secret in relation to the horse's foot, learning that the matter has been referred to you, have solicited an expression from me on the subject. In compliance with that request, and in concession of what I believe to be the merits of the matter, I have no hesitation in saying that Mr. Dunbar is the only man I ever saw or heard of, who thoroughly understands the horse's foot. All the professors and authors who have written on the subject are mere theorists, and in my opinion never could have investigated the subject practically. Their systems tend to lame horses; and that is the reason we have so many cripples all over the country. A few years ago, not more than ten or fifteen, all practical printers, machinists and printing-press manufacturers were of the opinion, that we never could make a printing-press to 'throw off' more than three or four thousand copies an hour; but Hoe came along with his rotary machine, and startled all the machinists by demonstrating its capacity to take 20.000 impressions of a given surface within the hour. Dunbar, in my opinion, is just as far ahead of all the Veterinary professors and surgeons as Hoe was of the old machinists, and further too, because the practice of the old veterinary surgeons tends to lame horses, while the old printing men were right as far as they went, only they were slow. I am impressed with the belief that the government ought to purchase the right to use the system at once, and they would purchase it, if they knew half as much of its advantages as two or three of our most experienced horsemen in this city." Dunbar, *Treatise*, pp. 112–13.

On March 18, Bvt. Maj. Gen. Daniel H. Rucker wrote to USG. "I have the honor to acknowledge the receipt of your letter of the 7th instant, asking an endorsement relative to the manner of treating 'Horses Feet,' as proposed by Doctor Alexander Dunbar. I have fully examined Doctor Dunbar's method of treatment as explained by him, and believe there is much merit in his system, and that it would be greatly to the interest of the Government to avail itself of his knowledge for the purpose of instructing such officers and employés as may be in charge of public animals. While thus acknowledging the merit of Dr. Dunbar's method of treatment, I cannot recommend that he should receive the excessive compensation asked for by him, viz: One hundred thousand dollars, and I cannot imagine that such was the intention of the Act of Congress authorizing his employment. The views of Genl. M. C. Meigs, Quartermaster General, in his report of November 26, 1866, to the Secretary of War, are concurred in. I would state, however, as an addition to this, that in my opinion the matter could be more fully tested by employing Dr. Dunbar under contract for a term of years at a stipulated remunerative salary, say three hundred dollars per month. That he be ordered on duty at one of the principal depots near the seat of active operations, where disabled horses are most likely to accumulate. I would respectfully suggest Fort Leavenworth as a suitable point, possessing already the necessary buildings and appliances. Dr. Dunbar could establish there a school of instruction for the education of the Army Farriers and such other persons ~~as~~ as it would be thought advisable to order there for that purpose." LS, DNA, RG 92, Miscellaneous Letters Sent (Press). On March 27 (possibly March 7, the letter answered above), USG wrote to Meigs. "Dr. Dunbar, who has spent the Winter here in the hope of having his method of treating the *horses foot* adopted by the Govern[me]nt, under the resolution of Congress authorizing the Sec. of War to appropriate money for that purpose, has met with no success so far. My own opinion is that this method has so much merit in it as to make it a matter of National importance, not that the government alone should be in possession of it, but that it become generally taught, so that wherever the horse is used the benefit of this treatment may be applied in case of need. How to secure this becomes the question! I would myself favor the establishment of a Veterinary College, under the patronage of government, where Army farriers could be taught, free, the whole secret and treatment, leaving the question of compensation to be made by outside persons wishing instruction in it, to be settled by the discoverer. It is not to be expected that any such measure as this will be adopted under present authority given to the Sec. of War, but if you feel the interest in this matter that I do, and can make any suggestion how to get this treatment adopted, either under present authority, or by asking further legislation, I will be obliged to you. . . ." Paul C. Richards, Catalogue 179 [1984], item 490. On June 29, USG wrote to Secretary of War Edwin M. Stanton. "Having been asked to state specifically whether I regard the secret possessed by Dr. A. Dunbar, for treating the 'Horses Foot' as worth to Government the amount asked by him towit: One-hundred Thousand Dollars I will say that taking a great interest in the horse I have examined his system closely and believe it of the greatest importance to the Country that his information should be diffused speedily. The amount asked bears no proportion to the Anual benefit which would follow an intelligent application of his treatment. The only question in my opinion should be as to the best method of introducing the information possessed by Dr. Dunbar." Copies, DLC-USG, V, 47, 60; DNA, RG 108, Letters Sent.

On July 17, 1868, Dunbar, New York City, wrote to Maj. and Bvt. Col. George W. Schofield, 41st Inf., asst. to Secretary of War John M. Schofield, accepting a one-year contract for $25,000 to teach his system. ALS, *ibid.*, RG 92, Consolidated Correspondence, Alexander Dunbar. On Sept. 8, 1869, USG wrote to Dunbar. "Learning that you are about visiting Europe for the purpose of introducing your system of treating the horse's foot, I take occasion to say that, before recommending its adoption in the United States service, I examined it clearly, and became thoroughly satisfied of its great value. Now after a year of trial under your instruction in the Army, I am satisfied that the system taught by you is destined to prove of inestimable value in prolonging the period of usefulness of the horse. I hope to see the knowledge which you possess, on this subject, generally diffused." Dunbar, *Treatise*, pp. 101–2. See *ibid.*, pp. 104–5, 114, 168, 172–73. On May 24, 1870, USG wrote to Secretary of War William W. Belknap. "The Sec. of War is authorized to settle with Dr. Alex. Dunbar for his services, beyond the year contracted for, at the same rate as he has already received for services. ~~w~~" ALS, DNA, RG 92, Consolidated Correspondence, Alexander Dunbar. On Feb. 23, 1871, Meigs wrote to Belknap. "I have the honor to return the letter addressed by Alexander Dunbar to the Presdident of the United States, dated 2d February Inst., and referred by the Secretary of War to the Quartermaster General for report. I seem to have fallen under the displeasure of Alex. Dunbar who, though his remarkable skill as a horse-shoer has gained him access to men of reputation and influence, seems willing to stop at nothing in his mad pursuit of money. Formerly, when seeking to impress me with the value of his skill, and to obtain my aid in his attempt to get from the United States $100,000 for a year's instruction of the Army Farriers, I could find no place sacred from his impudent and persevering intrusion. He intruded into my private quarters here, and having obtained a letter to me from Gen. Grant, speaking well of his system, he followed me when ill, to Philadelphia, and my physician informed me that it was with difficulty that he kept him out of my sick chamber. With great difficulty, from a sick bed, I wrote to the General a full statement of the reasons which appeared to me to have prevented his effecting a contract with Mr. Stanton. He has had the impudence even to ask me to change an official report—one made and forwarded—so as to enable him to get more money, for he is crazy with avarice, and now he plays Iago, and seeks to poison the mind of the President against one of his truest friends, who has stood with him under the Artillery of the enemy, and who has not been useless to him in the great operations which saved our country. He uses such language as, 'had you been controlled by Gen. Meigs', and other phrases as false and malignant, and as unjust. His cunning is of too low an order to do harm. It can, in any intelligent mind, create only disgust. His letter is rascally; but as it has been referred to me for report by such high authority I am obliged to report that I find it to be false, so far as it imputes to me any attempt or desire to set myself up against the will of my commander. . . ." Typescript, *ibid.* On Feb. 27, USG endorsed papers in the case. "If this Bill can be legally paid under any construction of law, I would like to have it paid." Copy, *ibid.* See letter to Robert C. Schenck, Jan. 12, 1867; *HED*, 40-3-63; *ibid.*, 41-2-302.

To Maj. Gen. William T. Sherman

Washington
Feb 10—1866:

To Maj Genl W. T. Sherman
St Louis Missouri
Sir

Captain B. R. Alden[1] and Mrs: Alden are intensely anxious for their son Robert's appointment as Cadet. Genl G. H. Thomas and myself have recommended it earnestly ~~to~~ and if you join us by letter and by telegraph to me—for the President, I think it will be granted.

Capt: Alden hesitated to apply for his son, because it might defeat the application of some soldiers son of the war—but Captain Aldens Oregon wound killed him for all military service. His sympathy for orphans and widows is well known. He has appropriated fifteen thousand dollars to widows and orphans of the war and has helped to raise $9000 for Genl: Charles F. Smiths family of Philadelphia and will continue all his life the friend and helper of widows of the army. This ought to interest the army for him.— His son will be 18 in March and this year is his only chance.

U. S. Grant
Lt. Gn.

LS (telegram sent), DNA, RG 94, Cadet Applications. On Feb. 11, 1866, Maj. Gen. William T. Sherman wrote to USG. "I received last night your telegram asking me to add my request to that of yourself and Thomas, for the President to appoint Capt Aldens son Robert a Cadet in the next Class for West Point. I answered by telegraph and now send you the letter to be used as you or Capt Alden may choose. If the Bill that we overhauled pass the present Congress, the President will have the appointmt annually of over 25, in order to keep the aggregate number of 75 full, and I hope it will pass for it will be in his power then to provide for the Sons of officers who have no chance of competition in the States. I got here yesterday at 1 P M & find things as quiet as a Country village. The River is clear of ice but the weather has been foul, and the ground is covered with snow—I find all my family well, and Mrs Sherman was delighted to learn from me how splendidly you were situated, and how Mrs Grant is able to realize all her fondest dreams. I have described as well as possible each room of your house, with its large yard and its surroundings. Mrs. Sherman used to be in Washington and comprehends perfectly the vast social labor that necessarily devolves on you & Mrs Grant. On my way out I spent two days at Detroit and Ord came with me as far as Chicago. I told him the substance of the Army Bills on which we had been engaged, and explained that he must look out for his own chances. The quicker we reduce all Military Establishmts in the Dept of the Ohio the better. All that is needed is the occupation of the permanent Posts on the Lakes. At present none are occupied but Fort Wayne near Detroit but Ord has a company of the 4th Infantry ready for Fort Brady as soon as the Lakes are navigable. It may be well for us to preserve a site for a Fort at the Outlet of Lake Huron, (Ft Gratiot) opposite a town in Canada, (Sarnia) from which a Railroad extends across Upper Canada. I will go on as soon as the lakes open and inspect the whole of that Frontier. At Detroit I saw many people who delighted in recalling anecdotes of you, when you were a Lt of the 4th Infy—especially of your drives along Fort Street with a certain pony. I wish you would present to Mrs Grant and the ladies of your family my best compliments and thanks for the many pleasant hours I spent under your roof at Washington, and I hope you will all live long to enjoy the fruits of your extraordinary but well merited position" ALS, USG 3. On July 6, 1865, Maj. Gen. George H. Thomas, Nashville, had telegraphed to Bvt. Brig. Gen. Edward D. Townsend requesting that President Andrew Johnson appoint Robert P. Alden to USMA. Telegram received (at 7:07 P.M.), DNA, RG 94, Cadet Applications. On Feb. 8, 1866, USG endorsed this telegram. "The Appointment of R. P. Alden to a Cadetship is earnestly recommended. The father of young Alden is an old Army officer of high character and worth. His services in the Army have been varied he having served on the frontier where he has been once wounded in maintaing order among the Indians. At various times he has served at West Point as Asst. Prof. Asst. Instructor of Tactics and as Comdt of Cades, &c. Every act and thought of his during the great rebellion the country has just emerged from has been in support of the Government and for the perpetuation of the Union. His charity to those who hav[e] been left destitute by the War has been great. Altogether I think he is of the class who should be specially favored in the distribution of these appointments, and I will feel gratified if this appointment can be given." AES, *ibid.* No appointment followed.

1. Bradford R. Alden, USMA 1831, resigned in 1853 after receiving a severe wound while fighting Indians in Ore. and later prospered drilling oil wells in Pa. On March 29, 1867, USG wrote to Governor Green Clay Smith of Montana Territory. "Capt. Alden . . . who was in the same regiment with me . . . has called on me in relation to J. R. Hodge, and son, of Montana, who are now in jail in the Charge of man slaughter. I know nothing of the case, but I can guarantee all that Capt. Alden may represent. His word . . . may be relied on . . ." Sotheby Parke Bernet, Elsie O. and Philip D. Sang Foundation sale, June 20, 1979, no. 698.

To Samuel H. Beckwith

HeadQuarters Armies of the U. S—
Washington D. C. Feb. 14 1866

S. H. BECKWITH
DEAR SIR:

Now that you are about leaving the service of the U. S., after more than four years of continuous duty, it affords me pleasure to bear testimony to the efficient manner in which you performed your duties

Enlisting early in the war as a private soldier, you were in 1862, if my memory serves me aright, detailed on special duty at my HdQrs as Telegraph Operator; Performing your duties faithfully you were discharged in 1863 as a soldier to take employment with the army as operator and were soon afterwards placed in over all other operators at HdQrs. Soon after the army cipher was entrusted to you: From that time to the close of the Rebellion no reason ever existed for ~~removing~~ releving you from the confidential position of Cipher Operator, thus entrusting to your knowledge every dispatch, order and information of such importance as to demand being communicated so that none should know of them but those for whom they were intended and hence you were continued in your position

Now that you leave the public service for private pursuits I wish you every success and in the position of Telegraph employee—any capacity—do not hesitate to recommend you.

Yours truly
U. S. GRANT
Lt Gen

Copy, DNA, RG 15, Pension Record SC-659-763; dated Feb. 19, 1866, in New York *Sun*, April 27, 1913. See *PUSG*, 10, 49*n*–50*n*; John Y. Simon and David L. Wilson, "Samuel H. Beckwith: 'Grant's Shadow,'" in *Ulysses S. Grant: Essays and Documents* (Carbondale and Edwardsville, 1981), pp. 77–139. On March 3, 1885, Samuel H. Beckwith, Utica, N. Y., wrote to Julia Dent Grant concerning USG's illness. ALS, USG 3.

To Charles W. Ford

Feb.y 14th 1866,

Dear Ford,

It has just occured to me that Judge Dent may have defered going south to commence planting for want of funds to take him. Under this supposition I wrote to him to-day if such is the case to call on you for $500 00 to be charged to me. If he calls please give him the money and draw on me at sight. I have purchased 86 acres of ground from him and by his direction I shall deposit the money with you to the credit of his wife. I hope this will not be troubling you too much! My family are all well and join me in regards for you.

Yours Truly
U. S. Grant

ALS, USG 3. See letter to Charles W. Ford, March 22, 1866.

To Andrew Johnson

Respectfully refered to His Excellency the President of the United States. The grandfather of this applicant was for many years the Professor of French at West Point. His son and grandson have grown up there and consequently have no Congressional representative to apply to for a Cadetship. If appointed therefore the appointment must be "at large."

U. S. Grant
Lt. Gn.

Washington D. C.
Feb.y 15th 1866.

AES, DNA, RG 94, Cadet Applications. Written on a letter of Feb. 5, 1866, from Blanche Berard, West Point, N. Y., to USG. "When I reflect upon the multitude of nearer and stronger claims upon your influence which you must needs have, I feel almost hopeless as to the success of this letter, and only write it because it seems to be my duty as well as my desire to do all that lies in my power to effect the object which it brings before you. I can but use this last means which seems pointed out to me, and leave the result with Him Who alone knows what is best to grant us of our heart's desires. We very much wish to obtain a cadets warrant for Claudius Berard, a lad of eighteen, of fair mental capacity, and of good honest principles. The only claims we can urge, are these. The boy is the grandson of the late Professor Claudius Berard, who after serving faithfully at the Military Academy for upwards of thirty years, literally died at his post, having been seized whilst in the Section room, with the attack which resulted, after a few hours of insensibility, in death. His last conscious words were those spoken to his section. The family have never received anything from Government, although the sons of every other Professor here, have either obtained, or have been offered commissions in the Army or the Navy. My brother is a poor and very hard-working man, with a family of seven children, and able to do little more than clothe and feed them. If, moved by these considerations, you should feel induced, (if, indeed, other and stronger claims do not prevent,) to obtain for Claude an appointment at the Academy, you may rest assured of the warmest gratitude on the part of the family. It occurs to me, dear Sir, that if, in justice to the appeals of others, you could not, however willing to do so, grant this request, perhaps you would kindly recommend the case to some other person of influence, who may have it in his power to obtain such a warrant and would do it for a worthy lad upon your recommendation. With sentiments of the highest esteem, praising God for the gifts He has bestowed upon you, and praying that He may evermore have you in His holy Keeping, . . ." ALS, *ibid.* No appointment followed.

To Henry Wilson

Washington D. C. Feby 15th 1866

HON. H. WILSON
CH. MIL. COMMITTEE
U. S. SENATE
SIR:

I have the honor of enclosing to you some papers referred to me on the subject of Legislation in behalf of "Military Storekeepers" of the Army. I have not been able to give the subject sufficient consideration to make any specific recommendation. The fact is however that some of the officers filling the position of Military Storekeepers have performed duties, particularly, during the war of great magnitude and pecuniary responsibility upon a salary less than is received by many clerks who have no responsibility. I believe something should be done for them

I have the honor to be
Very respectfully
Your obt. servt.
U. S. GRANT
Lt Gen'l

Copies, DLC-USG, V, 47, 109; DNA, RG 108, Letters Sent.

To Edwin M. Stanton

Washington, February 16th *1866*.

HON. E. M. STANTON,
SECRETARY OF WAR,
SIR:

I have the honor to submit herewith letters and instructions affecting the condition of affairs on the Rio Grande, but more particularly relating to the capture of Bagdad on January 5th 1866, by a party of filibusters among whom were some Union soldiers. The French Naval Commander protested in the name of his Government against the invasion of Mexican territory by Union troops. General Weitzel explains to General Mejia[1] the reasons governing him in sending troops into Bagdad. At the request of Escobedo[2] made in the name of humanity, two hundred men were sent to Bagdad, to preserve peace, protect private property and innocent lives until he could get a sufficient force of his own into the town, that it was therefore an act of pure humanity in the interests of the peaceful citizens of Bagdad, and had no relation to the cause for which the opposing armies are contending. The commanding officer of the troops sent was directed to execute the above orders, and to report to no one but his proper superiors and to receive no orders except from Weitzel, and under no circumstances to interfere between the contending parties, and not even to guard prisoners. Plundering continuing, Escobedo subsequently asked for one hundred men more, which were given him. The U. S. Forces remained in Bagdad until Monday the 22d January, when the Liberal leaders having failed to reenforce Bagdad with their own men, and to prevent further complications, General Weitzel withdrew his forces from Mexican soil. All the property taken was returned, Crawford[3] Reed,[4] and all the prominent leaders in the matter were arrested, and all armed parties in the vicinity disarmed.

Weitzel says that from the beginning to the end the Liberals managed the affair most disgracefully. Says his brigade and division commanders disclaim all knowledge or suspicion of the contemplated raid. The orders to preserve strict neutrality had been generally promulgated in his command. Brevet Major General Wm T. Clark, president of a commission of investigation has been ordered to hasten the examination and detect the guilty parties.

The course pursued by Generals Wright and Weitzel in the management of so delicate a matter, the promptitude with which they acted, and the determination with which they adhered to principle, is highly creditable to those gentlemen.

Mejia has ordered a forced loan upon the merchants of Matamoros, among whom are several Americans, and General Wright has notified Mejia that he will resist by force any attempted enforcement of the loan upon Americans, in which determination he is sustained by General Sheridan.

Very respectfully
Your obedient servant
U. S. GRANT
Lieutenant General.

LS, DNA, RG 94, Letters Received, 909A 1866. See telegrams to Maj. Gen. Philip H. Sheridan, Dec. 1, 1865; Jan. 25, 1866. On Feb. 3 (twice) and Feb. 5, 1866, Maj. Gen. Philip H. Sheridan, New Orleans, had written to Brig. Gen. John A. Rawlins transmitting papers relating to affairs on the Rio Grande. LS, DNA, RG 94, Letters Received, 909A 1866. The enclosures are *ibid.* On Jan. 27, Sheridan had written to USG. "I have the honor to enclose communications touch-

ing violations of Neutrality on the Rio Grande frontier by the Imperialists during the rebellion and since—I also respectfully call your attention to the extracts, cut from the Ranchero a paper published in Matamoras," LS, *ibid.*, 910A 1866. The enclosures are *ibid.* On Feb. 15, USG wrote to Secretary of War Edwin M. Stanton. "I have the honor to submit additional letters and directions given by Gen. Sheridan at various times to the commanding officers on the Rio Grande frontier; also miscellaneous correspondence between the Commanders on the respective sides of the river, and other letters bearing on the condition of affairs and our neutrality in Northern Mexico from May 1865 to the close of the year." LS, *ibid.*

On Feb. 19, Sheridan wrote to Rawlins transmitting the proceedings of a commission headed by Bvt. Maj. Gen. William T. Clark convened to investigate the capture of Bagdad, Mexico, by U.S. citizens. LS and copy, *ibid.*, 909A 1866. On March 1, USG endorsed this report. "Respectfully forwarded to the Secretary of War, attention being invited to the report of the Commission, in which they show that the City of Bagdad, Mexico, was attacked and capt[ur]ed by one R. Clay [Crawford] assisted by other [part]ies among them several U. S. soldiers—that the U. S. Soldiers were absent without the authority or consent of any U. S. Officer, and that the soldiers were in the employ and pay of Crawford and his Confederates during the attack and capture. That the U. S. Officers not only discountenanced and disapproved of any employment of their troops to attack Bagdad, but they used every precaution in their power to prevent the carrying away or destruction of property. The Revenue Officers and the ~~m~~Military showed the greatest diligence to preserve the strictest neutrality—That it was upon the urgent request of the proper authorities of the Republic of Mexico that U. S. troops were sent into Bagdad to restore tranquility preserve order and prevent outrage and promiscuous pillaging and that by the presence of these troops alone, order discipline and security to person and property was maintained. The Commission has been unable to implicate any U. S. Officer in the affair, and the U. S. Government was in no manner concerned in the matter other than that mentioned above" ES, *ibid.*

On Feb. 20, Sheridan endorsed papers protesting U.S. violations of Mexican neutrality. "Respectfully transmitted to the Lieut Gen'l. Commanding the Armies of the United States. Up to the time of the surrender of the Trans-Mississippi Department by E. Kirby Smith, Matamoras was a rebel post and should have been blockaded by our vessels of War, and all the merchants who have signed this paper were engaged with, or interested in, the blockade running vessels, and supplied the rebel Trans-Mississippi Army with material of war The Franco-Mexican commander of Matamoras, Genl Mejia, had a perfect understanding with the rebel authorities that arms and munitions of war should be supplied them by him, and was guilty of the entire suppression of the idea of neutrality. I myself found upon actual personal examination that hundreds of wagons were constantly engaged in hauling supplies to the rebel army and to disloyal Texans from Matamoras via Gonzales, and from both Lerado and Pidras Niegras, to San Antonia returning with Confederate Cotton. When I took command of this Military Division, about the (1) first day of June last, the troops of the so called Emperor occupied the line of the Rio Grande, holding Piedras Niegras, Camargo, Foller Matamoras, and Monterey. The Liberals or Republican forces since that time have compelled him to evacuate all excepting Monterey and Matamoras, the country between these points being held by them ('the

Liberals') all communication between these cities is cut off, and the Garrison confined, from necessity to the city limits. There has been no violation of neutrality on our part, on the contrary the greatest effort has been made to preserve it, and its effort has been successful. The capture of Bagdad cannot be attributed to officers of the U. S. Forces the investigation by the Military Commission having established this fact. I have the honor to enclose Genl Weitzels refutation of the charges herein made against him, and also copies of communications which prove complicity between the rebel forces and the representatives of Ma[x]amillian, and the consequent violation of neutrality." ES, *ibid.*, RG 108, Letters Received. On March 6, USG endorsed these papers. "Respy. forwarded to the Hon Sec. of War for his information with the request that these papers be transmitted to the Hon. Sec of State." Copy, *ibid.*, Register of Letters Received.

On May 9, Sheridan wrote to Stanton. "In reply to a communication from the Honorable Secretary of State, transmitting certain claims for artillery turned over to the Imperial authorities at Bagdad, Mexico, I have the honor to make the following report. On or about the 5th of January 1866, four lawless men at Clarksville, a small place opposite the insignificant town of Bagdad in Mexico, came to an understanding that they would capture and pillage the town of Bagdad, and employed from forty to sixty United States colored soldiers in the enterprise: some of these soldiers were armed and some were not. Their plans were well laid and successful. The capture of Bagdad was not in the interests of the Liberal Government of Mexico, but was a buccaneering expedition having plunder for its object. After the town had been captured and its Imperial garrison had become Liberal in their sentiments a plundering commenced, and some goods were transferred to the Texas side of the Rio-Grande, which were seized by the Customs authorities and held until afterwards returned to the owners. About one day after the capture of the town, a scoundrel named Crawford took command of it, styling himself Major General in the Liberal army, but he had no troops, so he left. Then, I believe, Cortina took command and having no troops, he too left. Then, I believe, Escobedo took command but having no troops, he also left, but, before leaving transferred some Ordnance and Ordnance Stores to our side of the river, which I thought I was justified in giving back, as per enclosed copy of directions to Major General Wright. I do not know whether any rights obtain from such or similar buccaneering expeditions The Emperor Maximilian is no more than a buccaneer in my opinion: a worthy successor of Morgan and the buccaneers of the West Indies. For instance he gets together a sufficient number of partizans or soldiers, captures a town or city and holds it, levying contributions on the unwilling inhabitants for the support of his soldiers or partizans, I have no doubt but a similar idea was in the minds of these lawless white men who captured Bagdad, and that they had as much right to capture Bagdad and hold it, levying contributions on the inhabitants for their support, as Maximilian has to do the same thing all over Mexico." LS, *ibid.*, RG 94, Letters Received, 399S 1866. On May 15, USG endorsed this letter. "Respectfully forwarded to the Hon. Secretary War." ES, *ibid.*

1. Tomás Mejía, born in 1820, commanded Mexican forces along the Rio Grande cooperating with Maximilian.

2. Mariano Escobedo, born in 1826, commanded Mexican forces along the Rio Grande opposing Maximilian.

3. R. Clay Crawford was appointed lt. col., 1st Battalion, Tenn. Light Art., as of Nov. 1, 1863, and mustered out as of Aug. 3, 1865. On Feb. 2, 1866, 3:00 P.M., Sheridan telegraphed to USG. "I have the honor to notify you that there is a very good, and quieter condition of affairs on the Rio Grande. There will be some question about captured artillery, which I presume can be settled here— The investigation of the affair so far, shows that there were about *thirty* (30) colored troops of the 118th U. S. infantry induced by Crawford and Company to participate. *Reed*, who was at the head of the party has been arrested—" Telegram received (at 6:25 P.M.), *ibid.*, RG 107, Telegrams Collected (Bound); *ibid.*, RG 108, Telegrams Received; *ibid.*, Letters Received; copies (two sent by mail), *ibid.*, RG 94, Letters Received, 909A 1866; *ibid.*, RG 108, Letters Received; DLC-USG, V, 54; DLC-Philip H. Sheridan. On Feb. 14, Stanton wrote to USG. "The President directs me to ascertain whether there are any charges against Crawford, arrested recently at New-Orleans by General Sheridan, for which he should be brought to trial; and if there are none, that he be released on parole, if not detrimental to the public service. You will please ascertain and report to me upon the subject." LS, DNA, RG 108, Letters Received. On Feb. 15, 12:30 P.M., USG telegraphed to Sheridan. "Relieve Gen H. Clay Crawford. and such other Officers of his party as you may have in confinement on their parole to appear for trial if called on by the President or under his authority" Telegram sent, *ibid.*, RG 107, Telegrams Collected (Bound); copies, *ibid.*, Letters Received from Bureaus; *ibid.*, RG 108, Letters Sent; DLC-USG, V, 47, 109. On Feb. 16, USG wrote to Stanton. "In pursuance to your directions of the 14th inst. I have examined and find that no specific charges have been made against H. Clay Crawford or his Confederates. I have therefore directed Gen. Sheridan to have them all released on Parole to appear for trial if proseedings are ever instituted against them by direction, or under authority of, the President of the United States." LS, DNA, RG 107, Letters Received from Bureaus. At 11:30 A.M., Sheridan telegraphed to USG. "I have the honor to report my return from the Rio Grande—Your dispatch in relation to R. Clay Crawford & Party has been received—He made his escape on the night of the 14th from Fort Jackson and is now at large—The rest of his party will be put on parole at once" Telegram received (at 9:00 P.M.), *ibid.*, Telegrams Collected (Bound); *ibid.*, RG 108, Telegrams Received; copies (one sent by mail, dated Feb. 17), *ibid.*, Letters Received; DLC-USG, V, 54; DLC-Philip H. Sheridan. On March 16, Sheridan forwarded to USG a report listing the individuals paroled. ES and copy, DNA, RG 108, Letters Received.

On Feb. 7, 3:30 P.M., Sheridan telegraphed to USG. "I will start for Texas today to see Gen. Wright. I think I can muster out some more colored troops in that Dept. and on my return in about ten days I will muster out some more colored troops in Dept. Louisiana." Telegram received, *ibid.*, RG 107, Telegrams Collected (Bound); *ibid.*, RG 108, Telegrams Received; copies, *ibid.*, RG 393, Military Div. of the Southwest and Dept. of the Gulf, Telegrams Sent; DLC-USG, V, 54; DLC-Philip H. Sheridan. On Feb. 17, 12:30 P.M., Sheridan telegraphed to USG. "I find affairs on the Rio Grande in very good condition, and order the muster out of the Sixty Second United States Colored Battalion, Battery B, Second U. S. Colored Artillery and the Thirty Eighth 38th Illinois Infantry, white. I now propose to muster out the four 4 white regiments at Brownsville. They are small and can be spared. Can I have your approval to muster out these regiments" Telegram received (at 4:15 P.M.), DNA, RG 107, Telegrams

Collected (Bound); *ibid.*, RG 108, Telegrams Received; copies, DLC-USG, V, 54; DLC-Philip H. Sheridan.

4. Arthur F. Reed, former lt. col., 40th Colored, had been cashiered from the U.S. Army on June 14, 1865.

To Andrew Johnson

Washington, D. C. February 17th *1866*.

HIS EXCELLENCY, A. JOHNSON,
PRESIDENT OF THE U. S.
SIR:

I have the honor to submit herewith for your information, reports from the Departments of South Carolina, North Carolina, Mississippi, Georgia and Tennessee, of outrages committed by Whites against Blacks and by Blacks against Whites, made in pursuance of the accompanying telegraphic instructions.

The following tabulated statement presents a résumé of the papers:

Departments	Assault & Batt'y Blacks	Assault & Batt'y Whites	Larceny Blacks	Larceny Whites	Murder Blacks	Murder Whites	Disorderly Conduct Blacks	Disorderly Conduct Whites	Drunkeness Blacks	Drunkeness Whites
South Carolina	123	60	605	90			45	25	55	135
North Carolina		68		29		13				
Mississippi	2	14		2		22		3		
Georgia & Tennessee	4	65		2		9				
	129	207	605	123		44	45	28	55	135

Assault & Battery, excess committed by Whites	78
Larceny, excess committed by Blacks	482
Murders, committed by Whites	44
Disorderly conduct & Drunkeness, excess by Whites	100

With great respect
Your obt. Servt
U. S. GRANT
Lieut Gen'l

LS, DLC-Andrew Johnson.

On Dec. 25, 1865, noon, USG had telegraphed to Maj. Gens. George H. Thomas, Thomas H. Ruger, Alfred H. Terry, and Daniel E. Sickles. "Send to these Hd Qrs. as early as possible a report of all known outrages occuring within your command since the surrender of the rebel Armies, committed by White people against the blacks and the reverse. It is desirable to have this information as soon as possible after the meeting of Congress." ALS (telegram sent), DNA, RG 107, Telegrams Collected (Bound); telegram sent, *ibid.*; telegram received (on Dec. 27, 10:00 A.M.), *ibid.*, RG 393, Army of the Ohio and Dept. of N. C., Telegrams Received; (on Dec. 26, 2:00 P.M.) *ibid.*, Dept. of Va. and N. C., 1st Military District, Telegrams Received. All four submitted lengthy and detailed reports to USG, filed *ibid.*, RG 108, Letters Received.

Endorsement

Headquarters, Armies of the United States.
Washington, February 17. '66.

The course of the "Examiner" in every number which I have seen has been such as to foster and increase the ill feeling existing towards the Government of the United States by the discontented portion of the Southern people. I believe it to be for the best interests of the whole people, North and South, to suppress such utterances where ever the power exists to do so. The power certainly does exist where martial law prevails and will be exercised.

Reluctant as I was to pursue the course I have felt it my duty to pursue in this instance, and as much as I dislike to interfere with the interests of individuals, I would deem it improper, and mischievous in tendency to revoke the order for the suppression of the Richmond "Examiner" at this time.

U. S. GRANT
Lieut. Ge[n.]

ES, DNA, RG 108, Letters Received. Written on a letter of Feb. 16, 1866, from H. Rives Pollard, Ebbitt House, Washington, D. C., to USG. "Referring to my request of this morning that the Examiner be permitted to resume its publication it is only necessesary, after our free and full conversation, to repeat what I then stated, that it is not my purpose to pursue a policy in any wise inimical to the Government, but to continue an earnest and cordial support of President Johnson. It remains only for me to remind you, General, that all my personal interests are involved in this matter, and that they would be hopelessly sacrificed by even a slight delay. As the President has promised me an interview on the subject at 3 P M. today I should be glad if you would see him previous to that hour." Copies (2), *ibid.* Pollard, born in Va. in 1833, was educated at the Virginia

Military Institute and the University of Virginia. During the Civil War, he served as news editor of the *Richmond Examiner*, and he revived the newspaper early in 1866. On Feb. 16, President Andrew Johnson wrote to USG. "I have sent H. R. Pollard Esqr of the Richmond Examiner, to you for the purpose of disposing of his case. I hope that if he makes satisfactory explanation, and promises to do better hereafter, you will be as moderate with him as possible." LS, *ibid.* On Feb. 17, Johnson wrote to USG. "H. R. Pollard, Esq, has been again to see me in reference to his case. I would not be considered importunate, but Mr. Pollard seems thoroughly penitent, and to give every reasonable promise for the future course of his paper, and I request that the order in regard to it may be suspended for the present. If such an order is made, the conditions upon which it is done should be clearly stipulated and expressed." LS, *ibid.* On the same day, Pollard had written to Johnson. "If the publication of the *Examiner* is permitted to be resumed it is my purpose to give a cordial support to the Union, the Constitution & the laws of the land. The policy of your administration will continue to receive the support of the journal." ALS, *ibid.*

On Feb. 9, 2:20 P.M., USG telegraphed to Maj. Gen. Alfred H. Terry. "Send me copy of Richmond papers tabbooing ladies for attending partys with Union Officers" Telegram sent, *ibid.*, RG 107, Telegrams Collected (Bound); copies, *ibid.*, RG 108, Letters Sent; DLC-USG, V, 47, 109. On Feb. 13, 5:30 P.M., Bvt. Col. Theodore S. Bowers telegraphed to Terry. "Lieut General Grant directs that your attention be called to the dangerously inflamatory course of the Richmond Examiner, a [n]ewspaper published in Richmond Va, and orders that you take immediate Military possession of said newspaper establishment and close it, and that you retain possession and prohibit the publication of the paper until further orders The Editor Mr Pollard, will not be restrained in his personal liberty unless his arrest is necessary to preserve order, or charges setting forth specifically his offenses are preferred" Telegram sent, DNA, RG 107, Telegrams Collected (Bound); copies, *ibid.*, RG 108, Letters Sent; DLC-USG, V, 47, 109. On Feb. 14, Terry, Richmond, telegraphed to Bowers. "I have closed the Examiner offices & placed it under guard. Will send by mail proof sheets found there of similar character to former articles & a further report" Telegram received (at 9:50 P.M.), DNA, RG 107, Telegrams Collected (Bound); *ibid.*, RG 108, Telegrams Received; copy, DLC-USG, V, 54. On the same day, Maj. Gen. Ethan A. Hitchcock wrote to Bvt. Col. Orville E. Babcock. "In answer to your note of this morning in reference to Pollard's parole, I beg to say that Pollard, as a civilian, never fell under my *official* notice, and I find no evidence in this office that he was taken up among the prisoners of war. I am under the impression that the orders in relation to him proceeded from the Sec.y of war directly, and were communicated by Telegram to Fort Monroe, from which point he went South (I believe), and before leaving the Fort he must have given his parole, unless he went South after the 3d of April '65.—I am causing a further search among some papers received from Richmond, and if I discover anything in relation to the case, will immediately send it—" ALS, DNA, RG 108, Letters Received. On Feb. 19, Bowers wrote to Terry. "Your order of date the 13th inst. taking military possession of the Richmond 'Examiner,' a newspaper published in Richmond, Va., and prohibiting its publication, made in pursuance of the directions of the Lieutenant General Commanding, is hereby temporarily suspended; and the Richmond 'Examiner' will be permitted to resume its publication upon the express condition that in future it will not pursue a course inimical to the Government, or to the growth or expression in acts or words of Union sentiments among the people of the States lately in rebellion, or to the cultivation of friendly relations between the people of these States, or any of them, and the other States of the Union; and that it will not in any wise fail in its editorials, correspondence, or transfer of articles from other newspapers, to give support, countenance and friendship to acts and expressions of loyalty to the Union and its supporters." Copies, DLC-USG, V, 47, 109; DNA, RG 108, Letters Sent.

On March 23, Terry wrote to Brig. Gen. John A. Rawlins. "In order to enforce the views which I have heretofore expressed in regard to the course and character of the 'Richmond Examiner', I enclose a copy of that paper of the issue of yesterday and I invite your attention to an article which it contains entitled 'A General of the U. S. A. in love &c'. There are two General Officers here, General Turner and myself. To one of us this article must refer. I trust that I need not assure you that neither of us has attempted to commit the crime of bigamy or any other felony. A more malicious or malignant slander never was uttered. I submit the point for the decision of Leiut. General Grant, whether Gen. Turner or I can remain with honor in this Department unless I be authorized to punish the slanderer." ALS, *ibid.*, Letters Received. On March 26, Bvt. Col. Adam Badeau wrote to Terry. "In reply to your communication of March 23d relative to the Richmond Examiner, a copy of which you forwarded, of date March 22d, Lieut. Gen. Grant directs me to instruct you to prepare charges against the editor, and forward them to these Headquarters for action." Copies, DLC-USG, V, 47, 109; DNA, RG 108, Letters Sent. On March 27, Terry wrote to Rawlins. "In obedience to instructions from Lieutenant General Grant I forward charges against H. Rives Pollard the Editor & Publisher of the Richmond Examiner. Since my communication of the 23d instant Bvt Major General Turner has called upon Mr Pollard to inform him who was the General Officer referred to in the article which is the subject of the charge. Mr Pollard has informed him that it referred to General Turner himself, & has since published a contradiction of the article. I enclose a copy of the paper containing the contradiction. It was *forced* from Pollard by General Turner" ALS, *ibid.*, RG 94, Letters Received, 205V 1866. The enclosures are *ibid.* On March 30, USG endorsed this letter. "Respectfully forwarded to the Hon Secretary of War for his consideration No action has yet been taken in this matter." ES, *ibid.*

On Feb. 17, Bowers wrote to commanding officers, Depts. of Va., N. C., S. C., Ga., Fla., Ala., Miss., La., Tenn., Tex., and Ark. "You will please send to these Headquarters as soon as practicable and from time to time thereafter such copies of newspapers published in your Department as contain sentiments of disloyalty and hostility to the Government in any of its branches, and state whether such paper is habitual in its utterances of such sentiments. The persistent publication of articles calculated to keep up a hostility of feeling between the people of different sections of the country cannot be tolerated. This information is called for with a view to their suppression, which will be done from these Headquarters only." LS, *ibid.*, RG 393, Dept. of Ark., Letters Received; *ibid.*, Dept. of Tenn., Unbound Materials, Letters Received; *ibid.*, Dept. of Miss., Letters Received; copies, *ibid.*, Military Div. of the Atlantic, Letters Received; *ibid.*, RG 108, Letters Sent; DLC-USG, V, 47, 109. On March 19, Terry wrote to Rawlins. "I have the honor to report that in order to enable me to obey the instructions contained in a letter from the Head Quarters of the

Army, I have directed that a copy of each issue of every newspaper published in this Department be sent by its publishers to these Head Quarters. It is manifestly impossible for me to exercise the supervision over the public press contemplated in the letter unless these copies are in someway obtained. My orders in this respect have excited much remark and the proprietors of several newspapers have demanded payment for the copies furnished. I have as yet made no reply to their demands: they seem to me to be absurd, but before replying to them I respectfully ask instructions as to whether I shall continue to require the papers and if so whether they should be paid for. I enclose copies of the Richmond Examiner for the 1st 10th 13th 15th 17th and 19th days of the present month in order to show the general character of the paper and to demonstrate how ill the editor of it complies with the conditions imposed upon him when his paper was reopened after its suppression, and I especially call the attention of the Lieutenant General to the articles in the issues of 10th 17th and 19th instant, reflecting upon the military authorities, both local and general. I respectfully submit that license to publish articles such as the last referred to is utterly inconsistent with the prevalence of martial law. Martial Law resting on power alone, ceases to be respectable when it ceases to shield from insult those who exercise it. Understanding that Major General Meade is absent from his Head Quarters, I address this communication to you directly." LS, DNA, RG 108, Letters Received. On March 23, Badeau wrote to Terry. "Lt. General Grant directs me to say in reply to your communication of March 19th that you will continue to require such copies of the issue of the various newspapers published in your Dept. to be sent to your head quarters as you may deem proper and that you will make no payment therefor. In regard to the other subjects mentioned in your letter of the 19th inst., Gen Grant has them now under consideration, and will apprise you of his determination." Copies, DLC-USG, V, 47, 109; DNA, RG 108, Letters Sent.

On March 21, Barry and Bernard, Wilmington, telegraphed to USG. "If the suppression of the Wilmington 'Despatch' has been recommended by the Assistant Superintendent of Freedmens Bureau at this point we respectfully ask that you suspend action until we can confer with you more fully Will be glad to hear from you immediately" Telegram received (at 7:45 P.M.), *ibid.*, RG 107, Telegrams Collected (Bound); *ibid.*, RG 108, Telegrams Received; copy, DLC-USG, V, 54.

On April 6, Bvt. Maj. Gen. Charles R. Woods, Mobile, wrote to USG. "I would respectfully lay before you this Copy of the Mobile Daily Times. containing a scurrilous, disloyal and unwarranted insult to the Government.—The Editor Henry St Paul is a half breed Frenchman with no common sense and a little superficial learning.—He and his paper have been persistently disloyal and insulting to the Military authorities and the Government during the past ten months.—I very respectfully ask your decision and instructions upon the matter" LS, DNA, RG 108, Letters Received. The enclosure is *ibid.*

On July 24, Maj. George K. Leet wrote to dept. commanders. "The Order of February 17 1866 from these Headquarters directing Department Commanders to forward copies of such newspapers published within their respective commands as contained sentiments of disloyalty &c is hereby revoked." LS, *ibid.*, RG 393, Military Div. of the Miss., Cav. Corps, Letters Received; *ibid.*, Dept. of Ark., Letters Received; copies, *ibid.*, RG 108, Letters Sent; DLC-USG, V, 47, 60.

On March 16, 1867, Edward McPherson, clerk, U.S. House of Representatives, wrote to USG. "I am preparing a Manual of Events of 1866–'67, connected with the military & political operations of the Government—and will be greatly obliged if you can furnish me a copy of the order revoking about August 1866, your Order of Feb. 17, 1866 respecting disloyal newspapers. The latter order is, in full, in my Political Manual for 1866; p. 123.—I desire to continue the record. Whatever orders, since July 4, 1866, you have issued, applying to the insurrectionary States and relating to Reconstruction, I would gladly have accurate copies of, for insertion in my forthcoming book.—I find newspaper copies too often inaccurate." ALS, DNA, RG 108, Letters Received.

To Bvt. Maj. Gen. Daniel Butterfield

Washington, D. C. Feb. 17 *1866*

DEAR GENERAL,

Your letter of the 15th inst. enclosing me the very handsome testimonial of the citizens of New York, with names of all the too generous contributors to it, is received. I feel at a loss to know how to express my appreciation of this substantial token of the friendship of the citizens named in your letter, and for the generosity of the citizens of New York generally, and especially towards those who they conceive have rendered service in maintaining the integrity of the whole Union. Suffice it to say that I shall always appreciate their generosity towards me and endeavor to pursue a course through life, and to make such use of the means thus unexpectedly placed in my possession, as will meet with their approval.

Through you I wish to thank the gentlemen whos names you have enclosed to me individually and collectively.

I have the honor to be,
Your obt. svt.
U. S. GRANT
Lt. Gen.

ALS (facsimile), IHi. On Feb. 15, 1866, Bvt. Maj. Gen. Daniel Butterfield, New York City, wrote to USG. "In accordance with the request of many citizens of New York whose names are herewith transmitted I have the honor to ask your acceptance of the enclosed testimonial of their appreciation of your services—. . . (Enclosed . . . $105.000.00" ALS (facsimile), *ibid.* On Feb. 19, Butterfield wrote a letter of acknowledgment. "I have the pleasure to enclose you (fac simile) copy of Lt. Genl Grants acknowledgment of the testimonial to which you were a contributor.—Also a list of the subscriptions & copy of the correspondence—In furnishing this information to contributors I am requested to ask that no copy of these documents may be allowed to be printed as many subscriptions were made with that understanding—Please consider this my reciept for your subscription . . . (please acknowledge)" ALS (facsimile), *ibid.* The list of 157 contributors is *ibid.* USG may actually have received the gift while visiting New York City, Feb. 21–27. See *New York Times*, Feb. 28, 1866. On Dec. 8, 1865, Butterfield had written to U.S. Representative Elihu B. Washburne. "*Private* . . . I notice with pleasure your bill reviving grade of '*General*' evidently intended for justice to Lt. Genl Grant—Can the action upon this bill be postponed until after Christmas? My object in asking is this—I am hard at work *quietly* & *privately* raising money for Gel. Grant to pay off the 30.000 mortgage on his (Washington purchase) house—balance if any to be given him in Govt. bonds I have already subscribed $37.000 I hope to get it to 50.000 before Christmas I am compelled to do it all myself personally & very quietly in consequence of Mrs Grants expressed wish that there should be no publicity about it—Every where I meet the inquiry—'*how much is Genl. Grants pay*'? my reply is 'not enough to support the position he holds at all'—I fear action on the bill before Christmas would cost me $10.000 of subscriptions which I should otherwise secure—You of course are the best judge as to the propriety of any delay—I make this statement to you in confidence & should like to know your views of the matter and to hear also whether action is likely to ensue soon upon your bill—" ALS, DLC-Elihu B. Washburne. See telegram to Maj. Gen. Joseph J. Reynolds, Oct. 16, 1865; letters to Charles W. Ford, Oct. 28, 1865, Elihu B. Washburne, Nov. 9, 1865; John Y. Simon, ed., *The Personal Memoirs of Julia Dent Grant* (New York, 1975), p. 161.

To Henry Wilson

Washington, D. C. Feb. 20th *1866*

HON. H. WILSON,
CH. MIL. COMMITTEE OF THE SENATE,
SIR:

Enclosed herewith I have the honor of returning Senate Bill No 138, left for me to examine, without further suggestion than that noted on margin of Sec. 18.

I also return the other enclosure without further remark than to say that, as a rule, I feel but little sympathy for Army sutlers and think generally that any legislation had on the subject should be for the protection of the soldier. In fact I have often thought that it would be better if the position of sutler was abolished altogether and the Commissary at posts remote from settlemen[ts] where there were private merchants, required to keep all the articles allowed to be kept by them, for sale to officers and men.

I have the honor to be,
Very respectfully,
Your obt. svt.
U. S. GRANT
Lt. Gn.

ALS, NHi.

To Hamilton Fish et al.

[*Feb. 22, 1866.*]

GENTLEMEN: The notice of your intention to present me with PAGE'S[1] portrait of Lieut.-Gen. WINFIELD SCOTT, was duly received. This is not the first token received by me of the friendship and generosity of the citizens of your metropolis, or of yourselves. It is, nevertheless, one which I will always cherish and value, both for what it is and for those who have done me this great honor.

The portrait of one who has rendered such vast service to the Republic, and whose services have continued through so many years, possesses a peculiar value to me.

Please accept my heartfelt thanks.

I have the honor to be, with great respect, your obt. servant,
U. S. GRANT, Lieut-Gen. U. S. A.

New York Times, Feb. 23, 1866. USG's letter was read at the Union League Club, New York City, during a reception on the evening of Feb. 22, 1866. James Wadsworth first read a letter from Hamilton Fish and twenty-nine others to USG. "With the desire of expressing, in an acceptable manner, that admiration which we have always entertained for your character and career, we have procured and now ask you to accept the portrait of your illustrious predecessor, in that high trust to which the favor of God and the discerning love of the American people have called you. We would fain hope that this token of our regard, painted by WILLIAM PAGE, will be deemed by you neither unfit nor unwelcome. Through an active military career of more than half a century, Lieut.-Gen. SCOTT adorned his profession by the cultivation of every sentiment that can honor a man, and the practice of every virtue that becomes a Christian. A soldier in every fibre of his being, he has been as conspicuous by his humanity as by his bravery, and has been as uniformly ardent and efficient in preserving peace as in conducting war. Trusting that your own career may be equally prolonged, we remain, yours devotedly, . . ." *Ibid.*; copy (unsigned), USG 3.

On Jan. 13, Simon Stevens, New York City, had written to USG. "(Confidential) . . . I have much pleasure in saying—that nearly all of the subscribers to the 'Scott-Grant Testimonial' have signed the letter presenting to you the portrait of Lt. General Scott.—I hope to have the matter entirely completed, in the coming week It is proposed to have the presentation made at the rooms of the Union Leage Club in this City, on Thursday Evening the 22d day of February, which shall be made the occasion of a Ladies reception, at which Mrs Grant will be expected to be present, to share your honors—I send you herewith a copy of the letter of presentation and some of the names of the subventors, to enable you prepare your reply—The complete list of names will be furnished you in due time. The whole matter will be turned over to the Club in the course of a few days, consequently it is desirable to know at an early day whether that day will suit the convenience of Mrs Grant and yourself. As soon as I have your reply on this point I will intimate the probabilities to the club, that the invitations and announcements may issue in a formal way—General Scott will be urged to be present It is purposed to invite the President of the United States and his Cabinet, the Judges of the Supreme Court of the United States, Senators and distinguished Members of Congress, Loyal Governors of States, distinguished officers of the Army & Navy President of Colleges & certain distinguished Citizens—The correspondence will be printed, 33 copies in book form, which will include a photographic copy of the Letter testimonial and your reply, one for each, one one for General Scott, one for Mrs Grant and one for the Artist Mr Page. I shall feel highly honoured if the originals fall to the lot of your friend & most humble servant" ALS, *ibid.* On Jan. 16, USG wrote to someone, probably Stevens, promising to be in New York City to accept a painting of Bvt. Lt. Gen. Winfield Scott. Carnegie Book Shop, Catalogue 142 [*1949*], no. 161. On Feb. 8, David Van Nostrand wrote to USG. "I write you now in behalf of the Union League Club in regard to the arrangements for the evening of the 22d inst when the presentation of the Portrait of Lt. Gen Scott to you is to be made I have your letter of the 16th Jany to Mr Simon Stevens accepting that day as convenient to you, but as we have extensive ~~arrangements~~ preparations to make, I desired to know a little more definetly if the time &c will suit you. We intend to make it as brillian[t] an affair as possible and therefore intend to have it a Ladies Reception and we trust that Mrs Grant will be able to accompany you. The presentation will be at 8 o'clock in the evening and supper will be ready at ten oclock. Will you have the kindness to drop me a line informing me if this is all right and if we can depend upon you for that time. Please let me know also what members of your Staff will accompany you." ALS, USG 3. On Feb. 17, Saturday, John W. Garrett, president, Baltimore and Ohio Railroad, Camden Station, Baltimore, telegraphed to USG. "I have received Col Badeaus communication and take pleasure in making the arrangement desired for Tuesday evening next" Telegram received (at 9:00 P.M.), DNA, RG 107, Telegrams Collected (Bound). USG arrived in New York City on Wednesday, Feb. 21, and left the city to return to Washington, D. C., on Feb. 27.

On Feb. 9, Simeon Draper, New York City, wrote to Bvt. Col. Adam Badeau. "I enclose a Letter to Lt Gen Grant, which you will please deliver and, give an early answer to; addressed to Govr King, and enclosed to me,—give us the members of his staff, that will honour us, that we may be ready for all" ALS, USG 3. On Feb. 10, USG wrote to John A. King concerning a dinner at the Union Club. *ABPC*, 1947, 534. USG dined at the club the evening of Feb. 21. See *New York Tribune*, Feb. 22, 1866.

On Feb. 16, C. J. Blauvelt wrote to USG. "The 8th Regiment, National Guard S. N. Y, will celebrate the Anniversary of Washingtons birthday at the Academy of Music in this city on the evening of the 22d Inst. The Officers and member[s] of the regiment have learned with much pleasure that you will be in our city on that day, and very earnestly request your acceptance of the enclosed invitation as it will afford many, an opportunity of tendering their congratulations to you who otherwise may be deprived of that pleasure" ALS, USG 3. On Feb. 17, Alexander T. Stewart wrote to USG. "I will consider it a great pleasure, to have the Company of Mrs Grant and yourself, at dinner, on any day that you will appoint, most agreeable to yourself, during your stay in our City on your proposed visit. Awaiting your answer, . . ." LS, *ibid.* USG dined with Stewart the evening of Feb. 23. *New York Times*, Feb. 24, 1866.

On Feb. 22, USG received another invitation. "Dr Osgood on behalf of the Harvard Club of New York asks the Honor of Lieut. General Grant's Company at the Reception this Evening to meet Presidents Sparks & Hill, Messrs Bryant, Bancroft & others this Evening at Delmonicos at 9½ oclock." AL, USG 3.

On Feb. 20, John C. Hamilton, Union League Club, wrote to USG. "A political meeting is called for Thursday evening next—expressly to support the P—ts policy as to the Rebel States. It has been got up, as welcome, by office holders here—and it is supposed that night was selected *expressly to secure your presence*. It will be a partizan meeting—& by persons of little weight in this community—A paper making the call for it was brought here on Saturday even'g, & *not one* member of this League would sign it. Your true friends here are anxious you would avoid it, as it will inevitably place you in an antagonistic position to Congress, I make this intamation after conversation with some of my friends & your friends. Nothing will be more easy than to regret you are engaged—& not only with our League—but with some military attraction for that evening—& if you write me authorizing it I will make such engagements for you which will not interfere with your presence here. You promised me your autograph—Merely answer you have recevd this note, & I will understand your wishes without any other words." ALS, *ibid.* Secretary of State William H. Seward was the principal speaker at a meeting held in New York City on Feb. 22 to support the Reconstruction policies of President Andrew Johnson. *New York Times*, Feb. 23, 1866. USG breakfasted with Hamilton on Feb. 23. *Ibid.*, Feb. 24, 1866.

On Feb. 21, Caroline W. Astor wrote to Julia Dent Grant inviting the Grants to dinner on Feb. 24. ALS, USG 3; *New York Times*, Feb. 24, 1866. Also on Feb. 21, Maria L. Daly wrote to Julia Dent Grant inviting the Grants to dine on Sunday, Feb. 25. ALS, USG 3. On Feb. 23, 1:00 P.M., James W. Beekman wrote to USG. "I called this morning to reply personally to Col. Badeau's note of last evening, but not finding you, I beg to thank you for giving me the pleasure of expecting to see you next Sunday morning—Shall I call for you in season to go to church with me, or would you prefer coming to my house after church, say at ½ past twelve?—I will do myself the honor in either case of calling for you in my carriage and bringing you to lunch with me at One O'Clock—And of then driving you back in good season for your dinner at Judge Daly's—You will meet no company, and I shall welcome you and Colo Badeau in a private and domestic way" ALS, *ibid.* On Feb. 24, 11:30 A.M., Beekman wrote to Badeau about the arrangements. ALS, *ibid.*

On Feb. 23, John H. Chambers, librarian, New York Free Academy, wrote to USG. "The Instructors and Students of the New York Free Academy not having enjoyed the pleasure of seeing you or paying you their respects, would most earnestly solicit you to visit the institution if it be only for a few moments, at any hour this day which would suit yr: convenience before 1. O.Clock P. M." ALS, *ibid.* On Feb. 23, M. Armstrong *et al.* wrote to USG. "Please bear in mind your appointment to meet your friends of the Leather Trade on Saturday 24th inst at 10 o'clock A. M. A Committee will have the honor of waiting upon you at that hour, for the purpose of accompanying you to the 'Swamp.'" LS (four signatures), *ibid.* See *New York Tribune*, Feb. 26, 1866. On Feb. 23, Theodore Roosevelt wrote to Badeau. "General Grant promised me to accompany Mr Wm E. Dodge Jr. and myself to look at some specimens of writing by those who have lost their right arm in the Service. This will gratify them more than the prize in money which we offered for the best specimen. General Grant appointed half past three, if through with the Swamp by that time, at which hour we will call for him if nothing has occured to change his plans. Please telegraph me to 94 Maiden Lane or send special messenger with reply tomorrow morning should you not be in when my messenger calls with this." ALS, USG 3. USG examined the manuscripts on Feb. 24 and exclaimed: "These boys write better with their left hand than I do with my right!" *New York Tribune*, Feb. 26, 1866. He also wrote a testimonial. "I have examined the large and exceedingly interesting collection of Left Hand Manuscripts written by our disabled soldiers who have lost their right arms. They are eminently honorable to the authors, and from the excellence of the penmanship, it would impose a task I would be sorry to accept to decide on the merits of the competitors." ADS, DLC-William O. Bourne.

On Feb. 24, Henry E. Pierrepont, Brooklyn Club, wrote to USG. "In accordance with the arrangement made by Mr Chittenden with Col. Badeau carriages will be in waiting for you and your Staff Monday evening at the Metropolitan Hotel at half past six O'Clock, to convey you to Brooklyn." ALS, USG 3. On Feb. 20, USG wrote to Bvt. Maj. Gen. Daniel Butterfield. "Mr. Pierrepont's dispatch to you is received. If you will do so you may telegraph to him that I remember my promise to Mr. Chittenden very well, and will be happy to see the citizens of Brooklyn on this visit. Every evening of this week is engaged however, but the days are not. I can spend either Friday or Saturday with them up to 4½ p. m. or Monday without limit. I would much prefer returning to Burlington N. J. in the Saturday night (12 o'clock) train if possible so to arrange but will stay over if specifically desired." Robert F. Batchelder, Catalogue 58 [*1986*], no. 64. On Feb. [*25*], Butterfield wrote to USG. "I have recieved a very long—earnest letter full of prayers & entreaties from Mr Chittenden begging me to surrender you to him for dinner to morrow—My intention had been to give three or four *very old* gentlemen warm friends of yours an opportunity to meet you quietly Gentlemen who could not get out to receptions or crowds & who do not go out evenings—I can arrange this otherwise very nicely. These gentlemen from Brooklyn—Chittenden Low Claflin & others have shewn much kindness & regard for you that I have felt it not only a duty on my part but the proper course towards you to yield to Mr Chittendens entreaties—You will by this be saved much personal inconvenience & hurrying about—& also meet undoubtedly many of the very best men of Brooklyn—I have therefore written a note to Mr Chittenden that I will yield to his entreaties with a good grace—Mrs Grant thinks it will be so inconvenient for her to go in travelling dress &c that I have at her request in my note to Mr Chittenden told him that Mrs Grant would not be able to accept—I will be down at ¼ before 10 in the morning when we will go to Commodore Vanderbilt stables—" ALS, USG 3. On Feb. 26, Simeon B. Chittenden wrote to USG. "If agreeable to you we propose to ferry you & your party direct from Brooklyn to Jersey City to night, to save time, and for your greater comfort. Our carriages will be at your hotel to bring you to my house ¼ before 4 o'clock this afternoon." ALS, *ibid.* See *New York Times*, Feb. 27, 1866.

On Feb. 24, Lucy Rushton wrote to USG. "Miss Lucy Rushton presents her respectful Compts to Lt Gl Grant and solicits the favor of a visit of himself & suite to her new Theatre any Evening he may be pleased to appoint—" AL, USG 3. On the same day, James Geddes Day wrote to USG. "Will you give me the honor of receiving yourself, Mrs. Grant, and your staff, at lunch at half past one o'clock, next Thursday, March 1st Trusting that I may have the pleasure of so doing . . ." ALS, *ibid.* On Feb. [25], 3:00 P.M., Theodore Tilton, editor, *The Independent*, wrote to USG. "As your Sisters (lately my guests in Brooklyn) mentioned that you would like to hear Mr. Beecher preach, it will give me pleasure to call for yourself and Mrs. Grant, in a carriage, to conduct you to church and return you to your rooms, without any annoyance from sight-seers. Of course I know how you are bored almost to death. This invitation is not for catching a lion in my own net, but simply for the sake of your *personal convenience*, if you should feel inclined to hear Mr Beecher this Evening. The carriage should leave at ½ past 6." ALS, *ibid.*

An erroneous report that USG had been accidentally wounded in the hand while examining a new rifle at the Metropolitan Hotel, originating in the *New York World*, Feb. 27, 1866, was widely noted in newspapers.

1. William Page, born in 1811 in Albany, N. Y., studied painting in Italy and established a studio in N. J. His brother-in-law, Simon Stevens, promoted his career and tried to obtain a commission for a painting showing USG entering Richmond in triumph before learning that he had not done so. Joshua C. Taylor, *William Page: The American Titian* (Chicago, 1957), pp. 178–80.

To Hugh McCulloch et al.

Washington, D. C. Feb. 28th *1866*

Mrs. Orpha Lawrence, a widow lady, is respectfully recommended to the Hon. Sec. of the Treasury, Judge Advocat[e] General or Sec. of the Interior, for a position as Copying Clerk. I have known Mrs Lawrence since she was a young girl and am aware that she, with one child, is dependent upon a retired officer of the

Army, Lt. Col. Whiting,[1] for support; Col. Whiting having at the same time two widowed daughters, and other children, dependent upon him.

If it is possible to give Mrs. Lawrence employment which will support her and relieve an old soldier of so much of his current expenses I will feel it as an obligation to myself.

Very respectfully
your obt. svt.
U. S. GRANT
Lt. Gn.

ALS, Victor Jacobs, Dayton, Ohio. President Andrew Johnson endorsed this letter. "It is hoped that the Secretary of the Treasury will find it consistent with the public interest to give Mrs Lawrence employment in the Treasury Dept—She is highly recommended as being worthy and well qualified to discharge the duties which may be imposed on by the appointment" AES (undated), *ibid.*

1. In Feb., 1866, Lt. Col. Daniel P. Whiting (retired), 6th Inf., USMA 1832, wrote a letter, referred to USG's hd. qrs. by Attorney Gen. James Speed, requesting relief for retired officers. DNA, RG 108, Register of Letters Received. On Feb. 20, USG endorsed this letter. "Respy. forwarded to the sec of war. I am of the opinion that the present law should be so modified as to allow an increase of pay to retired officer—when they have been retired on account of age—disability from long service and all causes not resulting from indiscretion—The number of rations allowed should, I also, think, be limited by the number allowed at time of retirement" Copy, DLC-USG, V, 58. On Feb. 26, Whiting, Philadelphia, wrote to Johnson requesting an appointment to USMA for his son. ALS, DNA, RG 94, Cadet Applications. On March 1, USG endorsed this letter. "Lt. Col. Whiting, the father of the applicant for a Cadetship, is an old Army officer, now retired after long service. He is one of a class who cannot expect such an appointment except 'At Large' and this is therefore respectfully refered to the Sec. of War for his concideration." AES, *ibid.* No appointment followed.

To Edwin M. Stanton

Washington, D, C, Feb. 28th *1866*

HON. E. M. STANTON,
SEC. OF WAR,
SIR:

Enclosed I send you copy of order which I propose to issue for the guidance of the Comd.g Officer of the Dept. of Ky. for approval of the President. If there is any point which you would change please make it before presenting to the President and the order will be issued as approved.

Very respectfully
your obt. svt.
U. S. GRANT
Lt. Gn.

ALS, DLC-Andrew Johnson. USG enclosed a draft of Special Orders: "Major General Jno. M. Palmer, Commanding Department of Kentucky, will at once issue and enforce orders protecting from prosecution or suits in the State, or Municipal Courts of the State of Kentucky, all officers and soldiers of the armies of the United States, and all persons thereto attached, or in any wise thereto belonging, subject to military authority, charged with offences for acts done in their military capacity, or pursuant to orders from proper military authority; and to protect from suit or prosecution all loyal citizens, or persons, charged with offences done against the rebel forces, directly or indirectly, during the existence of the rebellion, and all persons, their agents or employes, charged with occupancy of abandoned lands or plantations, or the possession or custody of any kind of property whatever, who occupied, used, possessed or controlled the same, pursuant to the order of the President, or any of the Civil or Military Departments of the Government, and to protect them from any penalties or damages that may have been, or may be pronounced or adjudged in said Courts in any of such cases." Copy, *ibid.* Secretary of War Edwin M. Stanton endorsed USG's letter. "Order approved." AE (undated), *ibid.* On Feb. 1, 1866, Maj. Gen. George H. Thomas, Washington, D. C., had referred papers to USG concerning civil suits in Ky. courts against Unionists. AES, DNA, RG 108, Letters Received. The papers are *ibid.* On Feb. 3, Thomas again endorsed these papers. "Respectfully referred to the Sec War, inviting attentention to a Communication from the Hon Green Clay Smith M. C. and others on the same subject (referred by me) to the Hon Sec though Lt Genl Grant Feby 1st Martial Law having been abrogated in Kentucky innumerable Suits of the nature of those named in the within communication have been already commenced against persons who have been in the Service of the Government, and the defendants are now at the mercy of the plaintiffs as the State Courts in Kentucky peremptorily refuse to consider the law of March 3, 1863, which provides for the removal of suits of this nature from the Civil Courts of States to the Fedral Court of the District. Believing this evil would be completely removed by an Act of Congress, Compell the States Courts to tranfer all such cases upon the application of the Defendant, to the Federal Court I have respectfully to request and urge that the question may be referred to the Judiciary Committee of the Senate for consideration & Such action as they deem proper" AES, *ibid.* On the same day, USG endorsed these papers. "Respectfully submitted to know whether it is competent to extend the provisions of General Order No. 3, (copy enclosed) to Kentucky, Missouri and other States" ES, *ibid.* See General Orders No. 3, Jan. 12, 1866. On Feb. 19, Maj. Gen. John M. Palmer, Louisville, wrote to the AG tendering his resignation. ALS, DNA, RG 94, ACP, 119P CB 1866. On March 10, Bvt. Col. Ely S. Parker endorsed this letter. "The resignation of General Palmer is approved, and Bvt. Maj. Gen. Jefferson C. Davis is respectfully nominated as his successor. It is also recommended that G. O. No. 3 and the substitute order relating to the same subject, be made to apply to the suits now pending against Gen. Palmer." AES, *ibid.*

To Maj. Gen. Philip H. Sheridan

Head Quarters Armies of the United States.
Washington, February 28th 1866.

MAJOR GENERAL P. H. SHERIDAN,
COMMANDING MILITARY DIV. OF THE GULF,
GENERAL:

By direction of the Secretary of War you will secure by such measures as may be necessary and proper to all the stockholders of the Buffalo Bayou, Brazos and Colorado Railroad, in whatever section of the country, their fair share in the reorganization and direction of the Company, and protect them in the assertion and resumption of any rights of which they may have been deprived by or under authority of any act of the so-called Confederate Government or of any of its agents, or by reason of any usurpation of control of the Company by any persons during the rebellion.

The Quarter Master General has directed that the suspension of payment of any dues to this railroad company from Government will be continued until it can be made to those authorized to receive it upon the legal reorganization of the Company.

Military possession of the road will not be taken unless the performance of transportation services required by it should render it absolutely necessary.

Very respectfully
Your obedient servant
U. S. GRANT
Lieut. General.

LS, DNA, RG 393, Military Div. of the Southwest and Dept. of the Gulf, Letters Received. On Feb. 26, 1866, Maj. Thomas T. Eckert, act. asst. secretary of war, wrote a letter received at USG's hd. qrs. "Submits matter of J. F. Barrett and Hiram Wellington in Buffalo Bayou, Brazos and Colorado R. R. now in possession of rebel stockholders Secty of War approves of the Q. M. Generals' recommendations and asks that orders be accordingly issued" *Ibid.*, RG 108, Register of Letters Received. On March 23, Maj. Gen. Philip H. Sheridan wrote a letter received at USG's hd. qrs. submitting a report stating: "that upon application of northern stockholders, action will be taken in the matter—not otherwise, as confiscation is a dead letter in Texas." *Ibid.* On March 30, USG endorsed these papers. "Respy. forwarded to the Hon Sec of War." Copy, *ibid.*

To Andrew Johnson

Washington, D. C. March 1st *1866*.

HIS EXCELLENCY, A. JOHNSON,
PRESIDENT OF THE UNITED STATES,
SIR:

I respectfully apply for the appointment of Cadet at West Point Military Academy for my son, Fred. Dent Grant. He will be Sixteen years of age the Thirtyeth day of May next, was born in St. Louis, Mo. and is now a resident of this City.

I have the honor to be
Very respectfully
your obt. svt.
U. S. GRANT
Lt. Gn.

ALS, DNA, RG 94, Cadet Applications. On March 3, 1866, Frederick Dent Grant wrote to Secretary of War Edwin M. Stanton accepting the appointment. LS (on printed form letter), *ibid.* USG endorsed the letter. "*I hereby assent to the above acceptance by my* son Fred *of his conditional appointment as Cadet, and he has my full permission to sign articles by which he will bind himself to serve the United States eight years, unless sooner discharged.*" ES (on printed form letter), *ibid.* USG's son became a cadet at USMA as of July 1.

On Feb. 17, USG had written to Capt. Edward C. Boynton, adjt., USMA. ". . . My boy will go to West Point nearly sixteen years of age and without many advantages of education. Before the war he was too young to have advanced much, and since my family have moved from place to place so often that the children have been to school in four different cities . . . the oldest has lost two full sessions by sickness and by being with me in the field. He is however a very strong healthy lad, full three inches taller than I was when I entered West Point and better prepared. I hope he will succeed though I have no expectation of him distinguishing himself in his studies . . ." Charles Hamilton Auction No. 162, March 8, 1984, p. 18. On Feb. 21, USG, Metropolitan Hotel, New York City, wrote to Boynton. ". . . The proposition you make to take Fred in your family is very kind and suits me much better than to send him to such a school . . . I will send him soon after the 1st of March and hope, before the examination comes on, he will give evidence that he will not only be able to enter the Academy but to remain there afterwards." ALS (incomplete facsimile), *ibid.*, pp. 18–19. USG, accompanied by Bvt. Col. Theodore S. Bowers, left Washington, D. C., on March 5, to take Fred to West Point, arriving the morning of March 6. On the same day, USG issued a check to Boynton for $200.00, presumably to pay Fred's expenses. DS (facsimile), Paul C. Richards, Catalogue No. 188 [1981]. USG left West Point that afternoon. See letter to Lorenzo Bowers, March 7, 1866. On May 7, USG wrote to Fred. "This will introduce to you Cadet Lovell H. Jerome who enters West Point with you this year. I hope you will be good friends, keep out of mischief, learn your lessons and both stand high in your class and become distinguished by your good deeds after graduation." ALS, USG 3.

On March 6, USG telegraphed to Stanton. "I respectfully recommend that orders be sent Gen Cullum to dismiss cadets Cunningham Full~~yer~~ Hyatt & Wallace all hopelessly deficient & doing nothing" Telegram received (at 4:15 P.M.), DNA, RG 94, Letters Received, 205A 1866; *ibid.*, RG 107, Telegrams Collected (Bound).

To Joseph E. Johnston

[*March 1, 1866*]

Your letter of the 28th of Feby in relation to John H. G[ee][1] who is now being tried in North Carolina by Military Court is just received. In all cases where Paroles have been given, and observed, under the Convention between Gen. Lee and myself, or between Gn. Sherman and yourself, I have always held and have so said in writing as well as by word, exempt the parties taking the Parole from future trial or punishment by Military or Government authority, for past offences, so far as these offences consisted in making war against the Government of the United States were concerned. . . .

G[ee] is charged with wilfully starving to death prisoners of War. Also of otherwise maltreating them to such an extent as constitute Murder in a very aggravated form. I know nothing of the circumstances myself and sincerely hope the evidence may disprove the charge. . . .

Dated Feb. 1, 1866, in Josiah H. Benton sale, American Art Association, March 12, 1920, no. 349. On Feb. 28, Joseph E. Johnston, Richmond, had written to USG. "I learn by the Newspapers, that John H. Gee, late a Major in the Confederate army, is unde[r] trial before a Military Commission. It appears from the record as published, that he belonged to the troops for whose benefit the convention of April 26th was Made—That he gave his 'obligation in writing not to take up arms against the government of the United States,' in obedience to article 3, & is therefore now under the protection of article 5, which guarantees him against disturbance 'by the United States authorities so long as he observes his obligation & the laws in force where he may reside.' This article, in my view, gives him full amnesty for past official acts. I respectfully Submit that he is not a prisoner of war, as the Military Commission Supposes. In the convention in question, the terms Surrender, prisoner, parole, exchange, do not occur. Soldiers become prisoners to Save their lives—The troops I commanded were in no immediate danger—being near eighty Miles from Major General Sherman's forces. They laid down their arms to reestablish peace, & prevent the further Miseries of a hopeless war—& in consideration, received promises of immunity for the past. I respectfully Suggest that the correctness of my interpretation of the convention of April 26th will be confirmed by considering it in connection with that of the 18th, & my letter of the 25th to Major General Sherman." ALS, Aurora College, Aurora, Ill. On March 1, USG endorsed this letter. "Respectfully [refer]ed to the Sec. of War. I am clearly of the opinion that J. E. Johnstons views are correct. It certainly was guaranteed to the officers and soldiers of the Southern Armies that they should be exempt from trial and punishment for past offences on condition they would surrender their ar[ms] and obey the laws. Unless they violate this obligation I think the good faith of the Govt. is pledged to protect them. Armies that could have escaped certainly never would have consented to a surrender which obligated them to a full observance of the laws and at the same time gave no [pro]tection." AES, *ibid.*

1. See *O.R.*, II, viii, 783, 819, 881–82, 956–60.

To William Coffin

Washington, D, C,
March 2d 1866.

DEAR SIR:

Your letter of yesterday enclosing check for $144 81/100 and receipt for taxes for this year is received. I am very glad the taxes for 1866 are paid and when the insurance runs out will be pleased to have that renewed also. I believe the policy is in my hands. If so it is at the house. I will examine it and see when the present risk expires and write in time.

Please present Mrs. Grant's and my compliments to your family and accept the same for yourself. I will probably be in Philadelphia Teusday or Wednsday next when I will do myself the pleasure of calling.

Yours Truly
U. S. GRANT

TO WM COFFIN, ESQ,
PHILA PA

ALS, Free Library of Philadelphia, Philadelphia, Pa. See letter to William Coffin, Nov. 3, 1865.

To Andrew Johnson

Washington D. C. March 3d *1866*

HIS EXCELLENCY, A. JOHNSON,
PRESIDENT OF THE UNITED STATES
SIR:

In connection with the subject upon which I had a conversation with you this morning, that of permitting the sale of Arms and Ammunition to the "Liberal Government of Mexico," without which aid their cause is in great danger, and an ultimate War of great magnitude between this Government and the usurpers of that iminent, I would respectfully ask if it would not be advisable for you to send for the accredited Minister of Mexico to get for yourself the information of the present situation? I ask this because I think the confidance of the Sec. of State is much more sanguine than mine is that the whole "Mexican" question will settle itself if not interrupted, and because the Minister refered to cannot see you except by invitation or through the Authority of the Sec. of State.

Very respectfully
your obt. svt.
U. S. GRANT
Lt. Gn.

ALS, DLC-Andrew Johnson. See letter to Edwin M. Stanton, March 28, 1866. On April 4 and 5, 1866, USG wrote to Matías Romero, Mexican minister, concerning a meeting between Romero and President Andrew Johnson. Translated into Spanish in Romero, comp., *Correspondencia de la Legacion Mexicana en Washington durante la Intervencion Extranjera 1860–1868* (Mexico, 1870–92), VII, 389. On April 5, Bvt. Lt. Col. Wright Rives, military secretary for Johnson, wrote to USG arranging the meeting. Translated into Spanish, *ibid.* See Thomas D. Schoonover, ed., *Mexican Lobby: Matías Romero in Washington, 1861–1867* (Lexington, Ky., 1986), pp. 120–28.

Circular

Washington, D. C. Mch 3d *18656*

To General[s] E R S Canby, Comdg Dept Louisiana
To General H. G. Wright Comdg Dept Texas
To General C R Woods Comdg Dept Alabama
To General J. G. Foster Comdg Dept Florida
To General J B Steedman Comdg Dept Georgia
To General Danl. E Sickles Comdg Dept South Carolina
To General Thos H Ruger Comdg Dept North Carolina
To General A H Terry Comdg Dept Virginia
Circular
General.

By direction of the Secretary of War you are hereby directed to establish in conjunction with the proper civil authorities, a rigid quarantine on all arrivals from the West India Islands, recent advices establishing the fact of the prevalence of Asiatic Cholera there

U. S. Grant
Lieut Genl

Telegram sent (in tabular form), DNA, RG 107, Telegrams Collected (Bound); telegram received (on March 4, 1866), *ibid.*, RG 393, Dept. of Va. and N. C., 1st Military District, Telegrams Received. On March 3, Brig. Gen. Joseph K. Barnes, surgeon gen., had written to Secretary of War Edwin M. Stanton. "I have the honor respectfully to recommend that the Commanding Generals of the Departments of Louisiana, Texas, Alabama, Florida, Georgia, South Carolina, North Carolina and Virginia be instructed (by telegraph) to establish, in conjunction with the proper civil authorities, a rigid quarantine on all arrivals from the West India Islands, recent advices establishing the fact of the prevalence of Asiatic Cholera there." LS, *ibid.*, RG 108, Letters Received.

On March 5, Maj. Gen. Alfred H. Terry, Richmond, telegraphed to USG. "Referring to your despatch of the third (3rd) inst. I think that the most effectual way of protecting the Department from Cholera would be to establish the Quarantine between Cape Henry and Cape Charles and take jurisdiction over all vessels entering the Chesapeake whether bound to ports in the Department or out Side of it—unless this be done I do not think that I can prevent vessels from entering the Rivers North of the James. If this Course should be authorized I Should need a Substantial Steamer for the health officer and it would be well to have a Naval Steamer to act as guard Ship" Telegram received (at 3:00 P.M.), *ibid.*, RG 107, Telegrams Collected (Bound); *ibid.*, RG 108, Telegrams Received; copies, *ibid.*, RG 393, Dept. of Va. and N. C., 1st Military District, Telegrams Sent; DLC-USG, V, 54. On March 10, USG endorsed a telegram received. "Respectfully forwarded to the Hon. Secy. of War." ES, DNA, RG 108, Telegrams Received. On March 15, 11:00 A.M., USG telegraphed to Terry. "Your telegram of the fifth 5th inst relating to quarantine is approved For further guidance in the matter you are referred to G O No 15 from these Hdqrs" Telegram sent, *ibid.*, RG 107, Telegrams Collected (Bound); telegram received, *ibid.*, RG 94, War Records Office, Dept. of Va. and N. C. On March 12, Bvt. Maj. Gen. Edward D. Townsend had issued General Orders No. 15. "~~In compliance with a joint resolution of congress~~ On the recommendation of the Surgeon Genl the Dept Commanders of Virginia North Carolina South Carolina Georgia Florida Alabama Mississippi Louisiana & Texas are instructed to cause; 1d all vessels arriving at ports within their Departmts from ports infected with the cholera, but having had no case during their passage, to be quantined for fifteen days & thoroughly fumigated; 2d all such vessels which have had cholera on board during the passage to be quarntined for fifteen days after the termination of the last case & thoroughly fumigated. In carrying out this ~~order quarantine~~ quantine Dept Commanders will consult & ask assistance from officers of the Navy in their vicinity & correspond direct with the Sec of the Navy in reference to such assistance & cooperation." ADf (in the hand of Bvt. Brig. Gen. Cyrus B. Comstock), *ibid.*, Letters Received, 203A 1866.

On March 7, Maj. Gen. John G. Foster, Tallahassee, Fla., telegraphed to USG. "I have the honor to acknowledge the receipt of your telegraphic order of March 3rd, 1866, relative to the Establishment of Quarantine, and will at once take steps to carry out your directions." Telegram received (on March 8, 6:20 P.M.), *ibid.*, Telegrams Collected (Bound); *ibid.*, RG 108, Telegrams Received; copy, DLC-USG, V, 54. On the same day, Maj. Gen. Daniel E. Sickles, Charleston, wrote to Bvt. Col. Theodore S. Bowers. "I have the honor to acknowledge the receipt of a telegram from the Lieut-General Commanding, directing me to maintain in conjunction with the civil authorities, a rigid quarantine on all arrivals from the West India Islands. This matter was the subject of a conference between His Excellency the Governor of South Carolina and myself, during the recent visit of the Governor to this City, in February, and in compliance with his request a thorough quarantine has been established, under the supervision of the Medical Director, at all the Ports of entry in this Department. Since the government of the City has been in the hands of the municipal authorities, the Medical Director has repeatedly had occasion to call the attention of the Mayor of Charleston to the insufficient measures taken to preserve the health of the

City, especially in view of impending epidemics; and I regret to find it my duty to report that these remonstrances have not been followed by such adequate and effective exertions as the emergency demands." LS, DNA, RG 108, Letters Received. On March 14, Bvt. Col. Ely S. Parker wrote to Sickles. "Referring to your letter of the 7th inst relating to the fact that the Medical Director had repeatedly called the attention of 'the Mayor of Charleston to the insufficient measures taken to preserve the health of the city, and that these remonstrances have not been adequately heeded the Lieutenant General directs that should the emergency arise you will assume the responsibility and supply any deficiencies neglected by the Municipal authorities of Charleston for a rigid qauarantine." Copies, *ibid.*, Letters Sent; DLC-USG, V, 47, 109. On March 21, 12:45 P.M., USG telegraphed to Bvt. Maj. Gen. John M. Brannan, Augusta, Ga. "Please give Surgeon Thos Sim, Health Officer of Charleston, facilities for carrying out quarantine restrictions in Savannah and throughout the Georgia Coast" Telegram sent, DNA, RG 107, Telegrams Collected (Bound); copies, *ibid.*, RG 108, Letters Sent; DLC-USG, V, 47, 109.

On March 5, Maj. Gen. Edward R. S. Canby, New Orleans, telegraphed to USG's adjt. "Telegram of the Lt Genl in reference to Cholera at the West Indies is recd. Orders for a rigid quarantine will be promptly issued." Telegram received (at 9:50 A.M.), DNA, RG 107, Telegrams Collected (Bound); (at 9:55 A.M.) *ibid.*, RG 108, Telegrams Received; copies (one sent by mail), *ibid.*, Letters Received; DLC-USG, V, 54. On March 12, John M. Courtney, agent, New-York Mail Steamship Co., New Orleans, telegraphed to USG. "A quarantine has been established to go into effect immediately by your order. The 'Evening Star' left New York four 4 days previous to your order with a large number of passengers, to touch at Havana to land mails and passengers. In case of no sickness and the sanitary condition of the ship being perfect will you please get her release? Answer" Telegram received (on March 13, 12:20 P.M.), DNA, RG 107, Telegrams Collected (Bound); *ibid.*, RG 108, Telegrams Received; copies, *ibid.*, Letters Received; DLC-USG, V, 54. On March 13, Barnes endorsed this telegram. "Respectfully returned. In case of no sickness and the sanitary condition of the ship being perfect, it is recommended that the passengers and cargo from New York be released and those from Havana subjected to quarantine regulations." ES, DNA, RG 108, Letters Received. At 5:45 P.M., USG telegraphed to Courtney. "In case the 'Evening Star' has no sickness and the Sanitary condition of the ship being perfect, the passengers and cargo from New York will be released but those from Havanna will be quarantined." Telegram sent, *ibid.*, RG 107, Telegrams Collected (Bound); copies, *ibid.*, RG 108, Letters Sent; DLC-USG, V, 47, 109. On March 14, 10:20 A.M., USG telegraphed to Canby. "A telegram has been sent to J M. Courtney Agt New York Mail S. S. Co that the passengers and cargo of the steamship 'Evening Star' taken from New York will be released from quarantine in case there is no sickness and the sanitary condition of the ship is perfect, but passengers & cargo from Havanna will be quarantined" Telegram sent, DNA, RG 107, Telegrams Collected (Bound); copies, *ibid.*, RG 108, Letters Sent; DLC-USG, V, 47, 109. On March 15, Courtney telegraphed to USG. "Your dispatch of thirteenth 13th received releasing New York passengers and cargo on steam ship 'Evening Star' Military here are at a loss to know if that order with its condition allows the 'Evening Star' to come to the city. The sanitary condition of the ship is perfect. Answer" Telegram received (at 5:45 P.M.), DNA, RG 107, Telegrams Collected (Bound); *ibid.*, RG 108, Telegrams Received; copy, DLC-USG, V, 54.

On March 14, Stanton wrote to USG. "The Steamship Cuba one of a recently established line from Baltimore to New Orleans via Havanna left the port of Baltimore on the 7th inst before the establishment of Quarantine regulations & is expected to reach New Orleans on the 18th inst. You will please issue an order in respect to her similar to the order in the case of the Evening Star viz that on her arrival at New Orleans 'in case of no sickness and the sanitary condition being perfect the passengers & cargo from ~~West~~ Baltimore be released & those from Havanna subjected to quarantine regulations'. The report of the Surgeon General on the case is herewith submitted with the application of the agents of Steamer Cuba." ALS, DNA, RG 108, Letters Received. At 2:30 P.M., USG telegraphed to Canby as Stanton had instructed. Telegram sent, *ibid.*, RG 107, Telegrams Collected (Bound); copies, *ibid.*, RG 108, Letters Sent; DLC-USG, V, 47, 109.

On July 20, Maj. Gen. George H. Thomas, Nashville, telegraphed to USG. "Gen C. R. Woods telegraphed yesterday from Macon that the San Salvador had arrived at Savannah with twenty eight (28) cases of cholera on board among recruits for seventh (7) Infantry bound for Florida.—He ordered the ship into Quarantine and to enforce the same telegraphed to Gen'l Sickles at Charleston asking for steamer Cosmopolitan—Gen Woods has since reported that Gen Sickles refuses to receive his dispatch" Telegram received (at 5:30 P.M.), DNA, RG 107, Telegrams Collected (Bound); *ibid.*, RG 108, Telegrams Received; copies, *ibid.*, RG 393, Dept. of the Cumberland, Telegrams Sent; DLC-USG, V, 54. At 8:00 P.M., USG telegraphed to Sickles. "Please direct the 'Salvador' with Cholera aboard to be placed in quarantine according to the request of Gen Wood" Telegram sent, DNA, RG 107, Telegrams Collected (Bound); copies, *ibid.*, RG 108, Letters Sent; DLC-USG, V, 47, 60. On the same day, Sickles telegraphed to USG. "Your telegram rec'd The only request I have received from Gen Wood was for a steamer to take off the troops which I have sent to him. I have offered him all the facilities of my quarantine station at Braddock's Point for the San Salvador troops passengers & crew. I understand the ship is in quarantine & the troops landed" Telegram received (dated July 21, received at 4:40 P.M.), DNA, RG 107, Telegrams Collected (Bound); (dated July 20) *ibid.*, RG 108, Telegrams Received; copies (one sent by mail), *ibid.*, Letters Received; *ibid.*, RG 393, 2nd Military District, Telegrams Sent; (dated July 21) DLC-USG, V, 54. At 8:00 P.M., USG telegraphed to Thomas. "Gen Sickles has been directed to comply with Gen Woods request in regard to Steamer 'Salvador.'" Telegram sent, DNA, RG 107, Telegrams Collected (Bound); copies, *ibid.*, RG 108, Letters Sent; *ibid.*, RG 393, Dept. of the Cumberland, Telegrams Received; DLC-USG, V, 47, 60. On Aug. 15 and 24, Bvt. Maj. Gen. Daniel Butterfield, superintendent, recruiting service, New York City, wrote to Brig. Gen. John A. Rawlins submitting reports on the matter. LS, DNA, RG 108, Letters Received.

On July 21, Mayor Jones M. Withers, Mobile, wrote to USG. "It is the opinion of the Corporate Authorities and of the Board of Health, that there is no valid reason for continuing the Quarantine, which was established in Mobile Bay some months since, by your order. If the City Authorities are permitted to exercise any discretion, the Quarantine will be abolished as an unecessary expense. Desirous however, of avoiding any conflict, I have been instructed to communicate with you for the purpose of ascertaining 'what powers the City Authorities possess in establishing and abolishing the present Quarantine System'" LS,

DNA, RG 108, Letters Received. On Aug. 1, Barnes endorsed this letter. "Respectfully returned to Head Quarters Armies of the United States with remark that the Quarrantine should be strictly enforced for the protection of the Troops." ES, *ibid.* On Aug. 2, Maj. George K. Leet wrote to Withers quoting Barnes. Copies, DLC-USG, V, 47, 60; DNA, RG 108, Letters Sent.

On Aug. 17, Maj. Gen. John M. Schofield, Richmond, telegraphed to USG. "The captain of the steamer 'Adelaide' was yesterday ordered by Gen Miles to land troops at Craney Island for quarantine This order he disregarded. I recommend that his pay be withheld until he gives satisfactory explanation" Telegram received (at 10:10 A.M.), DNA, RG 107, Telegrams Collected (Bound); *ibid.*, RG 108, Telegrams Received; copies, *ibid.*, RG 393, Dept. of the Potomac, Telegrams Sent; DLC-USG, V, 54. On the same day, Leet endorsed a copy of this telegram to Bvt. Maj. Gen. Montgomery C. Meigs. Copy, DNA, RG 108, Register of Letters Received. On Aug. 21, Meigs wrote to USG. ". . . It is supposed that this steamer belongs to the Baltimore Steam Packet Company, with which company the Quartermasters Department has an arrangement for the 'transportation of Government freight and troops between Baltimore, Fort Monroe, City Point and Richmond, and intermediate places.' The recommendation of General Miles will be carried into effect, and the amount due for the services referred to, be withheld until satisfactory explanation is given." LS, *ibid.*, RG 92, Miscellaneous Letters Sent (Press).

To Maj. Gen. William T. Sherman

Washington D. C. March 3d *1866*

GENERAL:

In pursuance of your recommendations of the 17th of Feb.y[1] I have recommended the Muster-out of all Volunteer General officers[2] with the exception of Department commanders and three Brigadiers, Allen, Rucker and Ingalls, and the division of the Dept. of Mo. into two Departments with Hd Qrs. at Leavenworth & Omaha, the territory comprising each Dept. to be designated by you. If the orders as recommended are approved Pope and P. St. G. Cooke[3] will be the Dept. Commanders. You and Sheridan will also be authorized to assign to duty, with their Bvt. Rank, such officers of your respective commands as you may deem necessary.

As early as possible in the Spring posts and lines of travel which it is necessary to hold with troops should be determined. To aid you in making the necessary inspection to determine this I propose to send two of my Staff officers, Babcock and either Comstock or Porter, to aid you. I would like to have Babcock take the Northern Route, from Minnesota to Puget Sound. These officers will report to you for instructions and information before starting, and to you, Gn. Halleck and myself, on their return.

General Cooke is a Brigadier in the regular Army. Otherwise I should not have selected him to command a Department. He has had experience on the plains however and may do well. One objection to retaining a Volunteer General for that service is that their desire to be retained in service may, even unintentionally, induce them to introduce hostilities where a mild course would be much more efficient. An officer whose rank is permanent has a personal interest in preserving quiet.

I am anxious to get some colored troops out on the plains and if Wilsons Bill passes in time will send you from four to six regiments of them in addition to the White troops you now have. In the absence of these I think you had better send about two regiments out and trust to recruiting most of them for the regular army afterwards.

Yours Truly
U. S. GRANT
Lt. Gn.

MAJ. GN. W. T. SHERMAN,
COMD.G MIL. DIV. OF THE MISS.

ALS, DNA, RG 393, Military Div. of the Miss., Letters Received. On March 7, 1866, Maj. Gen. William T. Sherman, St. Louis, telegraphed to USG. "Letter of March 3rd rec'd before making positive order for the plains, please await the receipt of a very full report on all the routes to be mailed you this day. My heartfelt sympathies in the death of Col Bowers." Telegram received (at 3:10 P.M.), *ibid.*, RG 107, Telegrams Collected (Bound); *ibid.*, RG 108, Telegrams Received; copies, *ibid.*, RG 393, Military Div. of the Miss., Letters Sent; DLC-USG, V, 54. On the same day, Sherman wrote to USG. "I have the honor to acknowledge receipt this day of your letter of March 3. I have given Gen Pope notice of such part as affects him, but I know him to be opposed to the division of his Departmt, but still Montana is growing daily into importance, and its interests and routes leading thereto in my judgmt require the Supervision of some one officer. NewMexico, Colorado and Utah, with routes leading thereto will give full employmt to another Departmt Commander. But that you may have all the facts spread before you, I have asked you by telegraph today to suspend action until you have in hand a valuable Report submitted by General Pope, and now being copied for transmittal to you. When Babcock and Comstock or Porter report to me, I can give them good maps, and much information, and can send the former up to Montana, via the Missouri River, and the latter across into Utah, by the travelled Road. Their personal presence will give great assurance that we are studying the subjects with a view to the permant interest of our People in those remote Regions. I have a Rgmt of Black troops at Cairo doing nothing, and have sent inquiries to ascertain if possible approximaty what proportn of the men would reenlist under the New Bill when it becomes Law—I have sent for similar data from one of General Reynolds Regimets at Helena. As soon as it becomes safe to draw in from Utah and NewMexico I will give these Regiments to General Pope for assignmt to NewMexico and Utah. They will have to march of course all the way from the Missouri River. . . . P S. I read with pain & sorrow of the sad & sudden death of the admirable staff officer and personal friend of yours, Colonel Bowers. He was invaluable to you, and you will find it difficult to replace him. I beg to offer you and his friends the assurance of my deep sympathy." ALS, DNA, RG 108, Letters Received. Enclosed was a letter of instruction of March 5 from Sherman to Maj. Gen. John Pope. Copy, *ibid.* See letter to Maj. Gen. William T. Sherman, March 14, 1866.

On March 3, Bvt. Col. Theodore S. Bowers wrote to Sherman. "Your endorsement on the paper of Generals Pope and St George Cooke in relation to recruits for regular regiments of your command has just been received. For your information I enclose copy of instructions sent to the Adjutant General yesterday. Since the receipt of your endorsement the order has been made imperative." LS, DNA, RG 393, Military Div. of the Miss., Letters Received; copies (attributed to USG), *ibid.*, RG 108, Letters Sent; DLC-USG, V, 47, 109. Bowers enclosed a letter of March 2 from USG to Bvt. Maj. Gen. Edward D. Townsend. "In view of the fact that Gen'l Sherman will replace all his Volunteers with Regulars as soon as they can be reached in the Spring, I think it advisable to send all recruits, especially Cavalry and Infantry, to him until the organizations with him are filled up." Copies, DNA, RG 108, Letters Sent; *ibid.*, RG 393, Military Div. of the Miss., Letters Received; *ibid.*, Dept. of the Mo., Letters Received; DLC-USG, V, 47, 109.

1. On Feb. 17, Sherman had written to Brig. Gen. John A. Rawlins. "I have been giving my whole attention to the subject of distribution of the Regular army subject to my command with a view to affording the largest amount of protection, proportioned to the force at my disposal, and will in a short time submit a 'projet' based on the official Reports and recommendations of Department Commanders. My own mind is made up, but I may modify it when I have more detailed reports. All volunteers will be mustered out as soon as we can reach them, and partially replace them with Regulars. I am now willing that the General officers of Volunteers still retained be mustered out at some prospective date say April 1, provided, the same course be pursued towards all and that all in the other Grand Military Divisions should be treated alike. In the Departmt of the Ohio there is no absolute necessity of Army troops, but to preserve the public property, and to maintain a mere show of force along the Canada Border, we should occupy Detroit with 2 Companies of the 4th Infantry Col Casey—& 1 Battery of Artillery, now there. At Fort Gratiot one Company of Artillery & 1 of Infantry, and at Fort Brady the two Companies of the 4th Infantry. I can send a

Battery of Artillery from here, and would merely suggest that another company of the 4th Inf be sent to Ft Gratiot. This would give for the whole Departmt two Companies of Artillery and half the 4th Infantry. (5 companies) In the Departmt of Arkansas I think the 19th Infantry now there *must* suffice, and I expect to draw therefrom the 3rd Regular Cavalry and send it to Colorado & New-Mexico, about June or July. The Departmt of Missouri is very large, and I sometimes think it would simplify it, by a division into two Departmts with their Head Quarters at Leavenworth, and Omaha, giving the one control of Kansas, Colorado, Utah & New Mexico, and the other Minnesota, Iowa, Nebraska Dacotah and Montana. The Mountain territories of Montana Utah & Colorado, are daily assuming more importance, and we will be forced to give them some military protection, and to cover the roads leading thereto as against the Wandering tribes of Indians who however friendly must live in part by depredations upon the White settlements, and Emigrant trains who always have, and always will act towards the Indians as hostile to them. We must guard two if not three Roads across the vast Plains,—viz from Riley to Denver & NewMexico,—from Omaha, by Kearney, Laramie and Utah, and some one of the other travelled roads further north, it may be from Minnesota by Fort Pierre, the Big Sheyenne, & north of the Black Hills to Montana. The best we can do this spring is to put the 3rd Infantry Col Hoffman in Minnesota & Westward: the 10th Infantry, along the Platte, the 13th Infantry in Colorado, and along the Smoky Hill.—The 5th Infantry for the time being had better remain in NewMexico, and we will have to send the 18th or some other to Utah.—The 2nd U. S. Cavalry will be used as auxiliary towards Montana; and the Third Cavalry on the Upper Arkansas towards Colorado & NewMexico. I could use a Negro Regimt in Utah, and another in NewMexico, but as the present Negro Regiments will doubtless have to be discharged, with a view to a reorganization into New Regiments I deem it imprudent at this time to send them beyond easy reach. These general dispositions are merely preliminary, and I make them now, that the Lt Genl Commanding may give me a full share of recruits for the Regiments destined to move far out, as soon as the spring will justify the order. The Condition of Peace that simplifies the military problems in all other parts of the United States, does not make a material difference in the Territories, for the Indians remain, and the natural Conflicts will be increased, by the greatly augmented number of Emigrants, who spite of all warning will move by different roads, and so strung out as to tempt the Indians to rob, plunder and kill. I of course prefer that the departmt commanders should not be changed as they are now familiar with their respective commands, yet I am fully aware that Generals Ord & Reynolds are held by their Volunteer Commissions and I cannot well replace them. But Regular officers can be found to replace all the other subordinate commanders." ALS, DNA, RG 108, Letters Received.

2. On Feb. 7, 11:30 A.M., USG telegraphed to Maj. Gens. George G. Meade, Philip H. Sheridan, Sherman, and George H. Thomas. "In all cases within your command where you can relieve General Officers of Volunteers by officers of the regular army assigned to duty according to brevet rank forward the names for assignment by the President, and upon the Officers reporting, relieve the General Officers and report their names to the Adjutant General for muster out" Telegram sent (Sherman not included among the addressees), *ibid.*, RG

107, Telegrams Collected (Bound); telegram received (incomplete), *ibid.*, RG 393, Military Div. of the Atlantic, Telegrams Received. USG's letterbooks include Sherman among the addressees. Copies, DLC-USG, V, 47, 109; DNA, RG 108, Letters Sent. On the same day, Meade, Philadelphia, wrote to Bowers. "In reply to the telegram, of this date, from the Lieutenant General, I have the honor to report that the following named General officers of volunteers, of this command, can be relieved by officers of regulars, as hereinafter set forth, provided that the latter be assigned to duty according to their brevet rank, by the President, viz: Major General J. C. Robinson, Command'g District of Northern & Southern New York, by Bv't Brig Genl. J. C. Robinson, U. S. Army, Bv't Major General R. B. Ayres, U. S. Vols, Comd'g District of the Shenandoah, Middle Department, by Bv't Brig Genl. R. B. Ayres, U. S. A. Major General N. A. Miles, U. S. Vols, Comd'g District of Fort Monroe, Virginia, by Bv't Brig Genl. H. S. Burton, U. S. A. Bv't Major General J. W. Turner, U. S. Vols, Comd'g District of Henrico, Department of Virginia, by Bv't Colonel J. W. Turner, U. S. A. Bv't Major General A. Ames, Commd'g District, Department of South Carolina, by Bv't Colonel A. Ames, U. S. A. The only other General officers of Volunteers in this command, are Major General Hooker, Comd'g Dep't of the East, Major General Hancock, Comd'g Middle Dep't Major General Terry, Comd'g Dep't of Virginia Bv't Major General Ruger, Brig Genl. Comd'g Dep't of No. Carolina, Major General Sickles, Comd'g Dep't of So. Carolina . . . P. S. The attention of the Lieut General is invited to the fact that the assignment of Major General Miles was a special one emanating from the War Dep't." LS, *ibid.*, Letters Received. On Feb. 13, Thomas, Nashville, telegraphed to USG. "In reply to your telegram of the 7th inst. I recommend as follows:—Brigadier & Brev. Maj. General J. C. Davis U. S. Vols. Brev't. Brig. Gen'l. U. S. army, commanding 1st Division Dep[a]rtment of Kentucky, be mustered out as volunteer & assigned to same command according to Bvt. rank in regular army with a view to his being assigned to command of Dept. of Kentucky upon acceptance of resignation of Gen. J. M. Palmer—*second*—Major Gen'l. George Stoneman [vo]lunteers Bvt. Brig. Gen. U. S. army to be mustered out as volunteer & assigned to command of Dept. of Tennessee which he now holds, according to Bvt. rank in regular army.—*Third.* (3d) ~~m~~Maj Gen'l A. C. Gillem volunteers, Bvt. colonel U. S. army Commanding District of East Tennesse to be mustered out as volunteer & assigned to the command according to his Bvt. rank—4th—Brig &. Bvt. Maj. Gen'l. John E. Smith Commanding district of west Tennessee to be mustered out of service & Bvt. Col. William H. Ca[r]lin Major 16th infantry to be assigned to that command according to Bvt. rank—*5th* Brig & Bvt. Maj Genl T. J. Wood, U. S. Volunteers Bvt. Brig Gen'l U. S. army Comd'g Department of Mississippi to be mustered out as Volunteer & assigned to same command according to Bvt. rank in regular army—*6th*—Maj. Gen'l Chas R. Wood Volunteers, Bvt. Brig. Gen. U. S. army Commanding Dept. of Alabama to be mustered out as volunteer & assigned to same command according to Bvt. rank in regular army—7th—Brig & Bvt. Maj Gen'l John M. Brannan U. S. Vol's. Bvt. Brig. Gen'l U. S. army Comd'g District of Savannah Ga.—to be mustered out as volunteer and assigned to same command according to Bvt. rank in regular army with view to his being assigned to command of Department of Georgia upon resignation of Gen'l Steedman—" Telegram received (at 7:45 P.M.), *ibid.*, Telegrams Received; copies, *ibid.*, RG 393, Dept. of the Cumberland, Telegrams Sent; DLC-USG, V, 54. On Feb. 20, Sheridan, New Orleans, telegraphed to USG. "I have the honor to acknowledge the receipt of telegram from the Lieut General of the 8th relative to the further muster out of general officers of Volunteers when their places can be supplied by officers of the Regular Army assigned to duty according to their Brevet rank. If officers in command of departments are understood to be included in these ends I have the honor to report for muster out. Maj Genl H. G. Wright commanding Dep't of Texas. Maj Gen'l E. R. S. Canby Com'd'g Dept of Louisiana Bv't Maj Gen T. W. Sherman Commanding Eastern Dist of Louisiana. Maj Gen J. G. Foster Com'd'g Dep't of Florida and Maj Gen G. W. Getty commanding District of the Rio Grande and to request that each of these officers may be assigned to duty according to his brevet rank. The list comprises all the general officers of Volunteers now under my command. The delay in reporting was owing to my absence in Texas during which time the despatch was received here." Telegram received (on Feb. 21, 9:15 A.M.), DNA, RG 107, Telegrams Collected (Bound); *ibid.*, RG 108, Telegrams Received; copies (one sent by mail), *ibid.*, Letters Received; *ibid.*, RG 393, Military Div. of the Southwest and Dept. of the Gulf, Telegrams Sent; DLC-USG, V, 54; DLC-Philip H. Sheridan.

On March 3, USG wrote to Secretary of War Edwin M. Stanton. "Enclosed I have the honor to submit orders which I respectfully recommend be published. If there are any General Officers named in the Musterout orders whos names should be omitted I would recommend that they be stricken from the order." ALS, DNA, RG 94, Letters Received, 250A 1866. The enclosed list is *ibid.*

3. On March 10, Sherman wrote to USG. "I am afraid that Gen P— St Geo Cooke is not the right man for the new and very important command of the Departmt of the Platte. We need a young General, who can travel and see with his own eyes and if need be command both whites and Indians to keep the Peace. General W. S. Hancock is the proper person. Cannot an exchange be effected? I think Hancock would not only consent but be gratified at the offer. Baltimore is no place for him, but is exactly the place for Cooke. Should the latter go up the Missouri I fear actual trouble, whereas with the latter I feel assured we can with our limited force not only avoid trouble, but lay the foundation for future peace & Safety. This earnest conviction will I trust warrant me in asking this change of detail." ALS, MoSHi. See letter to Maj. Gen. William T. Sherman, March 10, 1866.

To Lorenzo Bowers

Washington D. C., March 7th *1866*

DR. LORENZO BOWERS,
LEBANON, PA.

It is with heartfelt sorrow that I communicate to you the accidental death of your most estimable and beloved brother, Col. T. S.

Bowers, It occurred at 3 p, m, yesterday, opposite West Point. In attempting to get on the cars whilst in motion he fell between two of them and was instantly crushed to death. His funeral will take place tomorrow at West Point. Your brother had won more than esteem from all who knew him, and in his death the country sustains a great loss. His brother staff officers & myself leave here today to attend his funeral.

U. S. GRANT,
Lieut. General.

Telegram, copies, DLC-USG, V, 47, 109; DNA, RG 108, Letters Sent; *ibid.*, Letters Received. On March 6, 1866, USG, New York City, telegraphed to Bvt. Brig. Gen. Cyrus B. Comstock. "In getting on the cars at Garrison Station at three this afternoon Col. Bowers fell between the cars and was instantly killed." Telegram received, *ibid.*, Telegrams Received; copy, DLC-USG, V, 54. Bvt. Col. Theodore S. Bowers had accompanied USG and his son Frederick Dent Grant to USMA, arriving on the opposite side of the Hudson River from West Point, N. Y., the evening of March 5. Early on March 6, they crossed the river to USMA, leaving Fred (see letter to Andrew Johnson, March 1, 1866), and recrossed the river to Garrison Station. Upon being informed of the accident, USG stated: "Something told me he was killed." And after viewing Bowers's remains, "That is him. A very estimable man he was. He has been with me through all my battles." *National Intelligencer*, March 9, 1866.

On March 7, 9:00 A.M., USG, Washington, D. C., telegraphed to Brig. Gen. George W. Cullum, West Point. "Please postpone the burial of Col Bowers until tomorrow to enable some of the Staff to attend. Please answer." Telegram sent, DNA, RG 107, Telegrams Collected (Bound); copies, *ibid.*, RG 108, Letters Sent; DLC-USG, V, 47, 109. On the same day, Cullum telegraphed to USG. "As requested Col. Bower's funeral will be postponed till 4 P. M. tomorrow. Your son was much affected by the sad event. Capt. Dunn of your staff is here." Telegram received (at 11:00 A.M.), DNA, RG 107, Telegrams Collected (Bound); *ibid.*, RG 108, Telegrams Received; copy, DLC-USG, V, 54. At 11:40 A.M., USG telegraphed to Cullum. "Six Staff Officers leave here today and will reach West Point by the train leaving New York at 7.30 A M tomorrow to attend the funeral of Col Bowers." Telegram sent, DNA, RG 107, Telegrams Collected (Bound); copies, *ibid.*, RG 108, Letters Sent; DLC-USG, V, 47, 109. USG attended the funeral on March 8 and returned to Washington the morning of March 9. See *New York Times*, March 9, 1866; *New York Tribune*, March 9, 1866; *Galena Weekly Gazette*, March 13, 1866; Theodore G. Risley, "Colonel Theodore S. Bowers," *Journal of the Illinois State Historical Society*, XII, 3 (Oct., 1919), 407–11.

On March 15, George H. Stuart, Philadelphia, wrote to USG. "It was with feelings of great sorrow and surprise that I learned of the sudden death of your valued and intimate friend Adjutant Gen. Bowers. I am sure that the near relation which he sustained to you as one of your own family, and the associations which you have had with him in all of your campaigns as a tried and trusted companion in arms, make the stroke of Providence one of no ordinary sadness to you. The circumstances under which he was removed, as in a moment from the enjoyment of health, life, and vigor by a sad and distressing accident must make your loss more keenly felt. In the feeling of grief and sorrow which you have at this time, all who know and honor you for what you have done for the country, share, and it is my melancholy privilege to convey to you my personal assurances of sincere sympathy in this bereavement. While the memory of the virtues of the deceased is all that is left you to have, it is a comfort to know that even thus he may be said to live, especially if all that was good and imitable in a character so dear to you, is followed by those to whom his life and associations were precious. How impressive is the lesson thus taught to all of us, to be good soldiers in the cause of truth & God. With renewed expressions of condolence . . . P. S. My daughters join with me in this expression of sympathy, and remember with feelings of pleasant interest their intercourse with Adjt. Gen. Bowers at your residence." Copy, DNA, RG 108, Letters Received. Maj. and Bvt. Col. Michael R. Morgan, Fort Leavenworth, Kan., wrote to USG. "I was shocked and grieved to learn of the terrible death of poor Bowers. In him the Government has lost a conscientious and faithful officer. To you who had been so long associated with him his terrible fate must be deeply deplored, and it is to assure you that I sincerely join you in this feeling that I write" Copy (undated), *ibid.* Additional letters of sympathy are *ibid.* On March 9, Cullum wrote to USG. "Thinking it might be of interest to you, I directed Dr. Head, the Surgeon at this post, to prepare the enclosed statement of the condition of the body of the late Col. Bowers after his shocking death. I also enclose a letter for you received last evening. Hoping you returned safely to Washington, where you can take a little rest, . . ." ALS, *ibid.* The enclosed autopsy report is *ibid.*

On April 2, Maj. George K. Leet directed the AGO to issue General Orders No. 19. "The Lieutenant General with deep regret announces to the Army the decease, at Garrison Station, opposite West Point, N. Y., on the 6th inst., of Major Theodore S. Bowers, of the Adjutant Generals Department, and Brevet Colonel USA., at the age of thirty-four. Colonel Bowers began his military career as a private in Company "G" 48th Regiment Illinois Infantry Volunteers, in October 1861. He was commissioned first lieutenant of his company March 24th 1862; was made an aide-de-camp to General Grant April 26th 1862, and was appointed captain and aide-de-camp November 1st 1862. February 19th 1863 Captain Bowers was appointed Judge Advocate for the Department of the Tennessee with the rank of major. After the surrender of Vicksburg Major Bowers was assigned in orders assistant adjutant General with the rank of lieutenant-colonel. July 29th 1864 Colonel Bowers was made captain and assistant quartermaster in the regular army, and was transferred January 5th 1865, to the adjutant Gen'ls branch of the service with the rank of major. He was brevetted lieutenant-colonel and colonel USA. 'for gallant and meritorious services during the war' March 13th 1865. His duties were continuously in the field with the Lieutenant General until the surrender of General Lee at Appomattox Court House, and from that time forward at his Head Quarters at Washington, D. C. The Army generally has to mourn the loss of a brother officer whose virtues as a man and whose soldierly qualities are worthy of emulation. The officers of the Adjutant General's Department will wear the usual badge of mourning for thirty days." Df, *ibid.*, RG 94, Letters Received, 248A 1866.

To Thomas H. Dudley

Washington D. C. March 9th *1866*.

HON. T. H. DUDLEY,
AMERICAN CONSUL,
LIVERPOOL ENG.
DEAR SIR:

Your favor of the 16th of Feb.y kindly inviting me to become your guest whilst in Liverpool, in case I visit England as I had contemplated doing in the course of this year, is received. I feel highly flattered by this testimonial of your friendship and will avail myself of it when I do go to England. It is not now likely however that I shall get off this year. Public duties seem to confine me here for the present and it is impossible to foresee how long this state of affairs will continue.

Very respectfully
your obt. svt.
U. S. GRANT
Lt. Gn.

ALS, CSmH. Thomas H. Dudley, born in 1819 in N. J., trained as a lawyer, was appointed U.S. consul at Liverpool in 1861.

To Maj. Gen. William T. Sherman

Washington D. C. March 10th *1866*

DEAR GENERAL;

Whilst your Board[1] are in session I wish you would take up the subject of recommendations of officers of the Regular Army for the Field offices in the new regiments which it is supposed Congress will authorize, taking Wilson's Bill as your guide. Do not recommend for Cols. Lt. Cols. & Majors but for the Field offices placing the names in the order in which you would recommend them. I would suggest that your list should contain at least twice as many names as there will likely be places to fill.

The loss of poor Bowers is one that I feel more keenely than it is usually possible for anyone to feel for another not an immediate member of their own family. He had risen, by merit alone, whilst serving with me from the ranks to be a Major in the regular Army. His position, even by those who would liked to have had it for themselves, was acknowledged to have been well earned. He was one of the truest and most faithful of men and very efficient. The papers give very correctly the circumstances of his death. My family are all very well and desire to be remembered to you and Mrs. Sherman and the children.

Yours Truly
U. S. GRANT

ALS, DNA, RG 393, Military Div. of the Miss., Provost Marshal Gen., Miscellaneous Records. On March 14, 1866, Maj. Gen. William T. Sherman, St. Louis, wrote to USG. "I have yours of March 10 and as soon as the Board meets I will read the part requiring us to make up the list of recommendations for Field officers to the new Regiments, and have no doubt we can give the very best names. As to Poor Bowers I know how you will miss him. He was so patient & industrious, that no one could question his conduct. I was often struck with his remarkable dispatch of business and tact in fending off personal importunities. You may replace him in part but not entirely, for he spared you trouble in a thousand ways that never reached you. None of the Board is yet here, nor are the Records, although this is the day appointed to assemble. I expect all tomorrow and am ready to go to work. I sent you yesterday Popes orders for stationing his troops this summer All will soon be in motion. And as soon as General Cooke, or Hancock arrives I will part out the land and troops between them. I have ordered Reynolds to assemble the 3rd Cavalry, and one of his Black Regts about Fort Smith now that the Arkansas is up, and as soon as grass will permit to put them in motion up the Canadian to Anton Chico, and Fort Union thence to report to the Commanding officer in New Mexico. I have also selected the 125 U. S. Colored Inf now at Cairo to be ready by April 10 to embark for Leavenworth and thence to march to its destination. I have a Report from the Comdg officer Lt Col A Duncan, that his men will nearly all reenlist when the new Army bill passes. Our old Regular Regiments are nearly all sadly off as to Field officers, and I hope we will be able to amend them radically. Take the 3rd Cavalry—Howe its colonel is before the retiring Board—Stoneman absent comdg a Dept at Memphis, Benny Roberts better absent than present—Duncan on some fancy duty in Iowa, and Kenner Garrard with Pope as an Inspector Genl. I told Garrard that I should order him to duty, but he plead that for his present duty he had given up a leave of absence. I wish you would have Duncan relieved & ordered to duty also Colonel Alexander of the 10th Inf. now here on some mustering duty. We want him with his Regt in Minnesota. All mustering & Recruiting officers above the Rank of Lieutenant should now be with their Regular Regiments." ALS, *ibid.*, RG 108, Letters Received. See letter to Maj. Gen. William T. Sherman, March 3, 1866. On March 12, USG wrote to Sherman. "In the action of the board to revise brevets in the regular army, of which you are president, it is desirable in the case of officers recommended for or appointed to the brevet of general officers, but in which recommendation or appointment the board does not concur, that the board should specify the brevets, less than that of brigr general to which it deems the officer in question entitled, so that the board may make its recommendations in all the cases submitted to it, whether such recommendations are for higher or lower brevet rank than brigadier general. I also wish the board before adjournment to make out a list of recommendations for field officers in the regular army on its reorganization arranged according to their order of merit in the opinion of the board. The list should be much larger than the probable number of vacancies open to officers of the regular army." LS, DNA, RG 393, Military Div. of the Miss., Provost Marshal Gen., Miscellaneous Records; copies (dated March 10), *ibid.*, RG 108, Letters Sent; DLC-USG, V, 47, 109.

On March 20, Sherman telegraphed to USG. "Send us by mail as quick as you can the names of applicants for field officers of the new Regiments also names of the General officers of volunteers made since Genl Order No sixty five (65) of May twenty sixth Eighteen hundred and sixty five (1865)" Telegram received, DNA, RG 108, Telegrams Received; copies, *ibid.*, RG 393, Military Div. of the Miss., Letters Sent; DLC-USG, V, 54. On March 21, Bvt. Brig. Gen. Cyrus B. Comstock wrote to Sherman. "I am directed by the Lt Gen. Comdg. to say that the intention of his letter was to obtain a list of recommendations for promotion of regular officers to field officer's positions in the new regular regements, based on the opinions of the board of the several officer's merit, and not on papers Of the great number of regular officers who desire promotion comparatively few have made application for it, and to act only on such applications would do injustice to others. He did not wish a list of recommendations for promotion from the Volunteer service to the regular service as in his opinion such promotions depend mainly on the delegations from the state to which the officer belongs. The Adjt. Gen'l has been directed to send a list of the General Officers asked for in your telegram of the 19th inst." Copies, *ibid.*, V, 47, 109; DNA, RG 108, Letters Sent. On March 27, Sherman wrote to Comstock. "Yours of Mch 21. is received. The Board of Genl officers has concluded its labors, and the result i[s] in the hands of Col Dayton, who will transmit all the papers to Washington today at the hands of Col Asmussan who brought them out. Our action as to recommendation for Field officers corresponded with what you say, was Genl Grants wish. I am very anxious to secure the Services in the new army, of some of the best young volunteers, but that must be secured through the Members of Congress, to whom will doubtless be left the selection. This matter of Brevets and promotions will make much heart baring, but it is inevitable and we have done the best we could." ALS, DLC-Cyrus B. Comstock.

On March 24, Sherman and Maj. Gens. George G. Meade and George H. Thomas wrote to USG. "In compliance with the terms of your letter of March 12th 1866. in connection with our action under Special Orders No 92. from Head Quarters of the Army, A. G. O. current series, we have arranged our tables so as to cover all the grades from the highest to the lowest, of Officers whom we have recommended as Generals—We now send you lists of names recommended by yourself or the War Department, who are not embraced in our list of Major or Brigadier Generals, who in our judgment should be brevetted as Colonels—We also have computed that under Wilson's Bill, the Regular Army will be entitled to about thirty seven Colonels, Lieutenant Colonels and Majors; and we herewith submit a list of seventy four names (double that of computed vacancies), arranged in the order of merit. But you will observe in all these lists, when merit seemed about equal, we have given precedence according to the rank held in the Volunteer Army about the close of the War, and where according to the Army Register of 1865, officers have already been brevetted, we have treated their cases as disposed of—Hoping that these our recommendations may be of use to you in the difficult and delicate task of selection imposed on you, . . ." LS, DNA, RG 108, Letters Received; ADf, DLC-William T. Sherman. The lists are filed in DNA, RG 108, Letters Received. On April 2, USG favorably endorsed these lists to Secretary of War Edwin M. Stanton. Copies, *ibid.*; *ibid.*, RG 94, ACP, B1919 CB 1866. On April 4, USG wrote to Stanton. "I have the honor to forward herewith, approved, the report of the brevet board of which Gen. W. T. Sherman is President, and the lists of recommendations of the board for brevet major Generalcies and Brevet brigadier generalcies in the regular army." LS, *ibid.*, B282 CB 1866. On the same day, USG endorsed the list of officers for appointment to bvt. maj. gen. "Respectfully forwarded to the Hon. Secretary of War. Approved." Copies, *ibid.*; *ibid.*, RG 108, Register of Letters Received. On the same day, USG endorsed the list of officers for appointment to bvt. brig. gen. "Respy forwarded to the Sec of War. As in the case of some officers, the services are not specified to which the brevet (lower) are given; I would recommend that Captain Torbert receive his brevet for the battle of Gettysburg to date July 4, 1863—and Captain Comstock his brevet of major for seige of Vicksburg to date July 4 1863, and Lt Col for the battle of the Wilderness to date May 6, 1864—and that of Maj Carleton, his brevets of Lt Col & Col for services in New Mexico to date May 25,/65, and that of Major Beckwith receives his brevet of Lt Col for Atlanta Campaign to date Sept 1, 1864, the higher brevets in the cases remains as designated by the Board." Copy, DLC-USG, V, 58. See *SED*, 39-1-41; *HED*, 39-1-145.

On March 29, Sherman wrote to USG. "(private,) . . . What with the Board, and Genl Cooke I have been so busy of late as to neglect to write you on some points about which you feel interested. I think our action as to Brevets though somewhat hurried by reason of the impatience of Genl Meade to get through and our knowledge that another Board was waiting in Washington for our papers, our action was as fair as could be expected. The number of officers who deserve Brevets is so large that I think it would be impolitic to include Non Combatants. The line of distinction is broad, and well understood. Even as it is, we will be embarrassed in having too many officers of exalted Rank & expectations that we cannot give them satisfactory commands. I enclose you my letter of instructions to General Cooke. I feel sure he can do a great deal of good this summer, or at least prevent much mischief. There will be a very large emigration to Montana and the Upper Missouri River this year. Although the ice is not out yet, more than twenty Boats have started, and as many more are ready. Pope starts his troops on the 7th 10th & 13th of April. I can hardly suppose any mere band of Bushwhackers could attempt violence about Lawrence, for the reason that at the time indicated by Mr Babcock there will be assembling at Leavenworth all the Regulars, and the 125th Colored Infantry, and the 3rd Cavalry and another Regimt of Colored Infantry will be marching from Fort Smith Arkansas towards NewMexico, who would be sure to intercept this Band with their plunder. The Cry of Bushwhackers is raised as one of the political hobbies. Still I have sent your letter to Genl Pope with orders to send a Couple of Companies to Lawrence as precautionary. I have no doubt however that Govr Crawford could collect at Lawrence in two days notice, two thousand armed returned soldiers, who could beat the Missouri Bushwhackers at their own game. Every thing is working smoothly out here, and all I meet are engaged in useful work, or are preparing to migrate to one or other of the Frontier Territories. By the orders sent you, you will see I have made the Platte River—North Fork & Sweetwater the line of partition between the two Departmts. Pope will need that Road for the Present, as it is the chief one leading to Utah—and I want Cooke to give his whole attention to the Upper Missouri.—Reynolds has asked for a leave of absence and I have granted it. I rather think unless he is certain to receive a Colonels Commission in the New Army, he had better resign, when I would advise you to throw that Dept into this of the Missouri, and then give to the 'Dept of the Platte', all of the Platte Valley & Route as far as Laramie. I think the Indian Country west of Arkansas can be reached & controlled from Leavenworth quite as well if not better than from the Mississipi Valley. Every thing in the State of Arkansas is moving along so quietly, that if we could gradually draw off all troops but a Depot Guard at Little Rock, the People would hardly know or feel it.—By the 1st of May there will be no soldiers except recruits in Missouri." ALS, DNA, RG 108, Letters Received.

1. On March 1, Bvt. Maj. Gen. Edward D. Townsend issued Special Orders No. 92 appointing a board to meet in St. Louis to consider bvt. appointments of brig. gen. and maj. gen. in the U.S. Army. Copy, *ibid.*, RG 94, Letters Received, 174A 1866. On March 10, Bvt. Col. Ely S. Parker wrote to Townsend directing him to issue special orders assembling a board to consider bvt. appointments in the U.S. Army for the ranks of col. and below. ES, *ibid.*, 200A 1866.

On March 7, Bvt. Maj. Gen. Montgomery C. Meigs wrote to USG. "I see an Order for a Board upon Brevets of the Regular Army, which requires two classes only of Brevets, one for 'gallant and meritorious service,' the other for 'faithful service.' I trust that, on further consideration, the class of 'faithful and meritorious service' heretofore sanctioned will be maintained. There are services not on the field of battle of so much value in their ~~results~~ effects, of such great influence upon results, requiring so much talent, ability, exertion and zeal, that they are entitled, it seems to me, to some higher and different recognition than that of him who is faithful over a few things only. Of such are the services of those officers of the Quartermaster's Department, who, like Gen. Allen and the chiefs of important divisions of this office, have toiled and watched over the immense business and the innumerable details whose successful management went to keep the armies in condition to move at any moment ~~for~~ during months and years. I think Gen. Allen and others whom I have named for Brevet promotions in my own Department deserve recognition of the real value of their services to the cause, as well as of their fidelity to their trust. Fifty thousand men in battle do faithful service; it is to the lucky few, whom fortune favors with opportunity, that special distinction for gallant conduct is awarded by brevet. So among many faithful officers of the Staff Departments, I desire that those to whom much has been committed, and who have successfully achieved great results, something more than fidelity may be awarded—faithful and meritorious, or 'faithful and important' services, covers the ground." LS, *ibid.*, RG 108, Letters Received.

On March 11, Maj. Gen. Philip H. Sheridan, New Orleans, telegraphed to

USG. "I have just received the order detailing me on the Board at St Louis. Unless it is very important that I should go there I beg to be left off, It will interfere very much with a trip to the interior of Texas and over to Florida, which I wished to make to reduce expenses, and look after Government interests . . . Please answer immediately—" Telegram received (at 9:00 P.M.), *ibid.*, RG 107, Telegrams Collected (Bound); *ibid.*, RG 108, Telegrams Received; copies (one sent by mail), *ibid.*, Letters Received; DLC-USG, V, 54; DLC-Philip H. Sheridan. On March 12, 10:50 A.M., USG telegraphed to Sheridan. "You will first make the trip you suggest. Gen Sherman will be notified from these Head-Quarters of the cause of your absence from the Board" Telegram sent, DNA, RG 107, Telegrams Collected (Bound); copies, *ibid.*, RG 108, Letters Sent; DLC-USG, V, 47, 109. On the same day, USG wrote to Sherman. "General Sheridan has permission first to make a trip into Texas and Florida before meeting with the board at St Louis" Copies, *ibid.* On March 23, Sheridan telegraphed to Brig. Gen. John A. Rawlins. "I have the honor to report my return from Florida and to notify the Lieut Gen'l that I ordered the muster out of the Eighty second (82d) Colored infantry which leaves in that Department only one (1) regiment of colored troops. I found the military and civil affairs in very good condition reflecting much credit on the Department commander." Telegram received (at 8:00 P.M.), DNA, RG 107, Telegrams Collected (Bound); *ibid.*, RG 108, Telegrams Received; copies, DLC-USG, V, 54; DLC-Philip H. Sheridan. On March 24, 11:12 A.M., USG telegraphed to Sheridan. "Unless it is highly necessary for you to go to Texas in person I would like you to meet the Board in St Louis." Telegram sent, DNA, RG 107, Telegrams Collected (Bound); copies, *ibid.*, RG 108, Letters Sent; DLC-USG, V, 47, 109. On the same day, Sherman telegraphed to USG. "The Board will Close its work tomorrow Sunday & I will send on the papers Tuesday by Col Asmussen Better notify Sheridan that he need not Come unless he has started" Telegram received, DNA, RG 108, Telegrams Received; copies, *ibid.*, RG 393, Military Div. of the Miss., Letters Sent; DLC-USG, V, 54. At 4:25 P.M., USG telegraphed to Sheridan. "The Board in St Louis has completed its work. You need not go there." Telegram sent, DNA, RG 107, Telegrams Collected (Bound); copies, *ibid.*, RG 108, Letters Sent; DLC-USG, V, 47, 109.

On May 4, Sheridan wrote to Rawlins. "There is a great deal of dissatisfaction about Brevets. It seems to me that the action of the late Board in St Louis has increased it. The officers of the Board are charged with looking out for the interests of their own friends and not for the interests of all. Then it is alleged that they have sought to glorify their own campaigns, and have given brevêts for actions that were not so important, as other battles that officers had fought in under others. It appears to me that the best way to settle this subject, is to brevet all officers of the Regular army to a grade equal to the actual volunteer rank they held. The ruling of the board as to the character of services that should receive brevets, is satisfactory." LS, DNA, RG 108, Letters Received. On May 2, Sheridan had written a letter received at USG's hd. qrs. recommending Capt. and Bvt. Col. George Crook, 4th Inf., for appointment as bvt. brig. gen. *Ibid.*, Register of Letters Received. On May 12, USG endorsed this letter. "Respy. forwarded. Genl. Sheridan having been named as a member of the 'Board' to recommend brevet promotion but being detained by other duties from attending, I would give to his recommendations the same approval given to the action of the board itself." Copy, *ibid.*

On July 2, USG wrote to Stanton. "I would respectfully recommend that the dates of the last Brevets recommended by the St. Louis Board be changed to the 13th of March 1865. The reason for this is that Brevet commissions already confirmed bear the latter date. If the recommendations of the St. Louis Board are confirmed with date as recommended it would make Gn. Officers most distinguished for field service rank below all the confirmed list of same grade." ALS, *ibid.*, RG 94, ACP, G300 CB 1866. On June 28, USG had written to Stanton three times submitting lists of officers recommended for bvt. promotion and endorsed two other such lists. LS and ES, *ibid.*, B282 CB 1866; *ibid.*, 588 1872; *ibid.*, 589 1872. On June 30, USG endorsed to Stanton four lists of officers recommended for bvt. promotion and endorsed three other communications bearing on the subject. ES, *ibid.*, B524 CB 1866; *ibid.*, 588 1872.

Memorandum

[*March 10, 1866*]

HISTORICAL MEMORANDA, CONTINUED, Of the 21st *Regiment Illinois Volunteers, from the* Fifteenth *day of* June *1861, date of last report, to the* 7th *day of* August *1861* . . .

I was appointed Col. of the 21st Ill. Vol. Infantry by Governor Richard Yates some time early in the month of June 1861 and assumed command of the regiment on the 16th of that month. The regiment was mustered into the serv[ice] of the United States in the latter part of the same month. Being ordered to rendezvous the regiment at Quincy Ill. I thought for the purpose of discipline and speedy efficiency for the field it would be well to march the regiment across the country instead of transporting by rail. Accordingly on the 3d of July 1861 the march was commenced from Camp Yates, Springfield Ill. and continued until about three miles beyond the Ill. river where dispatches were received changing the destination of the regiment to Ironton Mo. and directing me to return to the river and take a steamer which had been sent there for the purpose of transporting the regiment to St. Louis. The steamer failing to reach the point of embarkation several days were here lost. In the mean time a portion of the 16th Ill. Infantry, under Col. Smith, were reported surrounded by the enemy at a point on the Hanibal & St Joseph rail-road, West of Palmyra, and the 21st was ordered to their relief. Under these circumstances expedition was necessary. Accordingly the march was abandoned and the rail-road was called into requisition. Before the 21st reached its new destination the 16th had extricated itself. The 21st was then kept on duty on the line of the H. & St. J. rail-road for about two weeks without however meeting an enemy or an incident worth relating. We did make one march however during that time, from Salt River Mo. to Floridas Mo. and return, in search of Thom. Harris who was reported in that neighborhood, with a handful of rebels. It was impossible however to get nearer than a days march of him.—From Salt River the regiment went to Mexico Mo. where it remained for two weeks, thence to Ironton Mo. passing through St. Louis on the 7th of August when I was assigned to duty as a Brig. General and turned over the command of the regiment to that gallant and christian officer, Col. Alexander, who afterwards yealded up his life whilst nobly leading it in the battle of Chickamauga.

U. S. GRANT
Lt. Gn.

ADS, ICHi. On Nov. 25, 1865, Ill. AG Isham N. Haynie, Springfield, wrote to USG. "I shall be exceedingly gratified to procure from yourself a historical memoranda—of the 21st Regt Ills Vols Infy during the period that you were its Commanding officer—beginning with your appointment by Gov Yates & ending with your promotion to Brigd Genl—I care not how brief (or how extended) you make it—What I desire is to have *in this office*—from *yourself*—this paper—We have as far as we could do so procured similar Memoranda from each regimental Commander—I trust you will gratify me and at the same time add a valuable historical paper to our records—" ALS, USG 3. Docketing indicates that USG answered Haynie on March 10, 1866.

To Maj. Gen. George G. Meade

Washington, D. C. March 12th *1866*

MAJ. GN. G. G. MEADE,
COMD.G MIL. DIV. OF THE ATLANTIC,
GENERAL:

In view of the threats of a Fenian invasion of Canada, from the United States, direct officers commanding troops on that frontier, within the limits of your command, to use all vigilence to prevent armed or hostile forces or organizations from leaving the United States to enter British Provinces. I do not feel authorized to direct any interferance with Fenian meetings within the United States; but as the intentions of the Brotherhood seem to be very public their proceedings should be closely watched, and advantage taken of this publicity to thwart their intentions if their object is to organize in the United States for the purpose of making War upon a foreign power with which we are at peace. During our late troubles neither the British Government or the Canadian officials gave themselves much trouble to prevent hostilities being organized against the United States from their possessions. But two wrongs never make a right and it is our duty to prevent wrong on the part of our people. The orders you issue in pursuance of these instructions please send me Copies of at once.

Very respectfully
your obt. svt.
U. S. GRANT
Lt. Gn.

ALS, DNA, RG 393, Military Div. of the Atlantic, Letters Received. On March 13, 1866, Bvt. Brig. Gen. Simon F. Barstow, adjt. for Maj. Gen. George G. Meade, Philadelphia, wrote to Bvt. Col. Ely S. Parker. "I have, in the absence of the Major General Commanding, to acknowledge the receipt of the Lieutenant General's instructions of the 12th inst; and in view of that absence, have not thought it advisable to take other action, than to give the Commanding Officer of the Department of the East, as closely as possible, the views of the Lieutenant General in a letter, a copy of which I enclose." LS, *ibid.*, RG 108, Letters Received. The enclosure is *ibid.* On March 16, 23, 26, Barstow forwarded to USG's hd. qrs. reports on Fenian activities in N. Y. *Ibid.* On March 31, Meade, Philadelphia, wrote to USG. "I forward herewith a copy of a report from the Comdg Officer at Fort Ontario N. York transmitted thro the Hd Qrs Dept. of the East.—I also transmit a copy of my ~~reply~~ letter to Maj. Genl Hooker written on receipt of the above report, by which you will observe, I have directed the seizure of any arms, munitions or other articles contraband of war, which are being collected on the frontier with a view to equipping forces for the invasion of Canada.—I take this occasion to call your attention to the small force now on duty, on that portion of the Northern frontier within the limits of the Military Division of the Atlantic—Enclosed I send an abstract from the latest return of the troops in the Department of the East, by which you will see there are only 357 officers & men, on the frontier of the State of New York, and none on the frontiers of N. Hampshire Vermont & Maine, coterminous with the boundary lines of Canada & New Brunswicke.—The small number of men in this department will permit of but few being sent to the frontier in an emergency—and if an invasion of Canada is seriously attempted in any force by the Fenians I do not see how the Comdg Genl. of the Dept. of the East, without very considerable re-inforcements, can offer any opposition. The report of the Comdg officer at Fort Ontario now sent, is the first official intimation I have received of any actual movement. and I think it well the position of the Govt should be made known and the fact made public, that all acts tending to a violation of neutrality will be discountenanced—And in this point of view, I think it would be advisable if there are any troops available, to increase the forces on the frontier, occupying particularly the lake harbors, from whence expeditions would be likely to sail, and assigning some reliable officer of energy & tact to the immediate command.—" ALS, *ibid.* The enclosures are *ibid.* On April 5, Parker wrote to Meade. "I am instructed by the Lieutenant General to acknowledge the receipt of your communication of the 31st ult. transmitting copy of report of Comdg Officer at Fort Ontario, and of your orders to Gen. Hooker relative to movements &c of Fenians on the frontier, and to say that your course is approved, and further that no troops are at present available to reinforce the troops on that frontier." LS, *ibid.*, RG 393, Military Div. of the Atlantic, Letters Received.

On April 16, Secretary of War Edwin M. Stanton telegraphed to Meade. "I ~~enclose~~ give below a copy of a telegram just transmitted to this Dept by the Secy. of Treasury. You will immediately ~~upon~~ proceed in person to Eastport Me and take such measures as may be proper to enf the neutrality laws of the U S You will please ack the receipt of this telegram. Genl Grant I am informed left this city for Philada to day. ~~if convenient~~ it would well to have an inter with him if you can before leaving and take such instructions as may be given you." ALS (telegram sent), *ibid.*, RG 107, Letters Received from Bureaus. Additional papers are *ibid.* On the same day, Meade telegraphed to Maj. George K. Leet. "The following telegram of this date has been received from the Com'dg Officer at Fort Sullivan Maine and is forwarded for the information of the Lieut General. 'A telegram has been received here today from Gov'r Gordon of New Brunswick stating that a steamer with men and arms has been chartered in New York to arrive here tomorrow morning. U. S. Gunboat "Winooski" arrived here today awaiting instructions. It is estimated that in this place & vicinity there are about three hundred strangers avowedly Fenians, among them B. Doran Killan (signed) D. R. RANSOM'" Telegram received (at 2:00 P.M.), *ibid.*, Telegrams Collected (Bound); (at 1:45 P.M.) *ibid.*, RG 108, Telegrams Received; copy (sent by mail), *ibid.*, Letters Received. On April 19, Meade, Eastport, Maine, telegraphed to USG. "Arrived at 7. a. m this day. Found a vessel loaded with arms Have directed her seizure: find there are numerous points on ~~co~~the Coast where Arms can be landed & therefore urge the immediate sending of several Naval vessels, not less than three, to prevent this. Special report by mail" Telegram received (at noon), *ibid.*, RG 107, Telegrams Collected (Bound); *ibid.*, RG 108, Telegrams Received; copies, *ibid.*, RG 393, Military Div. of the Atlantic, Letters Sent; DLC-USG, V, 54. On the same day, Meade wrote to USG. "I have the honor to report my arrival at this place at 7 a. m. this day, in compliance with the telegraphic order of the Hon. Secretary of War, received in Philadelphia, 6 P. M: of the 16th. I brought with me a company of Artillery from Portland, which I shall station at Calais, I have also ordered two additional companies, who will arrive by tomorrow morning. On my arrival I find the facts as nearly as I can gather them, as follows:—There are collected at this place some 400 men, Known to be

Fenians—a similar number is said to be at Calais—and it is understood that at all the towns in the vicinity—Lubeck, Pembroke, Robinson and others, there are collections of strangers Known to belong to the Fenian organization, These men are orderly and quiet, are believed to have side arms, but without any muskets, and as yet have assumed no military organization. Their leader, B. Doran Killian, publicly avers he has no intention of invading the provinces, that his object is to go on the banks fishing, and as the reciprocity treaty is abrogated & violation of the American fishermen's rights is to be anticipated, he claims the right to arm his parties. In my judgment this simply means, the Provincial authorities being prepared for any invasion, he expects either to be able to effect a landing at some unguarded point, or what is more probable to involve in some way the U. S. Gov't on the fishery question. I consider it therefore my duty to prevent the departure of any *armed* fishing party—and shall not permit any arms or munitions of war to be landed, or pass into the hands of private parties. It is understood that there are several vessels bound to this port with arms and that a vessel was purchased from some British subjects last night, with the intention of warning these vessels from this place and instructing them to land at some point not watched. I find the coast for some distance below here presents facilities for such landings, hence I telegraphed this morning asking that more naval vessels should be sent here to watch the coast points not occupied by the military. I consider this of the utmost importance & trust no time will be lost in sending them. I am in hopes my arrival, and the public expression of my determination, will have the effect of convincing these misguided people that the Government of the U. S. being determined to enforce the neutrality, it will be folly on their part to perservere in their illegal cause. I should be glad to receive any instructions and to learn at the earliest moment, by telegram, whether my course is approved." LS, DNA, RG 108, Letters Received. On April 20, 4:00 P.M., Meade telegraphed to USG. "Reported yesterday by mail—Have here four 4 companies of artillery—one at Calais, other three at this place. Having no means of transportation & there being several places in this vicinity requiring watching which can be reached by water, I have retained the small steamer that brought myself and one company from Portland. Everything quiet since my last report except the burning of a light last night on the British side charged to Fenians. The arms siezed were yesterday removed to Fort Preble, boxes contain carbines and muskets with the necessary equipments and ammunition; owner an Irishman from New York, disclaims any connection with Fenians, or any intention to violate neutrality laws but cannot explain grounds on which he, a stranger, expected to find a market in Eastport for such articles—nor the coincidence of his arrival with his goods simultaneously with the concentration here of the Fenians. Killian the acknowledged leader left yesterday in the Portland boat going, it is understood to Washington where I trust he will be clearly informed of the views and intentions of the Government. Had an interview this morning with Major Sinnott, a Fenian, who declared the object of the concentration here to be purely political and peaceful their object being to ferment a revolution in New Brunswick and to settle the Fishery question. Gave him distinctly to understand I should not permit any arming or organizing for these or any other purposes. I yesterday, while at Calais, received a visit from Maj Gen Doyle who is here with the Admiral of the Fleet and the Governor of New Brunswick. Much excitement and irritation on both sides of the line but I think my arrival with the troops & the decided attitude I have taken will in a short time quiet matters" Telegram received (at 5:30 P.M.), *ibid.*, RG 107, Telegrams Collected (Bound); *ibid.*, RG 108, Telegrams Received; copies, *ibid.*, RG 393, Military Div. of the Atlantic, Letters Sent; DLC-USG, V, 54. On April 23, Meade wrote to USG. "I send herewith the papers relating to the seizure (already reported) of the arms on board the schooner 'E H. Pray.' They consist of the statement of the Collector of this Port as to the circumstances of the seizure, and the inventory taken by the Commanding Officer of this Post of the property seized. There is also a copy of an application made by one Kerrigan, who claims the property, for its return. It will appear, by the admissions of the acknowledged leader of the Fenians collected here, and by the marks on the arms, that they were the property of the Fenian Brotherhood, and that the suspicions that led to their seizure were well-founded. Mr. Kerrigan, who claims this property, offers to guarantee to deliver it in New York, and to give bonds that it shall not hereafter be used to aid in any breach of the neutrality laws. If this be done, I would recommend that the property be delivered to him. But as many such cases are likely to occur, and this may form a precedent, I forward it for the final action of the highest authority." Copy, DNA, RG 393, Military Div. of the Atlantic, Letters Sent. On April 28, Leet endorsed this letter. "Respy. returned to MG. Meade, who is authorized to return the arms to Mr. Kerrigan upon his giving satisfactory bonds that they will not be used in any act which would be in violation of the neutrality laws." Copy, *ibid.*, RG 108, Register of Letters Received. On April 23, 8:00 P.M., Meade telegraphed to USG. "I have just received the following telegram; 'Calais Me. Apl 23. At sundown two citizens started across the bridge and were stopped by the British soldiers and refused passage as they were supposed by the British to be Fenians, Upon being refused one drew a pistol and fired upon the British soldiers, and then, both fled, My guard arrested them on this side, I have turned them over to the civil authorities on our side, Do you wish to give any order in the the case? Signed GUY V. HENRY, Brevet Colonel &c,' I have sent the following instructions, 'HdQrs Eastport Me, COL., HENRY, &c, &c, Maj. Gen. Meade directs me to ~~say~~ acknowledge your telegram and to say that your course is approved, You will sustain the civil authorities until the case is disposed of. Signed S. F. BARSTOW'" Telegram received (on April 24, 9:40 A.M.), *ibid.*, RG 107, Telegrams Collected (Bound); (at 9:50 A.M.) *ibid.*, RG 108, Telegrams Received; copies, *ibid.*, RG 393, Military Div. of the Atlantic, Letters Sent; DLC-USG, V, 54. On April 26, 7:00 P.M., Meade telegraphed to USG. "I yesterday received a communication from B. Doren Killian as agent, 'for the distribution of arms, of an association of American citizens &c' asking what my instructions were in regard to the seizure of such arms; To which I replied by referring him to my action in regard to arms seized on board Schooner, 'E. H. Pray,' and informing him that after such public notice and warning I should feel it my duty, not only to seize all arms, there was reasonable causes to believe were to be used in breach of the neutrality laws, but to take active measures against all persons instrumental in bringing them to the frontier for that purpose, The parties of fenians at Lubec and Calais have been called in, and this afternoon about one hundred and seventy (170) of the rank and file, leave in the steam packet for Portland, stating that they were to join Sweenys column moving on Canada—A small force with the leaders Killian, Sennett &c ~~are~~ is still here—" Telegram received (at 10:20 P.M.), DNA, RG 107, Telegrams Collected (Bound); *ibid.*, RG 108, Telegrams Received; copies, *ibid.*, RG 393, Military Div. of the Atlantic, Letters Sent; DLC-USG, V, 54. On April 27, 1:40

P.M., USG telegraphed to Meade. "Your despatches were received during my absence from the City. I am authorized by the Secretary of War to say that your course is fully approved" Telegram sent, DNA, RG 107, Telegrams Collected (Bound); telegram received (misdated April 26—received at 4:30 P.M.), *ibid.*, RG 393, Military Div. of the Atlantic, Telegrams Received. On May 1, Meade telegraphed to USG. "The greater portion of the Fenians having left this place and vicinity and everything quiet I purpose leaving to morrow or next day taking two out of the three companies I brought. The other has been ordered to remain at Calais for the present" Telegram received (at 5:00 P.M.), *ibid.*, RG 107, Telegrams Collected (Bound); *ibid.*, RG 108, Letters Received; copies, *ibid.*, RG 393, Military Div. of the Atlantic, Letters Sent; DLC-USG, V, 54.

On May 28, Meade wrote a letter received at USG's hd. qrs. submitting papers concerning Michael H. Kerrigan's "refusal to sign bonds that said arms will not be used against neutrality laws." DNA, RG 108, Register of Letters Received. On May 31, Leet endorsed these papers. "Respy. returned to Maj. Gen. Meade with directions to retain these arms until further orders, unless conditions prescribed are complied with." Copy, *ibid.* On June 4, Kerrigan, Putnam County House, New York City, wrote to USG. "I would beg leave to call your attention to papers relating to the seizure of arms now in possession of military authorities at Eastport, Maine, which I claim as my property. I was given to understand by General Hooker that the whole matter is now before you. I write to you for information in regard to how I shall proceed to obtain possession of the same. I would most respectfully state that while at Eastport I could not procure bonds (not knowing on what condition I was to receive my property before leaving this city for Eastport, I returned to New York, where I can give all necessary security) thinking I could arrange the matter with Genl. Hooker, when he informed me as above stated, that the whole affair was now before you. Having been already subject to great expense and inconvenience, I most respectfully request (if approved by you) that my property should be delivered to me at this city, where I can give ample security to the Government that the aforesaid property shall not be used in any act tending to violate the 'neutrality law' of these United States." ALS, *ibid.*, RG 94, Letters Received, 670W 1866. On Nov. 15, Richard Oulahan, former 1st lt. and bvt. maj., 164th N. Y., Washington, D. C., wrote to USG. "I beg leave, most respectfully, to forward the enclosed communication, with a note from Brig. Gen'l Halpin, which states that no answer has been yet received to Mr. Kerrigan's letter. If nothing has as yet been done in the case, may I respectfully and earnestly call your attention to it? and to hope that your action will be favorable? I shall be glad to receive, and communicate to the parties in NewYork, any communication on the subject." ALS, *ibid.* On Dec. 13, Meade endorsed this letter. "Respectfully returned to the Head Quarters, Armies of the United States. On my arrival at Eastport, Me., on the 19th of April last, I found a vessel in port laden with the arms in question ~~and directed their seizure~~ seized by the collector which action I confirmed. it afterwards appeared by the admission of the acknowledged leader of the Fenians, and by the marks on the arms that they belonged to the Fenian Brotherhood and that the suspicions that led to the seizure were well founded. The papers in the case together with the application of the within named Kerrigan for the return of the arms, he guaranteeing to deliver them in New York and to give bonds that they should not afterwards be used to aid in any breach of the neutrality laws, were forwarded to the Head Quarters of the Armies of the United States, on the 23rd April, and on the 28th of April authority was given to return the arms to the claimant on his giving satisfactory bonds as offered, and the Commanding Officer at Eastport, Me., who had the arms in charge was directed to deliver them to him on his complying with the conditions. Mr Kerrigan was unable or failed to give the necessary bonds, the fact was reported to the Head Quarters of the Army and on the 31st May instructions were received to retain the arms until the conditions prescribed were complied with, and the officer having the arms in charge was so instructed. The letter of Mr Kerrigan of June 4th referred from Head Quarters, Armies of the United States, to these Head Quarters was referred thro' General Hooker to the officer in charge of the arms and his attention called to endorsement from Head Qrs. Armies of U. S., of May 31st, for his guidance. Thus the matter has stood up to the present time, Mr Kerrigan having it in his power at any time to obtain the arms by complying with the liberal terms of the government, terms which were proposed by himself. I cannot recommend their delivery to him in New York as in my opinion he might as well set up a claim for the expense of their transportation to Eastport or for damages for interference with their sale or for interference with the use for which they were intended. The within named Kerrigan made this day personal applicacation at these Head Quarters for the return of the arms in question, and was informed that tho' there was no authority for the delivery of the arms to him in New York, a bond executed *there* and satisfactory to the District Attorney would be considered as satisfying the conditions preliminary to the return of the property to him at Eastport." ES, *ibid.* On April 18, 1867, Meade wrote to Bvt. Maj. Gen. Edward D. Townsend reporting that the arms had been restored to Kerrigan and enclosing a $10,000 bond signed by Kerrigan. LS and DS, *ibid.*

On Oct. 19, 1866, Col. and Bvt. Maj. Gen. William F. Barry, 2nd Art., Buffalo, wrote to Barstow concerning seized Fenian arms. ALS, *ibid.* On Oct. 24, Meade endorsed this letter. "Respectfully forwarded to the Head Quarters Armies of the U. S. for the information herein contained. Occasion is taken to invite the attention of the General Commanding to my endorsement of August 23rd, on the report of the Commanding Officer of Madison Barracks as to the insufficiency of his garrison to guard Fenian arms there stored, suggesting 'that some definite action be required of the civil department having control of these arms, or failing to obtain this that the War Department designate some Arsenal where the arms can all be sent, properly cared for and guarded. Prompt action is respectfully asked in this matter.' It will appear from the accompanying documents that the arms at Fort Porter will soon be, if they have not already been, restored to the claimants, those at Erie, Fort Ontario, Madison Barracks and Plattsburg, are still in the custody of the military authorities, and the sole obstacle to the removal of the Artillery Company at Erie, as was stated in my telegram to the General Commanding of the 8th instant, is the necessity of some troops being kept at that post to guard the Fenian arms stored there, as these arms being under the control of the civil authorities [a]nd subject to the jurisdiction of the U. S. Court in that district, can not be removed therefrom, without the highest authority." ES, *ibid.* Perhaps on Nov. 19, 1867, USG, secretary of war *ad interim*, noted on papers concerning Fenian arms: "Notify Commander at Watervleit Arsenal to restore Fenian arms on the order of the Atty Gn. given through Dist Atty." AN (docketed as received by the AGO on Nov. 19), *ibid.* Papers concerning the seizure of Fenian arms are *ibid.* See letter to Maj. Gen. George G. Meade, May 14, 1866; telegram to Maj. Gen. George G. Meade, May 30, 1866.

To Andrew Johnson

Washington, March 14th *1866*.

His Excellency A. Johnson
President of the United States.
Sir:

I have the honor to submit herewith for your information reports from the Department of Alabama of outrages committed by Whites against Blacks and by Blacks against Whites, made in pursuance of previous telegraphic instructions.

The following tabulated statement presents a resume of the papers, which papers also contain much other matter relating to the feeling and condition of society in Alabama.

Whites against Blacks.

assault and battery	larceny	assault with deadly weapons	murder	driven off without compensation for labor	retaining freedmen without compensation	arson
42	2	11	14	14	15	1

Blacks against Whites.

assault	larceny	assault with deadly weapons	murder	assaulting ladies	arson	rape
7	7	3	1	2	1	2

Assault and battery excess committed by whites	43
Murder excess by Whites	13
Larceny excess by Blacks	5

With great respect
Your obedt. servant
U. S. Grant
Lieutenant General.

LS, DLC-Andrew Johnson. See letter to Andrew Johnson, Feb. 17, 1866. On March 9, 1866, Bvt. Maj. Gen. Edward D. Townsend endorsed papers transmitted by Maj. Gen. George H. Thomas concerning treatment of Negroes in the Dept. of Ala. "Respectfully submitted to Lieut. Genl. Grant Comdg Armies of the U. S. for consideration in connection with previous papers in this case submitted March 6th 1866." Copy, DNA, RG 94, Endorsements.

To Edwin M. Stanton

Washington March 14th 1866.

HON. E. M. STANTON,
SEC. OF WAR,
SIR:

I would respectfully recommend that orders be given for a reduction of the present colored volunteer force of the United States, by Muster-out, to the following standard, towit: Leave one regiment in the District of Columbia; one regiment in N. Carolina; one in South Carolina; one in Georgia, one in Florida, Two in Alabama, Four in Mississippi, Four in Tennessee, and two in Ky. I would further recommend that Gen. Sherman, for the use of his Mil. Division, be directed to retain four colored regiments, mustering out all others, one of them for the State of Arkansas, or the Indian Territory, and three for the Plains

Within the Depts of La. & Texas, I would leave orders for the muster out of this class of troops until a report can be had from Gen. Sheridan[1] whether more can be spared.

I have the honor to be
Very respectfully
Your obt. svt.
U. S. GRANT.
Lieut. Gen'l

Copies, DLC-USG, V, 47, 109; DNA, RG 108, Letters Sent.

1. On March 28, 1866, 4:30 P.M., Maj. Gen. Philip H. Sheridan, New Orleans, telegraphed to USG. "On the 15th Col Foster telegraphed to know how many colored troops could be spared in the Dept of Texas for muster out—No

colored troops can be mustered out in Texas except on the Rio Grande frontier where there are seven colored regiments with an effective force of three thousand six hundred & sixty seven men—Unless the Govt desires to maintain this force for international reasons two or three Regts can be mustered out—I will say that this force is not much superior to the Imperial force now at Matamoras & Bagdad & there is some indication of increase to this force—I would therefore like your views before replying" Telegram received (at 11:05 P.M.), *ibid.*, RG 107, Telegrams Collected (Bound); *ibid.*, RG 108, Telegrams Received; copies (one sent by mail—misdated March 29), *ibid.*, Letters Received; DLC-USG, V, 54; DLC-Philip H. Sheridan. On March 29, 10:10 A.M., USG telegraphed to Sheridan. "Retain all colored troops on Rio Grande frontier for the present" Telegram sent, DNA, RG 107, Telegrams Collected (Bound); copies, *ibid.*, RG 108, Letters Sent; DLC-USG, V, 47, 109.

To Maj. Gen. William T. Sherman

Washington, D. C. March 14th *1866*

MAJ. GN. W. T. SHERMAN,
COMD.G MIL. DIV. OF THE MISS.
GENERAL:

The very admirable report of Gen. Pope upon the nature of the country embraced in the Dept. of Mo. the condition of the people and Indians within it, and the troops required to protect settlements and lines of travel, &c. has been read with interest.

The matter of first importance, in my opinion, for the economical and safe controll of Indian affairs depends upon getting the Indian Bureau transfered from the Interior to the War Dept. The next step then would be to deal farely with the Indians and protect them from encroachments by the Whites. I have spoken to Members of Congress on this subject and generally they agree with me. Whether anything will be done or not however I do not know.—In the event of no change in the management of Indian affairs we will have to do the best we can with the force at our disposal.—Without an increase in the regular army there is no more force to send to you than has already been assigned. Colored troops (volunteers) may be retained to the end of their enlistment and as it will take a long time to fill up the new regiments, if authorized, some of them will have to be so retained. I think therefore you had better supply present wants by the use of two or more regiments of colored troops.

The first thing in the Spring will be to replace all white volunteers with regular troops, or colored, and muster the former out. Give some temporary protection to the frontier settlements, as suggested by Gn. Pope, and to the mining and other settlements in the interior.

In the middle belt of country discribed by Gen. Pope, where the country is uninhabitable, select such of the traveled routes as you think ought to be protected and compell all travel to pass over them. With colored and regular troops I am in hopes that such respects for the rights of the Indian may be enforced as to avoid much of the difficulties with them heretofore experienced. Then too, in case of hostilities, the most that can be should be made of those tribes or parts of tribes remaining friendly to the Whites. I have always felt that a good part of our difficulties arise from treating all Indians as hostile when any portion of them commit acts that makes a campaign against them necessary.—I think peace with the Indian can be secured, in good part, by protecting them.

Authorize the retention of as many horses for the use of troops on the plains as you deem necessary. Select posts to be temporarily occupied on the best information at hand. Inspections to be made during the Summer will probably fix the points that should be permanently occupied and where all the troops on the plains would Winter.

This letter sifts down to leaving the management of affairs within your command to your own judgement with but very little in the way of suggestion. That is just where I have to leave it for with the exception of Gn. Pope's report, I have no data upon which I could base any specific instructions. Follow such of them as you deem most practicable and for the best interests of the service.

Very respectfully
your obt. svt.
U. S. GRANT
Lt. Gn.

ALS, DNA, RG 393, Military Div. of the Miss., Letters Received. On March 6, 1866, Maj. Gen. William T. Sherman, St. Louis, wrote to Brig. Gen. John A. Rawlins. "I have the honor herewith to send you a copy of Maj General Popes Report of Feb 25, 1866, with my Reply thereto of yesterdays date. The former contains the best, most clear, and satisfactorily condensed description of the country embraced in his Departmt, with its occupants and growing interests, and my letter sanctions in general terms the general policy proposed, and distribution of troops for the coming year. I would like the Lt General Commanding to read these papers carefully, at his leisure, and then to cause me to be informed of any modifications that may occur to him, as the country is so vast and roads so long that changes cannot be made at will. In general terms the settlements of Kansas, Dahcotah & Iowa have nearly or quite reached the Western limit of land fit for cultivation, Parallel 99°, of West Longitude. There begins the Great Plains 600 miles wide, fit only for nomadic tribes of Indians, Tartars or Buffalos, then the Mountain Regions, useful chiefly for precious metals. When all the volunteers are discharged, which must be as soon as the season will admit of their coming in, we will have only four Regiments of Infantry and one of cavalry available and will use them to the best advantage to protect the principal Routes of travel, trusting to increased enlistments, and new Regiments to cover the exposed frontiers, or to cover the new mining settlements against the Indians, who must as the Buffalos grow less, live in part by plunder and robbery, unless actually collected and fed by the United States. I will probably draw the 3rd u s cavalry out of Arkansas, and use it also on the Plains, and in case of the proposed increase of that arm of service will count on receiving a share of the new Regiments." ALS, *ibid.*, RG 108, Letters Received. On Feb. 25, Maj. Gen. John Pope, St. Louis, had written to Sherman reporting at length on frontier affairs. Copies, *ibid.*; *ibid.*, RG 94, Letters Received, 440M 1866. See *Calendar*, Nov. 11, 1865; *HED*, 39-1-76. On March 20, USG endorsed this letter. "Respectfully forwarded to the Hon. Secretary of War, and attention invited to the remarks on the transfer of the entire control of Indian affairs to the War Department." ES, DNA, RG 94, Letters Received, 440M 1866. On Feb. 15, Pope had endorsed papers concerning Indian affairs. "It is respectfully suggested to Maj Genl Sherman that these & others papers on the same subject which I will forward in a day or two be sent to the Genl.-in-chief for reference to the Committees on Indian affairs in Congress who are now examining the subject of our Indian management with a view to the transfer of the Indian Dept to the control of the War Dept" AES, *ibid.*, RG 108, Letters Received. On March 24, USG endorsed these papers. "Respectfully forwarded to the Hon. Secretary of War, attention being invited to the endorsement of Gen. Pope, hereon, which is approved and his suggestions concurred in." ES, *ibid.* On March 30, Secretary of War Edwin M. Stanton transmitted this material to the U.S. House of Representatives Committee on Indian Affairs. Copy, *ibid.*

On March 15, Secretary of the Interior James Harlan wrote to USG. "I herewith respectfully enclose to you a letter from Col. J. H. Leavenworth dated Feby. 22. 1866, in reference to employing the Kiowa and Camanche Indians to keep peace on the plains; prepared by him as he says at your request." LS, *ibid.* Harlan enclosed a letter of Feb. 22 from Jesse H. Leavenworth, Indian agent, former col., 2nd Colo., to Bvt. Col. Theodore S. Bowers. "At the request of Lieut. Genl Grant, I address this communication to you, for his information and action. The Indians of the plains, or the wild Indians of the Upper Arkansas, consist of the Comanches, Kiowas, Apaches, aArrapahoes and Cheyennes, These two last bands have heretofore ranged north of the Platte, as well as south of the Arkansas rivers. They are now divided, and have been since the Sand Creek massacre, some of them are north with the hostile Sioux, others are south of the Arkansas with or near the first three bands, all of whom are friendly. The Comanches are the most numerous and they, with the Kiowas, can, if they please, rule all the others, and it is well known that the Comanches are the best riders and the best fighters on the Continent. They are divided into nine bands, numbering from twenty five hundred to three thousand lodges. The Kiowas number about two hundred and eighty lodges, and are the most passionate Indians of my acquaintance. The Apaches only number about fifty lodges; the Arrapahoes about two hundred and twenty to two hundred and fifty lodges; the Cheyennes about the same, They will all average about four and one half individuals to a lodge. Little Raven's and Big Mouth's bands of Arrapahoes of near two hundred lodges, and Black Kettle's and Little Robe's bands of Cheyennes, of about one hundred lodges, are south of the Arkansas river, and are believed to be friendly, and were parties to the treaties in October last. From these figures it will be seen that the number of hostile Indians is quite insignificant, but it is not their number, but their activity that gives us so much trouble, and if they are not checked by prompt action before the Spring travel commences, there is great danger that they may induce the wild and reckless of the other bands and tribes to join them. I would therefore respectfully suggest that to match them at their own game, that friendly Indians be employed to compel them to cease their acts of violence, and to make peace. And from my long and intimate acquaintance with them, I am confident it can be done now, as well as it has been done heretofore. In 1862 I met the whole of these five tribes, except a part of the Comanches, at Fort Larned, when they were very much excited, and just about the time of the Minnesota Outrages, and when our whole frontier was threatened by a general Indian war, quieted them, and held them so for nearly two years. In 1863 one of the band of 'Dog Soldiers' of Cheyennes, was shot dead by a sentinel at Fort Larned, whilst I was in command there with only about one hundred and sixty men, and when there was from twelve to fifteen thousand Indians within ten miles of the post. Prompt and proper steps were taken and they were met and quieted. Again, in the Fall of 1864, I was sent to find and pacify, if possible, these same wild Indians, in which, after great hardships, and unparralled opposition, I succeeded, after having quieted them three times, once in February, once in May and the third time in August 1865 when preliminary treaties were signed on the 15th & 18th of that month, by all the bands and tribes then south of the Arkansas river, and fully ratified by them in the month of October last, for peace and amity with the Government of the United States. The Indians that are now hostile and raiding on our great lines of travel over the plains, are believed to be mostly of the band of Indians known as the 'Dog Soldiers' of the Cheyenne tribe. It is known that there is a small number of Arrapahoes with them, and some Sioux, the latter have never been known to have crossed the Arkansas river, but range mostly on the Platte and Smoky Hill. As soon as troops are sent into their range, they break up into small bands and scatter, making it almost impossible to capture them. This band of 'Dog Soldiers' has one white man with them by the name of Jo. North, but he is of no great account. They have also with them two half blood Cheyennes, George and Charles Bent, the former, so I have been informed, has become quite a chief in this band, and if so, it is well known how he has won his position and it is my opinion, as well as of many others, that we shall never have a permanent peace with these Indians until he is removed from them, and I feel myself fully justified in saying that if the present movements now being made at Fort Laramie by Lt. Col. Maynadier, and Major Wynkoop, at or near Fort Larned, fail to *obtain* the object desired, viz; peace with all the Indians on the frontier, and on all our great lines of travel over the plains, the object may be obtained, I believe, by employing the friendly Kiowas and Comanches. I have known them long and intimately and have always found them willing to listen to good council. I know that they want peace, and they entered into an arrangement with me last August, that if the Arrapahoe and Cheyenne Indians south of the Arkansas river, did not cease all acts of violence to the frontier settlements, and on the Santa Fé road, they would compel them to remove from their country. All that would be required would be for some one in whom they have confidence, to go to them, tell them what was wanted, be fully authorized and prepared to give them rations, a blouse, hat and feather to distinguish them, a Carbine and ammunition, and when they have given us proof that our great lines of travel over the plains, are safe, and no longer molested by hostile Indians, pay them as we would others for the services performed." ALS, *ibid.*

To Andrew Johnson

Respectfully forwarded to His Excellency the President of the United States with the recommendation that clemency be extended in this case or assurances given that no trial will take place for the offences charged against G. E. Pickett. During the rebellion belligerent rights were acknowledged to the enemys of our country and it is clear to me that the parole given by the Armies laying down their Arms protects them against punishments for act[s] lawful for any other belligerent. In this case I know it is claimed that the men tried and convicted for the crime of desertion were Union men from N. C. who had found refuge within our lines and in our service. The punishment was a harsh one but it was in time of war and when the enemy no doubt felt it necessary to retain, by some power, the services of every man within their reach. Gn. Pickett I know personally to be an honorable man but in this case his judgement prompted him to do what can not well be sustained though I do not see how good, either to the friends of the deceased or by fixing an example for the future, can be secured by his trial now.

It would only open up the question whether or not the Goverment did not disregard its contract entered into to secure the surrender of of an armed enemy.

U. S. GRANT
Lt. Gn

March 16th 1866

AES, DNA, RG 94, Amnesty Papers, Va. Written on a letter of March 12, 1866, from George E. Pickett, former C.S.A. maj. gen., Washington, D. C., to USG. "I have the honor to state that shortly after the Surrender of the Confederate Forces under command of General R. E. Lee to General U. S. Grant, Commander-in-chief, U. S. A. in the past year, being at the time paroled by the last named Officer, I made a communication to His Excellency, the President of the U. S., asking for his clemency. The papers in the case were presented by Ex Senator O. H. Browning, of Illinois, for the consideration of the executive. They consisted of the application above referred to, the required oath, a recommendation from Govr Pierpont of Va., and certain statements from Officers of the Confederate Service—members of a General Court Martial—in reference to the execution of a number of deserters from said service, whilst I was in command of the Department of North Carolina, in 1863. My object now, General, in presenting this paper is to ask your favorable consideration of my case, and that you will, if you believe in my Sincerity, for which I have pledged you my honor as an Officer and a gentleman, put such an endorsement upon it as will obtain from His Excellency the President, a guarantee that I may be permitted to live unmolested in my native State, where I am now trying to make a subsistence for my family, (much impoverished by the War,) by tilling the land. It has come to my knowledge that certain evil disposed persons are attempting to re-open the troubles of the past, and embroil me for the action taken by me whilst the Commanding Officer of the Confederate Forces in N. C. I acted simply as the General Commanding the Department. Certain men, deserters from a N. C. Regiment, were taken with arms in their hands fighting against the colors under which they had enlisted. Charges were preferred against them—a regularly organized Court Martial was assembled, composed of officers from N. C., Georgia, and Virginia, before whom the men were tried; the evidence in the cases being perfectly unmistakeable, the men being identified by numbers of their old Regtal comrades, they were found guilty & condemned to be hung—The sentences were approved by me, and they were duly executed according to the custom of War in like cases. My action was sanctioned by the then Confederate Government. If the time has not arrived for the Executive clemency to be extended to my case, (and which point I am not now pressing), I merely wish some assurance, that I will not be disturbed in my endeavor to keep my family from Starvation, and that my parole, which was given in good faith, may protect me from the assaults of those persons desirous of still keeping up the War which has ended in my humble opinion *forever*. Appealing to you as a soldier, and feeling confident you will appreciate my position, I sign myself with much esteem, . . ." ALS, *ibid.* On the same day, USG issued a parole. "Geo. E. Pickett, a paroled officer of the Southern Army is exempt from arrest by Military Authorities except directed by the President of the United States, Secretary of War, or from these Hd. Qrs. so long as he observes the conditions of his parole. The restriction requiring paroled officers to remain at their homes is removed in this case and Gen. Pickett will be allowed to travel unmolested throughout the United States" Copies, DLC-USG, V, 47, 109; DNA, RG 108, Letters Sent. See *HED*, 39-2-11.

To Maj. Gen. Philip H. Sheridan

Washington D. C. March 19th *1866*

MAJ. GN. P. H. SHERIDAN,
COMD.G MIL. DIV. OF THE GULF,
GENERAL;

I have ordered to you the 17th regular Infantry in the hope that it will enable you to muster out of service all the White Volunteers still remaining. This regiment has but few full companies at present but all the twenty-four companies are organized and I will send recruits to you as fast as possible to fill up. Unless you think security demands the retention of some of the White Volunteers muster the whole of them out as rapidly as possible. In the case of Colored troops musterout such of them as you think can be spared.

Yours Truly
U. S. GRANT
Lt. Gn.

ALS, DNA, RG 393, Military Div. of the Southwest and Dept. of the Gulf, Letters Received. On March 26, 1866, Maj. Gen. Philip H. Sheridan, New Orleans, wrote to USG. "Your letter notifying me that the 17th Infantry has been ordered to report to me has just been received. I feel so anxious to muster out all White Volunteer Troops that I will do so if possible on the arrival of this regiment, I hope you will fill it up as soon as possible. Recruits should be sent to the 1st Infantry, it is now only a handful of men." Copy, *ibid.*, Letters Sent. On April 22, Sheridan telegraphed to USG. "I have ordered the muster out of all white volunteers troops in Texas both Cavalry & Infantry and hope the Remaining portion of the 17th Infantry will be sent to me without delay." Telegram received (on April 24, 3:20 P.M.), *ibid.*, RG 107, Telegrams Collected (Bound); *ibid.*, RG 108, Telegrams Received; copies (one sent by mail), *ibid.*, Letters Received; *ibid.*, RG 393, Military Div. of the Southwest and Dept. of the Gulf, Telegrams Sent; DLC-USG, V, 54; DLC-Philip H. Sheridan.

On April 27, Sheridan telegraphed to USG. "I have the honor to report that I will be absent at Galveston Texas for seven 7 or eight 8 days" Telegram received (on April 28, 8:45 A.M.), DNA, RG 107, Telegrams Collected (Bound); *ibid.*, RG 108, Telegrams Received; copies (one sent by mail), *ibid.*, Letters

Received; DLC-USG, V, 54; DLC-Philip H. Sheridan. On May 4, Sheridan wrote to USG. "I have the honor to notify you of my return from Galveston and to report as follows. All white Volunteer troops are now being mustered out in the Department of Texas, and also the 10th Colored Infantry stationed at Galveston. The 3rd battalion of the 17th Infantry, I ordered on the line from Houston to Austin: this battalion has 8 companies present. The 2nd battalion was ordered to occupy the line from Victoria to San Antonio: this battalion has but 2 companies present. The 1st battalion I ordered to remain at Galveston, it having 3 companies present. The reason I hold this battalion at Galveston for the present, is this, If the colored troops on the RioGrande frontier are to be mustered out, I would put it on that line. If they are not to be mustered out I wish to open the line from San Antonio to ElPaso, I think this line could be opened by the reoccupation of two Posts, one at Fort Clark, the other at Fort Davis. Fort Davis should have not less than 6 companies, four of Infantry and two of cavalry, and Fort Clark about two companies. This would leave me but two companies for Fort Bliss, out of the 8 companies of the 1st battalion and this, perhaps, is not enough. I heretofore felt no particular inclination to open this line, or in the establishment of frontier Posts, as I had only volunteer organizations, and now when I am getting regular troops, I have to use them in the settled portions of the State, to make the people behave themselves. It is somewhat of a question in my mind, whether I should especially exert myself for the protection of the frontier of Texas, when the very troops which could be used for this purpose, have to be held to put down the disloyal acts of the people. However, I have not yet received the balance of the 17th Infantry and nothing can be done until it comes, and if ~~be~~ it does not come soon, it will be too late for this year. The horses of the 4th U. S. Cavalry have been allowed to run down, by the process of acclimation, or from hard service. I think a good deal from the latter. Since I gave up the personal command of the cavalry, at Austin and San Antonio, it has been used for all kinds of unnecessary purposes. I hope to be able to have it in good condition soon, as the grass is now very fine, and some good horses will be obtained from the Volunteer cavalry now being mustered out. I ordered two companies of the 4th Cavalry, dismounted, to Brownsville, to replace the 4th Wisconsin on that line. These companies will be remounted from horses of the 4th Wisconsin Cavalry I would suggest that if the colored troops are to remain in the service, a sufficient time to justify it, that Forts Clark, Davis and Bliss, be occupied by them; in fact they will make good garrison troops for such out-posts." LS, DNA, RG 108, Letters Received.

To Charles W. Ford

Washington, D. C.
March 19th 1866.

DEAR FORD,

Your letter in relation to my matters in Mo. was duly received. I hope Judge Dent's luck in escaping a conflagration with his property may prove the turning point in his affairs. I was fully aware of the Deed of Trust existing on Mr Dent's place. If it ever comes to be sold on that deed I expect to pay in proportion to the amount I may own of the land. In purchasing from the Judge I expect also to make the price correspond with the existing state of facts. Seventy-five dollars per acre is what I expected to pay him and now stand ready to pay up the balance the moment he has the deed for the land executed to me. I do not know where the Judge is to hurry him up in this matter. I do not want to sell the property under the ~~prese~~ present Trust Deed held by me.

Has the Judge's family gone south with him?—I have written to Sappington giving him directions what to do with my property also to sell a tract I have on the Iron Mountain road. I told to consult with you or John How about who to get to advertise and conduct the sale.

My family are all well. It is possible that I may get out to St. Louis in the course of a few weeks.

Has my suit come off with White yet?

Yours Truly
U. S. GRANT

ALS, USG 3.

To James W. Nesmith

Washington March 19th 1866.

HON J W. NESMITH U. S. SENATOR.
DEAR SIR:

Yours of the 17th inst. stating that it had been intimated that I had recommended the continuance of the Provost Marshal Generals Department and the transfer of the recruiting service to it is received. Some months since a paper was referred to me showing the great number of desertions from the Army and asking for suggestions to put a stop to them. To that paper I suggested a number of changes in orders governing the recruiting service and recommended that the whole matter be put in charge of the P. M. Gen. who could devote more attention to it than the Adjt. Gen. with all his other duties, could. I am opposed however to multiplying Bureaux and think there is no necessity for a Provost Marshal General—In fact If we had to organize the Army anew I would not have as many Bureaux as we I now have. In my opinion the country would be just as well, and much more economically, served if the Coast Surveying duties were added to the Eng. Bureau, and the Qr. Mr. Subsistence and Pay Depts. were merged into one. I would not recommend a change now however but would not make any increase of Bureausx

Very truly yours
U. S. GRANT
Lt. Gen'l

Copies, DLC-USG, V, 47, 109; DNA, RG 108, Letters Sent. See letter to Edwin M. Stanton, Dec. 14, 1865.

To Darius H. Ingraham

Washington, D. C. March 20th *1866*

D. H. INGRAHAM, ESQ.
CH. WIDOW'S & ORPHAN'S FAIR,
PORTLAND ME.
DEAR SIR:

Your letter of the 12th inst. enclosing a notice of a "Fair" to be held in Portland, Me. during the week commencing Apl. 23d, for the benefit of the Widows & Orphans of deceased soldiers is received. All well directed enterprises having for their object the relief of those who have been left destitute by the patriotic devotion of their natural protectors have my sympathy. The enterprize got up by the citizens of Portland is unquestionably such a one. I hope your highest expectations may be realized and many hearts made glad by the bounty of those who have received the benefits . . . of the human sacrifice which has caused the necessity for this charity.

AL (incomplete facsimile), The Rendells, Inc., Catalogue 150 [1980], no. 183. Darius H. Ingraham, born in Maine in 1837, entered the U.S. Naval Academy at Annapolis in 1853 and resigned in 1855 to study law.

To Edwin M. Stanton

Washington March 21st 1866

HON. E. M. STANTON,
SECY. OF WAR,
SIR:

I would respectfully recommend the appointment of Maj. Geo. K. Leet, A. A. G., of Volunteers to a Captaincy in the Quartermaster's Department, where there is now a vacancy. I ask this for the purpose of making Maj. Leet eligible for the appointment of Asst. Adjt. Gen. in the Regular Army in place of Col. T. S. Bowers deceased.

Should the recommendation be favorably considered. I would then recommend Capt. Leet for the above vacancy.

Very Respectfully
Your obt. servant
U. S. GRANT
Lieut. Gen'l

Copies, DLC-USG, V, 47, 109; DNA, RG 108, Letters Sent. On May 1, 1866, USG wrote to Secretary of War Edwin M. Stanton. "I would respectfully recommend the appointment of Capt. Geo. K. Leet, A. Q. M. United States Army, to the vacancy created by Col. T. S. Bowers, Maj. in the Adjt. Genl's Dept., death, to take rank from the 23d of March 1866." Copies, *ibid.* George K. Leet was appointed maj. and adjt. as of March 23. On July 5, USG wrote to Bvt. Maj. Gen. Edward D. Townsend. "Please muster Maj. Geo. K. Leet, A. A. Gen. Volunteers out of service under provisions of Gen. Orders, No. 79. May 1st 1865, to take effect from May 31st 1866." Copies, DLC-USG, V, 47, 60; DNA, RG 108, Letters Sent.

Also on March 21, USG wrote to Stanton. "I would respectfully recommend that Col. Ely S. Parker, and Col. Adam Badeau, both officers of my Staff, be appointed Lieutenants in the Regular Army. They have both served faithfully, and with credit to themselves, a longer period than is required, under existing rules, to entitle them to elegibility for such appointment. I make this also for the purpose of retaining them on my Staff after the Volunteers shall all be mustered out of service." ALS, *ibid.*, RG 94, ACP, G93 CB 1866. On May 2, USG wrote to Stanton. "I have the honor to respectfully request that 2d Lieutenant Ely S. Parker, 2d U S. Cavalry and 2d Lieutenant Adam Badeau 4th U S. Infantry be announced as Secretaries on my staff with the rank of Lieut. Colonel." LS, *ibid.*, G170 CB 1866.

To Andrew Johnson

Washington, D C., March 22d *1866*.

HIS EXCELLENCY A. JOHNSON,
PRESIDENT OF THE UNITED STATES.
SIR:

I would respectfully recommend the release, on parole, of D. L. Yulee,[1] late of the United States Senate, I make this recommendation on the supposition that no special charges have been made against him.

In making this recommendation I would give it as my opinion that no good is to be accomplished by confinement, without trial, or at least the prospect of a trial, and legal conviction, of conspirators against the Government, who are not directly charged with heinous offences, or with holding positions of great power or influence in the rebellion.

Mr. Yulee has already been long confined. I would urge this in his behalf unless, as before stated, charges exist against him of which I know nothing.

I have the honor to be
Very respy, Your obed't serv't
U. S. GRANT
Lieutenant General.

LS, DNA, RG 94, Letters Received, 210W 1866. President Andrew Johnson endorsed this letter. "Refered to the Secretary of War for consideration and action." AES (undated), *ibid.* See *O.R.*, II, viii, 893, 895.

1. David L. Yulee, born in 1810 in St. Thomas, West Indies, educated in Va., became a lawyer in Fla. in 1836. Active in promoting Southern railroads before the Civil War, he resigned as U.S. senator from Fla. on Jan. 21, 1861.

To Charles W. Ford

Washington, D. C. March 22d *1866*

DEAR FORD,

Enclosed I send check for $2,000 00 to be placed to the credit of Judge Dent. As soon as the deeds are made to me for the 86 acres of land I will forward to you the balance of the money that will still be coming to him. The Judge I see is now in St. Louis.

Yours Truly
U. S. GRANT

ALS, USG 3. On March 22, 1866, Lewis Dent wrote to USG. "I wrote you from below Cairo, which letter I suppose you have received. In that letter I informed you that John had not reached St Louis before I went below in February but had no doubt that during my absence he had arrived *and sent you the deed for the land.* What was my astonishment upon my arrival this morning to find that he has not yet come, but by a letter received by his wife, ~~he~~ informs her that he will leave in a few days. This is his way of doing business. I dont know when he will come. Relying confidently that his letter spoke the truth, I contracted to pay $2000 upon my arrival at St Louis being the rent for the plantation, supposing, that sum to be here to my credit from the Sale of land made to you. Now my mules, supplies, hands &c are on the place and we are hard at work but if I dont meet this payment these articles will all be seized for my violation of the contract, and I will be ruined utterly. Can I rely on you to indulge me until this deed can be sent which shall be done *on my honor* as soon as John arrives. Please inform me through Mr Ford at once that I may act accordingly—" ALS, *ibid.* At 2:50 P.M., USG telegraphed to Dent, Southern Hotel, St. Louis. "I will send money to Ford to-day to your credit." ALS (undated telegram sent), DNA, RG 107, Telegrams Collected (Unbound). On March 27, Dent signed a receipt for the money. ADS, USG 3. See letter to Charles W. Ford, March 28, 1866.

To Maj. Gen. John M. Schofield

[*March 24, 1866*]

I have never written to you since your departure, for two reasons: First, because I was afraid to send through the mails, lest the letter should fall into the hands of the French authorities. Second, because I could not say anything which would be agreeable to Mr. Seward, and did not like, therefore, to send by his mail.

I might add a third reason and say that Mr. S. keeps the whole question between the United States and Mexico so befogged that I know nothing really to write upon the subject that you do not learn from the papers of the country. It looks to me very much as if Mr. Seward's policy was to hold the Government and let the Imperial establishment take its chances for success or failure. If he has a partiality in the matter, I think it leans to Imperial success. In this matter, however, I may do him injustice. One thing is certain, however, with the present policy, and it looks as if it was to continue, the friends of the Liberal Government of Mexico can do nothing to help it. Under these circumstances I would say there is no necessity for your remaining longer abroad, unless your instructions require it. . . . If I was to try to give you any positive information in regard to our relations with Mexico, or with the man who keeps troops there, I could not do so. I could say nothing more consoling to the Emperor of the French than what I have here stated, nor nothing more distasteful to him than that the American people are united in their determination that his reign on this continent shall cease. Another election will probably bring this latter fact clear before his vision. I regret that his expulsion had not been the closing scene in the great struggle through which the country has just passed, and which he contributed largely to protract.

Adam Badeau, *Grant in Peace* (Hartford, Conn., 1887), pp. 183–84. On Nov. 8, 1865, 10:00 A.M., Wednesday, USG telegraphed to Maj. Gen. John M. Schofield, New York City. "Sickness in my family prevents my being able to say when I will be in New York. Probably not before Monday next." ALS (telegram sent), DNA, RG 107, Telegrams Collected (Bound); telegram sent, *ibid.*; telegram received, DLC-John M. Schofield. USG met with Schofield and Matías Romero, Mexican minister, in New York City on Nov. 14, the day before Schofield sailed for France. See letter to Maj. Gen. Philip H. Sheridan, July 25, 1865; John M. Schofield, *Forty-Six Years in the Army* (New York, 1897), p. 385; Thomas D. Schoonover, ed., *Mexican Lobby: Matías Romero in Washington, 1861–1867* (Lexington, Ky., 1986), pp. 104–5.

On Dec. 8, Schofield, Paris, wrote to USG. "The Emperor and the French Minister for foreign affairs being absent from Paris I have as yet made no progress. The Paris papers are having a lively discussion about the object of my visit and have created some public excitement. It will be necessary to let this excitment cool down a little before anything can be done. I shall however lose no time unnecessarily. Unless Napoleon has succeeded in completely decieving every body, the Mexican question admits of a satisfactory solution in a reasonable time. It is too early for me to form a decided opinion for myself, but I am strongly inclined to the belief that the whole thing can be peaceably settled before very long. In the mean time the best thing for our friends is a reasonable degree of patience. I will keep you advised of the progress of affairs here, and shall be glad if you will inform me of all that is specially interesting at home." Copy, USG 3. On Jan. 7, 1866, Sunday, Schofield wrote to USG. "Confidential . . . I take advantage of my brother's return to the United States to write you more fully than I have heretofore done, or thought it safe to do by the ordinary mails. You have doubtless learned from Mr. Seward or the President the progress that has been made in negotiations upon the Mexican question through the usual diplomatic channel. Hence it is not necessary for me to add anything on that subject. And if Mr. Bigelow is not deceived by the representations made to him the French Government proposes to do about all, and to do it about as soon, as the United States can reasonably demand. I am hardly in position to judge accurately as to the reliance to be placed upon those representations. But all the evidence I have been able to get from all sources tends to prove that Napoleon has decided to withdraw his troops from Mexico very soon. And I understand we are promised a public development of his policy upon the meeting of the Corps Legislatif which is fixed for the 22d of this month. We must therefore know it very soon if anything satisfactory is to be done. Under these circumstances I have not thought it proper to take any extraordinary means to carry out the objects of my mission to France, until the time for the promised development shall have passed. When if the promises are fulfilled, nothing will be left for me to do. If not fulfilled, then I must see what I can do. The French Government and some of the leading journals seem to have been informed of, or else to have very shrewdly conjectured, the character of my mission; only they probably attributed to it more of an official character than it has. Immediately upon my arrival in Paris these conjectures appeared in some of the leading journals and were denied by others, and the subject was discussed for several days by nearly all the papers of France and even other parts of Europe. The effect was very considerable public commotion and great fluctuation upon the stock exchange. Mr. Drouin de l'Huis, with other members of the French cabinet went at once to Compeigne, where the Emperor then was, and remained with him until about the time of his return to Paris, near two weeks. It is understood that during that time the Emperor determined to anticipate any demand from the United States by doing as an act of policy what he could not so well afford to do in compliance with the demand of any other power. Mr. Bigelow in his conversations with the Emperor and his Minister for foreign affairs has derived the decided opinion that the Emperor is very anxious, while promising to do substantially what we desire as to Mexico, to be left free to do it in his own way. This opinion of Mr. Bigelow I am bound to accept as correct. Indeed I have no good reason to doubt its correctness. You are aware that the usual mode by which foreigners obtain an audience with the Emperor, and generally the only practicable mode, is through the diplomatic representative of their country at the French Court. From considerations derived from the facts which I have stated above, and the fact that I was not officially accredited to the French Government nor to Mr. Bigelow, as charged with any mission, confidential or otherwise, from the Government of the United States, Mr. Bigelow has not considered himself authorized to ask for me an interview with the Emperor. And I have not thought it proper to resort to unusual means to obtain such an interview in face of Mr. Bigelow's opinion that the present satisfactory state of the diplomatic correspondence on the Mexican question renders such an interview unnecessary, and, to the Emperor, undesirable. Therefore I have not yet seen his Majesty. I expect to be presented at the Tuilleries next Wednesday, the first regular reception of the Emperor and Empress, and may then have an opportunity of conversing with Napoleon. If so I will be able to give you the substance of our conversation by this mail. I presume he will hardly expect any communication from me on the Mexican subject, since he has been told by Mr. Bigelow, in reply to a direct question, that I am here only as an officer on leave of absence and have no mission to this or any other government. This may make it difficult to introduce the subject at that time, but I hope at least to pave the way for a private interview if that shall seem necessary or desirable after the 22d of January. In any case, if the promised development of the 22d prove unsatisfactory I shall resort to whatever means that may be necessary to see the Emperor at once, and ascertain what can be done to accomplish the desired object. I have had long conversations with the Prince Napoleon, with Admiral de la Gradiére, Aide de Camp of the Emperor, and with Admiral Réno, assistant Minister of the Marine. They talk very freely upon the Mexican question and express decided opposition to the Emperors policy. They say he has been continually deceived by his agents as to the state of affairs in Mexico and as to the feeling existing in the United States. They all express a strong desire to have me see the Emperor and enlighten him on those subjects, but when I hinted something about the mode of obtaining an audience, they knew of no other but through the Minister of the United States. There the matter rests—It is not at all certain that these gentlemen are as well informed as Mr. Bigelow concerning the Emperor's knowledge or intentions. But their conversation shows how unpopular the Mexican intervention is both among the enemies and the friends of the Emperor and how general the belief that it must be abandoned Jan 10th The promised reception at the Tuilleries has been postponed. Therefore I shall not be able to see the Emperor for the present. From my later conversations with Mr. Bigelow I fear the intentions of the French Government have been represented to him as being more favorable than they really are. But we must know the truth in a few days, and I will inform you without delay." Copy, *ibid.* On Jan. 19, Friday, Schofield wrote to USG. "I was presented to the Emperor on Wednesday at a large ball given at the Tuileries. He conversed with me for some time about our late war, but being surrounded by a crowd from which it was impossible to escape there was no chance to talk on political subjects. But he expressed a desire to see me again, and will perhaps soon give me an opportunity to talk with him on the Mexican question. Meanwhile his address to the Corps Legislatif which meets next Monday will probably give us some idea of his policy and enable me to judge whether it is necessary for me to say anything to him. I will keep you informed of the progress made." Copy, *ibid.* On Jan. 24, Schofield wrote to USG. "You will get by this mail Napoleon's speech delivered at the opening of the French legislative session. I was present and heard the speech delivered. That part of it relating to Mexico and the United States was received with very general tokens of approbation, while most of the remainder met with rather a cold reception. I have since heard it discussed very freely by many prominent men of all shades of political opinion, among others the Prince Napoleon. All seem to recognize the falsity of the Emperor's assumptions where he says 'In Mexico, the government founded by the will of the people is consolidating itself, &c.' Yet his statements are no doubt believed by a large majority of the French people, and therefore afford him a very good reason for yielding to the demand made in common by the people of

France and the United States that his intervention in Mexico shall be brought to an end This is the logic of his position and his solution of his difficulty, viz: to assert that he has accomplished the object of his expedition to Mexico, and hence to end it. While we laugh at the absurdity of his premises we can hardly find fault with his conclusion and hence it is not worth while to criticize any part of his argument. Rather I think it well to let him make the most of his audacity in the creation of convenient facts. The opinion seems to be universal here that the Emperor is sincere in his declarations of intention as to Mexico. Indeed that he has adopted the policy of making the strongest possible bid for the friendship of the United States. It is certainly easy to derive such an opinion from his speech, and I am strongly inclined to believe it correct, yet we cannot forget the fact that in his speech of last year he used quite as strong language as to the speedy termination of his Mexican expedition. Hence I shall indulge in some doubt until I see the actual development of his present plans. I have no idea that Napoleon believes that Maximilian can remain long in Mexico after the French troops are withdrawn; but it is very important for him, in order to give some appearance of truth to his assumed grounds of action, that Maximilian be allowed to stay there for some time without French aid. And for this reason he wants some assurance of neutrality from the Government of the United States. Prince Napoleon and others with whom I have conversed express the decided opinion that Maximilian will come away with Marshal Bazaine in spite of all the Europeans may say to induce him to try to stand alone. This I apprehend will be the difficulty and may cause much delay unless the United States kindly lend a helping hand. Would it not be wise for us to abstain for a few months from all interference, direct or indirect, and thus give Napoleon and Maximilian time to carry out their farce? Mexico would thus be rid of the *French flag* in the least possible time. If the French *troops* come also Juarez can easily dispose of Maximilian at any time. If they succeed in getting the troops to remain as colonists, then the United States can easily find a good reason for disposing of the whole matter, and Napoleon will not dare to interfere. While waiting for instructions which Mr. Bigelow is now expecting from Washington, I shall let the Mexican question rest, so far as I am concerned, where it now is, and hope the whole thing will soon be arranged so that I can return to the United States. I forgot to say that an officer of the Emperors household left here about ten days ago with despatches for Mexico, which it is understood contains the Emperors declaration to Maximilian of his purpose to recall his troops. This will give you some idea of the time when the matter may possibly be arranged if all works well." Copy, *ibid.*

On April 26, Schofield, London, wrote to USG. "I have just learned from Mr. Geo. H. Stuart that before leaving home he was entrusted with an important letter for me by Col. Badeau which I presume was from you. Mr. Stuart stopping in Liverpool gave the letter to a Mr. Thos F. Page, who not finding me in Paris has carried the letter with him to Italy. I have just learned through his banker here Mr. Page's address in Genoa and have written him to send the letter to me here or to Paris by the first opportunity I presume it will reach me sometime but it is impossible to tell when. I write you about it at once, so that you may repeat the contents of the letter if you think it best to do so. I have been looking anxiously for a letter from you for some time and am greatly annoyed at the miscarriage of the one you sent. I wrote last week to Mr. Seward requesting his consent to my return to the United States; and if he gives it I shall expect to sail from Liverpool on the 19th of May—too soon for anything from you, written after the receipt of this, to reach me. I have made this request because I do not see that I can do any good by remaining longer. I did, soon after my arrival in Paris, all that could be done under my instructions, viz: to inform the Emperor, through his confidential subordinate with whom I was able to communicate, that the United States would not consent to his continual occupation of Mexico. His reply you know. I presume the time he has fixed for the withdrawal of his troops will hardly be satisfactory to the United States, and very likely he may be induced to shorten that time. I presume however Mr. Seward will not desire my services in any effort he may make to that end, and will therefore authorize me to return home. If it be otherwise, and I am to remain longer, I shall hope to hear from you soon. . . . Letters sent in the State Dept. Mail bag will now reach me safely, whether in London or Paris; for Mr Bigelow now has his mails sent in an official bag, by special messenger, between London and Paris, an arrangement which he has made only recently." Copy, *ibid.* The absence of USG's letter of March 24 in Schofield's papers suggests that the letter never reached him; Schofield left France early in May to return to the U.S. See Schofield, p. 393.

To Maj. Gen. William T. Sherman

Washington, D. C. March 25th *1866*

MAJ. GEN. W. T. SHERMAN,
COMD.G MIL. DIV. MO.
GEN.

A letter just received from Mr. Babcock of Kansas, a brother of Col. B. of my staff, shows a well grounded fear ~~of~~ from bushwackers from Mo. this spring. He states that the Gov. of Kansas was informed by the Gov. of Mo. that a large number of ~~r~~Rebel soldiers had returned to the Westn part of Mo. That finding the country uncomfortable for them they are organizing to go to Mexico and will pass through Kansas. Two reliable men were sent among them from Kansas to find out their intentions. This has brought out the fact that such organization is going on and that their intention is to pass through Kansas and recover, as they say, the plunder which was taken from them during the War. They will also probably try to release some of their comrades, Quantrel men, now in confinement in Lawrence. In view of these facts I think it will be well to forward some of the troops intended for the plains to

Kansas to await the opening of travel.—If about two companies of cavalry can be sent to Lawrence it will be well to have them there.

Very respectfully
your obt. svt.
U. S. GRANT
Lt. Gn

ALS, DNA, RG 393, Military Div. of the Mo., Letters Received. On March 29, 1866, Maj. Gen. William T. Sherman, St. Louis, endorsed this letter. "Referred to Genl Pope who will cause a couple companies to rendezvous at Lawrence to await the time of general movemt on the Plains." AES, *ibid.*

On March 19, 1:25 P.M., USG had telegraphed to Sherman. "Dispatches received this morning indicate trouble in Lawrence Kansas from bushwhackers Can you not send two or more companies of cavalry up there to keep the peace until they are wanted to go farther west?" Telegram sent, *ibid.*, RG 107, Telegrams Collected (Bound); copies, *ibid.*, RG 108, Letters Sent; (misdated March 14) *ibid.*, RG 393, Military Div. of the Miss., Telegrams Received; *ibid.*, Dept. of the Mo., Letters Received; DLC-USG, V, 47, 109. On the same day, Sherman telegraphed to USG. "I will instruct Gen Pope all sorts of reported troubles are [*designed*] to draw us into Collision with the Citizens in this quarrel. Cars run daily from here to Lawrence & no trouble there has been reported to me before" Telegram received, DNA, RG 108, Telegrams Received; copies, *ibid.*, RG 393, Military Div. of the Miss., Letters Sent; *ibid.*, Dept. of the Mo., Letters Received; DLC-USG, V, 54. On March 22, Maj. Gen. John Pope, St. Louis, wrote to Sherman giving reasons why troops should not be sent to Lawrence. LS, DNA, RG 108, Letters Received. On March 24, Sherman endorsed this letter. "Respectfully forwarded to the HdQrs of the Army for the information of the Comdg Genl. I dont believe there is any danger of Bushwhackers about Lawrence. If we yield to these expressions of fear by Civilians, our whole military force will be scattered and lost" AES, *ibid.* On March 30, Maj. George K. Leet wrote to Sherman. "The Lieut Genl. directs me to acknowledge the receipt of Gen. Popes report of 22d inst in relation to bushwhackers in Kansas with your endorsement of 24th inst. and to inform you that the action of Gen. Pope is approved." Copies, DLC-USG, V, 47, 109; DNA, RG 108, Letters Sent.

To Edwin M. Stanton

Washington, March 26th *1866*

HON. E. M. STANTON
SECRETARY OF WAR
SIR:

I respectfully recommend that the decision of the Retiring Board be reversed in the case of 2d Lieutenant John Elliott, Battery "A" 2d U S. Artillery, placed on the retired list by S O. 51 par 22, AGO. February 1st 1865, and that he be restored to his former position in his regiment.

Lieut. Elliott after having just graduated at the military academy, lost a foot while behaving very gallantly at the battle of the Weldon railroad. By the use of an artificial foot he is now capable of performing valuable service, and in consideration of his conduct it would seem but just to retain him in the line of promotion.

Very respectfully
Your obed't servant
U. S. GRANT
Lieut. General

LS, DNA, RG 108, Letters Received. Maj. George K. Leet noted on the docket: "Returned to the Lieut. General by Gen. Townsend, in person, with information that this recommendation cannot be carried into effect under existing laws." AN (undated), *ibid.* On May 17, 1865, USG had favorably endorsed a letter of May 5 from 2nd Lt. John Elliott (retired—USMA 1864), 2nd Art., Louisville, to the AG applying for a sixty-day leave of absence so that he could be fitted with an artificial foot. ES and ALS, *ibid.*, RG 94, ACP, R383 CB 1870. On Feb. 1, 1866, Elliott, Philadelphia, wrote to Bvt. Col. Theodore S. Bowers requesting restoration to duty with his regt. ALS, *ibid.* Probably some time before March 26, an endorsement had been prepared for USG's signature. "Respectfully forwarded to the Secretary of War with the earnest recommendation that Bt 1st Leiut John Elliott be restored to active duty." Copy (unsigned), *ibid.*

To Edwin M. Stanton

Washington, D. C. March 27th *1866*

HON. E. M. STANTON,
SEC. OF WAR,
SIR:

A misunderstangding seems to exist between officers who have been mustered out of the Volunteer service (regulars) and the Pay and Quartermasters Depts. as to their allowances during the interval of passing from one service to the other. My own opinion is that Regular officers holding commissions in the Volunteer service are clearly entitled to transportation from the place where they are on duty at the time of muster out to the place where assigned. Also that the time given them after muster out of the Volunteer service to join their appropriate duties in the regular service they are entitled to full pay according to the rank they hold in this interval. Where an officer is on voluntary leave of absence at the time of muster out the same rule should govern his allowances as governs other officers when on leave of absence.

I would respectfully recommend the publication of an order on this subject which will fix the rule to be observed.

Very respectfully
your obt. svt.
U. S. GRANT
Lt. Gn.

ALS, DNA, RG 94, Letters Received, 266A 1866. On April 5, 1866, USG wrote to Secretary of War Edwin M. Stanton. "A question has been raised by the Quartermaster General, or Third Auditor, as to whether officers of the Volunteer service, those of Veteran Reserve Corps for instance, are entitled to transportation from the place where relieved to the place where ordered. I am clearly of the opinion that they are entitled to such compensation same as an officer in the Regular Army when traveling under orders. I would respectfully suggest that an order be published requiring compensation to be paid from the place where the officer is on duty at the date of receiving his order to proceed to his home to await further orders, or order mustering him out of service, to the point where he was first mustered into the United States Service." ALS, *ibid.*

To J. Russell Jones

Washington, D. C. March 27th *1866*

DEAR JONES,

I bought to-day, and have mailed, a draft for $9585 76 payable to the Cashier of the Metropolitan National Bank of New York. The letter enclosing it directed that it should be placed to the credit of the Union National Bank of Chicago. If all does not come up right with the funds please notify me so that I may correct it. I have got my little means now invested as follows: Twenty thousand dollars in your "One horse rail-road. Forty thousand in 7/30 bonds Five thousand in 5/20 bonds Five Thousand loaned to Orvil One thousand stock in Galena National bank and one thousand rail-road bonds. Besides this I have rent from my Phila house $1600 per Annum. I do not care to speculate one dollar but so far as my bonds go am willing to transfer them to any other investment if I could see that they would do better.

Yours Truly
U. S. GRANT

ALS, IHi.

To Edwin M. Stanton

Private Washington, D. C. March 28th *1866*

HON. E. M. STANTON,
SEC. OF WAR,
SIR:

In forwarding you the enclosed official letter it is due that I should state that the object of furnishing arms to Messrs Juentes & Co. ~~it~~ is with the view of having them go into the hands of the Liberal party in Mexico. I am conscientious in the belief that all we do to keep the Republican Government of Mexico going now will save us men and money in the end. I have spoken to the President on the subject of furnishing these Arms and the subject seemed to meet his approval.

I would respectfully ask if the subject of my official communication can not be sanctioned without that it be refered to the President.

Very respectfully
your obt. svt.
U. S. GRANT
Lt. Gn.

ALS, DLC-Edwin M. Stanton. Also on March 28, 1866, USG wrote to Secretary of War Edwin M. Stanton. "I would respectfully ask that Five Thousand (5,000) of the most numerous class of Muskets or Rifles now in store be turned over to Messrs Juentes & Co. Commission Merchants at No 50 Exchange Place, New York City. Also that Two & a half Millions (2.500.000) rounds of Ammunition, suitable to the same, be turned over to the same parties with directions that their receipt be sufficient accountability to the Ordnance Dept. for their disposal." ALS, DNA, RG 94, Letters Received, 979A 1866. On the same day, Stanton wrote to USG. "I have received and will consider your confidential communication of this date & will either issue the order or confer with you on the subject" ALS, *ibid.*, RG 108, Letters Received. On March 29, Stanton wrote to USG. "After mature consideration of the request contained in your confidential letter of yesterday, I cannot see that it would be right for me to turn over Government arms to agents of the Juarez Government without the Presidents express authority. It seems to me that in doing so two grave offences would be committed—an unlawful interference with foreign political relations not entrusted to the administration of the War Department—and unlawful disposition of public property in charge of the Department. Sharing your anxiety as to the present condition of Mexican affairs, and agreeing to the importance of upholding the liberal Government, I will, if you desire, lay your letter before the President, & should it receive his sanction your request will be promptly gratified." ALS, *ibid.*; ADf, DLC-Edwin M. Stanton. See letter to Andrew Johnson, March 3, 1866.

On April 20, Andres Treviño, Washington, D. C., wrote to USG. "I desire to buy from the United States the following. 1.500.—muskets. 500. Sabres, cavalry. 300. rounds of ammunition for each musket. Or as many of these arms can be sold to me for ($—6.000 00) six thousand dollars in currency that I wish to invest in them. I wish these arms to be delivered to me in Brownsville—(txas.), or if this is not possible, at New Orleans" ALS, DNA, RG 94, Letters Received, 825T 1866. On April 25, USG endorsed this letter. "I would respectfully recommend that the Chief of Ordnance be directed to make the sale of Arms herein asked, receive the money, and direct the officer in charge of Arms in the Mil. Div. of the Gulf ~~be directed~~ to deliver themm to Mr. A. Treviño." AES, *ibid.* On April 30, USG wrote to Stanton. "Will you be kind enough to inform me if any decission has been made upon Mr. Treviño's application for the purchase of Arms, to be delivered in the Gulf Division?" ALS, DLC-Edwin M. Stanton. On the same day, Stanton wrote to USG, cancelling "War Department" on the stationery and using his home address. "On consideration of Mr Treviños application for arms I think in view of the recent correspondence upon Mexican affairs that the question should be submitted to the President before any action by the Department. This if there be no objection, I propose to do tomorrow at Cabinet meeting." ALS, DNA, RG 108, Letters Received. On May 1, Stanton wrote to USG. "The proposition of Armes Trevino received through you by this Department was submitted to the President in Cabinet to-day and is not approved." Copy, DLC-Edwin M. Stanton. On the same day, Stanton endorsed Treviño's letter. "The within proposition was this day submitted to the President in Cabinet and after full consideration was disapproved by the President and by each member of the Cabinet all being present but Attorney General Speed." AES, DNA, RG 94, Letters Received, 825T 1866. On April 12, 1867, Bvt. Maj. Gen. Alexander B. Dyer, chief of ordnance, wrote to Maj. Gen. Philip H. Sheridan explaining that 2,000 Enfield rifles had been sold to Treviño on the assumption that the sale had War Dept. approval; learning this was incorrect, an ordnance officer declined to deliver the remainder of the order. LS, *ibid.*, RG 156, Letters Received, 277WD 1867. On June 8, USG endorsed this letter. "I would respectfully recommend that the Chief of Ordnance be authorized to sell to Mr. Trevino the remainder of arms & ammunition, accoutrements &c. on his list for purchase and not yet rec'd." AES, *ibid.*

On March 27, 1866, 2:30 P.M., Sheridan, New Orleans, telegraphed to USG. "The Liberals without doubt have had some handsome success recently in Northern Mexico near Parras and Saltillo, and their cause is growing better every day. The column which marched from San-Louis-Potosi, towards the Rio Grande frontier was to have strengthened the garrison at Matamoras, and to have occupied Piedras Negras, and Camargo, so I am informed. It is doubtful if it can be done, The French do not realize the difficulty of holding such a country with its sparce population and long lines of communication" Telegram received (at 9:50 P.M.), *ibid.*, RG 107, Telegrams Collected (Bound); *ibid.*, RG 108, Telegrams Received; copies (one sent by mail), *ibid.*, Letters Received; DLC-USG, V, 54; DLC-Philip H. Sheridan. On March 28, USG wrote to Sheridan. "In view of the possible contingency of needing Arms on the Rio Grande I think it advisable that you should have from Ten to Fifteen Thousand stand, with ammunition for them, at Brownsville or Brasos which ever may be the most convenient for storing them. I do not know what number of Arms may be within your command outside of those in the hands of troops but presume you will find no difficulty in placing the number specified there either from those now in store or from those to be turned over by troops going out of service." ALS, DNA, RG 393, Military Div. of the Southwest and Dept. of the Gulf, Letters Received. On April 9, Sheridan wrote to USG. "I have the honor to acknowledge the receipt of your letter of Mar 28th and will put at Brazos Santiago or Brownsville *Ten Thousand* stand of arms. I will be obliged to send them from this place" ALS, *ibid.*, RG 108, Letters Received. See letters to Maj. Gen. Philip H. Sheridan, May 2, 19, 1866.

To Maj. Gen. George H. Thomas

Washington, D. C. March 28th *1866*

MAJ. GN. G. H. THOMAS,
COMD.G MIL. DIV. OF THE MISS.
GENERAL;

Enclosed I send you a copy of a dispatch from Macon Ga. to the President just refered to me as you will see by the note accompanying.

Orders were long since given for the withdrawel of Colored troops from the interior of the Southern states to avoid unnecessary irritation and the demoralization of labor in those states. How far it is practicable to carry out that order in Georgia you will have to be the judge. It is our duty to avoid giving unnecessary annoyance but it is a greater duty to protect troops acting under Military Authority, and also all loyally disposed persons in the Southern states.

In the spirit of these instructions then you will withdraw the Colored troops from the interior of the Country so far as you can replace them with White troops or so far as you can abandon the occupation of the interior without endangering the rights of loyal Whites and Freedmen. You will have to be the judge how far this can be done.

The dispatch sent you indicates danger to Colored Troops if allowed to remain where they are! It is your duty to see that no conflict shall be brought on by the acts of Government forces or Government agents. But if conflict does come the troops must be strong enough to resist opposition. All engaged in resisting the authority of the United States must be arrested and held for trial for their offence.

Very respectfully
your obt. svt.
U. S. GRANT
Lt. Gn.

ALS, DNA, RG 393, Dept. of the Tenn., Letters Received. On March 27, 1866, Bvt. Lt. Col. Wright Rives, military secretary for President Andrew Johnson, wrote to USG. "The President directs to forward to you for your consideration, the enclosed copy of a telegram that he receied to day." ALS, *ibid.* Rives enclosed a telegram of March 26 from Osborne A. Lockrane, Macon, to Johnson requesting that Negro troops be withdrawn from Ga. Copy, *ibid.* Also on March 28, Bvt. Brig. Gen. Cyrus B. Comstock wrote to Maj. Gen. George H. Thomas. "I am directed by the Lt. Gen Comdg. to say that in his opinion it is now practicable to muster the white volunteer troops remaining in the Mil. Div of the Tenn. out of service. If you should also think it practicable he wishes you to muster them out at once, and in any case to muster out all that can possibly be spared, reporting your action" Copies, DLC-USG, V, 47, 109; DNA, RG 108, Letters Sent. On April 3, Thomas, Nashville, wrote to USG. "I have the honor to acknowledge the receipt of your letter of March 26th and also that of Brt Brig Genl C. B. Comstock, A. D. C on your staff, of March 28th communicating your instructions for the muster out of the remaining White Volunteer forces under my command, if in my judgement they can be discharged with safety to the public peace. If,

Military supervision over the administration of the Civil Governments in the several States composing the Division of the Tennessee is to be discontinued and the duties of the Troops confined to guarding the Government property, Forts, Arsenals, Depots &c, I can at once muster out all the remaining Volunteer Force in this Military Division—I feel it my duty, however, to state that upon the discontinuance of military supervision over the civil affairs of these States, that the State Authorities will administer the laws directly or indirectly to the prejudice of all who are loyal to the constitution and Government of the United States—I have made arrangements to carry out your instructions, and will issue the necessary orders to that end on the 15th of this month unless countermanding instructions are received before that date. . . . P. S. Orders were given yesterday to prepare the Muster Rolls to be ready to commence this Muster out on the 15th." ALS, *ibid.*, Letters Received. On April 10, 12:45 P.M., USG telegraphed to Thomas. "My instructions of 28th March for muster out of Volunteer white troops were conditioned on your still giving proper protection to loyal persons in your military Division I thought you would be able by concentration to reduce the number and probably dispense with them entirely. Of the degree of reduction expedient I desire that you shall be the judge" Telegram sent, *ibid.*, RG 107, Telegrams Collected (Bound); copies, *ibid.*, RG 108, Letters Sent; *ibid.*, RG 393, Depts. of Cumberland and Tenn., Telegrams Received; DLC-USG, V, 47, 109.

To Charles W. Ford

Washington, D. C. March 28th *1866*

DEAR FORD:

Enclosed I send you check for One Thousand Dollars which please ~~place~~ keep to the credit of Judge Dent, settling what he owes you of course. Judge Dent never owned the land which I purchased so can make no deed himself. That comes from J. C. Dent and when received I will send to you the balance the deed comes.

All are well with me. I do not know positively yet that I shall be able to visit St. Louis but hope to.

Yours Truly
U. S. GRANT

ALS, USG 3.

To Maj. Gen. Alfred H. Terry

Washington, D. C., Mch 29th *18646*

MAJ GEN TERRY
RICHMOND VA

Your advice to the colored people of Richmond in relation to abstaining from a celebration on the third is for their interest If likely to cause disorder put a stop to it or take steps to suppress the disorder as you deem most advisable Do not leave Richmond until after the third yourself

U S. GRANT
Lieut Gen

Telegram sent, DNA, RG 107, Telegrams Collected (Bound); telegram received, *ibid.*, RG 393, Dept. of Va. and N. C., 1st Military District, Telegrams Received. On March 29, 1866, Maj. Gen. Alfred H. Terry had telegraphed to Brig. Gen. John A. Rawlins. "The negroes here propose to celebrate the 3rd of April by processions &c. I strongly advised that they should not do so for their own interest and supposed that I had convinced them that it was very unwise for them to carry out their plans. I now find that the great mass of them are determined to celebrate the day and that great numbers are coming in from the country to join them. The affair creates great excitement among the whites. I should not be surprised if disorder should occur. I respectfully ask instructions as to whether an order should be issued to suppress it. I have a leave of absence from Genl Meade and I expect to leave here tomorrow morning. I shall be glad of a reply today." Telegram received (at 2:20 P.M.), *ibid.*, RG 107, Telegrams Collected (Bound); *ibid.*, RG 108, Telegrams Received; copies, DLC-USG, V, 54; DLC-Edwin M. Stanton. On April 3, 11:00 A.M., USG telegraphed to Terry. "If the colored peoples celebration takes place to day close all drinking houses in the city and use patrols to arrest for the day, all parties black or white, who are threatening in their manner, or who are intoxicated" Telegram sent, DNA, RG 107, Telegrams Collected (Bound); telegram received, *ibid.*, RG 393, Dept. of Va. and N. C., 1st Military District, Telegrams Received. On the same day, Terry telegraphed to Rawlins. "The celebration today passed off in peace & quiet except a dubious report that the procession was fired upon by a white man from a window—I have heard of no disorders" Telegram received (at 8:15 P.M.), *ibid.*, RG 107, Telegrams Collected (Bound); *ibid.*, RG 108, Telegrams Received; copy, DLC-USG, V, 54.

On March 28, Joshua M. Bosley, Baltimore, wrote to Montgomery Blair. "Deeming the enclosed letter of the first importance to, not only the People of Richmond, but also to, the whole Country, and to the President in particular, I send it you, to be used as to you may seem best The writer I have known for a long time and believe him to intelegent, well informed, and truthful" ALS, DNA, RG 108, Letters Received. Bosley enclosed a letter of March 27 from R. Swan to Bosley concerning plans of Negroes to celebrate on April 3 in Richmond and alleging that Terry was encouraging the celebration. ALS, *ibid.* On March 30, Maj. George K. Leet referred these letters to Terry, who endorsed them on April 4. "Respectfully returned the allegations of the writer of the enclosed letter that I had encouraged the negroes to celebrate the the 3d of April is false" ES and AES, *ibid.*

To Andrew Johnson

Washington, March 30th 1866

HIS EXCELLENCY A. JOHNSON.
PRESIDENT OF THE UNITED STATES
SIR:

I understood from Bradley T. Johnson late of the Southern Army and who was included in the paroled officers under the convention between Gen W. T. Sherman and Gen. Joe E. Johnston, has been arrested in the State of Maryland on the charge of Treason for acts committed at the Battle of Gettysburg, Pa., in 1863. I have noticed the same thing from the Newspapers. There is nothing clearer in my mind than that the terms of the paroles given by officers and soldiers who were arrayed against the authority of the General Government of the United States prior to their surrender exempts them from trial or punishment for acts of ~~loyal~~ legal warfare so long as they observe the conditions of their paroles.

General Johnson was in Maryland by express authority from these Hd. Qrs.—I would now ask as a point of faith on the part of the Government, that proper steps be taken to relieve B. T. Johnson from the obligations of the Bonds which he has been forced to give in the State of Maryland

I have the honor to be
Very Respectfully
Your obt. servt.
U. S. GRANT
Lt. Gen'l

Copies, DLC-USG, V, 47, 109; DNA, RG 108, Letters Sent. On Feb. 12, 1866, Bradley T. Johnson, Raleigh, N. C., wrote a letter to President Andrew Johnson received at USG's hd. qrs. requesting an extension of his parole. *Ibid.*, Register of Letters Received. On Feb. 14, Bvt. Col. Theodore S. Bowers endorsed this letter. "The parole of B. T. Johnson, late of the Confederate Army, is hereby extended so as to permit him to proceed to and from all points within the limits of the U. S. until further orders from competent authority." Copy, *ibid.* On March 10, Bvt. Col. Ely S. Parker issued a parole for Bradley T. Johnson. Copies, DLC-USG, V, 47, 109; DNA, RG 108, Letters Sent. On April 2, USG wrote to President Johnson. "I would respectfully request that Bradly T. Johnson, late a General in the Rebel Army, be released from the Bonds under which he is now held by the state of Maryland for the part he took in the Battle of Gettysburg, as I understand, in 1863. B. T. Johnson was paroled under the Convention between Gens. Sherman and Johnston. At the time of his indictment he was in the state of Maryland by authority from these Hd Qrs." ALS, *ibid.*, RG 60, Letters Received from the President.

To Edwin M. Stanton

Washington, D. C. Apl. 2d *1866*

HON. E. M. STANTON,
SEC. OF WAR,
SIR:

I would respectfully suggest that Gen. Dodge's name be taken from the Order mustering out General Officers. He has tendered his resignation and I believe it has already been accepted.

I would suggest that Gen. Griersons name be added to the order.

Very respectfully
your obt. svt.
U. S. GRANT
Lt. Gen.

ALS, DNA, RG 94, ACP, G553 CB 1865.

On Jan. 13, 1866, Maj. Gen. William T. Sherman telegraphed to USG. "Genl Pope is very emphatic in his opinion that Gen G. M. Dodge ought not to be mustered out & says that he would like Dodge & T. C. H. Smith retained & to muster out Connor of Utah Upton & Wheaton instead—I do think Dodge is too va~~ul~~luable at his present post to be spared—Genl Dodges telegraphs me that it would incommodate him sadly to be mustered out before April next—Genl Pope also suggests that Genl Sully be mustered out & Gen Walcutt retained in his place. Genl Pope wants to send Genl T. C. H. Smith to Utah" Telegram received (at 6:45 P.M.), *ibid.*, D128 CB 1866; *ibid.*, RG 107, Telegrams Collected (Bound); *ibid.*, RG 108, Telegrams Received; copies, *ibid.*, RG 393, Military Div. of the Miss., Letters Sent; DLC-USG, V, 54. On Jan. 15, USG endorsed this telegram. "Respectfully forwarded to the Secretary of War, with the recommendation that the muster out of Maj. Gen Dodge be revoked" ES, DNA, RG 94, ACP, D128 CB 1866.

On July 16, Grenville M. Dodge, Omaha, wrote to USG. "I am now a citizen but still take great interest in the army, and shall always give it what aid there is in my power. I know that to your unfailing support and your confidence in me, I am greatly indebted for what little success I may have achieved, and I desire now to thank you. I hope I may be able some day to partly return it. Wherever fortune may hereafter place me, I shall never forget that all true soldiers owe to you more than they can ever repay, and that the country can never reward your successful labor for it in the army. I grew up under your's, Sherman's and McPherson's orders and guidance, and I shall take into civil life my lesson that will be of lasting benefit to me. I trust if I can ever be of service to you in any way that you will not fail to command me, and that you will visit our section of the country in some of your travels. We are fast civilizing this western country, and I believe our railroad will do more towards taming the Indians than all else combined. General Sherman was here to see me a short time ago." Grenville M. Dodge, *Personal Recollections of President Abraham Lincoln, General Ulysses S. Grant and General William T. Sherman* (Council Bluffs, Iowa, 1914), pp. 98–99. A draft of this letter includes a recommendation for the promotion of Maj. and Bvt. Col. Michael R. Morgan. ADfS, IaHA.

To Maj. Gen. Philip H. Sheridan

Washington, D. C. Apl. 2d *1866*

MAJ. GN. P. H. SHERIDAN,
COMD.G MIL. DIV. OF THE GULF,
GENERAL:

In the matter of restoring the Banks of New Orleans and Merchant's Bank, now held under orders from Gn. Canby in the hands of parties designated by him I would suggest the propriety of ~~restoring them to stockholders in at least~~ withdrawing all Military controll and leave the law to decide who should exercise controll. I do not know under what authority Gn. Canby has acted. If of his own volition his acts are sustained but it may now be concidered time to restore this property as the state laws may direct. If he has acted under orders of the President or Sec. of War direct the proper steps to be taken to get their authority for having the property restored.

If you know reasons why these instructions should not be carried out you need not act upon them until you communicate the objections here and get further instructions on the subject.

Very respectfully
Your obt. svt.
U. S. GRANT
Lt. Gn.

ALS, DNA, RG 393, Military Div. of the Southwest and Dept. of the Gulf, Letters Received. See letter to Maj. Gen. Philip H. Sheridan, Oct. 13, 1865.

To C. A. Eastman

Washington, D. C. Apl. 2d *1866*

DEAR EASTMAN:

This will introduce to you Col. John Riggin formerly of St. Louis, and during the first two years of the rebellion a member of my Staff.—Col. Riggin visits California for the first time and if you treat him well, or he likes the country as well as I did, he may settle among you.

Attentions shewn the Col. will be appreciated by him and will be regarded as a personal favor to me. Of your old Pacific Coast acquaintances I know none here except Ingalls and myself. Ingalls is well but a confirmed old bachilor with but little hare left on his head. My cappelary appendage still holds on without much sprinkling of Grey among it as yet. It will soon be time however to expect a change to come over it. My kind regards to Mrs. Eastman and all the little Eastmans. I believe I have heard as far along as young E the 2d.

Yours Truly
U. S. GRANT

ALS, James S. Schoff, New York, N. Y. See *PUSG*, 1, 297, 298*n*; letter to Maj. Gen. Philip H. Sheridan, Oct. 13, 1865.

To Andrew Johnson

Washington D. C. Apl. 3d *1866*

HIS EXCELLENCY, A. JOHNSON,
PRESIDENT OF THE UNITED STATES,
SIR:

I would respectfully recommend that pardon or Amnesty be extended to R. J. Castelbury, W. G. Lawrence and M. H. Van Dyke, all of Georgia. The two former come under the $20,000 clause of your Amnesty proclamation, if they come under it at all. ~~t~~The latter served in the Rebel Army as a Surgeon. They are represented to me by Col. Pride, who served on my Staff in the early part of the War, as being well disposed to the Government, in fact as having been rather obnoctious to ~~Secessionest~~ Secessionests on account of their Union proclivities during the War, particularly the two former.

The reason for asking Amnesty in these cases at this time is that Col. Pride, whos loyalty I vouch for, has purchased property from them, in the state of Georgia, which he desires to develope and make add to the general wealth of the country. Before laying out more money in the matter he wishes to feel himself secure.

I have the honor to be
Very respectfully
your obt. svt,
U. S. GRANT
Lt. Gn

ALS, DNA, RG 94, Amnesty Papers, Ga. Docketing indicates that the pardons were granted as of April 4, 1866.

On April 11, George G. Pride, Fifth Avenue Hotel, New York City, telegraphed to Brig. Gen. John A. Rawlins. "Tell Babcock, Porter, Parker & yourself if you want to go in telegraph or write me by Saturday" Telegram received (at 5:20 P.M.), *ibid.*, RG 107, Telegrams Collected (Bound). On April 13, Saturday, Rawlins telegraphed to Pride. "All wish to go in as suggested" Telegram sent, *ibid.*, Telegrams Collected (Unbound).

To Andrew Johnson

Washington, D. C. Apl. 3d *1866*

HIS EXCELLENCY, A. JOHNSON,
PRESIDENT OF THE UNITED STATES,
SIR:

Whilst in conversation with you this morning I forgot to mention a subject which I promised to speak to you upon the first opportunity. It is in relation to a Cadet's appointment for Steven A. Douglas, Jr. son of the late Senator Douglas. The boy is very desirous of entering West Point in September next. The claims the lad has upon this Govt. through the services of his father, it is not necessary for me to speak of.

It was not my intention to make a formal application for this appointment but to say to you that it was desired by the boy, and his stepmother, and if it could be given then it could be sent to him as a compliment due his family.

Very respectfully
your obt. svt.
U. S. GRANT
Lt. Gn.

ALS, DNA, RG 94, Cadet Applications. On June 9, 1866, Stephen A. Douglas, Georgetown College, D. C., wrote to President Andrew Johnson declining an appointment to USMA because he was under sixteen years of age. LS, *ibid.*

To Andrew Johnson

Washington, D. C. Apl. 3d *1866*

HIS EXCELLENCY, A. JOHNSON,
PRESIDENT OF THE UNITED STATES,
SIR:

The bearer of this is the mother of Charles W. Larned who I asked as a special favor, both in writing and verbally, should be appointed a Cadet at West Point.

Mrs. Larned is the widow of an officer who died in the service during the War. Her hopes, as well as that of her husband during his life time, has been centered in getting this son into the Army, through West Point, so soon as he should be old enough. So far back as 1863 I promised to give whatever influance I might have to procure it.

In the original application for C. W. Larned's I spoke more particularly of his claims to an appointment and need now only add my personal desire to see the appointment give if it can be done.

I have the honor to be
Very respectfully
your obt. svt.
U. S. GRANT
Lt. Gn.

ALS, DNA, RG 94, Cadet Applications. On Jan. 30, 1866, Charles W. Larned, Chicago, had written to President Andrew Johnson requesting an appointment to USMA. ALS, *ibid.* On Feb. 3, USG endorsed this letter. "This applicant is a bright inteligent boy whos father died in service during the rebellion leaving his family so destitute that this will be the only way in which the lad will be able to get an education. I feel a particular interest in securing it and therefore heartily endorse the application." AES, *ibid.* Larned graduated from USMA in 1870.

To Maj. Gen. Alfred H. Terry

Washington, D. C. April 3 *1866* [*1:55* P.M.]

MAJ GEN A H TERRY
RICHMOND VA

Complete the case referred to in your telegram of to day, unless you receive other orders The Judge Advocate General can determine the validity of the proceedings

U. S. GRANT
Lieut Gen

Telegram sent, DNA, RG 107, Telegrams Collected (Bound); copies, *ibid.*, RG 108, Letters Sent; DLC-USG, V, 47, 109. On April 3, 1866, Maj. Gen. Alfred H. Terry had telegraphed to Brig. Gen. John A. Rawlins. "The newspapers Contain the intelligence that the President has issued a proclamations, declaring the insurrection ended. I suppose this relieves all military Commissions. I have a very important case on trial before one, of a white man for the murder of a negro. I respectfully ask instructions whether this case should be completed or abandoned at once." Telegram received (at 11:00 A.M.), DNA, RG 108, Telegrams Received; copy, DLC-USG, V, 54. Bvt. Brig. Gen. Cyrus B. Comstock noted at the foot of the telegram received: "The Sec. thinks the case may go on, the effect on it of the proclamation to be determined by the Judge Advocate of the Army when the case comes up here" On April 2, President Andrew Johnson had issued a proclamation declaring an end to the insurrection in all Southern states except Tex. *O.R.*, III, v, 1007–9. On April 7, Bvt. Maj. Gen. John W. Turner, Richmond, telegraphed to Rawlins. "I respectfully request Official information whether Martial law has been removed in this Department, and the writ of Habeas Corpus restored. I understand that it is contemplated to sue out a writ for the Military prisoners in my custody Shall I surrender such prisoners?" Telegram received (at 5:30 P.M.), DNA, RG 107, Telegrams Collected (Bound); *ibid.*, RG 108, Telegrams Received; copy, DLC-USG, V, 54. On April 9, 9:45 A.M., USG telegraphed to Turner. "I do not understand Martial Law to be removed in Va, or the writ of Habeas Corpus to be restored. Obey no writ for taking out of custody any military prisoner without direct instructions to do so," Telegram sent, DNA, RG 107, Telegrams Collected (Bound); telegram received, *ibid.*, RG 393, Dept. of Va. and N. C., 1st Military District, Telegrams Received.

On April 9, Maj. Gen. George H. Thomas, Nashville, telegraphed to USG. "Does the President's peace proclamation abrogate martial law, and restore the writ of habeas corpus?—" Telegram received (at 5:20 P.M.), *ibid.*, RG 107, Telegrams Collected (Bound); *ibid.*, RG 108, Telegrams Received; copies, *ibid.*, RG 393, Depts. of the Cumberland and Tenn., Telegrams Sent; DLC-USG, V, 54. On April 10, 10:00 A.M., USG telegraphed to Thomas. "The Presidents proclamation as I understand it, does not abrogate martial law and restore the writ of Habeas Corpus" Telegram sent, DNA, RG 107, Telegrams Collected (Bound); copies, *ibid.*, RG 108, Letters Sent; *ibid.*, RG 393, Depts. of the Cumberland and Tenn., Telegrams Received; DLC-USG, V, 47, 109. On April 11, Maj. Gen. Philip H. Sheridan, New Orleans, telegraphed to USG. "The Presidents proclamation of April second (2nd) has not yet reached me officially—Have any orders based upon it been issued by the War Department? Does it involve the immediate muster out of all Volunteers?" Telegram received (at 5:10 P.M.), DNA, RG 107, Telegrams Collected (Bound); *ibid.*, RG 108, Telegrams Received; copies (one sent by mail), *ibid.*, Letters Received; (incomplete) *ibid.*, RG 393, Military Div. of the Southwest and Dept. of the Gulf, Telegrams Sent; DLC-USG, V, 54; DLC-Philip H. Sheridan. On April 9, Bvt. Maj. Gen. Edward D. Townsend had written to military div. and dept. commanders. "The Assistant Commissioner Bureau of Refugees, Freedmen &c for the state of Georgia having inquired whether the Presidents recent proclamation removes martial law, and stated that the Department Commander does not feel authorized to arrest parties who have committed outrages on freed people or Union refugees, the Secretary of War, with the approval of the President, directs me to inform you that the President's Proclamation does not remove martial law, or operate in any way upon the Freedmen's Bureau in the exercise of its legitimate jurisdiction. It is not expedient however to resort to military tribunals in any case where justice can be attained through the medium of civil authority." Copy, DNA, RG 108, Letters Received.

To Commander Benjamin M. Dove

Washington D. C. April 5th 1866.

CAPT. DOVE
U. S. NAVY
DEAR CAPT.

It affords me pleasure to bear testimony to that part of your record which fell under my observation; to wit: from the time you joined at Cairo Ill. in 1861, until after the fall of Fort Donelson.

During that time, I saw no reason, nor heard any given, by the Chief in your Arm of the public service, Adml Foote, why you should be superseded.

At Fort Donelson, where the Navy did all that it was in their power to do, no vessel was more exposed than the one commanded by you.

On the morning of the surrender, I found you at the town of Dover, within the lines of the enemy, on my arrival.

I then understood that you had declined receiving the surrender of the Water Battery, as you passed up, on the ground that you were not satisfied that the Navy had caused the surrender.

In this I thought you acted with great courtesy towards that branch of the service represented by myself, and just right under the circumstances; though with me it would have made no difference who received the surrender.

I understand that your course in this matter has been one of the principal grounds of your supersedure. If so, I think you have been ~~dealt with~~ unjustly dealt with.

My own ~~opinion~~ impression is, that at Donelson, at least, your conduct was highly commendable, instead of censurable.

very truly
your obt svt.
U. S. GRANT
Lt. Genl.

Copies, DNA, RG 46, Senate 39A–H12.1, Petitions and Memorials, Naval Affairs; *ibid.*, RG 108, Letters Sent; DLC-USG, V, 47, 109. Benjamin M. Dove, appointed midshipman as of Dec. 1, 1826, had retired as a commander as of Oct. 1, 1864.

To James C. Moodey

Washington, D. C. Apl. 5th *1866*

DEAR JUDGE,

Your letter of the 2d of this month is received. In relation to the Military Secretaryship the appointment is confined, by law, to officers holding Commissions in the Army. The number is limited to two. Sutlerships are given by the "Council of Administration" of each Military Post, confirmed by the Sec. of War. Such is composed always of the three officers next in rank after the Commanding officer. I know Johnny was a fine boy and a very smart one and would be glad to help him get a start in this world. If I could influance any "Council" to nominate him for a position of Sutler would do so with pleasure. I do not know where vacancies may now exist to recommend him to apply for a Sutlership but would suggest that he make up his mind where to go to (Little Rock or Fort Smith Arkansas would both be good places) and then make his application addressing it to "The Council of Administration" under cover to the Commander of the post, enclosing this letter with it as evidence of my endorsement of him.

Yours Truly
U. S. GRANT

ALS, DNA, RG 94, ACP, J79 CB 1866. On April 11, 1866, Maj. Gen. William T. Sherman endorsed this letter. "The Bearer of this note, the son of Judge Moody is recommended to the notice of Col Bonneville and the officers at Jefferson Barracks." AES, *ibid.* On April 26, Bvt. Col. Adam Badeau wrote to James C. Moodey. "Lt Gen Grant directs me to inform you that on the day after he last wrote you, he discovered that the Sec of War had made some appointments of Sutler, without the usually required recommendation of the Council of Administration; and that he immediately recommended your son for one of the sutlerships on the Overland route. If you will at once apprize Gen Grant for what sutlership you are now working for Mr. John Moody, the General will do his best to futher you wishes." ALS, *ibid.* On May 1, John W. Moodey, St. Louis, wrote to Secretary of War Edwin M. Stanton. "I respectfully apply for the appointment of 'Sutler' for some one of the Military posts on the *overland route*—I have a letter from Lieut Genl Grant and one from Major Genl Sherman recommending me—these I have sent to the Commander of the post at Fort Smith—as soon as I can procure their return I will enclose them to the War Department—" ALS, *ibid.*, M423 CB 1866. On May 4, USG endorsed this letter. "Respectfully forwarded. I know the applicant and would recommend him for a Sutlership when there is a vacancy existing. ~~but not~~." AES, *ibid.*

To Andrew Johnson

Washn April 10 *1866*

The President
Sir

I have the honor to forward herewith a copy of a letter from Robert Ould Commissioner of exchange for the confederacy to Jno. Mulford Asst. Commissioner of exchange for the U. S. dated Sept 12 1864, and of one to Gen Halleck from myself dated Jan 15 1865, in which an exchange of all prisoners of war held in close confinement or irons is arranged. The object, on our side, of the arrangement, was the relief of a class of union prisoners undergoing the severest suffering, even though in so doing some rebel prisoners should escape deserved punishment.

You will see that in this arrangement, prisoners of war, convicted by military courts on either side, were included.

Under it Frank Gurley convicted of the murder of Gen. McCook and sentenced to death was duly exchanged. Such exchange released him from his punishment precisely as it did the person or persons for whom he was exchanged, from their punishment or suffering

In my opinion after having obtained from the exchange the benefits which induced us to make the arrangement, we cannot honorably avoid fulfilling our part of the contract, although we now have the power to do as we please.

I recommend that Frank Gurley be released as having been duly exchanged.

I have the honor to be,
Very respectfully
your obt. svt.
U. S. GRANT
Lt. Gn.

LS, DNA, RG 153, MM 1326. On April 14, 1866, President Andrew Johnson endorsed this letter. "Respectfully returned to the Secretary of War Upon the recommendation of Lieut Gen Grant Frank B. Gurley is hereby released from confinement and will be placed upon his parole" ES, *ibid.* See *PUSG*, 9, 574–75; *ibid.*, 13, 266–67.

To Edwin M. Stanton

Washington, D. C. Apl. 13th *1866*

HON. E. M. STANTON,
SEC. OF WAR,
SIR:

Having been appealed to to recommend a further reduction of the Military Reservation at Fort Reiley, Kansas than that recommended by Gn. Sherman in his letter of the 15th of Feb.y 1866 so as to exclude from the Reservation the town site of Junction City, a place now said to have a population of five or six hundred people, I have no objection to leaving out of the Reservation all the land between the Kansas & Smoky Hill Rivers, and respectfully recommend such reduction. In fact Sections 28 & 29, and the land embraced in the Reservation South of the Kansas River, in my opinion, would embrace all that ever will be required for Military purposes, though it might be well for a few years yet to controll the land, and settlers, for some greater distance around the post. ~~for a few years yet~~.

Very respectfully
your obt. svt.
U. S. GRANT.
Lt. Gn.

ALS, DNA, RG 107, Letters Received from Bureaus. On April 12, 1866, U.S. Senator Samuel C. Pomeroy of Kan. had written to USG. "I beg leave most respectfully, to call your attention, to a recommendation, approved by you, of Maj. Gen. W. T. Sherman commanding Division of the Mississippi, for a change in the boundary lines of the military post of Fort Riley Reservation, in my State, a plot of which I hand you, together with a copy of the recommendation endorsed as aforesaid. By reference to the accompanying papers, you will see that the extension of the proposed new boundaries of the post Reserve to the Smoky Hill River, as recommended, would take into the Reserve full *two thirds of the villiage of Junction City, and*, as I know from personal knowledge, would include, all its business houses, churches, stores, dwellings &c. I cannot suppose General Sherman intended any such thing. What I suppose he did intend was, to recommend that the western boundary line should terminate on the *Republican* (instead of the Smoky Hill) fork of the Kansas river, and that it should follow that river, the Smoky Hill, & the present boundaries, to the place of beginning. An additional reason for believing that such was his intention, is found in the fact, that he has failed to mark the low bottom land between the rivers as 'Bottom Land' to be retained in the Reserve. As this matter is now before Congress & likely to be acted upon soon, I respectfully ask that you modify your recommendation so as to make the Republican river the terminus of the western line of the Resve, which change may be made without detriment to the usefulness of the post." ALS, *ibid.*, RG 233, 39th Congress, Committee on Military Affairs. U.S. Representative Sidney Clarke of Kan. endorsed the foot of this letter. "I concur in the above recommendation." AES, *ibid.*

To Maj. Gen. William T. Sherman

Washington D. C. Apl. 18th *1866*

Dear General,

Your letter of the 13th in relation to your proposed tour is just received. I favor the whole of it and will see the Sec. of the Treas. to-morrow and arrange for the use of a Revenue Cutter on Lake Superior as you request. There will be no difficulty about it I know so you may make your arrangements accordingly.

Yours Truly
U. S. Grant
Lt. Gn.

Maj. Gn. W. T. Sherman,
Comd.g Mil. Div. of the Mo.

ALS, DNA, RG 393, Military Div. of the Miss., Letters Received. See letter to Edwin M. Stanton, May 4, 1866. On April 13, 1866, Maj. Gen. William T.

Sherman, St. Louis, had written to USG. "I have several trips in view partly official, and partly personal, which I would not of course attempt without your full permission and approval—As soon as all the Regulars are off for their posts, and they are now moving—say early in ~~April~~ May I would go up to Fort Riley by the Pacific R. R. Then back to Fort Leavenworth—up the Missouri River to Omaha—out on that Pacific Road, & stages to Fort Kearney and back—up the Missouri to Sioux City and across land to Saint Paul, up to Fort Ripley & across to Fond du Lac of Superior, thence down the lakes to Detroit and back to Saint Louis. This would make me well acquainted with all questions of the Frontier, & enable me to give general assurances of future quiet and protection. On the Lakes I understand there are several new Steam Revenue Cutters, one of which I would like to get and use for a couple of weeks in looking to the Lake Frontier. If this meets your favor I would like you to get of Mr Secretary McCullough an order that some one of the Cutters should meet me at Fond du lac of Superior, at some date hereafter to be arranged. In July (17th) I am under a partial promise to attend the Commencemt Exercises of Dartmouth College New Hampshire, which would take me in going & coming ten days, this of course would be purely private at my own Cost. Generals Pope & Cooke will be absent from these HeadQrs in the Early Summer inspecting their Country, the former goes to NewMexico & the latter up the Missouri—In August Sept & October I propose to go out to Denver, the Middle Route, and it may be Utah, going out by the Smoky Hill route & returning by Laramie. Now if Babcock goes across by St Paul, Forts Berthold, Union, Benton, and Montana: and Sackett by Laramie & Utah, we ought this year to be so well informed of all facts and data, that next year, by the time the new army is fairly organised and filled we can post our troops to the best advantage. I dont like these 'little Posts' but dont see now how we can avoid them, but it may be we can arrange to keep our troops in cheap places in Winter, and send them out in Early Spring, and call them back as the Winter approaches. But for this year, I will stick to Popes distribution. I would like to have your general assent to this programme of mine this month, as I should then start early in May.—Babcock can hardly make the extreme northern tour by St Paul & the Upper Missouri, earlier than the 1st of June, though he would be safe in leaving here, by the Missouri River now or by the 1st of May. . . . Dispatch of this date about Babcock and Sackett just received." ALS, DNA, RG 108, Letters Received. See letter to Maj. Gen. Henry W. Halleck, April 19, 1866. On April 30, Monday, Sherman wrote to USG. "I received in due course of mail your letter approving of my programme for the summer, and telling me I might rely on getting a Revenue Cutter to meet me at Fond-du-Lac of Superior. I have nothing as yet more definite from you on this last point, but will start on Wednesday, relying upon you to have a Cutter waiting for me at the West End of Lake Superior say about the 5th of June. I would like its commander to be instructed to report to General Ord at Detroit in passing, and I will keep him informed at intervening dates of my progress, that the vessel may not be unnecessily detained. I understand there is a safe and good harbor in the River St Louis, at the mouth of which is the projected City of Fond du Lac, or Superior City. Since writing you, I have modified a little the route of travel. I will go direct to Fort Riley, thence by Land to Fort Kearney, where I will take the Overland Stage into Omaha, thence by Boat up to Sioux City thence across by Spirit Lake to Fort Ridgley and Saint Paul,—thence by boat up to Fort Ripley and by land across to the foot of Lake Superior. This Route will carry me across all the Emigrant Roads, and I can see for myself the relative proportion on each road and then form a judgmt as to how much military protection we should extend. I can travel pretty fast as far as Sioux City and am already ~~pretty~~ familiar with the Country and interests that far, but from Sioux City to St Paul & Lake Superior I may be delayed by various causes, and may not reach the foot of Lake Superior as early as I have named, but it will not be far from June 5 that I will turn up there. I want to spend ten days on the Lake Frontier, from the foot of Superior to Detroit, and my presence along that Frontier will show that we have an Eye to it. I take with me Col Bingham of the Quarter Masters Dept. and Maj McCoy my aid-de-camp—and should I find my route leads me through an Indian country will pick up a few soldiers as escort from Post to Post. Any orders or instructions sent to me will be forwarded or attended to by the Adjt Genl here." ALS, DNA, RG 108, Letters Received.

On May 7, Sherman, Fort Riley, Kan., wrote to USG. "Babcock came up with me to Lawrence where he stopped to see his brother, & will then strike across to Leavenworth & Atchinson whence the Regular Stage starts for Salt Lake. I saw his orders & instructions and advised him to stay in Salt Lake at least a month to learn and understand all the secrets of that Pandemonium. I have no doubt that little newspaper the 'Vedette' will involve the Country in trouble, for it rubs up the Mormons with just enough truth to irritate in the Extreme, and sooner or later it will make a collision between Jew and Gentile inevitable. Unless we have a right to regulate the 'Press' of a Country we cannot be responsible for its Peace, but the Freedom of the Press is our Corner stone, so that we cannot prevent the irritation of a polemical controversy, and had better take the ground that if the Gentiles will stir up strife they must take the consequences, but if they hold their tongues and mind their own business we will keep the present peace, and leave the Great questions of Polygamy and the sanctity of Religion to the Law making Power, Congress. I found the two companies at Lawrence, but am still of opinion that there is no danger whatever of the Bushwhackers of Missouri. Everybody seems busy in plowing & planting, but there is not as much increase of population hereabouts as I expected to find. All the land seems to be entered, but the owners are somewhere else. Davidson is here with two good companies of the 3rd Inf. and I hear that all the other changes are in rapid progress. I start in an hour with a small escort up the Republican for Kearney and expect to reach it in 5 days, and will write next from Omaha—There seems to be little or no emigration to Colorado or New-Mexico over this Road, but emigrants are taking up homesteads in the valley for thirty and forty miles above Riley. I came over the Railroad to a point 87 miles from Kansas City and found construction parties laying rail at the rate of ½ mile per day. The Superintendent says he will have 100 miles completed by June 1, but it will take into the fall to get the Rails laid to Riley 136 miles from the Missouri River. The grass is backward for the season, but good enough for ox trains. Mule Wagons must carry corn." ALS (misdated April 7), *ibid.*; copy (dated May 7), *ibid.*, RG 393, Military Div. of the Miss., Letters Sent. On May 14, Sherman, Omaha, wrote to USG. "I wrote you from Fort Riley, since which time I have travelled to Fort Kearney & to this place. We t[o]ok ambulances at Riley and travelled up the valley of the Republican one hundred miles, thence across the intervening high prairie Ridge to the Little Blue 40 miles, and then by the Main Road 52 miles to Kearney. The season is backward as to grass but we made the trip in 6 days. I found Col Carington with the 1st Battalion of the 18th

Regulars all ready to march by way of Laramie to the new Posts on the Road from that Place to Virginia City (Montana). Fort Kearney is made up of a set of old dilapidated frame buildings standing in the middle of a vast Plain without a tree, except on the Islands of the Platte, about a mile distant. It is a lonely desolate place, but convenient, as near it unite all the Roads west, from Leavenworth, Atchison, Nebraska City and Omaha. Farms or Ranches extend quite up to the Fort, and all the country east of it is considered safe against hostile Indians. After the 18th receives a detachmt of recruits now near Fort Kearney it will move out, and two companies of the 5th U. S. Vols. (Rebel Prisoners) will compose its garrison. There is no stone, timber or coal at or near Kearney. The ground looks fertile & produces good grass, but the drought of summer & severity of winter will prevent its being an inviting country to the Emigrant. After spending a day at Kearney—we crossed the Platte to its North Bank, by means of a boat, and a high wagon made on purpose, and took the stage which brought us in 24 hours, 125 miles, when we met the Railroad finished out from Omaha 75 miles, and got in today by 2. P M. (Since that time I have been around to the Machine & Work shops of the Union Pacific Railroad, which are certainly on a large scale exhibiting both the ability and purpose to push their work. The company has on hand here enough iron & ties to build 50 miles of Road, and Mr Durant assured me that he has contracted for enough for 150 miles of Road. Already 80 miles of Road are done, and he expects to complete the first hundred miles by the middle of June, and the second hundred miles in all 1866. This will make a continuous Railway to a point 5 miles beyond Fort Kearney. With Railroads completed to Forts Kearney and Riley our military question of supplies is much simplified, and I hope the President and Secretary of War will continue as hitherto to befriend these Roads as far as the Law allows. My own conviction is they will not come together at the 100th Parallel, but that the Kansas Road will go up the Smoky hill Route straight for Denver, and this one will keep on the north side of the Platte to a point above Fort McPherson, and its ultimate location will then depend on the interests of the Territories beyond. Expecting this summer & fall to go much further west I will not commit myself further at this time. I observed but little travel west by the Fort Riley Road, but a great deal by Fort Kearney. On the north side of the Platte I found no trains of heavily loaded wagons but a good many Emigrants. The great bulk of travel this season evidently leaves the Missouri River at Atchison, and Nebraska City and follows the Old Military Road by the south side of the Platte.) There being no boat here destined up the Missouri, I shall take the stage tomorrow for Sioux City & thence travel by land all the way to Lake Superior, crossing every Emigrant Road. Will write again from St Paul." ALS, *ibid.*, RG 108, Letters Received. On May 16, Sherman, Sioux City, Iowa, telegraphed to USG. "Gen'l Curtis objects to our establishing a post near the black hills, up the big Cheyenne, on the ground that the Indians with whom he is to treat will be alarmed at this occupation of their camping grounds. Please consult with the Secretaries of War and Interior and instruct Gen'l Cooke at Omaha, or Col. Reeve at Fort Sully, as troops are now moving up the Missouri for that destination.—Also impress it upon them that we are not prepared to feed any Indians at all, this year.—Our estimates and supplies are for the military alone and we can only ship at this season of the year." Telegram received (at 5:00 P.M.), *ibid.*, RG 107, Telegrams Collected (Bound); (on May 19) *ibid.*, RG 108, Telegrams Received; copy, DLC-USG, V, 54. On June 2, Secretary of the Interior James Harlan wrote to USG. "The receipt by your reference, of a telegram from General Sherman of the 16th ult in regard to the establishment of a military post near the Black Hills up the Big Cheyenne, is acknowledged and in reply I herewith transmit copy of a communication from the Commissioner of Indian Affairs of the 31st ult; to whom the subject was referred." LS, DNA, RG 108, Letters Received. The enclosed letter of May 31 from Commissioner of Indian Affairs Dennis N. Cooley to Harlan supporting the establishment of the post is *ibid.* On June 22, Sherman endorsed these papers. "Respectfully forwarded to Genl P St Geo Cooke for his information." AES, *ibid.*

On May 26, Sherman, St. Paul, Minn., wrote to USG. "I wrote you last from Omaha, after which I crossed to Council Bluffs on the east side of the Missouri river, and took stage for Sioux City. The going 110 miles consumed two days, and the road lay mostly in the valley of the Missouri river. The bottom lands are very fine indeed and most extensive, pretty well supplied with wood, and the farms look well. At Sioux City I found a Quartermaster and Commissary with the remains of General Sully's Head Quarters. Sioux City has been a kind of Depot for the country above, but is no longer of any use, and I gave orders to break it up absolutely, sending all available stores of all kinds up to Fort Randall where there are abundant storehouses, and all unserviceable animals and property to be sold or sent down to Leavenworth or St. Louis. I also found Col. Reeve of the 13th Infantry had stopped there by reason of that Depot, but I ordered him to proceed to the post hitherto assigned him further up the Missouri, viz. Fort Sully. Nearly all the 13th Infantry had passed Sioux City for their posts along the Missouri and all should reach their destination in late June. Gen. S. R. Curtis, and a Mr. Reed left a letter with Col. Reeve for my inspection, to the effect that they were Commissioners duly appointed to effect treaties with the Indians on the upper Missouri, and that they expected to meet large numbers of Indians at Forts Sully and Rice, and expected the army to feed them pending the negotiations, saying that they had assurance that such should be done, when they were in Washington. In sending our troops up the Missouri we took the precaution to send along with each detachment one years supply of stores for each post, and of course had no means of estimating or foreseeing such a demand. Thus at Forts Berthrand and Union, high up, where we have but one company, the Indians in council estimated by General Curtis at ten thousand would in one day eat out our little garrison. At Forts Rice and Sully we will have say four companies each, and their years supply would hardly supply one of these Indian talks and councils. I dont see why the Interior Department cannot foresee these wants and provide for them in time, and not at the eleventh hour appeal to our generosity on the score that evil consequences may arise unless the Indians are fed when invited to council. I gave Gen. Cooke instructions on no account whatever to diminish our army supplies on the upper river as there is no certainty of replacing them this season, but I suggested to him that on a formal demand of the Commissioners he might instruct the Post Commanders at Forts Sully and Rice to loan them one half their provisions, and to make immediate requisitions on the depot at St. Louis to replace this one half. I have no means of knowing if any understanding or agreement exists between the Secretaries of War and Interior on this point. All I know is that Commanding Officers of frontier posts are in the habit of relieving the pressing necessities of the Indians, but where an Indian Council is held by previous agreement and appointment it is quite as easy for the civilian agents charged with these matters to procure and send forward the necessary food in time as for us. It is extremely unpleasant for a Commanding Officer of a military post to have an agent of the General Government come to him at the last moment with a representation that he must have certain supplies for Indians invited to Council, or else the peace and security of the frontier will be be endangered. At Sioux City I also met a letter from Col. Sackett representing great danger of difficulty with the Indians on the upper Missouri about Fort Benton, we did not suppose we could spare troops for the purpose this year, but I sent Col. Sackett's letter down to Gen. Cooke at Omaha, with the expression of my opinion that sooner or later we would be forced to maintain a strong military post at or near Fort Benton, and if he could possibly spare four companies of Infantry it would be well to commence this year, trusting to get some Cavalry later. Of course it is utterly impossible to satisfy one tenth of the wishes of the Frontier People, or those who will emigrate across long lines of Indian country but we must keep every soldier we have in that vast and exposed country. General Cooke should have a Cavalry Regiment as soon as one can be possibly be spared or raised under the Army Bill when passed. I have seen your letter to the Sec. of War—on this subject and am very glad you made it. I don't see why Congress should hesitate one day in passing that Bill. At Sioux City I got three spring wagons carrying my party and a small escort, and started for Fort Ridgly on the Minnesota River 218 miles distant. The journey consumed six days travelling over a prairie country with settlements only on water courses about 40 miles apart. We travelled 15 miles up the valley of Floyd Cr. thence 40 miles without timber to the Little Sioux, thence up the little Sioux to Spirit Lake, thence 15 miles across to DesMoines River, thence 40 miles of flat uninteresting prairie to madelia on the Wantuwan, thence to New Ulm and Fort Ridgely. The moment we struck the territories of the Minnesota the land became good, and numerous settlements. It was in this region that the Indians in 1862 committed so much havoc and all events date from the massacre of 1862. We saw no Indians and heard of none, and though in conversations the people manifested fear lest the hostile Sioux might come down on them again, yet in their conduct I saw no signs of such fear. Wherever there is wood and water we found some sort of a settlement and men women and children were travelling about unarmed and alone without any serious apprehensions. On arrival at Ridgely I found it garrisoned by 1 Company of the 10th Infantry and heard that emigrants were passing daily up the valley of the Minnesota and taking up homesteads for sixty miles above the Fort. Fort Ridgley is of no use save as a point where the inhabitants would naturally rally in case of danger—but I could hear of no hostile Sioux nearer than James River, more than a hundred miles west. I think in a year or so we can give up Fort Ridgley, and station all the troops for the defences of Minnesota about Stone Lake, Fort Wadsworth, and Fort Abercrombie. It may be well to keep some scouts or patrols in the summer & fall months patrolling across to the Missouri River to give notice of the approach of any thieving or hostile bands. From what I observe and hear Forts Abercrombie and Wadsworth are well placed, but Forts Ridgely and Ripley will soon become unecessary, save as warehouses and depots of supply in transitu.) From Ridgely I came down to St. Paul in two days on a well travelled road and through a well settle country, meeting a Railroad twenty miles up the valley of the Minnesota. I learn that a Mr. Randall sutler claims the property of Fort Ridgely by a title of entry or purchase of the General Land Office and that by some omissions or neglect the Reservations for the Fort was never filed. It is well that we should know at once if the military authoritys have the lawful right to eject by force any persons who may attempt to enter or possess land within the limits of the reservation—I found at Fort Ridgely a good map of the reservation made by Capt. J. C. Kelton, some ten or fifteen years ago. I attach little importance to Fort Ridgely in a military sense, but its buildings are costly and they will serve all military uses on that Frontier for two or three years when there will be no use of a Fort there at all. Of course I instructed the Commanding Officer to pay no attention to adverse titles but to keep of all intruders, there being plenty of land open for settlement all round. But if Mr. Randall has a legal title the sooner we know it the better. The buildings are partly made of stone, and can never be removed, or used elsewhere. I also learn that Fort Snelling with its 6000 acres of Reserve was sold by Mr. Secretary Floyd to a Mr. Steele, that he has paid some thirty thousand dollars of the purchase money, but has failed to pay the balance. I understand that Mr. Steele is not anxious to fulfill the terms of his purchase, because the occasion is passed It is now too late for him to build a town there, which was the object of his purchase, for St. Paul below the Fort and Minneapolis above are established too well to be disturbed by a rival. The buildings at Fort Snelling are of no use except as a Fort, and the land is not worth for agricultural purposes anything like the price Steele contracted to pay for it. But Fort Snelling is valuable to us. The Government promptly took it back when the war revealed its use as a depot for the collection of volunteer troops and on all future occasions when troops are needed anywheres north or west of this Fort Snelling will be found the natural point. I therefore recommend its retention and that a compromise be effected with Mr. Steele. Fort Snelling will be a good point for the organization of a new regiment when the time comes. But it is of no use whatever for military defense because there is no Indian or hostile people within two hundred miles. Its only use is as a rendezvous for troops like Jefferson Barracks and Fort Leavenworth. I propose to remain in this quarter till the 1st of June, when I will cross over by land to Lake Superior, where on the 4th I expect to meet the Revenue Steamer John A. Dix that Gen'l Ord advises will meet me at that time. There is a marked degree of activity and seeming prosperity in all this quarter of our country and I have been agreeably surprised to find so busy a people and such a great variety of natural advantages for future wealth and developement" Copies, *ibid.*; *ibid.*, RG 393, Military Div. of the Miss., Letters Sent. On May 27, Sherman, St. Paul, telegraphed to USG. "Arrived today from Sioux City via Fort Ridgely. All well. Will start for Lake Superior June 1st If you wish me to do anything specific on the Lake Frontier advise me here within three days." Telegram received (on May 28, 9:40 A.M.), *ibid.*, RG 108, Telegrams Received; copy, DLC-USG, V, 54. On June 22, Sherman, St. Louis, wrote to USG. "Since my return, I find so many papers requiring my immediate attention, that I have not made anything a report of the latter part of my late tour of Inspection, and I doubt if one is necessary. In order that you may not have to read too much I give you the substance and conclusion in the form of a letter written yesterday to General Ord; Commanding that Department. I also send you, in a convenient shape, copies of General Pope's letters and notes to me, written as you will observe, as he progresses on his inland tour. You will perceive that he feels embarrassed and naturally too, by reason of the fact that the QuartermasterGeneral construes himself the judge of what improvements shall be made, and is in direct correspondence with Post Commanders and local Quartermasters. This is all wrong. We who cammand the troops must station them, and we must be the judge of the kind of structures needed. If General Meigs will simply tell me the maximum amount of money he can spare to enable me to quarter my troops, I can best judge what proportion of that money should go to each Department—then, in turn, each Department Commander could distribute his part according to the known necessities of the service. This is the only manner possible in which we can economize. Some of the Posts out on the Plains are really enough to make men desert, built years ago, of upright cottonwood poles, daubed with mud, and covered with mounds of earth, as full of fleas and bed-bugs as a full sponge is of water. Were it not for the intensely bitter winds of winter which force men to go in such holes, or perish, no human being, white man, Indian, or negro would go inside. Still, if there is no help for it, our officers and men will endure them, but we can help it, and must. Rather than deny our fellow soldiers the common deal boards that can be hauled out, (at terrible cost, I admit) if it becomes necessary to save the money the War Department should stop all other expenses, and give our troops on that bleak and dreary frontier, at least clean houses however coarse. When stone can be had the troops must build of that; but there are stretches of hundreds of miles without stone, or any building materials whatever, and there is no alternative but to buy boards and haul them out. I also send you Colonel Sacket's Inspection reports, and one from Colonel Otis, who is inspecting the cavalry. Many of the defects and irregularities, reported will cease as soon as the Regular garrisons arrive; but the great fact remains that the want of wood or materials will force us to neglect our troops or incur heavy expense. I would ask at once for a couple millions of dollars for Posts on the plains, and cCongress surely will give that. We cannot expect troops to be worth anything, if we winter them in holes, and force them to fight with rats, bed-bugs and fleas for existence. All these Posts were doubtless well selected at the time; but soon, what little wood there is, disappears, and the utter barrenness of the locality becomes repulsive so that every new Commander, or InspectorGeneral suggests a change, and, the change made, the new place becomes as bad as the old. The only safe calculation is to make good Infantry Posts along the routes of travel, and during the summer months, keep the cavalry in motion with orders to come into Fort Riley, Fort Leavenworth, or some other good place for the winter. Pope and Cooke have their troops now in hand, but should be informed, as soon as possible, just how much money they may expend to house and shelter their troops." Copy, DNA, RG 393, Military Div. of the Miss., Letters Sent. On the same day, Sherman endorsed an inspection report of May 14 from Col. Delos B. Sacket. "I want Genl Grant to read this as to the use of cottonwood for quarters, and then return to me. I will have Genl. Cooke to look into this matter of alkaline soil, and if Fort Randall is out of place, the quicker we know it the better" Copy, *ibid.*, Endorsements Sent.

On June 28, Sherman wrote a letter received at USG's hd. qrs. enclosing inspection reports of Bvt. Col. Orville E. Babcock and Maj. Gen. John Pope. *Ibid.*, RG 108, Register of Letters Received. On July 3, USG endorsed these papers. "Respy. forwarded to the Secretary of War, special attention being invited to the within reports, and I recommend that the sum of one million dollars be placed in the hands of Gen Shermans chief Q. M. to be expended in such manner in sheltering troops upon the Plains and within Genl S. Mil. Div. as may be directed by him." Copy, *ibid.* On July 18, Sherman, Hanover, N. H., wrote to Brig. Gen. John A. Rawlins. "I have today written the General a short note on the supposition that he is still there, but the enclosed papers should be ~~writt~~ read by him at his first leisure, because he will have to keep wide awake to keep up with the events in the Great West. Popes Reports are always well written and easily read, and I want the General to read these as Pope gives good reasons for adhering to his former Conclusion that Big Laramie is a better place for the 'New Post' than the Crossing of the North Platte, recommended by Babcock Of course I must sustain Pope for the Present, but even if a mistake occurs it is not all lost, for we must settle the Mountain District, the Middle Region of our Continent and even if the New Post becomes the nucleus of a hundred Ranches Uncle Sam is more than Compensated. Still I know that economy is now the order of the day and I will see to it myself in all September. I am glad that the QM Genl has given me a million for Easton is surely honest & competent and will disburse it with more exact proportion to the wants of the Army than can possibly be done from Washington. I came up here to attend the graduating exercises of Henry Sherman, and the Boston People have put me through. I am used up, and as soon as through will turn with a perfect sense of relief for the Desert Plains, where there is no handshaking or crowds of Curious people. When the Genl gets back lay these papers before him. He can file them away as they are copies. Sawyer has the originals and gives copies to Easton and all officers interested. The thing I apprehended is happening. The Pacific RR is going to keep north of the Platte,—all our posts & emigrant travel is south,—then I am asked to camp the troops on the North Side to protect the R. R. This I cannot do *now* because the Posts cannot be abandoned, and the emigrants have a promise of protection. This fact might be submitted to Congress as an additional reason for the speedy passage of the Army Bill. Hoping that you are enjoying reasonable health in that hot place, . . ." ALS, *ibid.*, Letters Received. The enclosures are *ibid.* See letters to Maj. Gen. William T. Sherman, July 12, 21, 1866.

On July 3, Sherman, St. Louis, wrote to Maj. George K. Leet. "I have the honor to acknowledge the receipt of the letter frm the Sec of the Interior, with copy of Gen Curtis communication to him of May 20, from the Yancton Agency, and repeat what I have heretofore reported, that on the former statemt of the two Commissioners General Curtis & Mr Reed, I had directed Gen Cooke Comdg Dept of the Platte, to send the troops destined for the Black Hills up to Fort Benton and that for the present we defer any military movemts up the Big Sheyenne. I also in my recent tour made diligent inquiry and could hear of no emigrants who wished to travel that way to Montana, so that the question remains now an open one, and I will gladly abide the action of the proper departmt. It is eminently proper that we should be kept advised in advance of the intentions of the Interior Departmt as to Indian Treaties, which when ratified are binding on us as the supreme Law, and unless advised at the earliest practicable time, we might compromise ourselves by promises to the Frontier's people, which we could not fulfil. All official information goes to the effect that the Country about the Black hills is only fit for Indians, and if the Commissioners will keep the Indians there, we should avoid it. We now have no troops North of the Platte, and West of the Missouri River, except along the course of the latter River, until about the parallel of Laramie, whence a road is being opened to Denver City along the Eastern slopes of the Rocky Mountains." ALS, DNA, RG 108, Letters Received.

To Maj. Gen. William T. Sherman

Washington, D. C. Apl. 18th *1866*

MAJ. GEN. W. T. SHERMAN,
COMD.G MIL. DIV. OF THE MO.
GENERAL:

In view of the Indian policy inaugurated by Gn. Carleton in New Mexico, and which seems to have been sucsessful so far as reports have reached these Hd Qrs. I think it will be well to retain him in command of that District, on his brevet rank, for the present at least. If you agree with me in this matter you may so retain him.

Col. Howe[1] should not, under any circumstances, be allowed to command a District. I believe his regiment goes to New Mexico where he will necessarily be the Senior line officer.

Very respectfully
your obt. svt.
U. S. GRANT
Lt. Gn.

ALS, DNA, RG 393, Military Div. of the Miss., Letters Received. On April 23, 1866, Maj. Gen. William T. Sherman, St. Louis, wrote to Maj. George K. Leet. "I have the honor to acknowledge receipt of Lieut General Grants letter of the 18th inst, and in pursuance therewith have made my special Orders retaining Genl Carleton on duty in NewMexico. Copy herewith. I will also furnish Gen Pope a copy of the letter itself, that he may be more fully possessed, with the views of the Lt Genl Commanding touching the subjects therein referred to." ALS, *ibid.*, RG 108, Letters Received. On Oct. 19, Sherman telegraphed to USG. "Genl Hancock is verry anxious to retain Genl Carleton until he settles the present *Ute* troubles We are so short of Officers that if Genl Carleton is not very much needed with his own Regiment I would ask to retain him until Genl A J Smith is ready" Telegram received (at 4:00 P.M.), *ibid.*, Telegrams Received; copies, *ibid.*, RG 94, ACP, 5058 1872; DLC-USG, V, 54. On Oct. 20, 1:00 P.M., USG telegraphed to Sherman. "You can retain Genl Carleton as requested" Telegram sent, DNA, RG 107, Telegrams Collected (Bound); copies, *ibid.*, RG 94, ACP, 5058 1872; *ibid.*, RG 108, Letters Sent; DLC-USG, V, 47, 60.

On Dec. 15, 1865, U.S. Delegate José Francisco Cháves of New Mexico Territory, Washington, D. C., wrote to USG. "I have the honor to request that Brig. Genl James H. Carleton U. S. V. be relieved from the Command of the District of NewMexico. This officer has been in command of that District since the month of September 1862 and has so conducted affairs as to destroy the confidence of the people in him and very materially impair his usefulness. Entirely cognizant as I am of the condition of affairs in NewMexico and fully advised of the wishes of a large majority of its bonafide citizens I assume the entire responsibility as the recently elected Delegate from that Territory of asking that General Carleton may be relieved by some officer in whose capacity integrity & fidelity to duty you may have entire confidence, and whose appointment will inspire confidence among the people. So far removed as NewMexico is from the Head Quarters of the Army, it appears to me to be the policy of the Government to place in command there an officer of the highest standing in the Army. Sincerely trusting that my request may meet the favorable consideration of the Lieut. General Comdg., . . ." ALS, DNA, RG 108, Letters Received. See telegram to Lt. Gen. William T. Sherman, Feb. 25, 1867.

1. On Aug. 23, 1866, Bvt. Maj. Gen. Edward D. Townsend wrote to USG. "On the Cadet Merit Rolls for 1825–6–7, *Marshall S. Howe*, now Colonel 3d U. S. Cavalry, is reported as nineteen years of age July 1, 1823. He should consequently be over sixty two years, and can be retired by the President's Order, under Section 12, of the Act approved July 17, 1862." ALS, DNA, RG 94, ACP, H767 CB 1866. On the same day, USG endorsed this letter. "Respectfully refered to the Sec. of War with recommendation that Col. How be retired from service under act of Congress authorizing the retirement of officers over Sixty-two years of age without examination." AES, *ibid.*

To Edwin M. Stanton

Hdqrs. Armies of the U. S.
April 19 1866.

Respectfully forwarded to the Hon. Secretary of War.

I cordially endorse the recommendation of General Sheridan for the transfer of Headquarters Department Louisiana to Baton Rouge. No sufficient implication is made against Gen. Canby to warrant the ordering of a court of inquiry. The fact is simply as stated by Gen. Sheridan. Gen. Canby has been in a diffrent school during the war, and has satisfied himself with looking at papers instead of men. He has been mistaken whilst Gen. Sheridan is probably right. It would be better therefore in my opinion to follow the views of the higher officer.

In making this recommendation I donot forget the high character of Gen. Canby, or the high estimation I have always placed upon his services

U. S. GRANT
Lieut. General.

ES, DNA, RG 94, Letters Received, 742G 1866. Written on a letter of April 5, 1866, from Maj. Gen. Philip H. Sheridan, New Orleans, to Brig. Gen. John A. Rawlins. "The enclosed application of General *E R S Canby*, for a court of Inquiry, was held by me for some days in the expectation that General *Canby* on reflection, would withdraw it. This was not done & I respectfully forward the communication with my endorsement. The whole thing is ridiculous on part of General *Canby*. Almost every place I have put my finger on in the Department of Louisiana, I have found fraud and abuses, much of which arises from want of personal attention from General *Canby*, who sits in his Office, looking up musty records, which are of no public value instead of exercising a little living force over his subordinates, throughout his Department. My relations with General *Canby* were very pleasent until I had the time to devote to correcting these abuses, and the result is an apparent desire on his part to embarras himself, and me also, by getting up a quarrel. I respectfully recommend that the Headquarters of the Department be removed to Baton Rouge, it will be to the interests of the public service, and put *Canby* in a place where he will not have an opportunity to meddle in Civil affairs, and give him more time to attend to his legitimate Military Duties." LS, *ibid.* Additional papers are *ibid.*

To Maj. Gen. Henry W. Halleck

Washington Apl. 19th 1866.

MAJ GENL H. W. HALLECK
COMD'G MIL, DIV, OF THE PACIFIC
GENERAL:

I am now about sending Inspectors from the Mo, to the Pacific, over all the travelled routes, with the view of determining permanent points to be occupied in future to secure travel and settlers on these routes. These officers necessarily pass through your's and Sherman's Commands. I have directed them to make a full report to me on their return and duplicate reports to you and Sherman of the portions that refer to you command.

Col Sackett;[1] and Col Babcock of my staff, are two of the Inspectors who go on this duty, but I do not know the route to be taken by any except Babcock. Nor do I know who the other Inspectors are. I left it for Sherman to name them and to give routes. Babcock, however, will leave the Mo River at Leavenworth and proceed to Salt Lake,[2] thence to Walla-Walla via Holliday's overland Mail route. From Walla Walla he will be guided by instructions from you. I wish you would send to him, as soon as you can after the receipt of this, addressed to Salt Lake City, a copy ~~a copy~~ of Maps from that point to the Pacific. Also send to him any instructions you may wish to give in regard to his inspections through your command. As soon as I get a list from Sherman of the names of his inspectors, and the routes they are to take, I will inform you.

Very Respectfully
Your Obt Servt
U. S. Grant
Lt Genl,

Copies, DLC-USG, V, 47, 109; DNA, RG 108, Letters Sent. See letters to Maj. Gen. William T. Sherman, March 3, April 18, 1866. On April 19, 1866, Maj. George K. Leet wrote to Bvt. Col. Orville E. Babcock. "You will proceed at once on a tour of inspection through the Military Division of the Mississippi and the Military Division of the Pacific, under the instructions verbally communicated to you by the Lieutenant General Commanding and such other instructions as may be given to you from time to time by letters or otherwise from these Headquarters. On reaching Saint Louis, Missouri, you will report in person to Maj Genl W. T. Sherman, and recieve from him such instructions, information, and orders as will enable you the more readily to comply with the foregoing orders, You will report from time to time to these Hd, Qrs, by letter~~s~~ and, when in your judgement it is necessary, by telegraph, sending copies of all such reports to Major General Sherman, if they in any manner relate to his command, When within the limits of the Military Division of the Pacific you will in like manner forward copies of your reports to Major General Halleck, All commanding Officers, Asst Quartermasters, commissaries of subsistance, or other officers of the army, are hereby directed to furnish, on your application, or requisition, such escorts, transportation, subsistance or other Stores, as you may deem necessary to the proper execution of these your orders, & instructed Upon the complition of the inspections herein directed, you will return to these Head-Quarters, via San Francisco and the Isthmus of Panama," Copies, DLC-USG, V, 47, 109; DNA, RG 108, Letters Sent. On May 21, Maj. Gen. Henry W. Halleck, San Francisco, wrote a letter received at USG's hd. qrs. "Relative to Col. O. E. Babcock's inspection tour and the establishment and breaking up of frontier posts. Recommends more troops. Starts on a tour of inspection in Middle of June, accompanied by Genls McDowell and Steele in their respective commands. He to be absent from Hdqrs 2 months." *Ibid.*, Register of Letters Received. On June 26, USG endorsed this letter. "Respy. forwarded to the Sec of War for his information." Copy, *ibid.*

On March 30, Babcock wrote to Maj. Gen. William T. Sherman. "The Lieutenant General directs me to communicate with you and ask whether it will be possible for you to furnish an escort for me to go out from Minnesota and go across to the vicinity of the mouth of the Yellow Stone. The General has been called upon by many gentlemen, especially by the entire delegation from Minnesota, asking this, and he desires me to start from there, provided it will not put you to too much trouble. The representations made are that many emigrants would go that route—say from St Cloud to the Missouri river—in preference to any other because they can take their cattle, wagons &c and march across, at but small expense, while to go from Minnesota to St. Louis and up the Missouri, will be so expensive that they cannot afford it. I wish this information so that I may make definite plans for my own action. If an escort can be furnished from Minnesota the General wishes all necessary orders issued to enable me to start as early as practicable. I shall of course go to St Louis on my way over either route. May I ask an early reply." LS, *ibid.*, RG 393, Military Div. of the Miss., Letters Received. On March 26, U.S. Representative Ignatius Donnelly of Minn. and six others had written to USG. "The undersigned Members & Senators from Minnesota and Wisconsin would respectfuly ask that the expedition which you are about to send out for the survey of an emigrant route, [under the command of Col. Babcock,] from the northern tier of States via Montana and Idaho to the Pacific Ocean *should start from some point in Minnesota or Wisconsin.* We understand it is proposed to ascend the Missouri River to the same latitude as St Paul Minn: and then move westwardly. This would leave the country between Minnesota and the Missouri unexplored by the expedition; and would be unjust to the Northwest by continuing to make it tributary to St. Louis—the very object sought to be avoided by the establishment of a northern line." LS (brackets in original), *ibid.*, RG 108, Letters Received. On March 31, Sherman, St. Louis, endorsed this letter. "All troops sent to the upper Missouri go by water, because of the manifest Economy. I have no Cavalry to escort a party by St Paul across to the Missouri, but Col Babcock could go from St Paul to Abercrombie, and thence to Fort Rice or Berthold along with some Emigrant party. I can only spare the 10th Inf for the Posts in Minnesota. Col Babcock will have about 500 miles more of land travel by this route than by the Missouri River, which is now navigable up to the mouth of the Yellowstone. Look at the maps." AES, *ibid.* On April 4, Babcock wrote to Donnelly. "Your communication requesting an escort of troops be sent across the country from St Paul was duly received and forwarded to Major Gen'l Sherman Comdg. the Mil. Div. of the Miss., to know if he could make such disposition of troops as you request. I send you this morning his endorsement on the same. The small number of regular troops to distribute over so extended a country renders it impossible for Gen'l Sherman to furnish the escort." Copies, DLC-USG, V, 47, 109; DNA, RG 108, Letters Sent.

On April 12, Sherman telegraphed to USG. "Col Sackett is here. Do you want him to inspect Via Laramie to Salt Lake & the Pacific or what route do you prefer he should take No instructions from you except those of March 3d in which you speak of Babcock & Comstock I infer Sackett is to take Comstocks place" Telegram received (at 3:20 P.M.), *ibid.*, RG 107, Telegrams Collected (Bound); *ibid.*, RG 108, Telegrams Received; copies, *ibid.*, RG 393, Military Div. of the Miss., Letters Sent; DLC-USG, V, 54. On April 13, 10:35 A.M., USG telegraphed to Sherman. "Col Sackett was sent in place of Gen Comstock. You may send Col Babcock Via Laramie and Salt Lake and Sackett any route you prefer" Telegram sent, DNA, RG 107, Telegrams Collected (Bound); copies, *ibid.*, RG 108, Letters Sent; DLC-USG, V, 47, 109. On April 14, Sherman telegraphed to Babcock. "When will you be here? I infer from Gen. Grant's dispatch of yesterday that you are going across to Salt Lake. In that event please send Sackett by Montana. If there be any error in this please advise me by telegraph." Telegram received (at 1:30 P.M.), DNA, RG 107, Telegrams Collected (Bound).

At 7:35 P.M., Babcock telegraphed to Sherman. "You are right I am to go to Salt Lake The General wishes you to send Col Sackett as you suggest I wrote today." Telegram sent, *ibid.*; copies (misdated April 10), *ibid.*, RG 108, Letters Sent; DLC-USG, V, 47, 109.

On May 4, Babcock, Lawrence, Kan., wrote to Brig. Gen. John A. Rawlins. "I arrived here yesterday; when in Galena I saw many inquiring friends, all of whom wished to be remembered to you. In St L. Genl S. and all his staff did likewise—I come from St L. to this place with Genl S. Col McCoy, and Col Bingham. The Genl is on his way to Forts Riley, Kearny, &c around to St Paul. He told me I need not go to F Laramie for his information is sufficient. He wants me to look after some of the forts down in the Denver Country, and then investigate the Morman question. In fact that is what he wishes me to look after particularly. He wants me to stay in Salt Lake valley at least one month, and get at the bottom of the question. So I shall go direct to Denver City by the Stage line and then look about a while and then go on to Salt Lake, and make the best of my time for a month or so—. And then I shall go on towards the Pacific. I shall keep you posted.—I saw Genl Mitchel, now Gov of New Mexico. He arrived here today from Santa Fea—He regrets very much that Carleton is to be releived—He says that he has examined into Carletons conduct there and he approves it all. He hopes he may be assigned by brevet so as to maintain the command—Gov Mitchell says the people are much disgusted at the idea of Negro troops being sent down there, He says he does not speak of this on his own account but the people do not feel any protection from the Indians if Negro troops are to have the place—He says the Indians Apachee's—(I spell Indian names so you can know what I mean not necessarily right) killed 15 men while he was there—He wants 5000 men, one year to force the Two Tribes now hostile into reservations and then they will agree to get along with 1000 men. He seems to talk as though he was in Earnest—and wished the good of New Mexico. He thinks the Negroes will be of very little service against those Indians—I told him I would write this to the Genl, so please tell him. He says the attacks on Carleton are wrong he is satisfied I cannot send word to Genl Sherman as he has gone on the inspection tour—Please give my kind regards to the Genl & family Mrs R— and children and the Staff—I shall be happy to hear from you, and hope you will be improving all summer so as to be well when I return" ALS, DNA, RG 108, Letters Received. On May 11, Babcock, Atchison, Kan., wrote to Rawlins. "You may begin to think I am delaying my journey. I have fallen a little behind my time, on severel accounts. The principal one is the advice of Genl Sherman not to be in too big a hurry, but wait until the weather was a little warmer, and beside the trops are all changing now. I am off though next Tuesday morning—and only six in the stage, Two ladies, I can endure it if they can—I was at the Fort yesterday. They are having a nice quarrel there about the sutlership. I tried to get at the truth of the matter. ~~and~~ I think they have not treated Dunn fairly. The council appointed a sutler and they wish to secure him the place—I think Dunn should have the right of his place, and at once. The building belongs to the old sutler, and if Dunn does not care to buy it (but he does) the old sutler can sell his building, but he should not be allowed to suttle—at all. He can sell his goods in Leavenworth. Dunn thinks Morgan has not been friendly to him, of course I could not tell. I had a long talk with Genl Dodge, and I am more than ever convinced that either the Q M. Dept should be put in command—or the Genl commanding, as it is the troops are simply attached to the

Q M Dept,—The best thing the Genl can do for econemy is to have some QuarterMasters put at the principal depots who have received some ideas during the war, and are not old ladies—Have this done and make all staff officers report through the Dept, Dist or Div Commanders, or furnish him (the Comdg officer), at the time copies of their report—and matters would soon assume a shape that would be comprehensible—As it is you cannot hold Pope, Dodge Sherman or anyone responsible when their Staff officers ~~when they~~ report direct and receive orders direct from the Chief, of their Bureaus in Washington—If any matter comes up—ten chances to one if it is not done on an order from the Chief Qr M or some other chief Send a live quarterMaster to Leavenworth at once—and things in my opinion will change a good deal for the better. The problem of transportation across the plains changes much as the rail road runs out. All freight should go next year from Ft Riley or beyond. Ft Leavenworth ceases to be of importance except from the fact that the government has storehouses there—This matter should be Considered this summer and temporary building or storehouses put up at Riley. Such a nature of storehouses as can be taken down and moved as the rail road extends west—Perhaps Genl Ingalls will be instructed to attend to it—I think our best quartermasters should be at St Louis and Leavenworth. Genl Hoffman is in command of the post of Leavenworth—He is not the man for the place. He is one of those ~~that~~ who never have men enough—to keep the post properly policed—We should have a live man there, one who knows what a soldier is. Sykes was much liked, Genl Dodge was much pleased with Sykes, but is not with Genl H.—I told Genl. Dodge that I thought the company of Infty now at Lawrence could as well be ordered away The company of Cavalry is sufficient, and that can be taken away in a few months, Though I think there are some bad characters down in Mo. but they will all be quiet in a little while. So much for business—Let me add a few lines of suggestion. Why dont you take a trip to Santa Fé New Mexico. Some one should go down there—You can be fixed off from Lawrence or Riley, so you will be as nicely as you wish—The climate, the air, the sights will all do you good. I know you think you cannot leave your family. I think you are wrong—If you can come back well, your family will be infinetely better off. You can take Mrs R. with you if you wish though it will be rather rough for her. I advise you by all means to go for pleasure and for benefit of your health. Please remember me kindly to Mrs Rawlins, and all of your family, also to all of the Staff. I hope to hear from you at Salt Lake." ALS, *ibid.*; copy (incomplete), *ibid.*, RG 94, Letters Received, 961A 1866. On June 7, Babcock, Denver, wrote to Rawlins. "There are a number of rumors of Indian troubles out here just now. I think they are sensational. I am going to start tomorrow for Collins, Big Laramie & Halleck, where they say the braves are and demand *rations* or *blood.* If they do not lift my hair I shall give you full information as I can get on the subject. On the south the Utes, 'they say' also are behaving badly. I think it is exagerated. I have been over into the Middle Park of the Rocky Mountains, and think I can give a plan to settle up this Ute question and better protect the route from here to Salt Lake. I had a pretty tough time in the Mountains, crossed over Vasquez Pass, and come back through Berthoud—Snow ten feet much of the way on the mountains. Things look better out here than they did last year—for food—Contracts just offered for beef bring in bids for beef at 7½ Cents where it was 19. cents last year, everything else in proportion. This post can be closed out as soon as the stores can be moved, the Commissary is ready to go. The Ordnance officer has about 150 tons of ordnance and stores here. ~~Much~~ Some of it good for nothing, and some good—His orders are to send it all back across the Plains to Ft Leavenworth—I telegraphed Pope today suggesting it be ~~sent~~ kept until he comes here, for I think he will sell the useless here and store the rest against any trouble—The servicable can be sent to Collins, for store—and save heavy rates here.—These are 530. Citizen Rifles, such as the freighters, pilgrims &c&c have brought out here, and are good for nothing but old iron—Not worth ¼th the freight to the Mo River. There are any number of rumors about Indians but I do not believe them reliable—Though I am more impressed with the error of this collecting the Indians in and making them presents. The presents are not made as expected and that is sufficient cause in the Indians opinion for a fight—. I shall try and give you a full account of Matters when I reach Salt Lake, where I shall remain some time." ALS, *ibid.*, RG 108, Letters Received. On June 12, Babcock, Stage Station, North Platte, Dakota Territory, wrote to Rawlins. "I have made a personal examination of the Reservation for a post at Big Laramie and am not at all pleased with it It will be easy to supply hay and water but will be bleak and very cold winters, no protection for stock at all, and no wood within ten or twelve miles and then on the mountain side of difficult access. The stage people now pay $12 a cord for wood for the post. When this is established as a post it will leave a distance of 335 miles between Fort Bridger and Big Laramie, the worst Indian Country, enterely unoccupied—and lying along the only traveled route to Salt Lake. I have examined the old Cherokee tribes Crossing of the North Platte 25 miles west of Ft Halleck. This you will see divides the distance more equally. The point has plenty of wood for fire for years, on the banks of the North Platte. Plenty of most excellent grazing about the point. I saw stock today that had wintered in here without a particle of feed except what they picked, and they (horses and mules) are in splendid condition. The stock of the post can find excellent protection under the bank of the river near the buildings of the post. Plenty of hay about the post, and fine meadows within eight and ten miles. Excellent building stone—sand stone (needing only to be split) within one mile of the proposed building place. Pine and cedar timber suitable for building within eight miles. In 62, troops passed the winter in the vicinity, in tents, and the officer commanding them informs me they were much more comfortable than those at Fort Halleck—The buildings at Fort Halleck can be moved here and be used for the coming winter if the troops do not have time to build their quarters. The passes of the Platte and its branches are the principal passes in the Rocky Mountains through which the Indians go either to fight each other or to steal from the whites—at Laramie (Big), the garrison would know nothing of the Indians where abouts until they had driven off all the stock along the road not mentioning the killing of the people. I am of the opinion you will agree with me in this, and have the garrison and store ordered to Big Laramie sent to North Platte. I think a party of 25 men, should be k~~a~~ept at Big Laramie in Camp this summer, and the line of this ro~~o~~ad should be patroled at least once a week, to intimidate the Indians if they come to make trouble—as soon as the cold weather sets in the Indians have to go to their villages and where they can feed their stock, as soon as this occurs, the detachment out patroling can all come in to winter quarters and remain until the grass grows in the Spring.—I have written or sent a telegram to Genl Grant on this subject. I am certain that if the post is established at Big Laramie another will have to be put in this country. I will write you more in a few days as soon as I get to Salt Lake. I have not sent any copy of this to Genl Sherman for I could not reach him. I have informed Genl Pope of the contents of my telegram and this letter. Will you telegraph me to Salt Lake whether this post is established on the North Platte . . . P. S. Remember and keep the letters" ALS, *ibid.* On June 13, Babcock telegraphed to USG. "I have examined Big Laramie and a position at crossing of old Cherokee trail on the north side of North Platte, Plenty of wood here on bank of Platte, fine building stone within one mile of point, and fine timber within eight miles, fine meadow about post, and within ten miles I saw stock that has wintered in valley and now fat, This point will divide distance between Denver and Fort Bridger, much better than Big Laramie, Big Laramie very cold and bleak winters & not a stick of wood within ten or twelve miles for fire or building. I think orders for Big Laramie should be immediately changed to North Platte. Wood now costs stage Company twelve dollars at Big Laramie, Letter by next mail." Telegram received (sent by mail to Denver—received on June 19, 3:00 P.M.), *ibid.*, RG 107, Telegrams Collected (Bound); *ibid.*, RG 108, Telegrams Received; *ibid.*, RG 393, Military Div. of the Miss., Letters Received; copy, DLC-USG, V, 54. On June 20, Leet referred this telegram to Sherman. AES, DNA, RG 393, Military Div. of the Miss., Letters Received. Sherman endorsed this telegram to Bvt. Col. John P. Sherburne, adjt. for Maj. Gen. John Pope, Fort Leavenworth. "The above despatch comes from Gen Grants Hd Qrs. Let the matter be well looked to, before any serious expenses are incurred in the New Post contemplated at Big Laramie." AES (undated), *ibid.*

On Aug. 16, Babcock, San Francisco, telegraphed to USG. "Gen Ingalls & myself arrived here last night & would recommend that Gen'l Steele be assigned to duty by Brevet rank and left in Dept of Columbia—Gen'l Halleck desires the same—Great scarcity of officers of the line here—I think officers belonging to regiments in the Division should be sent out here at once" Telegram received (on Aug. 18, 1:00 A.M.), *ibid.*, RG 108, Telegrams Received; copy, DLC-USG, V, 54. On Oct. 5, Babcock, Washington, D. C., wrote at length to Rawlins reporting on his inspection tour. LS, DNA, RG 94, Letters Received, 961A 1866. Printed as *HED*, 39-2-20. On Dec. 6, USG endorsed this letter. "Respectfully forwarded to the Secretary of War. Attention is invited to the following subjects: Mormons and their Territory—pages 19 to 25. Gen Connor's administration, for such actions as the Secretary of War may deem best. Transportation of Indian supplies and its abuse—page 52. Payment in Coin of Gov't Employes in California—page 57. Purchase of Stores at Ft Boise,—page 47. It is recommended that when this Post is broken up the buildings and reservation be given to the Territory, as requested by the Governor. Telegraphing—page 56. The recommendations for establishment of new Posts and Military Routes in the Military Division of the Mo. have been referred to the Lieut. Gen. Comdg. It is believed that the establishment of a Department with Hdqrs. at Salt Lake City, as recommended, is advisable, also that the reduction in size of the Military Reservation at Ft Bridger, U T. would be beneficial to the Government—page 18. I would recommend that authority be obtained from Congress to sell the land in lots of such size as will be most profitable to the Govt., where Military Posts are broken up, and until such authority be granted, that the officers authorized to sell public buildings be directed to lease the land so long as held as a Military Reservation, or for a period of years—see pages 48 & 49 It is recommended that Congress be asked for an appropriation to enable the Chief Engineer and the Coast Survey to make a proper survey of Puget Sound and the contiguous territory.—

page 51. In my opinion officers of the General Staff of the Army should not be independent of Division or Department Commanders. It leads to much trouble and expense and should be corrected.—page 53. The report of examination of the blankets sent to California—page 54, and the production of the woolen mills in Oregon and California, is called to the attention of the Secy. The best only of all articles should be transported to these very distant Posts. Where the manufactories in new States and Territories will supply articles as cheap and of as fine quality as Eastern manufactories it is believed expedient to purchase in those States or Territories. It is believed that one bonded officer—Commissary or Quartermaster—can do the business of Commissary, Quarter Mr and Ordnance Officer at any interior Post. This will leave the line officers to do duty with their cos.—p. 57. I would earnestly recommend that all troops serving in Indian Countries be as soon as possible armed with the latest improved repeating or breech-loading arms. Also that the transfer of supplies from one Staff Department to another be authorized as recommended—page 57 & 58. The Quarter Master General has already directed the rebranding of all public animals as recommended by Gen. Babcock." ES, DNA, RG 94, Letters Received, 961A 1866.

On Oct. 15, Babcock endorsed additional recommendations concerning the army in the West. "Respectfully submitted to the Genl in chief My observation across the continent was called often to the same difficulty in enforcing discipline where small garrisons are passed. I would recommend a Board be convened to report upon a system, and tabulated code of punishment, to cover all cases where Courts Martial cannot well be convened. I think this Board should be composed of officers who have been sering at these distant posts. I would suggest the following officers: Capt & Bv't Col Samuel Ross, 14th U. S. Inf'ty. Genl. Recruiting service; Capt & Bv't Col. John D. O'Connell, 14th Inf'ty Gen'l Recruiting service, and Col and Bv't Brig. Gen'l D. B. Sackett. Inspt. Genl U. S. A." ES, *ibid.*, RG 108, Letters Received; *ibid.*, RG 94, Letters Received, 723A 1866. The enclosure is *ibid.* On Dec. 7, USG endorsed these papers. "Respectfully forwarded with recommendation that a proper correction of the powers and formation of Courts Martial be introduced into the new regulations called for by Congress." ES, *ibid.*

1. See letter to Edwin M. Stanton, Dec. 11, 1866; *HED*, 39-2-23.

2. On April 7, Solomon P. McCurdy, associate justice, Utah Territorial Supreme Court, and three others, telegraphed to Secretary of War Edwin M. Stanton. "Learning the troops now in service in this Territory may soon be mustered out we wish to state in our judgement every interest public and private requires their services till their place is fully supplied and ask you will order accordingly, by telegraph if necessary. Gov Durkey is absent in the Southern part of the Territory." Telegram received (on April 8, 10:00 A.M.), DNA, RG 108, Telegrams Received; copy, DLC-USG, V, 54. On April 9, 10:00 A.M., USG telegraphed to Sherman. "Dont withdraw troops from Salt Lake until others are there to take their place. Alarm is felt lest a few days may intervene between the withdrawal of Volunteers and their replacement, in which case the Gentiles will all have to leave the country" Telegram sent, DNA, RG 107, Telegrams Collected (Bound); copies, *ibid.*, RG 108, Letters Sent; *ibid.*, RG 393, Dept. of Kan., Unentered Letters Received; DLC-USG, V, 47, 109. On the same day, Sherman telegraphed to USG. "Dispatch about Utah received will so instruct

Pope" Telegram received (at 3:35 P.M.), DNA, RG 107, Telegrams Collected (Bound); *ibid.*, RG 108, Telegrams Received; copies, *ibid.*, RG 393, Military Div. of the Miss., Letters Sent; DLC-USG, V, 54. See *Calendar*, May 4, 1865.

On March 16, 1866, Maj. Gen. Grenville M. Dodge, Fort Leavenworth, wrote to USG. "Br Gen P— E. Conner Comd. Dist of Utah is en route to Washington I have requested him to call on you as I know him to be well and fuly posted in all matters pertaining to that country—his views in relation to the policy to be pursued there I agree with and I believe is in accordn with the Govts—Gen Conner has served in Utah for three years he is thoroughly acquainted with the people—and I have no hesitatn in saying that he has commanded his Districts with great ability and prudence and to my entire satisfaction—I ernestly reccomdend that his services be recognized by Gvt—by suitable promotion" ALS, DNA, RG 108, Letters Received. On April 3, USG telegraphed to Pope. "Gen Connors leave is extended until further orders." Telegram sent (dated April 6, 10:45 A.M.), *ibid.*, RG 107, Telegrams Collected (Bound); copies (dated April 3), *ibid.*, RG 108, Letters Sent; DLC-USG, V, 47, 109. On April 6, USG wrote to Stanton. "I would respectfully recommend that Gen. P. E. Connor, be Brevetted a Major General of Volunteers." Copies, *ibid.* See *ibid.*, RG 94, Letters Received, 288A 1866. On May 8, Patrick E. Connor, former brig. gen., Washington, D. C., wrote to USG. "I have the honor to state, That the so called Gentile Citizens of utah, deem the present military force in that Territory inadquate, to their protection from Mormon assassination and persecution, desire to form themselves into independent volunteer military Companies, but for want of the necessary arms are unable to do so. Respectfully ask through me that they be furnished with arms, and accoutraments from the ordinance store at Camp Douglas utah I would state that there is a large surplus of arms and equipments at Camp Douglas, and if supplied with them, I am prepared to enter into bonds for their return when required, or their money value in Case of loss. my advi[ce]s from utah inform me that the late assassination of a Gentile in Salt Lake City, is Justified and extolled by the Mormon Leaders, and press, and a similar summary fate threathened to all who opposes or interferes, with their Cherished and unlawful institution, Polygamy, Most of the Gentiles in utah Imigrated to that Territory, during my military administration of that Dist. under assurances of protection from me, Hence my solicitude for their safety and welfare. I would respectfully suggest, That, the true way to avoid armed Conflict in utah, is to be prepared for it Trusting that my application may meet a favorable response . . ." ALS, *ibid.*, 307C 1866; copy (forwarded to Sherman), *ibid.*, RG 393, Military Div. of the Miss., Letters Received. On May 9, USG endorsed this letter. "Respectfully forwarded to the Secretary of War, with the recommendation that Gen. Sherman be authorized to issue arms to the companies in question, if he deems such a step necessary." ES, *ibid.*, RG 94, Letters Received, 307C 1866. On May 21, Lt. Col. W. Willard Smith, Great Salt Lake City, wrote to USG. "Private *unofficial* . . . I learn that interested parties are endeavoring to persuade you that it is necessary for the Govt. to send a brigade of troops to this Territory to preserve order. Knowing that your attention has been, for the past few years, called to more important matters & that the status of affairs here have been represented to you by those whom you would naturally believe. I deem it my duty as a loyal citizen & soldier to state, that, on my arrival here last summer, I was for a short time in command of the Distric of Utah & learned many unwarrantable & dishonest proceedings in this District & believe the sole & only object of certain persons now east is to procure said large force of troops that they may continue to defraud the Govt & enrich themselves The great cry 'that Mormons are arming to resist the Government' is simply absurd. I have had several conversations with Brigham Young, Heber. C. Kimball & their General of Militia, Daniel. H. Wells & am fully satisfied that it is a personal feude between the late Brig Genl Connor & the Mormons. In the Tabernacle, General Wells stated to the congregation that, 'there was not a Nation on the face of the earth, that could whip the United States.' The Indians, south, have been committing some depredations, Mr Head the Indian Agent called on the District Commander for troops, but did not get them, he then applied to the Mormons & obtained a small force for the protection of southern settlements. Brigham Young advises the people, in settlements thus threatened to throw up breast works for their protection against hostile Indians. I have traveled both north & south in the Territory & made every exertion possible to post myself with regard to the sentiments of loyalty of the Mormons & believe they will not fall much, if any, short in point of loyalty of those in the Northern States, With the exception of polygamy they are a law abiding & certainly the hardest working & quietest people I ever met & profess willingness to try the constitutionality of the act of Congress against polygamy. I am of opinion, unless the Indians become much worse, that the force, four companies, each at Camp Douglas & Ft Bridger, orderd here by General Pope is ample for the protection of all business in this Territory, but if the commanding officer is to give leaves of absence to a large number of soldiers to prospect & work mines on shares, as heretofore, a brigade will not be to many. . . . A secret detective sent here would discover many frauds & probably recover for the Government a considerable sum of money. I now hold a commission as LtCol 6th U. S. vols." ALS, *ibid.*, RG 108, Letters Received.

On June 23, Babcock, Salt Lake, telegraphed to USG. "One company 18th Infantry has arrived here—I think the Second California cavalry & first Nevada Cavalry should be mustered out at once and the third California Infantry soon as the other Co's of the 18th arrive—These men are of no use here—There is no need of them on account of Mormons & I think of no earthly use against Indians—They will demoralize our regular troops if left with them—They are all dissatisfied that they were not mustered out long ago" Telegram received (on June 28, 9:00 P.M.), *ibid.*, RG 107, Telegrams Collected (Bound); *ibid.*, RG 108, Telegrams Received; copies, *ibid.*, RG 94, Document File, B689 (VS) 1866; DLC-USG, V, 54. On the same day, Babcock wrote to Rawlins. "I promised you that on my arrival here I would give you a solution to the Ute Indian difficulty. I will now give you my idea on such information as I can gain from all sources. The Utes as a tribe are peacable, but some of the bands are marauders and kill if they cannot get the stock without. The only warlike band is under a Chief by the name of Black Hawk, who at first had but few men, but boldness and success in stealing has increased his force to, it is supposed, about three hundred braves. Their war is on the Mormons, and kill no gentiles unless they get in their way. The Indian Agent or Supt here has had runners out a long time trying to get Black Hawk to meet him but the Chief will not come in. He is afraid he says of treachery, for one of their Chiefs was killed by the Mormons. The Chief (Sand Pitch) had, the Indians say, been invited to come in and treat, and when he got in he was placed in jail, and when attempting to escape was killed. Black Hawk demands the men that killed him or blood and is taking blood. B Young told me they had killed about thirty of his people, mostly Danes. Brigham thinks or pretends to think that the Cupidity of the Danes has offended the Indians and they are taking their revenge. B. Young has sent some of the malitia (Church troops) He told me about 120 had gone from this place. He says they cannot reach the Indians as the disperse as soon as the troops appear. I think it a bad idea to have Mr Young's troops out but that is a thing for the Govenor to settle. I do not care much how many Mormons are killed but to protect the settlements generally and the new mining interest in the country, and the line of travel from Denver to their Valley which is about to be opened, I deem it very necessary that a Military Post be established in the Ute Country. The new line of road will pass over the Rocky Mountains probably at or through Berthoud Pass. Along through the Middle Park, through Goree Pass and along the valley of the White River crossing the Greene River about the intersection of the 110° degree of Lat, along the valley of the Uintah or Duchesne entering Salt Lake Valley opposite Utah Lake. This line has been put in passable order from Salt Lake Valley to the foot of the Rocky Mountains, It will shorten the distance from Denver here by 120, or not less than 80 miles. Plenty of fine grass, wood, and water. It has no alkali country at all. In my opinion the post should be in the vicinity of the Greene River near the mouth of the Uintah and White. There are I am informed by men who have been over the route (Bela M Hughes & Col John's, Col V. C) points where abundance of hay and grass can be obtained and good building material, It is from this valley that the Indians come to prowl and depredate on the white people. A post in their own country will put them into a position where they can be controled. The travel to the new silver mines, the Parkanayat Mines, is through the valley south of Salt Lake. The mines are some four hundred miles south and west, and according to all accounts bid fair to be among the finest in the world. The post I speak of will in my opinion serve to protect this line of travel. These mines if rich as reported—will attract a large number of miners, already it is said 700 people have gone to these mines. One gentleman, Capt Dahlgren (son of the Admiral), informs me that the miners have killed several Indians, such acts will lead to an Indian war, and the sooner posts are established the better. The line of travel from Denver to the New Mines will leave this place some fifty miles to the right—still the supplies for the mines will much of it go from here. The mines are said to be about 80 miles from the head of navigation on the Rio Colorado. Steamers are already on this river and advertise to furnish supplies from San Francisco via the Gulf of Calefornia. If this line of travel is opened supplies can be sent to this valley from San Francisco at much less expense than from the Mo River, even with a R R. much of the way, for it will have to be hauld but about 400 miles, and the route can be passed over most of the year, while freight can be hauled over the mountain road to this valley in but few months of the year. Troops can be supplied in this valley with all but clothing and a few quartermaster stores, cheeper than any point west of the Mo River and away from water navigation along the Pacific. So far, since I have been here, I have seen nothing to indicate any more trouble here, aside from the Indians, than in Mass. The Gentiles have no fear, and so far as the terror of the Mormons is conserned one company to represent the authority of the Govt is just as good as a regiment. This is the great half way place across the continent, I think the Army should have a substantial post here, bult of stone, and a large depot of supplies from the Country kept on hand, to supply troops passing, to winter troops on, and to supply the surrounding Country (Military Posts) in case of scarcity. The policy that has been practiced here under Genl Conner is in my opinion very bad, and if adopted by the government would in a few years make this valley a steril plain again. I think the religious views of a man should in no way exclude him from bidding for supplies to the government. These people will supply bread and meat and some other articles as cheep, to the U S Government as to their Church, but none but Gentiles, and certain one at that were allowed to furnish supplies under the command of Genl Conner. I am satisfied from what I have learned since I have arrived here that the Mormons are as innocent as yourself of the burning of the storehouses containing $2000,000.00 of stores. I think I shall be able to show evidence of many of these frauds. One company of the 18th Infty has arrived here. I have telegraphed the Genl recommending the immediate muster out (of the volunteers here). The men seem perfectly demoralized, and a mania for stealing seems to pervade the command. The sooner they are mustered out the better. If the Q M has to hire watchmen to take care of the property, I have met a number of the U. S. V. the galvanized rebels, and am satisfied they are of no use. Their officers seem of a poor class. I do not think them trusty, even after Indians. The sooner they are mustered out the better. I found Ft Bridger in a shameful condition. The garrison has at times burned up much of the flooring for bridges, storehouses and quarters. Under these officers here the garrison cannot and will not secure its own wood—I cannot see any use for more than two companies there, except because the Sutler there needs a guard for his stores, I have telegraphed to Col Maynadier at Ft Laramie for some information, but can get no reply. The sooner regular officers are responsible for these posts and military affairs the sooner the expenses will be reduced. I shall go on from here in about three weeks. My inspections will not be extensive after I leave here, for Genl Halleck thinks no permanent posts should be established except on the sea or large rivers. If you have any further instructions for me please send them to San Francisco. . . . P. S. I am looking up the subject of supplying this country by way of the Rio Colorado river of Col. The supplies will have to be hauled on waggons only about 485 miles, and 220 of that is through settled valleys. Teams can haul nine months of the twelve—The navigation of the river is the only question. I may go down there. I would but it will take me one month." ALS, DNA, RG 108, Letters Received. On June 25, Babcock telegraphed to USG. "The Company of eighteenth Inf'y now here can secure a number of recruits from discharged Vols if authority to recruit is given them immediately Only thirty seven men in the Co" Telegram received (on June 28, 9:20 P.M.), *ibid.*, RG 107, Telegrams Collected (Bound); *ibid.*, RG 108, Telegrams Received; copy, DLC-USG, V, 54. On June 30, USG endorsed this telegram. "Respy. referred to the Sec. of War requesting that the required authority be given to recruit from discharged volunteers" Copy, DNA, RG 108, Register of Letters Received. On July 7, Babcock wrote to Rawlins. "I have the honor to submit the accounts of the Union Vedette against the Govt. for printing and some evidence to show the manner in which US men and means have been employed for the benefit of this paper, said to be the private property of Gen. P. E. Conner. I donot think the accounts should be paid. I know soldiers are now at work in the Vedette Office. LtCol Johns comdg the post told me so yesterday. He says they have been on furlough since the Dist. was broken up, that he is waiting for Gen. Conner to return, when these men will be returned to their commands. To return them now would break up the issuing of the paper. You will please refer it to Gen. Grant for such action as he may wish. Please retain copies of all the papers as I have no copy books with me." Copy, *ibid.*, Letters Received. On Aug. 11, USG endorsed this letter. "Respy. forwarded to the Secretary of War, and the opinion of Bvt. Brig. Genl. O. E. Babcock that the enclosed account should not be paid—concurred in." Copy, *ibid.*, Register of Letters Received. On Feb. 18, April 5, 10, 1867, USG endorsed papers concerning the claim of Isaac M. Weston, former managing editor, *Union Vedette*. Copies, DLC-USG, V, 43. On June 29, 1868, USG wrote to Secretary of War John M. Schofield. "The payment of certain suspended vouchers payable to J. M. Weston for public printing done by the 'Union Vidette' at Salt Lake City, Utah Territory is respectfully recommended." Copies, *ibid.*, V, 47, 60; DNA, RG 108, Letters Sent.

Endorsement

[*April 26, 1866*]

Col Ihrie was relieved from duty on my staff for procuring a decision from the A G. of the Army, to the effect that a Department Commander was not entitled to a Commisary of Musters, a duty to which he had been assigned on my staff, without making his appeal to be relieved from such duties through Head quarters office. Col I[']s efficiency as an Army officer in any capacity in which he has ever been called to serve, I never have heard questioned. It is not my desire to take part against the confirmation of appointments made by the President, unless I am aware of facts, which in my opinion, were unknown to the President. In that case, I would concieve it my duty to go to the President and ask him to withdraw his appointmt before going to the senate. It was my feeling—that at this time all appointmts of Pay master in Reg. Army should be confined to those who have served as Paymaster creditably during rebellion. This is a matter of opinion.

U. S. GRANT
lieutenant General

Copy, DLC-USG, V, 58. Written on a letter of April 24, 1866, from George P. Ihrie to U.S. Senator James R. Doolittle of Wis. concerning a delay in the confirmation of his appointment as maj. and paymaster. *Ibid.*; DNA, RG 108, Register of Letters Received. Ihrie was appointed as of April 14.

To Edwin M. Stanton

Washington May 1st 1866.

HON. E. M. STANTON,
SEC. OF WAR,
SIR:

In the case of Cadet J. P. Walker, recently dismissed from the Military Academy by sentence of Court Martial I have taken the liberty of sending for the proceedings and have examined them. There is no doubt but guilt is proven of Cadet Walker having made the remark, "I can~~y~~ say nothing more now, but after graduation, I will," or words to that effect.

In view of the long arrest ~~of~~ Cadet Walker has undergone, and the promulgation of his sentence by the Court having been made public, I think he has been severely punished for all the offense charged.

I would therefore respectfully recommend that the sentence in the case of Cadet J. P. Walker be remitted and that he be restored to his place in his class.

I have the honor to be
Very respectfully
Your obt. servt
U. S. GRANT
Lt. Gen'l

Copies, DLC-USG, V, 47, 109; DNA, RG 108, Letters Sent. See *PUSG*, 10, 296–97, 382.

To Maj. Gen. Philip H. Sheridan

Washington, D. C. May 2d *1866*

DEAR GENERAL,

The bearer of this, Gen. Carvajal of the Liberal Army of Mexico goes to the Rio Grade frontier for the purpose of aiding his country in its struggle to uphold Republican institutions. I regret that we cannot give him direct aid. I know however you will cheerfully give him the benefit of advice and all the information you have concerning the situation South of the river.

My object in having Arms and Munitions sent to Brownsville was to have them handy in case anything should turn up in the future to justify interferance on our part. I do not believe that France, or any other foreign power, will be allowed to send more reinforcements to ~~m~~Mexico.

Yours Truly
U. S. GRANT
Lt Gn

TO MAJ. GN. P. H. SHERIDAN

ALS, DLC-Philip H. Sheridan. See Matías Romero, comp., *Correspondencia de la Legacion Mexicana en Washington durante la Intervencion Extranjera 1860–1868* (Mexico, 1870–92), VII, 466–67.

To Edwin M. Stanton

Washington, D. C. May ~~3~~4d *1866*

HON. E. M. STANTON,
SEC. OF WAR,
SIR:

Through you I would respectfully request of the Sec. of the Navy, or Treasury, that a Government steamer be sent to Superior City by about the 5th of June next to convey General Sherman on an Inspection tour along the southern shore of Lake Superior.

General Sherman has left St. Louis for a general Inspection of his command. He will go first to Fort Riley thence to Kearney, Omaha, Soux City, Spirit Lake, Fort Ridgeley, St. Paul, Fort Ripley and across to foot of Lake Superior, ariving at Superior City about the 5th of June or within a few days of that time.

General Sherman makes the request that the commander of the Steamer sent to convey him on Lake Superior be directed to report to Gen. Ord at Detroit as he will keep ~~g~~General Ord informed of his whereabouts and of the exact day when he will reach Superior City.

Very respectfully
your obt. svt.
U. S. GRANT
Lt. Gn.

ALS, DNA, RG 107, Letters Received from Bureaus. On May 8, 1866, Secretary of War Edwin M. Stanton wrote to USG. "In accordance with ~~your~~ the request of your letter of the 4th inst application was made to the Secretary of the Navy & Secretary of the Treasury to furnish to furnish a transport on Lake Superior for General Shermans proposed inspection. The Secretary of the Navy ~~inf~~ replied that he had no vessell ~~f~~ that could be used for that purpose. The Secretary of the Treasury has replied in a letter a copy herewith is enclosed and the arrangement he proposes will I trust accomplish the object of your letter. You will please advise me if any thing further be required" ALS, *ibid.* See letter to Maj. Gen. William T. Sherman, April 18, 1866.

To Andrew Johnson

Washington, D. C. May 8th *1866*

HIS EXCELLENCY, THE PRESIDENT OF THE UNITED STATES,
SIR:

W. H. Moore & Co. having been removed from the Sutlership at Fort Union, N. M. unexpectedly to them, and with a large stock of goods on hand and on the way out, thus subjecting them to heavy pecuniary loss, and this firm having always proven themselves friends of the Government at times when they had it in their power to be of material service, I would respectfully recommend that they be authorized to remain at Fort Union occupying their private buildings, on the public grounds, and to sell to all persons except the United States troops at the post.

All the regularly appointed Sutler can claim, under his appointment, is the exclusive right to sell to United States soldiers. This recommends competition in all other trade there may be at the post, and would give Moore & Co. the right to suttle for all Govt. employees, except the enlisted men.

I have the honor to be
Very respectfully,
your obt. svt.
U. S. GRANT
Lt. Gen.

ALS, DNA, RG 94, ACP, M274 CB 1870. On Feb. 27, 1866, U.S. Delegate José Francisco Cháves of New Mexico Territory had written a letter received at USG's hd. qrs. recommending the replacement of William H. Moore and Co. as post sutlers at Fort Union, New Mexico Territory, by Joseph R. West, former brig. gen. *Ibid.*, RG 108, Register of Letters Received. On April 20, USG endorsed these papers. "I would respectfy but earnestly recommend the retention of Moore and Mitchell as sutlers at Fort Union, N. M., at least until the expiration of the time for which they were nominated by the Council of Administration of the post. These parties are represented as having given great satisfaction In the early part of the rebellion they were of great service to the Governmen[t] in providing money and teams, without profit to themselves, at a time when this aid was of great service.—A furth[er] reason for asking that they should not be removed at this time grows out of the fact that they now must have their season['s] goods purchased and on their way to New Mexico This being true they would sustain a heavy pecuniary loss if removed." ES, *ibid.*, RG 94, ACP, M274 CB 1870. Charles W. Adams, former col., 12th Kan., had already received the appointment on the recommendation of U.S. Senator James H. Lane of Kan. *Ibid.* On May 14, USG wrote to Maj. Gen. John Pope. "You are authorized to give the same facilities and time to Moore & Co at Fort Union to dispose of and remove their goods and property that you were authorized to give in the case of the sutler at Fort Sumner N. M." ALS, *ibid.*, RG 109, Union Provost Marshals' File of Papers Relating to Individual Civilians. On March 30, 1867, Cháves wrote to USG. "I have the honor very respectfully to request that you will appoint under the Joint Resolution passed this day, Messers. W. H. Moore and W. C. Mitchell (under the style of W. H. Moore & Co.), as traders at Fort Union, N. M. My reasons for making this request are as follows.—These gentlemen have shown themselves among the most public spirited citizens in our Territory, they have erected large and extensive buildings involving great expense, on the Military Reserve at that Post; and, should it so happen that they fail to procure the appointment which I solicit at your hands, they will be compelled to leave that Post on the 1st of July proximo. with great and irreparable loss to themselves. Besides, I venture to think that they are entitled to the favorable consideration of the Government, for valuable services rendered in the past. In 1861—2— and 3—when the black cloud of rebellion hung over our beloved country, they were among the first and most prominent of the merchants of our Territory to sustain the credit of the Government, by boldly and patriotically coming forward, and accepting its indebtedness or vouchers at par. In a country situated as New Mexico, with but few facilities of communication, entirely surrounded by hostile elements, and with constant rumors of dis-aster to our arms, uncontradicted for considerable lengths of time, I respectfully submit was no mean service. In view of all these facts, I again renew my request for their appointment; confident, that should you be pleased to grant them that request, the result will conduce to the best interests of the public service, and to the satisfaction of that portion of my constituents who live in the vicinity of Fort Union.—" ALS, *ibid.*, RG 94, ACP, M274 CB 1870. On the same day, Moore and William C. Mitchell of St. Louis, Washington, D. C., wrote to USG. "We respectfully ask to be permitted, under the authority of the Joint resolution recently passed amending the act of July 28th 1866, to Continue our Trading Establishment at Fort Union N. M. Last year after we had been duly elected sutlers at Fort Union—C. W. Adams was appointed at the request of his father in Law the Late Genl. James H. Lane—he is still *nominally* sutler there, though he has no actual interest in the stores, having sold us all his privelege—present and prospective in the Business, which has been and still is mantained by us and with our means alone, we have on hand at Fort Union one hundred thousand dollars worth of goods, and our buildings which have cost us over twenty five thousand dollars, we have in addition seventy Five thousand dollars in goods, on the road to Ft Union, our trade with freighters and others not in the employ of of the government amounts to over seventy Five thousand dollars per year.—if we should be compelled to remove on the 1st July it would cause us a very heavy sacrafice and would seriously incommode the plainsmen on that great thoroughfare—our service to the government during the War has been made known to you by Genls Canby, Donaldson, Brice, McFerran & Nichols. Letters from them in regard to us are on file in the war department with the application made last year for the revocation of Mr Adams appointment, which application you did us the honor to reccomend to the President and the Secretary of War. Asking your early and favorable attention to our request . . ." LS, *ibid.* On May 1, Moore, Mitchell and Co., Fort Union, wrote to USG. "We have the honor to apply for the appointment of Traders at the Military Post and Depot of Fort Union, New Mexico, as provided for by Joint Resolution of the 40th Congress, authorizing the appointment of Traders at Military Posts West of the 100° longitude—" LS, *ibid.* On June 7, Maj. George K. Leet endorsed these letters and other papers. "Respectfully referred to the Adjutant General who will issue an order granting W. H. Moore and W. C. Mitchell, (W. H. Moore & Co.) permission to continue a trading establishment at Fort Union, N. M., under the Resolution of Congress entitled 'A Resolution to authorize the Commanding General of the Army to permit traders to remain at certain Military Posts.' " AES, *ibid.* See *HED*, 41-3-79; *HMD*, 43-1-63.

On May 7, 1866, USG had written to Pope. "Give Mr. J. A. LaRue, former Sutler at Fort Sumner, N. M., permission to remain at the Fort for a limited time to enable him to withdraw without too great a sacrifice of his goods on hand and private property. I think he should be allowed to remain for a stated period unless sooner bought out either by the new sutler or the ordinary trade of the post. He should however be restricted from selling to soldiers or Government Employes on credit." Copies, DNA, RG 75, Bureau of Indian Affairs, Central Office, Letters Received, New Mexico; *ibid.*, RG 108, Letters Sent; (2—one certified by Bvt. Col. Ely S. Parker) *ibid.*, RG 109, Union Provost Marshals' File of Papers Relating to Individual Civilians; DLC-USG, V, 47, 109. On Aug. 21, Oscar M. Brown, former col., 1st Calif., Metropolitan Hotel, Washington, D. C., wrote to USG. "I would respectfully state that I received from the *Secretary* of *War* a Warrant constituting me Sutler for the post of Fort Sumner New Mexico from the 19th day of may ult, That I proceeded to that post with a stock of goods and was ready to commence business on that day, That to favor the old Sutler J. A La Rue, as much as possible I offered to buy his stock of goods on hand his buildings and all else pertaining thereto at *cost*. After allowing him a week to consider he declined the offer, and I was forced to obtain a store room from the 'Post Commander,' in which to store and sell my goods, That the said La Rue continued to sell and dispose of his goods to soldiers employees and others at that post for *cash*, until the undersigned brought the matter to the attention of the Post Commander in the shape of a protest and demand for protection, That pending final action thereon the said La Rue, exhibited to the Post Commander a *certificate* from the *Indian agent* for the *Navajoe* tribe of Indians authorizing him to trade with the Indians at *that Post* and was allowed to continue and trade with said Indians within the limits of said Post until about the 27th day of June ult when the following order and endorsements were presented to and acted on by the said Post Commander.—Head Quarters Armies of the U. S. Washington D. C. May 7 1866 GENERAL Give Mr *J. A. La Rue* former Sutler at Fort Sumner N. M. permission to remain at the Fort for a limited time to enable him to withdraw without too great a sacrifice of his goods on hand and private property. I think he should be allowed to remain for a stated period unless bought out either by the new Sutler or the ordinary trade of the Post. He should however be restricted from selling to soldiers or government employees on credit. Very Respectfully Your Obt Servt Signed U. S. GRANT Lieut General MAJOR GENL. JOHN POPE Comdg Dept. of the Mo. Official Copy signed E. S. PARKER Brevet Col Mil Secretary.—That on the 3rd day of June nearly one month after the aforesaid direction of the Lieut General commanding the Armies of the United States, the said *La Rue* presented the same to *Maj Genl John Pope*, who made thereon the following endorsement 'Head Quarters Dept of the Mo Fort Leavenworth June 4 1866 respectfully referred to the Comdg Officer District of New Mexico, Santa Fé N. M, the within named sutler will be allowed a reasonable time to dispose of his property and close up his business, The Comdg. Officer of the Post will judge of the time necessary not to *exceed fifty* days By Command of Major Genl Pope (signed, JOHN T SHERBURNE Asst Adjt General Official CYRUS H. DE FORREST Brevet Major U S. Vols Aide de Camp That the foregoing copy of orders were by Brig Genl. *James H. Carleton* Comdg. District of New Mexico, sent to the Fort Commander of *Fort Sumner* New Mexico about the 27th day of June *Ult.*—who thereupon ordered that the said *La Rue* might have fifty days from that date to close up his business, and sell to *all persons whatsoever* during that time for cash—Thus giving to *La Rue* 90 days altogether in which he *might continue* to *trade* and *injure* the *business* of the Post sutler which he has done to the amount of $10.000—. The General will perceive that the spirit of his order has been violated by an *extension* of the time *beyond* the limit fixed That the *object* which was to prevent too serious a loss, by a *sudden* and *Summary* closing of his business was by La Rue made to cover a *speculative* and *trading* venture and also to break down if possible the *credit* of the undersigned. That he had no *intention* to close up his business as stated to the Lieut General Comdg is evidenced by the following Copy of a notice appearing in the Santa Fe Gazette on the 1st day of June Ult., which shows that he had not only no intention of leaving but that he is taking to Fort Sumner a large additional stock of goods. The *General* will thus perceive that statement made by '*La Rue*' on which the General order of the 7th of May, was based was erroneous if not *absolutely* and *willfully* false. In addition to this notice the undersigned has personal Knowledge of the fact of his (La Rue) purchasing and shipping a large stock of goods to *Fort Sumner*, since the date of the said order. The undersigned would respectfully state that the additional time expired on or about the 15th inst, that for the heavy loss sustained during that time he Knows of no remedy. But would most earnestly submit that until the *Indians* on the Fort *Sumner* reservation be turned over to the Interior Department no *Indian Trader* should *be allowed* to do business on *said Reservation* but that the trade should and of right ought to be done by the Post Sutler That unless the General Commdg the Armies of the United States should direct this to be done, the undersigned, whose term by recent Acts of Congress, expires in July 1867 will be a heavy loser— that the undersigned is not in a *pecuniary condition* to *sustain* a serious loss without *financial ruin* wheras *La Rue*, the former sutler might with ease have *lost all* his personal property at Fort Sumner, on the 19th day of May Ult. and yet be considered a rich man." ALS, DNA, RG 109, Union Provost Marshals' File of Papers Relating to Individual Civilians. On the same day, Leet endorsed this letter. "Respectfully reffered to Major General W S. Hancock U S A. Comdg Department of the Mo with directions to forbid J A La Rue & co former sutlers at Fort Sumner N M, remaining longer at that post as traders under my authority here tofore granted from these Headquarters." Copies, *ibid.*; *ibid.*, RG 108, Register of Letters Received. On March 30, 1867, Chāves wrote to USG. "A resolution of both houses granting you authority to appoint traders and to grant them permits on Military reservations passed the House this morning and has received the approval of the President of the U. S. I now respectfully request that under the provisions of that Resolution, you will grant such a permit to Col. O. M. Brown at present Sutler at Fort Sumner, ~~in~~ New Mexico.—The Col. has been Sutler less than one year, and has been quite unfortunate in his business, and should he be compelled to leave the Reservation under the 25th Section of the Army Bill it will be irretrievably ruined.—The Colonel was a prosperous business man in California, but he left *that* at the call of duty, he served his term with honor, and I think that should a favor such as I ask for him be granted the Government will be the gainer." ALS, *ibid.*, Letters Received. On April 1, Richard McAllister, attorney for Brown, Washington, D. C., wrote to USG. "I am advised that the Congress of the U. S. at its recent Session passed a joint resolution authorizing you to appoint traders or Sutlers between certain parallels of latitude for the benefit of citizens residing at points remote from the great centres of trade. As instructed I therefore desire to make application in behalf of Col: Oscar M. Brown the present sutler at Fort Sumner New-Mexico for an extension of his trade or Sutler's license from the 1st of July 1867 to such future period as under the discretion vested in you by the Said joint resolution you may deem advisable to designate. In behalf of Col: Brown (who is now at Fort Sumner N. M) I desire to state that he was appointed Sutler at Fort Sumner N. M. by the Secretary of War on the 19th of May 1866 for the usual period of three years; that on the   day of   1866 Congress repealed the law authorizing the appointment of Sutlers to take effect July 1st 1867 and that the present joint resolution was intended for the relief of certain Sutlers and citizens residing in remote regions of country; that Col: Brown at a very heavy expense has established himself at Fort Sumner and will sustain a ruinous loss unless he is permitted to continue a reasonable time to prosecute his present business; that Col: Brown was a gallant soldier in the Federal Army, is a thoroughly loyal and honorable citizen and entitled to the favorable consideration of his government. With this application I enclose you a letter from Col: J. Francisco Chaves Delegate from New-Mexico asking that a trade permit may be granted to Col: Brown. Hoping for a favorable answer . . ." ALS, *ibid.* On April 19, Brown, Fort Sumner, wrote to USG. "I would respectfully state that on the 19th of May last I re'c'd a Warrant from the Secretary of War as Sutler for the Post of Fort Sumner That I at once entered upon the discharge of my duties. To do so properly I was compelled to erect a Building for Store and Residence, at a cost of about ten thousand dollars. That for nearly three months after that date the former sutler was allowed to continue trading with the officers soldiers & employees of the Garrison for cash, and monopolized the cash trade by selling at greatly reduced rates That from various causes the undersigned has lost in his business up to this time about *twenty thousand* dollars That if allowed to continue his business until the expiration of his sutlers term (by Warrant May 19, 1869) he believes he will be able to pay off his liabilities which he cannot possibly do if his petition is not granted That he has a large Family depending on him for support, who must necessarily suffer in consequence of the heavy loss sustained as above stated, if the petition of the undersigned is not granted—That the building above mentioned is within the military Reserve, but outside the Garrison, and if required to remove there from he will sustain an additional loss of at least thirty thousand dollars ($30,000) That the undersigned is likewise a Licensed Indian trader and carries on his Indian trade in the same building—this latter trade however is not of much value" ALS, *ibid.* On May 7, McAllister wrote to USG. "I have the honor to submit for your consideration the Petition of Oscar M. Brown, the Sutler at Fort Sumner New-Mexico, for permission to continue his business at Fort Sumner after the 1st of July next in accordance with the Joint Resolution passed by Congress in March last authorizing you to permit trade within certain parallels of latitude. You will please notice the sworn statement of some eight citizens as to the necessity of a trading establishment at Fort Sumner for the accommodation of Travellers, Freighters and others—" ALS, *ibid.* On May 20, Lt. Col. and Bvt. Maj. Gen. George Sykes, commanding officer, Fort Sumner, wrote to Leet. "In conformity with the 'Circular' from Head Qrs Military Division of the Missouri C. S. April 30th. 67, I have the honor to nominate Mr J. A. LaRue of this Territory for the position of Trader at this Post under the Joint 'Resolution of Congress' Approved March 30th 1867. Mr LaRue is a gentleman long associated with the Officers serving here and in New Mexico, perfectly responsible as a Merchant, as well as experienced, was Sutler until the spring of 66, is now a Trader for Navajo Indians, and is both my own selection and that of the Officers of this Garrison for the position to which he is herein nominated, In this connexion it is proper to say, that before the 'Circular' refered to above was seen by me, or its provisions known, I had endorsed—favorably an Application both for Mr. LaRue, and Mr O. M. Brown Sutler, for the position of 'Trader.' Had I known the Appointment was to be Confined to one person I should have limited my recommendation to Mr LaRue." LS, *ibid.* On July 16, McAllister wrote to USG. "I have the honor to forward you the petition of Oscar M. Brown, late Col. 1st California Cavalry and now Sutler of Fort Sumner New-Mexico desiring the appointment of trader at that Post under the recent Act of Congress authorizing you to appoint traders between certain parallels of latitude. You will find this petition endorsed and approved by Bvt Maj. Genl. Geo. Sykes Comdg. at Ft: Sumner and by Bvt Maj. Genl. Geo W. Getty Com'dg. Dist of New-Mexico. Col. Brown brought this paper to Maj. Genl. Hancock but finding there that your Genl. Order No. 50 had obviated the necessity of this application he forwarded it to me to be placed on file with his other papers in your Department." ALS, *ibid.* Later, Col. and Bvt. Maj. Gen. Andrew J. Smith forwarded to USG's hd. qrs. Special Orders No. 60, Dept. of the Mo., appointing Joseph A. LaRue trader at Fort Sumner. *Ibid.* (undated), Register of Letters Received; DLC-USG, V, 52.

To Edwin M. Stanton

Washington, D. C. May 8th *1866.*

HON. E. M. STANTON,
SEC. OF WAR,
SIR:

In awarding brevet rank in the Regular Army the name of Brig. Gn. J. A. Rawlins, Chief of Staff, has been overlooked. He would probably have been recommended by the Board which met in St. Louis if a letter which I wrote some time since recommending him had been before them. Gen. Rawlins was appointed a Brevet Major General before that recommendation, without my knowledge, and when my letter went into the office to be copyed Gen. R. being present, and having just received his appointment, destroyed it. With the names sent for confirmation consequently his name did not appear.

Gen. Rawlins has served with me through the entire war from the Battle of Belmont to the surrender of Lee. No Staff officer ever before had it in his power to render as much service and no one ever performed his duties more faithfully or efficiently. He is eminently entitled to the Brevet rank of Major General and I earnestly but respectfully recommend that his name be yet sent in for confirmation.

Very respectfully
your obt. svt.
U. S. GRANT
Lt. Gn.

ALS, DNA, RG 94, ACP, R29 CB 1869. On May 9, 1866, Col. John C. Kelton, AGO, wrote to USG. "The Sec of War has ordered that General Rawlins be nominated for the brevet of Major General U S. Army and desires that you will assign the date the brevet should bear. Shall he be nominated with the date of the letter of appointment he holds viz March 13/65 or with some subsequent date corresponding with the recommendations of the St Louis Board?" ALS, *ibid.* On May 10, USG endorsed this letter. "The brevet should be given for the 'surrender of Lee', to rank from April 9th 1865." ES, *ibid.*

To Edwin M. Stanton

Washington, D. C. May 10th *1866*

HON. E. M. STANTON,
SEC. OF WAR,
SIR:

I would respectfully recommend the revocation of Par. 8, Spl. Orders No 91 of Feb.y 28th 1866 dismissing Bvt. Capt. D. E. Porter, 1st Lt. 1st U. S. Artilley.[1]

Capt. Porter is very young, and has been indiscreet, but he is brave and capable of becoming a valuable officer. He has served through the rebellion starting in whilst very yougng probably not over Seventeen years of age.

On account of the services of the father of Capt. Porter, Adm.l D. D. Porter, I would particularly ask this favor.

Very respectfully
your obt. svt.
U. S. GRANT
Lt. Gn.

ALS, DNA, RG 94, ACP, 552 1883. See letter to Brig. Gen. Lorenzo Thomas, May 1, 1865. 1st Lt. David E. Porter, 1st Art., was restored to duty as of May 23, 1866. Bvt. Brig. Gen. Cyrus B. Comstock wrote an undated note to Bvt. Maj. Gen. Edward D. Townsend. "Gen. Grant wishes me to say that Lt. Porters orders should be sent to care of Admiral D D Porter Annapolis Md." ANS, DNA, RG 94, ACP, 552 1883.

On July 30, 12:45 P.M., USG telegraphed to Vice Admiral David D. Porter.

"I have ordered Genl Hooker to send Essex home We will take into consideration what to do in his case afterwards" Telegram sent, *ibid.*, RG 107, Telegrams Collected (Bound); copies, *ibid.*, RG 108, Letters Sent; DLC-USG, V, 47, 60. At 12:50 P.M., Maj. George K. Leet telegraphed to Maj. Gen. Joseph Hooker. "Give Brevet Capt D. E Porter 1st Artillery permission to visit his father at Annapolis Md and send copy of charges against him to these HeadQrs" ALS (telegram sent), DNA, RG 107, Telegrams Collected (Bound); copies, *ibid.*, RG 108, Letters Sent; *ibid.*, RG 393, Dept. of the East, Telegrams Received; DLC-USG, V, 47, 60. On the same day, Hooker forwarded to USG's hd. qrs. charges preferred against Porter for "Absence without leave" on July 27 by Capt. and Bvt. Col. Guy V. Henry, 1st Art. ES and copy, DNA, RG 108, Letters Received. On Aug. 19, Henry, Fort Schuyler, N. Y., wrote to the AGO. "I would respectfully request that the resignation of Bvt Capt and 1st Lt D. E. Porter Co "G" 1st Arty be accepted, or he be sent back (being absent with leave (in arrest)), in order that I may prefer charges against him. He is so well known, for general worthlessness, and want of character, that it not necessary, to state it, in order, to impress the Department, with the urgent necessity for getting rid of him, not only for the good of the Army, but for example sake. I have only a 2nd Lt for duty with my company and would like to have Lt Porters place filled as soon as possible." ALS, *ibid.* On Oct. 2, USG wrote to Secretary of War Edwin M. Stanton. "I have the honor to recommend the transfer of 1st Lt. Jas. L. Sherman, 19th U. S. Infantry, to the Artillery branch of service. He is a graduate of the Class of 1865 and was recommended for the Artillery either by the Academic Board or by the Chief Engineer, or both. I would recommend his transfer to that regiment of Artillery which will give him nearest the rank he would now hold had he been placed in the Artillery on his first assignment." ALS, *ibid.*, RG 94, ACP, 3864 1873. On Oct. 3, USG endorsed this letter. "I respectfully recommend the transfer of 1st Lt. Jas. L. Sherman, 19th U. S. Inf.y and 1st Lt. & Bvt. Capt. D Essex Porter ~~3d~~ 1st Artillery." AES, *ibid.*

On April 14, 1869, Carlile P. Patterson, U.S. Coast Survey, wrote to Secretary of State Hamilton Fish seeking a consular appointment for young Porter. ALS, *ibid.*, RG 59, Letters of Application and Recommendation. On Dec. 10, Admiral Porter wrote to Fish. "I beg leave to acknowledge the receipt of a commission, sent through me, for Mr. David Essex Porter. I regret very much that circumstances prevent his acceptance of the position at this time, and beg leave to say that in my judgment Mr. Porter is too young a man to be entrusted with so important a place. It is one that requires more than usual ability and should be held by a person of mature judgment. If at any time a position of less importance for which Mr. Porter is qualified should become vacant, I should be much pleased if he could obtain it." LS, *ibid.*

1. On Dec. 29, 1865, Capt. Loomis L. Langdon, 1st U.S. Art., Brazos Santiago, Tex., reported Porter's desertion; on Feb. 7, 1866, USG endorsed papers concerning the case: "Dismissal approved" Copy, DLC-USG, V, 42.

To Edwin M. Stanton

Washington, D. C. May 10th *1866*

Hon. E. M. Stanton,
Sec. of War,
Sir:

I most respectfully recommend T. M. McDougall for the appointment of 2d Lieut. of Infantry, regular army. T. M. McDougall is now a Captain in the 5th Kansas Volunteers. He has served for a longer period than two years.

The father of Capt. McDougall is one of our oldes, most faithful and efficient Surgeons, Regular Army, and, in my judgement is entitled to receive favorable concideration in his effort to fix his son for life.

Very respectfully
your obt. svt.
U. S. Grant
Lt Gn.

ALS, DNA, RG 94, ACP, 2901 1872. On Dec. 2, 1865, Maj. Gen. John Pope, St. Louis, twice wrote to USG. "I send enclosed an official recommendation for an appointment in the regular Army of Capt T. M. McDougall now on service in Colorado—Aside from his own personal claims to such an appointment he is the son of Surgeon C McDougall of the Army an old & dearly loved friend of mine whom I would go a great way and sacrifice very much to serve—I am sure I need only present his case to you to secure as favorable action as your influence can obtain You will confer a very great favor upon me if you will use your influence in this matter" "I have the honor to present to your attention the record of the military services of Captain Thomas M. McDougall, 5th U. S. Vols. and to request that his claims to an appointment in the regular army be favorably considered. Captain McDougall was appointed Lieut. in a Louisiana Colored Regiment in 1863, served in Mississippi, served with distinction under General Steele in the investment and capture of Mobile, was appointed Captain in the 5th U. S. Vols. in 1865, served since with distinction on the Plains and is now Provost Marshal at Denver City. He is twenty years of age, well educated, of fine physique and in all respects high toned and honorable. He is eminently qualified for the duties of an officer of the regular Army and I know no young man who would do more credit to such an appointment as he asks, Viz: a 1st Lieutenancy in the regular Army—In addition to his own claims to such favorable action on the part of the Govt he is the son of Surgeon Charles McDougall an old and highly esteemed officer of the Army whose own services great and useful as they have been to his country, have left him an old man unrewarded by his

Government. On all grounds I earnestly ask, General, that you will interest yourself in Securing his appointment in the regular Army and I assure you that in doing so you will not only be doing an act of justice to a meritorious officer but will do that also which will secure to the Army an accomplished and efficient officer" ALS and LS, *ibid.* On Dec. 10, USG wrote to Secretary of War Edwin M. Stanton. "I have the honor to submit the name of T. McDougall (late Capt) for appointment in the regular army. He has served more than two years in the volunteer service & was appointed a Capt. in the 5th U. S. Vols. Kansas." LS, *ibid.* On Feb. 7, 1866, John G. Smith, St. Albans, Vt., wrote to USG. "Permit me to solicit for my much esteemed friend Dr C. McDougall the appointment of Captaincy in the new regiments now being organized, for his son Thomas Mower McDougall. I have not the pleasure of a personal acquaintan[ce] with the young man but I understand that he brings strong recommendations of his fitness for the position—The services rendered by Dr McDougall while connected with the Medical Dept of the East, in caring for our sick & wounded soldiers have endeared him to every friend of the soldiers, and having had from my official position while Governor of this state many opportunities to witness to his devotion and self sacrifice in their behalf, I feel it a great pleasure now to contribute in this form to the advancement of his wishes and interest—I hope therefore you may find it consistent to consider his application for his son with favor" ALS, *ibid.* On Feb. 15, John A. Dix, Union Pacific Rail Road Co., wrote to USG. "Capt. Thos McDougall of the 5th Regt. Kansas Vols. now on duty with Maj. Genl. Pope at St. Louis is desirous of being appointed in the Regular army, and I desire to unite with his friends in presenting his name to you. I do not know him personally but from information I have no hesitation in saying that on the score of his services during the war, his character as an officer and a gentleman, and his qualifications he is entirely worthy of the position he desires. His father, whom you no doubt know, is one of the most experienced, efficient and distinguished officers of the Medical Department, and it would be very Gratifying to him and his numerous friends to secure for his Son the appointment he desires." ALS, *ibid.* Thomas M. McDougall was appointed 2nd lt., 14th Inf., as of May 10.

To Maj. Gens. Philip H. Sheridan and John G. Foster

Washington, D. C., May 10th *18646* [*9:15* A.M.]

MAJ GEN P H SHERIDAN, NEW ORLEANS LA
" " J G. FOSTER TALLAHASSEE FLA

Reports received here indicate that the Steamer Virginia formerly a fleet blockade runner will leave the neighborhood of Pensacola to morrow with a cargo of negroes. Have this matter looked into, and if there is reasonable grounds for suspecting such attempt apply the proper remedy to prevent it. If there should be no design beyond voluntary expatriation on the part of parties intending to sail on the Virginia, you will not throw obstacles in the way of her going This report comes from Lawrence Warrell U. S Dist Atty Mobile who can give all information

U. S. GRANT
Lieut Genl

Telegram sent, DNA, RG 107, Telegrams Collected (Bound); copies, *ibid.*, RG 108, Letters Sent; DLC-USG, V, 47, 109. On May 11, 1866, 2:30 P.M., Maj. Gen. Philip H. Sheridan telegraphed to USG. "On yesterday evening I seized the blockade-runner-steamer 'Virgin' at this place—After a close inspection I released her as there was no visible indication that She was to go on a Slaving voyage—She was tied up at Algiers opposite the City—I released her on condition that she does not leave the City without my permission—Should any other evidence be received I can seize her again at any time" Telegram received (at 9:15 P.M.), DNA, RG 107, Telegrams Collected (Bound); *ibid.*, RG 108, Telegrams Received; copies (one sent by mail), *ibid.*, Letters Received; DLC-USG, V, 54; DLC-Philip H. Sheridan. Probably on May 11, Maj. Gen. John G. Foster telegraphed to USG. "Your telegram of the 9th has been received this moment There being no telegraphic communication with Pensacola I despatch at once an aid with instructions on the Steamer Ella Morse" Telegram received (dated May 14—received at 6:25 P.M.), DNA, RG 107, Telegrams Collected (Bound); *ibid.*, RG 108, Telegrams Received; copies, DLC-USG, V, 54; (dated May 11) DLC-U.S. Army: Civil War Miscellaneous.

On March 14, Sheridan had endorsed papers concerning rumors of kidnapping of Negroes in Fla. for sale as slaves in Cuba. "*Respectfully* forwarded for the information of the Lieut Genl For more than two months I have been diligently investigating this matter and have arrived at the conclusion that the various rumors concerning the kidnapping and running off of negroes to the West Indies Islands had no foundation in fact" ES, DNA, RG 94, Letters Received, 186G 1866.

To Edwin M. Stanton

Washington, D. C. May 12th *1866*

HON. E. M. STANTON,
SEC. OF WAR,
SIR:

Enclosed I send copy of a letter just received from Gen. Sheridan which I beg may be laid before the President and his special attention called to it. For myself I have never had any faith in Napoleon's promise to withdraw from Mexico. He has simply bound us over to keep the peace for Eighteen or twenty months to give him an opportunity of consolidating Maximilian's Empire. If he finds the Empire able to maintain itself without the aid of French Bayonetts he will be very glad to withdraw them; if not he will remain and claim that his duty, and previous engagements, compell him to remain. I do not look upon his promise to withdraw as meaning anything more than a promise to withdraw if the Empire can stand without his assistence.

Gen. Sheridan is deeply interested in Mexican Affairs and has been watching them very closely. His opinions therefore are entitled to more than ordinary weight on all questions connected with the situation there.

I have the honor to be
Very respectfully
your obt. svt.
U. S. GRANT
Lt. Gn.

ALS, IHi. On May 15, 1866, Secretary of War Edwin M. Stanton endorsed this letter. "Respectfully refered with General Sheridans letter to the President in Cabinet" AES, *ibid.* On May 7, Maj. Gen. Philip H. Sheridan, New Orleans, had written to USG. "*Private* . . . I see in the papers, the contemplated evacuation of Mexico by the French troops. This I presume means all foreign troops, now used by Louis Napoleon in his buccaneering expedition. Great care should be taken, to have a very clear understanding on this point. On the RioGrande frontier, there is more energetic action on the part of the Imperialists, than heretofore, and instead of giving up places, they are trying to occupy more and have advanced additional troops, and are contemplating more active hostilities. The time is long until the final evacuation, and I have not much confidence in the truth or sincerity of Louis Napoleon, Should the condition of our country, from party strife or any other cause, during this period, give him the slightest hope; we might say good bye to his protestations or present intentions. The sympathy of the whole south is with Maximilian; they know that there never can be a rebellion again against the Government except in connection with France and other European nations and it still gives them a hope, which they hold hidden. Then the catholic clergy, of the south who were disloyal during the Rebellion, have strong sympathies on account of the aggrandizement of the church, although they know that the clergy in Mexico are against Maximilian I also think that the most strenuous efforts will be made to change the latter body in Mexico, during the long period allowed for the evacuation. The Liberals are in good spirit and are doing very well. They are divided in Tamaulipas, and thus waste their strength, but all are contending against the common enemy." LS, DNA, RG 108, Letters Received.

To Frederick Dent Grant

Washington, D. C. May 12th *1866*

DEAR FRED,

I do not think I shall be able to be at West Point at your examination as I had expected but will be there with your Ma and brothers and sister during your encampment. Your Ma and me will be compelled to go to St. Louis early next month. We will be gone about two weeks. I have no idea that you will fail either in your examination for admittence ~~in~~ or in any subsequent . . . Capt. Boynton was recommended for was filled by Gn. Meigs Son-in-law.[1]

Your Ma, brothers and sister are all well.

Yours Affectionately
U. S. GRANT.

ALS (incomplete facsimile), Charles Hamilton, *American Autographs* (Norman, Okla., 1983), II, 485.

1. On April 7, 1866, President Andrew Johnson nominated Capt. Joseph H. Taylor (son-in-law of Bvt. Maj. Gen. Montgomery C. Meigs) for appointment as maj. and adjt. For Capt. Edward C. Boynton, see letter to Andrew Johnson, March 1, 1866.

To Maj. Gen. George G. Meade

Washn D. C. May 14 *1866*

GEN. G. G. MEADE
COMDG MIL. DIV. ATLANTIC
GENERAL

The papers of which the enclosed are copies have just been referred to me by the Sec. of War. You may direct military commanders nearest the points of deposit of munitions of war pointed out by the British Minister, to make immediate investigation and if there are reasonable grounds for suspecting that these stores are intended to be used unlawfully, seize and hold them until satisfactory security is given that they will not be used against any power with which the United States is at peace.

Very Respectfully Yr Obdt Svt
U. S. GRANT
Lt. Gn.

LS, DNA, RG 393, Military Div. of the Atlantic, Letters Received. The enclosures are *ibid.* See telegram to Maj. Gen. George G. Meade, May 30, 1866; letter to Maj. Gen. Edward O. C. Ord, June 7, 1866. On May 16, 1866, Maj. Gen. George G. Meade, Philadelphia, wrote to USG. "I have the honor to acknowledge the receipt of your letter of instructions of the 14th inst, enclosing a copy of a letter from Mr Seward, Secretary of State, to Mr Stanton, Secretary of War, and, also, a copy of an extract furnished the Secretary of State by Sir Frederick Bruce, British Minister, relative to munitions of war forwarded to points along the northern frontier &cc. I have, also, to inform you that I have given the necessary orders to the Commanding General of the Department of the East, to carry out your instructions relative to the cities of Buffalo and Dunkirk, and to the Commanding General of the Middle Department relative to the town of Erie. As Cleveland is beyond my military command, I have given no orders regarding it." LS, DNA, RG 108, Letters Received. On May 17, Meade forwarded to USG instructions of May 16 from Col. George D. Ruggles, adjt. to Maj. Gen. Joseph Hooker, New York City, to the commanding officer, Fort Porter, Buffalo, N. Y., concerning Fenian activity. ES and copy, *ibid.* On May 22, Capt. and Bvt. Lt. Col. Zenas R. Bliss, 8th Inf., Fort Porter, wrote to Ruggles reporting the absence of Fenian activity. Copy, *ibid.* On May 29, Meade forwarded this report to USG's hd. qrs. Copy, *ibid.* On May 18 and 25, Meade also forwarded reports to USG concerning Fenians. ES, *ibid.* The enclosures are *ibid.* On May 21, USG endorsed the papers submitted on May 18. "Respy. forwarded to sec of war for his information." Copy, *ibid.*, Register of Letters Received. On May 23, Meade wrote a letter received at USG's hd. qrs. "Submits matter of Genl Hooker of May 19th enclosing report of Lt Col. C. H. Carlton of May 16th concerning siezure of 3 cases containing 40 muskets, at Oswego, N. Y. (supposed for Fenians:) also the application of Patrick Reegan, a shoemaker, for return of said arms. . . ." *Ibid.* On May 23, Maj. George K. Leet endorsed these papers. "Respy. returned to Maj. Gen. G. G. Meade, comdg. Atlantic Military Division who is authorized to order the arms to be returned, when satisfactory bonds are given that they will not be used in violation of the neutrality laws." Copy, *ibid.* On June 2, Bvt. Brig. Gen. Simon F. Barstow, adjt. for Meade, forwarded a report to USG's hd. qrs. concerning the seizure of arms at Erie, Pa., intended for Fenians. ES and copy, *ibid.*, Letters Received.

On May 14, 9:00 A.M., USG telegraphed to Maj. Gen. Edward O. C. Ord. "The British Minister reports about fifty boxes sent to T Laven Cleveland weighing about 350 lbs each, and which he thinks contain rifles Have it investitgated and if there is reasonable grounds for believing they are to be used in violation of neutrality seize and hold them till proper security is given against such use" Telegram sent, *ibid.*, RG 107, Telegrams Collected (Bound); telegram received (misdated May 15), Ord Papers, CU-B. On May 18, Ord, Detroit, telegraphed to USG. "Genl Hoyt whom I sent to Cleveland has returned and reports that the boxes which were sent to T. Lavan there have not arrived All records of recent arrivals by Lake ~~and~~ or rail have been examined The Collector who is authorized by law to seize such boxes is on the lookout and will take them on arrival He reports no military needed at present He, the Marshall and the District Attorney are all on the que, vive" Telegram received (at 5:00 P.M.), DNA, RG 107, Telegrams Collected (Bound); *ibid.*, RG 108, Telegrams Received; copy, DLC-USG, V, 54. On May 19, Ord wrote a letter received at USG's hd. qrs. transmitting a report of May 18 from Col. and Bvt. Brig. Gen. Charles H. Hoyt, Detroit, to Bvt. Col. Placidus Ord, adjt. for Ord, stating that the arms reportedly en route to Cleveland for Fenian use had not yet arrived. DNA, RG 108, Register of Letters Received; the report is LS, *ibid.*, RG 94, Letters Received, 104O 1866. On May 24, USG endorsed the report. "Respectfully forwarded to Hon. Secretary of War for his information." ES, *ibid.*

On May 21, Secretary of the Treasury Hugh McCulloch wrote to Secretary of War Edwin M. Stanton concerning arms seized by the collector of customs at Rouses Point, N. Y. LS, *ibid.*, RG 107, Letters Received from Bureaus. On the same day, USG endorsed this letter. "I think the Arms should be held either by the Collector at Rouse's Point or turned over to the nearest Military commander to be held until claimants give proper security that they will ~~be~~ not be used against any powers with which the United States are at peace, by Citizens of the United States or by organizations fitting out from the territory of the United States. It seems as though the Atty. Gn. ought to define the legal course to be pursued against the Fenians who are supposed to be preparing to make War against Great Britten." AES, *ibid.* On June 4, 11:00 A.M., Bvt. Brig. Gen. Cyrus B. Comstock telegraphed to Meade. "The Engineer officer at Rouses Point (Ft Montgomery) reports that the Fenians threaten to seize arms detained there by Custom House Officer These arms are now stored in Ft Montgomery." Telegram sent, *ibid.*, Telegrams Collected (Bound); copies, *ibid.*, RG 108, Letters Sent; DLC-USG, V, 47, 109.

To Edwin M. Stanton

Washington, D. C. May 15th *1866*

HON. E. M. STANTON,
SEC. OF WAR,
SIR:

I would respectfully recommend that the States of North Carolina and South Carolina be consolidated into one Department, Maj. Gn. Sickles to command, Hd Qrs. Columbia, S. C. and that each of these two states ~~to~~ form a Military command, under Gens Ruger and Scott, who will, at the same time, act as Agts of the Freedmen's Bureau for these states.

I would recommend also the consolidation of Georgia & Alabama in like manner, Maj. Gn. Chas. Woods to command, Hd Qrs. Macon Ga. and these states respectively to be commanded by Gens. Tillson & Swayne who will in like manner perform the functions of Military Commanders and Agts. of the Freedmen's Bureau[.]

If this view is carried out I would recommend that Gn. Brannon be relieved from duty and mustered out of the Volunteer service to take effect May 31st 1866, giving three months to join his proper duties in the Regular Army.

Very respectfully
your obt. svt.
U. S. GRANT
Lt. Gn.

ALS, DNA, RG 94, Letters Received, 395A 1866. On May 16, 1866, USG wrote to Secretary of War Edwin M. Stanton. "Gen. Howard having been directed to arrest all the Officers of the Freedmen's Bureau in North Carolina I would respectfully recommend that Gen. Ruger be ordered, by telegraph, to assume the duties of Act. Com. for his Dept. at once, and that his Chief Qr. Mr. be directed to relieve the disbursing Officer of the Bureau now serving under Bvt. Brig. Gn. Whittlesey." ALS, *ibid.*, 382A 1866. See George R. Bentley, *A History of the Freedmen's Bureau* (Philadelphia, 1955), pp. 126–28, 130, 132–33.

To Julia A. Nutt

Washington May 15th 1866.

MRS. HALLER NUTT,
MADAM;

A statement of Quartermasters and Commissary's stores taken from your husbands plantations near Lake St. Joe, Louisiana, by the troops under my command in 1863, has been presented to me. Of the amounts taken I have no knowledge. I know that large quantities of both kinds were taken, and from my knowledge of your, and your husband's, loyalty, think that if any such claims where vouchers were not given for property taken, are allowed; yours should be so allowed, and I would recommend it under Gen.

Order, No. 109, of 1862. The prices I would recommend however would be the prices paid for the same articles by the Govt. at the time these were taken.

Very respectfully
Your obt. servt.
U. S. GRANT,
Lt. Gen.

Copies, DLC-USG, V, 47, 109; DLC-Nathaniel P. Banks; DNA, RG 108, Letters Sent. In 1860, Dr. Haller Nutt owned twenty-one plantations in La. and Miss. D. Clayton James, *Antebellum Natchez* (Baton Rouge, 1968), p. 156. On Sept. 21, 1863, Lt. Col. Loren Kent, provost marshal for USG, issued a safeguard for Nutt's property "on Lake St Joseph Tensas Parish Louisiana known as Winter Quarters." Copy, DNA, RG 56, Div. of Captured and Abandoned Property, File 276. See *SRC*, 48-1-325. On Oct. 2, Brig. Gen. Marcellus M. Crocker wrote to Brig. Gen. John A. Rawlins. "This will introduce to you Mr Haller Nutt a loyal Citizen of Natchez. Mr Nutt desires an interview with Gen Grant which if possable I wish you would obtain for him, This gentleman is one of the Natchez men who have always stood out against the rebellion" ALS, DNA, RG 56, Div. of Captured and Abandoned Property, File 276. Nutt's properties were badly damaged before his death on June 15, 1864. After the war, Julia A. Nutt pressed claims, and in Oct., 1865, traveled to Washington, D. C., to see USG, who ordered a military commission to meet to determine a fair settlement. Ina May Ogletree McAdams, *The Building of "Longwood"* (Austin, Tex., 1972), p. 116. On Oct. 24, USG endorsed papers in the case. "Soon after the fall of Vicksburg, Mr. Nutt of Natchez, Miss. with some three or four other gentlemen of the same place visited me at Vicksburg. My understanding was that Mr. N. had been loyal to the Government throughout. He was certainly a Citizen who conducted himself in such manner as to entitle him to protection from the Government instead of the seizure of his property. Of the claim which is now being made for the recovery of money taken from Mr. Nutt, I know nothing. I was not aware that money had been seized. I will state however that if investigation shows that money belonging to him has been seized and put into the United States Treasury, his family are as much entitled to its recovery as the most loyal in the South, for I believe the family are of that class." Copy, DNA, RG 56, Div. of Captured and Abandoned Property, File 276. See *HRC*, 40-1-7, pp. 874–77. The commission, which convened on Jan. 20, 1866, awarded Mrs. Nutt $112,472.16. On May 17, USG endorsed the report. "I am acquainted with the claimant, Mrs. Nutt, widow of Haller Nutt, deceased She has at all times been a loyal citizen of the United States, as I had every reason to believe, as was also her deceased husband up to the time of his death. I know that large quantities of supplies were taken, but cannot state quantities or value. I recommend the payment of this claim under General Order 109, of 1862, at the rates paid for the same articles by the government at the time they were taken." *HED*, 47-2-53. Because the q. m. gen. and commissary gen. ruled that the claim could not be paid under existing laws, Mrs. Nutt turned to Congress for relief with no success until the Southern Claims Commission awarded her $56,368.25, paid in 1873. *U.S. Statutes at Large*, XVII, 750. Dissatisfied with this amount, she continued to pursue her claim.

See *ibid.*, XXII, 734, XXIII, 586; XLV, part 2, 2014–15; *SRC*, 48-1-325; *HRC*, 52-1-1800; *SRC*, 56-1-685; *HRC*, 56-2-2169; *Congressional Record*, 70-1, 522.

To Edwin M. Stanton

Washington May 16th 1866,

Hon. E. M. Stanton,
Sec. of War,
Sir:

In view of the long delay in the Lower House of Congress in agreeing upon a plan of reorganization of the Army, suitable to our present requirements and the urgent necessity for early action, I am induced to present the matter to you, officially, and to ask the attention of Congress to it, believing that when they have the matter fairly before them they will do what should be done speedily.

At the present time settlements are springing up with unusual rapidity in the district of country between the Missouri river and the Pacific Ocean where heretofore the Indian was left in undisputed possession. Emigrants are pushing to these settlements, and to the Gold fields of the Rocky Mountains, by every available highway. The people flocking to these regions are citizens of the United States and are entitled to the protection of the Government. They are developing the resources of the country to its great advantage, thus making it the interest as well as duty to give them Military protection. This makes a much greater force West of the Mississippi necessary than was ever heretofore required.

A small Military force is required in all the states heretofore in rebellion and it cannot be foreseen that this force will not be required for some time to come. It is hoped that this force will not be necessary to enforce the laws either State or National. But the difference of sentiment engendered by the great war which has raged for four years will make the presence of a Military force necessary to give a feeling of security to the people. All classes disposed to obey the laws of the country will feel this alike.

To maintain order the Government has been compelled to retain Volunteers. All white Volunteers have become dissatisfied and claim that the contract with them has been violated by retaining them after the war was over. By reason of dissatisfation they are no longer of use and might as well be discharged at once—every one now remaining in service.[1]

The colored Volunteer has equal right to claim his discharge but as yet he has not done so. How long will existing laws authorize the retention of this force even if they are content to remain?

The United States Senate passed promptly a Bill for the reorganization of the Army, which, in my opinion is as free from objections as any great measure could possibly be, and which would supply the minimum requisite force. It gives but a few thousand additional men over the present organization, but gives a large number of additional Battalions and companies. The public service, guarding routes of travel over the plains and giving protection in the Southern States, demands the occupation of a great number of posts. For many of them a small company is just as efficient as one with more men in it would be. The Bill before Congress, or the one which has passed the Senate, gives increased number of Companies by diminishing the number, rank and file, of each company. It is an exceedingly appropriate measure in this particular for it provides for the increase when occasion requires more men. The Company is the smallest unit of organizations that can be used without materially injuring discipline and efficiency.

The belief that Congress would act promptly on this matter if their attention was called to it by the proper Government Official has induced me to respectfully ask your attention to it. If you agree with me in this matter I would also ask, if you deem it proper, that this, with such endorsement as you may be pleased to make, be laid before Congress, through the Speaker of the House.

Very respectfully
Your obt. servt
U. S. GRANT
Lt. Gen'l

Copies, DLC-USG, V, 47, 109; DNA, RG 108, Letters Sent. See *HED*, 39-1-113; letters to Henry Wilson, Jan. 12, Feb. 5, 6, 1866. The bill to reorganize the U.S. Army became law as of July 28, 1866. See *U.S. Statutes at Large*, XIV, 332–38.

1. On May 17, USG wrote to Secretary of War Edwin M. Stanton. "I would respectfully recommend the Muster out of all White Volunteer troops still remaining in service except the 1st or Hancock Corps." ALS, DNA, RG 94, Vol. Service Div., Letters Received, W2191 (VS) 1865.

To Edwin M. Stanton

Washington, D. C. May 16th *1866*.

HON. E. M. STANTON,
SEC. OF WAR,
SIR:

I have read a copy of the correspondence between Gen. Dyer, Chief of Ordnance, and Bvt. Col. Laidley of the same Corps, which lead to the removal of the latter from Springfield Arsenal. This Correspondence was laid before me by Col. Laidley with the view of obtaining for him an opportunity of submitting to you the same papers, in person, and to remove any unfavorable impression that may have been made upon your mind as to his course, and to correct, if possible the injury which he conceives has been done him by removing him from an important Arsenal to one of but little responsibility. I would respectfully ask for Col. Laidley the opportunity he desires. ~~but~~

Very respectfully
your obt. svt.
U. S. GRANT
Lt. Gn.

ALS, DNA, RG 107, Letters Received from Bureaus. USG enclosed correspondence between Bvt. Col. Theodore T. S. Laidley and Brig. Gen. Alexander B. Dyer concerning a quarrel over a breech-loading firearm designed by Laidley. *Ibid.*

To Matías Romero

Washington, D. C. May 16th *1866*

Dear Sir:

This will introduce to your acquaintance Gn. Custer who rendered such distinguished service as a Cavalry Officer during the War. There was no officer in that branch of service who had the confidence of Gn. Sheridan to a greater degree than Gn. C. and there is no officer in whos judgement I have greater faith than in Sheridans. Please understand then that I mean by this to endorse Gen. Custer in a high degree.

Gn. Custer proposes to apply for a leave of absence for one year with permission to leave the country and to take service whilst abroad. I propose to endorse his application favorably and believe that he will get it.

Yours Truly
U. S. Grant

To Sr. M. Romero
Minister &c.

ALS, USMA.

To Bvt. Maj. Gen. Charles R. Woods

Washington, May. 17th 1866.

Maj. Gen. Chas. R. Woods.
Comdg. Dept. of. Ala.
General:

Cause to be returned to Mrs. J. Kennedy her house and premises in the City of Mobile, now used as Provost Mar. Office and quarters.

As a rule private property should be returned to owners when it is not absolutely necessary for the public service, and then satisfactory contracts should be made with the owners to justify retention. This of course would not apply to the property of unpardoned rebels who have occupied conspicuous positions in the rebellion. As a rule both law and justice should be observed.

I do not say what is here said in reproof for any policy you have ever pursued either in this case or any other. There has never been a single complaint made to these Hdqrs. of your administration of affairs in any particular, but on the contrary your course has given satisfaction generally, or at least to those under whose orders and instructions you act, and to all higher authority. I write this merely as instructions in like cases should there be such.

Very respectfully
Your obt. Servt.
U. S. GRANT
Lt. Gen.

Copies, DLC-USG, V, 47, 109; DNA, RG 108, Letters Sent. On April 16, 1866, Thomas Kilby Smith, former brig. gen., Washington, D. C., had referred papers to USG's hd. qrs. concerning the case of M. E. Kennedy (Mrs. J. E.) who had contracted to rent her house in Mobile to the U.S. Army in Aug., 1865; the q. m. gen., however, had refused to pay rent while the local commander refused to vacate the house. *Ibid.*, Letters Received.

To Edwin M. Stanton

Washington, D. C. May 18th *1866*

HON. E. M. STANTON,
SEC. OF WAR:
SIR:

I would respectfully recommend Brevet Brig. Gn. Geo. D. Wise,[1] Asst. Qr. Mr. Volunteer service, for transfer to the Quarter-Master's Dept. Regular Army. I have recommended Capts. Belcher[2] and Webster[3] for similar transfer previously and would therefore ask that Gen. Wise come after these two officers, or that his appointment shall not prejudice their chances for appointment.

Gen. Wise has most unexceptionable recommendations now on file in the Adj's Office.

Very respectfully
your obt. svt.
U. S. GRANT
Lt. Gn.

ALS, DNA, RG 94, ACP, W1475 CB 1866.

1. On Aug. 14, 1867, the acting q. m. gen. wrote to the AGO recommending the muster out of Bvt. Brig. Gen. George D. Wise and Bvt. Maj. Joseph T. Powers, both q. m. of vols., as of Oct. 1. LS, *ibid.*, Q73 CB 1867. On Aug. 16, USG endorsed this letter. "Approved" AES, *ibid.* See *PUSG*, 13, 69*n.*

2. On May 6, 1866, Bvt. Maj. Gen. Jefferson C. Davis wrote a letter received at USG's hd. qrs. recommending Bvt. Maj. John H. Belcher, q. m., for appointment to the U.S. Army. DNA, RG 108, Register of Letters Received. On May 12, USG endorsed this letter. "I would respy. recommend Capt Belcher for one of the vacancies now existing in Q. M. Dep. I would, also, call attention to a previous endorsement made by me for Capt and Bvt Maj Amos Webster for same appointment." Copy, *ibid.* Belcher was appointed capt. and q. m. as of June 16.

3. See letter to Bvt. Maj. Gen. Montgomery C. Meigs, Oct. 28, 1865.

To Maj. Gen. Philip H. Sheridan

Confidential Washington, D. C.
May 19th 1866,

GENERAL;

I understand that Gn. Carvajal has succeeded in purchasing a quantity of Arms and Munitions of war which are about being shipped to Texas. There is no law or regulations against shipping these articles to any country nor will there be difficulty in starting them from New York. There may be however some regulation against such articles going into a state lately in rebellion. I was under the impression that all such regulations had been revoked but am now told that they were not, or if they have been have again been renewed. If this is the case I do not want to see the regulation enforced by Military authority.

I write you this confidentially but still for your protection if any is needed. There certainly can be no reason for using the Military force of the country as a police force to protect ~~the~~ a neutrality to build up a power that has done the United States so much harm and which contempla[tes] so much more.

If either of the belligerents in ~~m~~Mexico desire shipping through our territory I see no reason for preventing them, ~~S~~so ~~that~~ my instructions would be the same in either case.

This shipment will probably be for Brasos or Brownsville.

Very respectfully
your obt. svt.
U. S. GRANT
Lt. Gn.

TO MAJ. GN. SHERIDAN.

If I learn the name~~s~~ of the vessel having the consignment refered to I will inform you of it.

U. S. G.

ALS, DLC-Philip H. Sheridan. See letter to Maj. Gen. Philip H. Sheridan, July 20, 1866; Matías Romero, comp., *Correspondencia de la Legacion Mexicana en Washington durante la Intervencion Extranjera 1860–1868* (Mexico, 1870–92), VIII, 109–11. On July 13, 1866, Maj. Gen. Philip H. Sheridan, New Orleans, wrote to USG. " '*Personal*' . . . I have not written you for some time on Mexican affairs. After the arrival of General Caravajal with your letter to me, I thought the best way that I could assist him was to visit Brownsville, and pave the way for the surrender of Matamoros for him, which I did, by interviews with the merchants, and my advice to Caravajal to give protection to persons and property of all. This was all the people of Matamoros required. These negotiations were hastened by the defeat of the escort of the convoy near Camargo. I found the train had left Matamoros, on my arrival at Brownsville, and that it was to be passed through the Liberal lines by paying 'toll': this I advised against and urged the capture of the train; but, to protect it when captured, and I am happy to say this result was obtained. The possession of Matamoros is invaluable; and I have given Caravajal but six weeks to get all Northern Mexico. If he does not—do it I will be disappointed; because it is perfectly feasible. I am a little afraid of his military capacity and confidence, from the manner he talked to me in New Orleans of what he would require to capture Matamoros; however, he is a first rate man and I have much confidence in his sincerity. Since this success of the Liberals they are getting many friends in and about Washington. Men who would not, as you have done, help them when they were weak; but now, when assistance is not essential, Fremonts Dutch Generals and strikers, Congressmen and Heads of Bureaux, are all right on the Mexican question" ALS, USG 3. At 12:30 P.M., Sheridan telegraphed to USG. "Information to me from a private source from Vera Cruz says, all French troops at City of Mexico and vicinity, except a small garrison have marched to San Louis Potosi under Marshall Basin—

I presume they are going towards Monterey. One hundred and forty (140) French soldiers arrived at Vera Cruz by last French steamer, Much excitement among English & French shipping at Vera Cruz on receipt of surrender of Matamoras—" Telegram received (at 4:30 P.M.), DNA, RG 107, Telegrams Collected (Bound); *ibid.*, RG 108, Telegrams Received; copies, DLC-USG, V, 54; DLC-Philip H. Sheridan; USG 3.

On June 21, Sheridan wrote to Brig. Gen. John A. Rawlins. "I have the honor to report a very good condition of affairs on the Rio Grande frontiers. I find the troops at Brazos Santiago well quartered and comfortable and no sickness. At Brownsville the troops are in camps clean, comfortable and healthy. At Romo, Rio Grande City and Leredo, the same condition of affairs exists. The officers of the colored troops are desirous of being mustered out, but the men are not, and are contented and happy. As soon as the condition of international affairs will permit the muster out of these troops, I respectfully recommend, as the permanent garrisons for this line having in view our small army; two companies of Infantry for Brazos Santiago; four companies of Infantry and one Battery of Artillery for Brownsville; two companies of Infantry for Ringgold Barracks, and one company for Leredo. In addition to this, a small Cavalry force will, for the present, be required at Brownsville and Leredo. I have directed General Getty to make estimates for quarters &c for garrisons of this size at these points, with the view of submitting them to higher authority for the necessary orders." LS, DNA, RG 108, Letters Received.

On June 22, Sheridan telegraphed to Rawlins. "Please notify Lt. Genl. Grant for his information, that it is now my belief—that nine and nine tenths—of the people of Mexico, are against Maximilian, and this may be relied upon. Santa Anna will have to be looked-out for, He is in the interests of the traitors, and the French & English merchants of Mexico, who want to ring him in on account of his church proclivities to save them from their traitorous acts." Telegram received (at 7:40 P.M.), *ibid.*, RG 107, Telegrams Collected (Bound); *ibid.*, RG 108, Telegrams Received; copies, DLC-USG, V, 54; DLC-Philip H. Sheridan; DLC-Andrew Johnson; USG 3. On June 23, USG referred this telegram to President Andrew Johnson. ES, DLC-Andrew Johnson. On June 24, 12:30 P.M., Sheridan telegraphed to USG. "I have the honor to transmit to you the following reliable information—Gen'l Escobedo of the Liberal army captured near Camargo on the 16th a train of the Imperialists consisting of two hundred & fifty—twelve mule teams loaded with One & a half million of dollars worth of merchandize; also eleven pieces of artillery and ammunition and eight hundred prisoners—This success will, I think end French rule on the Rio Grande" Telegram received (at 10:30 P.M.), DNA, RG 107, Telegrams Collected (Bound); *ibid.*, RG 108, Telegrams Received; copies (one sent by mail), *ibid.*, Letters Received; *ibid.*, RG 393, Military Div. of the Southwest and Dept. of the Gulf, Telegrams Sent; DLC-USG, V, 54; DLC-Philip H. Sheridan; DLC-Andrew Johnson; USG 3. On June 25, USG referred this telegram to Johnson. ES, DLC-Andrew Johnson. On July 3, 3:30 P.M., Sheridan telegraphed to USG. "Matamoras surrendered to Carajaval on the twenty fourth 24 of June" Telegram received (on July 4, 12:30 A.M.), DNA, RG 107, Telegrams Collected (Bound); *ibid.*, RG 108, Telegrams Received; copies, DLC-USG, V, 54; DLC-Philip H. Sheridan; DLC-Andrew Johnson; USG 3. USG referred this telegram to Johnson. AES (undated), DLC-Andrew Johnson.

To Bvt. Maj. Gen. Montgomery C. Meigs

Washington, D. C. May 21st *1866*

Maj. Gn. M. C. Meigs,
Qr. Mr. Gn. U. S. A.
General:

I would recommend that before Gn. Ingalls[1] starts on his inspection Westward orders be given him to report for duty on his return in New York City, relieving Gn. Van Vliet.

Gen. Ingalls has performed more field duty during the War than any other Officer of the Dept. and has performed it well, and should therefore be entitled to a choice of station. He has expressed a choice for New York City.

I would also recommend a change in the Order assigning Capt. Rutherford to Jeffersonville, Ia, and would suggest ~~Capt. Belcher~~, the officer of your Dept who has had charge of clothing there and who has performed his duties so faithfully, in his stead.

Very respectfully
your obt. svt.
U. S. Grant
Lt. Gn.

ALS, DNA, RG 92, Letters Received.

1. On April 23, 1866, Bvt. Maj. Gen. Rufus Ingalls had written to Bvt. Maj. Gen. Montgomery C. Meigs proposing an inspection tour of western supply routes to ensure adoption of the most economical routes. ALS, *ibid.*, RG 94, Letters Received, 141Q 1866. On May 2, USG endorsed this letter. "Orders in accordance with the within recommendations is approved and recommended. I would further recommend that Gn. Ingalls instruction[s] authorize him to make any changes he may desire to reduce present cost of supplying Military Posts anywhere between the Mo. and the Pacific." AES, *ibid.* On Aug. 24, Ingalls, Copperopolis, Calif., telegraphed to USG. "Babcock Sackett & my self will be in San Francisco on the thirtieth. I return to Oregon during September, thence back to Washington" Telegram received (on Aug. 25, 9:00 A.M.), *ibid.*, RG 107, Telegrams Collected (Bound); *ibid.*, RG 108, Telegrams Received; copy, DLC-USG, V, 54. See letter to Maj. Gen. Henry W. Halleck, April 19, 1866.

On June 12, Maj. Gen. Joseph Hooker, New York City, wrote to USG. "In the event of the passage of a bill for the increase of the Army, and the creation of original vacancies in the quarter master General's Department, I have the honor to recommend that the claims of Brevet major General Rufus Ingalls be taken into consideration. Gen'l. Ingalls was my Chief quarter master while I commanded the Army of the Potomac, and displayed splendid administrative ability, and untiring zeal in the performance of his duties. I consider him eminently entitled to this preferment, both on account of his capacity and services during the war." LS, DNA, RG 108, Letters Received. On June 21, Maj. Gen. George G. Meade, Philadelphia, wrote to USG. "In view of the action of Congress, increasing the Army, I desire to place on record, my recommendation for promotion in the Quartermaster's Department of Brevet Brig. Genl. Rufus Ingalls. General Ingalls it is well known has been actively & conspicuously, employed *in the field*, since the beginning of the War. In the early part of the War, he was employed in creating & organizing the Department, & had charge of several of the most important depots in the field for supplying the troops. In the summer of /62, after the Peninsular operations, he was assigned as Chief Qr. Mr. of the Army of the Potomac, and served in this capacity, under Genl's. McClellan,—Burnside and Hooker.—On my taking command of the Army of the Potomac,—I found Genl. Ingalls, the Chief of his Department, which position he retained during the year /63 & 64, till he was transferred to the Hd. Qrs of the Armies, operating against Richmond, in June 1864.—In this latter high command, under your immediate supervision he remained till the close of the war. With this brief notice of the services of Genl. Ingalls, any one acquainted with the nature of the duties would be satisfied, but it is my wish to place on record, the high satisfaction, I experienced, from the support & co-operation I received from Genl. Ingalls. While he acted as Chief of his Department in the Army under my command,—In the discharge of those onerous & responsible duties, Genl. Ingalls exhibited great energy, zeal, and the highest executive & administrative qualities. At the Battle of Gettysburgh, and on numerous other fields he was distinguished for coolness & bravery.—I of course can not speak of the services of other officers, but from the knowledge I have of the services of Genl. Ingalls, his talents and capacity,—I should be suprised if in a fair comparison of his record, with those of others of his department, it is not ascertained, that in length & responsibility of service, and the fidelity and skill, with which the duties were discharged, Genl Ingalls stands second to no one, except the Quartermaster General. I therefore trust that in any increase of the Department, his claims will be promptly recognised." LS, *ibid.*

On Aug. 17, Bvt. Maj. Gen. Daniel Butterfield, New York City, telegraphed to Brig. Gen. John A. Rawlins. "Are you keeping a big Eye open for Rufus Ingalls in the new Colonels of the Qr Mrs Dept? Can I do anything—if I come on?" Telegram received (at 11:20 A.M.), *ibid.*, RG 107, Telegrams Collected (Bound). At 2:05 P.M., USG telegraphed to Butterfield. "There is no necessity for your coming here on the matter referred to in your despatch. It has been looked after" Telegram sent, *ibid.*; copies, *ibid.*, RG 108, Letters Sent; DLC-USG, V, 47, 60.

To Mrs. Lafayette S. Foster

May 23d *1866*

MY DEAR MRS. FOSTER;

Your letter of the 20th inst. asking for four Cartes de Visite, with autograph, is received. I have but three at present which I send cheerfully and will try to send the fourth when I get some more.

I was sorry to see that Connecticut failed to return Mr. Foster to the Senate. All agree I believe that he has reflected credit both upon his state and him self since he has been a member of that body. Mrs. Grant and myself will make a trip the coming Summer into New England and if we can do so it will afford both of us great pleasure to pay you a visit.

Mrs. Grant and family are well and desire to be remembered.

Yours Truly
U. S. GRANT

ALS, MHi. Martha Lyman married U.S. Senator Lafayette S. Foster of Conn. in 1860. Foster, a conservative Republican, had failed to receive the party nomination for a third term in 1866.

To Andrew Johnson

Washington, D. C. May 24th *1866*

HIS EXCELLENCY, A. JOHNSON, PRESIDENT OF THE U. STATES

SIR:

Col. M. M. Bane[1] of the Volunteer service having called on me for a statement of what I know of his services, probably with the view of making use of it with an application for some civil appointment, I cheerfully give it. I never knew Col. Bane prior to meeting him as Colonel of the 50th Ill. Inf.y Vols. His politcs I never knew but as a regimental and brigade commander he served directly under me in the early part of the War. In that capacity he was faithful and vigilent. At the battle of Shiloh he lost his right arm whilst gallantly performing his duties. Col. Bane is a gentleman of inteligence and education and a physician by profession prior to the War.

I have the honor,
Very respectfully, to be,
your obt. svt.
U. S. GRANT
Lt. Gn.

ALS, MH.

1. Moses M. Bane, born in Ohio in 1827, graduated from Starling Medical College in 1848, and moved to Adams County, Ill., in 1849. Appointed col., 50th Ill., as of Aug. 21, 1861, Bane resigned as of June 11, 1864. He attended Harvard Law School in 1865 and was appointed assessor of internal revenue, 4th Ill. district, as of June 18, 1866.

To Commander Daniel Ammen

May 29th *1866*

DEAR AMMEN,

Yours of the 26th is but just this moment received and as you speak of paying me a visit on Saturday next I hasten to answer. When you do come to town Mrs. Grant and myself will always be glad to have you stop with us and especially so when Mrs. Ammen is with you. I do not mean to be understood not to be equally glad to have you come when alone but to extend a special invitation to Mrs. A. On Thursday however Mrs. Grant and myself start for St. Louis to be absent probably three weeks. Don't let this prevent you from coming directly to my house to remain whilst you are in the City. Mr. Dent, Comstock and the children will all be there and housekeeping will go on as if we were at home. I agree with you perfectly about the impropriety of allowing the Miantenomah to go abroad and ~~have~~ had a conversation with the President on the subject last week. I supposed he would stop it and do not know that he has not done so. All is quiet on the Potomac

Yours Truly
U. S. GRANT

ALS, CLU.

On July 20, 1866, Commander Daniel Ammen, York, Pa., wrote to USG. "No doubt you have seen some if not all of the extracts from the London Times apropos of the visit of the Miantonemoh.—I nevertheless send you extracts of the 27th and 28th June and a slip of the 2nd July. I think after reading these Mr Fox might very well doubt whether he had 'served his country' even though it had never before been a question in his mind. Times 27th says: 'As these vessels resemble no other floating things, it follows almost inevitably that if the American ship builders are right ours must be wrong, and it is our imperative duty to investigate the subject without prejudice or delay.'—*To favor this end we have apparently sent that vessel abroad.* The remainder of the article suggests points of inquiry and states that 'we have hitherto been left in the dark about the actual power of the American guns . . . and we may possibly learn something from our neighbors in artillery as well as shipbuilding.' Times of the 28th—'One of the latest conceived and executed of these transatlantic prodigies is the two turret vessel Miantonomoh now anchored at Spithead, and in allowing this vessel to visit England at the present moment the Government of President Johnson has conferred upon this country a service only secondary to that so frankly rendered in the suppression of the miserable Fenian demonstration on the shores of the Canadian Lakes.'—[How much of a compliment should this be considered?] The turret question is just now one of vital importance with regard to the constitution of our iron clad Navy. . . . No opportunity for studying the whole subject with certain profit to ourselves can be afforded equal to a visit to the Miantomoh and other turret ships of the American Navy as they may visit our shores.'—*Thanks to Mr Fox.* The remainder of the article suggests points for examination with the view of improving the opportunity.—I think if the writer had been candid he would have put the visit of the Miantonemoh ahead of our suppressing the Fenian movement.—It was moreover *gratuitous* whilst the other was one of good faith and in the event of a War especially with England will cause us grave difficulties and untold cost. I enclose the slip of the 2nd July as a worthy finale to what preceded and we may note the significant presence of *Capt. Bythesea* of the English Navy and so long attached to the Embassy in Washington.—All of this is painful and we may doubt if ever before the great interests of a Country have been so betrayed. Admiral Davis at home appears to have been repairing the breaches making abroad.—After a laborious scientific investigation of some months he has come to the conclusion that the Isthmus of Darien should be examined at one or two points arrived at with the precision only arrived at by science.—You will I trust pardon a little scepticism as to the accuracy of these precise points resulting from some facts with which you are more or less cognizant but perhaps not in the order they came to me. You may remember my asking your permission to thank the Admiral in your name for the tracing of a map of the Isthmus compiled at the Observatory.—On making the acknowledgment to the Admiral I bore in mind a note he had written to Col. Biddle in which he stated that he felt satisfied that the only practicable route for a ship canal between the Oceans was in Honduras.—Therefore after returning your thanks I remarked that the map was valuable as a beginning to an extended and thorough survey of this almost unknown land.—This seems to have aroused the scientific nature a little as he favored me soon with a note of which the following is an exact copy: 'Saturday, Feby 17th '66. My dear Captain: Thank you for your Kind note. I know your great interest in the Isthmus but I am not fully informed as to the direction in which it tends. If you are studying the project of a ship canal I am inclined to think from the examination I made of the subject when last on the Isthmus and in Central America, that the only really *practicable* project would be to make an excavation on the line of the inter-oceanic railroad across the Isthmus of Honduras.' *etc* The admirals position as the head of the Naval Observatory very properly gave his opinion great weight so I thought it worth while that he should put it in a tangible form and also that in looking at the subject officially he could correct this great blunder based upon a pretended examination of the subject and that if he did not do so what he wrote could be readily controverted without officiousness. Therefore I gave to Judge Field of the Supreme Court a resolution presented by Senator Conness on the 18th March asking information through the Navy Dept and of the Sup't of the Observatory as to the various routes and whether the Isthmus of Darien is sufficiently Known, and if so, upon what authority and to furnish maps *etc.* As you are aware, the Admiral is no longer quite sure that the only practicable project is in Honduras and to which error, so persistently and as I supposed injuriously asserted, he owes the honor of being called upon to make a Report, instead of which I learn he has made a book, when one might suppose two or three columns of the Intelligencer would be ample in space. The Intelligencer of the 14th after a highly eulogistic introduction gives a synopsis of the Admirals Report of which I give an abstract: 'The *Honduras route* is also discussed in a few words since it has never been proposed to construct a Canal here.' Whether it had or had not been proposed, it is nevertheless certain that after a pretended examination of the subject the *Admiral did* regard the Honduras route as the only practicable project as his note to me shows without the shadow of a doubt.—Comment I would regard as a superfluity. In relation to the action of the Colombian Government I suspect none has taken place as Gen'l Salgar on an inquiry made by me by letter informed me that he Knew his papers relating thereto had reached Bogota and that his Congress were at the time considering and discussing the project of granting the right of way to an English company.—He expected advices by the steamer of the 9th July and informed me that if received he would write which he has not done. If the Colombian Government should be ugly what would we have a right to do?—So far as the body of the Isthmus is concerned beyond the vicinity of the paved roads lying between Porto Bello and Panama and also from Cruces to the latter place the Spaniards never established themselves and for the simple reason that the tribes were hostile.—Indeed this accounts for the actual want of Knowledge of the Isthmus.—The Admiral's Report says: 'Our really authentic information as to the Isthmus amounts to this, that at that part ~~of the~~ where the Oceans approach each other most nearly, nature has supplied harbors of unsurpassed excellence on both sides, and navigable rivers inviting the traveller to penetrate the interior, while on one side she has established a tidal condition favorable to a commerce which crosses the great seas.' If Colombia exists as a Nation by reason of having conquered her independence from the crown of Spain does she gain by it eminent domain never conquered by Spain, and which domain Colombia cannot now explore, much less construct a Canal across by reason of the continued hostility of the tribes, if for no other reason? In my note to Salgar I asked him if he thought my going to Bogota would correct any misapprehensions and hasten action; he replied that his advices by the steamer of the 9th would determine his opinion, since when he has not written. Years ago my wife Knew the family of President Mosquera and if you think it might be advantageous, pending your going abroad for me to go to Bogota on special duty I will be very happy to do so and take my wife along.—This of course would involve only an increase to 'other duty pay' and my travelling expenses. If I went I could communicate confidentially how averse our Government was to see a foreign company attempt the construction of a canal and indeed that without guerantees that no discriminating duties should exist we would not permit it or whatever it might be deemed advisable to say. Mrs Ammen begs to be most Kindly presented to you and to Mrs Grant to whom also I beg you to present my Kindest remembrances." ALS (brackets in original), USG 3.

General Orders No. 33

Head Quarters of the Army,
Adjutant General's Office,
Washington, May 30, 1866.

GENERAL ORDERS, No. 33.

With profound sorrow the General-in Chief announces to the army the death at West Point, N. Y., on the 29th inst., of its late illustrious commander, Brevet Lieutenant General Winfield Scott.

His history is a part of the history of the country,—it is almost needless to recall it to those who have venerated him so long. Entering the army as a captain in 1808, at the close of the war of 1812–14, he had already by the force of merit won his way to the rank of Brevet Major General.

In 1841 Major General Scott was assigned to the command of the army.

In the spring of 1847 the Mexican war having already begun he commenced, as commander in chief of the army in Mexico, the execution of a plan of campaign the success of which was as complete as its conception was bold, and which established his reputation as one of the first soldiers of the age.

A grateful country conferred on him in 1855 the rank of Brevet Lieutenant General as a token of its estimate of his brilliant services.

As the vigor of his life, whether in peace or in war, had been devoted to the service of the country he loved so well, so in his age his country gave to him in return that veneration, reverence and esteem which won by few, is the highest reward a nation can give.

Of most commanding presence, with a mind of great breadth and vigor, pure in life, his memory will never fade from the minds of those who have reverenced him so long.

As a testimony of respect the officers of the army will wear the usual badge of mourning for six months on the left arm and hilt of the sword.

Guns will be fired at each military post at intervals of thirty minutes from sunrise to ~~sunset~~ one o'clock P. M. on the day succeeding the receipt of this order. Troops will be paraded at 10 a, m, and this order read to them, after which all labor for the day will cease, and the flag will be kept at half mast during the day.

By command of Lieutenant General Grant:

E D TOWNSEND
asst. adjt. Genl.

ADfS (in the hand of Bvt. Col. Ely S. Parker), DNA, RG 94, Letters Received, 436A 1866. On May 30, 1866, Parker wrote to Bvt. Maj. Gen. Edward D. Townsend. "The accompanying is a draft of a General Order to the army which the Lieutenant General desires issued in compliance with instructions to him from the Hon. Secretary of War of this date." ALS, *ibid.* On May 29, 1:45 P.M., USG telegraphed to Bvt. Maj. Gen. George W. Cullum. "I hear unofficially that Gen Scott died this morning Please inform me if it is so and when and where the funeral takes place" Telegram sent, *ibid.*, RG 107, Telegrams Collected (Bound); copies, *ibid.*, RG 108, Letters Sent; DLC-USG, V, 47, 109. On the same day, Cullum, USMA, telegraphed to USG. "General Scott will be buried in West Point Cemetery at one P M on friday next with all the funeral honors which it is in our power to bestow" Telegram received (at 9:35 P.M.), DNA, RG 107, Telegrams Collected (Bound); copy, USMA. At 3:30 P.M., USG telegraphed to John W. Garrett, president, Baltimore and Ohio Railroad, Baltimore. "I will not go west Thursday as previously intended, but will go to New York to attend funeral of Gen Scott Will inform you of time for starting" Telegram sent, DNA, RG 107, Telegrams Collected (Bound). On May 31, 12:35 P.M. and 2:45 P.M., USG twice telegraphed to superintendent, Hudson River Railroad, New York City. "I go on the train to night to attend Genl Scotts funeral with my staff and party of Officers detailed by the Secretary of War Would be pleased to have a special car attached to any train leaving New York for West Point, between seven and ten tomorrow morning Please acknowledge receipt" "Having received invitation to go to West Point with Common Council in a boat, special Car requested in despatch of this morning will not be needed" Telegrams sent, *ibid.* Also at 2:45 P.M., USG telegraphed to Joseph B. Varnum, New York City. "Your despatch received I accept invitation of the Committee with many thanks for their politeness" Telegram sent, *ibid.* After attending the funeral on June 1, USG traveled to St. Louis via Buffalo and Chicago. See letter to Maj. Gen. Edward O. C. Ord, June 7, 1866.

On July 17, Cullum wrote to USG. "I have the honor to enclose, herewith, a bill of all the expenses incurred by me for the funeral of the late General Scott, under the telegraphic authority of the Secretary of War of May 28. 1866 that 'such measures as your [my] judgement may dictate will be sanctioned' Please cause the amount of $661.31 to be remitted by the proper Department to Mr O'maher or to myself at your earliest convenience, as the amount of the bill has already been advanced." Copy, USMA. On July 18, USG endorsed this letter. "Respy forwarded to the Sec of war." Copy, DNA, RG 108, Register of Letters Received.

To Maj. Gen. George G. Meade

Washington, D. C., May 30th *1866* [*11:55* P.M.]

MAJ GEN MEADE
PHILADELPHIA PA

The Mayor of Buffalo telegraphs that he has reliable information that six hundred Fenians have left Cleveland for that place. The Secretary of State has also sent copy of an order from Fenian Secretary of War directing Col Rice Fourth Fenian cavalry Boston to proceed to St Albans Vt. His orders for commencing hostilities are to be in these words "You may commence work" (signed) S. W. T." initials reversed Take the best steps you can to prevent these expeditions leaving the United States. I will send Sweeny's[1] order by mail

U. S. GRANT
Lieut Gen

Telegram sent, DNA, RG 107, Telegrams Collected (Bound); copies, *ibid.*, RG 108, Letters Sent; *ibid.*, RG 393, Military Div. of the Atlantic, Letters Sent; *ibid.*, Dept. of the East, Telegrams Received; DLC-USG, V, 47, 109. See letters to Maj. Gen. George G. Meade, March 12, May 14, 1866. On May 29, 1866, Secretary of State William H. Seward had written to Secretary of War Edwin M.

Stanton. "Your attention is invited to the accompanying communication, which purports to be a copy of a letter from T W Sweeney, Secretary of War F. B. to Colonel Edmund Rice &c., &c., &c. Boston, Massachusetts, and if genuine, shows a purpose to violate the neutrality of the United States" LS, DNA, RG 393, Dept. of the East, Letters Received. On May 30, USG endorsed this letter. "Respectfully forwarded ~~by~~ to Maj. Gn. Meade. Probably the best course to pursue will be to send a staff officer to each place, St. Albens & Buffalo to seize all Arms and equipments intended for Fenians, calling on civil authorities for such aid as can not be supplied by the Military" AES, *ibid.*

On June 1, Stanton telegraphed to USG. "The Secretary of State has just transmitted to this Department a telegram from the United States Distric[t] Attorney at Buffalo which indicates that the long threatened design to violate the neutrality laws of the United States is about to be carried into effect. An assemblage of Three hundred persons at St Albans to be reinforced by eight hundred more is also reported. You will please take any further ~~such~~ measures to prevent a violation of the neutrality laws and to aid the civil authorities ~~that you may deem proper as~~ as may be proper with the forces under your command. ~~may admit~~" ALS (telegram sent), *ibid.*, RG 107, Telegrams Collected (Bound); telegram received, *ibid.*, RG 108, Telegrams Received. Stanton transmitted to USG a telegram of the same day from U.S. District Attorney William A. Dart, Buffalo, to Seward. "Fifteen hundred men or more left this city about midnight and were passing Black Rock at last advice; have just learned two canal boats of arms with force enough to protect them have just landed Fort Erie." Telegram sent, *ibid.*, RG 107, Telegrams Collected (Bound); telegram received, *ibid.*, RG 108, Telegrams Received.

On June 2, USG, Buffalo, telegraphed to Maj. Gen. George G. Meade. "Gen. Barry is here. Assign him to general command from Buffalo to Mouth of Niagara. State autho[r]ities should call out M~~u~~ilitia on the frontier to prevent hostile expeditions leaving the United States and to save private property from destruction by mobs" ALS (telegram sent), Buffalo and Erie County Library, Buffalo, N. Y.; telegram received, DNA, RG 393, Military Div. of the Atlantic, Telegrams Received. On the same day, Bvt. Brig. Gen. Simon F. Barstow, adjt. for Meade, telegraphed to USG. "I have transmitted your telegram to General Meade, through General Hooker, as I do not know his address. He intended to return here from West Point this afternoon if he did not go to the frontier, and have read to Governor Curtin that part of the telegram relating to the action of the State authorities." Copy, *ibid.*, Letters Sent. On the same day, Meade, New York City, wrote to USG. "I enclose a copy of a letter this day addressed to the Commanding General Department of the East. In accordance with this letter, the troops of this Department, for the present, will be posted as follows: Nine (9) companies at Buffalo. One (1) companies at Fort Niagara. One (1) companies at Oswego. One (1) companies at Sackett's Harbor. Three (3) companies at Ogdensburgh. Five (5) companies at St. Albans. In addition to the above, the Commanding Officer of the company at Erie, Pa., in the Middle Department, has been temporarily included in the District of Ontario, and ordered to report to the Commanding Officer of that District." Copy (part in tabular form), *ibid.* Also on June 2, Barstow forwarded to USG's hd. qrs. copies of instructions to officers concerning Fenian activities. ES and copies, *ibid.*, RG 108, Letters Received. On the same day, Col. and Bvt. Brig. Gen. Israel Vogdes, 1st Art., Fort Hamilton, N. Y., telegraphed to Brig. Gen. John A. Rawlins. "I have just been informed by telegraph from Gen'l Hooker that Gen'l Barry has been assigned by the Lieut General to the District of Ontario—The original order of Gen'l Hooker directing the greater part of my regiment to garrison that District assigned me to the Command. As I am senior to Genl Barry I think that unless some very powerful reason exists to the contrary I am entitled to the command of the District of Ontario—I respectfully request that the original order so assigning me may be adhered to" Telegrams received (2—on June 3, 2:45 P.M.), *ibid.*, RG 107, Telegrams Collected (Bound); *ibid.*, RG 108, Telegrams Received; copy, DLC-USG, V, 54.

On June 5, Seward wrote to Stanton. "I have the honor to acknowledge the receipt of your letter of this date accompanied by telegrams from Lieutenant General Grant and General Sheridan and to inform you that they will receive attention. I would suggest that Major General Sheridan be instructed to report to the United States District Attorney any offenders for prosecution. I understand that the Attorney General has ordered the arrest of Sweeny and Roberts" LS, DNA, RG 107, Letters Received from Bureaus. On June 4, Maj. Gen. Philip H. Sheridan, New Orleans, had telegraphed to Rawlins. "Mr Donohoe the British consul at this place has addressed me a communication requesting steps to be taken to prevent a contemplated movement of Fenians from within the limits of my command, towards the Canadian frontier, but as there has been no Executive Proclamation or directions on this subject I am at a loss how to act in the premises I will thank you for instructions," Telegram received (at 8:40 P.M.), *ibid.*, Telegrams Collected (Bound); *ibid.*, RG 108, Telegrams Received; copies (one sent by mail), *ibid.*, Letters Received; DLC-USG, V, 54; DLC-Philip H. Sheridan. On the same day, Sheridan forwarded to Rawlins a letter of June 4 from Denis Donohue, British consul, to Sheridan concerning Fenian activities in New Orleans. ES and ALS, DNA, RG 108, Letters Received. On June 5, USG, St. Louis, telegraphed to Stanton. "I would recommend that orders be issued for the arrest of Sweeney, Roberts and a few others of the leading Fenians engaged in the present breach of our neutrality laws. It seems to me this course is demanded by a proper respect for our laws and National dignity." ALS (telegram sent), CSmH; telegrams received (2—at 2:00 P.M.), DNA, RG 107, Telegrams Collected (Bound). On June 6, 8:00 P.M., Stanton telegraphed to USG. "The President has issued a proclamation this evening against the violators of the neutrality laws, and authorised General Meade under the Act of 1818 to employ the land and naval forces to break up the armed expeditions against Canada, and has directed the arrest & prosecution of Sweeny Roberts and all engaged with them. This operates Substantially as a proclamation of Martial law, in the Military division of the Atlantic. If it should become necessary the same ~~power will be given~~ course can be taken in ~~the~~ other Military Divisions. General Meade is ~~ordered instructed directed~~ instructed that his powers under the Proclamation are to be exercised under your instructions. You will please give him such as you think proper, and also issue such as may be needed to General Sheridan or General Pope. ~~It~~ General Meade appears to be acting vigorously and will even ~~finish the job in~~ enforce the laws along the whole line unless the enterprise has larger proportions than have yet been developed. The Proclamation manifesting the Presidents determination, will probably ~~quench~~ exercise considerable influence. Nothing else of interest is transpiring here. Your friends are all well." ALS (telegram sent), *ibid.*; telegram received, *ibid.*, RG 108, Telegrams Received. On June 7, USG telegraphed to Stanton.

"Your dispatch of 6th recd Will give Ord necessary orders, Meade seems to be doing so well that I think nothing required more than to sustain his present course, The President's proclamation will I think, end the Fenian movement within a week so far as the Government is interested." Telegram received (at 2:30 P.M.), *ibid.*, RG 107, Telegrams Collected (Bound); copies, *ibid.*, RG 108, Letters Sent; DLC-USG, V, 47, 109. See following letter.

On Aug. 13, Col. and Bvt. Maj. Gen. William F. Barry, Buffalo, wrote to Meade's adjt. requesting that the capt. of the revenue cutter on Lake Ontario be instructed to cooperate in observing renewed Fenian activities. ALS, DNA, RG 108, Letters Received. On Aug. 15, Meade, Philadelphia, endorsed this letter. "Respectfully forwarded to Head Quars. Armies of the United States, for the information of the General Commanding: and I would request that in case the powers conferred on me by the President's Proclamation of the 6th June last are held to be no longer continuing and in force, that the Treasury Department may be directed to give the instructions applied for to the Collector at Ogdensburg." ES, *ibid.* On Aug. 16, USG endorsed this letter. "Respectfully forwarded to the Secretary of War." ES, *ibid.* On Aug. 17, Meade telegraphed to USG. "The following has just been received from Genl Barry, Attention is invited to my endorsement of the Fifteenth 15th as to my present powers, on his report of the thirteenth 'Buffalo N Y Aug 17th 1866 MAJ GEN MEADE U S A Phila Please cause orders to be sent to the collector at Erie Pa to hold the Revenue cutter "John Sherman" subject to my order that I may have occasion to send during the next five or six days (Signed) WM F BARRY Bvt M G'" Telegram received (at 2:15 P.M.), *ibid.*, RG 107, Telegrams Collected (Bound); *ibid.*, RG 108, Telegrams Received; copies, *ibid.*, Letters Received; *ibid.*, RG 393, Dept. of the East, Letters Sent; DLC-USG, V, 54.

On Oct. 8, 10:45 A.M., USG telegraphed to Meade. "If the Artillery company sent to Erie is no longer needed there send it back to Fort McHenry" Telegram sent, DNA, RG 107, Telegrams Collected (Bound); copies, *ibid.*, RG 108, Letters Sent; DLC-USG, V, 47, 60. On the same day, Meade telegraphed to USG. "The artillery Company at Erie is at present only needed there to guard the arms seized by the Civil authorities & which being under the jurisdiction of the Court in Pennsylvania I do not feel justified in removing. If these arms can be disposed of as suggested by me in my endorsement on a letter from Col Slemmer & forwarded to the Adjt Gen'l Aug twenty third, viz Storing them in some Arsenal, this company could be sent back to Ft McHenry—Unless these arms are disposed of in some way anther Co. must be sent to guard them" Telegram received (at 1:45 P.M.), DNA, RG 107, Telegrams Collected (Bound); *ibid.*, Letters Received from Bureaus; *ibid.*, RG 108, Telegrams Received; copies (one sent by mail), *ibid.*, Letters Received; *ibid.*, RG 393, Dept. of the East, Letters Sent; DLC-USG, V, 54. On the same day, USG endorsed this telegram. "Respectfully refered to the Sec. of War. It is desirable that the Company of Artillery at Erie, Pa should be returned to Ft. McHenry before Winter sets in. From the within dispa[tch] it will be seen that their detention is solely to guard Arms captured from the Fenians. I would recommend the return of the Arms to the parties from whom taken on bonds that they will not be made use of to make war against a Nation with which the United States is at peace." AES, DNA, RG 107, Letters Received from Bureaus.

On March 29, 1867, Maj. George K. Leet wrote to Meade. "The General-in-Chief directs me to acknowledge the receipt of your communication of 28th inst., with enclosures, relative to an apprehended renewal of Fenian operations on the Canada frontier; and to inform you that the papers will be submitted to the President for instructions. He also directs that you will continue to act under the President's Proclamation of June last until instructions are received countermanding it." LS, *ibid.*, RG 393, Dept. of the East, Letters Received; copies (dated March 30), *ibid.*, RG 108, Letters Sent; DLC-USG, V, 47, 60.

1. On Dec. 28, 1865, Bvt. Brig. Gen. Edward D. Townsend wrote to USG. "Referring to your order of this date to extend the leave of absence of Bvt. Colonel T. W. Sweeny, Major 16th Infantry, I am directed by the Secretary of War to inform you that he has been ordered by the President to be dismissed the Service." ALS, DNA, RG 108, Letters Received. On Dec. 9, Maj. Thomas W. Sweeny, 16th Inf., New York City, had written to Rawlins requesting a six-month leave of absence. ALS, *ibid.*, RG 94, Letters Received, 2648A 1865. On Dec. 28, Bvt. Col. Theodore S. Bowers endorsed this letter. "The Adjutant General will please extend the original leave so as to cover the time since its expiration, and order Major & Bvt Colonel T. W. Sweeny to comply with the order to join his regiment." ES, *ibid.* Sweeny was dismissed as of Dec. 29 for absence without leave, an action presumably connected to his activities as secretary of war for the Fenians. *Ibid.*, ACP, 1836S CB 1866. Probably on Oct. 24, 1866, USG endorsed papers concerning Sweeny's reinstatement in the U.S. Army. "Respectfully returned to the Secretary of War, disapproved. Gen. Sweeney's place has long since been filled, and to reinstate him would be unjust to officers who have remained in service and performed their duty since his dismissal." ES (torn), *ibid.* On Nov. 8, Stanton endorsed these papers. "The order dismissing Major Thos. W. Sweeney 16th Infty Dec 29. 65 will be revoked and he will be restored to the rank of Major in the 16th Infty as of his original date. By order of the President" ES, *ibid.* Sweeny was reinstated as of Nov. 8.

To Maj. Gen. Edward O. C. Ord

St. Louis,[1] Mo. June 7th 1866.

MAJ. GEN. E. O. C. ORD,
COMDG. DEPT. OF THE OHIO
GENERAL:

Under the President's proclamation of yesterday in support of the neutrality laws of the United States, you may use all power necessary to carry it out within your Department. If the civil authorities are taking the matter in hand it may not be necessary for you to do more than to give them such aid, as they may call on you for. Of this you are the best judge. The object is to see that United

States laws are not violated and if it becomes necessary for you to have the same powers, that of using the Military and Naval power of the United States, and the Militia of the States, same as extended to Gn. Meade by the Proclamation refered to, you may assume the power only reporting the necessity to the Chief of Staff, Washington.

Very respectfully
your obt. svt.
U. S. GRANT
Lt. Gn.

ALS (incomplete facsimile), Paul C. Richards, Presidential Catalogue [1982], p. 87; copies, DLC-USG, V, 47, 109; DNA, RG 108, Letters Sent. See preceding telegram.

1. On May 31, 1866, USG wrote to J. Russell Jones. "I start this evening for West Point to attend . . ." Paul C. Richards, Catalogue 179 [1982], no. 295. USG altered plans to go to St. Louis so that he could attend the funeral of Bvt. Lt. Gen. Winfield Scott. See General Orders No. 33, May 30, 1866. USG visited Jones in Chicago on June 4 (*Chicago Tribune*, June 5, 1866), and arrived in St. Louis on June 5. He had arranged his trip to St. Louis in connection with a lawsuit against Joseph W. White to regain possession of Hardscrabble. See *PUSG*, 2, 28*n*. USG appeared in court on June 13, but White's attorneys had the suit continued until Oct. on a technicality. See *Missouri Democrat*, June 12, 14, 1866. USG arrived in Louisville from St. Louis during Saturday morning, June 16, staying at the National Hotel and spending most of June 17 with Bvt. Maj. Gen. Jefferson C. Davis. He left Louisville at 4:00 P.M., June 18, taking a steamboat to Covington to visit his father. He met briefly with Maj. Gen. William T. Sherman in Cincinnati on June 19 and arrived in Washington, D. C., on June 21. See *ibid.*, June 20, 1866; *National Intelligencer*, June 20, 1866.

On June 17, 2:00 P.M., Bvt. Col. Adam Badeau telegraphed to USG, care of Jesse Root Grant, Covington. "Dr. Brenaman says that Mr. Dent is very low. He has been sick three days" ALS (telegram sent), DNA, RG 107, Telegrams Collected (Unbound). At the same time, Badeau sent a similar telegram to Jesse Root Grant. ALS (telegram sent), *ibid.* On June 19, 2:00 P.M., Bvt. Brig. Gen. Cyrus B. Comstock telegraphed to USG, "on train from Cincinnati via Bellaire to Balto." "Mr. Dent has had another attack today and Dr. Norris thinks his condition critical." ALS (telegram sent), *ibid.* On July 3, Emily Dent Casey, New Orleans, telegraphed to USG. "How is Papa?" Telegram received (at 12:45 P.M.), *ibid.*, Telegrams Collected (Bound).

On June 21, James F. Casey, St. Louis, telegraphed to USG. "Dispatch received—No letter yet—whose care did you direct?" Telegram received (at 4:50 P.M.), *ibid.* At 9:25 P.M., USG telegraphed to Casey. "I directed to you in St Louis" Telegram sent, *ibid.* Probably on June 22, 11:30 A.M., USG telegraphed to Casey. "I write again to day" Telegram sent (dated only 1866), *ibid.* See letters to Charles W. Ford, July 6, 9, 1866.

To Brig. Gen. John A. Rawlins

From St Louis Mo. June 7th *18656*

GN J. A. RAWLINS

Call attention of Secy of war Especially to Thomas [*Sherman's*] letter of 26th of May in regard to Indian Supplies called for by Genl Curtis.[1] Every act of Busy Indian Agents demonstrates the importance of transferring Indian Bureau to War Department. Call attention also to Randalls[2] claim to Ft Ridgely If he acquired title after becoming sutler I would recommend his immediate dismissal as sutler

U. S. GRANT
Lt Genl

Telegram received (at 2:40 P.M.), DNA, RG 107, Telegrams Collected (Bound); *ibid.*, RG 108, Telegrams Received; *ibid.*, RG 153, Military Reservation Files, Fort Ridgely, Minn.; copy, DLC-USG, V, 54. On June 9, 1866, Act. Secretary of the Interior William T. Otto wrote to Secretary of War Edwin M. Stanton. "In reply to a letter of yesterday from Inspector General Edmund Schriver, asking for information concerning B. H. Randall's entry of certain lands at Fort Ridgely Minnesota, I have the honor to inclose a letter from the Commissioner of the General Land Office on the subject to this Department, under date of Nov 22d 1865, which contains full details in regard to Mr Randall's entry." LS, DNA, RG 153, Military Reservation Files, Fort Ridgely, Minn. On July 3, USG endorsed this letter. "My recommendation for the dismissal of the sutler was based on the supposition that he had attempted to forestall the U. S. in getting a title to the land in question, knowing that the land was necessary to the Government. If this does not appear to be the case, my recommendation is revoked." ES, *ibid.* On June 8, 1867, Bvt. Maj. Gen. Edward D. Townsend wrote a memorandum for Stanton reviewing Benjamin H. Randall's claim to the land beneath Fort Ridgely. Through an oversight, the government had not filed a plat for the Fort Ridgely Military Reservation; consequently, Randall, post sutler since 1853, had secured title in 1861. DS, *ibid.*

1. See letter to Maj. Gen. William T. Sherman, April 18, 1866.
2. See William Watts Folwell, *A History of Minnesota* (Rev. ed., St. Paul, 1961), II, 127*n*–28*n*, 131*n*.

To James Harlan

Respectfully refered to the Hon. Sec. of the Interior[.] I am not personally acqua[in]ted with Mr. Wickersham[1] but I know the writer of this letter well and would give great weight to his endorsement. Mr. Crane[2] is a Methodist preacher and was the Chaplain to the regiment Commanded by me at the begining of the rebellion. So far as he entertained politics he was a Democrat but a staunch supporter of the War from the start.—Mr. Wickersham having served during the War I would not hesitate to recommend him above any one who had taken no part in it. Especially would I make this recommendation above that of a Sutler, a class who followed the Army solely to make money out of the War and but few of whom entertained a sentiment of patriotism. I understand a Sutler is one of the competitors for the office sought.

U. S. GRANT
Lt. Gn.

WASHINGTON, D. C.
JUNE 25 1866.

AES, CSmH. Written on a letter of June 4 from James L. Crane, Springfield, Ill., to USG. "My friend Col. Dudley Wickersham is an applicant for the pension office in this city I have known him for more than ten years, he is fully competant for the position, & is every way reliable. He is an old resident of this county & is a gentleman highly esteemed by all his acquaintances. He has been in the active service during the war & is faithful & true in every department that he undertakes. If you can do any thing for him, General, I will regard it as a personal favor, for he has been for years one of my most reliable & agreeable friends." ALS, *ibid.*

1. Dudley Wickersham, born in Ky. in 1819, moved to Springfield in 1843, becoming a merchant. Appointed lt. col., 10th Ill. Cav., as of Nov. 25, 1861, promoted to col. as of May 15, 1862, Wickersham resigned as of May 10, 1864. He was confirmed as assessor of internal revenue for the eighth district of Ill. as of July 23, 1866.

2. See *PUSG*, 2, 56.

To Bvt. Maj. Gen. George W. Cullum

June 25th *1866*

DEAR GENERAL:

Yours of the 23d announcing that Fred. is a full fledged Cadet, &c. is received. I supposed he would pass his first examination and hope he will be able to get through all succeeding ones. He is young and has had no advantages for his age.

I think of going to West Point about the 7th of July, with my family, to spend a few days.

Yours Truly
U. S. GRANT

ALS, James S. Schoff, New York, N. Y.

To Edwin M. Stanton

Respectfully forwarded.

The recommendations contained in the endorsement of the Chief of Ordnance are approved, except the proposition to place new patent arms in the hands of troops for trial.

There being such a large number of arms on hand capable of economical alteration, it seems unnecessary at present to experiment with new arms, many improvements in which will no doubt be made by the time they will be actually required

The superiority of the 45 calibr[e] in accuracy, range and [penetra]tion, seems to hav[e been p]laced beyond a dou[bt—bu]t a uniformity of [calib]re being so desirable, a[nd there] being such a large nu[mber of] arms of calibre 50 [on hand] it [may] be advisable [to a]dopt this calibre.

U. S. GRANT
Lieut. Gen

HDQRS. AUS
JUNE 26. 66.

ES, DNA, RG 156, Correspondence of Ordnance Boards, Special File, Entry 1012; copy (misdated June 27, 1866), DLC-USG, V, 58. *HED*, 39-2-1, p. 701. Written on an ordnance board report submitted on June 4 by Maj. Gen. Winfield S. Hancock. *Ibid.*, pp. 668–700. On June 16, Brig. Gen. Alexander B. Dyer, chief of ordnance, endorsed this report. "Respectfully submitted to the Secretary of War through the Lieutenant General commanding the army. The board is correct in its conclusions that, of all the calibres tested by it, that of .45″ will give the best results in accuracy, range, and penetration, with the same weight of powder and lead, but the superiority of this calibre over the .50″ calibre is not, in my opinion, sufficient to counterbalance the objections to so small a calibre arising from the great length of the cartridge. . . . A proper plan for the alteration of the Springfield rifle musket, of which there are about one million in the arsenals, is so great a desideratum that no one plan should be adopted until after it shall have been fully tested in the hands of troops. Several methods, appearing to possess great merit, have been brought to the notice of this department and of the board, of which the following are, in my opinion, worthy of being tested by troops, viz: 1. Berdan's, recommended by the board; 2. Major Yates's, presented after the adjournment of the board; 3. Remington's; 4. Roberts's; 5. Allin's, made at Springfield armory. . . ." *Ibid.*, pp. 700–1.

On Jan. 26, USG had written to Secretary of War Edwin M. Stanton. "I would respectfully request that the accompanying order be issued. . . ." Copies, DLC-USG, V, 47, 109; DNA, RG 108, Letters Sent. For War Dept. Special Orders No. 40, see *HED*, 39-2-1, p. 668. On May 27, USG wrote to Bvt. Maj. Gen. Edward D. Townsend. "When the Board now engaged in examining Arms is dissolved authorize Gens. Griffin and Buchanan to delay Ninety days before joining their line duties. After the Board reports it may be necessary to reconvene them to examine further into the subject they are now engaged on. I mention this because I am going to leave the city on Thursday next to be absent until about the 20th of June and during that time the Board will make their report." ALS, DNA, RG 94, Letters Received, 426A 1866.

On Oct. 6, Hiram Berdan, Washington, D. C., wrote to USG. "Having learned that you asked for the board to be appointed that recommended my gun for adoption, and having been informed by the Chief of Ordnance that he would not alter the muskets on the plan recommended by the board, and believing, as I do, that you are very anxious to get the best gun for your troops, I take the liberty of calling your attention to the defects in the plan about to be adopted, for the alteration of 25,000, muskets, with the request that you will use your influence with the Secretary of War, to have all, or a portion of the Old Board reconvened, or a new board appointed, to test the gun proposed by the Chief of Ordnance; also, to test my gun with or without the recent improvements, with orders to recommend one of the plans for adoption. . . ." ALS (misdated 1846), *ibid.*, RG 108, Letters Received. See *SRC*, 55-3-1653.

To Mrs. Crook

Washington, D. C. June 30th *1866*.

MRS. CROOK,
MY DEAR MADAM,
It affords me pleasure to testify to the services of Gn. Crook throughout the rebellion. In Western Va. in the early part of the rebellion, he did distinguished services which made it desirable to have him returned to that command. After a brief service in Tenn. he was returned to West Va. where his services gave entire satisfaction and for which he was given command of the Dept. which he retained up to his capture. In the last great struggle of of the War he commanded a Division under Gen. Sheridan, with distinguished gallantry, contributing largely to our crowning success.

There are but few officers who had it in their power to render more services than Gen. Crook or who performed their duties with more zeal and ability.

Yours Truly
U. S. GRANT
Lt. Gn.

ALS, ICarbS.

On Aug. 17, 1866, Maj. Gen. Philip H. Sheridan, New Orleans, wrote to USG. "General Crook has written to me several times in reference to his appointment as Colonel of one of the new regiments He is a good soldier and if anything can be done for him it would be gratifying to me. I have heretofore recommended him to favorable consideration on this subject." LS, DNA, RG 108, Letters Received. Bvt. Maj. Gen. George Crook was appointed maj., 3rd Inf., as of July 18, and lt. col., 23rd Inf., as of July 28.

To Andrew Johnson

WASHINGTON, D. C., July 4, 1866

His Excellency A. Johnson, President of the United States:

This will introduce to you Gen. G. H. GORDON, of Masaachusetts, an applicant, I believe, for a civil appointment. Gen. GORDON, being a graduate of West Point of about my own date, I have known him long, and can speak of his character from personal knowledge. He served gallantly in the Mexican War, was there twice wounded and brevetted for gallant and meritorious services. In the late rebellion he served throughout the conflict, rising from Colonel to Brigadier, and Brevet Major-General. While the army was holding LEE in Richmond and Petersburg, I found the latter was receiving supplies, either through the inefficiency or with the permission of the officer se[l]ected by Gen. BUTLER for the command of Norfolk from Norfolk, through Albermarle and Chesapeake Canal. Knowing Gen. GORDON to be honest and capable, I attached him to the Army of the James to take that command, knowing that no pe[rs]uasion could make him swerve from his duty. I can speak of Gen. GORDON knowingly, as being reliable in the [tru]est sense, and capable.

I have the honor to be, very respectfully, your obedient servant,

U. S. GRANT, Lieut.-Gen.

New York Times, Oct. 26, 1868. Publication of this letter occurred during a Mass. congressional contest between Republican Benjamin F. Butler and Democrat Richard Henry Dana when George H. Gordon and Judson Kilpatrick campaigned against Butler. On Dec. 14, 1866, Gordon was nominated as U.S. marshal for the district of Mass., but was not confirmed. On March 16, 1869, Edward W. Kinsley, Boston, wrote to USG. "In the scramble for office I am fearful that our friend Genl Geo H. Gordon (with whose military record you are familiar, and whose loyaly, honesty, and capacity are unquestioned) will be overlooked—. . . Genl Gordon is a modest man, and very likely will not ask for any office—He went into and came out of the war, *poor*. If he could have the consulate to London, or Havana, it would do him good, and he would well represent the United States—. . ." ALS, DNA, RG 59, Letters of Application and Recommendation. On Dec. 6, USG nominated Gordon for collector of internal revenue, 7th District, Mass.

To James R. Doolittle

Washington July 5th *1866*

HON. J. R. DOOLITTLE,
U. S. SENATE,
DEAR SIR,

Understanding that a few Gentlemen, among them yourself, are about to join in a recommendation for "Naval Officer" or "Agt." for the Port of New York induces me to say one word in favor of Col. Hillyer who is among the many applicants for that office. I will say in the begining that I do not desire to influance political appointments, ~~further~~ or recommendations, further than to give an opinion of individual applicants.

Col. Hillyer is an old St. Louis acquaintance of mine and one who I thought most highly of then as well as now. When first appointed Brigadier General the first two persons I thought of asking to take position on my staff were Col. Hillyer & Gn. Rawlins. Neither I suppose thought of such position until asked to accept, which both did. Col. Hillyer served in the capasity of a Staff officer near two years when he resigned for no reason of dissatisfaction either with the service, or of ~~mine~~ me with his services. I have taken frequent occations ~~of~~ to speak~~ing~~ of him favorably to the President ~~of~~ as a man of great ability and one well qualified for the position he sought, or all most any other within his gift. My personal attachment for Col. Hillyer is such as to induce me to go as far in his behalf as I am willing to go in the behalf of any one for an office where the contest is so great. I should be individually better pleased to see Col. Hillyer receive the appointment he asks than to see any other one whos name I have heard mentioned in connection with the office.

Very respectfully
your obt. svt.
U. S. GRANT

ALS, DNA, RG 56, Naval Officer Applications. U.S. Senator James R. Doolittle of Wis. forwarded this letter to President Andrew Johnson. AES (undated), *ibid.* On July 3, 1866, Bvt. Col. Adam Badeau had written to U.S. Representative

Elihu B. Washburne. ". . . You see by the enclosed scrap how even Gen Grant's staff are misrepresented. You know that most of us do not endorse or attack Col. Hillyer; and that at any rate we scrupulously abstain from any attempt at dabbling in personal politics. If you get a chance, wont you say so to Congressmen. It would not be desirable to make a public contradiction, but it is desirable, especially at this juncture, that we should not be represented as politicians, or partisans" ALS, DLC-Elihu B. Washburne. On July 12, USG, West Point, N. Y., wrote to William S. Hillyer. "Who ever informed the Editor of the Herald that I have in any manner opposed your appointment as Naval Officer told what was untrue and what there was no foundation for. As far as I allow myself to go in making recommendations I have gone in your favor for the appointment alluded to, civil appointments I mean. You are not the 'oldest inhabitant' but you have no other home but New York City and are unquestionably as eligible for office as any other citizen." ALS, Robert C. Hillyer, San José, Costa Rica. On July 13, George P. Ihrie referred a copy of this letter to Doolittle. AES, DNA, RG 56, Naval Officer Applications. No appointment followed.

General Orders No. 44

[*July 6, 1866*]

GENERAL ORDER NO.

Department, District and Post Commanders in the States lately in rebellion are hereby directed to arrest all persons who have been or may hereafter be charged with the commission of crimes and offences against officers, agents ~~and~~ citizens and inhabitants of the United States, irrespective of color, in cases where the civil authorities have failed, neglected, or are unable to arrest and bring such parties to trial; and to detain them in military confinement until such time as a proper judicial tribunal may be ready and willing to try them.

A strict and prompt enforcement of this order is required.

By command of Lieutenant General Grant

ADf (in the hand of Bvt. Col. Ely S. Parker), DNA, RG 94, Letters Received, 524A 1866; copy (printed as General Orders No. 44, July 6, 1866), *ibid.*, RG 107, Letters Received from Bureaus. See telegram to Maj. Gen. John G. Foster, Aug. 17, 1866; letter to Edwin M. Stanton, Nov. 22, 1866; following letter. On July 3, Maj. Gen. Oliver O. Howard, Bureau of Refugees, Freedmen, and Abandoned Lands, had written to USG. "I have the honor to state the case of the murder of Lt. J. B. Blanding 21st Reg't V. R. C. an officer of the Freedmen's Bureau, at Grenada, Miss, on the night of the 30th of April last. Lieut. Blanding was walking along a street; when a man stepped out from an alley, and fired upon him three times; one of the shots inflicting a fatal wound. Though the Lieutenant gave an accurate description of the murderer, the civil authorities have failed to apprehend any one up to the present time. I hear unofficially that a citizen who denounced the murder as infamous, has himself suffered a brutal outrage. Also the case of an assault upon Capt C. C. Richardson late agent of this Bureau at Thomasville Ga; He was shot at twice, and wounded, by a man named Lightfoot, on account of a fine imposed upon him by Capt Richardson while he was acting as agent of the Bureau. This fine had been imposed, for his unmercifully beating a freedman in his employ. Lightfoot has been arrested, but no further proceedings had transpired at last accounts. Again, more than a month since, I believe the 24th of May last, a freedman was shot by a man named Lovett, near Leesburg Va. The civil authorities have failed, and are afraid to act. The sheriff says he wishes the military authorities, would take the matter off his hands. The above are three sample cases, which may certainly be covered by a military order. The simple issuing of an order by yourself would go far to prevent the attacks upon officers of the Government on duty." LS, DNA, RG 108, Letters Received.

On Aug. 6, Maj. Gen. George G. Meade, Philadelphia, telegraphed to USG. "I forwarded telegram rec'd from Maj Gen'l Terry and my reply thereto for ~~your~~ such action as you may deem proper—I think it best to test the question whether the civil authorities of Virginia will or will not respect General orders number forty four 44—Please notify me of your decision in case my order to Gen'l Terry is countermanded . . . '*From* Richmond Va Aug 5th *186~~5~~6*. MAJ GEN MEADE, Two arrests have been made in General Miles District under General Grants order forty four 44—for shooting at & beating negroes—A Justice of the Peace caused the men to be arrested but was intimidated by them & stated the he could not try them—They were then arrested by military authority. They have been now sued out a writ of habeas corpus—I respectfully ask for instructions as to what course shall be taken as to this writ Will send full report by mail tonight (signed) ALFRED H TERRY Maj Gen Comdg' 'Philada Aug 6th 1866 MAJ GEN'L TERRY Richmond Va You will produce the bodies of the prisoners before the court making a full return showing the circumstances of the cases & the authority under which the arrests were made. This decision has been reported to the War Dept in Case superior authority deems it proper to overrule (signed) GEO G MEADE Maj Gen U S A" Telegram received (at 12:55 P.M.), *ibid.*, RG 107, Telegrams Collected (Bound); *ibid.*, RG 108, Telegrams Received; copies (one sent by mail), *ibid.*, Letters Received; *ibid.*, RG 393, Military Div. of the Atlantic, Letters Sent; (Meade to USG only) *ibid.*, Dept. of Va. and N. C., Letters Received; DLC-USG, V, 54. On Aug. 5, Maj. Gen. Alfred H. Terry, Richmond, wrote to Bvt. Brig. Gen. Simon F. Barstow, adjt. for Meade, enclosing additional reports. LS and copies, DNA, RG 108, Letters Received. On Aug. 7, Meade endorsed these papers. "Respectfully forwarded. On the receipt of General Terry's telegram announcing the serving the writ of Habeas Corpus, instructions were sent him to produce the bodies of the prisoners in court and make a return setting forth the facts of the case and the authority for the arrest. If the Court will not acknowledge this authority and the Civil Power is determined neither to act itself, nor permit the military to do so, I should then urge the proclamation of Martial Law as the only remedy for existing evils." ES, *ibid.* On Aug. 15, Terry wrote to Brig. Gen. John A. Rawlins. "I have the honor to forward herewith a copy of a report made by Lt. Col. *Mallory* of the Veteran Reserve Corps, an Inspector of the Freedmen's Bureau, in regard to the recent disturbances in Accomac County. I understand from Major General Meade, that he has already brought the matter to your attention and I now forward this report as containing a much fuller statement of the matter than the one heretofore sent. I have directed that a company of Infantry be sent to Drummondtown in that county for the purpose of overawing any who may be disposed to create further disturbance." LS, *ibid.* The enclosures, describing intimidation and disarming of Negroes by whites, are *ibid.*

To Maj. Gen. George H. Thomas

Washington, D. C. July 6th *1866*

MAJ. GN. G. H. THOMAS,
COMD.G MILL. DIV.
GENERAL:

This morning I sent despatch directing you to send three or four Companies of 5th Cavalry to Memphis for the purpose of operating in North Mississippi to suppress outrages in that section. It is probable that before these troops reach the scene of their operations orders will be issued which will clearly define their powers and duties. In the absence of orders however you may direct Stoneman to keep direction of these troops even though they act beyond the limits of his Department. If you think better however of these troops receiving instructions from the Dept. Commander where they are acting have it so.—The object to be attained is to suppress violence that is now being committed by outlawry in North Mississippi. If the Civil Authorities fail to make arrests for past violence let the troops make them and hold the parties in confinement until they, the Civil Authorities, give satisfactory evidence that justice will be done, or until you receive orders more clearly defining the course to be pursued.

Direct Stoneman to have collated the names and residences of the of the principle actors in the late disgraceful Memphis riots so that if orders are telegraphed to him to make arrests he can do so at once.[1] Of course it is not necessary to caution him as to the necessity of keeping this matter strictly from the ears of the parties interested.

Very respectfully
your obt. svt.
U. S. GRANT
Lt. Gn.

ALS, DNA, RG 393, Dept. of Tenn., Letters Received. See letter to Edwin M. Stanton, July 7, 1866. On July 6, 1866, 9:30 A.M., USG had telegraphed to Maj. Gen. George H. Thomas. "Send three companies Fifth Cavalry, the whole battalion if you can spare it to Memphis Tenn for the purpose of operating in North Miss, and stopping outrages in that section" Telegram sent (misdated July 5), *ibid.*, RG 107, Telegrams Collected (Bound); copies (misdated July 5), *ibid.*, RG 108, Letters Sent; DLC-USG, V, 47, 109. On the same day, Thomas, Nashville, telegraphed to USG. "Yours of 9.30 A. m. today rec'd. I will send three 3 Co's. as I think it essential to the peace of Tennessee that one 1 Co. should be retained here." Telegram received (at 7:00 P.M.), DNA, RG 107, Telegrams Collected (Bound); *ibid.*, RG 108, Telegrams Received; copies, *ibid.*, RG 393, Dept. of the Cumberland, Telegrams Sent; DLC-USG, V, 54.

On July 7, Bvt. Maj. Gen. Edward D. Townsend wrote to USG. "The Secretary of War directs me to send you the enclosed letter to Maj. Genl. G. H. Thomas, in relation to intervention in cases provided for in recent Act of Congress, which he desires you to forward to General Thomas." ALS, DNA, RG 393, Dept. of Tenn., Letters Received. On the same day, Townsend wrote to Thomas. "A copy of a letter of instructions to General T. J. Wood is herewith transmitted to you for information as to the President's views in such cases. I am instructed to add that, as the Act of Congress now affords jurisdiction to the Federal Courts, with ample means for judicial protection, it is not deemed necessary for military authority to intervene in such cases, or in any way interfere with the action of judicial tribunals having cognizance of them. You will therefore be governed by this view in your administration of affairs throughout the limits of your command." ALS, *ibid.* He enclosed a copy of a telegram of June 6 from Secretary of War Edwin M. Stanton to Maj. Gen. Thomas J. Wood, Vicksburg. "The attention of this Department has been called to the case of Portwood against Treasury Agent Harrison Johnson, pending in the Circuit Court of Lowndes County Miss., and to your telegram to Mr Johnson, dated at Vicksburg the 23d. of April, directing him to plead Genl. Grant's Order No. 3, in bar of said suit.—As the act of Congress now affords jurisdiction of such cases to the Federal Courts, with ample means for judicial protection, it is not deemed necessary for military authority to intervene in behalf of Mr. Johnson, or in any way interfere with the action of judicial tribunals having cognizance of his case. You will therefore abstain from interference in the case." Copy, *ibid.*

1. On Aug. 15, Thomas telegraphed to USG. "The names of the leaders in the recent Memphis riots have been clearly ascertained. Shall they be arrested in accordance with the requirements of General Order number forty four from your Headquarters? The grand jury has been in session since the riot and before

retiring for deliberation were especially charged by his Honor, Judge Hunter of the criminal court to require into the riot cases and indict the offenders, but notwithstanding the special charge of the judge the grand jury failed to take any notice whatever of the offenders or of the riot." Telegram received (at 4:45 P.M.), *ibid.*, RG 107, Telegrams Collected (Bound); *ibid.*, RG 108, Telegrams Received; copies, *ibid.*, RG 393, Dept. of the Cumberland, Telegrams Sent; DLC-USG, V, 54; DLC-Edwin M. Stanton. On Aug. 16, USG endorsed this telegram. "Respectfully refered to the Sec. of War for instructions. I do not feel authorized to order the arrest of the Memphis rioters but I think it ought to be done with a strong hand to show that where the civil authorities fail to notice crime of this sort there is a power that will do so." AES, *ibid.* On Aug. 18, 1:00 P.M., USG telegraphed to Thomas. "Your dispatch relative to arresting Memphis rioters has been submitted to the President. Instructions will be sent you on receipt of answer" Telegram sent, DNA, RG 107, Telegrams Collected (Bound); copies, *ibid.*, RG 108, Letters Sent; *ibid.*, RG 393, Dept. of the Cumberland, Telegrams Received; DLC-USG, V, 47, 60.

To Charles W. Ford

Washington D. C. July 6th *1866*

DEAR FORD,

Enclosed I send a note endorsed for the benefit of Jas. F. Casey to be negociated for his benefit. I believe in addition to this he is to send a Deed of Trust on some land which he has in St. Louis, Co. Probably he has explained the whole matter to you.

All are well here. In a day or two I start to West Point to spend a week and visit Fred. who is now a full fledged Cadet, full of ambition to go through the four years ordeal before him.

I promised Benton to send him a box of fine Cigars. If you receive one from Washington concider them from me for Benton. Every morning when I come to the office I forget to bring them down with me to express to him but will think of it some day. When they do reach you present them with my complements.

Yours Truly
U. S. GRANT

ALS, USG 3.

To Edwin M. Stanton

Washington, D. C. July 7th *1866*

HON. E. M. STANTON,
SEC. OF WAR,
SIR:

I have the honor of transmitting the report of the Commission appointed to investigate the causes and extent of the riot in Memphis Tenn. in May last. ~~F~~

From the evidence taken before the Commission it appears that on May 1st the first collission of any importance occured arising from an arrest made by the police of some disorderly negroes. Here, judging from the testimony, and the relative number of Whites & negroes killed, the outbreak on the part of the negroes ceased. But their massacre commenced and until the end of Wednesday night there was a scene of murder, arson, rape & robery in which the victims were all helpless and unresisting negroes stamping lasting disgrace upon the civil authorities that permitted them.

The testimony shews that two Whites were killed and two wounded while forty of the blacks were killed and fifty four wounded.

The negroes were robbed of an aggregate sum of $19.004.85 and the value of the negro churches, school houses and dwellings burned is estimated at $53.379.00. The mob seems, by the evidence before me, to have been composed of the lower class of Whites aided and abetted by policemen and firemen, while the City Recorder, Mr. Creighton, incited its begining. It does not appear that the city authorities took any efficient steps to suppress the riot. The only protection the sufferers had was from the Military force of the United States, stationed in Memphis, which was inadequate for putting down such a riot speedily.

Gen. Thomas, in transmitting this report, asks instructions upon several points which are mere matters of law and cannot be answered from these Hd Qrs. I would respectfully submit those questions for the decision of the Sec. of War or Atty. Gn. of the United States.

The civil authorities of Memphis having failed to make any arrests in this case I would recommend that the leaders in this riot be arrested by the Military, and held by them, until the civil authorities give evidence of their ability, and willingness, to take cognizance of their cases and to give a fare trial.—I would also recommend that legal proceedings be instituted against the city of Memphis for the payment of all damages accruing to the United States in consequence of the riot.

I have the honor to be
Very respectfully
your obt. svt.
U. S. GRANT
Lt. Gn.

ALS, DNA, RG 94, Letters Received, 412T 1866. On June 14, 1866, Maj. Gen. George Stoneman, Memphis, had written to Maj. Gen. George H. Thomas submitting a lengthy report of a military commission convened to investigate the Memphis riots. ALS and DS, *ibid.* On June 15, Thomas, Nashville, endorsed these papers. "Respectfully forwarded to the Adjutant General of the Army for the information of the Lieutenant General Commanding U S A and for instructions as to what course shall be pursued to secure indemnification to the United States for expenses incurred in suppressing the riot. What action shall be taken in case of attempts to release on writs of habeus corpus prisoners who may be arrested for participation in the riots; and should they be tried by Military Tribunal or turned over to the United States Court for that purpose? Also, what steps shall be taken to secure indemnity to private individuals for damages sustained at the hands of the rioters?" ES, *ibid.* On July 13, Attorney Gen. James Speed wrote to President Andrew Johnson. "Lieutenant General Grant's letter to the Secretary of War, of date July 7, 1866, which you have referred to me, with the papers that accompanied that letter, show that the riots in Memphis, Tenn., in the early part of May resulted in most disgusting scenes of murder, arson, rape and robbery, in which most of the victims were helpless and unresisting colored citizens. Gen. Grant well remarks that such a scene stamps lasting disgrace upon the civil authorities of Memphis. Inasmuch as the civil authorities have thus far failed to arrest the perpetrators of these wanton outrages, or to do anything towards redressing the injuries and damages sustained, he asks whether the military shall interfere. Whilst this conduct is so disgraceful to human nature, subversive of good order and peace, and derogatory to the dignity of the laws of the State of Tennessee, it constitutes no offence against the laws and dignity of the United States of America. Under our frame of government, the States are charged with the duty of protecting citizens from outrage, by public prosecutions, and the citizens themselves have the right to appear in the appropriate courts, State or national, for the redress of any private wrongs that they may have sustained. The military stationed at Memphis performed their duty in aiding to suppress the mob violence. Having done that, they have and can have nothing to do with the redress of private grievances, or prosecutions for public wrongs. The Courts, State and national, are open in Tennessee, and there is no war. Under the State laws, as well as United States laws, the injured party may appeal to the courts for redress." LS, *ibid.* See *HRC*, 39-1-101.

On May 12, 1:05 P.M., USG had telegraphed to Stoneman. "Please report by telegraph so far as you are able to do at once the circumstances of the recent riot at Memphis" Telegram sent, DNA, RG 107, Telegrams Collected (Bound); copies, *ibid.*, RG 108, Letters Sent; DLC-USG, V, 47, 109. On the same day, Stoneman telegraphed to USG. "Your telegram of this date received. The 3rd Colored Artillery has been stationed here since its organization and consequently were not under the best of discipline: large numbers of the men had what they call families living in South Memphis contiguous to the fort in which the soldiers were stationed. These soldiers had been used as the instruments to execute the orders of Government agents such as Provost Marshalls Bureau, agents &c and consequently had been more or less brought directly into contact with the law breaking portion of the community, and the Police which is far from being composed of the best class of residents here, and composed principally of Irishmen, who consider the negro as his competitor and natural enemy. Many negro Soldiers have from time to time been arrested by the police, & many whites including some of the police have been arrested by the negro soldiers, and in both cases those arrested have not unfrequently been treated with a harshness altogether unnecessary. These remarks and hints will lead you to reflections which will explain and indicate to you the state of feeling which existed between the negro soldiers and their sympathizers and the lower class of whites and their sympathizers, in which last are included agitators Demagogues and office seekers—The testimony before the commission which I have assembled to investigate the circumstances connected with the riot shows that at about 4. o'clock Monday afternoon April 30th four 4 policemen were walking down Cousey Street and met three or four negroes: they jostled each other on the sidewalk, an altercation occurred, one of the policemen struck a negro with a pistol and was in return struck by another negro with a cane. There was no further trouble though a good deal of excitement amongst the negroes during that night. Incident on this encounter about 4. o'clock P. M. Tuesday May 1st a crowd of from fifty to seventy five negroes, mostly discharged soldiers were congregated together near the corners of main and South Streets; the greater portion of these negroes were intoxicated. Six policemen approached the crowd and arrested two of the most boisterous of the negroes, the policemen proceeded to conduct these two negroes towards the station house being followed by the crowd of negroes which increased as they proceeded and who used very insulting & threatening language & accompanied their threats by firing pistols into the air: the police turned and fired upon the negroes wounding one, one of the negro prisoners escaped and the other was released by the police. The negros returned the fire wounding one of the police. The police force of the city together with a large crowd of citizens congregated together in the vicinity of South Street and being very much infuriated proceeded to shoot, beat, and threaten every negro met with in that portion of the city. This was continued until about midnight on Tuesday night when it was quelled by the interferance of a small detachment of U. S. troops. Wednesday morning arrived and found large crowds of people collected together in South Memphis most of whom were armed: they remained there until about 1-o'clock P. M when they were dispersed by a detachment of U. S. soldiers which had been employed during the day in keeping the discharged negro soldiers in and the white people out of the fort—During the day several negro shanties were burned down. About 10. o'clock Wednesday night a party of mounted men began to set fire to the negro schoolhouses churches & dwelling-houses. It is hoped that the investigations now being had will result in identifying the parties engaged. During Tuesday and Wednesday several inoffensive negroes were killed and many maltreated and beaten in different parts of the city. The number killed & wounded in the riot, as far as can be ascertained by the commission were one white man killed, shot by white man behind him,—one white man wounded, shot by negroes. The number of negroes shot & beaten to death has not yet been ascertained I will give you the information when procured. Frequent applications were made for arms and for permission to organize a militia force all of which were refused and Thursday I issued an order prohibiting any persons under what-so-ever pretext from assembling anywhere armed or unarmed. Great fears were entertained that other buildings, such as the Freedmen's Bureau buildings of the Memphis post, would be burned down, but if any such intentions were had the disposition made of the small force at my disposal prevented the realization. An attempt was made by some parties to gain possession of the muskets which a few days before had been turned in by the 3d Colored Artillery. Every officer and man here was on duty day and night during the riot. On the 4th they were relieved by a detachment, I had ordered over from Nashville. As before stated the rioters were composed of the Police, Firemen & the rabble and negrohaters in general with a sprinkling of Yankeehaters all led on and encouraged by demagogues & office hunters, and most of them under the influence of whiskey. It appears It appears in evidence before the commission that John Creighton, Recorder of the City made a speech to the rioters in which he said 'we are not prepared but let us prepare to clean every negro son-of-a-bitch out of town'. Very few parolled confederats were mixed up with the rioters on Tuesday and Wednesday, the large portion being registered voters. Who composed the Incendiaries on Wednesday night remains to be developed" Telegram received (on May 13, noon), DNA, RG 107, Telegrams Collected (Bound); *ibid.*, RG 108, Telegrams Received; copies, *ibid.*, RG 94, Letters Received, 328T 1866; *ibid.*, RG 393, Dept. of Tenn., Telegrams Sent; DLC-USG, V, 54. On May 18, Stoneman telegraphed to USG. "I have the honor to report that it appears upon investigation by the Commission that there were killed outright during the recent riots in Memphis Tenn, twenty four (24) negroes Eight (8) of whom were discharged soldiers" Telegram received (at 5:00 P.M.), DNA, RG 107, Telegrams Collected (Bound); *ibid.*, RG 108, Telegrams Received; copies, *ibid.*, RG 393, Dept. of Tenn., Telegrams Sent; DLC-USG, V, 54. See *HED*, 39-1-122.

To Rear Admiral Charles H. Davis

Washington, D. C. July 7th *1866*

REAR ADMIRAL, C. H. DAVIS,
U. S. NAVY,
DEAR SIR:

Your letter of the 3d of July alluding to the interest which I have heretofore expressed in favor of a canal to connect the Atlantic & Pacific Oceans is received. I firmly believe the scheme practicable and if it is there is no doubt but that in this age of enterprize the work will be done. I regard it as of vast political importance to this country that no European Goverment should hold such a work. For this reason I have endeavored, for the last year, to get such a thorough survey made, by the Goverment of the United States, through the territory of the Columbian Goverment, as would fully determine whether such a project is feasable; not doubting but that on the presentation of such feasability, American Capital and an American Company, under some treaty that could easily be arranged between the two Goverments, would undertake it.

To carry out this project an appropriati[on] by Congress, but what amount I could scarcsely say, would be necessary.

At the instance of Capt. Ammen, U. S. N. and myself, the Sec. of State has put himself in communication with the Columbian Government, with the view of obtaining the authority to make a survey through their territory for the purpose of determining the practicability of an interoceanic Canal.

Very respectfully
your obt. svt.
U. S. GRANT
Lt. Gn.

ALS, Free Library of Philadelphia, Philadelphia, Pa. On July 3, 1866, Rear Admiral Charles H. Davis, Washington, D. C., had written to USG. "I need make no apology for addressing you on the subject of Inter-Oceanic Communication through the American Isthmus; for I am well aware that you have, for a long time, given to this question a great deal of attention. It will interest you to learn that my recent study of the subject has led me to the conclusion, that our efforts towards the solution of this important problem must be directed to the Isthmus of Darien, which is, with the exception of one or two narrow lines of research, an almost unknown region. Enough however has been developed to justify a zealous expectation of finding a depression in the Cordilleras, such as will admit of the construction of a canal without locks and without a tunnel, at a cost of time, labor, and money, not exceeding those bestowed upon other great works of the day. On many accounts, which I need not repeat in this letter, the next season promises to be a particularly favorable moment for making the necessary explorations and surveys. Unless, however, some appropriation is obtained from Congress at this Session, a whole year must be lost before the surveys can be commenced. My maps and plans are nearly completed, and I expect to send in my report in the course of the week; and I venture to express the hope, General, that you will make known to others, as you have often done to myself, the favor with which you regard the further prosecution by the government of its surveys in this region." ALS, USG 3.

To Charles W. Ford

July 9th *1866*

DEAR FORD,

Enclosed I send deed from Mr. Dent to Mrs. Casey for price of land. Please have stamp put on it and have deed recorded and charge me with expense incured.

I sent last saturday a box of cigars to you for Benton. You can say to him that I know they are imported for I sent to Havanna for them myself.

Yours Truly
U. S. GRANT

ALS, DLC-Charles W. Ford.

To Maj. Gen. William T. Sherman

West Point[1]
July 12th 1866.

DEAR SHERMAN,

Your letter of yesterday is just received. If it was my intintion to be absent any time I would join you in your travels through the

East by all means. But I only run up here to spend the week with Fred. who has entered the present 4th class and shall not probably go any place else. I have never been to New Port and did think it possible that I might run up there Saturday night and remain until Monday night. It is not probable however that I will go. If the Army Bill passes Congress it will be necessary for me to remain at Washington until appointments are made, recruiting service organized &c.

I telegraphed to you yesterday to Boston advising you that $1.000.000 had been ordered transfered to Gen. Easton to be expended under your orders in sheltering troops, stores &c.[2]

I should enjoy the trip through New England with you very much and but for the fact that I do not think I should be away from Washington long at this time I would go—

Yours
U. S. GRANT

ALS, DLC-William T. Sherman. See letter to Maj. Gen. William T. Sherman, July 21, 1866. On July 5, 1866, Maj. Gen. William T. Sherman, Salem, Ill., telegraphed to USG. "I start this P m for New York & Dartmouth. attended here a large celebration but Logan & Oglesby spoke more politics than I think the national occasion warranted I do not wish to be compromised by their speeches." Telegram received (at noon), DNA, RG 107, Telegrams Collected (Bound); *ibid.*, RG 108, Telegrams Received; copy, DLC-USG, V, 54.

1. On July 2, Monday, George G. Pride, Fifth Avenue Hotel, New York City, telegraphed to USG. "Please telegraph me when I can see you at the Point" Telegram received (at 5:25 P.M.), DNA, RG 107, Telegrams Collected (Bound). At 6:10 P.M., USG telegraphed to Pride. "On Tuesday next." Telegram sent, *ibid.*, Telegrams Collected (Unbound). On July 3, USG wrote to Bvt. Maj. Gen. George W. Cullum, West Point. ". . . It would be very much more pleasant for me to be at a private house than at a crowded hotel and I will gladly accept the invitation if my family will not be too large for you to accommodate. Mrs. Grant and three children will be with me. If this is too much of a good thing please dont hesitate about saying so . . ." Sotheby Sale 5301, March 27, 1985, no. 170. On July 5, 10:15 P.M., USG telegraphed to Reverend Ten Broeck, Burlington College, Burlington, N. J. "Please send Ulysses home to-morrow with all his baggage. I go away and wish to take him with me." ALS (telegram sent), DNA, RG 107, Telegrams Collected (Unbound). On July 16, USG, New York City, telegraphed to Bvt. Col. Ely S. Parker. "We shall reach Washington at five & a half tomorrow morning. Order carriage & an early breakfast" Telegram received (at 6:15 P.M.), *ibid.*, Telegrams Collected (Bound).

2. On July 11, 3:50 P.M., Col. and Bvt. Maj. Gen. Edmund Schriver, inspector gen., telegraphed to USG, West Point. "The Secretary of War instructs me to acquaint you that the Quartermaster-General has been directed to carry

into immediate effect your recommendation in respect to the Shelter of troops at Western Posts; and to request you to notify General Sherman thereof" ALS (telegram sent), *ibid.* See letter to Maj. Gen. William T. Sherman, April 18, 1866.

To Hamilton Fish

West Point, N. Y.
July 13th 1866.

DEAR GOVERNOR,

Mrs. Grant & myself come up here for but a few days to visit our son who has just entered the Military Academy. We return to-morrow. It will therefore be impossible, on this occasion, to accept your kind invitation.

I hope to be able to visit here again during the encampment and should Mrs. Fish and yourself be at home I will take great pleasure in accepting your kind invitation to make your house my home at least for a portion of the time I may have to stay.

With great respect
your obt. svt.
U. S. GRANT

GOVERNOR H. FISH
GLENCLYFFE, N. Y.

ALS, DLC-Hamilton Fish.

To Edwin M. Stanton

Washington, July 18th 1866

HON. E. M. STANTON,
SEC. OF WAR,
SIR:

I would respectfully recommend that private Thomas Boucher Co. "F" 5th Cavalry now in confinement with his regiment for desertion, Thirty dollars having been paid for his apprehension, be pardoned and restored to duty, to make good, however, lost time and the money paid for his apprehension.

I make this recommendation because the mother of the boy (he is not yet eighteen years of age, I understand) came to me whilst he was said to be in Pittsburg, Pa. and applied for permission for him to return and give himself up without trial or punishment. I advised her to write to him to surrender himself and I would then intercede to make his punishment light. This was at the time I contemplated recommending the order, which was afterwards published, inviting deserters to surrender themselves.[1] He returned to Washington no doubt with a view of giving himself up for his company is on duty here, but was apprehended by a policeman for the reward before doing so.

Very respectfully
Your obt. servt.
U. S. GRANT
Lieut. Gen'l

Copies, DLC-USG, V, 47, 60; DNA, RG 108, Letters Sent.

1. On July 2, 1866, USG had written to Secretary of War Edwin M. Stanton. "I would respectfully recommend the publication of an order restoring to duty, without trial or punishment, all deserters from the Regular Army who join their regiments, or any Recruiting Rendezvous, voluntarily, before the 15th of August 1866. They should however make good the time lost by desertion, without pay or allowance for the time of their absence; and all those who surrender themselves at any other place than with their regiment should be subject to assignment same as unattached recruits." ALS, *ibid.*, RG 94, Letters Received, 514A 1866. USG's request was embodied in War Dept. General Orders No. 43. On Aug. 19, Thomas Brennan wrote a letter received at USG's hd. qrs. "Son Wm. Brannon deserted at Watertown Arsenal, but returned under order pardoning deserters. Is informed he returned too late—and is to be brought to trial—applies for pardon." *Ibid.*, RG 108, Register of Letters Received. On Sept. 17, USG endorsed this letter. "Respy. forwarded to the Sec of war with recommendation that the benifits of G. O. No 43, war Dept., of July 3d, 1866—offering pardon to deserters of the regular Army who should surrender themselves before the 15th August—be extended to the within named soldier, he having surrendered himself immediately upon learning of the offering of pardon—and within a few hours of the time to which it was limited" Copy, *ibid.*

To Edwin M. Stanton

Washington July 18th 1866.

Hon E. M. Stanton
Secretary of War,
Sir:

I would respectfully but urgently request for Allen Smith the appointment of 2d Lieut. in the present regular Army. I ask this as due to the memory of his father Maj. Gen. C. F. Smith, who died at Savannah, Tenn, in 1863 [*1862*]. The record of Gen. Smith is so well known that it is unecessary for me to recount it.

Allen Smith was born and raised in the Army. His mother has recently died,[1] leaving him, with one Sister, full orphans to get through the world almost destitute of means

Aside from rewarding the services of a meritorious deceased officer I believe the appointment of Allen Smith to the Army will be a good one.

Very respectfully
your obt. servt.
U. S. Grant
Lieut Gen'l

Copies, DLC-USG, V, 47, 60; DNA, RG 108, Letters Sent. Allen Smith was appointed 2nd lt., 1st Inf., as of July 18, 1866. See letter to Miss Smith, July 21, 1866; *PUSG*, 5, 83–84.

1. Fanny Mactier Smith had died on May 26. See DNA, RG 15, Pension Record 99888.

To Maj. Gen. George H. Thomas

Washington, D. C. July 18th *18656* [*1:50* P.M.]

MAJ GEN GEO H THOMAS
NASHVILLE TENN

The facts stated in your despatch of the Fourteenth do not warrant the interference of Military authority

U. S. GRANT
Lieut Gen

Telegram sent, DNA, RG 107, Telegrams Collected (Bound); copies, *ibid.*, RG 108, Letters Sent; *ibid.*, RG 393, Dept. of the Cumberland, Telegrams Received; DLC-USG, V, 47, 60. On July 14, 1866, Maj. Gen. George H. Thomas had telegraphed to USG. "Some of the members of the House of Representatives of the Tennessee General assembly conduct themselves in a very refractory manner,—absenting themselves to prevent a quorum, thus obstructing business,— The Governor cannot manage them with the means at his disposal and has applied to me for military assistance, Shall I furnish it?—" Telegram received (on July 15, 4:00 P.M.), DNA, RG 107, Telegrams Collected (Bound); *ibid.*, RG 108, Telegrams Received; copies, *ibid.*, RG 107, Telegrams Collected (Bound); *ibid.*, Letters Received from Bureaus; *ibid.*, Telegrams Sent by the President; *ibid.*, RG 393, Dept. of the Cumberland, Telegrams Sent; DLC-USG, V, 54; DLC-Andrew Johnson. On July 17, Secretary of War Edwin M. Stanton wrote to USG. "In reply to Major General Thomas telegram of the 14th, you will please instruct Genl Thomas that (the facts stated in his telegram do not warrant the interference of military Authority. The administration of the laws and the preservation of the peace in Nashville belong properly to the State Authorities and the duty of the United States forces is not to interfere in any controversy between the political authorities of the State; and General Thomas will strictly abstain from any interference between them" LS, DNA, RG 108, Letters Received; ADfS, DLC-Edwin M. Stanton.

To Maj. Gen. Philip H. Sheridan

Washington July 20. 1866.

MAJOR GENERAL SHERIDAN.
DEAR SHERIDAN.

Your despatch relative to selling the arms at Brownsville to the Liberals was referred by me to the President strongly recommended. I also saw the President in person about it, who said "Why can't we let them have them". The subject will be up before the Cabinet today, and as Seward is absent, I am in hopes it will be decided to let them go. Whether this ~~be~~ is done or not the Liberals are now getting arms. I got the Secretary of the Treasury to give clearance for a large lot of arms for Brownsville, for export beyond the limits of the United States. Some are now on the way, and others will follow.

There has been entirely too much lukewarmness about Washington, in Mexican affairs. I am afraid it may yet cause us trouble. It looks to me very much as if Napoleon was going to settle the European quarrel in his own way, thus making himself stronger than ever before. If he does will he not compel Austria to sustain the Imperial Government with such aid as he will give?

This looks to me to be the danger to apprehend. You and I should and we have done it, aid the Liberal cause by giving them all the encouragement we can.

A Minister to the Liberal Government has been confirmed but he is idling about Washington waiting for Mr S to give him his instructions.

Yours truly
U. S. GRANT.

Copy, DLC-Philip H. Sheridan. See letters to Maj. Gen. Philip H. Sheridan, May 19, July 30, 1866. On July 16, 1866, Maj. Gen. Philip H. Sheridan, New Orleans, had telegraphed to Brig. Gen. John A. Rawlins. "There is a quantity of surplus ordnance and small arms at Brownsville. If I was authorized to sell some of these to the Liberals say five thousand stand small arms with accoutrements and ammunition for same, it would benefit them very much, should the French make a movement towards the Rio Grande. Believe me General that the French in Mexico have not yet abandoned the idea that they have a strong sympathy in the Southern States." Telegram received (on July 17, 7:00 P.M.), DNA, RG 107, Telegrams Collected (Bound); *ibid.*, RG 108, Telegrams Received; copies, *ibid.*, RG 94, Letters Received, 747G 1866; DLC-USG, V, 54; DLC-Philip H. Sheridan; DLC-Edwin M. Stanton; USG 3. On July 18, USG endorsed a copy of this telegram. "Respectfully forwarded to the Secretary of War with recommendation that Gen. Sheridan be instructed to sell all surplus ordnance and ordnance stores at Brownsville to the highest bidder for cash. Should this recommendation not meet with approval, I would then recommend that on satisfactory information to the effect that a movement was on foot by the Imperialists of Mexico to recapture the Rio Grande frontier then Gen Sheridan shall cause all surplus ordnance stores to be disposed of to the Liberals." ES, DNA, RG 94, Letters

Received, 747G 1866. Also on July 16, Sheridan wrote to USG. "On the 13th instant I wrote to you in reference to condition of Mexican affairs on the line of the Rio Grande, and subsequently sent you news by telegraph just received from Vera Cruz. The reported movement of Marshal Bazaine on San Luis Potosi is probably correct; but, there has been, as yet, no means of confirming it. The French are fortifying near Orizaba on the mountain; also, some little island or point at Vera Cruz. Every encouragement should now be given to the Liberals; and if I could get authority to sell them some of the surplus Ordnance at Brownsville it would be a great help. I will be obliged to go over to Brownsville soon, to settle a little difficulty between Caravajal and Escobedo, and will set them up as much as possible." LS, USG 3.

On July 21, 8:30 P.M., Sheridan telegraphed to Rawlins. "I find it necessary to go over to the Rio Grande frontier for six days. Since the surrender of Matamoras there is the *diable* to pay over in Mexico. The Empress is on her way to Vera Cruz to leave the country, and there are general indications of a break up, or a stampede of the most alarming character—Fears are entertained of the ability of the French troops to get out of the country," Telegram received (on July 22, 12:15 A.M.), DNA, RG 107, Telegrams Collected (Bound); *ibid.*, RG 108, Telegrams Received; copies, DLC-USG, V, 54; DLC-Philip H. Sheridan. On Aug. 2, Sheridan wrote to USG. "I found everything quiet on the Mexican frontier, but some disposition on the part of Chieftains to quarrel among themselves. I would recommend that Mr Romero advise the President to come down as far as Monterey, if only on a visit: it would reconcile all strife. I think the French have by this time evacuated Northern Mexico, or if not they will be captured. The Empress has fled the country, and it would not surprise me if the Emperor did the same thing soon. I hope the Government will let me give the Liberals five thousand (5000) stand of Arms; it would be a valuable contribution to a good cause. I hope the Government will be firm, in case the strong position which Napoleon is now getting in Europe should cause him to again interfere in Mexican affairs." LS, DNA, RG 108, Letters Received. See Matías Romero, comp., *Correspondencia de la Legacion Mexicana en Washington durante la Intervencion Extranjera 1860–1868* (Mexico, 1870–92), VIII, 143–44.

On July 28, USG wrote to Secretary of War Edwin M. Stanton. "I would respectfully recommend a revocation of the order prohibiting the Ordnance Dept. fr[om] selling surplus Ordnance and Ordnance Stores to citizens, the occation, the Fenian excitement, no longer existing to make the prohibition necessary. The close of the War and the changes which will necessarily be made in Ordnance and fixed Ammunition leaves a large surplus on hand which can never be used and which requires large storage room." ALS, DNA, RG 107, Letters Received from Bureaus.

To Maj. Gen. William T. Sherman

July 21st *1866*

DEAR SHERMAN,

Your letter of the 18th is just rec'd. Your views about being a candidate for a civil office are exactly mine. It is a matter however which no one can come out publicly about. All that I can say to discourage the idea of my ever being a candidate for an office I do say.

Washburne, as you are aware, has been one of the warmest supporters of the Army, and my particular friend. You can well see that I feel a deep debt of gratitude to him. He has a young friend in the Army, young Atchison,[1] who is now on the Staff of Gen. Ord who he is very desirous of advancing the interest of by getting him a Staff position that will give him increase of pay. He has a mother to support and a sister ~~an~~ with two children to partially ~~to~~ support. If I had a vacancy on my staff, I would appoint him to it. If a vacancy occurs I will then give it. Now what I want to ask you is this. Under the bill which has just passed you will be promoted to Lt. Gn.[2] I was told to-day that the President would send my name in on Monday[3] and I made the request that yours should be sent in at the same time. This will give you three staff officers with the rank of Lt. Col. I want to ask if your staff is not already made up if you will not take Atchison until a vacancy occurs on my staff? I do not want you to do this if it trows off any one you have and wish to keep but if you can do it as well as not it would accomodate Washburne, and therefore me.

Your recommendation for the apt. of A. Gn. for Dayton[4] passed through my hands. There is no vacancy in the A. G. Dept. and to be eligible the applicant must be a Capt. in the regular Army. Supposing however that you was desirous of retaining him on your staff I recommended him for a 2d Lieut. to fill a vacancy now existing, and stated that you wanted to retain him. Write to me if this is so and I will endeavor to see that the appointment is given.

Yours Truly
U. S. GRANT

ALS, DLC-William T. Sherman. See letter to Maj. Gen. William T. Sherman, July 12, 1866. On July 18, 1866, Maj. Gen. William T. Sherman, Hanover, N. H., had written to USG. "I received your note from West Point at Boston, and have been so pulled about that till now I could not answer. I do hope the Army Bill will pass, for we have not enough men on the Plains to give security. It is such a vast Country, that our two Company Posts are far apart and I have no reserves at all. The Railroad Compy, Genl Dix & Dodge are telegraphing me, that they want military protection for their working parties beyond Kearney on the North of the Platte. I suppose the Indians may Construe the Cutting of ties as an invasion of their hunting grounds, but from all acounts the with drawal of the Posts along the Emigrant Road south of the Platte would be more dangerous than for the RR company to delay their work, west of Kearney, till their Rails are laid down that far. I will soon go out myself, and if I can find a small force that Can be spared will endeavor to make their workmen safe—NewMexico, though a poor misserable land absorbs too large a fraction of our troops. It always was the Case and always will be. Tomorrow will be the occasion for which I came here. It over, I will make the circuit round by the North to Montreal, Niagira Falls—Lancaster St Louis &c. aiming to be at Omaha Aug 15. A great many well meaning people still say that the faith of the masses is so shaken in politicians that you will have to be the Candidate for President whether you will or no—I always say that you would not act with your usual sense in taking such a temporary & unsatisfactory an office. Still if you ever yield, let me know—In no event will I ever let any person use my name for any political use or office, but should you your friends should have a hint in time. I prefer my present Command to any other that is possible, & would change with no one unless I had a fortune or some Civil employmt that would enable me to acquire property for my children—" ALS, USG 3.

On July 23, USG endorsed papers concerning a military post in Sioux Valley, Dakota Territory. "Respy. forwarded to Maj. Gen. Sherman—If it is possible to continue the occupation of the Military Post referred to—do so—The Army Bill will probably pass this week—As soon as it is possible I will give you increased force." Copy, DNA, RG 108, Register of Letters Received. On July 25, 12:30 P.M., USG telegraphed to Sherman, St. Louis. "Is it not imprudent in Gen Cook breaking up the post at Fort Berthold?" Telegram sent, *ibid.*, RG 107, Telegrams Collected (Bound); copies, *ibid.*, RG 108, Letters Sent; *ibid.*, RG 393, Military Div. of the Miss., Telegrams Received; DLC-USG, V, 47, 60. On July 26, Sherman, Niagara Falls, telegraphed to USG. "Dispatch in relation to Fort Berthold referred to me from St Louis. Fort Rice fulfills all the purposes & Berthold is of miner importance. I will soon be at Omaha & will report further" Telegram received (on July 27, 9:50 A.M.), DNA, RG 108, Telegrams Received; copy, DLC-USG, V, 54. On the same day, Sherman wrote to USG. "Am just arrived and congratulate you again on your promotion. You Cant get any higher Your Commission & office in every sense ~~is~~ are worth more than the Presidents. Will there be a scramble for the vacancy left by you? I have never said or written a word to any one and will not—Whatever Choice you & the President make will be acceptable to me, & my friends. I do hope the army Bill will pass, but lest it fail I have ordered one of the Regts of Blacks from Arkansas to Leavenworth and may post it at Kearney to cover the progress of the Pacific RR, and to make the great Central Route secure. Dodge seems to fear trouble to his parties at work west of ~~Riley~~ Kearney & North of the Platte. The location of that

Road North of the Platte, whilst all our posts and the Stage stations are south, may compel us to go to some trouble & expense, but I think the Railroad location right, and will in person look to the changes forced on us by this fact. Fort Berthoud was & is of minor importance, an old trading Post, & held by one company. Yet Genl Cooke should not have made any radical Change without Consulting me, and I have so instructed him through my Adjt Genl. If it be positively certain that Hancock is to succeed Pope, I would like to have it official that I may take him, Hancock up to Leavenworth & Kearney, and adjust any difficulty that may arise by the line of the Platte which is common to, and neccessary to each of the Depts of the Platte & Missouri. In a few days I will deposit my family at Lancaster Ohio, and will then give my whole time to these matters." ALS, USG 3. On July 27, Sherman twice wrote to USG. "I wrote you yesterday and now have yours of July 21, and am gratified beyond expression at what you say. In the event of being promoted I will give a place of reward to Atchison for the reasons you name, and I have very carefully abstained from making any promises at all. I dont like to have too many staff officers about me. They are jealous of each other & of every body else, and some are insatiable. I am under no obligations to befriend Dayton or McCoy further than that both began with me at Shiloh, and have clung to me all the time. They are willing & ready all the time & I have told them both exactly how their case stands, and both are applicants for Commissions in the New Army. If successful I will retain them for the reason that they are faithful. I suppose the nominations for all the vacancies—Lt Genl. Maj Genls &c will go in to the Senate together. As soon as I know positively that I am to be promoted I will send for Atchison & take him with me out on the Plains, and if he stand the test, he shall have a good place. You may so notify Washburn, & Atchison.—I will leave here tomorrow & spend Sunday at Cleveland, & by Teusday will be at Lancaster, Aug 5 at St Louis, and all my preperations are made to leave Omaha, Aug 15. It would gratify Washburn most, if you would write him, that he may see that you are watchful of his interests & wishes I am on the point of r[i]ding out, to show Minnie the Falls, and Canada Shore Barry & family are here & any quantity of all sorts of People, and one cannot but wonder where they come from, and who pays their Bills—" ALS, DLC-Elihu B. Washburne. "I wrote you this morning before breakfast since which time I have been across to Lundys Lane Table Rock &c. & back to Dinner where I met parties from Buffalo with a morning paper Containing the telegraphic announcemt of my Confirmation as Lieut General. I wont use words to express my personal thanks to you, but await a fitting time to prove it by acts. The fact that so firm a friendship & mutual confidence exist between us is often referred to as the Great Cause of our success. At all events I do attach a vital importance to it and will Continue my efforts to fulfil any thing you may desire. I want to remain in St Louis with my Command unchanged. I will make my trip as before arranged and will endeavor for the sake of economy to move the HeadQuarters of each Departmt inside of some Fort or Govt property. Reynolds is in Little Rock Arsenal—Pope in Fort Leavenworth, and as soon as the Pacific RR is at Fort Kearney I will with your approval move Cooke out there, with a Battery of Light Artillery & two cos of Cavalry, & shove all the Infantry beyond—I will try & discharge the two Regts of Vols—(Rebel prisoners of war, 5 & 6th) & replace them along the Platte by a Negro Regt ordered up from Arkansas. I also propose to Change the Line between the Depts of Mo & the Platte so as to give to the latter both sides of that valley as far out as

Laramie. I hope the Army Bill will pass as I think we will need more Cavalry. I want to make arrangemts for Mrs Sherman in my absence, and wish you would let your pay master make me up a set of pay accounts for a Lt Genl, to enable me to make my financial calculations & send it to me at Lancaster, as soon as possible. I must leave there about the 3rd of August—Also a list of staff officers that I will be entitled to with Rank &c." ALS, USG 3.

On Aug. 9, Thursday, Sherman, St. Louis, wrote to USG. "You remember that the President handed me some papers about matters in Missouri. I have made partial examination the result of which I report to the President direct as it is neither Military or Civil, but I transmit it through you, as you were present when he spoke to me. I cant see why the Politicians will not be quiet. Missouri is as prosperous as possible, the best sort of crops, and all classes reasonably prosperous, and so far as I can see all might do well if they would stick to their real interests—but if they cannot quarrel about one thing they will another. I want to keep out strictly and will only interfere save as a peace maker, by order of the President. I know that good ought to result from the interview of this morning, but no one can say, what ulterior designs these parties have. Conservatives accuse the Radicals of all sorts of Crimes & Criminal intentions, and the Radicals accuse their adversaries of bidding for Rebel Votes &c &c. I want to get up the Country next week. We are so late in getting to work on the New Army that I fear we cannot accomplish much this ~~Spring~~ year. I have put out all the orders, and will try and get recruits so that as soon as the Field officers are named they may arrange them into Companies I would like a Cavalry Regt in reserve as now every man is on one or the other of the terribly long lines to the remote territories and in the event of Indian hostilities I cannot call together a respectable force without abandoning public Forts and Stores. I as yet have not an inteligent idea of the troubles beyond Laramie, but the Indians evidently dont like the new posts being established by the 18th Infantry from Laramie to Montana. I have a long Report from Babcock, from which I infer we want in Utah rather a prudent Commander, than a large force. Major Lewis now out there has the reputation of being a good officer, and discreet gentleman. I have also a full report from Col Sackett at Virginia City—Matters seem to be assuming a good shape in every quarter but on the Road from Laramie to Virginia City. We will have to get a Cavalry Regiment at Laramie to be held there in reserve. I have ordered Genl Cooke to exercise general Command of all the troops now along the Platte, and as soon as I hear of the New Genl order dividing up the Departmts I will make this change permant, and give to Terry the managemt of affairs in Minnesota and as far West as Boats ply on the Missouri say Fort Benton. Hancock is down at his mother in law's—has a boil—carbuncle and has not yet been up. He no doubt expected to have the Command of this Military Division, but the Dept of the Missouri—well commanded will employ all his time. The Regt of colored Inf should be here at any time from Little Rock, and I will order it up to Fort Kearney as fast as possible. It has but a short time to serve, and can only be used to cover the working parties of the Rail Road—I want to start Sunday, and be at Omaha, by the 15.—" ALS, DNA, RG 108, Letters Received. On Aug. 13, USG wrote to Secretary of War Edwin M. Stanton. "I enclose to the President a report from Lt. Gn. Sherman on Missouri affairs, together with papers which were handed to Gn. Sherman by the President, and are now returned to him." ALS, DLC-Andrew Johnson. The enclosed letter of Aug. 9 from Sherman is *ibid.* along with additional papers.

Also on Aug. 9, Sherman telegraphed to USG. "The following dispatch just recd 'Ft Laramie Aug 8th Capt Haymond 18th Infy Just arrived at Horse shoe from Ft Reno telegraphs that Lieut Daniels 18th Infy was killed by Indians July 20th. Twenty four men have been killed since July 14th between Browns Springs & Tongue River (Signed) HENRY MAYNADIER Colonel' We must have more Cavalry from Laramie to Montana & I will push organizations as fast as possible but our troops are necessarily much scattered" Telegram received (at 4:30 P.M.), DNA, RG 107, Telegrams Collected (Bound); *ibid.*, RG 108, Telegrams Received; copies, *ibid.*, RG 107, Letters Received from Bureaus; *ibid.*, RG 393, Military Div. of the Miss., Letters Sent; DLC-USG, V, 54. On Aug. 10, USG endorsed a copy of this telegram. "Respectfully forwarded to the Secretary of War for his information." ES, DNA, RG 107, Letters Received from Bureaus. On the same day, Sherman telegraphed to USG. "News from Col Carrington beyond Laramie more satisfactory—no cause of alarm—He reports the loss of one Lieut & seven 7 men killed & wounded & seventy animals stolen" Telegram received (at 1:35 P.M.), *ibid.*, Telegrams Collected (Bound); *ibid.*, RG 108, Telegrams Received; copies, *ibid.*, RG 107, Letters Received from Bureaus; *ibid.*, RG 393, Military Div. of the Miss., Letters Sent; DLC-USG, V, 54. On the same day, USG endorsed a copy of this telegram. "Respectfully forwarded to the Secretary of War for his information." ES, DNA, RG 107, Letters Received from Bureaus.

Also on Aug. 9, Sherman telegraphed to USG. "Genl Reynolds is here I have told him of the proposed change that will give Ord the Department of Arkansas Before going he naturally wants to know if the order is certain He wants to be construed as an applicant for a Colonels Commission of white Infantry" Telegram received (at 4:45 P.M.), *ibid.*, Telegrams Collected (Bound); *ibid.*, RG 108, Telegrams Received; copies, *ibid.*, RG 393, Military Div. of the Miss., Letters Sent; DLC-USG, V, 54. On Aug. 10, USG telegraphed to Sherman. "The order is published assigning Ord to Dep't of Arkansas" Telegram sent, DNA, RG 107, Telegrams Collected (Bound); copies, *ibid.*, RG 108, Letters Sent; (2) *ibid.*, RG 393, Military Div. of the Miss., Telegrams Received; DLC-USG, V, 47, 60.

On Aug. 11, Sherman wrote to USG. "I have now cleaned my desk of the accumulation of new matter, and am closing my private business so as to start tomorrow for the Plains. I saw Hancock yesterday and had a long talk with him. He says he must return to Baltimore and cannot well replace Genl Pope till the middle of September, when he will meet him at Leavenworth, and have all the results of his Pope's inspection along the Mountains & New Mexico. I will also write fully to Genl Pope as to meeting Gen Hancock & imparting to him all he should know—Gen Ord will be here from Detroit today to meet General Reynolds to exchange views about affairs in Arkansas. Gen Reynolds has been most successful there in maintaining peace, Good order and the respect of the People. I will promise Ord one Company of light artillery now at Little Rock, four Companies of new Coloured Cavalry, and two of the Regts of Infantry made out of the present 19th serving in Arkansas. This will give me one of the Regts to be created out of the third Battalion for service elsewhere. Terry should come directly to see General Cooke at Omaha—he might then go up to Fort Rice by water and thence east by Fort Wadsworth, to Fort Snelling. This will at once give him the hang of his whole Dept. I can leave him the three Regiments made up out of the 13th—the present 10th Inf, and the two hundred mounted scouts already assigned, which will be an excellent command—I am assured parties in Minnesota are ready to put on a stage Line to Montana, as soon as we make the Line of travel across from Wadsworth to Rice—safe. I feel assured Terry is well suited to the new Departmt. I will spend Monday at Leavenworth at Popes HdQrs, and aim to reach Omaha on Wednesday. I shall advise Cooke to leave the Company at Fort Berthoud until Terry has time to look into the question. I want to strengthen Cooke all I can because it is all important to encourage and cover the operations of the R. R. now being pushed with so much energy and success. The Great Road from Omaha, to Great Salt Lake & Montana as well as Denver should be made as safe as the Old National Road used to be. It is the great link of connection East & West—I already know it as far as Kearney, and before winter I hope to know it quite as well to the Mountains, as far as I count on a Railroad in the next *four* years. Cooke must do the best with the troops now there, but I will reenforce him as fast as new Regiments are available. I will keep you well advised on all these points as we progress. Nichols is not here yet, but I will leave a letter of instructions for him, & Sawyer, and McCoy of my staff, with Easton Chief Qr Mr, & Haines Chief C. S. So that current business will not be interupted, I will also from time to time send back instructions. I have for some days, been embarrassed on the subject of staff. I promised you to provide for young Atchison of whom you wrote me, on the 21. of July. I then thought the number of my staff would be increased by my promotion, but the number is actually diminished—McCoy & Dayton have been with me since before Shiloh. Each is dependant upon this position and I could not without harshness & injustice displace them. Audenried has also been most devoted & faithful, and it would be wrong for me to overlook him, and I have felt constrained to retain these—It leaves out Sawyer who was assigned me by you at Young's Point. He has stuck to his post without a minute interruption hoping always to receive a Commission as Asst Adt Genl but now finds himself a Lt. in some unknown Regt. This may be the best that can be done now, and I have advised him to write fully & frankly to Rawlins that some one near the source of power may understand his wishes and interests—He has been so true to his duties, and has as you know filled an office far above his Rank & pay all the time, and by the Course of service should share my good fortune. I have done all I know how in his interest and must leave the rest to the War Dept & himself—I would like much to benefit young Atchison in the way of pay, but dont see how I can. If I am entitled to any other staff than the ones I have named I freely consent to give place to Atchison of whom I hear the best accounts. I see a notice in the newspapers that the Negro Regt in Route from Arkansas to the Platte, cut up some shines at Helena. I now have notice that five Companies passed north at Memphis yesterday. General Reynolds who is here waiting for Gen Ord discredits the statemt of misconduct as he speaks highly of the Regiment especially its colonel. He is in telegraphic communication with his HeadQrs at Little Rock, but has no information from that quarter of any such scenes. I must use that Regimt this fall & winter to cover the progress of the Railroad, as well as to replace the 5 & 6. U. S. Vols (Rebel prisoners) that are useless & should be got rid of as early as possible. The Regt will be pushed forward to Omaha as fast as possible, but our distances are so great that much time is consumed by transfers. You will probably next hear from me at Omaha." ALS, DNA, RG 108, Letters Received.

On Aug. 29, Sherman, Laramie, telegraphed to USG. "Accounts of Indian troubles much exaggerated. The telegraph is not interrupted. The mails travel regularly & no party that is properly organized has sustained a loss. There are some small parties of Indians stealing horses when they can do so with safety to themselves, still we must be careful as there are parties of whites who would be benefitted by an Indian war" Telegram received (at 4:35 P.M.), *ibid.*, RG 107, Telegrams Collected (Bound); *ibid.*, RG 108, Telegrams Received; copies, *ibid.*, RG 107, Letters Received from Bureaus; DLC-USG, V, 54. On Aug. 31, Sherman, Fort Laramie, wrote to USG. "Since my arrival here I have seen some things and have received Despatches of Generals Hancock and Cooke, which call for some explanation to you, as they may appeal to you. We are bound to afford approximate protection to parties residing along the Great Routes of travel westward, of which the Platte is one, and the Smoky Hill and Arkansas is another. The Posts and number of troops at each are well known to you, and you are also aware that the Indians are constantly engaged in stealing the horses, and in some recent cases have murdered the people along these Roads. In assigning troops I have given Genl Cooke the 18th Infantry and the 2nd Cavalry. A portion of this latter Regimt is now on the smoky hill and under my orders should come across the country to this Line—This will leave Gen Hancock for the other Road the ~~11th~~ 3rd Infantry, a part of the 3rd U. S. Cavalry sent last spring from Arkansas to Fort Union NewMexico and the new Regimt of Cavalry that you gave me to organise out of the Cavalry recruits from Carlisle, which I instructed should be sent to Fort Riley instead of Jefferson Barracks. From personal inspection I know that Ft Riley is admirably adapted to that end, and the Companies as fast as organised could be sent out on that Line. Genl Hancock, to ensure peace in Missouri thought that object more important than peace on the Plains and ordered some of his troops from Kansas into Missouri, and reported in Consequence his inability to spare all of the 2nd Cavalry. I have reversed that order and reiterated my command that the 2nd must come to the Platte and that troops should not leave the Lines of travel over the Plains to be in Missouri.— Not having troops ready for both purposes, Gen Hancock adjudges the peace of Missouri most important but my decision is that the Peace on the plains is most important and that if U. S. troops must be used in Missouri they must come from some other quarter or made up out of the new Regiments forming. Of Course my orders settle the Question, but I have given Genl Hancock authority to appeal to you and the President. If you could travel this long exposed Road, and see how difficult it is to defend the mails and telegraph I would not doubt your decision, but knowing how different, questions present themselves from diffnt stand points, I will abide your decision absolutely, & cheerfully. In like manner Genl Cooke wants to incur expense in building public quarters for his HeadQrs, and it may be one Company at Omaha. Omaha is as safe as Saint Louis. Had we public buildings there now, it would be prudent to occupy them, but to build de novo, is not necessary. The Pacific Railroad is done to abreast of Fort Kearney, and will be done to the forks of the Platte this year. In all next year it will probably reach Fort Sedgwick, and the Black Hills a spur of the Rocky Mountains, either at Laramie, Cheyenne Pass or Cache-la-Poudre Pass, at one of which points in my judgmt will be the true military Point from which to control Indian affairs.—Therefore Omaha is so ~~permant~~ temporary that I deem it unwise to expend money there, that should go to build a suitable Post, nearer the enemy.— I dont believe in conducting hostilities from the Rear. Still I am willing Gen Cooke should remain at Omaha in hind quarters, ready however to Come forward when his presence is necessary. I do not apprehend a Genl Indian War, but for years we will have a kind of unpleasant state of hostilities that can only terminate with the destruction of the hostile bands, only to be accomplished by putting our troops near where the Indians live, viz along the base of the Rocky Mountains.—I start tomorrow along down the mountains to the head of the Arkansas, via Denver." ALS, DNA, RG 108, Letters Received. See letter to Maj. Gen. Winfield S. Hancock, Aug. 8, 1866.

During his two-month inspection tour, Sherman wrote lengthy reports to Brig. Gen. John A. Rawlins on Aug. 17, 21, 24, 31, Sept. 12, 21, 30. ALS, DNA, RG 108, Letters Received. Printed in *HED*, 39-2-23. See letter to Edwin M. Stanton, Dec. 11, 1866.

1. See *PUSG*, 11, 300. On Aug. 4, USG wrote to U.S. Representative Elihu B. Washburne. "Sherman answered my letter in regard to the appointment of Atchison to his Staff promptly, telling me to say to you that he was not under promise to appoint any one in case of his promotion, and that he would take great pleasure in giving him a place." Copy (unaddressed and unsigned), DLC-Elihu B. Washburne. See letter to Elihu B. Washburne, Aug. 16, 1866.

On Dec. 7, 10:15 A.M., USG telegraphed to Bvt. Maj. Gen. Joseph Hooker, Detroit. "Change order sending Capt Atchison to his company to awaiting orders from Washington." Telegram sent, DNA, RG 107, Telegrams Collected (Bound); telegram received (at 10:40 A.M.), *ibid.*, RG 393, Northern Dept. and Lakes, Letters Received. On Dec. 18, Bvt. Maj. Gen. Edward O. C. Ord, Little Rock, Ark., telegraphed to USG. "I have applied for Col C B Atchison as asst Inspector General" Telegram received (at 8:45 P.M.), *ibid.*, RG 107, Telegrams Collected (Bound); *ibid.*, RG 108, Telegrams Received; copy (misdated Dec. 8), DLC-USG, V, 54.

2. See letter to Edwin M. Stanton, July 25, 1866.

3. July 23.

4. On March 26, Maj. and Bvt. Lt. Col. Lewis M. Dayton, adjt. for Sherman, St. Louis, had written to Rawlins requesting an appointment as adjt., U.S. Army. ALS, DNA, RG 94, ACP, D198 CB 1870. Sherman endorsed this letter. "I approve and recommend the above. Col Dayton has been all the time on duty Since Sh[i]loh—and is still a volunteer." AES (undated), *ibid.* On July 21, USG endorsed this letter. "I would respectfully recommend that L. M. Dayton be appointed a 2d Lt. to fill one of the existing vacancies in the regular Army. He has served long and faithfully on the Staff of Gn. Sherman and I know it is his desire to retain him." AES, *ibid.* Dayton was appointed 2nd lt., 2nd Inf., as of July 24, and assigned to duty as Sherman's military secretary with the rank of lt. col. as of Aug. 11.

To John A. Dix

Washington July 21st 66.

GEN. JNO. A. DIX,
PRESDT. UNION R. R. CO.

Yours of the 20th asking protection to working parties on the railroad West of Kearney is just received. I am also just in receipt of a letter from Gen. Sherman in which he informs me that he has received the same request both from you and Gen. Dodge. His present force will not justify him in promising the protection you ask in advance of the road being completed to Kearney. He is however going out to that country next month and if he can draw troops from other points to put a small force where you ask them he will do so.

The increase to the army which is now promised will enable me soon to send General Sherman more troops.

Very Respectfully
Your obt. servt
U. S. GRANT
Lt Gen'l

Copies, DLC-USG, V, 47, 60; DNA, RG 108, Letters Sent. See preceding letter. On July 20, 1866, John A. Dix, Union Pacific Rail Road Co., New York City, wrote to USG. "This Company has graded its road to a point five miles westwardly of Fort Kearney. It is laying track within 50 miles of that Fort and will reach it in September. A contract has been made to grade the 100 miles next west of that point, and we wish to commence work immediately so as to reach the 100th meridian of w. Longitude by 1. Dec. This we can do if our men can be protected; but we fear they cannot be kept to their work without a small covering military force. This great public enterprise ought not to be retarded by such a cause. I have a letter from Maj. Genl. Sherman today saying that he can spare us no troops, and I therefore, as the necessity is urgent, write to you to request that a small body of mounted men may be sent there for the protection of our working parties. Begging to ask your immediate attention to the subject, . . ." ALS, *ibid.*, Letters Received.

To Miss Smith

Washington, D. C.
July 21st 1866.

MY DEAR MISS SMITH,

I am very happy to be able to inform you that I have this day succeeded in getting the order for your brother Allens appointment of 2d Lieut. in the Army. I need scarsely assure you of the great pleasure it affords me to be able to serve in any way within my power the family of one who I so highly respected, I might say loved, as your father. My great respect for him commenced when he was Commandant of Cadets and I a *Plebe*. This respect ripened as I knew him better in later years.

My very kindest regards for yourself and assurance that it will always afford me the greatest pleasure to have you call on me for any thing within my controll to grant.

Yours Truly
U. S. GRANT

ALS, USMA. Probably Henrietta L. Smith, born in Philadelphia on Oct. 19, 1853, daughter of Maj. Gen. Charles F. Smith. See DNA, RG 15, Pension Record 99888; letter to John Tucker, Oct. 18, 1865.

To Maj. Gen. William T. Sherman

Washington, July 23d *1866*.

MAJOR GENERAL W. T. SHERMAN
COMDG. MIL. DIV. MISSISSIPPI.
GENERAL:

Information having been received at these Headquarters that unauthorized persons are frequently improperly selling arms and ammunition to Indians within your Military Division, and the Commissioner of Indian Affairs having instructed Indian Agents to prohibit traders from selling these articles to the Indians, it is deemed advisable for the military authorities to cooperate in the enforcement of this order. You will therefore issue such instructions to the various military commanders in your Mil. Div. as will prevent military traders from selling or disposing of arms or ammunition.

Very respy Your obedt servt
U. S. GRANT
Lieutenant General

LS, DNA, RG 393, Military Div. of the Miss., Letters Received. On July 23, 1866, USG wrote to Secretary of War Edwin M. Stanton. "The accompanying is a copy of communication sent to Gen. Sherman in relation to sale of arms and ammunition to Indians referred to in communication of Actg. Secy. of the Interior. W. T. Otto, dated June 26th 1866." Copies, DLC-USG, V, 47, 60; DNA, RG 108, Letters Sent. On June 26, Act. Secretary of the Interior William T. Otto had written to Stanton. "Herewith I have the honor to transmit an extract from a letter of Genl S. R. Curtis of the 10th inst. addressed to this Department, in regard to the sale of arms and ammunition to the Indians with which, as a Commissioner of this Department, he is now treating and to state that the Commissioner of Indian Affairs has been directed to instruct the Agents of the Indians to prohibit traders from selling arms to them and respectfully request that you will cause similar orders to be issued on the part of the military." LS, *ibid.*, Letters Received. The enclosure is *ibid.* See *ibid.*, RG 75, Miscellaneous Letters Received, Document W417.

To Ambrose E. Burnside

Washington, D. C. July 24th *1866*

DEAR GOVERNOR,

The bearer of this, Mr. F. Simmons,[1] Artist, has I believe been selected to make some statuary for your Capital. I take pleasure in introducing him to you as an artist of merit. I have sat to him, and others who are much more capable of judging of the merits of his work than my self pronounce the bust which he has made as excellent.

Very respectfully
your obt. svt.
U. S. GRANT
Lt. Gn.

TO GEN. E. A. BURNSIDE,
GOV. OF RHODE ISLAND

ALS, RPB.

1. Franklin Simmons, born in Lisbon, Maine, in 1839, studied sculpture briefly in Boston before opening a studio in Lewiston, Maine. USG's sitting led to an interview by the editor of the *Lewiston Journal*. "WASHINGTON, MAY 12, 1866.—We had the good fortune yesterday to meet General Grant at the studio of Maine's gifted artist, Simmons, and spent an hour in conversation with the Lieutenant General while he was giving Mr. Simmons the benefit of a 'sitting.' . . . 'I am breaking off from smoking,' remarked Grant. 'When I was in the field I smoked eighteen or twenty cigars a day, but now I smoke only nine or ten.' Seating himself, and turning towards the clay model of himself, which the artist was building up, Grant remarked: 'If you had been at Vicksburg when we were before that city, you would not have wanted for mud.' This naturally opened the way to a conversation on the events of the war, which we improved. Referring to the long struggle for possession of Vicksburg, Grant said he felt sure of that city the moment he had effected a landing below. 'I then clearly saw every step,' he remarked, 'but I didn't think the rebels would be such fools as to shut up thirty thousand troops there for me to capture.' Grant seemed to regard the series of battles which relieved Chattanooga and put that important strategic point securely in our possession, as one of the most satisfactory of his achievements in a purely military point of view. Pittsburg Landing he regarded as an important victory, and although he blamed the officers commanding our outposts for their negligence in allowing a surprise, yet he claimed that the battle did very much to dampen the ardor and break down the arrogance of the rebels. . . . The conversation turned to the Virginia campaigns of 1864 and 1865. 'I noticed,' remarked General Gant, 'that Mr. Swinton has published a history of the campaigns in the Old Dominion, in which he takes the ground that I gained nothing, but, on the contrary, lost many valuable lives uselessly, by moving my army from the Rapidan direct towards Richmond, rather than by taking it around by water to the Peninsula, as McClellan did.' 'This,' observed the General, 'is a revival of the old theory (referring to the McClellan policy) of subduing the rebellion by peace measures. A half a million troops might have been kept within sight of Washington till doomsday, and the rebellion would have flourished more and more vigorously day by day. Fighting, hard knocks, only could accomplish the work. The rebellion must be overcome, if overco[m]e at all, by force—its resources destroyed—its fighting material obliterated, before peace could be obtained.['] 'Now,' remarked the General, as he took another puff at his cigar, 'will anybody tell me what could be gained by moving my army by water a hundred miles further away from my base than was necessary to meet the foe against which all my blows must be directed? And then by marching overland I could keep my whole force together and protect Washington at the same time, whereas, had I moved by water to the Peninsula before Lee's army had been crippled, I should have been obliged to leave a large force behind to guard against raids on Washington It seems to me,' added the General, 'to be the simplest military truism to fight an enemy as near as possible to our base.' . . . In response to an allusion to the charge that little was accomplished by the tremendous loss of life from the Wilderness to the James, Grant remarked that he had little patience with those grumblers who expected that the rebellion could be put down without the loss of life. The problem given was to destroy the fighting material of the Confederacy, and that could only be done by a sacrifice of life on our side. It

was the constant pounding which we gave Lee's army from the Rapidan to the James that made possible the victories of April, 1865. In all the battles of 1864, except Coal Harbor, our loss was inferior to that of the enemy; and great as were those losses, yet they were not only necessary to secure the final result, but even less than they would have been by disease had we resorted to the Chickahominy warfare and the consequent prolongation of the war. . . . 'There were but two failures in the Virginia campaign of '64 which ought to have been successes,' said Grant, 'and those were the failure to capture Petersburg when we crossed the James, and afterwards at the mine explosion.' 'Blunders, and especially a failure to move with sufficient promptitude, lost us these two opportunities, which now it is clear might both have been successes.' 'But,' added Grant, 'it was all for the best that we failed in those two instances, for had we succeeded at either time Lee would have at once been obliged to abandon Richmond, and would have been able to secure a safe retreat into the interior of the South, where he would have prolonged the contest for years. Our failure then, and the determination of the rebels to hold on to their capital gave us time to extend our left southward, to, bring up Sherman from Georgia, and thereby made it impossible for Lee to escape.' . . . In reply to a question as to whether he was not surprised at the suddenness of the collapse of the rebellion, Grant said that he was, although he had always supposed that when it did break down it would go all at once. 'I thought, however,' he remarked, 'that it would hold out another season; and I am not sure,' he added, 'but that it would have been better for the country if it had. There were some parts of the country where our armies had never trod, particularly Texas, which needed to feel the blighting effects of war to bring their people to a realizing sense of the enormity of their crime and the necessity of a thorough repentance. I find,' said he, 'that those parts of the South which have not felt the war, and particularly those which have been within our lines and have therefore escaped the rebel conscription and taxes, are much less disposed to accept the situation in good faith than those portions which have been literally overrun with fire and sword.' . . . Referring to the temper of the Southern people, he remarked that they are much less disposed now to bring themselves to the proper frame of mind than they were one year since. 'A year ago,' said he, 'they were willing to do anything; now they regard themselves as masters of the situation. Some of the rebel Generals,' he added, 'are behaving nobly and doing all they can to induce the people to throw aside their old prejudices and to conform their course to the changed condition of things. Johnston and Dick Taylor, particularly, are exercising a good influence; but, he added, 'Lee is behaving badly. He is conducting himself very differently from what I had reason, from what he said at the time of the surrender, to suppose he would. No man at the South is capable of exercising a tenth part of the influence for good that he is, but instead of using it, he is setting an example of forced acquiescence so grudging and pernicious in its effects as to be hardly realized.['] 'The men who were in the rebel armies,' said Grant, 'acquiesce in the result much better than those who staid at home. The women are particularly bitter against the Union and Union men. Of course,' he added, 'there is some bitterness of feeling among all classes, but I am satisfied it would soon die out if their leading men had not somehow got the idea that treason after all was not very bad, and that the "Southern cause," as they phrase it, will yet triumph, not in war, but in politics. In my judgment,' said Grant, 'the tone of certain men and certain papers in the North is such as to do incalculable mischief in making the late rebels believe that they are just as much entitled to rule as ever, and that if they will only stand by what they are pleased to call their "rights," they will have help from the North. This,' significantly added Grant, 'is only playing over again the incipient stages of the rebellion.' He was confident that the large majority of the Southern people would smother their resentments and become good citizens if these mischief-makers at the North (the copperheads) would only let them alone. For himself, if he had the power, the first thing he would do would be to seize the New York News, and kindred sheets, which are giving the South so dangerous an idea of their own position and 'rights.' [']Dick Taylor,' added Grant, 'told me that the great body of the South would settle down quietly, and be satisfied with anything if it was not for this false idea of "their rights," and so called ill-treatment fostered by such sheets.' . . . 'Troops,' said General Grant, 'must be kept at all the principal points in the South for some time to come. This will be necessary to repress the turbulence of a class of the South very dangerous to all well-disposed persons, and also to protect the rights of the freedmen, who are looked upon with deep hatred by a very large proportion of the people. I am in favor, however,' he added, 'of not retaining our volunteers for this duty, because they very naturally think that they fulfilled their engagement one year since. Hence, whenever I have heard of any dissatisfaction in a volunteer regiment, I have at once ordered their discharge. I couldn't consent to the punishment for turbulence of brave men who had been through the war, and who regarded themselves as being wrongfully held. I have given orders for the immediate discharge of all the white volunteers.' . . . Grant spoke in high terms of Sherman, Sheridan, Howard, and other generals, and referred to our Mexican difficulties, forcibly adding that he believed the French invasion of Mexico a part of the rebellion, and he should have been glad to have seen a detatchment of our army sent there one year since. He would engage that Sheridan, with plenty of arms and two thousand American troops, and a goodly number of American officers, would, with the aid of the Mexicans, clean Maximilian out of Mexico in six months. . . ." *Missouri Democrat*, May 31, 1866. Later asked by a reporter about the authenticity of this interview, USG explained that "he had had a conversation with the editor of that paper, but that he had no expectation that it was to be published, and that if he had supposed the remarks which he then made were to get into the newspapers he should have refrained from making them. He was the General of the United States Army, and not a politician." *Chicago Tribune*, Sept. 14, 1866.

To Hugh McCulloch

Washington, D. C.
July 25th 1866.

HON. H. MCCULLOUGH,
SEC. OF THE TREAS.
SIR:

I would respectfully recommend to your favorable concideration to a clerkship in the Treasury Dept. Mrs. Sophie Curtis. Mrs. Curtis is the widow of Capt. Geo. Curtis who served in the Army from /61 to /66 and died a few days after his discharge. She is also the daughter of a Naval Officer, Commodore Casson, who died in the service as did also one of her brothers.

I hope it will be practicable to give this case favorable concideration.

Very respectfully
your obt. svt.
U. S. GRANT
Lt. Gn.

ALS, DNA, RG 56, Appointments Div. Vice Admiral David G. Farragut endorsed this letter. "I am well aware that Como Cassin & his son died in the Naval service & no doubt the Bearer is well known to Genrl. Grant as the Daughter of Como. Cassin & upon that I endorse the Genls letter." AES (undated), *ibid.* On July 28, 1866, Asst. Secretary of the Treasury William E. Chandler endorsed this letter. "Dismiss Miss Mary Middleton now employed in 4th Auditors Office, and whose father is a Fourth Class Clerk in 2d Auditors Office, and has not served in the Army, and appoint Mrs Curtis, the widow of a Union soldier and the daughter of the Naval Hero Comr. Cassin,—Recommended by Genl. Grant and Admiral Farragut." ES, *ibid.* On July 31, Chandler wrote to USG. "If you will instruct Mrs. Sophia Curtis, whom you recommended for a position, to report to the Appointment Clerk of the Department, she will receive her appointment." LS, ICarbS.

To Edwin M. Stanton

Washington, D. C. July 25th *1866*

HON. E. M. STANTON,
SEC. OF WAR,
SIR:

I would respectfully make the following recommendations for promotions in the regular Army, towit: Maj. Gen. W. T. Sherman to be Lieutenant General.[1]

Brig. & Bvt. Maj. Gen. W. S. Hancock to be Maj. General.

Lt. Col. E. O. C. Ord U. S. Artillery & Bvt. Maj. Gn. to be Brigadier General.

In making the recommendation of Gen. Hancock in preference to Gn. Schofield I do so solely on the grounds of present seniority. These two officers are each eminently qualified and deserving of the promotion and I make no distinction between them except that due to this seniority.

I have the honor to be
Very respectfully
your obt. svt.
U. S. GRANT
Lt. Gn.

ALS, DNA, RG 94, ACP, G660 CB 1866.

1. See letter to Bvt. Maj. Gen. Edward D. Townsend, July 28, 1866. On July 26, 1866, Bvt. Col. Ely S. Parker wrote to USG. "Genl Rawlins has been to see the Prest. and reports that he had a long & interesting interview with him. He desired the Genl to inform you that he had already sent in the names of Genl Sherman for Lt. Genl. Gen Hancock for Maj. Genl and Gen Ord for Brig. Genl." ALS, USG 3. On July 28, 11:20 A.M., USG telegraphed to Lt. Gen. William T. Sherman. "The President desires to present you your commission in person, and asks that you will come by Washington to receive it" Telegram sent, DNA, RG 107, Telegrams Collected (Bound); telegram received, DLC-William T. Sherman. On July 28, Sherman, Buffalo, telegraphed to USG. "Dispatch received. I will turn for Washington from Cleveland Sunday Evenig.—Please appoint some hour of Tuesday for me to call on the President.—" Telegram received (on July 29, 11:40 A.M.), DNA, RG 108, Telegrams Received; copy (dated July 29), DLC-USG, V, 54. On July 30, USG wrote to President Andrew Johnson. "A dispatch rec'd from Gen. Sherman in reply to mine requesting him to come by Washington to receive directly from the hands of the President his commission

of Lieut. General announces that he will be here ready to call at the Executive Mansion at any hour to-morrow that may suit the President." ALS, DLC-Andrew Johnson. Sherman arrived in Washington, D. C., on July 31 and, accompanied by USG, received his commission as lt. gen. from Johnson at the White House on Wednesday, Aug. 1, at 10:00 A.M. Sherman diary, July 31–Aug. 1, 1866, InNd.

To Edwin M. Stanton

Washington, D. C. July 25th *1866*

HON. E. M. STANTON,
SEC. OF WAR,
SIR:

I would respectfully but urgently recommend that Brig. & Bvt. Maj. Gn. R. Delafield, Chief Eng. be retired from the service, for long and faithful services, and that Maj. Gen. A. A. Humphries, U. S. Voluntee[rs], and Lt. Col. of Eng. be appointed to his place.

I look upon this change as important to the Army in view of the great work before us of changing our system of SeaCoast defences to meet the improvements of the last few years in appliances to use against such works. Gen. Delafield is too old for this work and has not had the field experience to properly qualify him for it. His age and services entitle him to retire now without discredit. Gen. Humphries, in my opinion, possesses every qualification requisite for the position of Chief Engineer.

I have the honor to be
Very respectfully
your obt. svt.
U. S. GRANT
Lt. Gn.

ALS, DNA, RG 94, ACP, G348 CB 1866.

To Bvt. Maj. Gen. Edward D. Townsend

Washington, D. C.
July 28th 1866.

BVT. MAJ. GN. E. D. TOWNSEND
A. A. GEN. U. S. A.
GENERAL:

I have the honor to accept the appointment of General, U. S. Army confered by Act of Congress, and the will of the President of the United States, on me.

I was born in the State of Ohio, April 22d [27] 1822 and was therefore Forty-four years of age last Apl.

You will please find also enclosed herewith the oath of office required by law.

I have the honor to be
Very repectfully
your obt. svt.
U. S. GRANT
Gen.l U. S. A.

ALS, DNA, RG 94, ACP, 4754 1885. On July 25, 1866, Secretary of War Edwin M. Stanton wrote to USG. "The President has signed the Bill reviving the Grade of General. I have made out and laid your nomination before him, and it will be sent to the Senate this morning." ALS, Justin G. Turner, Los Angeles, Calif. See *U.S. Statutes at Large*, XIV, 223. On July 28, USG signed his oath of office as gen. DS, DNA, RG 94, ACP, 4754 1885. USG's commission as gen. is reproduced in William H. Allen, *The American Civil War Book and Grant Album* (Boston and New York, 1894), p. [238].

Also on July 28, Maj. George K. Leet directed Bvt. Maj. Gen. Edward D. Townsend to issue General Orders No. 53. "The following named Officers are hereby announced as Aides-de-Camp to the General-in-Chief, with the rank of Colonel, to date July 25th 1866. Brevet Brig. Gen. Frederick T. Dent, Major 4th U. S. Infty. Brevet Brig. Gen. Cyrus B. Comstock, Major U. S. Engrs. Brevet Brig. Gen. Horace Porter, Capt. Ordnance U. S. A. Brevet Brig. Gen. Orville E. Babcock, Capt. U. S. Engrs. 2d Lieutenant Adam Badeau, 4th U. S. Infty. 2d Lieutenant Ely S. Parker, 2d U. S. Cavalry" AES and ADf (unnumbered, undated, and in tabular form), DNA, RG 94, Letters Received, 566A 1866; (printed) *ibid.*, ACP, 4754 1885.

On July 30, Bvt. Maj. Gen. Jefferson C. Davis, Louisville, wrote to USG. "Permit me to congratulate you upon your promotion—The compliment thus paid you is the universal verdict of the Country—All your companions in the Army during the War rejoice abit—this I am sure you will appreciate—And now

General after these few words of Compliment please permit me to introduce to you Bvt Brig. Gen. John Ely of vetran reserve Corps: Chief superintendant of the Bureau of freedme &c in this state who visits Washington on a little business: which he will make Known to you should you grant him his desired interview—Allow me to say that Gen. Ely is a faithful & intelligent officer & has performed his duties since he has been my assistant in the Bureau Affairs to my entire satisfaction—" ALS, USG 3. On Aug. 2, Vice Admiral David D. Porter wrote to USG. "Had I not been sick I would have written sooner to congratulate you on your promotion, and can only say now that not one of your many friends rejoices in it more than I do.—I knew three years ago that it would come, and felt that the Rebellion was doomed when you took the helm—I hope you may live many years to enjoy your honors and have higher ones if you desire it, but you would be consulting your own happiness and comfort be remaining in your present position, which is higher than any in the gift of the people" ALS, *ibid.*

On Aug. 27, USG endorsed to Stanton an undated draft order issued as General Orders No. 75. "Uniform of the General and Lieutenant General.—For the General.—The same as for Major General except that on the coat there shall be two rows of twelve buttons each on the breast, placed by fours, and on the shoulder-straps and epaulettes four silver stars. For the Lieutenant General.—The same as for a Major General, except that, on the shoulder-straps and epaulettes there shall be three silver stars." ES and Df (date and order no. in hand of Townsend), DNA, RG 94, Letters Received, 698A 1866.

On Sept. 24, USG wrote to Stanton. "I would respectfully renew my recommendation for the publication of an order fixing the Uniform of Officers holding Brevet Rank. The recommendation was submitted in the shape of an order and is now probably in the hands of the Adj. Gen." ALS, CSmH. On Aug. 2, USG had endorsed to Stanton an undated draft order. "The Regulation prescribing the uniform to be worn by officers of the Army holding brevet commissions is hereby changed so as to permit them to wear the uniform of the grade to which they are brevetted; those holding brevet commissions below the grade of brigadier general to retain the uniform perscribed for their respective Corps, Department or Arm of Service." ES and Df, DNA, RG 94, Letters Received, 785A 1866. On Oct. 18, Leet endorsed to the AGO an undated draft order issued as General Orders No. 86. "The following is substituted for paragraphs 1656 &, 1657 Revised General Regulations for the Army: Field and General Officers having brevets higher than their ordinary commissions will wear the uniform of their brevet rank; those holding brevet rank below that of Brigadier General retaining the uniform of their Corps, Department or arm of service. Captains and Lieutenants having brevets higher than their ordinary commissions will wear the uniform of their ordinary commissions, but with the shoulder-straps and epaulettes of their brevet rank" AES and Df, *ibid.* On March 21, 1867, Maj. and Bvt. Maj. Gen. (of Vols.) Henry E. Maynadier, 12th Inf., Russell Barracks, Washington, D. C., wrote to Bvt. Maj. Gen. Edward R. S. Canby's adjt. claiming the right to wear the uniform of his bvt. vol. rank while on regular duty, unfavorably endorsed by Canby on April 15. ALS and ES, *ibid.*, 570W 1867. On April 19, USG endorsed these papers. "Respectfully forwarded to the Secretary of War. I concur fully in the views of Gen. Canby, and recommend their adoption by the War Department in the settlement of questions of this character." ES, *ibid.*

To Samuel J. Crawford

Washington, D. C. July 29th *18~~5~~6* [*3:10* P.M.]

HON S J CRAWFORD
GOV OF KANSAS
TOPEKA KAN

The Secretary of War [i]nforms me that he has given the order for the distribution of arms and ammunition as you have requested. I have ordered troops to be sent at once to your relief. Fortunately a regiment of colored infantry was recently sent in your direction from Arkansas They may reach you in time.

U S GRANT
General

Telegram sent, DNA, RG 107, Telegrams Collected (Bound); copies, *ibid.*, RG 108, Letters Sent; DLC-USG, V, 47, 60. On July 28, 1866, Governor Samuel J. Crawford of Kan. had telegraphed to Secretary of War Edwin M. Stanton. "The Indians are murdering, robbing and driving the settlers from their homes on our western frontier, Will you immediately order troops to their protection? If not I shall be compelled to call out the militia for that purpose. Will you also direct the proper officers at Fort Leavenworth to turn over to the state two thousand stand of Cavalry arms, with ammunition? Prompt action is desired. Answer." Telegram received (at 2:00 P.M.), DNA, RG 108, Telegrams Received; copy, DLC-USG, V, 54. Stanton referred this telegram to USG. AES (undated), DNA, RG 108, Telegrams Received. On July 30, 1:20 P.M., USG telegraphed to Lt. Gen. William T. Sherman, St. Louis. "Governor Crawford reports the Indians murdering and driving off settlers from Western frontiers of Kansas If possible send troops to their relief Cannot colored regiment just ordered west by you be sent?" Telegram sent, *ibid.*, RG 107, Telegrams Collected (Bound); telegram received, *ibid.*

To Bvt. Maj. Gen. Benjamin W. Brice

Washington, D. C. July 30th *1866*.

BVT. MAJ. GN. B. BRICE,
PAYMASTER ~~U S~~ GEN. U. S. A.
GENERAL:

In filling the appointments created in your Corps by recent act of Congress I would like very much to get R. B. McPherson,[1] brother to Gen. McPherson, who was one of our ablest and best Generals, appointed to a vacancy created by the promotion of one of the present paymasters to a higher grade. McPherson, techn~~a~~ically speaking, may not be regarded as having served as a volunteer. He is very nearsighted which prevented him getting into the service at the begining of the War as such. But he entered the service in charge of Military rail-roads early ~~at~~ in the War, and continued in that service to the end of it. He is a man of fine capacity. It is out of personal regard for the merits and services of Gen. McPherson however that I particularly desire this appointment. I shall recommend it as strongly as I can and now write in hope that you may also concider it favorably. It is my desire to concur as far as possible in the recommendations of the Chiefs of Corps for appointments in their Corps.

Whilst on this subject I would mention the names of two Addl. Paymasters, Reese[2] and Stewart,[3] whose appointments I would like the pleasure of concurring in the recommendation of.

Very respectfully
your obt. svt.
U. S. GRANT
General.

ALS, DNA, RG 94, ACP, G332 CB 1866.

1. See *O.R.*, III, v, 993. Russell B. McPherson was not appointed. On April 13, 1871, USG nominated McPherson for asst. postmaster, Clyde, Ohio.

2. Henry B. Reese, appointed maj. and paymaster as of Jan. 17, 1867.

3. On March 27, 1866, USG wrote to Secretary of War Edwin M. Stanton. "I would most respectfully recommend the immediate appointment of Maj. I. S. Steuart, and Wm A. Rucker, Additional Paymasters, to the Pay Dept. Regular Army to fill the vacancies now existing in that Department. These officers have filled the position of Paymaster during the War with credit to themselves and honor to the service." ALS, DNA, RG 94, ACP, G434 CB 1866. William A. Rucker (as of April 16) and Isaac S. Stewart (as of Oct. 18, 1867) were both appointed maj. and paymaster.

To Maj. Gen. Philip H. Sheridan

Personal. July 30th *1866*

DEAR GENERAL.

Your dispatch recommending that a naval vessel be sent to the Rio Grande was referred to the President with recommendation not only that your recommendation should be complied with but that naval vessels, of the United States should be kept in the Gulf of California and on the Pacific Mexican sea coast. I am glad to let you know that it has had the effect to cause two or three vessels to be sent in compliance with your request. Orders have also been sent to the Commanders of the Pacific Squadron to place vessels in accordance with the other portion of my recommendation.

Since the repeal of our neutrality laws I am in hopes of being able to get authority to dispose of all of our surplus arms and munitions within your command, to the Liberals of Mexico.

Seward is a powerful practical ally of Louis Napoleon, in my opinion, but I am strongly in hope that his aid will do the Empire no good.

Yours Truly
U. S. GRANT
General

MAJ. GEN. P. H. SHERIDAN
NEW ORLEANS, LA.

Copies, DLC-Philip H. Sheridan; USG 3. On July 16, 1866, Maj. Gen. Philip H. Sheridan had written to Brig. Gen. John A. Rawlins. "Since the occupation of the RioGrande frontier by our troops, English and French War-Vessels have been constantly there, or at least made their appearance there occasionally, while not a single Vessel of ours has been there to my Knowledge, as a vessel of observation. Lately, when Metamoras surrendered, an English War Vessel started at once from Vera-Cruz to the mouth of the RioGrande. I recommend that one of our Vessels be sent there occasionally: in fact it would be very well if two occasionally went" LS, DNA, RG 107, Letters Received, S336 1866. On July 25, USG endorsed this letter. "I heartily endorse Gen. Sheridan's recommendation. I would also recommend that the United States should have War Vessels not only in the Gulf of Mexico but off the Coast of Mexico on the Pacific side." AES, *ibid.* On July 27, Secretary of War Edwin M. Stanton wrote to Secretary of the Navy Gideon Welles transmitting Sheridan's letter with USG's endorsement. Copy, *ibid.*

To Maj. Gen. George H. Thomas

Washington July 30th *1866.*

GENERAL:

Your letter of the 25th of July asking authority to go to Nebraska, and other places, in the month of August is received. It will not be necessary for you to take a leave of absence to carry out your plan. You can leave a Staff officer at Hd Qrs. with whom you can communicate by telegraph, when necessary, to administer your command during your absence.

Very respectfully
your obt. svt.
U. S. GRANT
General.

ALS, Mrs. Arthur Loeb, Philadelphia, Pa. On July 25, 1866, Maj. Gen. George H. Thomas had written a letter received at USG's hd. qrs. requesting a six-week leave of absence. DNA, RG 108, Register of Letters Received.

On July 28, Thomas, Nashville, wrote to USG. "The Summer being more than half gone, and the healthiness of this place not having, in the least, been affected, by the unusually hot weather, I respectfully recommend that the Cumberland General Hospital located on the outskirts of Nashville be broken up, and the Buildings be turned over to the Qr Master Dept to be used here after as Barracks for the Batn of the 16th US Inf as long as those Troops are stationed at this place. The site of the Cumberland Hospital is far preferable to the present Barracks of the Infty both on account ~~of considerations~~ of the discipline and sanitary condition of the troops In my opinion there is no longer any necessity for a continuance of the Cumberland General Hospital." ALS, *ibid.*, Letters Received; copy (misdated July 30), *ibid.*, RG 393, Military Div. of the Tenn., Letters Sent. On Aug. 2, Brig. Gen. Joseph K. Barnes, surgeon gen., endorsed this letter. "Respectfully returned. The Adjutant General has received from Major General Thomas information that Cholera has made its appearance at Nashville, as this is the contingency for which Cumberland Hospital was retained, its transfer now is not considered justifiable or expedient." ES, *ibid.*, RG 108, Letters Received. On July 31, Thomas had telegraphed to USG. "The cholera has broken out violently at Louisville in a detachment of recruits just arrived there From N York Taking ~~in~~ this in connection with the fact that the same disease broke out among the troops recently landed at Tybee Island I do not think it safe that any more recruits should be shipped from New York at present" Telegram received (at 11:20 P.M.), *ibid.*, RG 94, Letters Received, 582A 1866; *ibid.*, RG 107, Telegrams Collected (Bound); *ibid.*, RG 108, Telegrams Received; copies, *ibid.*, RG 393, Dept. of the Cumberland, Telegrams Sent; DLC-USG, V, 54. On Aug. 1, Maj. George K. Leet endorsed this telegram. "Respectfully referred to the Adjutant General who will give instructions to have no more recruits sent from N. Y. until abatement of the cholera there." AES, DNA, RG 94, Letters Received, 582A 1866. On the same day, Bvt. Maj. Gen. Edward D. Townsend wrote to USG. "I have the honor to acknowledge the receipt of your instructions endorsed upon a copy of a telegram from Major General George H. Thomas, Commanding Military Division of the Tennessee, reporting that the cholera had broken out at Louisville, Kentucky, in a detachment of recruits just arrived from New York, and in reply thereto, to respectfully inform you that when the recruits referred to left New York, not a single case of cholera had occurred among the troops there. As soon as a case was reported to this Office, instructions were sent to the Superintendent of Recruiting Service in New York City not to send any more men to, or from the General Depôt at Governor's Island, and to stop recruiting in New York City, and measures were at once taken by separating the sick from the well men, and in other ways to prevent a spread of the disease." LS, *ibid.*, RG 108, Letters Received. On the same day, USG telegraphed to Thomas. "Recruits sent from New York started before Cholera had broken out among troops. As soon as it was known that Cholera was among them recruiting was stopped in the City and it was forbidden to send any more away to any point" Copies, *ibid.*, Letters Sent; *ibid.*, RG 393, Dept. of the Cumberland, Telegrams Received; DLC-USG, V, 47, 60.

On July 30, Thomas wrote to USG. "The work of retrenchment in the Quartermaster, Subsistence, Ordnance and Medical Departments throughout my Command will be completed by the end of this year; all the large Depôts being broken up and the public property either disposed of at public sale or shipped to permanent depôts for storage. I have therefore respectfully to request that I may be permitted to make arrangements to remove my Head-Quarters to Louisville Ky on the first of January 1867." Copy, DNA, RG 393, Military Div. of the Miss., Letters Sent. On Aug. 3, USG endorsed this letter. "Respectfully forwarded to the Sec of war, approved." Copy, *ibid.*, RG 108, Register of Letters Received.

To Benson J. Lossing

Washington, D. C., July 30th, 1866:

DEAR SIR:—Among the subjects that occupied my mind when I assumed command at Cairo, in the fall of 1861, was the regular supply of mails to and from the troops; not only those in garrison, but those on the march when active movements should begin. When I commenced the movement on Fort Henry, on Jan. 7, 1862, a plan was proposed by which the mails should promptly follow, and as promptly be sent from the army. So perfect was the organization, that the mails were delivered to the army immediately upon its occupation of the fort. Within one hour after the troops began to march into Fort Donelson, the mail was being distributed to them from the mail wagons. The same promptness was always observed in the armies under my command, up to the period of the final disbandment. It is a source of congratulation that the postal service was so conducted, that officers and men were in constant communication with kindred and friends at home, and with as much regularity as the most favored in the large cities of the Union. The postal system of the army, so far as I know, was not attended with any additional expense to the service. The system adopted by me was suggested and ably superintended by A. H. Markland, special agent of the Post-office Department.

Respectfully, &c.,
U. S. GRANT, General.

Benson J. Lossing, *Pictorial History of the Civil War* (Hartford, Conn., 1868), II, 224*n*. Lossing, born in 1813 in N. Y., orphaned at twelve, moved to New York City in 1838 where he established himself as a wood-engraver, editor, and prolific author. On March 21, 1866, USG had written to "Officers Commanding Troops in Southern States" introducing Lossing who "visits the South for the purpose of seeing different battle fields and to illustrate them for the benefit of the future reader of the scenes through which this country has passed . . . all favors . . . will be appreciated by him and myself." Joseph Rubinfine, List 47 [*1976*], item 48. On Oct. 10, USG wrote a note: "Please give Mr. Lossing, historian, facilities for making such drawings of signals used in the late rebellion as he may desire to take, and it is not improper to have made public, in his 'Illustrated History of the Rebellion.'" Anderson Galleries, Sale No. 1347, April 1–5, 1918, p. 74. See *Pictorial History*, III, 547*n*–49*n*. USG also wrote a note to Julia Dent Grant. "Send my Medal down to the office by the Sergeant without delay. I want to get it Photographed for Lossing's History of the Rebellion." ANS (undated), USG 3. See *Pictorial History*, III, 561; Alexander Davidson, Jr., "How Benson J. Lossing wrote his 'Field Books' of the Revolution, the War of 1812, and the Civil War," *Papers of the Bibliographical Society of America*, XXXII, 57–64.

To Edwin M. Stanton

Washington, D. C. July 31st *1866*

HON. E. M. STANTON,
SEC. OF WAR,
SIR:

I would respectfully recommend that all General officers of volunteers be mustered out of the service, muster-out to take effect from the 31st of August 1866, except Maj. Gn. O. O. Howard and Maj. Gn. F. Steele. In the case of Gen. Howard I would recommend the retention of his volunteer rank so long as his present duties last and the law will permit.

In the case of Gn. Steele I would recommend his musterout to take effect thirty days after being relieved from the Command of his Dept.

I would further recommend that the Staff Depts of the Army be ordered to muster-out all volunteers still retained in their departments, (except such as it may be deemed absolutely necessary to retain in the Freedmens Bureau) by the 31st of August 1866.

I would further recommend that the Chief of the Freedmens Bureau be directed to relieve from duty, and report for muster out, as fast as their services can be dispensed with, or they replaced by other officers, all officers whos regimental organizations have been discharged from service.

The Chief of the Freedmens Bureau can be authorized to name any, or all, officers serving with troops in the Southern states to perform the duties of Asst. Commissioners of the Bureau in addition to their other duties. He could also be authorized to detail officers who may hereafter be appointed to the Veteran Corps provided for by recent act of Congress to relieve officers who should be mustered out.

Very respectfully
your obt. svt.
U. S. GRANT
General.

ALS, DNA, RG 94, ACP, G674 CB 1866.

Also on July 31, 1866, USG endorsed to Secretary of War Edwin M. Stanton draft orders, issued on Aug. 2 as General Orders No. 59. "The present arrangement of Military Divisions and Departments is hereby discontinued and the following division and commands substituted. 1st Department of the East, Headquarters Philadelphia, Penn., Major General G. G. Meade to command, will embrace the New England States, New York, New Jersey and Pennsylvania. 2d Department of the Lakes, Headquarters Detroit, Michigan, Brigadier & Brevet Major General J. Hooker to command, will embrace the States of Ohio, Michigan, Indiana, Illinois and Wisconsin. 3d Department of the Potomac, Headquarters ~~Baltimore~~, ~~Md~~., Richmond Va, Brigadier & Brevet Major General J. M. Schofield to command, will embrace the States of ~~Delaware~~, ~~Maryland~~, Virginia and West

Virginia. 4th Department of the South, Headquarters Charleston, S. C., Brigadier ~~& Brevet Major General W. S. Rosecrans~~ Major General Sickles to command, will embrace the States of North Carolina and South Carolina. 5th Department of the Tennessee, Headquarters Nashville, Tenn., Major General G H Thomas to command, will embrace the States of Kentucky, Tennessee, Georgia, Alabama and Mississippi. 6th Department of the Gulf, Headquarters New Orleans, La., Major General P. H. Sheridan to command, will embrace the States of Florida, Louisiana and Texas. 7th Department of the Arkansas, Headquarters Little Rock, Ark., Brigadier & Brevet Major General E. O. C. Ord to command, will embrace the State of Arkansas and Indian Territory West. 8th Department of the Missouri, Headquarters Leavenworth, Kan., Major General W. S. Hancock to command, with the same boundaries as now constituted except such as may be detached to form a new Department to be created. 9th Department of the Platte, Headquarters Omaha, Neb., Brigadier General P. St. G. Cooke to command, with same boundaries as now constituted except such as may be detached to form a new Department to be created. 10th Department of California, Headquarters San Francisco, Cal., Brevet Major General I McDowell to command, same as now constituted. 11th Department of the Columbia, Headquarters Portland, Or., Brigadier & Brevet Major General J. Pope to command, same as now constituted. 12th Brigadier & Brevet Major General A. H. Terry will report to Lieut. Gen. W. T. Sherman to take command of a Department to be created out of the Departments of the Missouri and the Platte according to his judgment, subject to the approval of the Secretary of War. 13th Lieutenant General W. T. Sherman is assigned to the general command of the Departments of the Arkansas, the Missouri, the Platte, and the new Department to be created. The style of Lt Gen. Sherman's command will be the Military Division of the Missouri, Headquarters St Louis, Mo. 14th The Departments of California and the Columbia will constitute a Military Division under Major General H. W. Halleck, Headquarters San Francisco, Cal. 15th The Department of Washington, with its present limits, Brigadier & Brevet Major General E. R. S. Canby to command, will be continued until further orders, with Maryland and Delaware added." Df (alterations and additions in nos. 3 and last five words of 15 in USG's hand; in no. 4 in Stanton's hand), *ibid.*, Letters Received, 598A 1866.

To J. Russell Jones

July 31st *1866*.

DEAR JONES,

The President withdrew Norton's[1] name at my request but it seems afterwards sent it in without my knowledge. It will not be proper for me to interfere any further in the matter nor do I suppose I could do any good by doing so. I do not suppose you will be be interfered with, but politicians are so uncertain that I think I will have to decline sending you the grey horse. The horse railroad would have to suffer for his keeping you know if you should be turned out of office.

Yours Truly
U. S. GRANT

ALS, USG 3.

1. Jesse O. Norton, born in Vt. in 1812, graduated from Williams College in 1835, started to practice law in Joliet, Ill., in 1840, and served three terms as a Whig and Republican U.S. representative (1853–57, 1863–65). On July 3, 1866, President Andrew Johnson nominated Norton as U.S. attorney for northern Ill., withdrawing the nomination on July 5. Norton was renominated on July 20 and confirmed on July 26. J. Russell Jones then served as U.S. marshal for northern Ill.

To Edwin M. Stanton

Washington, D. C. JAug 1 *1866*.

HON. E. M. STANTON,
SEC. OF WAR,
SIR:

I would respectfully recommend that authority be given to Lt. Gen. W. T. Sherman to organize Six Hundred (600) Indian scouts, Maj. Gn. Sheridan Two Hundred (200) and Maj. Gn. Halleck Two Hundred, (200) as provided for by the Act of Congress reorganizing the regular Army, to be used within their respective command. In view of threatened hostilities and the meagre force now in the Indian Territories I would respectfully suggest that this authority be communicated by telegraph.

Very respectfully
your obt. svt.
U. S. GRANT
General.

ALS, DNA, RG 94, Letters Received, 575A 1866.

To Edwin M. Stanton

Washington, August. 2d *1866.*

HON. E. M. STANTON
SECRETARY OF WAR.
SIR:

As an increase to the force on the plains before the beginning of winter is almost a necessity I would respectfully recommend the immediate organization of the colored force authorized by the "Act" reorganizing the army.—I would suggest that Gen. Sheridan[1] be authorized to raise two of these regiments, one of cavalry and one of infantry, and that Gen. Sherman[2] be authorized to raise the other two. In each case I would recommend that colored volunteers still in service be authorized to receive their discharge where they enlist in the new organizations. There are now three regiments of colored volunteers on the plains; a fourth on its way. From this force it is believed the two regiments for Gen. Sherman's command can be raised. To carry out this plan I would recommend the immediate appointment of all the field officers for these regiments, and instruct them to select one officer for each company to be organized from the officers serving with colored troops. Officers so selected need not be mustered out whilst retained for duty, even though their regiments may be. Their names should be reported to the Adjutant General at once, with such recommendation as to their merits, whether fitted for permanent appointment in the regular army or not.

The following are my recommendations for the appointments of field officers for colored troops, towit:

Infantry—

Capt. & Bvt Maj. Gen. W. B. Hazen to be Colonel.
Capt. & Bvt Maj. Gen. J. A Mower to be Colonel.
Maj. & Bvt Maj. Gen. C. Grover to be Lieut. Colonel.
Capt. & Bvt Maj. Gen. J. W. Turner to be Lieut. Colonel.

From Volunteer Service:

N. A. Miles to be Colonel.

C. J. Paine to be Colonel.
E. W. Hincks to be Lieut. Colonel.
J. W. Sprague to be Lieut. Colonel.

Cavalry—

Capt. & Bvt Maj. Gen. G. A. Custer[3] to be Lieut Col.

From Volunteer Service:

E. Hatch to be Colonel.
B. H. Grierson to be Colonel
C. C. Wolcott to be Lieut. Colonel.

Very respectfully
Your obed't. serv't.
U. S. GRANT
General.

P. S. To this list I would add as Major of ~~Infantry~~ Cavalry (Colored) 1st Lt. & Bvt. Brig. Gn. Jas. F. Wade, 1st Cavalry and as Maj. of Infantry, (Colored) Bvt. Brig. Gn. Howard, U. S. Vols.

U. S. GRANT
General.

LS, DNA, RG 94, ACP, G661 CB 1866. On July 28, 1866, U.S. Senator Henry Wilson of Mass. had written to USG. "Private and *unofficial* . . . I have had a hard fight over the army bill, but have carried it nearly as I wished, & I believe generally satisfactory to the army, and as there are a few colored regiments provided for, I take the liberty of saying a few words to you about them. You will of course be consulted, and will have considerable influence, in the appointment of officers to command them, and I trust your influence may be used to secure men whose sympathies are with our institutions—men who always did and do yet believe that the negro could fight, and that he 'has some rights' &c. Such men are Russell, Ames, *Brisbin* and others, as you and I well know. In their hands the negroes will be moulded into good soldiers, and citizens, and such, and only such as they, should be placed over them. The bill as passed, is free from any body's *eccentricities* or oddities, though it was hard work in the conference to keep them out, as certain parties not in the Senate seemed determined to make a raid on the *army*, which *I* would not permit. The bill is as near as I expected to what I wanted: *I* would not have had any veteran reserve, but took four regts rather than lose the bill. Please consider my suggestions about officers of colored troops, & if possible get the three I have named made Colonels—Brisbin in cavalry." ALS, USG 3. On Aug. 1, Maj. Gen. Oliver O. Howard, Bureau of Refugees, Freedmen, and Abandoned Lands, wrote to USG. "I have the honor to renew recommendations formerly made as follows: For *Colonel* of a colored regiment—Bvt. Maj. Genl. *J. W. Sprague*—Brigadier General U. S. Vols. For *Lieutenant Colonel*—Bvt. Brig. Genl. *C. H. Howard*, Col.

128th U. S. Colored Troops. For *Major*—Lieut. Colonel *Wm M. Beebe*—128th Regt. U. S. Colored Troops. For Captain of one of the Companies—Capt. *A. P. Ketchum* 128th Regt. U. S. Colored Troops—Bvt. Major U. S. Vols. The above officers have my unqualified recommendation." LS, DNA, RG 94, ACP, H702 CB 1866.

1. On Aug. 6, Maj. Gen. Philip H. Sheridan, New Orleans, telegraphed to Brig. Gen. John A. Rawlins. "From my observation in the Rio Grande while there I can recommend the muster out of three 3 regiments of Colored troops in Dep't Texas can I have permission" Telegram received (on Aug. 7, 8:30 A.M.), *ibid.*, RG 107, Telegrams Collected (Bound); *ibid.*, RG 108, Telegrams Received; copies, *ibid.*, RG 393, Military Div. of the Southwest and Dept. of the Gulf, Telegrams Sent; DLC-USG, V, 54; DLC-Philip H. Sheridan; USG 3. On Aug. 7, USG telegraphed to Sheridan. "Two regiments of colored regulars will be raised out of troops in your command. When that is done you may muster out of service all others colored troops you can spare" Telegram sent, DNA, RG 107, Telegrams Collected (Bound); copies, *ibid.*, RG 108, Letters Sent; DLC-USG, V, 47, 60.

2. On Aug. 7, Lt. Gen. William T. Sherman, St. Louis, telegraphed to USG. "Dispatches all on hand on my arrival I will at once instruct as to the two 2 regiments of blacks and the scouts The Indians are made restless by the travel over the new road beyond Laramie I want to start out early next week" Telegram received (at 5:30 P.M.), DNA, RG 107, Telegrams Collected (Bound); *ibid.*, RG 108, Telegrams Received; copies, *ibid.*, RG 393, Military Div. of the Miss., Letters Sent; DLC-USG, V, 54. On Aug. 13, Bvt. Maj. Gen. Edward D. Townsend telegraphed to Sherman. "General Grant directs that in raising new colored regiments, recruiting from volunteer regiments now in service be first exhausted, before taking men from Civil life. That then, care be taken not to disturb labor contracts to get recruits. That the depôts for regiments be chosen with regard to places where recruits are made, so that new regiments shall replace the volunteer regiments, to be discharged when reduced by enlistment in regulars. Acknowledge receipt." LS (telegram sent), DNA, RG 107, Telegrams Collected (Bound); copies (2—one dated Aug. 14), *ibid.*, RG 393, Dept. of Ark., Letters Received; (2—one dated Aug. 14) *ibid.*, Dept. of the Mo., Letters Received. Also on Aug. 13 and 14, Townsend sent identical telegrams to Maj. Gen. George H. Thomas and Sheridan. LS (telegrams sent), *ibid.*, RG 107, Telegrams Collected (Bound). On Aug. 17, Sherman, Omaha, telegraphed to USG. "Dispatch as to recruits for new Cavalry regiment rec'd. I can organize the regiment best at Ft Riley Kansas where we have good quarters & stables & can use other Cavalry now there. I start for Laramie tomorrow a m" Telegram received (at 9:45 P.M.), *ibid.*; *ibid.*, RG 108, Telegrams Received; copy, DLC-USG, V, 54.

3. On Aug. 13, Capt. and Bvt. Maj. Gen. George A. Custer, 5th Cav., Washington, D. C., wrote to Townsend requesting assignment to duty in Mich. on account of the death of his father-in-law. ALS, DNA, RG 94, Letters Received, 712A 1866. On the same day, USG endorsed this letter. "Gen. Custer has been recommended for a Lieut. Colonelcy of a Colored regiment which, if he gets, woul[d] preclude the possibility of giving him the detail he asks. I would be willing however to see his appointment transfered from a colored

regiment to a white one and the Volunteer officer recommended for the same grade in the white Cavalry transfered to take his place." AES, *ibid.* Docketing indicates that Custer had been appointed lt. col., 9th Cav. *Ibid.* On Aug. 18, Lt. Col. John C. Kelton, AGO, endorsed this letter. "Respectfully returned to the Genl in Chief for his recommendation as to the regiment to which Lt Colo Custer should be transferred Capt Merritt is proposed as the Lt Colo of the 7th Cav'y. No one has been decided upon yet for the 8th cavy" AES, *ibid.* On Aug. 20, USG again endorsed this letter. "I have no further recommendation to make in case of Gn Custer." AES, *ibid.* Later, Secretary of War Edwin M. Stanton endorsed this letter. "Genl Custar thinks the reccommendation of Genl Grant implies that being assigned to a White regt his application ~~to~~ ~~be~~ within can be granted. General Grant will please report his recommendation in that particular" AES (undated), *ibid.* On Sept. 24, USG wrote a note. "The regiment to which Gen. Custer has been appointed is already recruited and assembled at Jefferson Bks. Mo. He can not therefore be of service to the Government if assigned according to his request. Further, no officers have been appointed to the 7th Cavalry, as yet, except the Field officers. It is therefore very important that these officers should be on duty with it without delay. All the Field officers to the 7th Cavalry, who have received their appointments, have been ordered to join it." ANS, *ibid.* On the same day, USG wrote to Townsend. "In view of the 7th Cavalry being at Fort Reily Gn. Custer's orders may be changed to 'joining his regiment without delay, with authority to go to Fort Monroe for his horses and other Military equipments.' He can also have transportation for two horses, and necessary baggage, to his regiment." ALS, *ibid.*, 714A 1866. On March 1, 1867, Col. Andrew J. Smith, 7th Cav., St. Louis, telegraphed to USG. "I hope Custer may be confirmed as Lieut Col. of the seventh (7th) Cavalry. He is a worthy officer and an accomplished cavalry soldier. I cant well do without him." Telegram received (at 2:00 P.M.), *ibid.*, ACP, 1239 1871; *ibid.*, RG 108, Telegrams Received; copy, DLC-USG, V, 55. On the same day, USG endorsed this telegram. "Respectfully forwarded to the Secretary of War" ES, DNA, RG 94, ACP, 1239 1871.

To Edwin M. Stanton

Washington Aug. 3d *1866.*

HON. E. M. STANTON,
SEC. OF WAR.
SIR.

I would respectfully recommend the following promotions in the Inspector Generals Department towit.

Major & Bvt. Maj. Gen. Absalom Baird to be Lieut. Colonel.

Major Nelson H. Davis to be Lieut. Colonel, and
Maj. & Bvt. Brig. Gn. James Totten to be Lieut. Colonel.

In making this recommendation I have selected Gen. Baird and passed him over the heads of his senior, Major Roger Jones, because I think his services during the rebellion entitle him to promotion which he would not get, in his Corps, if the rule of promoting by Seniority is adhered to.

Maj. Davis and Gn. Totten are the Senior Inspectors of the rank of Major.

Very respectfully
your obt. svt.
U. S. GRANT
General,

ALS, DLC-Edwin M. Stanton. All four officers named were promoted to lt. col. and asst. inspector gen. as of June 13, 1867.

To Alexander W. Randall

Washington, D. C.
August 4th 1866.

HON. A. W. RANDALL,
POSTMASTER GENERAL,
DEAR SIR:

Permit me to recommend as a most worthy lady for employment in the P. O. Department Mrs. Dixon[1] of Va. now a resident of this city. Mrs. Dixon is the widow of a loyal Virginian who was driven out of the state at the begining of the rebellion, on account of his loyalty. He took service in the Union Army, as paymaster, and continued in it until the close of hostilities. Last year he was murdered by a Virginia ex-rebel officer leaving a widow and eight children who found their home so unpleasant for them, even dangerous, that I sent Goverment teams to move them to this city. They are dependent for a support upon what they can earn. I regard this as a very deserving case and shall feel glad if suitable employment can be given to Mrs. Dixon.

Very respectfully
your obt. svt.
U. S. Grant
General.

ALS, DLC-USG, I, B. Alexander W. Randall, born in N. Y. in 1819, moved to Wis. in 1840 to practice law, and was elected governor (1857–61). He was confirmed as asst. postmaster gen. on Jan. 9, 1863, and as postmaster gen. on July 25, 1866.

1. Annie E. Dixon, widow of Henry T. Dixon, who was appointed maj. and paymaster as of June 1, 1861, mustered out on July 31, 1865, murdered on Nov. 10. See *SRC*, 40-2-17.

To Edwin M. Stanton

Washington August 6th *1866*.

Hon. E. M. Stanton,
Sec. of War;
Sir:

I would respectfully recommend that the organization of the four regiments of "Invalid" troops authorized by "Act of Congress" be commenced at once. I would suggest that one regiment be formed in this City, one in New York Harbor, (as soon as the health of that harbor will permit) one in New Port Ky. and one at Jefferson Barracks, Mo. Recruits can be received by all recruiting officers for these regiments and forwarded, ~~thence~~ by detachments, to the nearest points where "Invalid" Regiments are being organized.

The Field officers of these regiments can all be appointed at once and the regiments organized under them. I respectfully recommend the following officers for promotion to these regiments; towit:

Maj. & Bvt. Maj. Gn J. C. Robinson, 2d U. S. Inf.y to be Colonel.

Maj. & Bvt. Brig. Gn. Joseph H. Potter, 19th Inf.y to be Colonel.

Maj. & Bvt. Brig. Gn. Thos. G. Pitcher, 16th Inf.y to be Colonel.

Brig. & Bvt. Maj. Gn. Wager Swayne, U. S. Vols to be Colonel.

Maj. & Bvt. Col. Louis H. Marshall, 16th Inf.y to be Lt. Colonel.

Capt. & Bvt. Brig. Gn Alex. S. Webb, 11th U. S. Infantry to be Lieut. Colonel.

Capt. & Bvt. Maj. Gn. Francis Fessenden 19th U. S. Inf.y to be Major.

1st Lieut. & Bvt. Brig. Gn. Martin D. Hardin to be Major.

Very respectfully
your obt. svt.
U. S. GRANT
General.

ALS, DNA, RG 94, ACP, G790 CB 1866. On Aug. 5, 1866, USG had written to Secretary of War Edwin M. Stanton. "I would respectfully recommend Capt. J. B. McIntosh, Brevet Brig. Gen. in the regular Army, for Lieut. Col. of Invalids. He is a gallant officer and lost a leg in the service. In making this recommendation I would take the name of Gen. Webb from the recommendations sent in this morning; and if but two Colonelcies are given to the regular Army, in the Invalid Corps, I would take the name of Gen. Potter off also. ~~the~~" ALS, *ibid.*, 4214 1873.

Also on Aug. 6, 7, 17, and 22, USG wrote to Stanton transmitting lists of officers recommended for appointments. LS, *ibid.*, G658 CB 1866; *ibid.*, G659 CB 1866; *ibid.*, G815 CB 1866; *ibid.*, G816 CB 1866. See *ibid.*, G346 CB 1866. On Aug. 24, USG wrote to Stanton. "In my list of Aug 22d I recommended R. B. Potter of N. Y. for a Lt. Colcy. I now recommend that he be appointed Colonel vice Duncan, that J. J. Bartlett be made Lt. Col instead of Major & that Gen. J. E. Hamblin be appointed Major from NewYork to fill Bartletts place. NewYork is fairly entitled to this additional Colonel." LS, *ibid.*, G819 CB 1866. On Feb. 1, Jeremiah T. Boyle, Louisville City Railroad Co., had written to USG recommending Capt. and Bvt. Brig. Gen. Horatio G. Gibson, 3rd Art., for appointment. ALS, *ibid.*, G127 CB 1863. On Dec. 29, USG wrote to Stanton. "I have the honor to renew my recommendation of Aug. 7th for filling the majorities of artillery, substituting Captain H. G. Gibson for Capt.ain W. M. Graham; so that the list will now stand: . . ." LS, *ibid.*, G753 CB 1866.

On Aug. 6 and 14, Maj. George K. Leet had written to Maj. Gen. Philip H. Sheridan and other gen. officers, first requesting promotion recommendations for U.S. Army 1st and 2nd lts., and second asking for recommendations of vol. officers for appointment as field officers. LS (2—addressed to Maj. Gen. George

G. Meade), *ibid.*, RG 393, Military Div. of the Atlantic, Letters Received; (the second addressed to Maj. Gen. George H. Thomas) *ibid.*, Dept. of the Tenn., Unbound Materials, Letters Received; copies (of the first dated Aug. 4), *ibid.*, RG 108, Letters Sent; DLC-USG, V, 47, 60. On Aug. 15 and 23, Sheridan responded directly to USG. LS, DNA, RG 94, ACP, S1906 CB 1866; *ibid.*, S1907 CB 1866.

On Sept. 18, 21, 22, Oct. 1, and 13, USG transmitted additional lists for appointment to Stanton. ES, *ibid.*, 789G CB 1866; LS, *ibid.*, G749 CB 1866; *ibid.*, G430 CB 1866; *ibid.*, G818 CB 1866; *ibid.*, 824G CB 1866. On Sept. 17, USG wrote to Stanton. "I have the honor to recommend the following appointments. Lt. Col. C. C. Walcutt 10 U. S. Cavalry to be Colonel 32d Infantry vice Force, declined. Maj. J. W. Forsyth to be Lt. Col. 10th Cavalry vice Walcutt. W. Redwood Price of Ohio to be Major 9th Cavalry vice Forsyth. R. De Trobriand of New York to be Colonel 31st Infy vice Slocum, declined." LS, *ibid.*, 814G CB 1866. On Oct. 8, USG wrote to Stanton. "I have the honor to recommend that Chas. C. Wolcott, appointed Lt. Col. of Cavalry, regular Army, be transfered to the Infantry, same grade, vice J. W. Sprague declined. I make this recommendation because I doubt the elegebility of Col. Wolcott for the cavalry in consequence of his not having served with the Cavalry during the War." ALS, *ibid.*, 817G CB 1866. On Oct. 23, USG endorsed an AGO memorandum concerning the assignment of Lt. Col. Charles C. Walcutt. "In my opinion, Gen'l. Walcutt having served more than two years as a General Officer, thereby rendering himself eligible to command troops of all arms of the service, is under the spirit of the law eligible to a commission in the cavalry service." ES, *ibid.*, W1009 CB 1866.

On Aug. 11, U.S. Senator Henry B. Anthony of R. I., Providence, had written to USG. "You may not remember that I represented to you the case of Capt. William H Walcott, retired from the 17th Infantry, on account of the loss of a leg in battle; but now fully competent for active duty. You told me that if the army bill should pass you would take him into favorable consideration for one of the new commissions. His papers are on file with the Secretary. I feel an especial interest in this case, because he is a gallant fellow, full of zeal and has approved himself an excellent officer; just the kind of man you would select, and who would vindicate your selection." ALS, *ibid.*, 1683 1871. On Oct. 9, USG wrote to Stanton recommending William H. Walcott and eight others for appointment to the Veteran Reserve Corps. LS, *ibid.*, 791G CB 1866.

On Oct. 17, USG wrote to Stanton. "In view of the facts that the 7th Regt. of Cavalry is already nearly full, and yet is almost without Company Officers, that the men will desert rapidly unless Company Officers are appointed; and that the regiment is needed at once for service against the Indians, I would urgently recommend that the Company Officers be appointed without delay. I submit a special list of recommendations for Company Officers of this regiment herewith." LS, *ibid.*, G454 CB 1866.

On Oct. 29, Nov. 15, 30, Dec. 28, and Feb. 15, 1867, USG wrote to Stanton transmitting additional lists for appointment or promotion. LS, *ibid.*, G792 CB 1866; *ibid.*, G747 CB 1866; *ibid.*, G825 CB 1866; *ibid.*, G758 CB 1866; *ibid.*, G56 CB 1867. An additional list, dated Dec., 1866, is *ibid.*, G701 CB 1866.

On Oct. 30, USG wrote to Stanton. "I have the honor to recommend Maj. & Bvt. Maj. Gen Frank Wheaton, for the appointment of Lt. Col. of Infantry to fill the original vacancy declined by Gen. Brannan or Howe." Copies, DLC-USG, V,

47, 60; DNA, RG 108, Letters Sent. On Dec. 11, USG wrote to Stanton. "I have the honor to recommend Jas. W. Latta for the appointment of 1st Lt. in the 40th U. S. Inf.y vice Jas. T. Bates declined. Address; care Hon. Chas. O'Neill, M. C. Washington, D. C." ALS, *ibid.*, RG 94, ACP, V21 CB 1865.

To Maj. Gen. Winfield S. Hancock

Washington, D. C., Aug. 8th, 1866.

MAJ. GEN. ~~H. W. HALLECK~~ W. S. HANCOCK
ST. LOUIS, MO.
GENERAL:

The President with whom I have just had a conversation, desires that I should send an officer of discretion to Jefferson City, to consult with the Governor of the State on Mo. affairs. From accounts received here there seems to be danger of collision between the different factions (political) about election times. This should be avoided if possible. It is understood that the Governor is organizing militia which he may use on that occasion. If there is danger of violence would it not be better to call on the Government to place troops, under his control of the District Commander at the most threatened points to keep the peace and preserve law and order? Is there not danger of a force called out by the Governor and under the exclusive control of the Governor, in the present antagonistic state of public feeling, being regarded by those opposed to the present party in power as a force not intended to protect the purity of the ballot but to control the election?

Peace, good order and observance of the law is what is wanted. I want you to see the Governor and influential citizens and do what you can to secure this object by advice, and report what you find to be the state of public feeling, and the danger, if any, you may apprehend. I do not know that the military can be used in the State except at the instance of the Governor. It can be stationed however where we please to put it, and if riots do occur it will be on hand to suppress such riots. This is not to be regarded in the light of official instructions to you, but rather as private and confidential instructions to get information upon which official action may be based if it becomes necessary.

Very respectfully
Your obt. servt.
U S GRANT
General.

This letter is strictly private and confidential, not to be shown to the Governor of Missouri, or any other person.

U. S. GRANT.
General.

Copies, DLC-USG, V, 47, 60; DNA, RG 108, Letters Sent. On Aug. 11, 1866, Maj. Gen. Winfield S. Hancock, Carondelet, Mo., wrote to USG. "Your communication of August 8th has just been received. I understand the matter to which you refer, in its general bearings, and will proceed to Jefferson city, by the first train leaving here after I have had interviews with prominent persons here, in whose judgement I have confidence. To morrow, being Sunday, no trains leave for Jefferson city, and I shall not be able I fear, to see the persons referenced to, in time to take the last train of today, Still that will not be important. I will advise you by letter as to my views So Soon as I return. My impression now is from what I have observed that the organization of troops at this time, by the Governor, tends to produce fear and excitement and will possibly interfere with the freedom of the elections—Certainly So if they are used on the day of election. I am now inclined to believe that with the present temper of the people of both parties, and the nervousness incident to the Situation, that a firm body of good troops placed at the proximate center under the direction of discreet District Commanders, to preserve the peace in case of riots, would have a tendency to prevent them and to check the partizan use of the State troops by unwise commanders. Still I am perfectly free to give you [disinterested] advice, and I know that it would be hurtful to give advice which would cause action that afterwards might seem to have been unnecessary. I Saw General Sherman yesterday; I believe he has left (today) for Omaha. As General Pope is far distant on the plains, exercising the command of the Department to a useful purpose, it was thought advisable by Genl S. and myself that I should not proceed to Leavenworth to relieve him until his return—which it was understood would be about the 15th of September. I have been unwell for Several days and was only waiting until I felt perfectly well, to proceed to Baltimore and to wind up the affairs of the Middle Department: I shall not now go to Baltimore, and in view of matters here (in this State) and in consideration of General Sherman's understanding of matters, I think it would be well for you to telegraph me or him—to the effect that I should take command here at once. I need not interfere with Indian matters—leaving those to General Pope until his return. Considering that Genl Sherman proposes to be absent three months (or less), if it is thought necessary to Send troops here, it would be better that I should be directed to establish my Head Quarters here and not in Kansas—certainly until Genl Sherman's return or until further orders. I might indeed press upon you the fact that the proper place for the administrative commander of this Dept, is always in St Louis: but as the order is issued to the contrary, and I believe Genl Sherman does not wish it otherwise, I do not desire to press the matter upon your attention unless I should do So through him. As I have already conversed with him on the subject and learned from him that the designation of Leavenworth as Head Quarters—was pronounced at Washington, I shall make no further comment in reference to it even through him, except So far as relates to the matter in point: and it is well known that the Commander should be near the Sources of transportation and Supply: The troops will come here—And will not proceed to Leavenworth: That is the proper post I conceive for a District Commander: Leavenworth has lost its former importance from the fact that there is a Rail road to Kearney &c. as one Route and one to Riley, daily progressing, as the other. I have no staff with me—not an aide even, (Graham at Fort Benton or vicinity, had not at latest advices: recd his orders). Should Bvt Brig Gen Mitchell be appointed in one of the new Regiments, I request he may be ordered to report to me. I will make him an Aide. Should he be appointed in the Staff ~~officer~~ or as a Field officer, I should like to have him, as a. a. G. or a. I. G. and you will do me a favor by complying with my request. I understand the nature of your letter as confidential and unofficial and will So act in reference to the matters in point: and the letter will be shown to no one. . . . In reading over my letter I have thought from its wording in one or two cases, you might think I had some what misinterpreted your letter: but such is not the case. I understand the point to be obtained if possible: is to have Federal troops at hand under the Regular commanders, to preserve order in case of necessity, instead of the irresponsible partizan state troops under the control of the Governor: and in speaking of troops arriving here, I do not forget that there are troops in the Dept: Some no doubt available: As yet I do not know their numbers or disposition," ALS, DNA, RG 108, Letters Received. See letter to Maj. Gen. William T. Sherman, July 21, 1866.

On Aug. 16, Hancock wrote to USG at great length about the meeting with Governor Thomas C. Fletcher of Mo. ALS, DNA, RG 108, Letters Received.

On Aug. 18, 12:30 P.M., USG telegraphed to Hancock. "Take immediate command of Department of Missouri with Head Quarter at St Louis, until the return of Genl Sherman." Telegram sent, *ibid.*, RG 107, Telegrams Collected (Bound); telegram received, *ibid.*, RG 94, Generals' Papers and Books, Winfield S. Hancock. On Aug. 20, Hancock wrote to USG acknowledging USG's telegram. Carnegie Book Shop, Catalogue 300 [*1968*], no. 226; DNA, RG 108, Register of Letters Received.

On Aug. 26 (twice) and Aug. 28, Hancock wrote to USG about affairs in Mo. ALS, *ibid.*, Letters Received. On Aug. 29, Hancock twice wrote to USG transmitting additional documents. LS, *ibid.*

On Aug. 30, adding a postscript on Aug. 31, Hancock wrote to USG. "I send some communications between myself and Lieut Genl Sherman, numbered according to date of receipt or issue; I have felt bound to send the troops from Riley and Leavenworth as directed by Genl Sherman, although I wanted them here. The Battery from Jefferson Barracks Genl Cooke did not want at present so I was enabled to retain that. (I have two Companies of Infantry, at Independence.) All the troops possible to be had for Service here are those remaining at the following posts, Two Companies of Infantry at Fort Riley which is the whole garrison—one Company of artillery at Leavenworth all the Garrison not previously ordered away—and one Company of artillery temporarily at Jefferson Barracks Mo the entire garrison. By Genl Shermans letter it will be seen that I have no certainty of obtaining the 3d Battns of 19th Infantry from Arkansas—soon and have no troops in case of emergency—There are about four hundred recruits for the 8th Cavalry at Fort Riley—but they have no arms and are not available. . . . P. S. The following Official copy of telegram has been rec'd. since the above communication was written, but it does not materially affect the order." LS, *ibid.* The enclosures are *ibid.* On Aug. 30, Lt. Gen. William T. Sherman, Fort Laramie, telegraphed to USG. "General Hancock is using some troops in Missouri it may be by order of the President If so tell him that we need every man we have & more too on the plains but by November we may have some new troops ready" Telegram received (on Aug. 31, 12:30 P.M.), *ibid.*, RG 107, Telegrams Collected (Bound); *ibid.*, RG 108, Telegrams Received; copy, DLC-USG, V, 54. On Sept. 5, 21, and 22, Hancock forwarded additional papers to USG. ES and copies, DNA, RG 108, Letters Received.

On Sept. 3, noon, Bvt. Brig. Gen. Cyrus B. Comstock telegraphed to USG, Buffalo. "*Cipher* . . . Hancock writes August 28th, that the governor promises to disband the partisan troops already raised and organize the militia. Says he has but four companies available and the registration begins Sep't 20th. He was however in communication with Sherman at Laramie on Aug 30.—Sherman reiterating the order to send troops to Cooke, fearing a general Indian war and not fearing trouble in Missouri. Mr Dent was very ill yesterday but is quite well again this morning, having had a convulsion" Telegram sent, *ibid.*, RG 107, Telegrams Collected (Bound); copies, *ibid.*, RG 108, Letters Sent; *ibid.*, Letters Received; DLC-USG, V, 47, 60. Also at noon, Comstock telegraphed to Hancock. "Your letters are recieved. Genl Grant now on his way to Chicago will probably not be back here before the 9th. inst. when he will see them. If any action is necessary before that time you had best communicate with him direct" Telegram sent, DNA, RG 107, Telegrams Collected (Bound); copies, *ibid.*, RG 108, Letters Sent; *ibid.*, Letters Received; DLC-USG, V, 47, 60. On the same day (Monday), Hancock, St. Louis, twice wrote to USG. "Private, . . . I enclose you the last letter of the Governor of this state, to me, together with my reply—I also enclose a telegram from the Acting Adj' General of the State. The Governor promised to furnish me with a list of his Military organizations which he has not yet done (unless this telegram is considered to furnish the information). The promise to me however related to armed *and* unarmed organizations—and there are understood to be many of the latter as classified by the Governor. I have a witness of this promise. The Governor left for Philadelphia, the day after the interview in question—and I suppose will not be back for Some days to come. The understanding between the Governor and my self at our last interview, was that the partizan organizations should be disbanded at once—To defer it until after the day of Registration—or until that time, would be a clear violation of the Spirit of the Governors promise. I have a witness that it would also be hostile to the letter of said promise. I have daily reports in writing and otherwise, of Secret transfer of Arms to different portions of the State: I fear these statements are true: It is probable that the organizations to be Armed are *Leagues* of the Radical party, not under state authority: but the facts can Scarcely be unknown to the Governor: Where the Arms are obtained from I do not know: They may belong to the State or they may be contributed. I surmise that the State Arms without being issued to organizations other than those admitted in the enclosed Telegram, are being placed at points convenient of access in case it is deemed necessary to use them by Leagues or other organizations: If the Governor disbands and disarms at once, all armed organizations and disbands all those not ~~dis~~armed, instead of delaying to do So until the proper time has passed (22d Sept or the commencemt of the Registration), we may have no disturbance of the peace. otherwise, I believe we will have collisions of armed men. It must be recollected too, that I have no troops to fulfil my obligations, should the Governor demand them. (at the Same time I am inclined to think he will not ask for many) Lt General Sherman forbids me using any troops on the plains, for Service in Missouri. As I only [wished] to use those at Riley, Leavenworth and Jefferson Barracks—and So expressed it, the two former are in question of course, under his orders, I consider the two companies of Infy at Independence, should be on the Plains road; but I shall not dispatch them until I hear from you. (I have Sent you official papers concerning all these matters)—I would suggest that Some troops be sent here at once: otherwise if we want them, they will not be at hand. . . . I learn from Mr Blow that the Govr will not be back until the 12th. Mr B. says the Governor will without doubt disband at once all the partizan organizations—and that the order will be given this week. I think it probable—but if it is not done by the 12th we should conclude it will not be done at all. The Registration commences on the 22d and continues every Saturday" "I have just learned that the President, with yourself and others—are expected in St Louis: on the coming Saturday, and that it is expected you will remain until Monday: I have written to Mr Seward and to the President—(the former in Some detail) asking that the President and party—visit me in the Country on Sunday: should the President desire quiet and wish to leave the city on that day or night: I can give the party luncheon—and invite Such friends as may be desired by the President, if any, and if they desire to remain in the Country all night—I have three chambers or more at their disposal: I write also to you, trusting that you may also come down: There is a good road—from the city: (eight miles)—or it is one half hour by rail. We cannot do much in the military way in the city: I shall order up Gibson's Battery from the Barracks, to fire a salute on the Presidents arrival: the Engineer company at the Barracks—can Serve as a guard of honor during this stay of the President in the city." ALS, DNA, RG 108, Letters Received. On Sept. 7, Hancock wrote to USG. "I have the honor to forward the enclosed Order, issued by the Acting Adjutant General of the Mo. for your information" Copy, *ibid.*, RG 393, Dept. of the Mo., Letters Sent.

On Sept. 4, Sherman's adjt. wrote to USG enclosing copies of correspondence between Hancock and Sherman concerning troop movements in Mo. Copy (unsigned), *ibid.*, RG 108, Letters Received.

To Edwin M. Stanton

Washington. Aug. 9th 1866.

HON. E M. STANTON
SEC. OF WAR
SIR:

I have the honor to recommend Maj. Gen C. C. Augur, U. S. Vols. and Col. 12th U. S. Infantry for the Superintendency of the Military Academy at West Point. Gen. Augur has been Commandant of Cadets and understands the wants of the institution as well probably as any officer who could be selected. Before making this recommendation I have considered well the qualifications of all the Colonels and Lieutenant Colonels of the line of the Army and have taken the views of a number of officers whose judgment in this matter, I regard highly and have come to the conclusion that no better selection can be made for the place

I have the honor to be
Very respectfully
Your obt. servt.
U. S. GRANT
~~Washin~~ General

Copies, DLC-USG, V, 47, 60; DNA, RG 108, Letters Sent.

To Edwin M. Stanton

Washington Aug. 10, 66

HON. E. M STANTON,
SEC. OF WAR,
SIR:

I have the honor to enclose to you Mail Copies of Gen. Sheridan's dispatches on the New Orleans Riots and to ask their publication in full. Already a garbled version of one of these dispatches and an incomplete copy of another have appeared in the public prints. These publications put Gen. Sheridan in the position of taking a partisan view of the whole question, and what is still worse of being one day on one side of the question and again on the other. His dispatches given in full show that he takes no partisan view but that he reports what he conceives to be the facts without regard to who is hit.

I am just in receipt of a dispatch from Gen'l Sheridan, showing displeasure at his dispatches getting into print in a mutilated or incomplete form.[1]

I have the honor to be
Very respectfully
Your obt. servt
U. S. GRANT
~~Lieut~~ General

Copies, DLC-USG, V, 47, 60; DNA, RG 108, Letters Sent. See following letter; telegram to Maj. Gen. Philip H. Sheridan, Aug. 16, 1866. On Aug. 11, 1866, Secretary of War Edwin M. Stanton twice wrote to USG. "Your note of yesterday respecting General Sheridans despatches has been referred to the President for his instructions, which will be communicated to you when they reach me." ALS, DNA, RG 108, Letters Received. "Will you please to furnish me for the use of the President, copies of all despatches received at your HeadQuarters from New Orleans relating to the recent riot—if there be any beside those enclosed to me with your note of yesterday." Copy, *ibid.*, RG 94, Letters Received, 536G 1866.

On Aug. 1, first at 1:30 P.M., Maj. Gen. Philip H. Sheridan, New Orleans, had twice telegraphed to USG. "You are doubtless aware of the serious riot which occurred in this City on the 30th—A political body styling itself the Convention of 1864 met on the 30th for, as it is alleged, the purpose of re-modelling the present Constitution of the State—The leaders were political agitators & revolutionary men and the action of the Convention was liable to produce breaches of the public peace—I had made up my mind to arrest the head men if the proceedings of the Convention were calculated to disturb the tranquility of the Dept but I had no cause for action until they committed the overt act—In the mean time official duty had called me to Texas & the mayor of the City during my absence suppressed the Convention by the use of the police force & in so doing attacked the members of the convention & a party of two hundred negroes with fire-arms, clubs & knives in a manner so unnecessary & atrocious as to compel me to say it was murder—About forty whites & blacks were thus killed & about One hundred & Sixty wounded—Everything is now quiet but I deem it best to maintain a military supremacy in the City for a few days until the affair is fully investigated—I believe the sentiment of the general community is great regret at this unnecessary cruelty and that the police could have made any arrest they saw fit without sacrificing lives" "You need feel no uneasiness about the condition of affairs here I think I can arrange matters without difficulty" Telegrams received (the first at 6:15 P.M., the second at 6:40 P.M.), *ibid.*, RG 107, Telegrams Collected (Bound); *ibid.*, RG 108, Telegrams Received; copies (two of the first, one of the second), *ibid.*, Letters Received; (the second only) *ibid.*, RG 393, Military Div. of the Southwest and Dept. of the Gulf, Telegrams Sent; DLC-USG, V, 54; DLC-Philip H. Sheridan; DLC-Andrew Johnson. On Aug. 2, USG forwarded these telegrams to President Andrew Johnson. ES (2), *ibid.* At 11:30 A.M., Sheridan telegraphed to USG. "The more information I obtain of the affair of the 30th in this City, the more revolting it becomes. It was no riot, it was an absolute masacre by the police which was not excelled in murderous cruelty by that of Fort Pillow. It was a murder which the mayor and police of this perpetrated without the shadow of a necessity. Furthermore I believe it was premeditated, and every indication points to this—I recommend the remov~~aling~~ of this bad man. I believe it would be hailed with the sincerest gratification by two thirds of the population of the city There has been a feeling of insecurity on the part of the people here on account of this man, which is now so much increased that the safety of life and property does not rest with the civil authorities but with the Military" Telegram received (at 6:00 P.M.), DNA, RG 107, Telegrams Collected (Bound); *ibid.*, RG 108, Telegrams Received; copies (2—one sent by mail), *ibid.*, Letters Received; DLC-USG, V, 54; DLC-Philip H. Sheridan; DLC-Andrew Johnson. A note of Aug. 3 on a telegram received reads: "Copy forwd to Secy 'with recomn that the city of N. O. be kept under martial law until the causes of the riot are ascertained and the guilty parties brought to punishment'.—3d Aug also to President" AN, DNA, RG 108, Telegrams Received. On the same day, Stanton wrote to USG. "You will please transmit to General Sheridan the following instructions 'Continue to enforce martial law so far as may be necessary to preserve the peace, and do not allow any of the civil authorities to act if you deem such action dangerous to the public safety. Lose no time in investigating and reporting the causes that led to the Riot and the facts which ocurred' " ALS, *ibid.*, Letters Received. At 5:00 P.M., USG telegraphed these instructions to Sheridan. Telegram sent, *ibid.*, RG 107, Telegrams Collected (Bound); copies, *ibid.*, RG 108, Letters Sent; DLC-USG, V, 47, 60; DLC-Andrew Johnson. On Aug. 4, Sheridan telegraphed to USG. "I have the honor to acknowledge the receipt of your despatch of the date of August Third 3rd. five 5 P. M." Telegram received (at 5:05 P.M.), DNA, RG 107, Telegrams Collected (Bound); *ibid.*, RG 108, Telegrams Received; copies (one sent by mail), *ibid.*, Letters Received; *ibid.*, RG 393, Military Div. of the Southwest and Dept. of the Gulf, Telegrams Sent; DLC-USG, V, 54; DLC-Philip H. Sheridan; DLC-Andrew Johnson.

Also on Aug. 3, 3:30 P.M., Sheridan telegraphed to USG. "I have the honor to report quiet in the city but considerable excitement in the public mind—There is no interference on the part of the Military with the civil government which performs all its duties without hindrance I have permitted the retention of the Military Governor appointed during my absence, as it gives confidence and enables the Military to know what is occurring in the City. He does not interfere with civil matters—Unless good judgement is exercised there will be an exodus of northern capital and union men, which will be injurious to the City, and to the whole country. I will remove the Military Governor in a day or two—I again strongly advise that some disposition be made to change the present Mayor, as I believe it would do more to restore confidence than any thing that could be done. If the present Governor could be changed also, it would not be amiss—" Telegram received (at 10:30 P.M.), DNA, RG 107, Telegrams Collected (Bound);

ibid., RG 108, Telegrams Received; copies, *ibid.*, RG 107, Letters Received from Bureaus; (2—one sent by mail) *ibid.*, RG 108, Letters Received; DLC-USG, V, 54; DLC-Philip H. Sheridan; DLC-Andrew Johnson. On Aug. 4, USG referred this telegram to Stanton. ES, DNA, RG 107, Letters Received from Bureaus. On Aug. 5, 6:30 P.M., Sheridan telegraphed to USG. "I have the honor to report quiet in the City yesterday and today but some unfounded rumors afloat which Excite the timid—The exciting reports will be in circulation for a day or two yet" Telegram received (on Aug. 6, 8:50 A.M.), *ibid.*, Telegrams Collected (Bound); *ibid.*, RG 108, Telegrams Received; copies, *ibid.*, RG 107, Letters Received from Bureaus; (sent by mail) *ibid.*, RG 108, Letters Received; DLC-USG, V, 54; DLC-Philip H. Sheridan; DLC-Andrew Johnson. On Aug. 6, USG referred this telegram to Stanton. ES, DNA, RG 107, Letters Received from Bureaus. On Aug. 7, 12:30 P.M., Sheridan telegraphed to USG. "I have the honor to report a rapid change for the better throughout the city. There was much excitement on Sunday & Monday in consequence of an unfounded rumor that there would be a collision between the whites and blacks yesterday There was no good reason to expect such an event however—" Telegram received (at 4:10 P.M.), *ibid.*, Telegrams Collected (Bound); *ibid.*, RG 108, Telegrams Received; copies (one sent by mail), *ibid.*, Letters Received; DLC-USG, V, 54; DLC-Philip H. Sheridan; DLC-Andrew Johnson. A note on a telegram received indicates that this telegram was forwarded to Stanton on Aug. 8. AN, DNA, RG 108, Telegrams Received.

On Aug. 13, noon, Sheridan telegraphed to USG. "The military board called by Gen'l Baird to investigate the occurrences in this City of July 30th is progressing as rapidly as possible—I see in the ~~reports~~ papers by reports of officials here an attempt made to cast blame on the military for not being present on the 30th—There could have been no object in its being present except to keep the police from perpetrating a revolting massacre—Its absence for this reason I regret—From the accounts of my own scouts who saw the affair from first to last, from my own officers & from disinterested & truthful persons I believe that at least nine tenths of the casualties were perpetrated by the police & citizens stabbing and smashing in the heads of many who had been already wounded or killed by policemen" Telegram received (at 3:30 P.M.), *ibid.*, RG 107, Telegrams Collected (Bound); *ibid.*, RG 108, Telegrams Received; copies (one sent by mail), *ibid.*, Letters Received; DLC-USG, V, 54; DLC-Philip H. Sheridan; DLC-Edwin M. Stanton. On Aug. 14, USG referred this telegram to Stanton. ES, *ibid.* On Sept. 6, Sheridan wrote to Brig. Gen. John A. Rawlins. "I have the honor to transmit herewith the proceedings of a Board convened by Maj General Baird to investigate the occurrences in this city of July 30th last, with a brief of the proceedings there of: also an affadavit of certain parties charging Mayor Monroe and other city officials with the conception and perpetration of crimes which they alledge as having been perpetrated on that day" LS, DNA, RG 94, Letters Received, 536G 1866. On Sept. 21, USG forwarded these papers to Stanton. ES, *ibid.* The enclosed report is *ibid. HED*, 39-2-68. See also *ibid.*, 39-2-46; *HRC*, 39-2-16. On Sept. 8, Sheridan wrote to Rawlins. "At the request of Major General F. J. Herron I have the honor to transmit herewith the accompanying revised statement of his evidence before the Military Board convened by General Baird to investigate the occurrences in this City on the 30th of July last. General Herron desires to have this substituted for that given in the regular proceedings: Will you have the kindness to comply with his request." LS, DNA, RG 94, Letters Received, 536G 1866. The enclosure is *ibid.* On Sept. 21, USG transmitted these and related papers to Stanton. ES, *ibid.* On Oct. 9, Bvt. Maj. Gen. Edward D. Townsend wrote to Stanton. "I have the honor to report that the Report of General Baird, and Proceedings of the Military Commission in relation to the riot in New Orleans on the 30th July last, which were forwarded to the Office of General Grant by Major General Sheridan, were received by General Grant the 13th September 1866, and retained in his own desk until the 21st September, when they were sent over to the Office of the Secretary of War, after 3 o'clock P. M.—They were kept in an iron safe by the Clerk who received them, until they were handed to me the morning of the 22d September, with instructions to deliver them to the President, which I did in person within the same hour. The papers were not meantime out of my sight. General Grant informs me that no authority, or opportunity, was given by him, or within his knowledge by any one else, while the papers were in custody in his office, to any person whatever, to take copies or extracts from any part of the papers, for publication, or for any other purpose; and that it is hardly within the range of probability that any one but himself and one or two of his Staff Officers could have known that such papers were in his possession. The papers were again delivered to me by Colonel Moore from the President, on the morning of the 3d October 1866. I learned the same morning that a portion of them was published in the New York Tribune of the previous day. It is absolutely certain that they were not obtained for that purpose at any time while in my custody." ALS, DLC-Edwin M. Stanton.

Probably in early Aug., A. M. Winship wrote an undated and unaddressed letter describing conditions in New Orleans. Copy, DLC-Andrew Johnson. USG endorsed this letter. "The enclosed is respectfully forwarded to the President as giving the views of an eye witness to the New Orleans riot, and probably as impartial a version as will be received." AES (undated), *ibid.*

1. On Aug. 9, 1:00 P.M., Sheridan telegraphed to Rawlins. "I see that my despatch to General Grant of August first is published with one paragraph suppressed Can you tell who was guilty of this breach of Military honor?" Telegram received (at 5:00 P.M.), DNA, RG 107, Telegrams Collected (Bound); *ibid.*, RG 108, Telegrams Received; copies, DLC-USG, V, 54; DLC-Philip H. Sheridan. A note on a telegram received indicates that this telegram was referred to Stanton on Aug. 10. AN, DNA, RG 108, Telegrams Received. On Aug. 9, USG telegraphed to Sheridan. "Your despatches did not get into print from these Head Quarters. If you do not object I will ask to have your despatches published in full. Answer" Telegram sent (marked as sent on Aug. 10, 11:40 A.M.), *ibid.*, RG 107, Telegrams Collected (Bound); copies, *ibid.*, RG 108, Letters Sent; DLC-USG, V, 47, 60. On Aug. 11, noon, Sheridan telegraphed to USG. "I did not for a moment suppose that my dispatch of August first (1st) was published by authority from your Head quarters I think I have a right to feel justly indignant at the person who gave the authority As to the publication of my other dispatches, it is not for me to say They were not written for publication unless my lawful superiors chose to make them public" Telegram received (at 4:30 P.M.), DNA, RG 107, Telegrams Collected (Bound); *ibid.*, RG 108, Telegrams Received; copies (one sent by mail), *ibid.*, Letters Received; DLC-USG, V, 54; DLC-Philip H. Sheridan. See *Personal Memoirs of P. H. Sheridan* (New York, 1888), II, 235–37; *HRC*, 40-1-7, pp. 535–40.

To Maj. Gen. Philip H. Sheridan

Washington, August 12th *1866*

DEAR GENERAL,

I am just in receipt of copy of your letter to the President, in reply to his despatch of the 4th inst.[1] It is certainly a very clear statement of the cause and effect of the riot and in my judgment it is due to the public, to you and even to the President that it should be published—I have requested from the President the publication of all your dispatches on the subject of the New Orleans riot on the ground that the partial publications which have appeared put you in the position of taking a partisan view of the matter whereas the dispatches given in full, show that you never dreamed of extenuating faults no matter which side they occur on. One thing you may rely on; the purity of your motives will never be impeached by the public no matter what capital the politicians may attempt to make out of garbled or partial publications of what you say or write officially. Persevere exactly in the course your own good judgment dictates. It has never yet led you astray as a military commander nor in your administration of the affairs of your military division.

Yours truly
U S GRANT

TO MAJ. GEN. P. H. SHERIDAN

Copies, DLC-Adam Badeau; DLC-Philip H. Sheridan. See preceding letter.

1. On Aug. 6, 1866, Maj. Gen. Philip H. Sheridan, New Orleans, wrote to USG. "I have the honor to transmit herewith a copy of a telegraphic dispatch forwarded President Johnson, as it gives a brief synopsis of the occurrence of the 30th ultimo, with my opinions concerning the same." LS, DNA, RG 108, Letters Received. Sheridan enclosed a copy of his telegram of the same day to President Andrew Johnson. "I have the honor to make the following reply to your dispatch of August 4th A very large number of Colored people marched in procession on Friday night, July 27th, and were addressed from the steps of the City Hall by Doctor Dostie, ex-Governor Hahn, and others. The speech of Dostie was intemperate in language and sentiment; the speeches of the others, so far as I can learn, were characterized by moderation. I cannot give you the words of Dostie's speech, as the version published was denied, but from what I have learned of the man I believe they were intemperate. The Convention assembled at twelve O'clock on the 30th ultimo; the timid members absenting themselves because the tone of the general public was omenous of trouble. I think

there were about Twenty six (26) members present. In front of the Mechanic's Institute, where the meeting was held, there was assembled some Colored men, women and children, perhaps Eighteen (18) or Twenty (20); and in the Institute a number of Colored men, probably One hundred and fifty; among those outside and inside there might have been a pistol in the possession of every tenth man. About one o'clock a procession of say from Sixty to One hundred and thirty Colored men marched up Burgundy Street and across Canal Street, towards the Convention, carrying an American Flag. These men had about one pistol to every tenth man, and canes and clubs in addition. While crossing Canal Street a row occurred. There were many spectators on the street, and their manner and tone towards the procession unfriendly. A shot was fired, by whom I am not able to state, but believe it to have been by a policeman, or some Colored man in the procession; this led to other shots and a rush after the procession to the Institute. On arrival at the front of the Institute, there was some throwing of brickbats by both sides. The police, who had been held well in hand were vigorously marched to the scene of disorder. The procession entered the Institute with the flag; about six or eight remaining outside. A row occurred between a policeman and one of these Colored men, and a shot was again fired by one of the parties which led to an indiscriminate fire on the building through the windows by the policemen; this had been going on for a short time when a white flag was displayed from the window of the Institute, whereupon the fireing ceased, and the police rushed into the building. From the testimony of wounded men and others who were inside the building, the policemen opened an indiscriminate fire upon the Audience until they had emptied their revolvers, when they retired, and these inside barricaded the doors. The door was broken in and the fireing again commenced, when many of the Colored and white people either escaped through the door and out, or were passed out by the policemen inside, but as they came out, the policemen who formed the circle nearest the building fired upon them, and they were again fired upon by the Citizens that formed the outer circle. Many of those wounded and taken prisoners, and others who were prisoners and not wounded, were fired upon by their Captors and by Citizens. The wounded were stabbed while lying on the ground, and their heads beaten with brickbats. In the yard of the building, whither some of the Colored men had partially secreted themselves, they were fired upon and killed or wounded by policemen. Some were killed and wounded several squares from the scene. Members of the convention were wounded by the police while in their hands as prisoners, some of them mortally. The immediate cause of this terrible affair was the assemblage of this Convention. The remote cause was the bitter and antagonistic feeling which has been growing in this Community since the advent of the present Mayor, who, in the organization of his police force, selected many desperate men and some of them known murderers. People of clear views were overawed by want of confidence in the Mayor and fear of the 'Thugs', many of which he had selected for his police-force. I have frequently been spoken to by prominent citizens on this subject, and have heard them express fear and want of confidence in Mayor Monroe. Ever since the initiation of this last Convention movement, I must condemn the course of several of the City papers for supporting, by their articles, the bitter feeling of bad men. As to the merciless manner in which the convention was broken up, I feel obliged to confess strong repugnance. It is useless to attempt to disguise the hostility that exists on the part of a great many here towards Northern men, and this unfortunate affair has so precipitated matters that there is now a test of what shall be the status of Northern men; whether they can live here without being in constant dread, or not; whether they can be protected in life and property, and have justice in the Courts. If this matter is permitted to pass over without a thorough and determined prosecution of those engaged in it, we may look out for frequent scenes of the same kind, not only here but in other places No steps have as yet been taken by the Civil Authorities to arrest Citizens who were engaged in this Massacre, or policemen who perpetrated such cruelties. The members of the Convention have been indicted by the Grand Jury, and many of them arrested and held to bail. As to whether the Civil Authorities can mete out ample justice to the guilty parties on both sides, I must say, unequivocally, that they cannot. Judge Abil whose course I have closely watched for nearly a year, I now consider one of the most dangerous men that we have here, to the peace and quiet of the City The leading men of the Convention King Cutler, Hahn, and others, have been political agitators, and are bad men. I regret to say that the course of Governor Wells has been vacillating, and that during the late trouble he has shown very little of the man." LS (copy), *ibid.* On Aug. 7, 4:00 P.M., Secretary of War Edwin M. Stanton telegraphed to Sheridan. "The President directs me to acknowledge your telegram of the sixth (6th) in answer to his inquiries of the fourth (4th) inst. On the [th]ird (3d) instant instructions were sent you by General Grant in conformity with the President['s] directions authorizing you to 'continue to [e]nforce martial law so far as might be necessary to preserve the public peace and ordering you not to allow any of the civil authorities to act if you deem [s]uch action dangerous to the public safety, and also that no time be lost in investigating the causes that led to the riot and the facts, which occurred' By these instructions the President designed to vest in you as the chief military commander full authority for the maintenance of the public peace and safety and he does not see that any thing more is needed pending the investigation with which you are entrusted. But if in your judgement your powers are inadequate to preserve the peace until the facts connected with the riot are ascertained you will please report to this Department for [t]he information of the President." LS (telegram sent), *ibid.*, RG 107, Telegrams Collected (Unbound); ADfS, DLC-Edwin M. Stanton. See *HED*, 39-2-68, pp. 13–14.

To Edwin M. Stanton

Washington D. C. August 13th *1866*.

HON. E. M. STANTON,
SEC. OF WAR:
SIR:

I have the honor to recommend that three Boards be convened to examine officers to be appointed in the regular army, in accordance with the law for the re-organization of the Army, to be convened at the following places: Chicago, Ill. Governor's Island,

New York Harbor, and Washington City. I would recommend that these ~~b~~Boards consist of three officers and a recorder each, two to be composed of Infantry officers, those at Governor's Island and at Chicago, and the other of Cavalry officers. All officers named for the Cavalry service will have to come before the Board composed of Cavalry officers; all others from the state of Ohio, and states West of that, can be required to go before the Chicago Board, and all others before the New York Board.

In addition to the Boards here recommended it might be advisable, in view of the great number of officers to be examine, to order an additional Board for the examination of Field officers of Infantry.

For the Cavalry Board I would recommend Bvt. Maj. Gn. David Hunter, Bvt. Maj. Gn. W. H. Emory, & Bvt. Brig. Gn. L. P. Graham, ~~and Bvt. Maj. J. W. Mason for Recorder~~.

For Infantry Board, New York Harbor,
Bvt. Maj. Gn. W. S. Ketchum,
Bvt. ~~Col. Wm Chapman~~ Maj. Gn. C. C. Augur,
Lt. Col. Seth Eastman.
For the Chicago Board.
Bvt. Brig. Gn. Sidney Burbank,
Lt. Col. T. L. Alexander,
Lt. Col. Wm Chapman,

This leaves the Recorders to be selected who can be taken from officers on duty near where the Boards are to set.

I have the honor to be,
Very respectfully
your obt. svt.
U. S. Grant
General,

ALS, DNA, RG 94, Letters Received, 693A 1866. On Aug. 14, 1866, U.S. Senator Henry Wilson of Mass., Natick, wrote to USG. "I have received several letters from officers in regard to the act of the 28th of July in relation to the army. It is said that instead of making promotions provided for by Senority—it is to be done by selection. I write simply to say that if the Latter policy is adopted it will not be in accordance with the intentions of the committee, nor do I think it will be in accordance with the intentions or wishes of Congress" ALS, *ibid.*, ACP, W1422 CB 1866. On Aug. 16, USG endorsed this letter. "Respectfully refered to the Sec. of War. I presume Senator Wilson only intends to be understood as confining promotions by Seniority to the increase given to the Staff Corps and Artillery regiments. All the appointments for new regiments created by the Act of Congress are original vacancies, to be filled by selection, unquestionably." AES, *ibid.*

On Sept. 17, Lt. Col. Henry W. Benham, U.S. Engineers, Boston, wrote to USG. "*Unofficial*, . . . As reports continue to reach the Officers of Engineers here that efforts are still being made for the sanction of the promotions by selection for the increased rank constituted in the corps by the late law of Congress—I have felt I might properly send to you a copy of a letter to an Engineer Officer here, from Senator Wilson—who I beleive drew up—and was principally instrumental in carrying that law through Congress—a law, that, by a published letter from yourself General, appeared to have your sanction also—Not knowing whether a former letter of mine upon this subject has reached your notice I feel you will not object to the consideration of this enclosed letter—which is respectfully offered—with the belief that I have, that it is your earnest wish to carry out all laws in their true intent and meaning—which laws I think are only best explained by those who draw them up and pass them. While at the same time I am unwilling to beleive that the rumored action on this subject of promoting others over me, can have your sanction to such injustice to myself—after as I beleive the most ample evidence can shew my long continued faithful and efficient service in my own Corps' duties both in peace and War—as well as other and effective service in every way I was permitted, in command of troops on several occasions in the field. And in view of this I must feel that you will not, that you cannot permit the injustice of my being overslaughed—if your action can prevent it." ALS, *ibid.*, B447 CB 1864. The enclosure is *ibid.* On Sept. 19, USG endorsed these papers. "Respectfully refered to the Sec. of War." AES, *ibid.* On Nov. 26, USG wrote to Secretary of War Edwin M. Stanton. "I have the honor to recommend that Bvt. Brig. Gn. H. W. Benham be breveted Maj. Gen. from March 13th 1865, in accordance with the rule that has been generally adopted, that of breveting officers of the regular Army to the highest grade held by them in the Volunteer service either by brevet or otherwise." ALS, *ibid.*

To Jesse Root Grant

Washington, Aug. 14th *1866*.

DEAR FATHER,

There is no vacant Cadetship which the President has the power to fill except on the nomination of a member of Congress The Southern vacancies he is expressly prohibited from filling by a resolution of Congress. I do not know whether there are vacancies in the Naval Academy or not. There was not a few weeks ago.

I hope Jennie has made up her mind to spend next Winter

with us! I shall be in Galena on the 9th of November and will come by Covington if she wishes to come on here. Gen. Babcock is to be married on that day.[1]

The family except Jesse are well. It may become necessary for Julia to go some place on the Sea shore for a few weeks on his account.

My love to all at home.

ULYSSES.

ALS, deCoppet Collection, NjP.

1. See letters to Elihu B. Washburne, Aug. 16, Oct. 23, 1866.

To Maj. Gen. Philip H. Sheridan

(*Cipher*) *Washington, D. C.*, Aug 16th *18646* [*10:30* A.M.]

MAJ GEN P. H. SHERIDAN
NEW ORLEANS LA

In view of the threat contained in an anonymous letter you send to me I advise increasing your force about the city from other parts of your command. As soon as they can be organized two more companies will be sent to each of your Infantry Battalions, besides the three companies that have never yet joined will be sent as soon as the cholera disappears

U. S. GRANT
General

Telegram sent, DNA, RG 107, Telegrams Collected (Bound); copies, *ibid.*, RG 108, Letters Sent; DLC-USG, V, 47, 60. On Aug. 9, 1866, Maj. Gen. Philip H. Sheridan had written to USG. "I enclose to you an anonymus letter. I believe I know the author and he is a very worthy man. I regard the letter as I do all letters of this kind but wheather the circumstances related are correct or not, it shows the animus of the persons whos names are mentioned—better than I could tell you." ALS, USG 3. Sheridan enclosed an anonymous letter of Aug. 3 from a "*Business Man of Canal St*" to Sheridan concerning the role of John T. Monroe, mayor of New Orleans, and others in the riot of July 30. AL, *ibid.* On Aug. 17, 11:00 P.M., Sheridan telegraphed to USG. "I am in receipt of your telegram of the 16th Everything is very quiet and in fine condition here—As soon as it was found that the military would be allowed to maintain the supremacy in the city there was a general backing down—I have no fear of my ability to take charge of the city and consider the force here adequate unless there was some very great disturbing cause—As to the anonymous threats I am not afraid of them and as to idle threats of driving the troops out of the city there would not be much of the city left when it was done—I am all right & will take care of myself" Telegram received (at 4:35 P.M.), DNA, RG 107, Telegrams Collected (Bound); *ibid.*, RG 108, Telegrams Received; DLC-USG, V, 54; DLC-Philip H. Sheridan. Possibly sent at 11:00 A.M. and marked in error.

To Elihu B. Washburne

August 16th *1866.*

DEAR WASHBURNE,

I enclose you a letter from Sherman on the subject of Atchison's appointment on his Staff and also an extract from a Semi-official letter of a subsequent date on the same subject.[1] Sherman feels every disposition to accommodate both you and me. But it is a hard test to ask a man to dismiss a Staff officer who has been with him through the war, and who he likes, to take one who has done no service with him. I do not know that McCoy or Dayton have received commissions in the regular Army. If they have not, or do not, they will not be eligible for their Staff positions long.

My family with the exception of Jesse are quite well. Jesse has been confined to bed for several days with a fever.

Campbell has invited me to be present in Galena on the 9th of November.[2] This date seems to be fixed with the view of having me there at the election. I have no objection to being in Galena at that time but I do not think it proper for an Army officer, particularly the Army commander, to take part in elections. Your friendship for me has been such that I should not hesitate to support you on personal grounds, on the ground that there is no one who cannot recognize great acts of friendship.

My family join me in desiring to be rembered to your Me. friends.

I will not get away from Washington for many days at one time this Summer.

Yours Truly
U. S. GRANT,

Atchison is recommended by me for one grade of promotion in the re-organization.

ALS, IHi.

1. See letter to Maj. Gen. William T. Sherman, July 21, 1866.
2. See letter to Elihu B. Washburne, Oct. 23, 1866.

To Maj. Gen. John G. Foster

Washington, D. C., Aug 17th *18646*. [*11:30* A.M.]

MAJ GEN J. G. FOSTER
TALLAHASSEE FLA.

Genl Order No 44.[1] is not intended to apply to offences committed prior to the close of hostilities. As a rule no arrests should be made under it except when the civil authorities refuse to make them. Release all prisoners you may now have whose offences were committed previous to May/'65

U. S. GRANT
General

Telegram sent, DNA, RG 107, Telegrams Collected (Bound); copies (misdated Aug. 7, 1866), *ibid.*, RG 108, Letters Sent; (dated Aug. 17) *ibid.*, RG 393, Dept. of the South, District of East Fla., Telegrams Received; DLC-USG, V, 47, 60. See letter to Elihu B. Washburne, Nov. 9, 1865. On Aug. 20, 1866, Maj. Gen. John G. Foster wrote to USG. "I have the honor to acknowledge the receipt of telegram of the 17th inst., directing the release of Prisoners whose offences were committed previous to May '65.—I respectfully report, that I had four Prisoners of that kind; three of whom had been released before the above telegram was received, and are now held under bail by the Civil authorities; the fourth one was sent to Fort Jefferson, but I have ordered him now to be released at once, in compliance with directions contained in said despatch." LS, DNA, RG 108, Letters Received. On Aug. 26, Wilkinson Call, New York City, wrote to USG. "Information reaches me that an order: has been issued by Some Military Authority in Florida. supposed to be Col Zulanski. Commdg in West

Fla. for the arrest of J L Dunham of Apalachicola, one of the gentlemen from Florida who recently waited on you in Washington, Mr Dunham has been guilty of no offence since the surrender and none previous except such as belongs to all who bore arms. against the Gov't of the U S, He has been quietly pursuing his business & beyond some personal feeling towards Col Zulanski, & a subordinate officer from whom he conceived he had received personal wrong—I presume his Conduct has been without any cause of objection Col Dunham is a merchant of large business & his presence is required at home. You will oblige me very much if you can properly do so. by instituting such means as will prevent the arrest of Col Dunham by the local Military Authoritys. until the charges if any there are can be investigated by you or some other authority—designated by you. The statements I here make in regard to Mr Dunham & his Conduct are Correct & may be relied on—I will thank you if some immediate action can be taken in the premises & beg that you will Communicate to me the result of your decision. address Care of Gilliss & Harney. 35. Broad St. N. Yk." ALS, *ibid.* On Sept. 24, Foster endorsed this letter. "Respectfully returned to Hd. Qrs. Army of the U. S. with the following report. Mr J. L. Dunham, was ordered to be arrested by me, for insulting the American Flag, and causing it to be hauled down on the 4th July last, at Apalachicola, Fla. The circumstances were these: A Citizen of that town, named Antonio Messina, master of a sloop employed as lighter in Apalachicola Bay, hoisted the American Flag on the 4th July, in honor of the day, and in accordance with my Gen. Ord. No 39.—Mr Dunham (late a Captain in the Confederate Army) ordered Messina to take it down threatening not to employ him any more if he did not do so.—Mr Messina who depended chiefly upon Mr Dunham for employment, yielded to his order and hauled down the flag. The report of the Comm of Officers reached me on the 25th July, when I ordered Mr Dunham to be arrested for the offence, but as he has departed for Philadelphia, as a Delegate to the Convention of Aug 14th, the arrest was not made. Subsequent telegraphic orders dated Aug 17th from the Genl Commdg the Armies of the U S—caused me to revoke my order for his arrest, which consequently has never been made." ES, *ibid.*

On Nov. 12, USG wrote to Secretary of War Edwin M. Stanton. "At his own request I have the honor to recommend that Bvt. Maj. Gn. J. G. Foster be relieved from duty as Comd.g Officer of the District of Florida and that he be ordered to report to the Chief Engineer for assignment. I would also recommend that Gen. Sheridan be directed to name the officer who shall relieve Gen. Foster from his duties as District Commander & Agt. of the Bureau of Refugees & Freedmen, with authority if he does not select the senior officer on duty in the district, to assign such officer to duty with his brevet rank." ALS, *ibid.*, RG 94, Letters Received, 343F 1866. Additional papers are *ibid.*

1. See General Orders No. 44, July 6, 1866; letter to Edwin M. Stanton, Nov. 22, 1866.

To Andrew Johnson

Washington, D. C. August 20th *1866*.

His Excellency, A. Johnson,
President of the U. States,
Sir:

I take great pleasure in giving General M. L. Smith, late of the Volunteer service, the highest testimonials I know how to give. He was one of the first to turn out from the state of Mo. to raise forces to put down the rebellion. He served directly under me in all the early part of the War and was promoted to a Brigadier Generalcy[1] on my recommendation given purely for the services he rendered and his great fitness for the command which that rank would give him. He has served under no General Commanding an Army in this War who did not regard him as among the very best of Division Commanders they had. It gives me great pleasure to endorse him thus and to say that I would be pleased to see him receive any appointment he may desire at the hands of the Government he has served so faithfully, and in whos services he has been wounded and permanently disabled.

With great respect,
your obt. svt.
U. S. Grant
General.

ALS, DNA, RG 59, Applications and Recommendations, Lincoln and Johnson. On Aug. 13, 1866, Lt. Gen. William T. Sherman, Fort Leavenworth, had written to President Andrew Johnson recommending Morgan L. Smith for a consular appointment. ALS, *ibid.* Smith was confirmed as U.S. consul gen., Honolulu, on Feb. 6, 1867.

1. See *PUSG*, 4, 357; *ibid.*, 5, 184.

To Andrew Johnson

Washington, D. C. Aug. 22d *1866*.

His Excellency, A. Johnson,
President of the United States.
Sir:

In regard to the requisition of the Gov. of Va. refered to me by your direction, in relation to furnishing arms for the Va. Mil. Institute, and 10,000 stand of arms for the use of the state, I have refered the papers to Gen. Schofield, Comd.g Dept. of Va. requiring him to have an interview with the Governor of the state on the subject refered to in the papers presented by W. H. Richardson,[1] Adj. Gn. of the State, and to report the necessity and expediency of making such issue. I am inclined to doubt the expediency for making such issue for reasons which I have explained to Gn. Richard[son] but have invited the opinion of Gn. Schofield who has a better opportunity of judging of the Matter. I would approve however the issue of arms for the use of the Military Institute of Virginia without reference to the Department Commander.

I have the honor to be,
Very respectfully
your obt. svt.
U. S. Grant
General.

ALS, DLC-Andrew Johnson. On Aug. 22, 1866, Maj. Robert Morrow, adjt. for President Andrew Johnson, had referred papers received at USG's hd. qrs. concerning procurement of arms for the Va. militia and the Virginia Military Institute. DNA, RG 107, Letters Received from Bureaus; *ibid.*, RG 108, Register of Letters Received. On the same day, Maj. George K. Leet endorsed these papers. "Refered to Maj. Gen. Schofield, Comdg Potomac Dept. who will advise with the Governor of Virginia on the subject referred to within—and report upon the necessity and expediency of issuing arms to the state of Virginia." Copies, *ibid.* On Aug. 25, Va. AG William H. Richardson, Richmond, wrote to USG. "I failed to see the Presidents private Secretary with reference to the 150 Cadet muskets & accoutrements which you recommended to the President should be ordered for the Military Institute, and, was compelled to return home the next morning—leaving a short (& I apprehend) scarcely legible note at your head quarters—I ought to apologise for troubling you again with this matter, when doubtless so many of more importance claim your attention—but feel assured the circumstances will excuse it—These arms will have to be sent from here to Lexington, 150 miles west, and it is very desirable should be received there some days prior to the 10th September—The decision of the President will I suppose, if favorable, go to the War Department and might be delayed beyond the time when it would be possible to get them to their destination. This I feel well assured you will guard against if it be in your power—The four light bronze field guns may be sent to this place with the muskets, or remain for the present at the arsenal—They are not mounted and we have no means of building carriages for them—Among the munitions of war captured here, were more than 100 iron field guns, chiefly 6. prs, which were fabricated at the Virginia Armory many years ago under the supervision of Major John Clarke afterwards of the Bellona Arsenal. I have often heard it said that all the arms manufactured by the state were of the best gun metal that had ever been discovered, and within a few years past, looking over a folio volume of public documents of the U S, met with a correspondence of Major Clarke, in which he mentioned the discovery of the iron ore from which the metal used at the Virginia Armory was obtained, as the best by far he had ever seen. I am not positive, but my impression is that he had had it tested in England—It has occurred to me that the Ordnance Departmt. may find the guns referred to, of much more value then mere old iron, indeed I am confident that the metal is valuable, and if it be found so it may be of some importance to the Government—I sincerely hope that nothing will occur to prevent your being present at Lexington on the 10th September, and can confidently assure you of a cordial reception—It is quite probable that you will meet there some of our best and most reliable citizens, whose information upon the most important matters of public interest will command your confidence—" LS, *ibid.*, Letters Received. On Aug. 27, Maj. Gen. John M. Schofield, Richmond, wrote to Leet. "I have received and duly considered the letter from Governor Peirpoint to the President, enclosing one from the Adjutant General State of Virginia, asking for arms and amunition for the State militia, which was referred to me August 22.nd. by command of General Grant, with directions to confer with the Governor and report upon the necessity and expediency of issuing arms to the State of Virginia. I have conversed with Governor Peirpoint and others upon the subject and have formed the following opinion concerning it. The white people throughout the State are almost totally destitute of arms of all kinds, while a considerable portion of the colored men have arms of various kinds, many of them of a military character. This causes a general feeling of insecurity among the whites, which feeling may very likely prove to be well founded, unless the cause of it be, in some way, removed. The Constitutional right of the colored people to bear arms being guaranteed by the Act of Congress of July 16. 1866 there seems no way to remove the difficulty referred to but by arming enough of the white people to give them a feeling of security. The best mode of doing this which has occurred to me, is for the Governor to cause to be organized a certain number of Volunteer Militia Companies, distributed throughout the State, under Officers to be previously named for the purpose, with instructions to enroll only men who are loyal to the U. S. Government, and properly disposed toward the freed people. Upon satisfactory proff that these instructions have been followed in the organization of a company, arms may be issued to it, with propriety and general benefit. If the above views meet with the General's approval, I would advise that a moderate supply of arms and ammunition be placed subject to my orders, either in Richmond or at Fortress Monroe, to be issued from time to time upon the Governor's requisition, made upon the proof of proper organization of companies as suggested above. Governor Peirpoint expresses himself entirely satisfied with the above proposition." LS, *ibid.*, RG 107, Letters Received from Bureaus. See letter to Andrew Johnson, Nov. 9, 1866.

On Sept. 22, 1865, Caleb G. Forshey had written to Maj. Gen. Horatio G. Wright requesting permission to reopen the Texas Military Institute. Copy, DNA, RG 107, Letters Received, F1099 1866. On Oct. 15, USG endorsed this letter. "Respectfully returned. I disapprove of authorizing the re-opening of Military Schools in any of States that passed the Ordinance of Secession until they are recognized and treated by the Government as upon the same footing as States that were always loyal" Copy, *ibid.*

1. Richardson, born in Va. in 1795, appointed Va. AG in 1841, served on the board of the Virginia Military Institute. See Charles W. Turner, "William H. Richardson: Friend of the Farmer," *Virginia Cavalcade*, XX, 3 (Winter, 1971), 14–20.

To Bvt. Brig. Gen. Cyrus B. Comstock

From Phila Aug 28, *1866*

To Gen C. A. Comstock
Care G. W. Baldwin
Am'n Tel Officer

Howard can name some one else for agent in La without him commanding Dist—If he declines telegraph Sheridan to name Dist Commander

U S Grant
General

Telegram received (on Aug. 29, 1866, 9:15 A.M.), DNA, RG 107, Telegrams Collected (Bound); *ibid.*, RG 108, Telegrams Received; copy, DLC-USG, V, 54. On Aug. 22, Maj. Gen. Philip H. Sheridan, New Orleans, had written to USG. "I have just received a telegram from General Howard, which informs me that as I have kept the State of Louisiana under my immediate command I am appointed Assistant Commissioner of the Freedmens Bureau If General Howard by his telegram means to apply a censure on me, I can make a District out of Louisiana with great ease; but; as the posts in Louisiana reported directly to Department Headquarters, under the then existing status of military affairs, when the Department of Louisiana was abolished by General Orders No 1, these posts would, naturally, report to my Headquarters, and consequently in the changes made this rule was followed. I do not much like to perform the duties of Assistant Commissioner; but, my objection is only on account of the additional labor it will bring on me. I can assure you I have had no sinecure position since I left the field of actual hostilities. I think now that I ought to be made the

Commissioner of Indian affairs for the numerous hostile Indian tribes of Texas. Then I shall be well saddled, and cinched tight." LS, DNA, RG 108, Letters Received. On Aug. 28, 11:30 A.M., Bvt. Brig. Gen. Cyrus B. Comstock telegraphed to USG, Philadelphia. "Sheridan in abolishing Dept. of Louisiana has its posts report direct to him and accordingly Howard telegraphs him that he is appointed Ass't commissioner Freedman's Bureau. Sheridan writes objecting to the additional labor. Could it not be avoided by having a District of Louisiana and its commander the Ass't commissioner? He also says Carvajal was driven out of Matamoras because the people thought he and Lew Wallace intended to establish an independent Republic of Sierra Madre" Telegram sent, *ibid.*, RG 107, Telegrams Collected (Bound); copies, *ibid.*, RG 108, Letters Sent; DLC-USG, V, 47, 60. See letter to Maj. Gen. Philip H. Sheridan, Oct. 9, 1866. On Aug. 29, 11:15 A.M., Comstock telegraphed USG's instructions to Sheridan. Telegram sent, DNA, RG 107, Telegrams Collected (Bound); copies, *ibid.*, RG 108, Letters Sent; DLC-USG, V, 47, 60. On Aug. 30, Secretary of War Edwin M. Stanton telegraphed to Sheridan. "Your telegram respecting the Freedmants Bureau has been received. After much consideration by General Grant & myself as to [t]he administration of that Bureau it was concluded a short time ago, to make Department Commanders the Commissioner & Superintendant [i]n their respective Commands, where no reason to the contrary existed. In pursuance of that view you were assigned in your Department. General Howard informed me he had done so, [a]nd it met my approval. The assignment was not an order, but an authority to act, and if you can do so without great inconvenience & [i]nterference with other more important duties I hope you will assume the burden." ALS (telegram sent), DNA, RG 107, Telegrams Collected (Bound).

On Oct. 4, 10:30 A.M., Sheridan telegraphed to USG. "I am in receipt of your letter of the [*20th*] ultimo and will constitute Louisiana into a District as soon as I can get some one suitable to command it. At present I have no suitable officer available in my Department and am anxiously looking for new regiment appointments which may give me a suitable officer. It requires a decisive and shrewd officer here" Telegram received (at 1:30 P.M.), *ibid.*; *ibid.*, RG 108, Telegrams Received; copies (one sent by mail), *ibid.*, Letters Received; DLC-USG, V, 54; DLC-Philip H. Sheridan.

On Aug. 20, Maj. Gen. Oliver O. Howard, Bureau of Refugees, Freedmen, and Abandoned Lands, wrote to Maj. Gen. George H. Thomas concerning assignment of officers for duty with the Freedmen's Bureau. Copy, DNA, RG 94, ACP, H1291 CB 1866. On Sept. 20, Thomas, West Point, endorsed this letter. "Respectfully refered to Genl U S Grant with the request that Maj Genl T J. Wood Bvt Maj-Genl D Tillson & Bvt Maj Genl Wager Swayne be retained as Asst Comrs Freedmens' Bureau for the states of Miss—Ala & Ga—" AES, *ibid.* On Sept. 24, USG endorsed this letter. "Respectfully forwarded to the Secretary of War. In my opinion there are plenty of officers of the regular army who could take the places of volunteer officers, now on duty in the Freedmens Bureau, and I would therefore recommend the immediate muster-out of the latter, their places to be filled by the Commanding Officers of Departments from among the regular officers serving in their respective commands. Gen. Wood should rejoin his reg't without delay. If other agents are required than such as can be selected from officers of the army, the law authorizes their employment from the appropriation for the Bureau. I am opposed to paying the expenses of this Bureau out of the Army appropriation." ES, *ibid.*

To Julia Dent Grant

Albany, N. Y.
August 31st 1866.

DEAR JULIA,

We arrived here after dark last night and were pulled and hawled about until late so that I had no oppertunity of writing to you just a few minuets before starting We stopped about one hour at West Point yesterday. I did not see Fred though Gen. Rawlins did. He is in hospital on account of granulated eyelids. The Dr told me they were not bad and that he had only taken him to hospitle to keep him out of the Sun a few days. I went to the hospitle to see Fred. and found that he had gone to Camp to see me. I looked for him the whole of our stay at the Point and was the only one of the party who did not see him.

Love and kisses to you and the children.

ULYS.

ALS, DLC-USG. USG had begun the tour arranged by President Andrew Johnson to dedicate the tomb of Stephen A. Douglas in Chicago, a tour better known as the "Swing Around the Circle." On Aug. 25, 1866, USG wrote to William A. Short, chairman, Soldiers' and Sailors' Union. "The invitation of the committee of which you are the chairman, to me to be present and participate in the celebration of the first anniversary of that body to be held Sept. 10, is received. If I am in the city on that day it will afford me great pleasure to join your Union on that occasion. Previous to receiving your invitation however, I had accepted another invitation, which if I keep, will take me out of the city at that time. All I can say now, is that it will afford me great pleasure to be with you on the 10th of September if it is so that I can." *Galena Weekly Gazette*, Sept. 4, 1866.

To Julia Dent Grant

Auburn, N. Y.
August 31st/66

DEAR JULIA,

I am getting very tired of this expedition and of hearing political speaches. I must go through however.

I only write now to give you a letter each day as near as I can. Love and kisses to you and the children.

ULYS.

ALS, DLC-USG.

To Julia Dent Grant

Detroit, Sept. 4th *1866.*

DEAR JULIA,

Gen. Rawlins, Dr. Barnes and myself switched off from the party at Cleveland last night and come here by boat.[1] The balance of the party staid over night there and will reach here this evening. This has given me a fine chance for a rest.—I received your letter on my arrival here. The race you saw reported is almost without foundation Mr. Jarome took me from the Hotel to Manhatten-ville, above Central Park where all the party took the boat to go up the river, in his four-in-hand team, the same you drove with when you were in New York, and when we got into the Park he asked me to drive, which I did. But there was no fast driving nor talk of it.[2]—Kisses to you and the children.

ULYS.

ALS, DLC-USG.

1. Secretary of the Navy Gideon Welles, present on the tour, and Post-master Gen. Alexander W. Randall, who was present part of the time, stated that USG left the party in Cleveland intoxicated. Howard K. Beale, ed., *Diary of Gideon Welles* (New York, 1960), II, 591, 593; Theodore Calvin Pease and James G. Randall, eds., *The Diary of Orville Hickman Browning* (Springfield, 1925–33), II, 115. See Sylvanus Cadwallader, "Four Years with Grant," IHi, pp. 786–87. In his speech at Cleveland, Sept. 3, 1866, President Andrew Johnson said that USG was "extremely ill," and at Detroit the next day a reporter stated that USG had been "quite ill." *New York Times*, Sept. 5, 1866.

2. On Aug. 30, two carriages filled with dignitaries on the tour went for a drive in Central Park, New York City. According to newspaper report, USG seized the reins from Leonard W. Jerome, financier and noted horseman, challenged the driver of the other carriage to a race, and won. *Ibid.*, Aug. 31, 1866.

To Julia Dent Grant

St. Louis, Mo,
Sept. 9th/66

DEAR JULIA,

To-morrow morning the party starts on its course East and will reach Washington on Saturday I will be glad enough to get there. I never have been so tired of anything before as I have been with the political stump speeches of Mr. Johnson from Washington to this place. I look upon them as a National disgrace. Of course you will not shew this letter to anyone for so long as Mr. Johnson is President I must respect him as such, and it is the country's interest that I should also have his confidence.

This is Sunday morning and it is raining very hard. If it stops before 1 O'Clock Ford and I will drive out to see Anna. Lewis Dent has gone South.

Love and kisses to you and the children.

ULYS.

ALS, DLC-USG.

On Sept. 5, 1866, Wednesday, Julia Dent Grant telegraphed to USG, Chicago. "I shall certainly expect you back Saturday. Father has not recovered from his stroke of paralysis. Please answer." Telegram sent, DNA, RG 107, Telegrams Collected (Unbound). On Sept. 6, 10:25 P.M., Bvt. Brig. Gen. Cyrus B. Comstock telegraphed to USG. "Telegram recieved. Mr Dent is physically better, mentally he is not much improved. His memory is affected and he talks a good deal at random. Everybody else very well" Telegram sent, *ibid.*, Telegrams Collected (Bound).

On Sept. 11, while USG was at Wood's Theatre in Cincinnati, a group planning to demonstrate support for him approached, and USG responded with his only substantive speech of the tour. "SIR: I am no politician. The President of the United States is my Commander-in-Chief. I consider this demonstration in opposition to the President of the United States, ANDREW JOHNSON. If you have any regard for me you will take your men away. I am greatly annoyed at this demonstration. I came here to enjoy the theatrical performance. I will be glad to see you all to-morrow when the President arrives." *New York Times*, Sept. 13, 1866. A second version of USG's remarks also circulated: "I am not a politician. The President of the United States is my superior officer, and I am under his [c]ommand. I beg of you, if you, have any regard for me, to march your company away, as I do not wish to be thus annoyed. I consider this a political demonstration for a selfish and political object, and all such I disapprove of. I came here to enjoy the performance, but I shall be glad to see you all to-morrow at the Burnett House." *Ibid.*, Sept. 14, 1866. See *Chicago Tribune*, Sept. 14, 1866.

To Edwin M. Stanton

Washington, D. C. Sept. 18th *1866*

HON. E. M. STANTON,
SEC. OF WAR.
SIR:

I have the honor to recommend that Maj. Isaac Lynde, who was sumarily dismissed from the Army in 1861, without trial or investigation of his conduct, be appointed Colonel of Infantry to fill one of the vacancies now existing, and that he be immediately retired. Major Lynde, had he been permitted to remain in service, would now hold the rank of Colonel. He is now over Sixty-two years of age and can therefore be retired from service. I respectfully refer you to the statement of Bvt. Maj. Gn. Canby for the justice of this recommendation.

I have the honor to be,
Very respectfully, your obt. svt.
U. S. GRANT
General.

ALS, DNA, RG 94, ACP, L736 CB 1866. Additional papers are *ibid.* Isaac Lynde, USMA 1827, promoted to maj., 7th Inf., as of Oct. 18, 1855, had been dismissed from the U.S. Army on Nov. 25, 1861, for abandoning Fort Fillmore, New Mexico Territory, on July 26 and surrendering to C.S.A. forces on July 27 without a fight. See A. F. H. Armstrong, "The Case of Major Isaac Lynde," *New Mexico Historical Review*, XXXVI, 1 (Jan., 1961), 1–35. Lynde's daughter Helen had married USG's brother-in-law Frederick T. Dent. On Nov. 27, 1866, Lynde was restored as maj., 18th Inf., to date from July 28, and immediately retired.

To William S. Hillyer

WASHINGTON, D. C., September 19, 1866.

I see from the papers that you have been making a speech in which you pledged me to a political party. I am further in receipt of a letter from General Gresham of Indiana, in which he says that his opponent for Congress had published an extract from a letter received from you, in which you pledged me to the support of President Johnson, and as opposed to the election of any candidate who does not support his policy. You, nor no man living, is authorised to speak for me in political matters, and I ask to desist in the future. I want every man to vote according to his own judgment, without influence from me.

Yours, etc., U. S. GRANT.

TO BREVET BRIGADIER GENERAL W. S. HILLYER, NEW YORK.

New York Tribune, Sept. 29, 1866. On Sept. 19, 1866, Col. Adam Badeau wrote to Walter Q. Gresham. "General Grant directs me to acknowledge the receipt of your letter of September 10th, and to forward you the accompanying copy of a letter sent by him this day to General Hillyer. You are at liberty to make what use you please of the inclosed." *Galena Weekly Gazette*, Oct. 2, 1866.

On Sept. 28, William S. Hillyer wrote to USG. Carnegie Book Shop Inc., Catalogue 307 [*1969*], p. 13. On Oct. 15, Hillyer drafted a letter to "General," possibly USG. "I herewith enclose a copy of a letter received this day from Mr Kerr and my letter to him concerning which Gen Gresham wrote to you. I have already sent you a copy of my speech and now you have before you the speech and the letter—to which you refer in yours of the . I have waited silently and patiently for the reception of this letter feeling well assured that when you had the whole facts before you and saw how grossly I had been misrepresented and you imposed upon that you would so far as you could repair the great wrong done me—I ask your early reply—. . . P. S. Please send me a copy of Greshams letter which you promised me" ADfS, Hillyer Papers, ViU.

To Robert C. Schenck

Washington, D. C. Sept. 19th *1866*

HON. R. C. SCHENCK,
MEMBER OF CONGRESS,
DEAR SIR;

Your letter of the 17th inst. in which you say you think it proper to inform me that my Chief of Staff, Brig. Gen. Rawlins, *is known* to have declared to a gentleman who is understood to sympathize with him in hostility to Congress, "that in Ohio, Schenck must be beaten if we have to take Valandingham to do it," is received. Your assertions, both as to what Gen. Rawlins said and as to his hostility to Congress, are positive and leave no room for denial except in a flat contradiction of your statements. Notwithstanding your statement to the contrary General Rawlins, who has been shewn your letter, denies ever having given utterance to such language or to such sentiment. I believe him and know that he condemns Valandingham['s] disloyalty as bitterly as you do. Whilst an officer of the Army he has not, nor will he, interfere with elections.

Your assertion of Gen. Rawlins hostility to Congress is too broad and too sweeping. He is not hostile to Congress though he may entertain different views from them on some points.

I have the honor to be,
Very respectfully
your obt. svt.
U. S. GRANT

ALS, deCoppet Collection, NjP. On Sept. 17, 1866, U.S. Representative Robert C. Schenck of Ohio, Dayton, had written to USG. "I think it right & proper to inform you that your Chief of Staff, Brig. Genl Rawlins, is known to have declared, a few weeks ago, to a gentleman in Washington, who is understood to sympathise with him in hostility to Congress, that 'in Ohio, Schenck must be beaten, if we have to take Vallandigham to do it.'" ALS, USG 3. On Oct. 8, Schenck wrote to USG. "Absence from my house, & continuous engagments, have prevented an earlier acknowledgement & notice of your letter of the 19th of Septr As you inform me that Brig Genl Rawlins, your chief of staff, 'denies ever having given utterance to such language or to such sentiment' as was imported to him in my letter of the 17th Septr it is due to him to state that the communication made to me was positive, & therefore I said that he was 'known' to have made the declaration;—that the gentleman to whom it was averred that the declaration was made is Genl Thomas Ewing;—that the place indicated was Genl Ewings office in Washington;—& that I shall take the earliest possible opportunity to apply to the gentleman who said he heard that remark made by Genl Rawlins, for authority to give his name." ADfS, OFH. On Oct. 15, USG wrote to Schenck. "Your second letter received. Gen. Rawlins says he never was in Gen. Ewing's office in his life nor did he ever talk politics to him elswhere. The mistake has unquestionably been made by taking J. A. Rollins, who was member of Congress from Mo. for J. A. Rawlins of my Staff. Before this a Conservative speech, if you would characterize it by no harsher term, of the former was attributed to the latter by parties in high place in this City." ALS, deCoppet Collection, NjP.

To Maj. Gen. Philip H. Sheridan

Washington, D. C., Sept. 21st *1866* [*1:00* P.M.]

MAJ GENL SHERIDAN
NEW ORLEANS LA.

Despatch of 20th received. Your cours in regard to riot in Brenham Texas right, only I think troops to defend themselves should be sent there without delay. If arms are used against peaceable soldiers disarm citizens

U. S. GRANT
General

Telegram sent, DNA, RG 107, Telegrams Collected (Bound); copies, *ibid.*, RG 108, Letters Sent; DLC-USG, V, 47, 60. See *HED*, 40-2-57, pp. 31–32. On Sept. 20, 1866, Maj. Gen. Philip H. Sheridan had telegraphed to USG. "Two soldiers of the 17th Infantry were wantonly shot at Brenham Texas on evening of the 7th of this month; they were unarmed and inoffensive. On that night a party of four or five persons broke into a store of Mr Compton and about 4 a. m it was found to be on fire and a small block of buildings burnt. Lieut Col C. E Mason commanding at Galveston at the request of the governor proceeded to Brenham and made an open investigation in the Court House, the result of which is that Brevet Major Smith took every precaution to keep his men in camp during the night—that he himself was not out of camp after 12. midnight, and the examination does not fix the crime of arson on any of the soldiers—Notwithstanding this writs were issued for the arrest of Major Smith and four of his men, not one of whom, it is the belief of Lt Col Mason, could have committed the crime. Since the occurrence the town of Brenham has been held at night by a Sheriffs Posse of fifty men, no soldiers allowed to come into the town, and the threats against Bv't Major Smith and his command have been such as to cause him to inclose his camp by a field work. I have sent orders to Bv't Major Smith to not deliver himself nor any of his men up, meantime I will assemble a Military board to ascertain if any of the soldiers were guilty of the act of arson. The manner of the civil authorities at Brenham is insolent and threatening, the language towards the soldiers insulting and menacing—unless it subsides I will move troops from Austin and San Antonio to that point. I will forward by mail the report of Lieut Col Mason. I have delayed reporting on this case until the facts were received. Two more of our soldiers were shot near Jefferson sometime ago which I have not yet reported as I am awaiting the receipt of the official evidence" Telegram received (on Sept. 21, 10:00 A.M.), DNA, RG 107, Telegrams Collected (Bound); *ibid.*, RG 108, Telegrams Received; copies, DLC-USG, V, 54; DLC-Philip H. Sheridan. On Sept. 21 and Sept. 22, 11:00 A.M., Sheridan telegraphed to USG. "I telegraphed you yesterday about the difficulty at Brenham Texas—I think it will subside without serious trouble—I am inclined to think there was a good deal of bluff intended—I will make every endeavor to get at the parties who fired the store of Mr Compton if they are soldiers, and there is a strong probability that they were" "Your despatch of the 21st has been rec'd—I think the force at Brenham will be able to maintain itself—I will go over in a few days and look the affair up still further—I transmit you by mail copies of my telegrams to the Governor of Texas and copy of the communication from the Sheriff of the County to the District Commander for the delivery of Brevet Major Smith and his soldiers" Telegrams received (on Sept. 21, 7:10 P.M., and Sept. 22, 8:25 P.M.), DNA, RG 107, Telegrams Collected (Bound); *ibid.*, RG 108, Telegrams Received; copies (one sent by mail), *ibid.*, RG 94, Letters Received, 626G 1866; DLC-USG, V, 54; DLC-Philip H. Sheridan.

On Sept. 23, Sheridan wrote to Brig. Gen. John A. Rawlins transmitting papers in the case. LS, DNA, RG 94, Letters Received, 626G 1866. The enclosures are *ibid.* On Sept. 24, Sheridan telegraphed to Rawlins. "I respectfully notify the General that I leave for Texas this morning & will be gone five 5 or six 6 days—Gen' Getty who is in Command of the District has not reached Galveston as there was no communication between that point & Brazos Santiago" Telegram received (at 4:00 P.M.), *ibid.*, RG 107, Telegrams Collected (Bound); *ibid.*, RG 108, Telegrams Received; copies, DLC-USG, V, 54; DLC-Philip H. Sheridan. On Oct. 1, 11:00 A.M., Sheridan telegraphed to Rawlins. "I have the honor to report my return from Texas—I visited Brenham and affairs are now arranged so that no difficulty will occur—The men who shot the soldiers have been held to bonds—The Sheriff has given up the attempt to arrest innocent men & if the guilty parties are found I will not screen them—The Charge that the town of Brenham was fired is exaggerated—One small square of houses separate from any others, about One hundred and fifty feet front by sixty feet deep was burned—The buildings and their contents not very valuable" Telegram received (at 5:25 P.M.), DNA, RG 94, Letters Received, 626G 1866; *ibid.*, RG 107, Telegrams Collected (Bound); *ibid.*, RG 108, Telegrams Received; copies, DLC-USG, V, 54; DLC-Philip H. Sheridan. On Oct. 3, USG forwarded to Secretary of War Edwin M. Stanton papers regarding the matter. ES, DNA, RG 94, Letters Received, 626G 1866.

Also on Oct. 1, Sheridan wrote to Rawlins. "I have the honor to transmit a report of the circumstances connected with the murder of two soldiers of the 80th U. S. Colored Infantry, stationed at Jefferson, Texas, On the 29th of August last. I doubt very much if any redress can be obtained in this case, but will follow it up. This section of the State of Texas is very lawless from all I can hear, and the injustice done to Freedmen very great, but I can cover but few of the cases as I have not the troops to spare." LS, *ibid.*, 738G 1866. On Oct. 10, USG forwarded these papers to Stanton. ES, *ibid.*

To Bvt. Brig. Gen. Cyrus B. Comstock

Washington, D. C. Sept. 24th *1866*.

~~B~~ GENERAL:

You will proceed with as little delay as possible to Nashville, Tenn. and through the State officials, Civil and Military, ascertain all you can with reference to secret Military organizations that are rumored to be forming within the state. If such organizations are being formed ascertain the object of them and on your return to Hd Qrs. report whether they are for political purposes, and whether, in your judgement, they threaten the safety of the lives and property of peaceable citizents.

If you should find it necessary to travel through the state of Tennessee, to satisfy yourself on the subject of your investigation, you are authorized to go wherever, in your judgement, you think it needful, within the state.

Very respectfully
your obt. svt.
U. S. GRANT
General.

TO BVT. BRIG. GEN. C. B. COMSTOCK, A. D. C.

ALS, DLC-Cyrus B. Comstock. On Oct. 7, 1866, Bvt. Brig. Gen. Cyrus B. Comstock, Indianapolis (although content indicates Tenn.), telegraphed to USG. "Neither the Authorities nor the people so far as I can learn expect any serious trouble here on election day Indeed it has not even been deemed necessary to ~~menace~~ increase the ordinary police force there has been some talk here of troops being sent independent of the State Authorities The Governor thinks this would create very bad feeling and that then if a slight Collision with them should occur the Most serious Consequences might follow" Telegram received (at 9:15 P.M.), DNA, RG 107, Telegrams Collected (Bound); *ibid.*, RG 108, Telegrams Received; copy, DLC-USG, V, 54.

On Oct. 12, Comstock, Washington, D. C., wrote to USG. "On the 24th ult. you directed me to visit Nashville Tenn., to ascertain all I could 'with reference to secret military organizations . . . In compliance with these instructions I visited Nashville, and on calling on the military authorities, found that they not only had no knowledge of such arming of either of the parties that would be most likely to arm, but entirely discredited it. The negroes were represented as entirely quiet and not in the least threatening—those formerly in the rebel service as having no inclination for further difficulties with the United States,—and the government of the state as without any militia or troops whatever. Having failed to obtain from the U. S. authorities any information of the rumored arming, I then visited many prominent citizens of both parties, believing that either party would be ready in making charges against the other; but none of the gentlemen I met gave credit to the belief of the existence of armed organizations of any party, as now existing. It seems that the negroes have some charitable societies established among themselves, but no one stated that they were armed or credited it, though one gentlemen had seen what looked like a company marching. Among the gentlemen with whom I had free conversations on these points, I will mention; Mr Fletcher Sec. of State of Tenn., ex Gov. N. S. Brown, Mr Lindsley Postmaster of Nashville, Judge Trimble, R. B. Cheatham Esq. G. M. Fogg Esq. Maj. W. B. Lewis, A. J. Duncan Esq Presdt. Bank of the Union. I asked the opinion of these gentlemen, as to the causes which would produce future difficuties—few thought there was any danger of trouble before the elections for governor, next summer, and that time was too far distant, for any one to form an opinion of value, now. I was told that some of the ultra democrats had broached the question of a convention of the people to be held independently of the present state government, and with the intention of superceding it. All persons of both parties who spoke of this, thought it possible or probable that such a step would result in civil war. But the general opinion among those I saw, was, that no such convention would be initiated. As to the prospective arming of any class within the state, the only information I could obtain was that derived from Gov. Brownlow's speeches. I did not learn of the arrival of any unusual quantity of arms within the state or of any unusual demand for arms, at the hardware stores. In conclusion, I am of the opinion that there now exist no armed organizations within the state (except a few guerilla parties that are being suppressed by the military authorities), that endanger the lives, or property of peaceable citizens." ALS, DLC-Andrew Johnson. On the same day, USG wrote to President Andrew Johnson. "Enclosed please find report of Bvt. Brig. Gen. C. B. Comstock of the result of his inspection to ascertain whether any Military Organizations were forming, or being designed, in the state of Tennessee threatning the peace or security of the inhabitants of the State. I am pleased to see that no cause for apprehension exists, at least for the present." ALS, *ibid.* See diary, Sept. 22–Oct. 12, 1866, DLC-Cyrus B. Comstock.

To Edwin M. Stanton

Washington, D. C. Oct. 1st *1866*.

HON. E. M. STANTON,
SEC. OF WAR,
SIR:

I would respectfully recommend Geo. S. Bensen, late of 2d Vt. Infantry, Vols. for the appointment of 1st Lt. if there is such a vacancy, 2d Lt. if the other is not vacant, in the 12th U. S. Infantry under the act reorganizing the Army. Lt. Bensen is from South Carolina but being North when the War broke out he Volunteered, as a private in the 1st Vt Three Months Vols. At the expiration of his time he re-enlisted in the 2d Vt Vol. Infantry, Veteranized at the expiration of three years more, and continued in service until the regiment was mustered out of service after the surrender of the rebel Armies. He rose to the rank of Commissioned officer in the service and was on the Staff of Gn. L. A. Grant at the close.

If there is no vacancy in the 12th Infantry (to which two new companies are to be added) I would then ask the appointment to any Infantry regiment.

The address of Lt. Bensen is Washington City P. O.

Very respectfully
your obt. svt.
U. S. GRANT
Gen.l

ALS, DNA, RG 94, ACP, B1044 CB 1866. On Oct. 18, 1866, George S. Benson, Washington, D. C., wrote to Bvt. Maj. Gen. Edward D. Townsend accepting his appointment as 1st lt., 12th Inf., enclosing his oath of office. ALS and DS, *ibid.* The appointment, however, was canceled when Benson failed the examination; he later was arrested for falsely presenting pay accounts. *Ibid.*

To Jesse Root Grant

Oct. 2d *1866*

DEAR FATHER;

I am going to Galena to attend the wedding of Col. Babcock, of my Staff, on the 9th of November. If Julia goes with me I shall go by Cincinnati to take Jennie on with us, and return that way to be present at the meeting of the "Society of the Army of the Tennessee" on the 14th of that month. If Julia does not go, and I do not think she will, I shall go direct to Galena and return by Cincinnati. I should like very much to see Aunt Rachel but I know the object of her seeing me is to secure a claim which she has made out against Government not one cent of which do I think should be allowed In time of war people living and holding property in regions occupied by Armies must expect to sustain losses without recourse upon Government even when their sympathies are with the Government. In her case sympathy, and all the fighting element of her family, were the other way. I will probably spend five days in Cincinnati from the 14th of November.

Yours Truly
U. S. GRANT

ALS, Mr. and Mrs. Philip D. Sang, River Forest, Ill. Presumably for an autograph collector, USG's mother added her signature below that of her son, and on Nov. 15, 1866, Jesse Root Grant added a note. ANS, *ibid.* See letter to Elihu B. Washburne, Oct. 23, 1866; letter to Manning F. Force, Nov. 11, 1866.

To Edwin M. Stanton

Washington, D. C. Oct. 5th. *1866*,

HON. E. M. STANTON,
SEC. OF WAR;
SIR:

I have the honor to recommend that all promotions in the Staff Corps of the Army, to fill original vacancies, created by the "Act of Congress re-organizing the Army," be by Seniority except in the Quarter Master's Department. My reasons for this are that in no Staff Department of the Army, except the Quarter Master's, have any officers demonstrated any special preeminence over others of their Corps in the line of their special duties. Many Officers of Staff Corps have won distinction as commanders of troops. For such distinction all original vacancies, in new regiments created, are as open to them as to line officers. A number of Staff Officers have received such appointments. My reccommendation would be that when officers are advanced for distinguished services, as commanders, or with troops, it be in the line of the Army. If the advancement is for distinguished services in one of the Staff Corps of the Army it be in that Corps where their services were rendered. Following this rule I could only make the recommendations in the one Corps alluded to.

I have the honor to be,
Very respectfully
your obt. svt.
U. S. GRANT
General.

ALS, DNA, RG 107, Letters Received from Bureaus.

To Maj. Gen. Philip H. Sheridan

Cipher *Washington*, D. C., Oct 8th *18~~64~~*66 [*1:30* P.M.]
MAJ GENL P H. SHERIDAN
NEW ORLEANS LA.

Your despatch of 3d inst just received. Your views about not authorizing volunteers to be raised in Texas ostensibly to put down Indian hostilities are sustained. With the military at your command as full protection can be given to the people of Texas as to any other exposed settlements You may so instruct Governor Throckmorton[1]

U. S. GRANT
General

Telegram sent, DNA, RG 107, Telegrams Collected (Bound); copies, *ibid.*, RG 108, Letters Sent; DLC-USG, V, 47, 60. See telegram to Maj. Gen. Philip H. Sheridan, Oct. 11, 1866; letters to Maj. Gen. Philip H. Sheridan, Oct. 12, 1866; letter to James W. Throckmorton, Oct. 20, 1866. *HED*, 40-2-57. On Oct. 3, 1866, Maj. Gen. Philip H. Sheridan had written to USG. "I have the honor to forward the enclosed telegram from Governor Throckmorton of Texas. I have no reason to believe that there is any necessity for these volunteers, except the reports found in the Texas newspapers, and the representations of Governor Throckmorton. There has not been a single military commander in Texas, who has reported Indian difficulties, Except in the case of a few Kickapoo's, who came over on our side of the RioGrande two or three times, and in parties not numbering more than five or six So far as my judgement is concerned, it is opposed to the acceptance of these troops, and I have been led to believe, from what I have heard and seen, that the mainspring of the whole movement, is, to get the United States troops from the interior of the State. There is no one who would hail such an event with greater pleasure than myself; but, so long as the Government pursues its present policy, I would not advise their removal, until there is a practical illustration of a better sentiment among the people of Texas. I have, indirectly, been contending with the Governor of Louisiana, to prevent him from raising troops in this State, for the alleged purpose of protecting Union people, (but most probably for other and more selfish motives) but, if the Governor of Texas can call out troops, the Governor of Louisiana has the same right, and, there will be this strange anomaly—The troops raised in Texas would be of the element which fought against the Government; those in Louisiana of the element which fought for it, and so it goes. I have sent the 4th Cavalry to the region of alleged Indian troubles General Wright informed me that Governor Throckmorton was going to make a great effort to remove the troops from the interior of Texas; This may be a part of the programme." LS, DNA, RG 108, Letters Received. Sheridan enclosed a copy of a telegram of Sept. 26 from Governor James W. Throckmorton of Tex., Austin, to Sheridan. "The Legislature requests me to call out One thousand (1000) mounted men to defend the frontier, unless immediate relief is offered by the Government. If their services are accepted by the Federal Government, they are at the disposal and service of the Federal authorities for such term as they may desire, They can be put in the field and supplied in three weeks from the order. Necessity requires prompt action." Copy, *ibid.* On Oct. 9, USG forwarded these papers to Secretary of War Edwin M. Stanton. Copy, *ibid.*, Register of Letters Received. On Sept. 28, Stanton had telegraphed to Throckmorton. "Your telegram of the 26th inst., has been referred by the President to this Department. Major General Sheridan, Command—the Military Division of which Texas forms a part, is now on a visit to that state, and upon his report being received the action of the Government on your request for troops will be communicated to you. In the mean time it would be well for you to confer with General Sheridan on the subject." Copy, *ibid.*, Letters Received.

On Sept. 8, Sheridan had written to Brig. Gen. John A. Rawlins. "I have recently received a communication from the Governor of Texas addressed to Maj Gen H. G. Wright, representing and complaining of Indian troubles in the Camanche county in that State, and at other points on the northern frontier and asking for the requisite protection from the military. I have also seen articles in the news papers of Texas about Indian depredations at different points on the frontier; but, while these reports come from the sources enumerated, there is not a single military report to sustain them. Howeve[r] Capt Claflin of the 6th U. S Cavalry is now out investigating these reports and I will depend more upon what he says than on any of these reports, which may be originated for some special purpose. I have ordered a portion of the 4th U. S. Cavalry to take post at Camp Verdi and at Fredericksburg, which will cover that country and also Camanche county. While these reports are being made to me and published in the Texas newspapers, the Legislature is passing acts to raise citizen troops, and it may be that this cry is gotten up to help along the passage of these acts to raise citizen soldiery for frontier service. General Wright said to me that the Governor of Texas would make a great effort to have the troops removed from the interior of the State, and this excitement about Indian difficulties may be based on this object. There would be no person more willing than I am, to remove all troops from points where their duties are more of a civil than a military nature; but, under the present policy of the Government, to give protection to Freedmen and men who were not disloyal during the rebellion, I cannot see how that change can at present occur. I want to go to the interior of Texas very much; but, am so tied down here for the present that I cannot get off." LS, *ibid.* On Sept. 18, Throckmorton wrote at length to Sheridan concerning the need to raise Tex. troops to stop Indian depredations on the frontier. Copy, *ibid.* On Oct. 6, Sheridan endorsed this letter. "Respectfully referred to the General-in-Chief for his information. There is no doubt in my mind that the Indian troubles on the frontier of Texas are very much exaggerated. There have been troubles on this frontier always, and always will be, and I doubt if they are much greater now than heretofore. I will have all my arrangements made by early spring to establish Posts, as by that time I hope to have an adequate force of Regular troops to establish them. I am opposed to the use of the mounted force the Governor proposes to call out. With reference to the good sentiment, and the desire to do justice to every class of citizens in Texas; there are so many intelligent officers and citizens, who differ from the Governor in his views, that I am compelled to believe he only represents one side of the question" ES, *ibid.* On Oct. 13, USG forwarded these papers to Stanton. ES, *ibid.* On Oct. 8, Sheridan endorsed papers received at USG's hd. qrs. "Gov Throckmorton's letters are rather 'Bunkum' I have not replied to them—silence is the best policy." Copy, *ibid.*, Register of Letters Received.

On Oct. 15, Col. Ely S. Parker wrote to USG. "I have the honor to submit the following as a correct history in part, if not of all, of the Indian troubles now raging along the western frontier of Texas, and causing so much anxiety to the authorities and people of that State. The primary cause of the feud originated previous to the breaking out of the late rebellion, by the citizens of Texas forcibly expelling the Indians from their reservations in that State, and forcing them to seek safety by fleeing to the plains North and west of Texas. During the rebellion, the ~~Confederate~~ Rebel Army & citizens of the southwest attempted to ally the Plain Indians (many of whom had been driven out of Texas) in arms with them against the United States. The Indians declined, and preparations were made by the southwestern whites to force them into a compliance with their wishes. The Indians (some 300 or 400 in number) then fled into Mexico to avoid being mixed up, in what they called, the 'white man's war'. After remaining there, as they supposed, long enough for reason to resume its sway in the bosoms of their persecutors, they determined to return to their homes by way of Texas. The Texians however, met them, drove them back and killed many of their number.

This at once created the most intense feeling of hostility in the Indian mind to the native Texians, and they immediately commenced a system of warfare and plunder upon the inhabitants of the frontier, resulting so seriously as to compel the state authorities to call upon the general Government for aid and protection from their incursions and depredations. The United States have no treaties with many of these people, for they are composed of wild Indians of several tribes, viz; the Camanches, Kiowas, Caddos, Wichitas and others. They are all desirous and aniious to get back to their ancient homes among their people, and in my opinion the most speedy method of quieting these troubles & reassuring the Indians of the good will of the Government towards them, is to invite them out of Mexico to a peace conference on American soil, and if they will consent to return to their northern homes, to give them safe military Escort, locating them upon the country known as the 'Leased Land,' west of Arkansas, (they can never live peaceably in Texas) where they could be easily, and I believe willingly supported by the Interior Department, and also be fully under the protection and surveillance of the military, which must necessarilly be maintained in that Country." ALS, *ibid.*, Letters Received. On the same day, USG endorsed this letter. "The enclosed statement of the cause for the Indian hostilities which now exercise the mind of the authorities of Texas to such an extent is respectfully submitted to the Sec. of War and the attention of the Interior Department is respectfully invited to the suggestions of Col. Parker, which I endorse, for the settlement of these difficulties." AES, *ibid.*

1. Throckmorton, born in Tenn. in 1825, moved to Tex. in 1841 where he practiced medicine and law. Although opposed to secession, he served in the C.S. Army and was elected governor in 1866.

To Maj. Gen. Philip H. Sheridan

Confidential Washington, D. C. Oct. 9th *1866*

DEAR GENERAL:

Enclosed I send you two letters furnished me by the Mexican Minister. One is from the Agt. of the Liberal Government of Mexico and the other is an intercepted letter fully explaining itself. How far the Agt. may judge the objects of Santa Anna and Mr. Seward correctly I do not know. But I do not belive that either of these parties are favorable to the Liberal cause. My own opinion is that the interest of the United States, and duty, is to see that foriegn interference with the affairs of this continent are put an end to. There is but one Government in Mexico that has ever been recognized by the United States and *we* must respect the claims of that Government and advance its interests in every way we can. It is probable that you may have an opportunity of judging the designs of Santa Anna should he attempt to send a force to the Rio Grande. Should his designs be inimical to the Government of Mexico, with which we are at peace, the same duty in obedience to our own neutrality laws compells us to prevent the fitting out of expeditions hostile to that Government that existed in the case of the Fenian movement against our Northern neighbor. There is but one party, one Government, in Mexico whose complaints or wishes have claim to respect from us. No policy has been adopted by our Government which authorizes us to interfere directly on Mexican soil with that country, but there is nothing that I know of to prevent the free passage of people or materiel going through our territory to the aid of the recognized government. Our neutrality should prevent our allowing the same thing where the object is to make war upon that Government so long as we are at peace with it.

Yours Truly
U. S. GRANT
General.

TO MAJ. GN. P. H. SHERIDAN,
COMD.G DEPT. OF THE GULF

ALS, DLC-Philip H. Sheridan; (variant copy) *ibid.* See letter to Maj. Gen. Philip H. Sheridan, Oct. 31, 1866. On Oct. 22, 1866, Maj. Gen. Philip H. Sheridan, New Orleans, wrote to USG. "I am in receipt of your letter of the 9th instant, and cordially coincide with all your views. I have sent a Staff officer to the Rio Grande, to definitely announce that I will support the Juarez Government in Mexico against all factions, and to notify the adherents of Ortega and Santa Anna to get out of the way, That no protection or security would be given to such parties on our side of the river. I also, sent word to Canales that his conduct had been disgraceful and unfaithful. I have been obliged to neglect affairs over there for some time past on account of being anchored here, but will give more attention to them from this time out Maximilian has gone over to the Church party without doubt, or at least has made the offer, and if accepted, it will give him the backing of Catholicism in Europe and, perhaps, in all the Southern States; but, the church party in Mexico has lost its wealth to a great extent, and is not so powerful as formerly. The calculation of the adherents of Maximilian, in Mexico and out of it, is, an expected disturbance of the peace of our country: and they are calculating largly upon it. I think myself, that the foreign merchants of Matamoros have been the principal instigators of the conduct of Canales, and I learned recently, that they have sent a petition to Maximilian to re-occupy the place, I do not believe this, but doubtless some have sought to give publicity to this impression. There has been a total disregard of commercial interests in the conduct of Mr Seward, in reference to the Rio Grande line, which, it seems to me, can only be attributed to butt-headedness or the indifference or vanity of old age. The trade which would flow through the channels of Monterey, Matamoros, Brownsville and Brazos Santiago, will amount to nearly twelve (12) millions of dollars per year, as soon as there is a settlement of Mexican difficulties, in the establishment of a Government there, friendly to the United States, and that can give security to trade. I will tolerate no violations of neutrality on the part of factions opposed to the Juarez Government." LS, USG 3.

On Aug. 15, Sheridan had written to USG. "I have the honor to report that the Imperial troops have been driven from Northern Mexico. Caravajal is not doing well and I am afraid it is not in him to do well. I strongly advise that President Juarez be urged to come down to Monterey. General Lew Wallace and some other sharks have arrived off Brazos, where their services are not regarded: I doubt if they can do much good." LS, DNA, RG 108, Letters Received. On Aug. 22, Sheridan twice wrote to USG. "There is much trouble over on the Rio Grande. Lew Wallace and Caravajal were chased out of Matamoros. I think it was induced from the impression that the people got that Caravajal and Lew Wallace intended to establish an independant republic under the name of the 'Sierra Madre'. I am unable to go over there, and regret it, as perhaps I could regulate affairs again; it is bad to have these dissensions. When I was over in Matamoros, Caravajal put me in mind of a race horse, who shows he has broken down by throwing up his tail while on the run: He has got too much weight on his shoulders certain, and for that reason I advised that Mr Romero prevail on President Juarez to come down, if only on a visit, to reconcile dissensions." "In accordance with General Orders No. 59 from the War Department I have made the following changes in my command: Texas a District; Florida a District; and each District a Seperate Brigade. Making them Districts was a necessity, from the difficulties of communication, and everything will work well so long as they can be regarded as Seperate Brigades; but, as their condition as Seperate Brigades is limited by the final termination of the Rebellion, I do not know how soon Seperate Brigades will end; when they do end all General Courts will have to be ordered from this point to cover cases originating at posts so remote, that it will require two months for communications to pass to and fro. The fact is, General, Texas should be a Department and it will be a very important one. As to Florida it is difficult only from the long time it takes to communicate,—some sixteen days. I would suggest that Texas be made a Department. That Florida be annexed to General Thomas' command, as it adjoins Georgia and is more easily communicated with by overland or by Mobile; that Mississippi be given me in lieu of Florida; and that Louisiana and Mississippi be made a Department, which, together with the Department of Texas, shall constitute a Military Division. These two Departments, so formed, will make a Military Division having more difficulties in it, in the way of communicating and controlling, than any Military Division now existing; but still, the difficulties will be less than now exist in the Department of the Gulf with its present geographical limits. As the Department commander I am now handcuffed to New Orleans, although my presence is required in Texas, on the Rio Grande and on the rout to El Paso, a trip which I contemplated taking, and which it seems necessary I should make in order to establish Posts. They will have to be established as soon as troops come out to occupy that line, and I wished to get the necessary knowledge by this trip to locate them at the proper points. Should my suggestions be approved I would recommend that the headquarters of the Department formed of Louisiana and Mississippi be established at some point on the Mississippi river; leaving New Orleans for my headquarters. The Military Division thus created will be one of more importance than any other, for it has Indian difficulties in it, Freedmen also; the political troubles, and the Mexican troubles on the Rio Grande: whereas the present Military Divisions have only Indian difficulties, and those difficulties of communication which also exist here." LS, *ibid.*

On Oct. 8, Sheridan wrote to USG. "On August 22nd last, I wrote you in reference to the difficulties of communication from remote sections of my command, stating that I could get along very well, so long as Seperate Brigades were authorized by law, but that after they ceased and Courts-Martial had to be convened by me, there would be much delay in the transaction of some of my public duties. It appears from the enclosed copy of endorsement of the Judge Advocate General that Seperate Brigades have ceased to exist" LS, *ibid.* The enclosure is *ibid.*

On Sept. 15, Sheridan wrote to USG. "Confidential . . . I respectfully communicate the following information regarding Mexican affairs. The Imperialists have withdrawn from Guaymas and Mazatlan, and I believe have only two ports left to them in Mexico.—Vera-Cruz and Acapulco.—The Liberals hold the roads between Vera-Cruz and the City of Mexico: in fact the French are on the defensive. There is much quarrelling and alarum among Imperial and French officials. It is rumored that Marshal Bazaine will go to France on the next steamer, if he can get to Vera Cruz without moving a large part of his army to escort him. There are also other rumors that Maximilian would leave and that he packed up to leave; but, Bazaine would not let him go. From the Rio Grande frontier I have information to the 6th instant; and from Monterey up to the 26th ultimo: Escobedo was about to march on San Luis Potosi, with about (12,000) twelve thousand Liberals, expecting to be joined by other commands. Everything east of Sierra Madre is in the hands of the Liberals. At Matamoros and in the whole State of Tamaulipas, there is a mixed and disgraceful state of affairs, between Caravajal Canales, Tapia, Cortina, Hinojosa and Lew Wallace: it is all about the Custom House at Matamoros, and this quarrel has deadened the commerce of the country so much, that it is a quarrel about a bone. I am sorry I cannot get over, as I might be able to exercise some influence towards a settlement; but it is impossible just now. Negrete is in Brownsville aggravating this quarrel. He is in the interest of the Ortega faction, and also, it is said, of Santa Anna." LS, *ibid.* On Sept. 18, Sheridan wrote to USG. "Confidential . . . I have advice to day from Vera-Cruz up to the 12th instant. The French have been trying to charter such light draft steamers as might sail along the coast to Tampico or Matamoros. One hundred and fifty seven men of the legion of honor have just arrived on the French steamer 'Panama'. One battalion of the 81st regiment of the line it is said will come to Vera Cruz to embark; the balance of the regiment.—from 1500 to 2000.—are willing to change colors and join Maximilian. My information points very strongly to an insincerity in complying with the terms of evacuation, and I again caution the Government on this point. I sometimes believe that the least hope given by the political condition of this country, would cause a breach of faith in respect to the evacuation; and it looks *tricky now* by a *change* of *flag* on the part of the *French regiments.* Maximilian appears to be disgusted, and if report speaks true, is substantially a prisoner in the hands of the French. French money is now being expended on French organization in the country, and there is no tangible evidence of evacuation; except by force. The forces of the Liberals skirmish around the walls of Vera Cruz, and Jalapa is about being attacked. The feeling of the Liberals in Vera Cruz is not to say very favorable to any foreigners, even Americans. There has been some handsome successes by the Liberals in Mechoacan, but no details." LS, *ibid.*

To Maj. Gen. Philip H. Sheridan

Cipher *Washington, D. C.*, Oct. 11th *18~~64~~*66 [*4:00* P.M.]

MAJ GEN P. H. SHERIDAN
NEW ORLEANS LA.

Despatches from the governor of Texas to the President and Newspaper extracts show Indian hostilities to exist on the frontier of that State to an extent requiring immediate attention. Your despatches on the same subject have been received and shown to the President Please report again the latest information you have on the subject and in the mean time give such protection as you can with the means at hand. If it is necessary to break up any Interior posts take such as you think may be best spared.

U. S. GRANT
General

Telegram sent, DNA, RG 107, Telegrams Collected (Bound); copies, *ibid.*, RG 108, Letters Sent; DLC-USG, V, 47, 60. See telegram to Maj. Gen. Philip H. Sheridan, Oct. 8, 1866. On Oct. 11, 1866, Secretary of War Edwin M. Stanton had written to USG. "I enclose to you for your consideration and such action as you deem proper a communication ~~addressed by~~ dated Austin Sept 29, 1866 addressed to this Department by J W Throckmorton Governor of Texas in relation to Indian outrages committed in that state, ~~and~~ accompanied by a copy of an Act of the Legislature of Texas providing for raising troops for defence, together with sundry newspaper extracts and a statement of the Hon Mr Black a member of the Legislature all of which ~~accompany~~ are referred to in the Governors communication. A telegram from ~~the~~ Governor Throckmorton dated the 26th of September addressed to the President & the answer thereto relating to the same subject are also herewith submitted. ~~herewith~~. The papers above mentioned have been laid before the President and considered by him in connection with the report of Major General Sheridan to you dated at Head Quarters New Orleans Oct 3 1866 enclosing a telegram to him from Governor

Throckmorton dated Sept 26, 1866 and your telegraphic reply addressed to General Sheridan dated Oct 8. 1866. ~~The President is deeply impressed with by~~ The representations of ~~the~~ Governor Throckmorton & the statements that he transmits deeply impress the President with the obligation & necessity of affording relief and protection to the people of Texas from ~~such~~ indian outrages to the utmost ~~exp~~ extent within the power of the Federal Government and he is of opinion that if troops ~~are~~ stationed in the interior can be advantageously employed for that purpose on the frontier it should be promptly done. He desires therefore that you take ~~measures~~ such proper measures and give such instructions as may verify the actual condition of ~~th~~ affairs in Texas and afford ~~and afford the necessary~~ immediate and adequate protection to the people on the frontier of Texas. If this protection can be afforded by the regular Military forces of the United States he deems it preferable to calling out and organizing a local military force. ~~But if it cannot be done~~ With this expression of his wishes the subject is referred to you for the prompt investigation and action which the urgency of the case seems to require." ADf, DLC-Edwin M. Stanton. See following letters. On Oct. 12, 11:00 A.M., Maj. Gen. Philip H. Sheridan telegraphed to USG. "I have the honor to acknowledge the receipt of your dispatch of the 11th I have no additional news regarding hostilities on the Texas frontier and still believe that there is a great deal of Bunkum in the reports. I have a company of cavalry stationed within a few miles of where an alledged massacre took place but have no reports from it and doubt whether it realy occurred. I will however send additional troops to the frontier without delay and hope that the nine (9) companies of the 17th Infantry now at the north will be sent me at once. I have notified the Governor of Texas that I would send an inspector to the frontier and that I would render such protection as the forces within my control would admit of and would establish posts in the early spring. I do not doubt but that the secret of all this fuss about Indian troubles is the desire to have all the troops removed from the interior and the desire of the loose lazy adventurers to be employed as volunteers against the Indians under the act of the State Legislature." Telegram received (at 5:00 P.M.), DNA, RG 107, Telegrams Collected (Bound); *ibid.*, RG 108, Telegrams Received; copies (2—one sent by mail with enclosures, including a copy of a telegram of Oct. 9 from Sheridan to Governor James W. Throckmorton of Tex. stating that "I am directed by the General in Chief to inform you that the volunteers authorized by the Legislature of Texas will not be accepted. . . ."), *ibid.*, Letters Received; DLC-USG, V, 54; DLC-Philip H. Sheridan. On Oct. 13, USG endorsed a copy of this telegram. "Respectfully referred to the Sec. of War for information. More troops will be sent to Gen. Sheridan immediately, if indeed some are not already on the way, which will enable him to give all the protection that troops can give against Indian hostilities. Occasional murders will take place on our frontiers and would if our people were all soldiers." AES (incomplete), DNA, RG 108, Letters Received; copies, *ibid.*; *ibid.*, Register of Letters Received.

On Oct. 15, 4:00 P.M., Sheridan telegraphed to Brig. Gen. John A. Rawlins. "I have directed General Heintzleman Commanding the District of Texas to concentrate all the available force of the fourth and sixth Cavalry, twenty one companies, at such remote points on the frontier of Texas as are most suitable for its protection against Indians—The movement of this mounted force will depend upon the necessity for its actual presence for the protection of the frontier people—Should it appear from truthful accounts that this force is inadequate, additional troops will be sent—Great difficulty will be encountered in maintaining this force at remote points and Genl Heintzleman is put on his good judgement before occupying these remote places—The movement of troops in Texas is a fat job for contractors and the pressure to get up Indian difficulties very great" Telegram received (at 7:30 P.M.), *ibid.*, RG 107, Telegrams Collected (Bound); *ibid.*, Letters Received from Bureaus; *ibid.*, RG 108, Telegrams Received; copies (one sent by mail with enclosure), *ibid.*, Letters Received; DLC-USG, V, 54; DLC-Philip H. Sheridan. On Oct. 16, USG forwarded this telegram to Stanton. ES, DNA, RG 107, Letters Received from Bureaus. On the same day, USG forwarded to Stanton a list summarizing Indian depredations since Sept. 1 compiled in the Tex. governor's office from letters and newspapers. ES and copy, *ibid.*, RG 94, Letters Received, 824T 1866.

On Oct. 16, 11:30 A.M., Sheridan telegraphed to Rawlins. "The twenty one (21) Companies of Cavalry which I have authorized to be concentrated at points on the frontier of Texas are mounted, and those at Carlisle reach the Regiments be about two thousand strong. This force I consider amply sufficient but if not I can strain a point & send more. Much unnecessary delay has occurred in the purchase of Cavalry horses in Texas on account of the system adopted by the Quarter Master Genera[l] in this purchase. Can you hurry him up?" Telegram received (at 3:40 P.M.), *ibid.*, RG 107, Telegrams Collected (Bound); *ibid.*, RG 108, Telegrams Received; copies (one sent by mail), *ibid.*, Letters Received; DLC-USG, V, 54; DLC-Philip H. Sheridan. On Oct. 18, Bvt. Maj. Gen. Montgomery C. Meigs wrote to USG. "I have received a copy of Gen. Sheridan's despatch, stating that . . . Gen. Sheridan desires greater speed. No new system has been adopted by the Quartermaster General. Instructions were given to the Chief Quartermaster, who is under Gen. Sheridan's orders, to purchase the horses upon the system established by law and regulations and perfected by experience after the organization of the Cavalry Bureau, and under which the armies of the United States were supplied during the later years of the war. If Gen. Sheridan will point out any defect in the system, and a remedy therefor within the legal competence of this office, I shall be happy to apply such remedy promptly upon its being suggested. The law for the better organization of the Quartermaster's Department requires all purchases to be made upon public notice, in order to prevent fraud and favoritism, and to secure the best supplies on public competition. That law points out the mode to be pursued in case of emergency requiring purchase in open market, and making it impossible to take time for the ordinary precautions against favoritism, fraud or waste. Section 4, chapter 253, act of July 4th, 1864, provides that in such case 'it shall be lawful for the commanding officer of such army or detachment to order the chief quartermaster of such army or detachment to procure such supplies during the continuance of such emergency, but no longer, in the most expeditious manner, and without advertisement; and it shall be the duty of such quartermaster to obey such order,' &c. . . . Gen. Sheridan has, under this law, a power to dispense with advertisements, and to hasten purchases, not vested in this office. If a sufficient emergency exists, he should exercise this authority. I am of opinion, however, that emergencies interfering with the usual precautions for securing honest and fair contracts ought seldom to arise in the service in time of peace." LS, DNA, RG 108, Letters Received. On Oct. 20, noon, Sheridan telegraphed to USG. "I am very much embarrassed by the delay of the Qr Master General in approving the bids for the horses for the 4th & 6th

Cavalry ordered to be purchased in Texas. Can he be hurried up?" Telegram received (at 2:25 P.M.), *ibid.*, RG 107, Telegrams Collected (Bound); *ibid.*, Letters Received from Bureaus; *ibid.*, RG 108, Telegrams Received; copies (one sent by mail, misdated Oct. 23), *ibid.*, Letters Received; DLC-USG, V, 54; DLC-Philip H. Sheridan. On Oct. 23, USG forwarded this telegram to Stanton. ES, DNA, RG 107, Letters Received from Bureaus. At 1:00 P.M., Sheridan telegraphed to USG. "Information from Comd'g Officer at Jacksboro Texas & also from Comdg Officer at Sherman Texas mention some Indian depredations on that line of frontier. Capt Cram followed with two Companies of Cavalry from Jacksboro & ran the Indians across the Wachita River but could not overtake them They apparently came from The Indian Territory but it is not certain Maj Forsyth is now Enroute to that line of frontier & will if possible ascertain what tribes these Indians belong to" Telegram received, *ibid.*; *ibid.*, Telegrams Collected (Bound); *ibid.*, RG 108, Telegrams Received; copies (one sent by mail), *ibid.*, Letters Received; DLC-USG, V, 54; DLC-Philip H. Sheridan. On Oct. 24, USG forwarded this telegram to Stanton. ES, DNA, RG 107, Letters Received from Bureaus. On Oct. 26, Meigs wrote to USG. "I have just received the letter of General Sheridan, in regard to purchases of horses, referred to me. I enclose a copy of a dispatch sent on the 24th, to Col. Sawtelle, instructing him to make contracts or purchases at once. I regret to see that a mistake has been made causing delay reported by General Sheridan, and justly complained of. It was not necessary, nor was it ever my intention to require these bids to come here from New Orleans before concluding contract. The contract should have been made, and purchases concluded as soon as the bids, received under the advertisements required by law, were opened and examined and satisfactory to the Chief Quartermaster at New Orleans. The law requires the bids to be finally deposited in Washington, but the Chief Quartermaster there was competent to make a contract upon the bids received, subject to after correction, if he made any great error. If he was instructed to the contrary it was an error in this office, made without my personal knowledge. I acknowledge my responsibility for the acts of the officers who assist me, and can only say that the business is so large that occasionally a mistake will occur. I rectified it as soon as I was aware of it, and much regret the delay. I have telegraphed General Sheridan on the subject as enclosed." LS, *ibid.*, RG 108, Letters Received. The enclosure is *ibid.* On Oct. 30, Sheridan wrote to Rawlins. "I am in receipt of the letter addressed to the General in Chief by the Quartermaster-General on the subject of the delay in the purchase of horses in Texas. I cannot well see how the Quarter Master General could write such a letter, in the face of the copy of instructions to my Chief Quartermaster, herewith enclosed. Attention is also invited to the enclosed copy of a telegram from the Quartermaster General dated 26th inst" LS, *ibid.* The enclosures, including Meigs's letter of Oct. 18 to USG, are *ibid.*

On Oct. 29, 1:30 P.M., Sheridan telegraphed to USG. "The question of raising volunteer troops in Texas is settled—None will be called out" Telegram received (at 7:00 P.M.), *ibid.*, RG 107, Telegrams Collected (Bound); *ibid.*, RG 108, Telegrams Received; copies (one sent by mail), *ibid.*, Letters Received; DLC-USG, V, 54; DLC-Philip H. Sheridan. On Nov. 8, Sheridan telegraphed to Rawlins. "I report my return from Texas Indian difficulties satisfactorily arranged with the Governor" Telegram received (at 3:00 P.M.), DNA, RG 108, Telegrams Received; copy, DLC-USG, V, 54. On the same day, Sheridan wrote to USG. "*Confidential* . . . I have the honor to enclose a copy of instructions, given to Brevet Major General Heintzleman Commanding the District of Texas; which fixes the position of the troops in his command until early spring. The arrangement on the Indian frontier will be satisfactory to the State authorities, and will give protection to the settlers. It should be born in mind, however, that a straggling white man will be occasionally killed on an Indian frontier, in spite of the best system of defence that can be adopted. Each regiment in the State is now in position to be very easily concentrated." LS, DNA, RG 108, Letters Received. The enclosure is *ibid.*

To Maj. Gen. Philip H. Sheridan

Washington D. C. Oct. 12th 1866.

GENERAL:

My dispatch of yesterday was sent to you on receipt of the enclosed which is forwarded for your information. Great care will have to be observed to see that no just cause of complaint can be urged against the army for not giving proper protection to the Citizens of Texas against Indian hostilities at the same time it is equally important that loyal and law abiding citizens should have protection against the violently disposed in their midst. I am satisfied that you have done and are doing the very best that can be done. Your attention however is called to the enclosed that you may know the apprehensions and desire of the President, and cause such inspection as will enable you to report satisfactorily on the points that give him uneasiness.

Very respectfully
Your Obt. Servt.
U. S. GRANT
General

TO MAJ. GEN. P. H. SHERIDAN
COMDG. DEPT OF THE GULF
NEW ORLEANS, LA

Copies, DLC-USG, V, 47, 60; DNA, RG 108, Letters Sent. See preceding telegram; following letter. On Oct. 20, 1866, Maj. Gen. Philip H. Sheridan wrote to Brig. Gen. John A. Rawlins. "I have the honor to acknowledge the receipt of the letter of the General in Chief dated 12th instant, enclosing report of Governor Throckmorton of Texas in reference to Indian depredations on the frontier of that State. I have already given orders for the movement of the 4th and 6th Cavalry, to points on the frontier most suitable for its protection, and can and will send additional force, if these regiments (which will number about two thousand when filled up) are not deemed adequate to give entire security. I have despatched Major G. A. Forsyth, a capable and intelligent officer, to the frontier, with instructions to stop *en route* and consult with General Heintzleman and Governor Throckmorton. I will go over to Galveston next week and see General Heintzleman in person on the same subject. I have notified Governor Throckmorton of the action which I have taken; and if he still desires to call out troops, I will be compelled to say, it will be unnecessary. I will, within two months, have two regiments organized, and ready for active service, in New Orleans.—the 9th Cavalry and the 39th Infantry." LS, DNA, RG 108, Letters Received. Sheridan enclosed a letter of Oct. 16 from himself to Governor James W. Throckmorton of Tex. concerning the stationing of troops on the frontier and stating: ". . . In reference to the points at which Colored troops shall be placed; it will be governed by the interests of the public service. While I have no disposition to give annoyance to the Community; it might as well be understood at once, that no distinction will be made, in reference to Color of soldiers, wearing the uniform of the United States:" LS (duplicate), *ibid.* On Nov. 8, USG endorsed these papers. "Respectfully forwarded to the Secretary of War for his information" ES, *ibid.* On Nov. 11, Sheridan transmitted to Rawlins a report of Nov. 2 from Maj. George A. Forsyth. *HED*, 40-2-57, pp. 129–30. On Dec. 10, USG endorsed to Secretary of War Edwin M. Stanton a report of Nov. 10 from Forsyth. ES, DNA, RG 94, Letters Received, 731G 1866. On Dec. 20, Sheridan transmitted to Rawlins a report of Dec. 16 from Forsyth. *HED*, 40-2-57, pp. 45–48.

To Maj. Gen. Philip H. Sheridan

Confidential Washington, D. C. Oct. 12th *1866*

DEAR GENERAL:

I regret to say that since the unfortunate differences between the President and Congress the former becomes more violent with the opposition he meets with until now but few people who were loyal to the Government during the rebellion seem to have any influence with him. None have unless they join in a crusade against Congress and declare their acts, the principal ones, illegal and indeed I much fear that we are fast approaching the point where he will want to declare the body itself illegal, unconstitutional and revolutionary. Commanders in Southern states will have to take great care to see, if a crisis does come, that no armed headway can be made against the *Union*. For this reason it will be very desirable that Texas should have no reasonable excuse for calling out the Militia authorized by their Legislature. Indeed it should be prevented.

I write you this in strict confidence but to let you know how matters stand, in my opinion, so that you may square your official action accordingly.

Very respectfully
your obt. svt.
U. S. GRANT

TO MAJ. GN. P. H. SHERIDAN,

P. S. I gave orders quietly two or three weeks since for the removal of all Arms in store in the Southern states to Northern storehouses. I wish you would see that those from Baton Rouge, and other places within your command, are being moved rapidly by the Ordnance officers having the matter in charge.[1]

U. S. G.

ALS, DLC-Philip H. Sheridan. See preceding letter. On Oct. 20, 1866, Maj. Gen. Philip H. Sheridan, New Orleans, wrote to USG. "I thank you for your letter of the 12th inst which has just come to hand. It gives shape to many thoughts which I have had, and which have urged me so far as to order to this city two additional regiments from the Rio Grande. I had also strenghtened the regiment at Baton Rouge by four companies of the 10th Heavy Artilley, and have urged on the recruiting of the 9th Cavalry & 39th Inf While I have had these thoughts on my mind I have allowed no one to know them for I sincerely hope that the President may not take a stand which would be so liable to jepordize the peace of the country. I feel but little security from profession of Texian loyalty, & have been very reluctant to scatter the troops beyond their ability to concentrate for their own protection. The moral standard in Texas is best elustrated by the noise they make over the occaisonal murder of a white man by Indians on the extreme frontier while nothing is said or done over the murder of very many negroes in the settled potions of the state. I will try and arrange affairs in Texas so as to give no excuse to the governer' to call out troops. I wish you would occaisonally, write to me and alway's rely on my unwavering support" ALS, USG 3.

1. On Sept. 22, USG had written to Brig. Gen. Alexander B. Dyer, chief of ordnance. "You will please direct the officers of your Corps, in charge of Ordnance and Ordnance Stores &c. at Augusta, Ga., Baton Rouge, La., Charleston, S. C., Harpers Ferry, Va., Mt. Vernon, Ala., and Galveston, Texas, to remove, without delay, to New York Harbor, all small arms, of every description, in their charge, with the exception of three thousand (3000) muskets, fit for

issue to troops, at Baton Rouge, and fifteen hundred (1500) of like quality at Charleston, SC. On the arrival of such arms in New York Harbor give such directions for the storage of serviceable arms as you may think proper to secure them. For all others submit recommendation, before removal from New York, for their disposal either for repairs or sale as you may deem most advantageous to Government." Copies, DLC-USG, V, 47, 60; DLC-Edwin M. Stanton; DNA, RG 108, Letters Sent. On the same day, USG endorsed this letter. "Respectfully forwarded to Secretary of War for his information." ES, DLC-Edwin M. Stanton. On Oct. 2, Bvt. Maj. Gen. James A. Hardie, inspector gen., Washington, D. C., wrote to Secretary of War Edwin M. Stanton concerning permanent fortifications in the South. LS, DNA, RG 94, Letters Received, 884H 1866. On Oct. 4, USG endorsed this letter. "I agree with the recommendations of the 'Board' in all their recommendations, and would advise that the Chief of Ordnance be directed to carry them out without delay. This of course excepts the sales of property at Charleston and Augusta, which can only be authorized by Act of Congress. In regard to the ammunition at Baton Rouge, I think the Board recommend the retention of more than it may be advisable to keep there, but this matter can be taken under advisement hereafter. With regard to the ammunition at Fortress Monroe, I would leave it for the present where it is in accordance with the suggestion of Gen. Dyer. After all the other suggestions of the Board are carried out it can be disposed of as may then be deemed advisable. In regard to the disagreement between the 'Board' and the Chief of Ordnance on the subject of removal North for repairs and storage of infantry accoutrements, the 'Board' seem to have made their recommendation upon a knowledge of the fact that about two-fifths of the equipments are rendered serviceable with but very little expense. In this particular then I would agree with the 'Board.' The question of the disposition of small arms has been disposed of by ordering all North for storage with the exception of a limited, specified amount for issue to troops. I would not recommend any change in orders already given on that subject. Where the Board have recommended special places for deposits of stores removed from Southern Arsenals, I would suggest that instead of carrying out their recommendation to the letter that the Chief of Ordnance be authorized in all instances to designate where they shall be sent for storage." ES, *ibid.*

To Orville H. Browning

Washington, Oct. 13th 1866

SIR:

Your communication of this date acknowledging receipt of communication from me containing extract from a letter from Lt. Gen. Sherman[1] relative to the Indians now held and fed by Govt. at "Bosque Redondo" is received The season is now so far advanced that I do not deem it practicable to relieve the Government of the burden of their present charge before Spring without manifest injustice, and great suffering to the indians who cannot properly be held responsible for their present position But orders for their disposal should be matured as soon as possible, and they should be carried into effect so soon as the season will admit of it. When released from nominal imprisonment these Indians, become a charge upon the "Indian Bureau." For this reason I asked the views of the Interior Dept. in order that the army could aid in carrying out these views. It seems from all the information that I get that it is impracticable to protect the Indians from adventurers in search of mines on any reservations in the mineral regions. The very Indians in question, I believe, were practically driven from a reservation assigned them in New Mexico. I would recommend their removal therefore with the consent of the removed, to the Indian Territory, west of Arkansas. I am not familiar with the terms of existing treaties relative to this territory but suppose the Government could give them lands on it or contiguous to it, where they would be comparatively safe from encroachments of white people.—I will endeavor to have an interview with you on this subject early next week at your office, or at mine at any time it might suit your convenience to call.

I have the honor to be
Very respectfully, your obt. servt.
U. S. GRANT
General

TO O. H. BROWNING
SEC. OF THE INTERIOR

Copies, DLC-USG, V, 47, 60; DNA, RG 108, Letters Sent. On Oct. 16, 1866, USG wrote to Secretary of the Interior Orville H. Browning. "I will call at the Interior Dept. to-morrow between 10 & 11 a. m. if the hour suits your convenience. If not any other hour during the day, or the day following, will suit my convenience equally well." ALS, IHi.

1. On Sept. 21, Lt. Gen. William T. Sherman, Fort Garland, Colorado Territory, had written in part to Brig. Gen. John A. Rawlins. "I learn also that he (Gen. Carleton,) has collected at the Bosque Redondo, Fort Stanton, all the Navajos, 8000 in number, who are held as prisoners of war and are to be fed as such. This is a matter of some importance, and is most costly. I think we could

better afford to send them to the 5th Avenue Hotel to board, at the cost of the US. Gen. Pope recommends they be removed to the Indian Territory west of Arkansas, where they could be fed at less cost. This whole subject of the maintenance of the Indians who wont work, and must be fed or turned loose, is one that should be solved at Washington and not thrown on us. I have called for full and specific reports for General Carleton, which with those of General Pope, I will digest and send to the General some time this winter, that we may begin next year with some intelligble system." Copy, DNA, RG 108, Letters Received. On Oct. 10, USG endorsed this letter. "The within extract is respectfully forwarded to the Secretary of War. In my opinion, the subject matter of the extract should receive prompt action and decision, and while I have my own views as to the course which should be pursued by the Governm't, I would respectfully request that the subject be submitted to the Hon. Secy of the Interior, for his decision." ES, *ibid.*

On Sept. 30, Sherman, Fort Lyon, Colorado Territory, wrote in part to Rawlins. "Craig, '(formerly a Colonel or Captain in the Army, and owner of a large ranch on the Huerfano,)' may be taken as the best sample of the class of men who are settling along the east base of the mountains. He has thoroughly proven the ability to produce, but then comes the more difficult problem of consumption. Who is to buy his corn? The miners of Colorado in the mountains two hundred miles distant will take some, but the cost of hauling is enormous. The few travellers and stage companies will buy a little, but he and all situated like him look to our military for a market, and that is the real pressure for garrisons and an Indian war. The Utes are harmless and peaceable, and the Cheyennes and Arrapahoes are off after the Buffalo, God only knows where, and I dont see how we can make a decent excuse for an Indian war. I have travelled all the way from Laramie without a single soldier or escort. I meet single men unarmed travelling along the road as in Missouri. Cattle and horses graze loose, far from their owners, most tempting to a starving Indian, and though the Indians might easily make a descent on these scattered ranches, yet they have not done so, and I see no external signs of a fear of such an event, though all the people are clamorous for military protection. I received at Pueblo a petition to that effect, signed by so many names that I could not help answering that the names to the petition exceeded in number the strength of any of our small garrisons. Still I do think that the efforts of these people to transform the desert into productive farms is worthy of encouragement of the General Government, and I will treat of the subject again at length. After spending part of a day and the night at Craig's I resumed the journey down the Huerfano twenty miles to its mouth—there forded the Arkansas and turned up five miles to the house of Colonel Boone, a man of note in this quarter. He also has a good two-story frame house with his family, embracing the wife of Colonel Elmer Otis, but she happened to be away on a visit to some neighbor and I did not see her. Colonel Boone was at home and I talked with him freely on the above and all other points of interest. He is an old Indian man, was on the Plains with General Ashley as early as 1824, and has been more or less connected with the Indians ever since. He also made the treaty with the Cheyennes and Arapahoes in 1860. He cultivates a farm and lives seemingly as little apprehension of danger from Indians as the rest of the people. After camping a night near his house, we turned down the Arkansas, and travelled in three days one hundred miles to this post, Fort Lyon. I did not see or hear of an Indian the whole distance though we passed through the whole length of the Cheyennes and Arapaho Reservation." Copy, *ibid.* On Oct. 18, USG endorsed this letter. "Respectfully forwarded to the Secretary of War with request that this extract be forwarded to the Secretary of the Interior, for his information." ES, *ibid.* Both Sherman letters are printed in full in *HED*, 39-2-23.

In Dec., USG favorably endorsed Special Orders. "I . . . Agreeably to instructions from the Secretary of War, the Commanding General, Department of the Missouri, will immediately give orders to turn over the control of the Navajo Indians now held as prisoners at the Bosque Redondo Reservation, New Mexico, to such agent of the Indian Department as may by that Department be designated to receive and take charge of them. II . . . The Indian Agent is authorized to make requisitions on the Subsistence Department for such supplies as can be ~~furnished~~ spared in the Territory of New Mexico for the use of these Indians, settlement for cost of such supplies to be made between the Departments of War and of the Interior III . . . The Commanding Officer in New Mexico will afford the necessary and usual military aid to the Indian Agent in his control of these Indians, but without going beyond the strict duties and administration of the military service, or interfering with those which belong to the Indian Department" AES (undated) and copy (printed—dated Dec.), DNA, RG 94, Letters Received, 91I 1866; (printed—issued as War Dept. Special Orders No. 651, Dec. 31) *ibid.*

To Charles W. Ford

Washington, D. C. Oct. 15th *1866.*

DEAR FORD:

Judge Irvin[1] of Texas, who has been absent from St. Louis for near twelve years and who holds a Deed of of Trust for $5,000 00 on Mr. Dent's place, with 10 prct. int. for all that period, has at last turned up. I own about 200 acres of the land included in the deed of trust and am ready to pay my part. I do not want to pay the whole however without being secured. I shall send $11.000 00 in a draft to L. A. Benoist for you to deposite to my credit to settle this matter with in a few days. What I want to ask you to do is to get some good lawyer to settle this matter so that I will be I will either pay my part, and that of General Dent, who owns 100 acres of the land, and have those portions cleared or I will pay the whole and either have the land sold and bought in for me, or have the deed of trust secured to me. If I purchase the land I will either pay the balance of the owners all it is worth or I will deed the land back to them on payment of their part.

I have written to John Dent to see you in this matter.

Yours Truly,
U. S. GRANT

ALS, USG 3. See following letter; letter to Charles W. Ford, Oct. 25, 1866; letter to John W. Garrett, Dec. 9, 1866.

1. On Sept. 28, 1866, David Irvin of De Witt County, Tex., Washington, D. C., wrote to President Andrew Johnson requesting a pardon. ALS, DNA, RG 94, Amnesty Papers, Tex. Docketing indicates that Irvin was pardoned on the same day. AN, *ibid.*

To Charles W. Ford

Oct. 17th *1866*.

DEAR FORD,

Enclosed I send draft for $11.000 00 which please deposite with L. A. Benoist subject to my draft. I send it out so as to have the money ready to relieve that land I wrote to you about a few days ago.

I got your letter about Ten Eyck[1] some time ago and forgot from time to write to you about it. The fact is since the Phila Convention I cannot intercede in the matter of appointments. If they were confered for merit, or services in the War, I could do so to a reasonable extent, but where opinions of policy are to be taken into account I can not. I would like very much to do you a favor in any other way however.

Yours Truly
U. S. GRANT

ALS, USG 3. See preceding letter.

1. On July 5, 1866, Anthony Ten Eyck, former maj. and paymaster, Detroit, had written a letter received at USG's hd. qrs. applying for the position of Mich. pension agent and enclosing a letter of recommendation from Charles W. Ford, St. Louis. DNA, RG 108, Register of Letters Received. On July 17, USG endorsed these papers. "Respy. referred to the President—Maj Ten Eyck served honorably as a Paymaster during the rebellion—Mr Ford, the writer of the accompanying letter, I have known for many years." Copy, *ibid.*

To Edwin M. Stanton

Washington, D. C. Oct. 18th *1866*.

Hon. E. M. Stanton,
Sec. of War;
Sir:

I have the honor to recommend that Bvt. Maj. Gen. R. C. Buchanan be Breveted Colonel for the battle of Gaines Mills, June 27th 1862. Gen. Buchannan has received two brevets, that of Brigadier and Major General, but being only a Lieut. Colonel in full rank at the date of the battle of Gaines Mills a brevet for that battle would be but just to him and would place his relative rank among brother officers, who have also been breveted to the rank of Major General, where his relative full rank places him. As matters stand now officers who did not happen to reach the full rank of Colonel before brevets were given, and have since been breveted up to Major General, have received brevets for all the intermediate grades between their real and the brevet rank given. In this way Gen. Buchanan, and possibly other officers of his rank, will loose brevet rank in consequence of having gained real rank before the subject of brevets was taken up.

I have the honor to be
Very respectfully
your obt. svt.
U. S. Grant
General.

ALS, DNA, RG 94, ACP, B333 CB 1870.

To Lt. Gen. William T. Sherman

Private Washington, D. C. Oct. 18th *1866*.

Dear General:

Yesterday the President sent for me and in the course of conversation asked if there was any objection to you coming to this

City for a few days. I replied of course that there was not. I wish therefore that you would make your arrangements to come on with me from Cincinnati after the meeting of the "Society of the Army of the Tenn."—The President shewed me a letter which you wrote to him about the 1st of Feb.y the contents of which you will remember, and stated that some people had advised its publication and asked my advice. I told him very frankly that Military men had no objection to the publication of their views as expressed upon official Matters, properly brought before them, but that they did not like expressions of theirs which are calculated to array them on one or other side of antagonistic political parties to be brought before the public. That such a course would make, or was calculated to make, a whole party array itself in opposition to the officer and would weaken his influance for good. I cannot repeat the language use by me but I gave him to understand that I should not like such a use of a letter from me nor did not think you would. Taking the whole conversation to-gether, and what now appears in the papers, I am rather of the opinion that it is the desire to have you in Washington either as Act. Sec. of War or in some other way. I will not venture in a letter to say all I think about the matter or that I would say to you in person.

When you come to Washington I want you to stay with me and if you bring Mrs. Sherman and some of the children we will have room for all of you.

Yours Truly
U. S. GRANT

TO MAJ. GN. W. T. SHERMAN,
ST. LOUIS, MO.

ALS, DLC-William T. Sherman. See letter to Andrew Johnson, Oct. 21, 1866; letter to Edwin M. Stanton, Oct. 27, 1866.

On Oct. 20, 1866, Saturday noon, USG telegraphed to Lt. Gen. William T. Sherman. "Come to Washington without delay. Leave St. Louis by Tuesday if you can" Telegram sent, DNA, RG 107, Telegrams Collected (Bound); copies, *ibid.*, RG 108, Letters Sent; DLC-USG, V, 47, 60. At 3:00 P.M., Sherman telegraphed to USG. "Dispatch received—I can, of course, start for Washington tuesday at 3 P M if absolutely ordered but if possible spare me the most unpleasant duty, suggested in the newspapers—The Military ought to keep out of quasi-political offices—I will await your receipt of my letter of yesterday and in case of no countermand will start for Washington as you order on tuesday P M" Telegram received (at 4:45 P.M.), DNA, RG 107, Telegrams Collected (Bound); *ibid.*, RG 108, Telegrams Received; copy (misdated Oct. 22), DLC-USG, V, 54. On Oct. 19, Sherman had written to USG. "I got back yesterday, and found all my folks reasonably well, and at the office enough to occupy me pretty close for a few days. At Riley I found a despatch from the President asking my consent to the publication of some letter I wrote him last Winter. Of course I consented if it would do any good, and did not involve me in controversy. But I cannot imagine what the letter is as I have no copy. I remember you & I called one day the time Meade Thomas & I were there on that Board, and that I neglected to call to see the President again, for which I wrote him an explanatory and apologetic note, in which I doubtless expressed some general wish that he should succeed in his efforts to restore our Country to Political Peace. I also see notices of some vague intention of Mr Stantons going abroad leaving the War office vacant and that I am to be invited to fill it pro tempore. This cannot be. The President or no one ever breathed such a thought to me, and I should of course decline. I doubt in our country whether the Secretary of War can even be ~~any~~ purely a Military officer. He must be a member of the Cabinet mingling with the other Political questions, and sharing the fate of the administration, whereas we are Commissioned for life, and must serve in succession every administration. If you ever hear such a thought broached as to me, fend it off, and spare me the unpleasant task of declining. As to approving or disapproving the individual acts of the administration I have never thought of it.—It is none of my business. I surely do approve of any honest, sincere effort to reestablish the States so that Civil law may relieve the Military of their present doubtful duties of police, but I do not love a Rebel, or Copperhead today one whit better than I did in 1864, nor do I approve of mob law in any manner, shape or form. I hear also that you talk of going to Europe. Let me beg you to defer it for the present, even up to the conclusion of the Next Presidential Election. Genls Hancock & A. J. Smith have just called, and I will close this, intending in a very few days to complete the series of letters I have been making to Rawlings—Are you *surely* going to attend the aniversary meeting of the Army of the Tennessee at Cincinati? If you do, I will." ALS (misdated Aug. 19), DNA, RG 108, Letters Received. See Maj. Gen. William T. Sherman to Andrew Johnson, Feb. 2, Oct. 16, 1866, DLC-Andrew Johnson.

On Oct. 22, Sherman telegraphed to USG. "Your letter of Eighteenth rec'd Cannot you excuse my coming to Washington now? Answer today as your telegraphic order is peremptory" Telegram received (at 6:00 P.M.), DNA, RG 107, Telegrams Collected (Bound); *ibid.*, RG 108, Telegrams Received; copy, DLC-USG, V, 54. At 8:05 P.M., USG telegraphed to Sherman. "The order for you to come to Washington was by direction of the President. Stay with me while in the city." Telegram sent, DNA, RG 107, Telegrams Collected (Bound); copies, *ibid.*, RG 108, Letters Sent; DLC-USG, V, 47, 60. On Oct. 23, Sherman telegraphed to USG. "Dispatch of yesterday rec'd I will start this afternoon & reach Washington thursday at five fifty P M Will be most happy to accept your hospitality" Telegram received (at 10:00 P.M.), DNA, RG 107, Telegrams Collected (Bound); *ibid.*, RG 108, Telegrams Received; copy, DLC-USG, V, 54. On Oct. 26, Sherman, Washington, D. C., wrote to Mrs. Sherman. "I got here punctually at 5.15 yesterday, and took a hack for Genl Grant, meeting him on the way to the Depot on the Supposition that we would arrive at 5.50—We found dinner waiting—and afterwards talked over matters of common interest and then went to the Theater. This morning as soon as breakfast was over we went to his office and at 10 a m we called on the President—Grant supposing the President wanted to talk to me in private left us alone. I waited for Mr Johnson to do the talking which he did in a circuitous way, first of England—then France and then Mexico. I learned that he wanted to do something in Mexico to influence her when the French with draw, which they are sure of doing soon—and he wants Grant to go there along with Our Minister Lew Campbell of Ohio—but Grant *wont* go and rightfully too in a mere subordinate diplomatic Capacity.—I kept very quiet—only asking incidentally what sort of Govt Mexico would have when Maximilian withdraws—what means were left to support [a]nother; and what reason he had to know or believe our interference unasked, without Money and without an Army would be more welcome than that of the French—Our conversation was very general, and it being Cabinet day & the Secretary of the Treasury—McCullough having arrived I asked when I should call again and tomorrow at 10 I again go. Unless Grant goes away, and I know he will not in which he is emphatically right—I do not believe the President will do more than consult with me on the General status of affairs out West, and then let me off— . . . I have no doubt there is some plan to get Grant out of the way, & to get me here, but I will be a party to no such move—There may be trouble ahead—but I shall steer clear of the breakers if I can, and in my own way. . . . The letter about which so much has been said has not been published, and doubtless is in so general terms that it may mean any thing or nothing but if published I will ask Mr Johnson to publish two others which are not so paleatable. But I repeat I will keep as mild and gentle as a dove, till I find what use is to be made of me, and then will begin the game whether I can be used by others as a plastic piece of Clay. . . ." AL (signature clipped), InNd.

On Oct. 30, Secretary of War Edwin M. Stanton wrote to Sherman. "I am directed by the President to communicate to you a copy of a letter addressed by him to the Secretary of War, dated the 26th instant, and of my letter transmitting the same to General Grant and, also, a copy of instructions by the Secretary of State to the Honorable Lewis D. Campbell, Minister of the United States to Mexico, referred to in the Presidents' letter, which papers are herewith enclosed. The President has relieved General Grant from the duties referred to and transmits through me the assignment and instructions to you, set forth in the enclosed letter addressed by him to the Secretary of War of this date. You will please favor me with an acknowledgment of the papers and your answer to be communicated to the President, stating at what time it will suit your convenience to enter upon the specified duty." Copy, DLC-Edwin M. Stanton. On Oct. 31, Maj. George K. Leet forwarded to the AGO undated draft orders issued on the same day as War Dept. Special Orders No. 543. "During the absence under instructions from the President of Lieut. Gen. W. T. Sherman from his command, reports and routine papers will be forwarded by his subordinates to the Asst. Adjt. Gen'l., Hd. Qrs., Mil. Div. of the Mo. In important cases, requiring immediate action, Department Commanders in the Mil. Div. of the Mo. will correspond direct with Hd. Qrs. of the Army during Gen. Sherman's absence. Lieut. Gen. Sherman will report direct to the General-in-Chief in reference to the execution of the duties entrusted to him." Df, DNA, RG 94, Letters Received, 809A 1866.

On Nov. 2, Sherman, Cincinnati, telegraphed to USG. "Juarez ought to be notified by the earliest possible means to expect the U. S. Minister & Myself at Vera Cruz on board the Susquehanna He should follow the retiring French quickly into the City of Mexico. Sherridan could send a messenger via Matamoras." Telegram sent, DLC-William T. Sherman; telegram received (at 12:20 P.M.), DNA, RG 107, Telegrams Collected (Bound); *ibid.*, RG 108, Telegrams Received. On Nov. 3, Sherman, St. Louis, wrote to USG. "I got home last night, and have already put in motion all things looking to my departure early next week for the Mission to which I am assigned. The Kioways having delivered up the two women they held, relieves us from the necessity of making active War on them this Winter. By Spring I feel assured we will be ready for any event likely to transpire on the Plains. In connection with the Mexican projet I am fully aware that my duties will be mostly advisory, but in advance I suggest two things. 1st. That General Sheridan be instructed by telegraph to send at once to Juarez where ever he may be, a messenger charged to tell him all that it is proper he should know—viz of the projected departure to Vera Cruz of the U. S. Steam Frigate Susquehannah, with the U. S. Minister & Myself on board prepared to extend to him our Friendly offices, that he may as fast as the French retire follow up as far as the City of Mexico and thence open communication with us. That same messenger should if possible come to us at Vera Cruz. 2nd. In as much as the French on leaving Vera Cruz, may prefer to deliver into our Custody the most important Forts on the Island of San Juan d'Ulloa, I would like Gen Sheridan to hold in New Orleans two Companies of Artillery, without guns, ready to come should I send for them. Of course our occupation should be temporary and to be relinquished as soon as Juarez is in Condition to take the Fort off our hands. If there be any impropriety in our using land forces for such a purpose, these two Companies should be loaned to the Navy as Marines, and then could be used with propriety for the purpose. A similar mode of transfer of the important Fort at Acapulco might also be accomplished by General Halleck, on the Pacific side. Orders to him could go by the Overland Telegraph. Please cause me to be informed on these points at NewYork, say next Thursday." ALS, *ibid.*, Letters Received. On Nov. 4, Bvt. Brig. Gen. Cyrus B. Comstock wrote to Maj. Gen. Philip H. Sheridan. "Confidential. . . . By direction of Gen. Grant I enclose an extract of instructions to Hon. L D Campbell by the Sec. of State made under the supposition that Gen. Grant would accompany him to Mexico. By the President's direction the duties therein entrusted to Gen Grant have been transferred to Lt. Gen Sherman with full power to act in Gen. Grants place. You will therefore comply with any request as to location of troops in your Dept. that Lt. Gen. Sherman under these instructions, may make." Copies, DLC-USG, V, 47, 60; DNA, RG 108, Letters Sent. On Nov. 5, Sherman telegraphed to USG. "Have finished my report No fears entertained by Gen Hancock as to a peaceful Election tomorrow I propose to Start tomorrow afternoon for NewYork Ready to Embark Nov eighth (8th)" Telegram received (at 4:20 P.M.), *ibid.*, RG 107, Telegrams Collected (Bound); *ibid.*, RG 108, Telegrams Received; copy, DLC-USG, V, 54. See letter to Lt. Gen. William T. Sherman, Nov. 7, 1866; *Memoirs of Gen. W. T. Sherman* (4th ed., New York, 1891), II, 414–20; Rachel Sherman Thorndike, ed., *The Sherman Letters* . . . (New York, 1894), pp. 277–87.

To Lewis S. Felt

Oct. 18th *1866*

Dear Sir:

Yours of the 15th inviting Mrs. Grant & my self to make your house our home during our proposed visit to Galena is received. We would both be very glad to stay with you (and will manage to see a goodeal of you) but we have accepted a previous invitation from Mr. Washburne & lady.

Galena is not so large now but that we will get all over town during our stay.

Mrs. Grant joins me in desiring to be rembered to your self and family.

Your Truly
U. S. Grant

To L. S. Felt, Esq.
Galena, Ill.

ALS, James A. Bultema, Westlake Village, Calif.

To Edwin M. Stanton

Respectfully forwarded to the Secy. of War.

The records in the A G O. show that two of the members of the Court stood at the time of the Court dishonorably dismissed the service, (their pay having been previously stopped) on the evidence furnished in part by Capt. Sokalski.

The records of the Court show a number of severe, if not unjust, rulings ag'st the accused—in cross-examinations—on subjects allowed by the prosecution; that the person preferring the charges had, previous to the assault, personal difficulties with the accused. Said prosecutor had, previous to the trial, sent for the servants of Capt. Sokalski and in presence of other officers questioned them about the treatment of Mrs. Sokalski by her husband.

The records also show that the prosecutor did use language to this effect—in the presence of officers and enlisted men—about Captain & Mrs. Sokalski, "By God, when women get to target practicing it is time to quit soldiering." As to the 3d Charge, viz: Conduct unbecoming an officer and gentleman, and its specification: "Taking from P. O. and opening an official letter addressed to Commanding Officer Co. "B" 2d U. S. Cavalry," the evidence shows this letter was not taken from the office, nor sent for by him, but given by some officer at the office to the servant or orderly of Capt. Sokalski; that Capt. S. was the Commanding Officer of the Squadron to which this Company belonged, and ha[d] been in charge of Co. "B" as well as Co. "A", and still claimed the control of Co. "B"; and that the document open'd was the promulgation of a Gen. C. M. in the case of a soldier—the records of the case being in the possession of Capt. S., who immediately notified the Post Adjutant—(the prosecutor) and informed him where the papers were.

Second specification—same as in 1st and 2d Charge. Third Specification: "Not Guilty"—

The records also show that the proceedings of the Court were not reviewed by the Dept. Comr, but reviewed and "forwarded, approved" by the A A Gen. of the Dep't. This is contrary to law.

All this with an unblemished record of five years in the field, participating in eighteen hardly contested battles, and a great many smaller engagements, earning by his gallantry and efficiency the promotion to Lt Col. and Inspr Gen. of an Army Corps; and believing the punishment already received commensurate with the offence, I would respectfully recommend he be reinstated, or if the vacancy created by his dismissal has been filled, that he be given a commission of equal grade in a new regiment.

U. S. GRANT
General.

HDQRS. A U S
OCT. 19. '66.

ES, DNA, RG 94, ACP, A22 CB 1869. Written on a letter of Oct. 18, 1866, from George O. Sokalski, Washington, D. C., to Brig. Gen. John A. Rawlins.

"I have the honor to submit the following statement and request: I was dismissed the Service of the United States as Capt. 2d U. S. Cavalry, by a Gen. Court Martial convened by order of Maj. Genl. Wheaton at Ft Kearney May 1st 1866. Two members of the court Capt. L. P. Gillette 1st Nebraska Vol. Cav. judge advocate, and Lieut. B. F. Giger, Q. M. 7th Iowa Cav. stood at the time of sitting of the court dishonerably dismissed the service of the U. S. their pay having been previously stopped, both these on information I was instrumental direct or indirect, in furnishing the War Dept. I made challenge against several members of the court, none were entertained, I was not allowed time to procure my most important witness, though I made affidavit to this effect. I submit also a statement of one of the members of the court, showing that the word 'dishonerable' was not in the verdict of the Court. I have made application to Brig. Genl. Vincent Asst. Adjt. Genl. and a statement of my military service, and the personal trouble existing between Genl. Heath and myself at the time the charges were preferred. I would also call your att[ention] to the reports of Maj Genl Steele on whos[e st]aff I served over two years. I was educated for the service, and believe my punishment too severe for any offence committed by me. I have been in the field during the entire war, participated in fifty-six fights, eighteen of which were pitched battles. I cannot but deeply feel the dishonor and injustice that I believe has been done me. It is the first blot on my record either as an officer or an honest man. I most earnestly request you may have my case investigated, and see if I am not right in asking a removal of this stain upon my character, and a reinstatement in the Service of the United States." ALS, *ibid.* Sokalski, USMA 1861, had been promoted to capt., 2nd Cav., as of Sept. 19, 1864, and dismissed as of July 10, 1866. On Aug. 9, Maj. and Bvt. Col. William Winthrop, act. judge advocate, had written to USG. "I have the honor to advise you, in response to the inquiry conveyed to this Bureau this morning by Col. Badeau, A. D. C., that the case of Captain George O. Solaski, 2nd U. S. Cavalry, was recently disposed of in Gen. Court Martial Orders, No. 177 of the War Department (A. G. O.) of July 10th last; in which the conviction and sentence (of dismissal) of this officer were approved and confirmed. The charges and specifications are fully set forth in the order. This case was formally reviewed and reported upon by this Bureau (on June 28th.) to the Secretary of War. The opinion formed therein by the Judge Advocate General was a most unfavorable one. This Bureau has had no evidence that the trial of the accused was other than fair and impartial." Copy, *ibid.*, RG 153, Letters Sent. Sokalski, reinstated as of Sept. 26, was soon in trouble again, and on Feb. 1, 1867, Col. Ely S. Parker endorsed papers in this case. "Respectfully returned. Capt. Sokalski, being in arrest on 'very disgraceful charges,' will be tried by a G. C. M. and not ordered before a Retiring Board." AES, *ibid.*, RG 94, Letters Received, 49P 1866. Sokalski died on Feb. 12.

To James W. Throckmorton

Washington, Oct. 20th 1866.

HIS EXCELLENCY J. W. THROCKMORTON
GOVERNOR STATE OF TEXAS
AUSTIN, TEXAS,
SIR;

I have the honor to acknowledge the receipt of your communication of 5th inst., urging upon the General Government the acceptance of a regiment of volunteers from the State of Texas, to be used in defending the frontier of that State against the incursions of hostile Indians, &c., In reply thereto I would state that Gen. Sheridan has already sent as large a force to the portion of the Frontier of Texas, infested by Indians, as can probably be supplied with forage and provisions during the coming winter. If a larger force should still prove necessary, there are enough United States troops on their way, or under orders to report to Gen. Sheridan to supply the deficiency. It is deemed therefore unadvisable to accept the service of volunteers whose pay and maintenance would have to be provided for hereafter by a special appropriation of Congress—

I have the honor to be
Very Respectfully, Your obt. servt.
U. S. GRANT, General

Copies, DLC-USG, V, 47, 60; DNA, RG 108, Letters Sent. On Oct. 5, 1866, Governor James W. Throckmorton of Tex. had written to USG. "Some time since I had the honor to forward to Genl Sheridan, also to the Secretary of War, copies of a recent Act of the Legislature, requiring me to call out one thousand mounted men for the defense of the frontier of this State. The act referred to requires that I should tender the service of the Regiment to the General Government, which I have done. I address you with a view to urge upon you the acceptance of these troops for such length of time as you may think necessary; and for the further purpose of asking you to order vigorous measures against the wild tribes of Indians now depredating upon the border of Texas, New Mexico and Kansas. In a communication to the com'd'g officer of this Military District, I have urged the concentration of one thousand men on upper Red River, about the mouth of the Witchita, to move, this fall, through the Witchita Mountains and West of them through the Texas, and Indian Territory, North of Red River, in two columns, uniting high up on the Canadians, and sweeping up those streams. This Section is the great resort of these Indians. I also suggested, if it could be so arranged, that at the same time these two columns move, that a column should move from Kansas, and one from New Mexico, all converging towards the Canadians, and the sources of Red River and Pecos. The head waters of these streams, and especially along the two Canadians, are the sections of country where the wild tribes principally resort and retreat to with their plunder. A body of troops moving from Texas is easily evaded by the Indians, and they flee towards the borders of New Mexico or towards the Arkansas river, and troops are broken down before they can strike a blow. But if a simultaneous movement is so made, the columns converging to their hiding places, they might be made to feel the power of the Government in one campaign. I have been on the frontier of this state for twenty-five years, and I assure you, General, there has been more depredations within the last few months than in years before. Last October these wild tribes, (Cheyennes, Arrhapahoes, Comanches, Kiowas and Lipans) made a treaty with the Government Agents, and delivered up ten captives they had carried from our border. Since that time they have killed not less than one hundred of our people, and quite a number of women and children carried into captivity. Within the last month, I have positive information of the murder of seven citizens, and ten persons carried off. The loss of property has been very heavy. The Indians have swept the frontier of ~~the~~ immense herds of cattle, and now they are penetrating into interior counties stealing large numbers of horses. The scenes of misery and desolution are truly appauling. As the commanding officer of the army, I make this appeal to you with the hope that you will direct at once a vigorous campaign to be made. The grass is better this season than usual on the plains, and perhaps no more favorable time than this fall will present itself for active measures. I trust you will not deem me presumptuous for writing so freely and making the suggestions I have submitted. I should not have done so, were it not for the urgent necessities of those who look to me to see that the Government is made acquainted with their condition I have written fully on these subjects to the com'd'g officers of this Department and District. But upon reflection I have thought it my duty to address you at once, and call your immediate attention to the condition of affairs here." ALS, *ibid.*, Letters Received. See telegram to Maj. Gen. Philip H. Sheridan, Oct. 8, 1866.

To Andrew Johnson

Washington, D. C. Oct. 21st *1866*.

His Excellency, A. Johnson,
President of the United States,
Sir:

On further, and full, reflection upon the subject of my accepting the mission proposed by you in our interview of Wednesday,[1] and again yesterday, I have most respectfully to beg to be excused from the duty proposed. It is a diplomatic service for which I am not fitted either by education or taste. It has necessarily to be conducted under the State Department with which my duties do not connect me. Again then I most urgently but respectfully repeat my request to be excused, from the performance of a duty entirely out of my sphere, and one too which can be so much better performed by others.

I have the honor to be,
with great respect,
your obt. svt.
U. S. GRANT
General,

ALS, DLC-Andrew Johnson. See letter to Edwin M. Stanton, Oct. 27, 1866.

1. Oct. 17, 1866.

To John W. Garrett

October 21st *1866*.

J. G. GARRETT, ESQ,
PRES. B & O. R. R.
DEAR SIR:

I have been requested by the Society of Methodists who are engaged in building a large Church in this City to write to you requesting a deduction upon the usual rates of freight over the B & O road for the material of their church, a large portion of which comes from West Va. They tell me this is usually done for the benefit of institutions intended for the public good. I know nothing of your custom in such cases but at the request of the Minister who has the work in charge make this request.

Yours Truly
U. S. GRANT

ALS, DLC-John W. Garrett.

On Jan. 4, 1866, Thomas Kelso, Baltimore, wrote to USG. "I am an old

Man—more than Four Score Years of Age—Born in Ireland, but have Resided in this City more than Seventy Years. I am a Member of the Methodist Episcopal Church—the Same church to which your honored Parents belong—I am Sincerely Attached to the church, in which I have long enjoyed the inestimable benefits of the Holy Sacraments and of Christian Communion and Fellowship with very many persons eminent for Wisdom and Piety. It having pleased God, greatly to prosper me in my worldly affairs—I desire before I go hence to invest some of my Means in Such a Way as shall be of permanent Service to His Cause. I judge that it would be for His Glory and the Moral and Religious benefit of my fellow men, to have erected at the Capitol of our Country, a permanent, Spacious and Elegant House of Divine Worship. The foundations of Such a House—Called the Metropolitan Church—were laid Several Years Since—But for want of means the work has been, for Some time, Suspended. I propose, General, by your leave, to give to Said church—*Five Thousand Dollars* in your Name—Designing in this way to Connect your Name with this Godly undertaking: and also to evince the Gratitude—which in Common with all Loyal Citizens—I cherish toward you for the Signal Services, which, under God, you have rendered to our beloved Country. With earnest prayer to the Father of Mercies, that you may be permitted to enjoy a long, useful and happy life . . ." LS, USG 3. Kelso donated $14,000 to the Metropolitan Methodist Episcopal Church, Washington, D. C., of which $5,000 was given in USG's name. *Baltimore Sun*, Feb. 1, 1866; *New York Times*, July 27, 1878.

To Edwin M. Stanton

October 23d *1866*.

HON. E. M. STANTON,
SEC. OF WAR;
SIR:

Gen. Brooks is in command at Ft. McHenry. Lt. Col. J. Roberts is the Lt. Col. of his regiment and would be no improvement on Brooks as commander should there be difficulty in Baltimore. Bvt. Maj. Loder, a good officer, commands the troops at Ft. McHenry.

The Lt. Col. of Burton's regiment, Col. B. H. Hill, is in Florida. F. N. Clarke, one of the Majors, died recently, Getty, another, is just promoted. The third is Gen. Hayes who is, I believe, at Ft. Monroe. Gen. Schofield is now in my office. I will give him verbal directions to give such directions about Ft. Monroe as will secure the nonadmission of the mass of visitors to the Fort. He may send

Hd Qrs. of an Infantry regiment there to secure a good commanding officer.

Respectfully &c.
U. S. GRANT
Gn.

ALS, RPB.

To Elihu B. Washburne

October 23d *1866*.

DEAR WASHBURNE,

I will not be able to go to Galena to the wedding. I cannot fully explain to you the reason but it will not do for me to leave Washington before the elections. This is a matter of great regret to me but you will appreciate my staying.

Mrs. Grant joins me in regards to yourself, Mrs. Washburne and children.

Yours Truly,
U. S. GRANT

ALS, IHi. On May 4, 1866, Bvt. Col. Orville E. Babcock, Lawrence, Kan., had written to Bvt. Col. Adam Badeau concerning his impending marriage to Annie Campbell of Galena and his hope that the Grants would attend. ALS, MH. On July 18, Babcock, Salt Lake City, telegraphed to USG. "When will you be in Galena? I want to be with Ingalls long as possible. Answer here." Telegram received (on July 19, 9:00 A.M.), DNA, RG 107, Telegrams Collected (Bound). At 10:05 A.M., USG telegraphed to Babcock. "Will not be in Galena until you go there." Telegram sent, *ibid.*; copies, *ibid.*, RG 108, Letters Sent; DLC-USG, V, 47, 60. On Oct. 5, Babcock, Washington, D. C., wrote to U.S. Representative Elihu B. Washburne. "Your note reached me in N. Y. I could not answer it for I could not tell when Genl Grant would go, but I now know; he will be there on the 8th for the wedding. . . ." ALS, DLC-Elihu B. Washburne. See letter to Annie Campbell, Nov. 2, 1866.

To Andrew Johnson

Washington, D. C. Oct. 24th *1866*.

His Excellency, A. Johnson,
President of the United States
Sir:

After the conversation of Saturday[1] last in which you expressed apprehension of riots and bloodshed in Baltimore City at the approaching election

I have the honor to enclose to you the within report from Gen. Canby, Commander of this Military Department, upon the threatened violence in the City of Baltimore ~~at~~ previous to the approaching elections. ~~After~~ Upon receiving your verbal instructions of the 20th inst. to look into the nature of the threatened difficulties in Baltimore ~~and~~ to ascertain what course should be pursued to prevent ~~them~~ it I gave Gen. Canby, whos Dept. embraces the State of Md. instructions, also verbal, to proceed to Baltimore in person ~~and~~ to ascertain as nearly as he could ~~of~~ the cause which threatened to lead to riot and bloodshed. The report submitted is given in pursuance of these instructions.

Since the rendition of ~~this~~ Gn. Canby's report I had a long conversation with him and also with Governor Swann[2] of the State of Maryland. It is the opinion of Gn. Canby, and the ~~admission~~ statement, of Gn. Swann, that no danger of riot need be apprehended unless the latter should find it necessary to remove the present Police Commissioners of Baltimore from office and to appoint their successors. No action in this direction has been taken yet nor will there be until Friday next, ~~and~~ when the trial of the Commissioners, before the Governor is set to take place. I can not see the possible ~~pretext~~ necessity for calling in the aid of the Military in advance of even the cause, (the removal of said Commissioners) which is to induce riots. ~~unless the case of the Commissioners has been prejudged and it is determined to remove them if the aid of the Government can be had to make the operation a safe one.~~

The principal charge against the police Commissioner seems

to be that at the late election in the City of Baltimore ~~the~~ some of the Judges of Election, appointed by the Commissioners, failed to have an additional Ballot Box, provided for by law, in which to place the votes of all persons who might attempt to vote but whos votes the Judges might determine were illegal. The Commissioners inform Gen. Canby that the additional boxes were furnished all the Judges and if they failed ~~then~~ to have them at the polls it was a violation of the law for which the law provides a punishment. The Governor holds the Police commissioners responsible for the delinquency of their appointees. There is a countercharge against Governor Swann that in appointing Registrars for the state at least some men were selected who ~~were~~ received and registered the names of all persons who would take the oath required by law even though it could be shewn that they were disfranchised by the laws of the state in expres terms. In this way they claim that from Forty to Fifty per cent of the increase of registration this year over that of last is made up of men who are not legal voters and whos votes cannot be taken without violation of the statute laws of the state of Maryland. Governor Swann contends that the Registrars are sworn officers and that by a decission of the Court of Appeals the Judges of Elections can not go behind the registry. They must accept the vote of man registered who presents his ballot. The Police Commissioners say, and the law says, for I have taken the pains to look at it, that the Judges as well as the Registrars can, and are required, to jude of the qualification of voters. ~~as well~~ ~~The followin~~ Indeed it would be difficult to understand the object of having a second ballot box in which to receive rejected votes if this were not the case. The following is the exact phraseology of the law: "It shall be the duty of the judges of election in each of the precincts herinbefore provided for, so soon as any person shall present himself to vote or offer to vote therein, to take from him the ballot which he may tender before they shall examine him or any other person touching his qualifications, and before they shall determine in regard ~~to the ballot~~ thereto; and the said judges in each precinct, in addition to the ballot box or boxes to be used for the reception of votes which they shall receive as legal, shall provide another box wherein all ballots which they shall reject shall be separately deposited by the said judges, each in sealed or closed envelope, with the name of the party offering the same endorsed thereon, which said box shall be sealed up immediately after the said election, and deposited with the Board of Police aforesaid until the end of twelve months next ensuing, when if the ballots shall not have been or shall not be required for the purposes of any election contest or judicial investigation (in which case they shall be produced and opened if necessary) they shall be ~~determined~~ destroyed by the said Board, without being opened."

The conviction is forced on my mind that no ~~reasonable~~ ~~exists~~ ~~excuse~~ reason now exists for giving or promising the Military aid of the Government to support the laws of Maryland. The tendency of giving such aid or promise would be ~~calculated~~ to produce the very result intended to be averted. So far there ~~is~~ seems to be merely a very bitter contest for political ascendency in the state. Military interference would be interpreted as giving aid to one of the factions no matter how pure the intentions or how ~~just~~ garded and just the instructions. It is a contingency I hope never to see arise in this country whilst I occupy the position of General-in-Chief of the Army to have to send troops into a state *in full relations with the General Goverment*, on the eve of an election, to preserve the peace. If ~~the~~ insurrection does come the law provides the method of calling out forces to suppress it. No such condition seems to exist now.

ADf, IHi. On Oct. 24, 1866, USG rewrote the letter to President Andrew Johnson. "I have the honor to enclose to you the within report from Maj. General E. R. S. Canby, Commander of this Military Department, upon the threatened violence in the City of Baltimore previous to the approaching elections. Upon receiving your verbal instructions of the 20th inst. to look into the nature of the threatened difficulties in Baltimore to ascertain what course should be pursued to prevent it I gave Gen. Canby, whos Department embraces the state of Maryland, instructions, also verbal, to proceed to Baltimore in person to ascertain as nearly as he could the cause which threatened to lead to riot and bloodshed. The report submitted is given in pursuance of these instructions. Since the rendition of Gen. Canby's report I had a long conversation with him and also with Governor Swann of the State of Maryland. It is the opinion of Gen. Canby, and the statement of Governor Swann, that no danger of riot need be apprehended unless the latter should find it necessary to remove the present police commissioners of Baltimore and to appoint their successors. No action in this direction has been taken yet nor will there be until Friday next when the trial of the commissioners, before the Governor, is set to take place. I can not see the possible necessity for calling in the aid of the Military in advance of even the cause (the removal of said commissioners) which is to induce riot. The conviction is forced on my mind that no reason now exists for giving or promising the Military aid of the Government to support the laws of Maryland. The tendency of giving such aid or promise would be to produce the very result intended to be averted. So far there seems to be merely a very bitter contest for political ascendency in the state. Military interference would be interpreted as giving aid to one of the factions no matter how pure the intentions or how guarded and just the instructions. It is a contingency I hope never to see arise in this Country whilst I occupy the position of General-in-Chief of the Army to have to send troops into a state *in full relations with the General Government*, on the eve of an election, to preserve the peace. If insurrection does come the law provides the method of calling out forces to suppress it. No such condition seems to exist now." ALS, DLC-Andrew Johnson. On Oct. 23, Bvt. Maj. Gen. Edward R. S. Canby, Washington, D. C., had written to USG. "I have the honor to report that I have visited Baltimore for the purposes indicated in your verbal instructions of Saturday the 20th. inst. The controversy now pending grows out of a provision in the present State Constitution which disfranchises persons who gave aid to, or sympathized with the late rebellion. Effect was given to this provision by very stringent laws but it is alleged that during the past year attempts have been made to evade these laws by including in the registry of voters persons who are not under the constitution entitled to vote. This on the ground that the oath required is illegal and void and not binding in conscience or in law. The correction of the registry is required by law to be completed on the 31st of October of each year. For this reason and under an opinion of the Attorney General of the State the registry of 1865 controlled at the late municipal election and the issue now presented was not so prominently exhibited. About 14,000 names have been added in the registry of 1866 for the City of Baltimore and about 10,000 in the remaining parts of the State or about 28000 in the entire State. Of this increase forty or fifty per cent is due, it is alleged, to the registration of persons who under the constitution and laws of the State are not entitled to vote. It is contended by the one party that the simple registration is conclusive as to the right to vote and by the other that it is only a *prima facie* evidence of that right; that it is subject to challenge and upon proof of disqualification to rejection. The new registry becomes effective after the 31st instant and will of course control at the coming State election, and the present contest divested of all side issues is for the power to admit to vote or to exclude from voting persons who are, or who are alleged to be, disqualified by the State Constitution I know nothing of the charges against the Police Commissioners beyond what is stated in the public prints and these relate mainly to duties that are committed by the constitution and by law to the Judges of elections. As these officers are amenable under the law to heavy penalties and can easily be reached by ordinary legal proceedings, the present attempt appears to be an effort to secure political power by indirect means and through that power to admit persons to vote who are disqualified by the State Constitution and must remain disqualified until that constitution is changed. It is so regarded by a large part of the population of Baltimore who look upon it as an attempt to subvert the Constitution of the State by indirect means and are prepared to resist it. The city was quiet but the feeling upon this point is deep and intense. I had no means of ascertaining the extent of any organization for this purpose, ~~have~~ but I have no doubt that they exist as I was informed by the Police Commissioners that they had been offered support in the city but had declined it because they relied upon their innocence of the charges against them and believed that the Governor would be convinced of this so soon as he ascertained their true character." ALS, *ibid.* On Oct. 18, Bvt. Maj. Gen. Edward D. Townsend had endorsed papers to USG. "The report of Bvt. Lieut. Colo Martin, upon certain organizations in Baltimore with endorsement of Major General Canby, is respectfully [r]eferred to General Grant" AES, *ibid.* The papers are *ibid.* On Oct. 22, Capt. and Bvt. Lt. Col. James P. Martin, 7th Inf., wrote to Maj. and Bvt. Col. Joseph H. Taylor, adjt. for Canby, reporting that there was no evidence to support assertions that illegal military organizations existed in Cumberland, Md. ALS, DNA, RG 94, Letters Received, 760W 1866. On Oct. 31, USG endorsed this letter. "Respectfully forwarded to the Secretary of War for his information." ES, *ibid.*

On Oct. 25, Johnson wrote to Secretary of War Edwin M. Stanton. "From recent developments, serious troubles are apprehended from a conflict of authority between the Executive of the State of Maryland and the Police Commissioners of the City of Baltimore. Armed organizations, it is alleged, have been formed in the State, and threats have been made that should a collision occur, organized bodies from other States would enter Maryland, with the view of controlling its people in the settlement of questions exclusively local in character. The Governor of Maryland has therefore deemed it expedient and proper to issue a proclamation, bearing the date the 22d instant, warning all persons against such unlawful and revolutionary combinations. In the event of serious insurrectionary disorders, the Government of the United States might be called upon to aid in their suppression; and I therefore request that you inform me of the number of Federal troops at present stationed in the city of Baltimore, or vicinity, that would be available for prompt use should their services be required to protect the State from invasion and domestic violence, and to sustain the properly constituted authorities of Maryland." LS, DLC-Andrew Johnson. On Oct. 27, USG endorsed this letter. "Respectfully returned. When the President mentioned to me, one week ago, his apprehension of difficulties in the City of Baltimore at, or previous to, the election, I caused an investigation to be made into the origin of the troubles, with the view of recommending such action as I might think should be taken by the military branch of the Government. The direction, if what was said in conversation might be regarded as directions, coming directly from the President, my report on the subject was made directly to him, without sending copy to the War Department. For information of the Secretary of War, I therefore now attach copy of that report. A return of all the troops in this Military Department shows the aggregate to be 2224, of which 'For duty' 1550, every one of whom may, in view of facilities by rail and steamer be regarded as in *the vicinity* of Baltimore, and full two thirds of them 'would be available for prompt use, should their services be required to protect the State from invasion and domestic violence.'" ES, *ibid.* On the same day, Canby had written to USG. "I have the honor the honor to transmit a weekly statement of the effective force in this Department. It differs from the trimonthly statement by including in the 'effectives', the special extra and daily duty men." ALS, *ibid.* The enclosure is *ibid.* On Nov. 1, Johnson wrote to Stanton. "In the report of General Grant of the 27th ultimo, enclosed in your communication of that date, reference is made to the force at present stationed in the Military Department of Washington, (which embraces the District of Columbia; the Counties of Alexandria and Fairfax, Virginia; and the States of Maryland and Delaware;) and it is stated that the entire number of troops comprised in the command is 2,224, of which only 1,550 are enumerated as 'effective.' In view of the prevalence, in various portions of the country, of a revolutionary and turbulent disposition, which might at any moment assume insurrectionary proportions and lead to Serious disorders, and of the duty of the Government to be at all times prepared to act with decision and effect, this force is not deemed adequate for the protection and security of the Seat of government & I therefore request that you will at once take such measures as will ensure its safety, and thus discourage any attempt for its possession by insurgent or other illegal combinations." Copy, *ibid.* See letter to Bvt. Maj. Gen. Edward R. S. Canby, Nov. 2, 1866.

1. Oct. 20.
2. Thomas Swann, born in Va., left the University of Virginia in 1827 to study law and moved to Baltimore in 1834. Elected governor of Md. in Nov., 1864, he assumed office in Jan., 1866.

To Charles W. Ford

October 25th *1866*

DEAR FORD,

Your letter and John Dent's on the subject of attending to the Irwin matter is received. I had written to John Dent more fully on the matter in a letter which he probably had not received when your letters were written. I want the matter settled. If the law gives Irvin the full amount the place had better be sold on the Deed of Trust and bought in for me. I have had letters written to the other owners of the land and give them to understand that if they wish me to I will pay the Irvin debt and they can either refund their proportion or I will take land contiguous to mine for it. If I buy in the place I will deed back to them all the land on the payment of their part or will deed back the balance taking out only so much as we agree upon.

In the matter of the Irvin debt if it outlawed I want to pay the principle with 10 pr. ct. interest for the first year, and 6 pr. ct. from that time to the breaking out of the rebellion. Nothing after that date. Irvin was in the southern Confederacy and if he had owed me the laws which which he held obedience to would have confiscated the debt to the support of that bogus government. I do not pretend that there is any law in this: only equity. It is only a settlement proposed in case the law gives him nothing. John Dent says lawyers have told him that the debt is outlawed. But in his letter he states that the note was given to Irvin in 1843. This is true but Mr. Dent paid interest on the note up to the 1st of Jan.y 1854 and the question is whether it would not have to run from that date the whole period of time ~~to~~ necessary to outlaw it. I wish you would shew this letter to John Dent, and some good lawyer, and settle according to his advice and these instructions.

Your letter in regard to Gn. Bonneville[1] is just received. Government has some fine buildings at Harrodsburg which it is necessary to keep some careful officer in charge of. It is probably a permanent place. I selected Gen. B. for it because I know him to be a very careful officer and supposed it likely to prove a place where he would not likely be disturbed from again. I do not know however but what I can select some other retired officer for it.

Yours Truly
U. S. GRANT

ALS, DLC-Charles W. Ford. See letter to Charles W. Ford, Oct. 15, 1866.

1. On Oct. 22, 1866, Bvt. Brig. Gen. Benjamin L. E. Bonneville, St. Louis, had written to USG. "It is with sincere regret I find myself ordered to Harroddsburg Ky. For fifty years I have obeyed all orders most cheerfully, and for the first time in my life, I beg to be indulged. I feel mortified at the necessity, but request some modification of the order may be made so as to permit me to remain on duty in this Department. Here I lost *all* my family, and here desire to remain if possible. Cannot your feelings of friendship interpose in my behalf; or must I request to be relieved from all duty, and fame to the alternative of a retired officer. Soliciting your favorable consideration for my appeal to your friendship—" ALS, DNA, RG 108, Letters Received. On the same day, Lt. Gen. William T. Sherman endorsed this letter. "I appreciate Col Bonnevilles position so highly, that I venture to add my name to his paper. All I will venture to say is, that he is one of the oldest and most faithful of the Officers of the Old Army, and too much cannot be done for him" AES, *ibid.* On Nov. 30, USG

wrote to the AGO. "Please relieve Col. Easton [*Eastman*] from the duties he is now on and send him to Harodsburg." ALS, *ibid.*, RG 94, Letters Received, 884A 1866.

To Edwin M. Stanton

Washington, D. C. Oct. 27th *1866*.

HON. E. M. STANTON,
SEC. OF WAR,
SIR:

Your letter of this date enclosing one from the President of the United States of the 26th inst. asking you to request me "to proceed to some point on our Mexican frontier most suitable and convenient for communication with our Minister; or—(if Gen. Grant deems it best)—to accompany him to his destination in Mexico, and to give him the aid of his advice in carrying out the instructions of the Secretary of State," is received. Also copy of instructions to Hon. Lewis D. Campbell,[1] Minister to Mexico, accompanying your letter is received.

The same request was made of me one week ago to-day, verbally, to which I returned a written reply copy of which is herwith enclosed.[2] On the 23d inst. the same request was renewed, in Cabinet Meeting when I was invited to be present, when I again declined, respectfully as I could, the mission tendered to me, with reasons.[3] I now again beg most respectfully to decline the proposed mission for the following additional reasons, towit: Now, whilst the Army is being re-organized, and troops distributed as fast as organized, my duties require me to keep within telegraphic communication of all the Department Commanders, and of this city from which orders must emanate. Almost the entire frontier between the United States and Mexico is embraced in the Departments Commanded by Generals Sheridan and Hancock, the command of the latter being embraced in the Military Division under Lt. Gen. Sherman, three officers in whom the entire country has unbounded confidence. Either of these General officers can be instructed to accompany the American Minister to the Mexican frontier, or the one can through whos command the Minister may propose to pass in reaching his destination. If it is desirable that our Minister should communicate with me he can do so through the officer who may accompany him, with but very little delay beyond what would be experienced if I were to accompany him myself. I might add that I would not dare counsel the Minister in any matter beyond the stationing of troops on United States soil without the concurrence of the Administration. That concurrence could be more speedily had with me here than if I were upon the frontier. The stationing of troops would be as fully within the control of the accompanying officer as it would of mine.

I sincerely hope I may be excused from undertaking a duty so foreign to my office, and taste, as that contemplated.

I have the honor to be,
with great respect,
your obt. svt.
U. S. GRANT
General,

ALS, DLC-Andrew Johnson. On Oct. 27, 1866, Secretary of War Edwin M. Stanton had written to USG. "I am directed by the President to communicate to you the request contained in the accompanying letter of the President, dated Oct. 26th, 1866, addressed to the Secretary of War, and also a printed copy of the instructions of the Secretary of State, dated Oct. 25th, 1866, addressed to the Hon. Lewis D. Campbell, United States Minister to Mexico, referred to in said letter: both papers being herewith enclosed. You will please favor me with your answer, to be communicated to the President." LS, DNA, RG 108, Letters Received. Stanton enclosed a letter of Oct. 26 from President Andrew Johnson to Stanton. "Recent advices indicate an early evacuation of Mexico by the French expeditionary forces, and that the time has arrived when our Minister to Mexico should place himself in communication with that Republic. In furtherance of the objects of his mission, and as evidence of the earnest desire felt by the United States for the proper adjustment of the questions involved, I deem it of great importance that General Grant should, by his presence and advice, co-operate with our Minister. I have therefore to ask that you will request General Grant to proceed to some point on our Mexican Frontier most suitable and convenient for communication with our Minister; or—(if General Grant deems it best)—to accompany him to his destination in Mexico, and to give him the aid of his advice in carrying out the instructions of the Secretary of State, a copy of which is herewith sent for the General's information. General Grant will make report to the Secretary of War of such matters as in his discretion ought to be communicated to the Department." LS, *ibid.* On Oct. 25, Secretary of State William H. Seward had written to Lewis D. Campbell, minister to Mexico, concerning his mission and discussing USG's role. Copy, *ibid.*; DS (printed), *ibid.*, RG 84, Mexican Legation.

On Oct. 30, Johnson wrote to Stanton. "General Ulysses S. Grant having Found it inconvenient to assume the duties specified in my letter to you of the 26th instant, you will please relieve him from the same, and assign them, in all respects, to William T. Sherman, Lieutenant General of the Army of the United States. By way of guiding General Sherman in the performance of his duties, you will Furnish him with a copy of your special orders to General Grant, made in compliance with my letter of the 26th instant together with a copy of the instructions of the Secretary of State to Lewis D Campbell, Esquire, therein mentioned. The Lieutenant General will proceed to the execution of his duties without delay." LS, DLC-William T. Sherman. On the same day, Stanton wrote to USG. "The President, by the accompanying letter addressed to the Secretary of War, has relieved you from the duties specified in his letter of the 26th instant, which was transmitted to you, and has assigned them to Lieutenant General Sherman. You will please transmit to the Lieutenant General the President's instructions of this date together with the accompanying papers, viz: a copy of the President's letter of the 26th instant to the Secretary of War and of my letter transmitting the same to you, also, a copy of the instructions by the Secretary of State to the Honorable Lewis D. Campbell, Minister of the United States to Mexico. You will please favor me with the answer of Lieutenant General Sherman, stating when it will suit his convenience to enter upon the specified duty." LS, DNA, RG 108, Letters Received. See letters to Lt. Gen. William T. Sherman, Oct. 18, Nov. 7, 1866.

1. Campbell, born in Ohio in 1811, trained as a newspaper editor and lawyer. He was elected U.S. representative (1849–58), opposed the repeal of the Missouri Compromise, and served briefly as col., 69th Ohio. Confirmed as minister to Mexico in May, 1866, he was also a delegate to the Philadelphia Union convention.

2. See letter to Andrew Johnson, Oct. 21, 1866.

3. Johnson asked USG to attend the cabinet meeting of Oct. 23. After Seward read to the cabinet his proposed instructions for the Mexican mission, Johnson again asked USG to accompany Campbell. USG again refused. Adam Badeau, *Grant in Peace* (Hartford, Conn., 1887), pp. 53–54; Howard K. Beale, ed., *Diary of Gideon Welles* (New York, 1960), II, 621–22; Theodore Calvin Pease and James G. Randall, eds., *The Diary of Orville Hickman Browning* (Springfield, 1925–33), II, 103–4; St. George L. Sioussat, ed., "Notes of Colonel W. G. Moore, Private Secretary to President Andrew Johnson, 1866–1868," *American Historical Review*, XIX, 1 (Oct., 1913), 99–102.

To Maj. Gen. Philip H. Sheridan

Washington, D. C. Oct. 31st *1866*.

DEAR GENERAL.

Since the publication of your letter of the 23d inst. to Bvt. Brig. Gn. Sedgwick it may be possible that you or I may be called on for a copy of the instructions under which you gave such instructions. As my letter of the 9th of October contained some passages which it would not be well to give to the public, and was confidential though it gives authority for just the instructions you have given to Gen. Sedgwick, barring perhaps calling Maximilian a buccaneer, I have thought it proper to renew my letter to you, for official record, leaving out the objectionable passages.

Do not understand me as shrinking from the responsibility of the letter I wrote to you. On the contrary I was delighted with your letter. It will have a great effect in sustaining the cause of Juarez both by encouraging his adherents and by discouraging other factions. In view of the fact that Max. and the French, are about going out of Mexico it might have been well to have left out the term buccaneer. If however no explanation is called for I will be glad even of the use of that expression.

Yours Truly
U. S. GRANT

TO MAJ GN. P. H. SHERIDAN
NEW ORLEANS, LA,

ALS, DLC-Philip H. Sheridan. See letter to Maj. Gen. Philip H. Sheridan, Oct. 9, 1866. On Oct. 29, 1866, Maj. Gen. Philip H. Sheridan had written to USG. "I enclose a copy of a letter which I addressed to Brevet Brigadier General T. L Sedgwick, Commanding the Sub District of the Rio Grande. I found it necessary to take some stand to better the condition of affairs on that frontier and believe that the public announcement of this policy will do much in favor of the Juarez Government. This letter contains nothing more than you foreshadowed to me in your letter of the 9th instant. The immediate necessity of the issuing of my instructions to General Sedgwick was, the expected arrival of General Ortega,—some of his adherents having already reached New Orleans,—and the existence of secret societies here having the object of the invasion of Mexico, in the interests of any party in Mexico in preference to the Juarez Government because that Government sympathised with the United States during the late Rebellion. Then there are the French English and Rebel interests of

Matamoros, all working against the Juarez Government for the same reason Upon the arrival of Ortega in this city I sent him an official copy of my letter to General Sedgwick, and, should he still persist in his attempt to violate our neutrality laws by continuing his voyage to Brownsville, I will arrest him at Brazos Santiago." Copy, DLC-Philip H. Sheridan. Sheridan enclosed his letter of Oct. 23 to Bvt. Brig. Gen. Thomas D. Sedgwick (never confirmed in rank). "I am satisfied that there is only one way in which the state of affairs on the RioGrande can be bettered, and that is by giving the heartiest support to the only Government in Mexico recognized by our own, and the only one which is really friendly to us. You will therefore warn all adherents of any party or pretended Government, in Mexico or in the state of Tamaulipas, that they will not be permitted to violate the neutrality laws, between the Liberal Government of Mexico and the United States; and also, that they will not be permitted to remain in our territory and receive the protection of our flag, in order to complete their machinations for the violation of our neutrality laws. These instructions will be enforced against the adherents of the imperial buccaneer representing the so-called Imperial Government of Mexico; and also, against the Ortega, Santa Anna, and other factions. President Juarez is the acknowledged head of the Liberal Government of Mexico." Copies, *ibid.*; DNA, RG 108, Letters Received.

On Oct. 31, Sheridan wrote to Brig. Gen. John A. Rawlins. "To show you how tender the French of this city are on Mexican affairs I forward you the enclosed translations from city papers It should be understood that a considerable portion of the city French still think they belong to France, and also, that the word 'buccaneer', in French means a man who smokes bacon 'or some such sort of a thing' " LS, *ibid.* The enclosed translation from a French language newspaper (*Avenir*) of New Orleans, a part of an anonymous letter of Oct. 30 to Sheridan, attacked Sheridan for his letter to Sedgwick and also assailed USG and President Andrew Johnson. Copy, *ibid.*

On Nov. 3, 12:30 P.M., Sheridan telegraphed to USG. "How would Jos A Mower do for the Command in the District of Louisiana? I should have more freedom to visit other portions of my Command than I now have. He is the Senior Officer and in fact the only one I have who is available Griffin is ordered down but his Reg't is in Texas" Telegram received (at 3:00 P.M.), *ibid.*, RG 107, Telegrams Collected (Bound); *ibid.*, RG 108, Telegrams Received; copies (one sent by mail), *ibid.*, Letters Received; DLC-USG, V, 54; DLC-Philip H. Sheridan. At 6:00 P.M., USG telegraphed to Sheridan. "You could have no better Commander for Louisiana than Mower" Telegram sent, DNA, RG 107, Telegrams Collected (Bound); telegram received, *ibid.*, RG 393, Dept. of the Gulf, Telegrams Received. On Nov. 10, 11:35 A.M., USG telegraphed to Sheridan. "How would you like the assignment of Griffin to his Brevet rank and command of Texas?" Telegram sent, *ibid.*, RG 107, Telegrams Collected (Bound); telegram received, *ibid.*, RG 393, Dept. of the Gulf, Telegrams Received. On the same day, Sheridan telegraphed to USG. "Your telegram of today rec'd I would very much like the assignment of Griffin as you suggest" Telegram received (at 8:00 P.M.), *ibid.*, RG 107, Telegrams Collected (Bound); *ibid.*, RG 108, Telegrams Received; copies, DLC-USG, V, 54; DLC-Philip H. Sheridan. On Nov. 12, USG wrote to Secretary of War Edwin M. Stanton. "I have the honor to recommend that Col. & Bvt. Maj. Gen. Chas. Griffin be assigned to duty with his Bvt. rank to enable him to command the District of Texas. General Sheridan desires this assignment to enable him to give the command to Gen. Griffin instead of Gen. Heintzelman who is the Senior officer in the State of Texas by full commission." ALS, DNA, RG 94, ACP, G216 CB 1863.

On Nov. 8, 10:00 A.M., Sheridan telegraphed to USG. "While at Galveston on the Sixth (6th) Capt McCarr of the Navy who left Tampico on the 2nd informed me that Maximillian had abdicated I think that his foreign troops had substituted the french establishment for the imperial & that the french forces in Mexico are now an Army of Occupation" Telegram received (at 5:00 P.M.), *ibid.*, RG 107, Telegrams Collected (Bound); *ibid.*, RG 108, Telegrams Received; copies (one sent by mail), DLC-USG, V, 54; DLC-Philip H. Sheridan; DLC-Andrew Johnson. On Nov. 13, USG endorsed the mail copy. "Respectfully forwarded to Secretary of War, for information of the President." ES, *ibid.*

To Bvt. Maj. Gen. Edward R. S. Canby

Washington D. C. Nov 2 *1866*

GENERAL

Enclosed I send you orders just received from the President of the United States. They fully explain themselves. As Commander of the Military Department including the State of Maryland, you will take immediate steps for carrying them into execution. There are now six or eight companies of Infantry ready organized in NewYork that have been ordered to Baltimore on their way to their regiments here in Washington and in Va. Either visit Baltimore yourself or send a staff officer there to stop the~~m~~se at Fort McHenry until further orders. Also hold one of the Infantry regiments on duty in this City in readiness to move at a moments notice. By having cars ready to take a regiment all at once they will be practically as near Baltimore, here, as if in camp a few miles from that city.

These are all the instructions deemed necessary in advance of troops being legally called out to suppress insurrection or invasion.

Having the greatest confidence however in your judgement and discretion I wish you to go to Baltimore in person and to remain there until the threatened difficulties have passed over.

Proper discretion will no doubt go farther towards preventing conflict, than force

Very Respectfully Yr Obd St
U. S. GRANT
General,

P. S. The orders referred to have not as yet been received, when received they will be forwarded to your address which you will please communicate.

U. S. G.

LS, DNA, RG 393, Dept. of Washington, Letters Received. Probably on Nov. 2, 1866, Attorney Gen. Henry Stanbery drafted a letter for President Andrew Johnson to USG. "There is ground to apprehend ~~that there is~~ danger of an insurrection in the City of Baltimore, on or about the day of the election ~~about~~ soon to be held there, against the constituted authorities of the State of Maryland and that ~~the I may be the I may be called upon~~ the ~~authority~~ aid of the United States may be invoked, under the Acts of Congress on that subject, to suppress such insurrection—~~Th~~ It seems proper to be prepared for such an emergency should it arise—Whilst therefore I am averse to any military demonstration that would have a tendency to interfere with the free exercise of the elective franchise in that city, or be construed into any ~~espousal of~~ interference in ~~the~~ local questions, I feel great solicitude that preparations be ~~qu~~ made ~~as quietly as~~ to meet ~~the~~ & promptly put down ~~the~~ such insurrection if it should break out—I accordingly desire to call your attention to the subject leaving to your own discretion and judgement the measures of preparation and precaution that ~~may~~ should be adopted—" ADf (undated), DLC-Andrew Johnson. A copy of this letter, readdressed to Secretary of War Edwin M. Stanton and dated Nov. 2, is *ibid.* On Nov. 3, Bvt. Brig. Gen. Cyrus B. Comstock telegraphed to Bvt. Maj. Gen. Edward R. S. Canby. "I enclose herewith a copy of the President's instructions referred to in Gen. Grant's letter to you yesterday." Copies, DLC-USG, V, 47, 60; DNA, RG 108, Letters Sent; *ibid.*, Letters Received. See letter to Andrew Johnson, Oct. 24, 1866.

On Nov. 1, USG, accompanied by Comstock, traveled to Baltimore to investigate the crisis created by the replacement of two police commissioners by Governor Thomas Swann of Md. USG urged the old commissioners not to resort to force and the new commissioners to obey the law. See *New York Times*, Nov. 2, 1866; diary, Nov. 1–2, 1866, DLC-Cyrus B. Comstock. On Nov. 2, Comstock wrote to Maj. Gen. George G. Meade. "Confidential . . . General Grant desires me to say that there is in Baltimore very high political feeling which may possibly result in collision & bloodshed. It is reported that organizations of ex-soldiers called 'Boys in Blue' exist there, and threats have been made that similar organizations from Penna would pour into Baltimore if there should be in that city a serious collision between the two political parties. Such an invasion would inevitably cause serious bloodshed and might lead to the most deplorable consequences. The general desires that you obtain all the information you can in reference to such movements if any should be contemplated, using your influence in the way you deem most efficient to prevent such organizations from entering Maryland from Pennsylvania and reporting at once by telegraph for orders as to the use of troops, in case such attempt should be made." ALS, Meade Collection, PHi.

On Nov. 3, Canby, Baltimore, twice telegraphed to USG. "The troops from NewYork five hundred & ninety arived at one oclock today only fifty of them were armed" "There is a good deal of excitement in the City but it appears to be subsiding. The new police Commissioners were arrested today & in default of bail have been Committed They are charged with inciting a riot This will bring the Case at once before the Superior Court & Court of appeals both of which are now in session My Office is number twelve (12) North Calvert St" Telegrams received (at 5:00 P.M.—one of the first, two of the second), DNA, RG 107, Telegrams Collected (Bound); *ibid.*, RG 108, Telegrams Received; copies, *ibid.*, Letters Received; DLC-USG, V, 54.

On Nov. 4, 2:30 P.M., Canby telegraphed to USG. "I have directed Gen Emory to hold four (4) companies of the remaining Battalion of the 12th in readiness to come to this city—This is not done from any greater indications of trouble, but because the recruit[s] from New York are entirely inexperienced.—The troops ordered from Washington will arrive this evening. The commissioners appointed by the gov[er]nor will it is understood be released tomorrow on a writ of habeas corpus." LS (telegram sent), DNA, RG 107, Telegrams Collected (Unbound); telegram received (at 4:30 P.M.), *ibid.*, Telegrams Collected (Bound); *ibid.*, RG 108, Telegrams Received. At 3:00 P.M., USG telegraphed to Canby. "I will be at the Eutaw House at 8.30 this evening. Would like to see you, Judge Bond, the Police Commissioners and one or two leading members of the Governors party" Telegram sent, *ibid.*, RG 107, Telegrams Collected (Bound); copies, *ibid.*, RG 108, Letters Sent; *ibid.*, Letters Received; DLC-USG, V, 47, 60. USG had met with Johnson and Swann that afternoon to discuss the situation in Baltimore. USG agreed to return to the city, meeting with representatives of one faction that evening and with the other side the following morning. See *New York Times*, Nov. 5–6, 1866. On Nov. 5, 12:30 P.M., USG telegraphed to Stanton. "This morning collision looked almost inevitable. Wiser counsels now seem to prevail and I think there is strong hopes that no riot will occur. Propositions looking to the harmonizing of parties are now pending" Telegram received (at 1:30 P.M.), DLC-Andrew Johnson; DNA, RG 107, Telegrams Collected (Bound); copies, *ibid.*, RG 108, Letters Sent; DLC-USG, V, 47, 60.

On Nov. 6, Canby telegraphed to USG. "The election has passed off quietly no disturbances of any kind have been reported" Telegram received (at 6:00 P.M.), DNA, RG 107, Telegrams Collected (Bound); *ibid.*, RG 108, Telegrams Received; copies, *ibid.*, Letters Received; DLC-USG, V, 54. On Nov. 7, Canby telegraphed to USG. "I propose to send the recruits for the Department of Virginia to Fort Monroe by the steamer city of ~~Baltimore~~ Albany which is here under my orders and the others to Washington by rail as originally intended,—~~taking~~ sending with them the Ordnance and camp equipage issued to them here and returning the remainder to the depôts at Washington. The only contingency in which trouble may possibly occur depends upon the action taken by the Governor's Commissioners if they are released from custody upon the return of the writ of habeas corpus tomorrow. I do not anticipate any, and will instruct General Emory to re-establish the troops at Washington in their usual positions. If you should have any other dispositions to direct will you please advise me this evening. If you have not I will return to Washington this evening or tomorrow morning." ALS (telegram sent), DNA, RG 393, Dept. of Washington, Letters Received; telegram sent, *ibid.*, RG 107, Telegrams Collected (Unbound); telegram received (at 11:00 A.M.), *ibid.*, Telegrams Collected (Bound); *ibid.*, RG 108, Telegrams Received. At 1:30 P.M., USG telegraphed to Canby. "You may return to Washington and the troops here may be restored where they were and the Rail Road men relieved from readiness to transport troops to Baltimore. Leave directions for sending the troops at Fort McHenry as suggested in your despatch on Friday or Saturday. It may be well to retain them where they are for a day or two to guard against accident" Telegram sent, *ibid.*, RG 107, Telegrams Collected (Bound); copies, *ibid.*, RG 108, Letters Sent; *ibid.*, RG 393, Dept. of Washington, Letters Received; DLC-USG, V, 47, 60. On the same day, Canby telegraphed to USG. "The troops at Fort McHenry had moved prior to the receipt of your dispatch & it was not practicable to recall them I have directed Gen Emory to hold in readiness to move the third (3rd) Battalion & four (4) Companies of first Battalion twelfth Infantry I shall remain in Baltimore for the present" Telegram received (at 8:30 P.M.), DNA, RG 107, Telegrams Collected (Bound); *ibid.*, RG 108, Telegrams Received; copies, *ibid.*, RG 393, Dept. of Washington, Letters Received; DLC-USG, V, 54. On Nov. 8, 9:50 A.M., Comstock telegraphed to Canby. "Gen Grant directs me to say that you may now return everything to its condition before the recent election in Baltimore" Telegram sent, DNA, RG 107, Telegrams Collected (Bound); copies, *ibid.*, RG 108, Letters Sent; DLC-USG, V, 47, 60.

To Annie Campbell

Nov. 2d *1866*,

MY DEAR MISS ANNA,

This is probably the last opportunity I shall have of addressing you by so affectionate a title. I had expected, and very much desired, to be present on the interesting occasion when that privilege should pass from all others to the exclusive privilege of the one of your chose. Permit me to say however that I think you will never regret the choice you have made and if it were not that I do not like to flatter people to their faces I would say the same thing of Gen. Babcock's wisdom in making his selection.

Give my kindest regards to your father, Mother and the balance of the family.

Yours Truly
U. S. GRANT
General

ALS, Galena Historical Society, Galena, Ill. Annie Campbell married Col. Orville E. Babcock on Nov. 8, 1866, at Galena. Probably on the same day, USG and eight staff officers telegraphed to the Babcocks. "We tender you our hearty congratulations." Newspaper clipping (printed as received at 7:00 P.M., dated Nov. 9, in *Galena Gazette*, Nov. 9, [1866]), Babcock Collection, ICN. See letter to Elihu B. Washburne, Oct. 23, 1866.

To Capt. Daniel Ammen

November 6th *1866*.

DEAR AMMEN,

Your letter was duly received. Of course I read your article in the Army & Navy Journal as was deligted with it. Fearing that Grandfather Welles might not get up to the Journal of the 27th ult. during his term of office if left to his ordinary course of reading I had the article cut out and sent to him. Knowing our intimacy he will judge you to be the author but it will take until the 4th of March /69 to draw this inference. As he will likely cease to be Sec. of the Navy about that time you are secure. Mr. Dent was delighted with your invitation to him and he may be able some time to make you a visit for a few days. We will not go away without providing him a home however with one of his children. I shall not be able to leave Washington this Winter. It is a great disappointment to me but affairs here have taken such a turn as to make this course necessary. I can not explain in a letter the reasons for this course. My going to Europe next Spring, in fact my going at all during this Administration, will depend on the course affairs take this Winter.

My family, including Mr. Dent, all send love to Mrs. Ammen.

When ever you come to this City we will expect you and your wife to stop with us.

Yours Truly
U. S. GRANT

ALS, IHi. The article is printed in Daniel Ammen, *The Old Navy and the New* (Philadelphia, 1891), pp. 534–36.

To Lt. Gen. William T. Sherman

Washington D. C. Nov. 7th *1866*.

DEAR GENERAL;

Your letter of the 7th[1] is just received. Your suggestions in regard to informing Juarez of the Mission of our Minister to Mexico and yourself have been carried out. The President, Mr. Seward being absent from the City in conciquence of family affliction, left me to inform Minister Romero of all that is being done and to advise him what to do. Juarez has been advised in accordance with your telegraphic dispatch by the way of Denver, to the latter place by telegraph, as fully as is convenient to send by that mode. Full information has been sent to him through General Sheridan who will send the despatches by special Messenger to Gn. Tapia[2] at Matamoras by whom they will be sent to Juarez without any delay.

If is should be desirable that we should occupy any of the seaports I have no doubt but the Navy could furnish sufficient men for that service until word could be sent back and the men to replace them sent from here. We have sufficient Artillery in Florida for the purpose. I will submit your letter to the President to-day and if he has any suggestion to make I will telegraph it to you.

Yours Truly
U. S. GRANT
General

TO LT. GN. W. T. SHERMAN
NEW YORK, N. Y.

ALS, DLC-William T. Sherman. See letter to Edwin M. Stanton, Oct. 27, 1866. On Nov. 9, 1866, Lt. Gen. William T. Sherman telegraphed to USG. "Arrived last night—Ready to start but Mr Campbell has set twelve (12) oclock tomorrow saturday to be on board. Any thing for me will reach me at the sShip tomorrow or at the Metropolitan Hotel today" Telegram received (at 1:10 P.M.), DNA, RG 107, Telegrams Collected (Bound); *ibid.*, RG 108, Telegrams Received; copy, DLC-USG, V, 54. At 2:20 P.M., USG telegraphed to Sherman. "I wrote to you directing to City Post Office. Nothing further to direct. Mr Seward is back and will probably send further directions" Telegram sent, DNA, RG 107, Telegrams Collected (Bound); telegram received, DLC-William T. Sherman.

On Nov. 18, Sherman, *U.S.S. Susquehanna*, Havana, wrote to USG. "We have just come to anchor in this harbor, and it being sunday will lie close today and circulate tomorrow. We have had a pleasant trip and have no doubt that in a few days we shall anchor close to San Juan d'Ulloa. Thus far we hear nothing new from the Quarter of Mexico, and therefore I will not allude to the subject till we have something definite and precise. I will be sure to lay in for you five thousand cigars of good quality trusting to bring them to you in due season. If anything occurs before we leave I will make it the subject of an official letter." ALS, DNA, RG 108, Letters Received. On Nov. 24, Sherman wrote to USG. "I wrote you last per the Liberty for Baltimore, and now find the Regular Mail Steamer Columbia about to sail for NewYork, and must report ourselves here yet although I expected to be by this time half way hence to Vera Cruz. We went out on Tuesday to the plantation of Señor Miguel Aldamas, about 70 miles out, and saw one of the very best samples of a sugar estate, and came back on Wednesday by Matanzas, expecting to start Thursday: but found on our return that the engineer had discovered a burst place in the Boilers which had to be patched, and that will delay us until tomorrow Sunday when Commodore Alden assures me we will be off. There seems no real need for haste, as we do not know for certain that Maximilian is out of Mexico, or that the French are really ready to embark, but I have seen an extract from a paper in Paris said to be the official organ, to the effect that The French troops will embark, at the 'same day, and at the same hour,' exactly as they should do, and if by the agreement they are to embark one detachment in November, all should be ready to quit when we get there. Even if the French still hold the City on my arrival, I may go up in person, before the Minister, but he can do nothing till the country is clear, and Juarez is established in the City of Mexico. I have been received here in a very friendly way by all—have called twice on the Captain Genl Manzaus, and dined once in state, all the Grand officials being present. There seems a deep feeling of hatred between the Cuban Creoles, and the Spanish the latter monopolizing all the offices of honor and profit. I think I have detected several efforts to complicate us with reference to the Creoles, who seem to look on the United States as their natural friends and ultimate benefactors. Strange to say the natives who own the land & *slaves* would favor abolition whilst the Spaniards favor slavery, because slaves produce the sugar, which makes Cuba, so valuable to Old Spain. It is alledged that Spain collects thirty three millions of taxes of this Island alone.—Of course I am careful to say nothing and to do nothing that looks like an interest in this question. It is for them to solve. We have enough trouble of our own. I hope soon to write you from Vera Cruz, something more definite on the subject of Our Mission. . . . I keep no copies of these letters which are private unless you want to use the information—Please let Badeau keep them, that I may have copies" ALS, *ibid.*

On Dec. 1, "off Vera Cruz," Sherman wrote to USG. "We reached our anchorage under Isla Verde about 4 miles out from the Castle of San Juan d'Ulloa, the day before yesterday, it blowing heavy from the north. We had no communication with shore until yesterday morning, the wind subsiding a steam yawl came out from Vera Cruz, with a Lieutenant Claire of the French Navy, who paid the usual call of courtesy from the French Commodore Clouet, to our Commodore Alden. He inquired for Mr Campbell and myself, and stated that they had heard of our coming, and had telegraphed to Marshal Bazaine at the City of Mexico, who had replied that we should be received with the utmost courtesy, and further that if we desired to come up to the City we should have every facility and welcome. After Lieut Claire had left, our Consul Mr Lane came off, and he is now on board detained by a heavy Rain storm which now prevails. Things in Mexico are mixed. Maximilian is at Orizaba whence he is carrying on a Government, but he has here an Austrian Frigate the Dandolo, and a sailing Barque on which he is stowing an immense lot of stuff from the City as many as eleven hundred packages according to our Consul so that the impression is that he is going away. Lieut Clare said without concealment that he thought that if we had waited (8) eight days more, we would have found him gone Marshal Bazaine and General Castelnau are at the City of Mexico, and have about 28.000 french troops in all, for which it is said transports are coming from France. The mode and manner ~~is~~ of going seems the great problem, and doubtless the French would be glad to have us step in. We cannot hear of Juarez but the English Mail Steamer is today expected from Tampico, from which quarter the Consul ~~the Consul~~ Mr Lane expects to hear of Juarez. The French hold only the country hence to Mexico, where it is said they are collecting all their troops prior to moving down to Vera Cruz, but then begins the purely Mexican Imbroglio. I believe the French could and would be willing that Juarez should come in, and take their place: but between them there is no intercourse, and the difficulty is or will be, how Juarez will regard the foreign residents and the Mexicans who have given their adherance to Maximilian and the French occupation. I suppose we must go up to Tampico and it may be to the Rio Grande to search for Juarez. I believe good would result from my meeting Marshal Bazaine by and through whom could be effected the change without shock or loss of property to the Mexican People, but Mr Campbell can have no intercourse with the French, or any faction but that of Juarez, and consequently I can do nothing until we make the connection with Juarez. I think therefore after gaining more information from the City of Mexico, and hearing from Tampico by the English steamer we will probably go up to Tampico. If Juarez can be reached from that quarter Mr Campbell may go out to him, but I shall not go along. I do not see that I can do any good till the New Regime is established in Mexico City. My position is anomalous and if the President wants me to meet the French Military Authorities in anticipation of the probable change, and before Diplomatic intercourse is fully established I should have specific instructions to that effect. Whether right or wrong the French are the real Power in Mexico at this instant of time, and the probabilities are that their withdrawal will result in another contest between the Liberals and Reactionists. Under present instructions I would not commit the Government to any promise of aid other than what is contemplated by the recognition of Juarez as the Legitimate President, but if on with drawal the French would do the same, Juarez could take possession as the French leave and would thereby avoid the conflict that ~~would~~ will necessarily ensue if they simply withdraw. There is little or no commerce at Vera Cruz. The French occupy the Castle and town with Turco or Egyptian troops, but the Civil Governmt is nominally with Maximilian. We can hear of no Liberal Army near, nor that they act by or under authority of Juarez still they are said to occupy the towns of Perote & Jalapa, and their Guerillas attack the coaches, and come within ten miles of Vera Cruz. I will keep you fully advised by any and all chances. This will come to Mobile by a propeller now in Port, to sail as soon as she can discharge." ALS, *ibid.* At 1:00 P.M., Sherman wrote to USG. "Since closing my letter a boat has come off from town with a note to the consul still on board, enclosing a Proclamation dated today to the effect that Maximilian intends to stay and shed the last drop of his Blood in defence of his Dear Country. The note says that he left Orizaba at 11. oclock last night for Mexico City." ALS, *ibid.* Also on Dec. 1, Sherman wrote to USG. "We are now at anchor under Isla Verde, the U. S. Consul on board. I have written you a long letter to go to Mobile by a propeller, and as the English Mail goes tomorrow to Havanna, I write this by her. Matters in Mexico are statu quo. Maximilian at Orizaba, and the French still in Mexico to the number of 28000. The French & Austrian officers have called to pay the usual visits of etiquette but there have been no salutes. We expect today, news from the City of Mexico and from Tampico. Our arrival was telegraphed to Marshal Bazaine, who replied we should be received in the most friendly way, and that if we wanted to come up to the City he would welcome us in person. But until we hear from Juarez, and know what he is about, it would not be right to have much to do with the French as it would be misconstrued by the People, but it is manifest the French control all this section of Mexico. Of course our first business is to get in communication with Juarez, and with that end we shall probably go up to ~~Ve~~ Tampico and it may be the Rio Grande. The first place where he will likely turn up will be San Luis Potosi which can be reached from Tampico, but if Mr Campbell chooses to go there I shall not under present circumstances go there, but if Juarez can reach the City of Mexico I should go up. There is no Regular Line from the U. S. to Vera Cruz, but you can communicate to Havannah, whence our consul can send by the English, French & Spanish steamers to this place, but the probabilities are that we shall watch events in this quarter and communicate the first authentic news from NewOrleans. We are all well and comfortable on board—" ALS, *ibid.*

On Dec. 7, Sherman, Brazos Santiago, Tex., wrote to USG. "I wrote you fully from Vera Cruz, and lest my letter may not have reached you I reiterate that we found the French in possession. None had gone, but it was universally reported & believed that they were collecting at the City of Mexico preparatory to embark all at once. I felt disposed to accept a General invitation of Marshal Bazaine to go up to the City and see for myself, but judged it would not be proper until Mr Campbell had found Mr Juarez and could assure him of the determination of the United States to recognise his Authority. Maximilian had come as far as Orizaba with it is thought a determination to return to Europe but all at once he seems to have changed, and whilst we were at Vera Cruz, and after he must have heard of our arrival he resolved to return to the City of Mexico and stand by his Empire. We then sailed for Tampico, stopping en route at the Island of Lobos, the only place on the Coast where any shelter can be had in the Northers. The next day we steamed up to Tampico Bar, & fortunately met the U. S. Gunboat Paul Jones which took us on board and carried us over the Bar to Tampico. We were received very kindly by all the People, & our Consul Mr Chase. This Place is in possession of local troops commanded by two Generals Gomez, and Cuesta, who for a time are reported to have been disposed to side with Canales, but latterly have taken strong sides with Juarez. The Panuco River is deep, and an excellent harbor, but the Bar like all others on this Coast is bad. We crossed it finding 9. feet of Water, but Mr Chase our Consul, says when during our Mexican War, the frequent passage of vessels deepened the Bar to eleven feet—In any event Tampico is the place on the Coast next in importance to Vera Cruz, and if Mr Juarez has to fight, he should look to its security and should fortify. At present there are no Guns or Forts at the Bar, and a single Gunboat of the French, or Maximilian could enter, and Tampico would cease to be liberal. At Tampico we could hear nothing of Juarez this side of Chihuahua, and therefore have come here, where we learn that there has been a fight at Matamoras between Escobedo, & Canales, that General Sheridan has been up there, and is now en route coming down. We shall await his coming, and will probably go tomorrow up to Brownsville and Matamoras where probably we can hear of the whereabouts of Juarez. If he be up about Monterey, I will accompany ~~him~~ Mr Campbell that far, and seeing him once well established will return and report. The only possible way of getting at all the facts that interest the Govt of the U. S. is for me to go straight to the City of Mexico under an invitation of Marshal Bazaine but as this might be misconstrued I will not do it without the specific orders of the President. I wish you would be ready to answer me, on this the only point in about ten days, by which time I hope that Mr Campbell can find his ~~Japhet~~ Post and that I will be at liberty to come for further orders to Berwicks Bay, or New Orleans." ALS (misdated Nov. 7), *ibid.*

Probably on Dec. 7, Sherman telegraphed to USG via New Orleans. "Susquehannah arrived from Vera-Cruz via Tampico—All well—French and Maximillian still at Mexico and Vera Cruz—Tampico held by Liberals in the interest of Juarez—Have been unable to hear of or from Juarez, though he seems to be expected at Monterey, to which point we shall go if of any use—Gen. Sheridan now coming down from Brownsville may have some news on this point and may advise you" Copy (unaddressed and misdated Nov. 7), DLC-William T. Sherman. On the same day, Sherman wrote to USG. "Private & Confidential . . . When at Havannah I bought you (5) five thousand segars, three thousand at $57, and two thousand at $34. Finding here a steamer waiting for Genl Sheridan, I have sent off to the Susquehannah for them, and will give them to Genl Sheridan to send you by express. In this way they will reach you sooner than if I hold on. This buffeting about in Northers is no fun, and I am as anxious to find Juarez as Japhet was to find his father that I may dispose of this mission. I never did have faith in Mexicans, and feel certain that the French will go.—Maximilian must follow, and then a general scramble for what little is left—I dont want to get mixed up in their broils, which will be all pay and no profit, all loss & no glory I have read my instructions over & over and see in them nothing but advice, and this I give full & gratis, but as soon as Mr Campbell stops his search for Juarez—My Mission Ends, and I hope soon so to report and to ask leave to go home. I am perfectly willing to go up to the City of Mexico, not in a Diplomatic Capacity—but as an officer goes to others, in which I doubt not Marshal Bezaine would tell me every thing we want to know—viz, are they sincere in saying that they propose to go?—If not my own eyes would detect the fact—I believe they will go, simply because they are fools for staying, after the Great Idea of Napoleon failed—by reason of our success in maintaining our Union. I feel as bitter as you do this meddling of Napoleon, but we can bide our time & not punish ourselves by picking up a burden they cant *afford* to carry" ALS (misdated Nov. 7), DNA, RG 108, Letters Received.

On Dec. 16, Sherman, "at Sea," wrote to USG. "We were delayed much about Brownsville and Brasos Santiago by a heavy storm that cut us off from the Susquehannah, but last night the wind moderated, so that Mr Campbell got off his Baggage and started this morning to return to Brownsville, whence he ~~would~~ will go inland as far as Monterey; in the hopes to meet President Juarez: and I have resolved to proceed to New Orleans to confer with you by telegraph. On Sunday December 9, at Matamoras I had a long & free conversation with General Escobedo, who is recognized as the Military Commander of the Northern Departmt of the Republic of Mexico, acting of course in the interest of, and in subordination to the authority of President Juarez. He claimed that by January 15 next, all the military forces of the Republic (Northern Part) acting on a common plan would move concentrically towards the City of Mexico from the North, aiming by that date to be on the southern Line of the State of San Luis Potosi, Juarez moving from Chihuahua and Durango, Zacatecas, and San Luis Potosi, and he (Escobedo) moving by Monterey direct to San Luis, thus effecting a Junction thereabouts on the 15 of January. He named to me in detail the strength of the several bands or bodies of troops, all as he contended recognizing the authority of President Juarez, to the number of 40,000 men,—but some of these would have to remain behind to guard against the chances of insubordination so that he reckoned to have about 25,000 men in San Luis by January 15, 1867. That is about as far ahead as he could look, but he seemed confident that so much could be relied on. In the event of a General concentration of the Military forces of the Republic, he Escobedo, would be only a Division Commander, and he supposed that a General Dial of Oajaca would be Commander in Chief, and that Juarez would remain at the City of San Luis Potosi, until the military Problem could be settled. Of course all agree that Mexico is exhausted of money, & moveable wealth, and all ask help in some shape. I cannot advise the granting of men or money, but as the President & Congress may concur in granting some more substantial assistance than what is termed 'moral', I advised General Escobedo to consult with his staff officers, and to put down on paper, over his official signature a list of such arms amunition & clothing as he would want to equip the Army designed to establish the Juarez Governmt firmly as against Maximilian, or any reactionary or revolutionary Party. He did so, and I enclose it herewith. The ~~three~~ Four heavy 100 Pr Rifled Guns are for the defence of the Bar at Tampico, and if granted should ~~be~~ of course be provided with carriages—Traverse circles—pintle blocks—and every thing needed to put them in position ready for use & service, for the Mexicans have nothing at all—absolutely nothing of Modern Artillery. The other articles enumerated are for Armies in the Field, and Genl Escobedo was very anxious to get a portion of the arms ~~&~~ and clothing delivered at Matamoros as early as possible. I saw enough to know that his troops are poorly clad for the high and cold plateaus of Mexico, and that cartridges & equipments are with them very scarce. All the muskets I saw were English Enfields, and yet officers & escorts had Colt's pistols and Sharps and Spencer Carbines. All I said to Genl Escobedo was that our Congress had to be consulted in grants of money or property; but that I believed if the Mexican People would drop their petty quarrels, and unite in some general way to satisfy us that they meant to build up a stable Republican Government, that our President & Congress would gladly aid them by grants of clothing arms, & amunition of which we possessed so vast a supply. In this sense I prepare in advance of my arrival at New Orleans, to be forwarded to you this paper of General Escobedo, of which I retain a copy. It is in Spanish, but you can make it out. Doubtless before you receive this by mail, you will have instructed me by telegraph to return to my Post at St Louis, in which case General Sheridan will be the proper person to advise of the positive action of our Govt: of which I beg you will also convey to Mr Campbell the earliest possible notice, that the Mexican Liberal Generals may know the resources on which they are to rely, for the execution of their plans. . . . Excuse bad writing—the sea is *up*." ALS, *ibid.* The enclosures are *ibid.*, RG 94, Letters Received, 1584M 1866.

On Dec. 20, Sherman, New Orleans, telegraphed to USG or President Andrew Johnson. "Just arrived—left Mr Campbell last Sunday at Brasos Santiago to start same day for Monterey Mexico with the expectation to meet President Juarez about 25. inst. General Sheridan is out and I find nothing for me here.—At the time we seperated Mr Campbell had not seen the Presidents Message or received any communication from Washington since our departure. I will write fully from here. Is there any further necessity of my remaining Can I not return to Saint Louis. Would like to start up River Saturday evening—please answer on Friday. Nothing new in Mexican affairs since I wrote by Genl Sheridan, except Escobedo asks for arms, clothing &c of which I write in detail." ALS (telegram sent), DLC-William T. Sherman; telegram received (marked as sent at 6:00 P.M., received at 7:40 P.M.), DNA, RG 94, Letters Received, 1593M 1866; *ibid.*, RG 107, Telegrams Collected (Bound); *ibid.*, RG 108, Telegrams Received. On Dec. 21, noon, Bvt. Brig. Gen. Cyrus B. Comstock telegraphed to Sherman. "General Grant is now absent from the city but is expected back today. In answer to your despatch the Secretary of War thinks you had better wait at New Orleans till you hear from General Grant" Telegram sent, *ibid.*, RG 107, Telegrams Collected (Bound); telegram received, DLC-William T. Sherman. On the same day, Sherman telegraphed to Comstock. "Dispatch rec'd will await further orders" Telegram received (at 7:05 P.M.), DNA, RG 107, Telegrams Collected (Bound); *ibid.*, RG 108, Telegrams Received; copy, DLC-USG, V, 54. On the same day, Sherman wrote to USG. "I wrote you on the ship coming over from Brasos Santiago, on the subject of General Escobedos request to be supplied with certain articles therein enumerated. I now beg to submit with my hearty approval the verbal request of the Hon Mr Campbell that the Post Master General or Secretary of the Navy will arrange for a semi monthly mail to Tampico from NewOrleans, via Brasos Santiago. If as now seems probable President Juarez will make San Luis Potosi his Capital till the French are out of the way, Tampico will be its natural Sea Port, and the proper place of residence for our Minister. But at present it has no means of communication with the rest of the world except by the English Mail steamer that arrives there twice a month from Havanna & Vera Cruz—For the present I have arranged with General Sheridan to have a casual Boat that runs from NewOrleans to BrasosSantiago continue on to Tampico in the event that Mr Campbell makes a written request to that effect of the Commanding officer there. I do not think Mr Campbell will be back from Monterey much before the 15 of January but by that date we should have a Regular line of mail steamers between NewOrleans and Tampico, connecting there on the 1st & 15 of each month with the English Mail. If the Post Master General cannot do this, it should devolve on the Navy Departmt and not the Army to supply the Boats, as these transient Boats are not fit to be risked on that stormy and dangerous Coast. Without such a Line it would be folly to keep up Mr Campbells mission as the Consul assured us at Tampico that he was sometimes five and six weeks without his letters from Washington." ALS, DNA, RG 108, Letters Received. The enclosures, identical to those in the letter of Dec. 16, are *ibid.* On Dec. 22, Sherman telegraphed to Secretary of War Edwin M. Stanton. "Despatch received. Am glad the little I was enabled to do gives you and the President satisfaction I have a despatch from Mr Campbell from Galveston. He will be here this afternoon and wants to see me. I will therefore remain here till Monday 5. P M—" ALS (telegram sent), DLC-William T. Sherman. On Dec. 23, Sherman probably telegraphed to Stanton or USG. "Mr Campbell arrived at 7 P M—and called on me at Gen Sheridan this forenoon—He has nothing to warrant my detention, and I will start for St. Louis tomorrow afternoon—" AL (unaddressed telegram sent), *ibid.* On Dec. 27, Comstock wrote to Sherman. "General Grant requests me to enclose the within check for the cigars, for $210 in coin. The cigars have arrived but I don't believe the general who has been under the weather has opened them yet. He sends his thanks. With Escobedo's death, affairs on the Rio Grande look mixed. Nothing new here." ALS, *ibid.* On Jan. 2, 1867, Sherman, St. Louis, wrote to USG. "I now enclose you copies of a note from Marshal Bazaine to our Consul at Mexico, with his to me & my reply. These copies conclude all my official papers on the subject of the Mission to Mexico." ALS, DNA, RG 108, Letters Received. On Feb. 2, Sherman wrote to USG. "I have just received the enclosed letter of Jan 3, 1867, from General Escobedo, at Monterey Mexico. It is in Spanish, and I shall simply acknowledge its receipt. I construe it as saying that he now does not feel in need of the arms and clothing he asked for at Matamoras copies of his requisitions being already in your hands." ALS, *ibid.*, RG 94, Letters Received, 137M 1867. The enclosure is *ibid.* On Feb. 8, USG endorsed these papers. "Respectfully forwarded to the Secretary of War" ES, *ibid.*

1. For Sherman's letter of Nov. 3, 1866, received by USG on Nov. 7, see letter to Lt. Gen. William T. Sherman, Oct. 18, 1866.

2. Governor Santiago Tapia of Tamaulipas, born in 1820, commanded Mexican forces at Matamoras before his death in 1866. On Nov. 11, Maj. Gen. Philip H. Sheridan, New Orleans, had written to Bvt. Brig. Gen. Frederick T. Dent. "I have the honor to notify you of the safe arrival of the package forwarded through military channels to Gen Tapia. Governor of Tamaulipas, Mexico. It will be forwarded in safe hands by the first opportunity" LS, DNA, RG 108, Letters Received.

To Jesse Root Grant

Nov. 7th *1866*

DEAR FATHER,

Some two weeks ago I wrote a letter to Uncle Samuel, directed to Bantam P. O. making propositions for hiring Ellrod[1] to go on my farm in St. Louis, Co. to take charge of it for me. As I have heard nothing from him I fear he has not received the letter. I now have some six or seven hundred acres of the Dent farm. It is my intention to stock it in a small way and keep about three men on it to put the place in meadow and to cultivate but very little beyond the orchards. There is now about twenty acres or more young orchard and with a few acres more set out in strawberries and other small fruit the principle work will be marketing hay and fruit and hawling manure to replace what is taken off the ground. I believe Ellrod is honest and will do what I tell him. I expect to spend two or three weeks each year on the place and in that time can give directions for the year. I wish you would send Uncle Samuel word about the letter I have written him and say that I would like to have an early answer because if I do not get E. I must look out for some one else.

The family are all well. Jesse has learned to tell the time of day by the watch and is talking of writing to his Grandpa to remind him of his promise. Jesse is learning more rapidly than either of the other children did. He commenced going to school later than the others but I believe at ten years of age he will be further advanced then they were besides will be speaking French and German.

We expect Jennie to come on with Rawlins about the last of next week to spend the Winter with us.

Yours &c
U. S. GRANT

ALS, DLC-USG, I, B.

1. In 1854, William Elrod married Sarah Simpson, daughter of Samuel Simpson, USG's uncle. See letter to William Elrod, Jan. 15, 1867; LeRoy H.

Fischer, ed., "Grant's Letters to his Missouri Farm Tenants," *Agricultural History*, 21, 1 (Jan., 1947), 28.

To Andrew Johnson

Washington, D. C. Nov. 9th *1866*.

HIS EXCELLENCY, A. JOHNSON,
PRESIDENT OF THE UNITED STATES,
SIR;

The enclosed letter has been left with me by the Adj. Gn. of the State of Va. who has been prevented from presenting it in person and stating his business by this being Cabinet day. He desires me to present it with the object of his visit to Washington.

Some two months or more ago application was made by the Governor of the State of Va. for 10.000 stand of arms to arm the Militia of the state and for the return of two hundred Cadet Muskets and one battery of small guns, entirely unsuited for field service, taken from the Military institute of that state. These latter were wanted to continue the instruction in the Va. Military Academy. The matter was refered to me for my endorsement. Enclosed I send copy of that endorsement.

I would not recommend the issue of arms for the use of Militia of any of the states lately in rebellion in advance of their full restoration and the admission of their representatives by Congress. But I would recommend the immediate restoration to the Va. Military Institute the Two Hundred Cadet Muskets and Four small pieces of Artillery taken from them during the rebellion. The latter are now in the arsenal in this city.

I have the honor to be,
Very respectfully
your obt. svt.
U. S. GRANT
General,

ALS, DNA, RG 107, Letters Received from Bureaus. See letter to Andrew Johnson, Aug. 22, 1866.

To Manning F. Force

Washington, D. C., *November 11, 1866.*

Dear General:—It is with great disappointment that I have to announce, at the last moment, my inability to attend the meeting of the "Society of the Army of the Tennessee" on the 14th inst. I find that it will be impossible for me to be absent from this city, for the present, for so long a time as it would take to go to Cincinnati and return. I regret not being able to attend the first meeting of a Society composed in whole of officers of the Army which formed my first command in the late terrible rebellion, and with which I felt myself identified to the end of its service. When my command was less than an "Army," it was composed of troops which formed the nucleus of the Army of the Tennessee in its organization into an Army. It was the first Army I had the honor to command, and, to the end of the rebellion, it was an integral and important part of the force which I had the honor to direct, though through the ablest and most distinguished officers of any service. It is a proud record the Army of the Tennessee gained during the rebellion. As an Army, it never sustained a single defeat during four years of war. No officer was ever assigned to the command of that Army who had afterwards to be relieved from duty, or reduced to a less command. Such a history is not by accident, nor wholly due to sagacity in the selection of commanders. Again permit me to express, through you, to the Society of the "Army of the Tennessee" my deep regret at not being able to be with it on the interesting occasion of its first meeting. I have the honor to be, with great respect,

Your obedient servant,
U. S. Grant,
General.

To Brevet Major-General, M. F. Force,
Chairman Com. of Arrangements, Society of the Army of the Tenn.

Report of the Proceedings of the Society of the Army of the Tennessee (Cincinnati, 1877), pp. 10–11. Manning F. Force, born in 1824, graduated from

Harvard Law School in 1848, and moved to Cincinnati in 1849. He was appointed maj., 20th Ohio, as of Aug. 26, 1861, and brig. gen. as of Aug. 11, 1863 (see *PUSG*, 9, 124, 125*n*). At war's end, he commanded the 3rd Div., 17th Army Corps, Army of the Tenn., and was mustered out as of Jan. 15, 1866. On Sept. 11, Force *et al.*, Cincinnati, had written to USG. "The Society of the Army of the Tennessee hold its annual social meeting at Cincinnati on the 14th of November next. The gathering will not be complete without you, its first commander and instructor in that art which most of us have happily laid aside. It was your first army, and was so trained by you in the beginning that no jealousy or ill-feeling ever marred the cheerfulness with which every order was obeyed, or the universal cordiality which made every one take pride in honors bestowed upon any of its members. We hope for written assurance that you will share in the gathering of your old family." *New York Times*, Oct. 22, 1866. On the same day, USG, Cincinnati, wrote to Force. "I have the pleasure to acknowledge reciept of invitation from your committee to be present at the meeting of the Society of the Army of the Tennessee, to be held in this city on the [1]4th of November next—It will afford [me] great pleasure to be present on that interesting occasion and I know nothing [no]w to prevent it. I therefore accept [wi]th pleasure." Copy, MeB. On Nov. 7, Wednesday, Brig. Gen. John A. Rawlins wrote to Force. "... Please engage ~~a~~ rooms for myself Col Parker & Capt Dunn at the Burnett House. Shall leave here Sunday night next There is some doubt whether the General can get off from here to be with he still has hopes to, Sherman's Mission of course takes him away This is too bad." ALS, Force Collection, University of Washington, Seattle, Wash. On Nov. 9, Force telegraphed to Rawlins. "Meeting will be killed [if] the General does not come." Telegram received (at noon), DNA, RG 107, Telegrams Collected (Bound). At 2:05 P.M., Rawlins telegraphed to Force. "The General will be at the meeting if possible" Telegram sent, *ibid.*; telegram received, Force Collection, University of Washington.

To Bvt. Maj. Gen. John M. Schofield

Washington, D. C., Nov. 15th *18~~64~~66*. [*10:15* A.M.]

MAJ GEN J. M. SCHOFIELD
RICHMOND VA

You may send a company to Union West Virginia. when you deem it proper to withdraw the company do so without further directions. There is no special orders for the troops going to Union but they are sent on account of the reported unsettled condition of affairs there

U. S. GRANT
General

Telegram sent, DNA, RG 107, Telegrams Collected (Bound); copies, *ibid.*, RG 108, Letters Sent; DLC-USG, V, 47, 60. On Nov. 9, 1866, Maj. George K. Leet had written to Bvt. Maj. Gen. John M. Schofield. "The General-in-Chief directs that upon the request of the Governor of West Virginia or Judge N. Harrison, of the 9th Judiciary District of that State You will establish military posts at either or both Lewisburg & Union W. Va." Copies, *ibid.*

In Dec., James C. Spotts *et al.*, Lewisburg, West Va., wrote to USG. "A body of United States soldiers having been recently quartered ~~among us~~ in the adjoining County of Monroe, as it is said by your orders: we citizens of Greenbrier Co. W. Va deem it an appropriate occasion, to make to you, a fair and truthful representation of our feelings and condition. We believe that you were induced to send these troops among us by falsehood and mis-representation and a candid statement, supported if need be, by incontrovertible evidence, will secure the favor, good will and protection of the generous, honest and brave every where. The people upon the Eastern border of this state, including the Counties of Greenbrier, Monroe, Pocahontas and Mercer, by a majority amounting almost to unanimity, were southern in their feelings, and sympathy: and in the late war took sides with the 'Confederacy.' At the close of the war, with one accord they renewed their allegiance in good faith, to the Government of the United States, and though without being in any manner consulted they were included within the bounds of the New State of West Virginia, yet they in good faith submitted to the laws of the New State, and gave to the State Authorities their support and influence in the enforcement of the Constitution and all laws made in pursuance thereof. In every respect whatever did the people of these counties yield to the situation, and have from the day that Genl Lee surrendered to the present ~~time~~ hour, honestly and patriotically, and with promptness and cheerfulness given a hearty support to the Government, of the United States, and to all Constitutional measures of the State of W. Va Whatever difficulty or disturbance, there may have been, can be directly traced to the lawless conduct of an unscrupulous and an unprincipled radical faction, supported by about 1/10 of the voting population, and 1/20 of the whole population. Laws have been passed by the State Legislature most cruel and oppressive towards those who are termed 'Rebels:' yet the protection afforded by even those laws is denied by state officials. Our Courts of Justice are a mere farce. The Judge (N. Harrison), who stands publickly charged with almost every crime mentioned in the Decalogue, before the Legislature of the State, and an investigation of which he has studiously avoided, avails himself of his position as Judge, to gratify his revenge and personal animosities; and by fraud, duplicity and falsehood as we believe, has induced you to send troops to this section of the State to sustain him in his petty acts of tyranny, too annoying and too oppressive to be quietly submitted to by an honest, brave and patriotic people. As an evidence of his fairness and integrity as Judge, we instance the following: But recently, a man by name Newlin, brought here as a Lawyer from Philadelphia by Mr Harrison, and appointed by him as the Attorney for the State throughout his entire Circuit of five Counties, shot, without sufficient provocation a plain Farmer, who was intoxicated, and who used, as we admit, improper language towards Mr Newlin, inflicting a very serious and dangerous wound. Newlin was imprisoned for a felony. Judge Harrison without an investigation of the case discharged him, requiring bail for his appearance. The Grand Jury (all Harrisons friends and Radicals) refused to take any notice of the case. About the same time a late

Confederate Soldier, accidentally shot a small negro boy, slightly abrading the skin upon the arm. He was immediately indicted for a felony: warrants were issued for his arrest, and had he been apprehended and tried, we believe he would have been sentenced to the Penitentiary for that which was accidentally done. His only safety was in flight from the State.—No Conservative although a consistent Union man, 'ab initio,' is safe either in person or property, when in the hands of the law officers of this section of the State. Test oaths are resorted to in such endless profusion and variety, as to prevent justice, defeat right and protect vice and iniquity. A Registration act secures the power of the State in the hands of the minority. The large Majority in these border Counties have no voice in any election, they are unrepresented, yet they pay nine tenths of the taxes, and are the peaceful, honest, substantial, patriotic and truly loyal portion of the people, though they were the friends of the South in her late struggle. We therefore, respectfully request: That an Inspecting Officer, or some Army Officer of standing and ability, may be sent among us, who shall freely mix among, and converse with the People, and shall report to you the result of his observations.—That the troops herein before alluded to may be withdrawn, and that such protection be afforded us by the General Government as we have a right to expect and demand. We have refrained from going into detail: Hoping this may receive your favorable notice, . . ." LS, DNA, RG 108, Letters Received. On Dec. 12, William G. Moore, secretary to President Andrew Johnson, forwarded to USG a similar letter addressed to Johnson. ES and LS, *ibid.*

On March 25, 1867, Judge Nathaniel Harrison, Salt Sulphur Springs, West Va., wrote to USG. "On my arrival here from Washingn last friday, I found Captn Joseph Conrads Co. K (29th Regement, comfortably quartered at Union, where they arrived on the 17th Feby. The Union & Freedmen of this Section are entirely satisfied with Captn, Conrad, and I am convinced from what I have seen & heard of him, that he is admirably fitted for the present post which he occupies, and that he will render to me all the aid which is necessary, to the enforcement of Civil law and the protection of Union ~~me~~ men throughout my circuit. The necessity for such aid still continues, and I have no idea that it will cease for at least twelve months to come. ~~Captn Conrad's Co. has been recently transf~~ The State of West Va, has been lately transferred to the Department of the Cumberland & Captn Conrad, is now under the Command of Genl Pope at Louisville. General, I am sure, I express but the interest & wish of the whole Union party of my Circuit, as well as ~~that~~ the desires of Govr Boreman of my state, when, I ask you, so to order it as to permit Captn Conrad & his Company to remain in Union where they are—Our people, have learned to know & esteem him as a gentleman & good officer, ~~whose~~ and would have cause to regret his removal at any time, especially now, when the Spring Courts throughout my Circuit are just Commencing." ALS (marked as copy), *ibid.*, RG 393, Dept. of the Cumberland, Letters Received.

To Maj. Gen. Philip H. Sheridan

Washington, D. C. Nov. 15th *1866*,

DEAR GENERAL;

General Taylor of the rebel army has been in this city a good deal since the close of the War. Having served under his father and having known him when a young man I saw more of him than I have of any one else of the leaders in arms against the Government. Taylor is a candid and truthful man and a very correct observer. Having failed in War he now advocates peace and has sense enough to acknowledge that those who were victorious in war will not only dictate the conditions of peace but that they have the right to do so. He has been here on what I think a good mission and only hope that his advice in high quarters may have the right effect. As Taylor has now gone back to his home in Louisiana and may see you, I know he is anxious to do so, I write this to you. I would like you to become acquainted with him because it may be of mutual advantage to both of you in the changes that will necessarily take place from time to time in civil controll of the State. Taylor knows all the leading men of La. what they have been and what their influence amounts to.

Things have changed here somewhat since the elections. I do not like to commit to paper what has taken place though I would like you to know.

Your action on the Rio Grande suits me exactly, the arrest of Ortega and all. I believe its exactly agrees with the Presidents notion also but whether that will be officially acknowledged or not I do not know. Your dispatch asking approval was received yesterday and was forwarded with an endorsement asking its approval and expressing mine.[1]

Yours Truly
U. S. GRANT

TO MAJ. GN. P. H. SHERIDAN,
NEW ORLEANS, LA.

ALS, DLC-Philip H. Sheridan. See letter to Richard Taylor, Nov. 25, 1866. On Nov. 23, 1866, Maj. Gen. Philip H. Sheridan wrote to USG. "*Confidential* . . . I am in receipt of your letter of the 15th instant. I will with great pleasure call on General Taylor. I have met him here once or twice but did not follow up the acquaintance. I have been so situated on account of the bitter political animosities and the anomalous condition of affairs, that I have not sought the society or acquaintance of any one outside of army circles. I found it necessary to pursue this course after my arrival here, and it has turned out fortunately for me; for when the time came for me to differ in my official actions from the sentiment of the community I had no embarrassments, and neither party could claim that the other was running me. Had I been intimate with secessionists, the Union men, many of whom fought during the Rebellion, would have raised a howl that I had turned my back upon them, and *vice versa*; the other party would have cried out that I was run by fanatics: The result is that both sides here fear me and respect me, and I grow stronger every day. There was an additional reason for this course—the fact that I have not been invited to the houses or families of a single secessionist since I came to this city, and as a consequence, if gentlemen of secession proclivities call on me without inviting me to their homes, they are not welcome a second time to my house, and for the same reasons I decline outside restaurant acquaintance with such men. I have declined many invitations of this kind. In pursuing this course I am getting stronger every day and I do not lose my own respect. I can assure you, General, from close observation that in a community where the social standard has been formed by contact with slaves, and not by contact with intelligent white people, it leads that community to believe they are a little better than others, when actually they are much inferior, and that there is nothing gained by concession. We must make them realize that where they have five per cent of intelligent people, we have forty per cent to come up to the same standard. I think General Taylor a very clever gentleman and will try and cultivate his friendship I have had some troubles—Military political and social, but they have all been cheerfully met and most of them overcome by the confidence I put in you, and the support I know you have given me; and I will never forget it." LS, USG 3.

1. On Nov. 14, 10:00 A.M., Sheridan had telegraphed to USG. "Colonel Gillispie of my Staff has just returned from Brownsville. Ortega was arrested at Brazos Santiego for attempted violation of our neutrality laws. My letter to Sedgwick and this arrest were opportune as Canales in Matamoras and Negrete and adherents in Brownsville were just awaiting his arrival to assert his claims by an appeal to arms. He has no adherents in Mexico except French & English merchants who heretofore supported Maximilian. There is no trouble in all Northern Mexico except in Matamoras and Tampico & those merchants are at the bottom of it. My letter and the arrest of Ortega will settle everything on the Rio Grande line and I think within a few days then Ortega can go without violating neutrality. I hope the Government will support me in this simple and just method of restoring pleace to our border and trade and commerce to our people. There will be a trade through Brownsville and Brazos Santiago with Northern Mexico of twelve million dollars yearly as soon as those Mexico troubles subside" Telegram received (on Nov. 15, noon), DNA, RG 107, Telegrams Collected (Bound); *ibid.*, RG 108, Telegrams Received; copies (one sent by mail), *ibid.*, Letters Received; DLC-USG, V, 54; (2) DLC-Philip H.

Sheridan; DLC-Andrew Johnson; USG 3. On Nov. 15, USG endorsed this telegram. "Respectfully forwarded to the Sec of War for his information. I think Gen. Sheridan has done right and that the government should sustain him." Copy, DNA, RG 108, Register of Letters Received. See letter to Maj. Gen. Philip H. Sheridan, Oct. 31, 1866.

On Nov. 27, Sheridan telegraphed to USG. "I am just in receipt of news from Brownsville and fear that Gen Sedgewick Commanding the Subdistrict of the Rio Grand will for some unaccountable & unjustifiable reason demand of Canales the Surrender of the town of Matamoras on the plea of preventing the pillage of houses of Americans &c The situation there is this Gen Escabedo is in front of the City with about three thousand five hundred (3500) men & Canales offered to Surrender if the Liberal Government would pay the Merchants who have been supporting him in his illegal & infamous acts, This Escabedo would not agree to I very much fear that these very Merchants have in some way gotten around Sedgwick who is I fear not a strong man & have prompted him to this action Which he contemplates I have heretofore notified you that these very Merchants were at the bottom of all troubles over there. There is perfect harmony between Sedgwick & Gen Escabedo & no objections are made to the Contemplated act of Gen Sedgwick, Should Gen Sedgwick act as I have some reason to expect I will at once disapprove of his action & relieve him from his Command. I have telegraphed to Gen Sedgwick disapproving his Contemplated act or any action he may have taken in view of it" Telegram received (at 4:30 P.M.), DNA, RG 107, Telegrams Collected (Bound); *ibid.*, RG 108, Telegrams Received; copies, DLC-USG, V, 54; DLC-Philip H. Sheridan. See *HED*, 39-2-76, p. 544. On the same day, Sheridan wrote to USG. "I have the honor to enclose herewith a copy of the communication from General Sedgwick Commanding the SubDistrict of the Rio Grande on which my telegram of this date is founded. Although the contemplated action of General Sedgwick will not make any complications, still it is disapproved by me as against my orders; and so far as I know unjustifiable. Instructions are in possession of General Sedgwick that American citizens (if any are in Matamoros deserving to be called such) that their grievances could not be settled by the military authorities, but that they must seek the proper avenue—the State Department—for redress. I very much fear that General Sedgwick has allowed himself to be influenced by Matamoros shrewedness. Those who have furnished supplies to Canales to sustain him in his acts, since they cannot have the debts acknowledged by General Escobedo nor personal security given to Canales, now find some means to influence this bad judgement on the part of General Sedgwick. The act contemplated by General Sedgwick may not take place, but if it does I will regret it. I will remove him whether it does or not. He fell to the command by virtue of seniority" LS, DLC-Andrew Johnson. The enclosure is *ibid.* On Dec. 5, USG endorsed this letter. "Respectfully forwarded to the Secretary of War for his information." ES, *ibid.*

On Nov. 30, Sheridan wrote to USG. "*Confidential* . . . The report in the newspapers that General Sedgewick had crossed the Rio Grande is premature. He certainly had not crossed or demanded the surrender of the town on the 23rd instant, and I hope he has not made this blunder There is no doubt in my mind but that General Sedgewick has had some influence brought to bear on him. (Do you think there could be any double-dealing at Washington?) Sedgewick went over to Matamoras and took breakfast with the merchants on the morning he wrote the letter which I enclosed to you. There is something wrong about this transaction. Escobedo was about to take the place by assault and was able to do it, when Sedgewick apparently adopted his course to prevent it and save the merchants. The whole affair, should it take place, will not complicate things, and my disapproval of it must have reached Brownsville yesterday 29th instant—" LS, DNA, RG 108, Letters Received. On Nov. 5, Jesús Gonzáles Ortega, Brazos Santiago, Tex., had written to Capt. John Paulson, 117th Colored, protesting his arrest. ALS (incomplete), *ibid.* Printed in *HED*, 39-2-76, pp. 483–85. On Nov. 30, Sheridan endorsed this letter. "Respectfully forwarded for the information of the General in Chief. On or about the 24 June 1866 the city of Matamoros was surrendered by the Imperialists to the forces of the Lib[e]ral Government of Mexico and soon thereafter the city of Monterey and all of Eastern and Northern Mexico. In process of time, the Imperial forces were driven to the Valley of Mexico and line connecting the city of Mexico and Vera Cruz, and it became reasonable to suppose that the Imperial Government would be driven out of the country The acknowledged head of the Liberal Government of Mexico, during all these important, events, was President *Juarez*, and it is well known that General *Ortega* fled his country and took no part in bringing about these events, but on the contrary, he while in a foreign country, did as much as he could to counteract them by creating political divisions, and by the publication of real or pretended rights as Constitutional President of Mexico So far as this went it did not interfere with my command and there was no violation of our neutrality laws; but this did not satisfy Gen *Ortega* or his schemers, but an appeal to arms must be made to enforce his claims, and combinations were formed in New York and Brownsville, within the United States, for an armed assertion of his claims at the expense of a violation of our neutrality laws To counteract these machinations and to prevent our neutrality laws from being violated, my letter of October 23rd to General *Sedgwick* was written, and a copy of it placed in the hands of General *Ortega* in the city of New Orleans. Not heeding this, but under the belief that we gave directions in our country for buncombe, General *Ortega* was about to cross the line of our frontier and was arrested, on the same principle that the Fenians were arrested in attempting to violate our laws by the invasion of Canada Since the termination of the Rebellion, the people of the United States have suffered in trade from the disturbed condition of affairs on the Rio Grande line, about twelve millions (12,000,000) of dollars yearly. First, by Imperialism; then by the hostility of foreign merchants in Matamoras, who set up such men as *Canales* and *Ortega*; supporting them and reimbursing themselves, by passing goods out from the city free, or nearly free, of duty" ES, DNA, RG 108, Letters Received. On Dec. 8, USG endorsed these papers. "Respectfully forwarded to the Secretary of War. I concur in the views expressed by Gen. Sheridan in his endorsement hereon." ES, *ibid.*

On Dec. 1, 10:00 A.M., Sheridan telegraphed to USG. "I have an opportunity to go over to the Rio Grande this evening and by going I think I can settle the Ortega affair, also ~~that~~ the Sedgwick trouble if any has occurred and put things on a good footing but I would like to have your approval of my absence. Affairs are in good condition here and Genl Forsythe communicates to me from Texas frontier no Indian troubles" Telegram received (at 1:00 P.M.), *ibid.*, RG 107, Telegrams Collected (Bound); *ibid.*, RG 108, Telegrams Received;

copies, DLC-USG, V, 54; DLC-Philip H. Sheridan. At 1:30 P.M., USG telegraphed to Sheridan. "Your going to the Rio Grande in person is highly approved." Telegram sent, DNA, RG 107, Telegrams Collected (Bound); copies, *ibid.*, RG 108, Letters Sent; DLC-USG, V, 47, 60. On Dec. 10, Sheridan telegraphed to USG. "I have the honor to notify you of my return from the Rio Grande frontier. I have the honor to report affairs there in very good condition—On the 28th of November Genl Sedgwick demanded and obtained the surrender of the City of Matamoras from General Canales occupying it with about one hundred men—On the 30th he received my orders disapproving his action and withdrew his men to our side of the river—The object of the occupation was for the alleged purpose of protecting american citizens but the real facts are that he was made the cats paw of shrewd merchants of Matamoras who wanted to secure the liabilities which were due to them from Canales before he was obliged to give up the city to Liberal forces. General Sedgwick's action was without authority and in violation of written instructions as to manner in which the grievances of American citizens in Matamoras should be redressed—I have releived him from his command in obedience to orders from the Secretary of war and placed him in arrest subject to further orders from the President Matamoras passed into the hands of Escobedo on the 30th November and a better condition of affairs now exists on the Rio Grande frontier than has for the last eighteen months A detailed report will be forwarded by tomorrows mail" Telegram received (on Dec. 11, 2:00 P.M.), DNA, RG 107, Telegrams Collected (Bound); *ibid.*, RG 108, Telegrams Received; copies (one sent by mail), *ibid.*, Letters Received; DLC-USG, V, 54; DLC-Philip H. Sheridan; USG 3. On Dec. 11, 1:00 P.M., Sheridan telegraphed to USG. "I telegraphed you last evening of the good condition of affairs on the Rio Grande—The act of Gen'l Sedgwick gave rise to no complications; in fact General Escobedo called on me to ask me not to hold him responsible for it—The Canales faction having been *submerged* I was enabled to release Gen'l Ortega upon Escobedo promising that he would look out for him—There is not a City or State in Mexico which takes issue against Juarez' Government—On my return I met Gen Sherman at Brazas Santiago—He had just come from Vera Cruz and was enroute with Mr Campbell for Matamoras" Telegram received (at 7:00 P.M.), DNA, RG 107, Telegrams Collected (Bound); (torn) *ibid.*, RG 108, Telegrams Received; copies (one sent by mail), *ibid.*, Letters Received; DLC-USG, V, 54; DLC-Philip H. Sheridan; DLC-Andrew Johnson; USG 3. On the same day, Sheridan wrote to Brig. Gen. John A. Rawlins. "I have the honor to make the following report of my recent trip to the RioGrande frontier I arrived at Brownsville at 4 oclock on the morning of the 6th instant and found that on the 24th of November General Sedgwick, Commanding the SubDistrict of the RioGrande had demanded and received the surrender of the city of Matamoras from Canales, who arbitrarily held possession of the city against the legitemate authority of his Government. That on the 30th ultimo the few United States troops (about fifty) holding the city had been withdrawn, in obedience to instructions sent by me disapproving the act of occupation or any action arising from it. The motives which influenced Brevet Brigadier General Sedgwick in this act are unknown to me; but the alleged one of protecting American Citizens and their property, was in violation of a decision made by the Honorable Secretary of State on this subject, which decision is on file in his office. The case presents itself to my mind in this way: After the surrender of Matamoras to General Caravajal the merchants of Matamoras—most of them foreign born and some claiming American citizenship, but ultra Maximilian adherents, and blockade runners during the Rebellion—induced Canales (a noted character,) to pronounce against the authority of the Liberal Government. They had two objects in this: first, to help the Imperial cause by creating as much dissension as possible among the Liberal leaders: second that they might pass out goods from the city free of duty, or nearly so. This worked well for them and goods said to amount to a large sum of money were so moved out. This condition of affairs continued until General Escobedo, in command of the Liberal forces, advanced troops against Matamoras for its recapture. Pending this event Ortega was sent for, and as Canales was a usurper, it was necessary to support him by a more noted character like Ortega; but Ortega having been arrested at Brazas Santiago and Escobedo having laid seige to the city, these merchants were obliged to change their plans. They then proposed that Canales should surrender the city to Escobedo, if Escobedo would agree to pay them the money given, or said to have been given, to Canales, the amount being some ($600 000) six hundred thousand dollars. This Escobedo refused and fearing that they would lose their claim and perhaps their property if the city was taken; they brought their influence to bear on Brevet Brigadier General Sedgwick and made him their 'cats paw' to protect their interests. This is the point of the whole affair. The occupation of the city was a mere matter of form and had the consent of General Escobedo, who made no objections and since the city passed into his hands has called on General Sedgwick in the most friendly manner, and asked me to forgive his action. There is little doubt but that this unauthorized and harmless intervention does much to reconcile and bring about the very good condition of affairs that existed in Matamoras when I left Brownsville, which condition of affairs enabled me to release General Ortega, as he had but few friends on the Mexican side after the suppression of the Canales usurpation." LS, DNA, RG 108, Letters Received.

On Dec. 20, Sheridan wrote to Rawlins. "I have the honor to respectfully request the release from arrest of Brevet Brigadier General T. D. Sedgwick, so that he may be enabled to command his regiment. No complications have occured or will occur from the foolish act of which he was guilty, but much benefit has come from it as it had an important influence in the suppression of the Canales faction which enabled me to release Ortega and enabled the friends of the Juarez Government to recover Matamoros and receive Lieutenant General Sherman and minister Campbell in that city" LS, *ibid.*, RG 94, Letters Received, 730G 1866. On Dec. 29, USG endorsed this letter. "Respectfully forwarded to the Secretary of War, approved." ES, *ibid.* On Jan. 16, 1867, 1:45 P.M., USG telegraphed to Sheridan. "Is Sedgwick's regiment to be mustered out of service? If so release him from arrest and place him on duty" Telegram sent, *ibid.*, RG 107, Telegrams Collected (Bound); copies, *ibid.*, RG 108, Telegrams Sent; DLC-USG, V, 56. On Jan. 18, Sheridan telegraphed to USG. "General Sedgewicks regiment will be mustered out. I have released him from arrest" Telegram received (at 8:00 P.M.), DNA, RG 107, Telegrams Collected (Bound); *ibid.*, RG 108, Telegrams Received; copies (one sent by mail), *ibid.*, Letters Received; DLC-USG, V, 55; DLC-Philip H. Sheridan.

On Jan. 4, Sheridan wrote to Rawlins enclosing information on Mexican affairs. LS, DNA, RG 108, Letters Received. On Jan. 8, 11:00 A.M., Sheridan telegraphed to USG. "General Charles Griffin has just returned from the Rio Grande frontier—He reports affairs there in good condition—The reports heretofore published untruthfull" Telegram received (at 5:15 P.M.), *ibid.*, RG 107, Telegrams Collected (Bound); *ibid.*, RG 108, Telegrams Received; copies, DLC-USG, V, 55; DLC-Philip H. Sheridan.

To Edwin M. Stanton

[*November 21, 1866*]

HON. E. M. STANTON,
SEC. OF WAR:
SIR:

Since my report for 1865 the Volunteer force then in service has been almost entirely replaced by the regular Army, mostly organized under the "Act of Congress" ~~of~~ ~~the~~ approved 28th of July 1866. The report of the Adj. Gen. of the Army gives exact statistics on this subject.

Passing from Civil War of the magnitude of that in which the United States has been engaged, ~~in~~ to government through the Courts, it has been deemed necessary to keep a Military force in all the lately rebellious states ~~which were engaged in rebellion against the government~~ to insure the execution of law, and to protect life and property against the acts of those who, as yet, will acknowledge no law but force. This class has proven to be much smaller than could have been expected after such a conflict. It has however been sufficiently formidable to justify the course ~~that~~ which has been pursued. On the whole the condition of the States that were in rebellion against the Government may be regarded as good enough to warrant the hope that but a short time will intervene before the bulk of the troops now occupying them can be sent to our growing territories where they are so much needed.—I respectfully refer you to the reports of Gens. Sherman, Halleck, Meade, Sheridan, Thomas, Sickles, McDowell, ~~&~~ Pope Steele, herewith for full information of the condition of the states and Territories under their command.

The last of these reports is but this moment received. The time has passed when they should be in the hands of the printer to prepare them for presentation to Congress on its assembligng. To make a full report I would have to get my facts from these reports. Time not permitting I beg to refer to them in lieu of their condensation by me.

With the expiration of the rebellion Indian hostilities have diminished. With a frontier constantly extending and encroaching upon the hunting grounds of the Indian hostilities, opposition at least, frequently occur. To meet this, and to protect the emmigrant on his way to the Mountain Territories troops have been distributed to give the best protection with the means at hand. ~~But~~ fFew places are occupied by more than ~~Two companys~~ and many but by a single company. These troops are generally badly sheltered and are supplied at great cost. During the past Summer inspections were made by Gens. Sherman, Pope, Ingalls, Sackett & Babcock to determine the proper places to occupy to give the best protection to travel and settlements, and to determine the most economical method of furnishing supplies. The labor of putting up temporary quarters is performed by the troops intending to occupy them. In the course of the next season more permanent buildings will have to be erected however which will entail an expense for material at least. I would respectfully suggest therefore that an appropriation for this special purpose be asked.

The present peace establishment being much larger than has been hertofore provided for an appropriation for building barracks, storehouses &c. to meet present wants seems to be required. The reports of the heads of the Staff Departments of the Army, particularly that of the QuarterMaster General, may cover this point.

I would respectfully suggest for the concideration of Congress the propriety of transfering the Indian Bureau from the Interior to the War Department, and the abolition of Indian Agencies, with the exception of a limited number of Inspectors, The reason for this change seem to me both obvious and satisfactory. It would result in greater economy of expenditure and, I think, diminution of conflicts between the Indian & White races.

I have the honor to be,
Very respectfully,
your obt. svt.
U. S. Grant
General.

ADfS, DLC-USG, III; LS, DNA, RG 94, Letters Received, 933A 1866. *O.R.*, III, v, 1045–46. The enclosures are in DNA, RG 94, Letters Received, 933A 1866. See *HED*, 39-2-1.

On Oct. 3, 1866, Maj. George K. Leet had written to Maj. Gen. George G. Meade *et al.* "You will forward to these HeadQuarters as soon as practicable a report of military operations during the present year, and the condition of affairs generally within your command, to enable the General-in-Chief to prepare his annual report to the Secretary of War." ALS, DNA, RG 393, Dept. of the East, Letters Received; telegram sent (dated Oct. 4, 10:40 a.m.—addressed to Maj. Gen. Henry W. Halleck), *ibid.*, RG 107, Telegrams Collected (Bound); copies (dated Oct. 4—addressed to Meade, Halleck *et al.*), *ibid.*, RG 108, Letters Sent; DLC-USG, V, 47, 60. On Nov. 11, 12:30 p.m., USG telegraphed to Maj. Gens. Philip H. Sheridan, George H. Thomas, and Daniel E. Sickles. "Your report called for by letter of October 4th from these Head Quarters not yet received. It must be forwarded at once in order that my report may be ready before opening of Congress" Telegram sent, DNA, RG 107, Telegrams Collected (Bound); telegram received (addressed to Sheridan), *ibid.*, RG 393, Dept. of the Gulf, Telegrams Received. Telegraphic replies from all three to USG are *ibid.*, RG 108, Telegrams Received; DLC-USG, V, 54.

To Edwin M. Stanton

Washington, Nov. 22d *1866*.

Hon. E. M. Stanton
Secretary of War
Sir:

Enclosed please find copy of a communication addressed to Maj. Gen. Sheridan under date of Oct. 17th 1866, giving my construction of the effect of the Presidents Proclamations[1] upon certain military orders. The construction is the same that I understood you to entertain at the time. The orders referred to have not yet been revoked, nor has my construction of the effect of the

President's Proclamations upon these orders been officially announced to any but Gen. Sheridan's command. I would therefore submit whether my construction of the Proclamations as above stated is correct, so that we may have a uniformity of action upon this matter throughout the different commands.

It is evident to my mind that the provisions of the Civil Rights Bill cannot be properly enforced without the aid of Order No. 44 or a similar one. Even in the State of Kentucky Gen. Jeff. C. Davis states that he cannot enforce it.

I have the honor to be
Very respectfully
Your obedient servant
U. S. GRANT
General,

LS, DNA, RG 107, Letters Received from Bureaus. USG enclosed a letter of Oct. 17, 1866, from Maj. George K. Leet to Maj. Gen. Philip H. Sheridan. "Referring to your endorsements upon communications of Gen. J. G. Foster, Command'g District of Florida, of date September 18th and 20th, relative to the effect of the President's Proclamations &c., I am directed by the General in Chief to enclose you a copy of the same, and to say that he construes these Proclamations as nullifying General Order No. 3 War Department, A G O., January 12th and General Order No. 44, Head Quarters of the Army, July 6. 1866" Copies, *ibid.*; *ibid.*, RG 108, Letters Received; *ibid.*, Letters Sent; DLC-USG, V, 47, 60. On Oct. 19, USG endorsed this letter. "Respectfully forwarded to Secretary of War for his information." ES, DNA, RG 108, Letters Received. See General Orders No. 3, Jan. 12, 1866; General Orders No. 44, July 6, 1866. On Sept. 18, Bvt. Maj. Gen. John G. Foster, Tallahassee, Fla., had written to Bvt. Maj. Gen. George L. Hartsuff, adjt. for Sheridan. "I have the honor to request to be instructed as to the effect of the Presidents Proclamation of August 20th 1866. Does it in effect, restore the priviledges of the Habeas Corpus Act, in all cases: and if not in all cases, to what extent does it operate to restore the privileges of the law. Does it deprive me in the exercise of my command, of the supremacy of Martial law in cases of conflict between the authority of acts of Congress and orders of my Military Superiors, and the State or Municipal Authorities The immediate cause of this request is the action of the Municipal Authorities of this town, who, in the temporary absence of troops, have essayed to arrest Officers, Soldiers, and Employees, for trifling infractions of the Municipal Ordinances, and this too, while the latter were in the discharge of their special Military duties: and in most cases to fine them and require the fine to be paid or go to Jail. I resisted this at once, and have forbidden the Mayor to arrest any Officers, Soldiers, or Employees while in the discharge of their duties, but requested him to notify me of any of them who may offend, against the law, so that I may investigate each case and punish the offenders. . . ."

LS, DNA, RG 108, Letters Received. On Oct. 6, Sheridan, New Orleans, endorsed this letter. "Respectfully forwarded to the General-in-Chief for his decision. As the Proclamation of the President has never been received by me, and as there has been no official promulgation of his Proclamation, and as General Orders nos *3* and *44* from Army Headquarters have not been rescinded; I have not regarded the Proclamation as intended to affect the present military *status* of my command, and have gone on maintaining it as heretofore In this I may be wrong but there was no other course left to me. Conflicts come up in *Florida* and *Texas* regarding the Proclamation; but none in *Louisiana*, where none have arisen, although I have to supercede the action of the civil authorities in many cases. It would be but justice, however, to more remote portions of the command that some *decision* should be made and I respectfully refer to you this communication of General *Fosters*. If there is no *restraint* on the Civil authorities in reference to actions that they will bring, we will have a bad condition of affairs I am afraid. The number of outrages which occur in the State of *Louisiana* against *Freedmen*, which we cannot reach, are numerous, even under the present restraint, and if the civil authorities are to be looked to for justice, I fear that the condition of affairs will become alarming" ES, *ibid.* On Sept. 20, Foster wrote to Hartsuff concerning civil affairs in Fla. and on Oct. 6 Sheridan endorsed this letter. "Respectfully forwarded for the information of the General-in-Chief. There has been increased insolence on part of the functionaries of the Civil Law in Florida and Texas, growing out of the Proclamation of the President. In Louisiana it has not been so, as the Proclamation has never been officially promulgated, and as General Orders Nos 3. and 44 from Head Quarters of the Army have not been rescinded, I have gone on, in Louisiana, as though no Proclamation had been issued" ES, *ibid.*

On Sept. 15, Maj. Gen. Wager Swayne wrote a letter requesting instructions endorsed on Oct. 20 by Leet. "Respectfully returned to Major General Thomas Comdg. Dept. of the Tenn. It is deemed entirely unsafe to permit, in all cases, the arrest of Officers, soldiers or Government employes on duty within the ten States not yet fully restored to their former relations with the general government by the civil authorities and Courts. In many cases without doubt, the Courts would do justice, but it can not be concealed that in many instances the civil control of affairs is in the hands of men who are hostile to the military authorities in their vicinity. By declining to suffer arrests of Officers or men, save in cases where it is evidently proper, their is much less danger of inflicting wrong on a citizen than there is of inflicting great wrong on the soldier by surrendering him. Of course when the representative from any State is admitted into Congress, the same rule will govern as in States that have always been loyal. Until that time you will instruct your District Commanders not to surrender Officers or soldiers in the States referred to, to the civil authorities when in your opinion or theirs, justice would not be done." Copies, *ibid.*, RG 393, Subdistrict of Ga., Letters Received; DLC-USG, V, 42.

On Oct. 18, Wilkinson Call, Baltimore, wrote to President Andrew Johnson concerning affairs in Fernandina, and on Nov. 13, USG endorsed this letter and other papers. "Respectfully returned to the Secretary of War inviting attention to the enclosed copy of letter from these Headquarters to Gen. Sheridan on this subject." ES, DNA, RG 107, Letters Received from Bureaus. USG enclosed a letter of Nov. 1 from Leet to Sheridan. "You will instruct Gen. Foster to refrain from interference with the execution of civil law in Florida when the laws of the State are not in conflict with laws of the United States. It is alledged that orders given by Colonel Sprague to officers in Fernandina practically prevent the execution of civil law. The duty of the Military is to encourage the enforcement of civil law and order to the fullest extent." Copies, *ibid.*; *ibid.*, RG 108, Letters Sent; DLC-USG, V, 47, 60. See letter to Elihu B. Washburne, Nov. 9, 1865. On Nov. 9, 1866, Foster wrote to Sheridan's adjt. ". . . The politicians are much interested in affairs in Washington. All warmly endorse the President's Proclamation and firmly believe that it reestablishes the entire supremacy of Civil law in the Southern States. Many of them take every public opportunity to denounce the actions of Congress, which are stigmatized as usurpations. As an illustration I enclose extracts from the charge of Judge Long of the Supreme Court of this State to the Grand Jury in Levy County. . . ." LS, DNA, RG 94, Letters Received, 737G 1866. In Nov., Sheridan endorsed these papers. "Respectfully forwarded for the information of the Gen'l in chief The cases of arrests & judgments against ex officers & citizens connected with the union army during the rebellion, are now being presented here and without my ability to give redress. Since the proclamation of Aug 20th 66 the charge of Judge Long to the Grand Jury is a fair index of the genl feeling in my command" AES, *ibid.* On Dec. 5, USG endorsed these papers. "Respectfully forwarded to Secretary of War for his information" ES, *ibid.*

1. Johnson's proclamation of Aug. 20 declaring the insurrection terminated is in *O.R.*, III, v, 1009–12.

To Maj. Gen. George H. Thomas

Washington, Nov. 24th *1866*

General:

A good deal of apprehension is felt about Dahlonega, where much northern capital is being expended in opening up the gold-mines of Georgia lest all their efforts, capital, and even their lives, may be lost at the hands of bushwhackers and lawless persons. It is an out of the way place, well calculated to invite the desperate, particularly if mining should prove successful. As troops are kept in the Southern States to protect the law-abiding against the acts of the lawless, they should be stationed where this end will be best secured. I think it advisable therefore that one company at least should be sent to Dahlonega at once—cavalry if you can spare it—

and if circumstances demonstrate that more is necessary they can be sent afterwards.

Very respy, Your obt. svt.
U. S. GRANT
General.

MAJ. GEN. G. H. THOMAS,
COMDG DEPT TENNESSEE, LOUISVILLE, KY.

ALS, DNA, RG 393, Dept. of the Tenn., Unbound Materials, Letters Received. On Nov. 28, 1866, Maj. Gen. George H. Thomas wrote to USG. "I have the honor to acknowledge the receipt of your letter of the 24th inst., advising that troops be sent to Dahlenega Ga., and giving reasons therefor. Upon the receipt of your despatch on same subject I communicated with Gen'l. C. R. Woods and Gov. Jenkins and on information received from them, have ordered one company of Cavalry to Morgantown Ga. which appears to be the Head Quarters of the 'bushwhackers' and lawless persons who are disturbing the peace, and disorganizing society in Northern Georgia. If this force prove not sufficient, Infantry will be sent to take post there, and enable the Cavalry to move to disturbed districts Your attention is respectfully called to the copy of a letter from Gov. Jenkins, in answer to my enquiries, herewith enclosed. Recent difficulties in Mississippi and Kentucky, requiring Cavalry, have, with this, left me but one company for any service that may be required in Tennessee, and I am constantly hampered for want of Cavalry." LS, *ibid.*, RG 108, Letters Received. The enclosure is *ibid.*

On Nov. 17, George G. Pride, Dahlonega, Ga., had telegraphed to USG. "A company of bushwhackers & Robbers one to two hundred strong & increasing in numbers near Murdering & robbing. Will you at once order one or two Companies of Infantry and some Cavalry with a competent Officer here to hunt them & ~~protect~~ remain here for protection of the interests here It is absolutely necessary to be done immediately I send this upon consultation with Genl Dick Taylor who arrived last night Please answer" Telegram received (sent via Atlanta on Nov. 20—received at 10:00 P.M.), *ibid.*, RG 107, Telegrams Collected (Bound). See following letter. Probably on Nov. 21, 9:45 A.M., USG telegraphed to Pride. "Despatch of 17th only just received—Will be attended to." Telegram sent (dated Nov. 20), DNA, RG 107, Telegrams Collected (Bound); copies (variant text—dated Nov. 21), *ibid.*, RG 108, Letters Sent; DLC-USG, V, 47, 60. At 9:40 A.M., USG had telegraphed to Thomas. "Bushwhackers are said to be infesting Northern Ga. particularly in the region of about Dahlonega. Ascertain if this report is true and if so station troops to prevent depredations by them." Telegram sent, DNA, RG 107, Telegrams Collected (Bound); copies, *ibid.*, RG 108, Letters Sent; *ibid.*, RG 393, Dept. of the Cumberland, Telegrams Received; DLC-USG, V, 47, 60. On Nov. 23, Thomas telegraphed to USG. "Gen'l. C R Woods Comdg Dist of the Chattahoochie reports that he has no information of depredations committed by bushwhackers recently in the vicinity of Dahlonega or other parts of Northern Georgia except a letter of complaint sent him in Oct last which is now being investigated. I have made the same inquiry of Gov Jenkins but as yet have rec'd no reply from him" Telegram received (at 3:30 P.M.), DNA, RG 107, Telegrams Collected (Bound); *ibid.*, RG 108, Telegrams Received; copies (one sent by mail), *ibid.*, Letters Received; *ibid.*, RG 393, Dept. of the Cumberland, Telegrams Sent; DLC-USG, V, 54. On Nov. 24, Thomas telegraphed to USG. "Gov Jenkins telegraphs me that there is much disorder accompanied with bloodshed near Morgantown Fanin Co Georgia. I have ordered a Company of Cavalry to make post at Morgantown to assist the civil authorities in arresting and bringing to trial the disturbers of the peace" Telegram received (at 2:15 P.M.), DNA, RG 107, Telegrams Collected (Bound); (2) *ibid.*, RG 108, Telegrams Received; copies, *ibid.*, RG 393, Dept. of the Cumberland, Telegrams Sent; DLC-USG, V, 54.

On Nov. 26, Thomas wrote to USG. "I have the honor to make the following report for your information, relative to proceedings connected with the funeral of the late rebel General Roger. W. Hanson at this place. For some days prior to the day of funeral a number of articles on the subject appeared in the newspapers, among others the articles marked "A"—These caused much comment and some excitement. On the 9th inst., the day before the funeral, the articles marked "B" appeared in the Louisville Courier; from this it was evident that a demonstration was intended which would be insulting to loyal citizens; and by meeting together and acting as organizations of the late rebel army, in violation of the parole accepted by these men, would tend to a breach of the peace Much feeling and indignation was evinced. I was appealed to, to prohibit such demonstrations; and to prevent any military display on this as well as on future occasions, I directed the notice marked "C" to be published. On the day of the funeral the articles marked "D" were published, showing still further the intention of these people The effect of the notice has evidently been good: it has tended to allay fears on the part of loyal citizens; and has prevented subsequent demonstrations of the kind. Some of the papers were, however, violent, as you will see by the articles marked "E." From the remarks in these, in regard to Brevet Major General Jeff C. Davis, he was called upon for a statement as to their truth or falsity. He promptly replied, a copy of which is marked "F" A number of papers still continue to do all in their power to bring odium on the Military Authorities; and as an evidence of the animus of their conductors, your attention is respectfully called to the article marked "G," in relation to a subsequent matter" LS, DNA, RG 108, Letters Received. The enclosures are *ibid.* On Dec. 7, USG endorsed these papers. "Respectfully forwarded to the Secretary of War for his information." ES, *ibid.*

To Richard Taylor

Washington Ill, [*D. C.*] Nov 25 *1866*

DEAR GENERAL,

Your letter of the 20th is just received. My letter to Pride, with which this is enclosed, answers a part of yours.

The day after you left here the President sent for me as I expected he would after my conversation with the Atty. Genl I told him my views candidly about the course I thought he should take, in view of the verdict of the late elections. It elicited nothing satisfactory from him, but did not bring out the strong opposition he sometimes shows to views not agreeing with his own. I was followed by Gen. Sickles who expressed about the same opinions I did.

Since that I have talked with several members of Congress who are classed with the radicals; Schenck & Bidwell[1] for instance. They express the most generous views as to what would be done, if the constitutional amendments proposed by Congress were adopted by the Southern states. What was done in the case of Tennessee was an earnest of what would be done in all cases. Even the disqualification to hold office imposed on certain classes by one article of the amendment would, no doubt, be removed at once, except it might be in the cases of the very highest offenders, such ~~persistence~~ for instance as those who went abroad to aid in the Rebellion, those who left seats in Congress &c. All or very nearly all would soon be restored, and so far as security to property and liberty is concerned, all would be restored at once. I would like exceedingly to see one Southern state, excluded state, ratify the amendments to enable us to see the exact course that would be pursued. I believe it would much modify the demands that may be made, if there is delay.

Yours Truly
U S GRANT

TO GEN R. TAYLOR

Copy, DLC-Adam Badeau.

1. John Bidwell, born in 1819 in Ripley, N. Y., went to Calif. in 1841 and eventually acquired the huge Rancho Chico. A prewar Democrat, he was elected a U.S. representative (1865–67) as a Unionist. Bidwell visited USG in June, 1864, and on Oct. 3, USG wrote to Bidwell. "I have the pleasure of acknowledging the receipt of two boxes of very superior segars sent by you. Please accept my thanks for this mark of your esteem and recollection of your visit to this Army. Many a hard day's fighting we have had since you left us on the Chickahominy; but this Army is not discouraged. It feels that it has the rebellion by the throat and shows no disposition to let go until the thing is dead. The

rebels feel the same thing and are now hanging their last hope on Northern aid and succor. In this they will be disappointed I hope." Rockwell D. Hunt, *John Bidwell: Prince of California Pioneers* (Caldwell, Idaho, 1942), p. 185. On April 16, 1868, USG attended Bidwell's wedding to Annie Kennedy, daughter of Joseph C. G. Kennedy, superintendent of the censuses of 1850 and 1860. *Ibid.*, p. 298. On Sept. 7, 1869, Kennedy wrote to USG requesting (unsuccessfully) Bidwell's appointment as minister to China. ALS, DNA, RG 59, Letters of Application and Recommendation.

To Edwin M. Stanton

Washington, D. C. Dec. ~~4~~5th *1866*.

HON. E. M. STANTON,
SEC. OF WAR,
SIR:

I would respectfully recommend that the name of Fred. E. Trotter[1] be withdrawn as Maj. of the 44 Inf.y and that the name of John R. Lewis,[2] ~~late~~ Col. 1st V. R. C. be substituted. It seems that Vermont has not got a single Field officer among all the Army appointments. Col. Lewis lost an arm in the service which prevents him taking up his profession, that of a Dentist. Maj. Trotter, who has received the appointment, is not disabled though from the fact that he received a wound during the rebellion he is elegible for the appointment given him.

I think there are circumstances attending the manner which Maj. Trotter used to obtain his appointment which would warrant the withdrawel of his appointment.

I have the honor to be,
very respectfully
your obt. svt.
U. S. GRANT
General.

ALS, DNA, RG 94, ACP, 2423 1881.

1. Frederick E. Trotter's appointment as maj., 44th Inf., as of July 28, 1866, was canceled on Dec. 8, and he was appointed capt., 45th Inf., as of July 28. On Aug. 13, 1867, John H. James, Washington, D. C., wrote to President Andrew Johnson recommending Trotter for bvt. promotion. ALS, *ibid.*,

T578 CB 1866. On Oct. 11, USG endorsed this letter. "Respectfully returned. It is not deemed just to other officers to brevets Capt. Trotter to a higher position than that of Lieut. Col., for faithful and meritorious service during the war." ES, *ibid.* On Nov. 4, 1875, Edward W. Serrell, New York City, wrote to USG. "There is a worthy gentleman in the Army, Capt Trotter of 14th Infantry, and I want very much to serve him—You will see by his record that he was Col. Vet. Res. & Bt. Brg. Genl.: that he lost his rank through no fault of his and has suffered uncomplainingly ever since. I have never asked the government to do anything for me, personally, since the war, which perhaps I might have properly done, but I do now ask you for my sake to restore Cap. Trotter to his rank if you can do so—I ask this as if I was asking. it for myself, believing that you never turn your back on a worthy man when in your power to help him. It is with great pleasure Mr President I congratulate you on the result of the recent elections—Such an endorsement of the government will go a long way, and as I have before said to you I hope you will be President as long as you live and that you may live many, many years, is the wish of your sincere friend . . ." ALS, *ibid.*

2. On Nov. 6, 1866, Lewis A. Grant, former brig. gen., Moline, Ill., wrote to the AGO recommending Col. John R. Lewis, 1st Veteran, for an appointment in the U.S. Army. ALS, *ibid.*, 2423 1881. On Dec. 1, USG endorsed this letter. "Respectfully forwarded to the Secretary of War, recommending Gen. Lewis for a field appointment in the Veteran Reserve Corps, if a vacancy exists." ES, *ibid.* Lewis was appointed maj., 44th Inf., as of Jan. 22, 1867. On Dec. 11, Maj. Gen. Oliver O. Howard, Bureau of Refugees, Freedmen, and Abandoned Lands, wrote to USG, secretary of war *ad interim*. "I have the honor to request for Major John R. Lewis, 44th U. S Infantry, promotion to the rank of Lieut. Colonel and Colonel by brevet. Major Lewis lost an arm in the service, and his military record is highly honorable. His faithful services as an officer of this Bureau deserve also the recognition herein solicited." LS, *ibid.* On Dec. 23, USG (as gen.) endorsed this letter. "Approved for brevet of Lieut.-Col. for White Oak Swamp, and brevet of Colonel for Wilderness." ES, *ibid.*

To Edwin M. Stanton

Washington, Dec. 6th *1866*.

HON. E. M. STANTON
SECRETARY OF WAR.
SIR:

I have the honor to renew a recommendation made by me in December[1] last, which I deem of great importance both to the service and to the individual officers of the Army.

Without some stimulus, experience has shown that many officers donot even in time of peace give that attention to obtaining a thorough knowledge of their profession which adds so much to their efficiency and ability to serve the Government.

I therefore recommend that Congress be asked to provide by law that "Hereafter no officer of the regular army below the rank of field officer shall be promoted to a higher grade before having passed a satisfactory examination as to his fitness for promotion before a board of three officers senior to him in rank; and should the officer fail at said examination he shall be suspended from promotion for one year, when he shall be re-examined, and upon a second failure shall be dropped from the rolls of the Army."

This law already applies to certain parts of the Army; in my opinion it will be a great benefit if extended to the whole.

Very respectfully
Your obt. serv't.
U. S. GRANT
General.

LS, DNA, RG 233, 39A–H15.4.

1. See letter to Henry Wilson, Jan. 12, 1866, note 1.

To Bvt. Maj. Gen. Edward O. C. Ord

Washington, D. C. Dec. 6th *1866*.

DEAR GENERAL;

A dispatch was received this morning from Gov. Murphy[1] asking a suspension of orders removing your Hd Qrs. to Fort Smith.[2] I was so much pleased with the tone of the Governor's message to the Legislature that I acseeded to his request at once. I now send Gen. Porter[3] out to consult with you about the permanent location of Hd Qrs. and Military posts, and also to see the general condition of the country.

Give my best respects to Mrs. Ord and the children.

Yours Truly
U. S. GRANT

TO MAJ. GN. E. O. C. ORD.

ALS, Brigham Young University, Provo, Utah. See following letter.

1. Isaac Murphy, born in 1802 in Pa., moved to Ark. in 1834 and became a lawyer. A Unionist, he was elected governor in 1864. On Dec. 7, 1866, Murphy, Little Rock, wrote to Secretary of War Edwin M. Stanton. "On the 5th inst, I telegraphed you, requesting a suspension of the execution of the order for the removal of Head Quarters Department of the Arkansas, to Fort Smith, until I could more fully Communicate with you by mail, and was gratified to receive this morning your telegram of yesterday. . . . As Little Rock, where Head Quarters now are, and where the operations of the Freedmen's Bureau, can best be directed, is also the Capital of the State, I regard it as highly important, that in the present juncture of our affairs, the facilities for Communication between this office and other Departments of the State Government, and the General Commanding the Department of the Arkansas, should be the best that the nature of the case will allow. The Legislature of the State is now in session, and will be for some time to come, and while its general relations to the Executive are amicable, its action upon the proposed Constitutional amendment is still Withheld, and the disposition of the body is not favorable to the ratification. What complications will yet arise I Know not, but in view of the probable action of Congress, as foreshadowed by the events of the last four days, and being familiar with the attitudes of those citizens of the State, who were implicated in the rebellion, some of whom have accepted the situation in good faith, while others are still disposed to engender strife, I desire to be in as close Communication as possible with General Ord. . . ." ALS, DNA, RG 108, Letters Received.

2. On Nov. 10, Bvt. Maj. Gen. Edward O. C. Ord, Detroit, wrote to Lt. Gen. William T. Sherman requesting permission to locate his hd. qrs. at Fort Smith. LS, *ibid.*, RG 94, Letters Received, 860A 1866. On Nov. 21, Col. Ely S. Parker endorsed this letter. "Respectfully returned. The Adjutant General will issue an order transferring Headquarters Departmt Arkansas from Little Rock to Fort Smith, and authorizing General Ord to move the band now at Little Rock to the post within his command having the largest permanent garrison." AES, *ibid.* On Nov. 16, Ord wrote to "General," presumably USG. "Lieut. General Sherman gave me verbal instructions to move my Department Head Quarters to Fort Smith—which finding my troops were required principally in the Indian Country west of Fort Smith, and there were not proper buildings for storage or quarters at Little Rock—except at extravagent rents I had arranged to do, when I left Little Rock about two weeks since—but General Sherman did not issue the necessary order in accordance with his verbal instructions, nor do I know if he has asked that the order should issue from Washington, and though I wrote to him to that effect I fear my letters did not reach him before his departure. Besides the expense of maintaining Head Quarters at Little Rock,—(where I do not propose to keep more than two or three Companies of troops) it is so sickly there, that four fifths of the men were sick during last fall and summer of fevers—and many died thereof—and over one fourth those remaining died of Cholera, so that for the safety of the Command and on the recommendation of the Medical Director I had the Garrison removed to the country during the sickness. I hope therefore General that you will order the change already authorised—and give me authority to locate the Band at such post as may have the largest permanent garrison. The wild Indians in my Department are very

numerous—and those north of it—Comanches and Koways—pass through it to Texas continually in their hostile and horse stealing expeditions,—To check this I have reoccupied Fort Arbunckle and propose building a new post near Fort Cobb for cavalry and scouts. The Kansas Indians are by treaty, about to be removed to my Department; so that with the already unsettled condition of things there I cannot restrain or capture outlaws or depredators—whites or Indians without some cavalry. There is such a demand for colored labor that I have not been able to enlist a single soldier of that kind. I have asked Lt. General Sherman to apply for authority to enlist in my Department one hundred more Indian scouts, which can be done with much ease and good results provided (as I believe is the case) General Halleck cannot obtain the number allowed him by one hundred. I made application on the 13th by telegraph from here to the Secretary of War to be ordered to Washington to see him in regard to the policy required in the Freedmans Bureau, and other important matters; he has not replied to my application—from which I conclude that he don't want to see me. General Howard is absent from Washington so much that I cannot get replies from him in regard to matters—and I doubt if he can act on them—such for instance, as to how far I can restrain white parties from removing their cotton who owe the Freedmen for raising or picking it? What system of penalties can be adopted to enforce contracts with freedmen under the civil rights bill and what I should do when civil courts take action under State laws which I might consider in violation of the civil rights bill? To what extent claims of late rebel parties for the restoration of their property in use by the military should be granted? And how far I could interfere with civil courts—if at all—when they bring judgment against parties not officers—for acts done in conformity with military orders? during War These questions and others of a military character in regard to arrests of civilians for outrages upon Union men apparently on account of their opinions—have all been pressed upon me for action, so that I should have some knowledge of the policy it is expedient for me to pursue upon such questions—and I presumed the Secretary could give it, Peace with the Indians in some instances depends upon the establishment of Military Posts in certain localities and the prompt pursuit by Cavalry and severe punishment if possible of ma~~u~~rauders: besides the Indian agents and military commanders should always act in accord, and with a careful understanding, so that the roving bands of murdering and robbing Indians might not be receiving presents and permits to purchase arms and powder of Indian Agents in one section of the Country, after having been pursued by the military away from some other section on account of their murders and depredations, which I am informed is now sometimes the case: I therefore wished to consult with the ~~c~~Commissioner of Indian Affairs and if possible have him instruct his Agents in certain localities not to make presents or buy captives of the same Indians who were fighting us elsewhere.—The bands of Commanches and Kioways on the forks of the uper Arkansas—with whom Agent Leavenworth—I am informed—treats and to whom he makes presents, are continually engaged in forays upon Texas. Some of the provisions of the Treaty recently made with the Choctaws and Chickasaws are particularly severe upon the freedmen who fled from the Indian Country to the North during the War, and who are in large numbers and destitute ~~and~~ around Forts Gibson and Smith; they are by the recent treaty not allowed to return to the Indian Country. Perhaps the Commissioner of Indian Affairs might have relieved the Military of the care of these people—Could I have conferred with him. The extent to which the government wishes to encourage the opening for a Rail Road of the short, easy and genial route, to NewMexico near the 35th parallel—by the reestablishment of Military Posts, once considered important on that route, and in regard to which Generals Emory and Marcy could give much useful information. The matter of locating some of the wild Comanches, Caddoes, Witchitas and others, who were at old Fort Arbunckle recently to see about it, but found no Indian Agent there or near there. The feasibility of keeping them from stealing other peoples horses and cattle; by settling them with horses and cattle of their own, and thus making them as stock raisers, liable to suffer if stealing were not discouraged—were subjects of interest in the same connection and about which I would have been glad to have consulted with you and the Secretary. I have so far I believe, satisfied the best men in Arkansas, but unless I can have the assurance that I shall be supported by the government in pursuing a certain line of policy—I shall be compelled to submit all doubtful and difficult questions as they arise to the Secretary of War, or yourself for action; which besides producing delay might result sometimes in loss of life. Most questions can be best settled in a remote Department by the Commander thereof, who has all the facts before him provided he has the confidence of the Government. I hope General you will lay my letter before the Secretary of War so as to make him aware of my position as well as my anxiety to discharge my duties in accordance with instructions from the wisest and highest authority—and let me know if possible if I am to expect to be sustained—provided I take responsibilities. At present I have some doubts which you can see I ought not to have. . . . P. S. I start back for my Command about the 20th will you please write or direct Genl Rawlings to write to me covering my questions as near as may be and oblige . . ." LS, *ibid.*, RG 108, Letters Received. On Nov. 21, Bvt. Brig. Gen. Cyrus B. Comstock wrote to Ord. "General Grant desires me to acknowledge the receipt of your letter of the 16th inst. and to reply as follows. Orders will be issued transferring the Headquarters of your Dept to Fort Smith and authorizing you to move the band now at Little Rock to the post within your command having the largest permanent garrison. It is impossible for the General-in-Chief to give instructions which shall guide you in all extraordinary and exceptional cases; whenever such cases come within the provisions of the Civil Right's Bill, Freedman's Bureau Bill, or other laws, these laws must be your guide. In other cases, you must exercise a wise discretion acting wherever it is possible in concert with the civil authorities. Property belonging to private persons seized as a military necessity while in a state of war and held only because it had been once seized should, now that a state of war no longer exists, be restored to its owners. Claims for the rent of such property will undoubtedly be made and perhaps held to be rightful—Those claims would in most cases exceed the value to the Government of the use of the property. It is reported that there are in your Dept. organized bands of robbers or bush-whackers persecuting all alike. You should consult with State authorities in reference to these and suppress them at once. In the exercise of the discretionary powers possessed by you, you will wherever it is possible be supported by the General-in-Chief." Copies, DLC-USG, V, 47, 60; DNA, RG 108, Letters Sent. On Dec. 1, Ord, Little Rock, wrote to Comstock. "I have the honor to acknowledge the receipt of your note of the 21st ultimo, which is very satisfactory.—In regard to the suppressing bands of robbers, allow me to call your attention to the enclosed instructions and reports on this very subject, which show what I have done and am doing;—but I received a letter from General Townsend, calling my attention to my having '*mounted*' infantry, when authority to do so, was only vested in the President. I might as well attempt to clear the Mississippi of snags with a teaspoon, as to suppress robbery and murder in Arkansas with Infantry on foot. . . . I have made this subject a speciality since taking command & have worked up the evidence in some of the worst cases procured the issue of writs by civil authority, and made arrests in *every* case where complaints to me ~~are~~ were well founded of murders of union men—and now have the accused (except one who died of cholera there—in the pinitentiary; which is under my control—I would have caught 'west' had I have had mounted force to send for him—please say to the General that the western part of my department the Indn Country & is of *very great* importance, and the matter of proper posts of mounted men being established there should be acted on at once—" LS, *ibid.*, Letters Received.

On Dec. 6, 10:20 A.M., USG telegraphed to Ord. "Suspend the change of Department Head Quarters from Little Rock until further orders" Telegram sent, *ibid.*, RG 107, Telegrams Collected (Bound); copies, *ibid.*, RG 108, Letters Sent; DLC-USG, V, 47, 60. At 1:00 P.M., Ord telegraphed to USG. "Telegram Suspending Change of Headquarters received. Self and portion Staff have secured quarters there and the move is part~~y~~ly made. Can I expect to complete it after adjournment of Legislature if all quiet" Telegram received (on Dec. 7, 9:00 A.M.), DNA, RG 108, Telegrams Received; copy, DLC-USG, V, 54. On Dec. 7, 10:15 A.M., USG telegraphed to Ord. "It is probable you will be allowed to change Head Quarters soon. Genl Porter starts to see you tomorrow" Telegram sent, DNA, RG 107, Telegrams Collected (Bound); copies, *ibid.*, RG 108, Letters Sent; DLC-USG, V, 47, 60.

On Jan. 9, 1867, 1:00 P.M., USG telegraphed to Ord. "You are authorized to remove the Head Quarters, of your Department to Fort Smith immediately after the adjournment of the Arkansas Legislature." Telegram sent, DNA, RG 107, Telegrams Collected (Bound); copies, *ibid.*, RG 108, Telegrams Sent; DLC-USG, V, 56. On Jan. 25, Ord wrote to USG. "The Banker of this town and some of the merchants anxious to retain the expenditures of the Qur Mrs Dept: and the hundred or two employess: the rents—&c of Hd Qurs, and offices, stores &c,—which amount to from 2 to 5 thousand dols per month—are getting up a petition & trying to interest the Legislature to get the President to countermand your order moving Hd Qurs to Fort Smith—I would not like to go there and have to return—the Depot must go there anyhow as this place will supply no other,—& no trains will be needed here—& large ones will be needed at Ft Smith—I propose with your consent keeping Hd Qurs of the Freedmens Bureau here and spending most of the time here during the session of each Legislature but I want to look after the Indian Country & its Post during the summer and want to cease paying heavy rents for every Store house, office, or shantee built on privt property in this town—which we are doing now—I also want to get away, at times from the Hd Quarters of politicians of any stamp—which I can not do here—will you state these facts to the President so as to secure us from further interference" ALS, DNA, RG 94, Letters Received, 121M 1867. On Jan. 31, Sherman endorsed this letter. "The HeadQrs of the Dept of Arkansas were changed from Little Rock to Fort Smith when I was away. In a military sense a city or town is a bad place for soldiers, and there can be no necessity for the hiring of any private building in Little Rock, because the arsenal should suffice. Inasmuch as the order was made for the HdQrs to go to Fort Smith I would not change now, but leave Genl Ord to move in person to that point of his Dept which he judges necessary to control the Military interests of his Dept." AES, *ibid.* On Feb. 1, Murphy telegraphed to Stanton protesting the removal of Ord's hd. qrs. Telegram received (at 3:40 P.M.), *ibid.*, RG 108, Letters Received. USG noted on the docket of this telegram. "The Military in Ark. will be as effective with Hd Qrs. at Little Rock as elswhere in the state." AN (undated), *ibid.* On Feb. 2, 10:00 A.M., USG telegraphed to Ord. "Do not move Head Quarters from Little Rock without further authority You had better make your preparations to remain there purmanently" Telegram sent, *ibid.*, RG 107, Telegrams Collected (Bound); telegram received, *ibid.*, RG 393, Dept. of Ark., 4th Military District, Miscellaneous Records.

On Jan. 5, Ord wrote to the AGO requesting authority to mount inf., enclosing a report on the growing number of outrages committed against Negroes in Ark. LS, *ibid.*, RG 94, Letters Received, 49M 1867. On Jan. 14, Sherman endorsed these papers. "Respectfully forwarded to the HeadQrs of the Army with the request that permission be given to mount the two (2) companies of Infantry until they can be replaced by Cavalry in process of enlistmt. If there be Power in our Governmt to assess damages to a County for a murder which is not punished by the organized courts it would stop this practice of killing negros. If it is decided that the military can do this I can soon put a stop to the practice." AES, *ibid.* On Jan. 16, Sherman had endorsed papers forwarded by Ord. "Respectfully forwarded to Hdq. A. U. S. These papers are sent me by General Ord, to strengthen his application for more Cavalry. I cannot give him Cavalry, because all I have is needed against the Indians.—He is to have 4 Cos of the 10 Cavalry Colored as soon as they can be enlisted. I doubt if the Military can do all the police work of the South." AES, *ibid.* On Jan. 8, Ord wrote at length to Brig. Gen. John A. Rawlins concerning his dept., concluding: ". . . In addition to the posts in this state already named, occupied by troops, I have issued a Circular to the Agents of the 'Freedmens Bureau,' promising them each a detachment of mounted troops—See Circular No 30—and reports of murders and outrages for two weeks enclosed—I apprehend these difficulties will increase rather than diminish, the Corn Crop being not enough to last through the year—To carry out my promises mounted troops are necessary—As for the four (4) Companies of Colored Cavalry, which I am authorized to raise, there are none so poor in this Department as to be willing to accept the pay clothing &c. of the United States, when they can enjoy freedom and 25 dollars per month and found and the society of the fair—I therefore must have some white Cavalry or I cannot protect setlers—freedmen—or loyal citizens; and the United States, will gradually loose in this region the prestige acquired at such an immense cost during the last six years—" LS, *ibid.* On Jan. 10, Ord wrote to Sherman that ". . . the danger of a general colission and an attempt to kill all the negroes in certain sections is imminent—. . . ," and requested reinforcements. ALS, *ibid.* Additional papers are *ibid.* On Jan. 16, Sherman endorsed these papers. "Respectfully forwarded to the HdQrs of the Army. It is impossible to draw troops from Genls Cooke and Hancock to reenforce Arkansas. There is evidently a dead-set on Gen Ord for more Cavalry, and I can only refer it to General Grant—" AES, *ibid.* On Jan. 12, Ord, Pine Bluff, wrote to "General," presumably USG. "I have written to Genl Sherman enclosing a few of the complaints—I am almost daily recieving from the agents of the Freedmans Bureau—of the treatment by the lower class of brutal whites of the Freedmen—Planters are now coming in who inform me that this treatment is due to a determination to run the negroes out of the State (or the portions of it under control of these men—) and that they the lower class of whites are opposed to freedmen's labouring on the large plantations—they want these planters broken up—many murders have been committed and in some counties the white inhabitants are in great terror of the outlaws—I have asked Genl Sherman several times for cavalry—without it or mounted troops I can do nothing—I should have at least five companies of cavalry and one more Regiment of ~~mounted~~ Infantry—now I have in the state only about 400 infantry—the companies being reduced to about 40 men each for duty—these are much scattered—and I cannot catch well mounted outlaws on poorly mounted raw infantry in detachments of three or four men I hope General you will present the circumstances of the bitter feeling growing up between the blacks and low class of whites in this state to the President—If I have no more troops than at present, serious and wholesale collisions between them can not be prevented—I am recieving intimations to this effect from the most bitter of the late Rebels—Such men as R W Johnson late senator of Arkansas—Dr Stout—&c—in many parts of the state the roads are infested by highwaymen, and it is dangerous to travel without a force—one of my Freedmens Bureau agents has been shot & lost his arm—another had to run for his life, and mobs have threatened others—all because they attempted to protect the freedmen—and I have not troops to protect *them*—this state of things has grown much worse recently, owing perhaps to the fact that the ~~poor~~ worst whites have not worked, have no crop & the freedmen have worked and have made a good deal of money—are being educated and do in places hold up their heads pretty high I enclose you slip from yesterdays paper giving one of the many instances of the roberies I refer to—The paper is rebel—. . . P. S. There has just been another freedman murdered in this county making two killed without excuse in the last ten days and this is one of the most orderly counties in the state—" ALS, *ibid.* On Feb. 7, USG wrote five identical endorsements forwarding these papers to Stanton. ES, *ibid.* On Jan. 12 and 16, USG had forwarded to Stanton papers detailing murders and outrages committed against freedmen in Ark. ES (2), *ibid.*, 963A 1866.

On Feb. 1, Ord, Little Rock, telegraphed to USG. "I want field officers to command important posts and districts such as Washn Ark and Fort Arbuckle Indian Nation Cannot Bvt Maj. Gen Ayres be directed to report to me the comdr at Washn has had a difficulty and been badly beaten The comdr at Arbuckle is ordered to another dept. Cannot Maj. Geo P Andrews of the Artillery now in Boston Harbor be ordered to me He desires it Also Maj Jno Hamilton of the Artillery I have need for all three of these officers" Telegram received (at 8:40 P.M.), *ibid.*, RG 107, Telegrams Collected (Bound); *ibid.*, RG 108, Telegrams Received; copies, *ibid.*, RG 393, Dept. of Ark., Telegrams Sent; DLC-USG, V, 55. See letter to Bvt. Maj. Gen. Edward O. C. Ord, March 1, 1867.

3. On Dec. 6, 1866, Maj. George K. Leet wrote to Col. Horace Porter. "You will proceed without delay to Louisville, Ky, Memphis, Tenn., Little Rock & Fort Smith, Ark., Vicksburg, Miss., Chattanooga, Tenn., Atlanta & Dahlonega, Ga., and make investigations in accordance with the instructions verbally communicated to you by the General-in-Chief. Upon the completion of this duty you will rejoin these Hdqrs." Copies, DLC-USG, V, 47, 60; DNA, RG 108, Letters Sent.

To Bvt. Maj. Gen. Edward O. C. Ord

Washington, D. C. Dec. 6th *1866*.

DEAR GENERAL:

I am just in receipt of a dispatch from Gov. Murphy asking to have the order for the removal of your Hd Qrs. from Little Rock suspended for the present. Feeling that Gov. Murphy, of all the Southern Governors, is the only one who has recommended a course calculated to restore political peace to the country, I have acceeded to his wish. I hope the Governor may be sucsessful in procuring the adoption of the Constitunal Amendments proposed by Congress. I believe that if one single Southern State should adopt them Congress would establish a precedent that would induce all others to adopt them. The South ought to see that these amendments have been ratified by the peopl who sustained the Government in its hour of trial, and those alone who have the power to fix the terms of political reconstruction. I have nothing to say of the merits of the terms propose: it is a final decission from which there is no appeal. Delay may cause further demands but it is scarcely within the range of possibility that less will be accepted. Certainly not within the term of this and the next Congress.—It looks important to me that the South should get their political status settled whilst we have an inflated currency and abundence of money. The South is poor and wants capital to develop their resources. The North has it now in great abundence, but capital is always sensitive to danger. It will not flow into territory with such a political uncertainty before it as now exists in ten of the Southern States. Any settlement is better for them than the existing state of affairs.

I hope you will talk to the Governor, and such members of the Legislature as you may have influence with, on this subject. It is not proper that officers of the Army should take part in political matters. But this is hardly to be classed as a party matter. It is one of National importance. All parties agree to the fact that we ought to be united and the status of every state definitely settled. They only differ as to the manner of doing this. It ought to be seen that no way will sucseed unless agreed to by Congress.

This letter will be handed to you by Gn. Porter of my Staff who goes into your Dept. on a tour of inspection.

Yours Truly
U. S. GRANT

ALS, DLC-Horace Porter. See preceding letter. On Dec. 19, 1866, Bvt. Maj. Gen. Edward O. C. Ord, Little Rock, wrote to USG. "General Porter leaves to night—I have mentioned to him & repeat here that events may occur which it would be proper I should communicate to you by telegraph and confidentially—but I have no cypher—can you not send me one—I did not know that you wished this Legislature to take any action of a special nature or I might have intervened to have prevented a rejection of the constitutional amendment—I think it is not too late to get them to reconsider and perhaps pass it—shall write to you in case of such an event—and telegraph—My Quarter Master Maj Montgomery is somewhat uncertain—his long retirement during the war makes him timid—and slow he will do for a chief when there is no hard out of door work but I want an active young officer—for the work & I can put montgomery in general charge—I shall remain here until I hear that I can move west—in any event I proposed keeping Hd Qurs of the Freedmans Bureau here and spending most of each Session of the legislature here—Genls Reynolds & Sprague both were absent all last summer at the north I shall *have* to take a look at the indian country in the spring & summer it requires a thoro overhauling & several new posts among the Indians of the plains especially on the upper Arkansas—whom Genl Sherman says must be kept south—and the only way to do it is to keep posts among them—I shall have from 30 to 50 thousand Indians to look after—a pretty wild set of white men and no cavalry unless you send me some—" ALS, USG 3.

To Edwin M. Stanton

Washington D. C. Dec 8th *1866*.

HON. E. M. STANTON
SEC. OF WAR
SIR;

I have the honor to return herewith a Resolution of the House of Representatives, Congress of the U. S., asking to be informed "whether any portion of Mexican Territory has been occupied by troops of the United States, and if so by what authority and for what purpose," which Resolution was referred to me for report.

In compliance therewith I would respectfully state that no official information of the occupation of any portion of Mexican Territory has been received at these Headquarters and no authority has been given either by the Major General Commanding Department of the Gulf or myself for any movement of troops into said territory.

Attention is respectfully invited to the communication of Maj. Gen. Sheridan dated Nov. 27th ultimo. and enclosing letter of Gen. Sedgwick, Comdg. Sub District. Rio Grande, which was forwarded to the Sec. of War for his information, Dec. 5th, 1866; also to the enclosed copy of his letter of Nov. 30th; copies of telegrams bearing upon this subject.

Very respectfully
Your obt. servt.
U. S. GRANT
General

Copies, DLC-USG, V, 47, 60; DNA, RG 108, Letters Sent; USG 3. On Dec. 27, 1866, USG wrote to Secretary of War Edwin M. Stanton. "I have the honor to return herewith the Resolution of the House of Representatives, Congress of the U. S., calling for further information in regard to the occupation of Mexican territory by U. S. troops, &c., referred to me for report. The only information on this subject received at these Headquarters since my report of the 8th instant is contained in the enclosed copies of a report and telegrams from Maj. Gen. Sheridan ~~from Maj. Gen. Sheridan~~ of date Dec. 10th and 11th inst." Copies, *ibid.* See letter to Maj. Gen. Philip H. Sheridan, Nov. 15, 1866; *HED*, 39-2-8; *ibid.*, 39-2-17.

On Dec. 15, Maj. Gen. Philip H. Sheridan, New Orleans, wrote to Brig. Gen. John A. Rawlins. "Confidential . . . Please find enclosed the substance of the last dispatch of Napoleon to his Aid de Camp in Mexico. It is not a literal translation but embodies the substance of the dispatch. We have been working on the '*cipher*' since the despatch sent to Napoleon dated mexico Dec 3d which despatch & the enclosed reply fell into my hands. Should we be able to get the cipher worked out & my present arrangemts continue I will be able to give the General the corresponde[nce] passing by the cable There is undoubtedly a 'new deal' being made with the church party, but it is as poor as a church mouse, and, as for the merchants giving any large amount to help Maximillian it is 'bosh' there is too much risk in it." ALS, USG 3. The enclosed dispatch concerning the evacuation of Mexico is *ibid.* On Dec. 17, Charles A. Keefer, cipher clerk, New Orleans, wrote to USG. "Napoleon sent a cable message on the 13th to Gen Castelneau Mexico to the care of the ~~f~~French Consul in this city and I happened to be in the telegraph office at the time and I copied it and translated it & gave Genl Sheridan a copy of it. General Sheridan told me yesterday that he sent you a copy of it. I have now in my possession a cipher cable message dated Mexico 3rd December and addressed to Napoleon I have been trying to work it out but it is impossible the only intelligible words in it are Campbell and Sherman. If our Minister or Consul at Paris can secure a copy of this dispatch if it is ever published in France I can work it out and understand the key Napoleon & Maximilian use & work out any of their ciphers in the future. They have sent several telegrams through this office since I have been here. Please be good enough to call the attention of Mr Seward to this matter and to acknowledge the receipt of this letter It will be better not to mention my name in connection with this matter because the Telegraph Lines in the south are controlled by Southern men and if they suspected my intentions they would not allow me to come any wheres near where I could hear the instrument clicking I am stationed here to take charge of Gen Sheridans Cipher telegraphic correspondence and I consider it my duty to furnish such information as this . . . P. S, The Cipher I refer to is signed Marshall Bazaine and Gen Castelneau and contains 375 cable words" ALS, Seward Papers, NRU. On Dec. 20, Sheridan wrote to Rawlins. "I enclose you for the information of Genl Grant a cable telegram of yesterday." Copies, DLC-Philip H. Sheridan; (2) USG 3. The enclosed cable of Dec. 19 from the Austrian cabinet instructing the commander of an Austrian corvette to remain in Vera Cruz until further orders is *ibid.*

On Jan. 12, 1867, Sheridan telegraphed to USG. "I respectfully transmit the following telegram for your information 'Paris Jany 10th French Consul New Orleans for General CASTLENO at Mexico—Received your despatch of the 9th December—Do not compel the Emperor to abdicate, but do not delay the departure of the troops; bring back all those who will not remain there—Most of the fleet has left. (signed) NAPOLEON' The above is genuine" Telegram received (at 2:30 P.M.), DNA, RG 107, Telegrams Collected (Bound); *ibid.*, RG 108, Telegrams Received; copies (one sent by mail), *ibid.*, Letters Received; DLC-USG, V, 55; DLC-Philip H. Sheridan.

To John W. Garrett

Washington, D. C. Dec. 9th *1866*.

J. G. GARRETT,
PRES. B & O. R. R.
DEAR SIR:

I am going to presume again on your good nature, and kind offers, to ask you for a place on the B. & O. cars, for Teusday[1] evening next, to the Ohio river. I shall leave here in the 8 p. m. train on that day for St. Louis as direct and quick as I can go. If you will do me the kindness to have reserved for me one section on the sleeping car, from the Relay House, you will place me under renewed obligations.

I shall take but one person with me so that I prefer not taking a separate car.

From the Ohio river I do not know the best route to take but would like to go as expeditiously as possible. If there is any difference in them, and it is not too much trouble for you to telegraph me, I will take the one you suggest. I am sorry to give you so much trouble; but it is your own fault. You have invited by your uniform courticy.

Yours Truly,
U. S. GRANT
General.

ALS, DLC-Garrett Family. For the business taking USG to St. Louis, see letters to Charles W. Ford, Oct. 15, 17, 25, 1866, March 24, 1867. On Dec. 15 and 17, 1866, USG negotiated with William B. Napton, attorney for David Irvin, offering $8,000 to settle Irvin's claim for $13,000. Napton diary (typescript), MoSHi. On Dec. 21, Charles W. Ford, St. Louis, telegraphed to USG. "I closed that matter with Napton yesterday and paid him eighty thousand dollars Please send me your check for that amount Answer" Telegram received, DNA, RG 107, Telegrams Collected (Bound).

1. Dec. 11.

To George B. McClellan

Washington, D. C. Dec. 10th *1866*.

DEAR GENERAL,

I have the honor to acknowledge receipt of your letter of the 24th of Nov. In reply I enclose you copies of all letters addressed to Gen. Marcy on the subject of papers supposed to be in your possession. These letters contain a full explanation to yours and, as you will see, do not imply an intention on your part to withhold any paper properly beloning to Hd Qrs. of the Army.

Trusting that this letter, with enclosures, will relieve you of any misapprehension you may have felt from Gen. Marcy's letter, and with the assurance that the Gn. kindly offered to furnish anything we might want from papers retained in your possession,

I remain,
Very Truly yours
U. S. GRANT

To GN. G. B. MCCLELLAN.

ALS, DLC-George B. McClellan. On Nov. 24, 1866, George B. McClellan had written to USG. "In a letter received yesterday from Gnl Marcy he says—'I had a note yesterday from a member of Gnl Grant's staff in which he says it had been officially reported to the General that he (McClellan) had retained in his possession certain records pertaining to the Hd Qtrs of the Army, which were loaned to him while preparing his Report in 1862–3.'—I desire to state that I have not knowingly retained or caused to be withheld any document whatever, whether important or unimportant, belonging to the Hd Qtrs of the Army or to any other Dept of the Government. When my Report was completed I caused all the original subordinate reports, and all other documents belonging to the Govt. to be boxed up, & sent them to the Adjt Gnl of the Army in Washington, I think at the same time with my Report. My recollection is that they were sent by the hands of my aide de Camp Capt A. McClellan. I do not think it possible that any document can have been overlooked, because in examining my papers subsequently my attention would in all probability have been attracted to it, and as a matter of course I would at once have forwarded it to Washington. I shall be under especial obligations to you, General, if you will cause me to be informed what documents are alluded to in the report referred to, also by whom the report was made to you. To such a general statement as that made to Gnl Marcy—at least as it has reached me—I can only return a general reply as I have already done. Desiring the favor of an early reply, directed to the care of 'Mssrs J. S. Morgan & Co—22 old Broad St—London'—" ADfS, *ibid.* Probably on Dec. 25, McClellan drafted a letter to USG, later adding a note that it was never sent. "I have to day received a letter from Gnl Marcy informing me that he had examined my papers in order to ascertain if there were among them any documents belonging to the Hd Qtrs of the Army, & that he had forwarded to you certain telegrams from Gnl Halleck to me, which he found there. I was not aware that those telegrams were among my papers. From their nature I was naturally unwilling that they should meet the eye of any whom they did not concern & presume that for that reason I took them to my house where they became *mixed up with other papers & were lost sight of.* Soon after the capture of Ft Donelson I, on a Sunday morning the date of which I have forgotten, caused all business to be suspended on the wires leading from Washn to St Louis & Louisville, desired Gnls Halleck & Buell to go to the tel. offices in the two cities last mentioned, & went myself to the tel. off in the Hd Qtrs of the Army of the Potomac, with the intention of promptly checking the measures to be taken by the respective commands of H & B. One of my first questions was as to the condition, position, numbers etc of their troops at the moment. This interrogatory called forth Gnl H's reply in which he states that he had not heard from you for more than a week, that you had gone to Nashville without authority, that you deserved removal etc etc. I have nothing but recollection to guide me as to what my reply was to this & to his subsequent despatch in which he stated that you had ~~frequently~~ ~~repeated~~ neglected his repeated orders, that he did not deem it advisable to arrest you at that moment, & that he had placed C F Smith in command of the expdn up the Tenn etc.—My recollection is that I stated that must have ~~at~~ ~~this~~ immediately the information I required & that if he deemed it advisable he might [a]rrest or remove you & replace you by some one who would give the information so imperatively necessary to me & obey his orders. I am quite confident that this was the tenor of my reply, & I know that [i]t was based entirely upon the representation contained in his official telegrams to me for I was in communication with no one else on the subject. . . . I was much surprised by the contents of his dispatch I am also confident that I did not press Grant's arrest, & I do not now even remember that he was arrested at all. My impression is that the matter passed over without action altho' I may be mistaken as to this point . . ." ADf, *ibid.* This correspondence resulted from Col. Adam Badeau's research for an official biography of USG, which involved an effort to explain USG's suspension from command in March, 1862. At that time, Maj. Gen. Henry W. Halleck led USG to believe that McClellan originated the suspension; Badeau learned that McClellan had acted solely on the basis of accusations made by Halleck. Adam Badeau, *Military History of Ulysses S. Grant* (New York, 1868–81), I, 60–65; *Memoirs*, I, 326–28. On Oct. 29, 1866, Badeau wrote to Col. and Bvt. Maj. Gen. Randolph B. Marcy. "General Grant directs me to say that it has been officially reported to him that a number of papers pertaining to the records of the Headquarters of the Army, are probably now in the possession of Gen'l McClellan, and that you having been Chief of Staff for Gen'l McClellan, can doubtless state what those papers are, and where. It is desired to obtain possession of any such documents now in existence and Gen'l Grant directs me to call upon you for any information you may be able to furnish on the subject. You will please state what records were kept, while Gen'l McClellan was in command of the Army, and what you may know of their history. as well as what relates to any particular papers loaned to Gen'l McClellan while he was engaged in making his report in New York in 1862 & 1863" Copies, DLC-USG, V, 47, 60; DNA, RG 108, Letters Sent. Additional letters from Badeau to Marcy on this subject dated Nov. 13, Dec. 1, and Dec. 10 are *ibid.* Marcy's replies of Nov. 4 and Dec. 6 are *ibid.*, Letters Received.

On Dec. 26, McClellan, Vevey, Switzerland, wrote to Marcy. "Yours of the 24th Nov. and 6th December were received. Yesterday, I had a letter from Grant in reply to mine of Nov. 24th. . . . Unless I am laboring under a mental hallucination, I remember distinctly the very appearance of the cipher telegraph books, and I am positive that they never came into my possession. General, you remember that about the time my report was made we were more than once told that Stanton had made a huge collection of *all* my telegraphic correspondence with which he had intended to spring a mine upon me; also that he showed it to certain parties. Where did the Committee on the Conduct of the War get my telegrams if not from Stanton? . . . When I return I shall make it a point to see Grant and do not doubt that I may aid him materially in what he desires. Whenever there is a new Secretary of War so that I can have access to the papers of the War Department, I think that I can unravel all the secrets of the prison-house. In regard to the I enclose a copy of an extract from a note which I had intended to send to Grant, but which I am not sure yet whether I will or not. It will at least serve to explain the matter to you and place you au courant of any questions upon the subject. When did Eckert send that box of telegrams? . . ." Copy, DLC-George B. McClellan. On the same day, McClellan wrote to USG. "Yours of the 10th inst reached me yesterday, and I now fully understand what is wanted. When called to the command of the U. S. armies in 1861, I left unchanged the organization of the Army of Potomac, & its Hd Qtrs, & in no manner merged them with those of the Hd Qtrs of the U. S. A—the Staff for each being distinct, except with regard to my personal Aides de Camp. Thus: Gnl Marcy, the Chf. of Staff of the A. of P. had nothing to do with the Hd Qtrs of the U. S. A.: Gnl S. Williams was Adjt. Gnl of the A. of P., while Gnl L. Thomas was my A. G. in my capacity as Comdr of the U. S. A—etc. The papers & records of the two offices were entirely distinct I had in the War Dept building two rooms for my office as Comg. Gnl of the U. S. A, & thither Gnl Thomas brought to me all papers & matters requiring my action, received my orders thereon, carried back the papers to his own office, where they should be found, together with the orders & letters issued by him thereon in conformity with my instructions. You will the more readily comprehend the state of affairs when I remind you that my predecessor—Gnl Scott—had an office—first in N. Y. afterwards in Washn.—entirely distinct from that of the Adjt. Gnl of the U. S. A, where he had his own A. G. & entirely distinct records; the A. G. of the U. S. A. being then simply the A. G. of the Secty of War. I changed the arrangement; dispensed with the machinery of a separate office, & merged all the routine service & records of the command in Chief with those of the A. G.'s office. The only papers, to the best of my recollection, kept in my office were the retained copies of my own letters on subjects of an important nature requiring more or less secrecy—such as letters of instruction in regard to military movements. As the telegraph was much used these letters were not numerous. Col A. O. Colburn had charge of these letters, & I am not sure whether they were copied into books or simply filed. I kept nothing for myself but the original rough drafts either in my own hand writing or that of the Aide to whom they were dictated. All written reports received went finally to the Adjt Gnls Office, or that of the Secty of War, none were retained in my office, which, after all, was simply a place for the transaction of business & not a place of record. When I left Washn in March 1862 to accompany the A of P. on its march towards Manassas, I was still the Comg Gnl of the U. S. A, had no reason whatever to suppose that any change was contemplated by the Presdt, left at a few hours notice, & expected to return in a few days, preparatory to the final movement to the Peninsula. I therefore made no special arrangements ~~in~~ in regard to my office in the War Dept, & left everything as it happened to be, all my personal Aides accompanying me. Two or three days after, while at Fairfax C. H., I, to my complete surprise, learned *through the newspapers* the order *relieving* me from the command of the U. S. A, & never afterwards entered the office in Washn. I was informed that it was *immediately* taken possession of by the War Dept for its own uses, & have no knowledge of what disposition was made of the papers etc found there, further than that it was about the same time stated to me that the War Dept had taken possession of everything in the office, as the function of Comg Gnl was assumed by the Secty. All telegraphic dispatches of any importance were sent & received in cipher, & were handed to me translated; the work of deciphering & the reverse being executed in the teleg. office. My recollection is that the cipher copies, *at least*, were recorded in books, which were kept in the Chief Teleg. Office; these books were never in my personal possession—This chief office, originally organized under my direction, was in the building occupied as the Hd Qtrs of the A of P. on Penna Avenue & Jackson Sq. Soon after the accession of the present Secty of War to office, & during my absence from the city, on duty, for two or three days, the entire establishment with all its records, apparatus & personnel, was removed to the War Dept building, without my knowledge, by order of the Secty of War; & from that time I ceased to have the slightest control over it. When I returned to the city I found the removal accomplished;—which was the first intimation I had of it. In that office should be found copies of all the messages that passed through it. With regard to the books containing the original duplicates of my messages sent, I have now no means of learning what ones were left in my War Dept office when it passed from my possession. I do not think there are any in my possession (among my papers in the U. S.) except that sent to you by Gnl Marcy. As that was simply my private memorandum, I would be glad to have it returned to Gnl Marcy when you have done with it. I was not aware that the telegrams of Feby & March 1862, from Gnl Halleck, were among my papers—I have requested Gnl Marcy to forward to you whatever copies of telegrams etc he may find. From his letters to me I think that he has examined all my papers, for all that I know of are at Orange. I will do my best to aid him in making a thorough search. When I return to the U S—probably in the course of a few months—I will most cheerfully aid you in any possible way to carry out your wishes, but I am at present inclined to think that a close search in Washington will be productive of much better results than one conducted elsewhere. I must apologize for inflicting so long a letter upon you" ADfS (2), *ibid.*

To Edwin M. Stanton

Washington, Dec. 11th 1866.

HON. E. M. STANTON,
SEC. OF WAR
SIR:

In reply to Resolution of Congress of Dec. 6th 1866, Copy herewith returned. I have the honor to return a copy of inspection report made by Bvt. Brig. Gen. D. B Sackett,[1] Inspector General's Department and also copies of letters from Lt. Gen. W. T. Sherman, written from different parts of the "Plains" whilst he was inspecting that part of that Territory during the last summer, as furnishing the most of the information called for.

In respect to the additional force required to the Regular Army to "thoroughly protect" communication by two great routes,

&c. I have to say that I do not believe additional protection would be given by additional force. When the Regular Army is filled to the standard now allowed, and as it becomes practicable to withdraw a portion of the troops from States lately in rebellion, as much force can be put upon the "plains" as it is practicable with any view to economy to support them.

A standing army could not prevent occasional Indian outrages, no matter what its magnitude. It is to be hoped however that the number of these outrages will materially diminish from this time forward until finally travel will be as secure through the "Far. West" as though the old states. Information derived from last summer's inspections will materially aid in producing this result, the construction of railroads over the "Plains" now rapidly progressing will naturally draw all travel to those lines and will further aid in giving security to communications through and with all the Territories of the United States.

I would not recommend any increase to the present Regular army.

I have the honor to be
Very respectfully
U. S. GRANT
General

Copies, DLC-USG, V, 47, 60; DNA, RG 108, Letters Sent. See letters to Maj. Gen. William T. Sherman, April 18, July 21, 1866; letter to Maj. Gen. Henry W. Halleck, April 19, 1866.

1. On Aug. 16, 1866, Bvt. Col. Roswell M. Sawyer, St. Louis, wrote to Brig. Gen. John A. Rawlins. "In accordance with instructions received from Lieutenant General Sherman at the moment of his departure from Saint Louis for the plains, I have the honor to forward herewith an official copy of a report received from Colonel D. B. Sacket, Inspector General, U. S. Army, dated Virginia City, Montana, July 20, 1866. The General directed me to add his recommendation that the report be published, as it is to our military interests to encourage settlers in the mountains." LS, DNA, RG 94, Letters Received, 1585M 1866. The enclosure is *ibid.* On Aug. 21, USG endorsed these papers. "Respectfully forwarded to the Secretary of War—Lt Gen Sherman's recommendation approved." ES, *ibid.* On Oct. 26, Col. and Bvt. Brig. Gen. Delos B. Sacket, inspector gen., Cape Vincent, N. Y., wrote at length to the AGO reporting on his inspection tour. *HED*, 39-2-23. On Dec. 11, USG forwarded this report to Secretary of War Edwin M. Stanton. Copy, DNA, RG 108, Register of Letters Received.

To Edwin M. Stanton

Washington, D. C. Dec. 11th *1866*.

HON. E. M. STANTON;
SEC. OF WAR;
SIR:

I have the honor to recommend that Col. & Bvt. Maj. Gn. R. Ingalls, Quartermaster U. S. A. be assigned to duty in New York City.—This is Gen. Ingalls choice. It is one of the most important stations under the Qr. Mr. General. Gen. Ingalls demonstrated qualifications in his department during the war equal to every call upon him, and his field services stand unequaled by any other Quartermaster.

Very respectfully
your obt. svt.
U. S. GRANT
General.

ALS, DNA, RG 94, Letters Received, 962A 1866.

To Edwin M. Stanton

From St Louis Mo. Dec 17, *1866*

To HON E M STANTON
SECY WAR

In view of the troubles threatened in Lexington I have thought it necessary to Send 1 company of troops there, Copy of the orders are Sent you with this

U S GRANT
Genl

Telegram received (at 11:00 P.M.), DNA, RG 107, Telegrams Collected (Bound); (torn) DLC-Andrew Johnson; copies, DLC-USG, V, 47, 60; DNA, RG 108, Letters Sent. On Dec. 17, 1866, USG telegraphed to Governor Thomas C. Fletcher of Mo. "I send you the following orders sent to Major Gen'l Hancock: 'Headquarters Military Division of the Missouri St. Louis, Mo. Decr.

17th 1866 Major General Hancock Fort Leavenworth, Kansas. General Grant desires you to send a company of Infantry to Lexington, Lafayette County to remain there until otherwise ordered and instructed simply to maintain the peace.' L. M. Dayton Lieut. Col. & Military Secretary There is no intention of interference with civil proceedings." Copies, *ibid.* On the same day, Lt. Col. Lewis M. Dayton wrote to USG. "Enclosed I have the pleasure of sending you copies of the telegrams dictated by you and which have been sent" ALS, *ibid.*, Letters Received. The enclosures are *ibid.* On the same day, Maj. Gen. Winfield S. Hancock, Fort Leavenworth, telegraphed to USG. "Your dispatch directing a Company of Infy to be sent to Lexington Mo to remain there until otherwise ordered simply to maintain the peace has been recd & will be executed at once— ~~Is~~ A Communication on this subject was sent you under Cover to General Nichols by the mail whch left here at twelve twenty (12 20) P M today" Telegram received (at 9:00 p.m.), *ibid.*; *ibid.*, Telegrams Received; copy, DLC-USG, V, 54.

On Dec. 18, Fletcher wrote to USG. "The condition of Lafayette and Jackson counties has required that I should take some steps to compel a united action of the people in support of the civil authorities. A law of this State authorizes me to send militia to any county in the State where a posse will not respond to the call of the Sheriff. There have been roamings at large in these two counties bands of outlaws, robbing and murdering at will and without fear of arrest; people were afraid to take writs for them; the officers could not arrest them; they came into the county towns and taunted the Sheriffs. Under the law I had offered rewards for some of them. One of those for whom a reward was offered, for murders committed by him, was killed at Lexington recently in an attempt to arrest him. The people of these counties can give security to life and property by arresting these outlaws, and they will do it when they find that they are to be taxed to pay troops for that purpose. The people of Jackson county have moved in the matter, and I am now so well satisfied that they are in earnest that I will withhold militia in that county. In Lafayette county I can attain the same desired end—the union of all parties to enforce the law, and thus give security to the men of all parties, negroes included (the latter of whom have recently been robbed and killed in Lexington with perfect impunity.) The wealthy and influential citizens of Lafayette have persistently encouraged the outlaws; they will desist from this when it costs them large taxes. I will have the most discreet and reliable men in command of the Militia—men who will do no unlawful thing, and preserve the peace. No man shall be molested in person or property without due process of law These outlaws are taught by a portion of the press and people that the U. S. Government will protect them in their robbing and killing of radicals and negroes, and that impression was confirmed by the course of a captain of U. S. troops stationed at Lexington before election who fraternized with the Bushwhackers in the streets of Lexington. The troubles there are purely local. The late Confederate soldiers, I am glad to be able to say, are not in sympathy with the lawless portion of the people. There is no danger to the peace of that county. The troops will be armed with writs as well as muskets. All men of every party who respect the laws will unite in the objects I have in view. The sending of a company of U S troops there by your order will be taken as a confirmation of the oft-repeated assurances given to the outlaws by the Conservative leaders that they would be protected by the United States, and will greatly augment the difficulties in making them fear and obey the law. This is a subject to which I have given great care and attention, and I am acting with a full understanding of all the surrounding circumstances. Two years of constant labor in reducing the bad elements of a population just emerging from civil war to obidience to civil law, has given me experiences of the best means to use in the various localities. I have deferred the application of the proper remedy to Lafayette county until the election was over, and no partisan purposes could be charged upon me: The sending of U S troops to Lexington will just now be productive of the worst effects, and of no good to any person whatever. I will see that the peace is kept there, and I will make the people themselves keep the peace among themselves if my plans are not interfered with. I did not call on Genl Hancock for troops, because, to effect what I desired, it was necessary to have troops known to be under my command. If you fully understood the condition of affairs in Lafayette county, I am very certain you would not do a thing calculated to defeat the objects for which I am working The whole thing is of such a purely local nature, and so entirely within the exclusive jurisdiction of the State authorities, that I feel assured the facts have been very greatly misrepresented to you to induce the doing of a thing which, unintentionally on your part, will defeat my objects, and instead of preserving peace, will have a tendency to embolden the only party from whom breaches of the peace are to be anticipated" ALS, DNA, RG 108, Letters Received. On Dec. 19, Fletcher telegraphed to USG. "I hope you will not send troops to Lexington until after you receive my letter tomorrow" Telegram received (at Cincinnati, 6:15 P.M.), *ibid.*; *ibid.*, Telegrams Received; copy, DLC-USG, V, 54. On Dec. 21, USG, Columbus, Ohio, telegraphed to Hancock. "If you have not sent a Company to Lexington you need not ~~send~~ ~~it~~ do so—If it has been sent withdraw it." Telegram received, DNA, RG 393, Dept. of the Mo., Telegrams Received; copies, *ibid.*, RG 108, Letters Sent; DLC-USG, V, 47, 60. At 12:40 P.M., Hancock telegraphed to USG. "Your dispatch recieved I have ordered the withdrawal of the troops from Lexington at once" Telegram received (at 1:40 P.M.), DNA, RG 108, Letters Received; *ibid.*, Telegrams Received; copy, DLC-USG, V, 54. On the same day, Hancock wrote to Brig. Gen. John A. Rawlins. "I have the honor to enclose herewith several Despatches received and sent to day, concerning affairs at Lexington, Lafayette County, Missouri, and the withdrawal of the United States Troops from that point. I also transmit the Despatch received by me from L. M. Dayton, Military Secretary, dated StLouis Mo, Decr 17th at 7.20 p. m, stating that General Grant desired me to send a Company of Infantry to Lexington, Mo. It will be observed that among these Despatches, there is one, No five (5), received from Colonel Nugent, after the order was sent to him to withdraw his detachment, by which it appears that an application was made to him by the United States Marshal for the Western District of Missouri, for United States Troops, to assist in serving a warrant on Colonel Bacon Montgomery, the Commander of the State Troops at Lexington. As the Troops were sent there merely to preserve the peace, and I presume were directed to be withdrawn in order to avoid a conflict with the State Troops, I have taken no action in the matter, except to request that the application should be forwarded to these Headquarters. When it is received, it will be transmitted to you. I look upon the question of Jurisdiction in this case, as one that should be decided by the highest authority. . . . The enclosed Despatches are numbered, from (1) one to (9) Nine." LS, DNA, RG 108, Letters Received. The enclosures are *ibid.*

On Dec. 23, USG, Washington, D. C., telegraphed to Fletcher. "The order sending U. S. troops to La-Fayette County was countermanded on receipt of your dispatch." Copies, DLC-USG, V, 47, 60; DNA, RG 108, Letters Sent. On Dec. 24, Fletcher telegraphed to USG. "Thanks Lafayette will now come to terms & all parties will unite to uphold the law" Telegram received (at 12:40 P.M.), *ibid.*, RG 107, Telegrams Collected (Bound); *ibid.*, RG 108, Telegrams Received; copies, *ibid.*, Letters Received; DLC-USG, V, 54. On Dec. 26, Hancock wrote to Rawlins. "I have the honor herewith to enclose copies of four (4) Warrants by B. F. Hickman, Commr of Circuit Court of the District of Missouri, dated St Louis Mo, the 19th inst. issued to the United States Marshal of the Western District of Missouri, for the apprehension of Colonel Bacon Montgomery, and others. The originals of these Warrants were brought to me by Thomas B. Wallace Esqre U. S. Marshal of the Western District of Missouri, in person. On the morning of the 21st inst before Colonel Nugent had received the orders which I sent him to withdraw his detachment from Lexington, Missouri), he was called upon by the United States Marshal of the Western District of Missouri, to aid with his troops in serving these Warrants upon Colonel Bacon Montgomery, Commanding the State Militia at that place. As soon as I received notice of this demand upon Colonel Nugent, I directed him to take no action in the matter, as the orders had gone to him, (in accordance with instructions received from General Grant) to withdraw his Troops; and as the detachment was sent there solely to preserve the peace, I supposed the order for withdrawal was given to avoid a conflict with the State Troops. I therefore directed Colonel Nugent to forward the application of the United States Marshal, for the assistance of the United States Troops to these Headquarters. These Warrants are understood to be under the civil-rights bill; As this is a matter of importance, and one in which a decision of the highest authority should be had, I respectfully refer the same." LS, DNA, RG 108, Letters Received. The enclosures are *ibid.*

To Lt. Gen. William T. Sherman

Washington, D. C., Dec. 31st *18646*

LT GEN'L W. T. SHERMAN
ST LOUIS MO.

Authority has been given to fill the 2nd and 3d Cavalry to the maximum. There are now three hundred Cavalry recruits that can be sent to you. Where will you have them?

Do you think an Infantry regiment sent from here this winter can be made available? If so where will you have them sent to?

U. S. GRANT
General

Telegram sent, DNA, RG 107, Telegrams Collected (Bound); copies, *ibid.*, RG 108, Letters Sent; DLC-USG, V, 47, 60. On Dec. 31, 1866, Lt. Gen. William T. Sherman telegraphed to USG. "Dispatch of today received Please order the Recruits to be sent to Omaha via Chicago and Clinton Iowa The Infantry Regiment should take the same direction as there is now RailRoad all the way from Chicago to the forks of the Platte excepting a break of about fifty (50) miles east of Omaha which must be marched The simple fact that these reinforcements are expected will enable Gen Cook to use all the men now in his Dept" Telegram received (at 5:10 P.M.), DNA, RG 107, Telegrams Collected (Bound); *ibid.*, RG 108, Telegrams Received; copy, DLC-USG, V, 54. On Dec. 29, 1:30 P.M., USG had telegraphed to Sherman. "Could you make use of more Infantry against the Indians this winter? Would it be of use to you to send Cavalry recruits to fill companies to a higher standard?" Telegram sent, DNA, RG 107, Telegrams Collected (Bound); copies, *ibid.*, RG 108, Letters Sent; DLC-USG, V, 47, 60. On the same day, Sherman telegraphed to USG. "Your dispatch just rec'd It is an excellent plan to increase the strength of the second U S Cavy for the Indian Campaign say one hundred men to a company if you have a single Regt of white Infantry it will be enough till we recruit the Black Regt belonging to Hancocks Dept" Telegram received (at 5:00 P.M.), DNA, RG 107, Telegrams Collected (Bound); *ibid.*, RG 108, Telegrams Received; copy, DLC-USG, V, 54. On Jan. 2, 1867, Maj. George K. Leet wrote to the AGO. "The Adjutant General will issue an order directing Brevet Major General E. R. S. Canby, Commanding Department Washington, to put the 30th U S. Infantry en route for Omaha, Nebraska, via Chicago, Illinois, and Clinton, Iowa, to report to Lt-Gen. Sherman, the Q. M. Dept to furnish necessary transportation and General Sherman to receive timely notice of the movement." ALS, DNA, RG 94, Letters Received, 3A 1867. At 1:35 P.M., USG telegraphed to Sherman. "Genl Canby has been directed to send the 30th Infantry to Omaha by the route you suggest. You will be notified when it leaves here" Telegram sent, *ibid.*, RG 107, Telegrams Collected (Bound); copies, *ibid.*, RG 108, Telegrams Sent; DLC-USG, V, 56. On Jan. 3, Bvt. Maj. Gen. Philip St. George Cooke, Omaha, Nebraska Territory, telegraphed to Brig. Gen. John A. Rawlins. "I wish much thirteenth (13) Regt be armed with breech loaders before they leave Washington" Telegram received (at 5:45 P.M.), DNA, RG 108, Telegrams Received; copy, DLC-USG, V, 55. On Jan. 4, Leet wrote to Bvt. Maj. Gen. Edward R. S. Canby. "Gen. Grant desires that you arm the 30th Infy. with the Spencer Carbine previous to its starting, calling upon the Ordnance Dept. for the arms, &c." Copies, *ibid.*, V, 47, 60; DNA, RG 108, Letters Sent. At 1:30 P.M., Bvt. Brig. Gen. Cyrus B. Comstock telegraphed to Cooke. "The 30th Infantry will be armed here with Spencer Carbines" Telegram sent, *ibid.*, RG 107, Telegrams Collected (Bound); copies, *ibid.*, RG 108, Telegrams Sent; DLC-USG, V, 55.

On Dec. 21, 1866, Col. Henry B. Carrington, 18th Inf., Fort Phil Kearny, Dakota Territory, twice telegraphed to USG. "I send copy of dispatch to Genl Cooke simply as a case when in uncertain Communication I think you should know the facts at once. I want all my officers I want men. Depend upon it as I wrote in July no treaty but hard fighting is to assure this line I have had no reason to think otherwise I will operate all winter whatever the season if supported but to redeem my pledge to open and guarantee this line I must have reinforcements and the best of arms up to my full estimate." "Do send me reinforcements forthwith expedition Now with my force is impossible—I risk everything but the post & its store I venture as much as any one can but I have had today a fight unexampled in Indian warfare My loss is ninety four (94) Killed I have recovered forty nine bodies and thirty five more are to be brought in in the morning that have been found. Among the Killed are Bvt Lt Col Fetterman Capt F. H. Brown and Lt Grummond—The Indians engaged were nearly three thousand (3000) being apparently the force reported as on Tongue River in my despatches of the 5th of November and subsequent thereto. This line so important, can and must be held It will take four times the force in the spring to reopen if it be broken up this winter I hear nothing of my arms that left Leavenworth Sept fifteenth additional Cavalry ordered to join has not reported their arrival would have saved us much loss today The Indians lost beyond all preceedent I need prompt reinforcements and repeating arms I am sure to have as before reported an active winter & must have men & arms every officer of this battallion should join it today I have every teamster on duty & best [*but*] one hundred & nineteen left at post I hardly need urge this matter it speaks for itself Give me two 2 Cos of Cavalry at least forthwith well armed or four Co's of Infantry exclusive of what I need at Reno and Ft Smith I did not overestimate my ~~party~~ early application a single Co promptly will save the line but our Killed show that any remissness will result in mutilation & butchery beyond precedent No such, mutilation as that tody is on record Depend on it that this post will be held so long as a round or man is left. Promptness is the vital thing Give me officers and men. only the new Spencer arms should be sent. The Indians desperate and they spare none" Telegrams received (marked as sent by courier to Fort Laramie—received on Dec. 26, 3:15 P.M.), DNA, RG 107, Telegrams Collected (Bound); *ibid.*, RG 108, Telegrams Received; copies (printed), *ibid.*, RG 46, Senate 40A–G7, Reports, Interior; *ibid.*, RG 107, Letters Received from Bureaus; DLC-USG, V, 54. On Dec. 27, USG forwarded copies of these telegrams to Secretary of War Edwin M. Stanton. ES, DNA, RG 107, Letters Received from Bureaus. On Dec. 26, Cooke telegraphed to Rawlins. "On the twenty first. inst three 3 of officers & ninety (90) men Cavalry and Infantry were massacred by Indians Very near Ft Philip Kearney—Indians reported near three-thousand probably from Completeness of the massacre I order up four 4 Companies of Infantry and two 2 of Cavalry from Laramie. I order Col Carrington to Caspar Haad Qrs of the New eighteenth ıIf not approved I request the assignment of Gen Wessells at Reno at his rank to command Dist Just recd at least five leaves of absence of officers of these troops It is important that all these officers be ordered to join Send direct in Gen Shermans absence Bt Lt Col Fetterman Capt Brown and Lieut Grummond are the officers Killed. Not a man was left alive. Shall report by mail" Telegram received (marked as received at 3:25 P.M.), *ibid.*, Telegrams Collected (Bound); *ibid.*, RG 108, Telegrams Received; copies (one sent by mail), *ibid.*, Letters Received; *ibid.*, RG 107, Letters Received from Bureaus; DLC-USG, V, 54. On Dec. 27, USG forwarded a copy of this telegram to Stanton. ES, DNA, RG 107, Letters Received from Bureaus. On Dec. 26, 3:15 P.M., Comstock telegraphed to Cooke. "Gen'l Grant desires me to say that your despatch of today is received. Your action in Col Carrington's case is approved and if you deem it still necessary you are authorized to assign Gen'l Wessels as proposed. Suspend all leaves of absence until you think they can be safely granted" Telegram sent, *ibid.*, Telegrams Collected (Bound); copies, *ibid.*, RG 108, Letters Sent; DLC-USG, V, 47, 60. On Dec. 27, Cooke wrote to Rawlins. "I communicated yesterday by telegraph the disastrous news from Fort Philip Kearny: I enclose a copy of Col. Carrington's telegram—an officer's letter states not one escaped!—Dec. 6th a severe skirmish occurred a few miles from that post,—where Lt Bingham 2d Cav.y, Sergt Bowers 18th Inf. were killed, & 1 Sergt and 4 privates were wounded (and 8 horses killed & wounded)—Dec. 11th a private soldier was killed in sight of Fort Reno—I shall enclose several messages of instruction to Col Carrington, as bearing on my subject matter Col. C's. statement that with teamsters he had Dec. 21st 'but 119 men left in the fort', requires the statement that his Dec. 10th report shows an aggregate present of 475.—My special orders to meet this occasion have been mailed to you (as in usual course.) The six companies ordered forward will have the duties of reinforcing perhaps Fort Reno,—opening communication with C F Smith,—reinforcing that, beside Fort Philip Kearny. Deficiency of troops, the season, & amount of supplies at the upper posts, together,—do not admit of ~~further~~ more being sent; I *hope* they will do, and be able to carry out my telegraphic instructions to Genl Wessells; viz, 'I expect you to make Reno safe, with power to forward mails, and to proceed with all other of the six companies ordered to you, above; I hope regular communications can be kept with Fort C F Smith; and that we may be able to chastise indians who may insult the posts; but with great caution; the officers are not equal to their stratagems in the broken ground they know so well; their numbers, it seems now certain, are so very superior.' Col. Carrington is very plausible; an energetic industrious man in garrison: but it is too evident that he has not maintained discipline and that his officers, have no confidence in him;—some of his acts *officially reported*, such as shelling woods where indians had appeared on a previous day, may have by this time, settled his appreciation by indians—Major VanVoast volunteered to lead a short winter expedition of some five companies which I approved, in the abstract; but when he communicated his information, places &c I found it would be too far—(100 miles beyond Reno)—his force too small; all too uncertain for the risk & sufferings. I have always understood that about the first grass, the indian ponies, are unserviceable;—I think it will be practicable to attack them about the 1st of May:—that an additional regiment both of Cavalry and infantry will be the *least* needed; and that they can be placed at Fort Laramie about the 1st of April. at that time they will be able to go by steam, within about 150 miles. I think it will be practicable—as wel as very important, that the migration to Montana—our best new Territory, of arrable land, as well as precious metals—should not be interrupted, by this best route—You will observe Col. Carrington asks for *Spencer* arms—for infantry some of his men have used them—monted—and have since felt the inferiority of the muzzle loading arms: in fact I have had an official report of a cattle guard excusing themselves for not firing on attacking indians, that if they fired, the indians having *revolvers*, they would be defenceless: They *have* revolvers; & it comes to this, that the savages are better armed than the troops!—I therefore earnestly recommend that breech loading Springfield Muskets be now furnished for all these troops:—I found that even the cavalry were generally unfurnished with revolvers: and a telegraphic requisition for a supply for five companies,—with an implied consent of Genl Dyer—of November 6th, has not yet resulted in there being received,—

or heard from." ALS, DNA, RG 108, Letters Received. On Jan. 5, 1867, USG forwarded a copy of this letter to Stanton. ES, *ibid.*, RG 107, Letters Received from Bureaus.

On Dec. 27, 1866, 2:30 P.M., Comstock telegraphed to Sherman, sending a copy of Cooke's telegram to Rawlins. "Gen'l Grant desires me to forward the accompanying telegram from Gen'l Cooke and to say that Gen'l Cooke's action in Col Carringtons case has been approved: that Gen'l Cooke has been authorized to assign Genl Wessels as proposed if he still deems it necessary; and also to suspend all leaves of absence" Telegram sent, *ibid.*, Telegrams Collected (Bound); copies, *ibid.*, RG 108, Letters Sent; DLC-USG, V, 47, 60. On Dec. 28, noon, Comstock telegraphed to Sherman. "Gen'l Grant requests that you will furnish him with any additional information you may receive in reference to the Ft Philip Kearney massacre, and if there has been fault in the matter that you will have it strictly investigated" Telegram sent, DNA, RG 107, Telegrams Collected (Bound); copies, *ibid.*, RG 108, Letters Sent; DLC-USG, V, 47, 60. On the same day, Sherman telegraphed to USG. "Just arrived in time to attend the funeral of my Adjt Gen'l Sawyer—I have given general instructions to Gen'l Cooke about the Sioux—I do not yet understand how the massacre of Col Fettermans party could have been so complete—We must act with vindictive earnestness against the Sioux even to their extermination, men women & children nothing less will reach the root of this case" Telegram received (at 4:45 P.M.), DNA, RG 107, Telegrams Collected (Bound); copies (printed), *ibid.*, RG 46, Senate 40A–G7, Reports, Interior; *ibid.*, RG 108, Letters Sent; DLC-USG, V, 54. On Dec. 29, Sherman telegraphed to Comstock. "Your despatch of yesterday is rec'd—I have another despatch from Gen Cooke but nothing more definite as to the Ft Phil Kearney massacre. A heavy snow storm is prevailing west of Omaha & cuts off communication. I will have the matter fully investigated. In the meantime the Indians must be pursued—and punished. Gen'l Cooke asks for a regiment of Cavalry & one of Infy I will see if the two new Colored Regts now organizing in Gen'l Hancocks Dept can be made available by April 1st—if, not I may have to ask some help from Gen'l Grant. Please ascertain of him if he has any troops he could spare this Spring as we must not overlook this case but must pursue & punish at all hazards—The posts in that quarter are strong and well supplied but it is reported the Sioux have three thousand (3000) warriors well armed and their country is very difficult to operate, in" Telegram received (at 3:00 P.M.), DNA, RG 107, Telegrams Collected (Bound); *ibid.*, RG 108, Telegrams Received; copies (printed), *ibid.*, RG 46, Senate 40A–G7, Reports, Interior; DLC-USG, V, 54. On Dec. 30, Sherman wrote to USG. "As you know, I got back home last Thursday night just in time to attend Sawyers funeral. I had not even heard of his sickness. His father was here, but had arrived too late, to see him alive. He died of typhoid fever, which I am told is now prevailing. I came up from NewOrleans by Rail, passing through Jackson Canton, Grenada, Grand Junction and Jackson Tennessee. Of course all these places looked familiar, and our old marks of Chimneys, twisted rails and blown up locomotives stood at each station & depot. At first I thought it imprudent to risk the trip lest some one might say or do something not agreeable, but wishing to get here so as to spend some of the Holiday Week with the children I concluded to risk it and am glad I did so. I sayw any number of Ex Rebels all the way, and saw or heard nothing that was at all disagreeable. At Jackson Tennessee we missed the Connection and I had to lay over all of one day. A great many people called to see me, and it was hard to realize that only two years ago we were such bitter enemies. A great many people called among them Dr Jackson, and his son Genl W. H. Jackson of the Rebel Cavalry. At NewOrleans I saw Bragg, Dick Taylor, R O Hebert & others, but Hood Longstreet & Beauregard did not call. At first I went to the St Louis Hotel but Sheridan insisted on my & Commodor Alden going to his house which we did. He has a beautiful place, and lives most comfortably, to the envy of all the marriagiable girls of his acquaintance I am very sorry I was not at home when you were at St Louis, and that you did not see Mrs Sherman—She is in that Condition when she did not like to be seen, and that is one reason why I ought to be home in *all* January. After that month if the President wants me to go to the City of Mexico I can easily go, and can reach NewOrleans in two days by Rail, or 5 by Boat—Please say as much to him incidentally as he may suppose I took less interest in the Mexican question than he thinks it merits. Mr Campbell is not exactly the right man in that place—He drinks, and loses all self control when in that Condition—after being at sea two days I made a pledge of abstinence with him which he observed very well and improved amazingly. But as I left him in NewOrleans I saw the signs of a relapse. I think he will not have the patience to see the thing out—but that is none of my business. I would prefer of course to lay low a year or so to recuperate in finances, and next spring I am satisfied both Hancock and Cooke will have an Indian War on hand—It seems inevitable—We Cannot overlook the affair at Phil Kearney, but I am not satisfied with Genl Cooke—or the two officers now up there, Carrington & Wessels.—I think if you can give me a white Regt of Inf—and fill up the 2nd & 3rd Cavalry to 100 privates each we will have troops enough. Of Course every body will call for more men—but I shall insist on seeing what they have fully employed. The Rail Road can now enable us to feed & supply the troops with more ease, it is finished 300 m west of Omaha. If I can be of any use to you in your farm, I can run out there almost any day.—At this momnt I have a bad cold, but hope to shake it off by NewYears.—Give to Mr Dent—Mrs Grant and the children my best wishes for their present & future happiness." ALS, USG 3. See letters and telegram to Lt. Gen. William T. Sherman, Nov. 7, 1866, and Jan. 13, 14, 1867.

Calendar

1866, JAN. 4. Warren Leland, New York City, to USG. "By permission of Gen Van Vleit I shall ship the wine on Govt steamer Louisburgh I hope it will arrive in time for the opening of your new house I wish yourself & family a happy new year"—Telegram received (at 6:00 P.M.), DNA, RG 108, Telegrams Received; copy, DLC-USG, V, 54. Sent by the brother of Capt. William W. Leland, who served USG as commissary before his discharge as of June 24, 1862. Warren, Charles, and William W. Leland operated the Metropolitan Hotel in New York City and later the Grand Union Hotel, Saratoga, N. Y.—*New York Tribune*, Aug. 11, 1879.

1866, JAN. 5. USG endorsement. "Respy. forwarded to the Sec of war with the recommendation that Gen. Mulford be directed to turn over funds & property in his possession belonging to prisoners of war, both kinds, to the AG. of the Army, or Provost Marshal Generl, who will hold the same for further directions, requiring Gen Mulfords reciept for money & property delivered . . . P. S. I would recommend the adoption of General Mulfords views with regard to packages in which there is neither money or valuables—that is, that they be turned over to the Freedmen Bureau in Richmond, where these packages now are"—Copy, DLC-USG, V, 58. Written on a letter of Dec. 30, 1865, from Bvt. Brig. Gen. John E. Mulford, U.S. exchange agent, concerning property taken by C.S.A. authorities from prisoners.—*Ibid.* On Aug. 21, Mulford had written to Bvt. Col. Theodore S. Bowers accounting for funds taken by C.S.A. authorities from U.S. prisoners, funds taken from C.S.A. prisoners by U.S. authorities, and other valuables.—LS, DNA, RG 108, Letters Received. *O.R.*, II, viii, 721–22. See *ibid.*, pp. 722–23. On Aug. 23, Mulford wrote to Bowers. "I have the honor to inform you that in pursuing the examination of prisoners accounts and claims against Confederate Officials I have discovered the names of some of those Federal prisoners who deserted our service and joined the Enemy, enlisting in what was called the 'Foreign Battalion'; all such received their money and other valuables at the time of entering the rebel service. Thinking this information should affect their claims for back pay, bounties &c., I will immediately make a list together with such information as I may be able to gather and forward the same to you."—LS, DNA, RG 108, Letters Received.

1866, JAN. 6. USG endorsement. "The Adjutant General will make the orders within suggested."—ES, DNA, RG 94, Letters Received, 1056G 1865. Written on a letter of Dec. 16, 1865, from Maj. Gen. Philip H. Sheridan, New Orleans, to USG. "I respectfully recommend that the Twenty fifth (25th) Army Corps be discontinued: it is found exceedingly difficult in a place like Texas where communications are so difficult to get timely returns and manage this body of troops under a Corps or Division orginazation. It is best that they should make their reports from the Posts where stationed direct to the District commander. The dissolution of this Corps will be economy to the government and great convenience to the public

Service. Genl Weitzel has made repeated applications to be relieved from his present command and also requests that upon the discontinuance of the Twenty fifth Corps, which he has commanded Since its orginization, he may be ordered to his home in Cincinnati to report by letter to the Adjutant General of the Army. He is anxious to have this done & if my request is acceded to I can then relieve him."—LS, *ibid.*

1866, JAN. 6, 1:10 P.M. To Bvt. Maj. Gen. Charles R. Woods, Mobile, Ala. "You will order the Judge Advocate to be present in New York at the deposition of citizen Jno. F. Collins—"—LS (telegram sent), DNA, RG 107, Telegrams Collected (Bound); telegram sent, *ibid.*; copies, *ibid.*, RG 108, Letters Sent; DLC-USG, V, 47, 109. On Jan. 3, Woods had telegraphed to Brig. Gen. John A. Rawlins. "The defence in the Dexter case pending in this Dept have applied for postponement of fifteen 15 days to obtain the deposition of Jno F. Collins Citizen at N Y City It is necessary that the Judge advocate of the commission be present when each evidence is taken—Shall I order him to N Y for that purpose—Collins has neglected to obey subpoena served on him"—Telegram received, DNA, RG 108, Telegrams Received; (press) *ibid.*, RG 107, Telegrams Collected (Bound); copy, DLC-USG, V, 54.

1866, JAN. 8. Bvt. Col. Theodore S. Bowers to Maj. Gen. William T. Sherman. "L[ieut]enant General Grant directs me to call your attention to the marked paragraph in the accompanying newspaper, relating to an expedition under Gen. Heath against Indians, and to say that he desires no offensive operations to be undertaken against the Indians unless in your judgment such a campaign is absolutely necessary. He also desires to suggest that if Gen. Heath is a (full) Brigadier General, he should be relieved and ordered home; and that if he is a Brevet Brigadier General, serving with his regiment, you muster out his regiment at the earliest practicable date."—Copies, DLC-USG, V, 47, 109; DNA, RG 108, Letters Sent; *ibid.*, RG 393, Military Div. of the Mo., Letters Received. On Jan. 15, Sherman wrote to Bowers. "I had the honor to receive your letter without signature of Jan 8. enclosing a newspaper, calling my attention to a paragraph therein. The General Heath therein referred to is a Colonel of Volunteers, & Bvt Brig Genl of Vols, temporarily assigned to duty with his Brevet Rank, on the Special application of Maj Genl Wheeton in Command of the Sub. District of the Platte. I had seen the paragraph before, but construed it to be the usual & popular mode of creating a little cheap glory that is too common in our country. If got up by himself, and it results in his summary discharge, he will find it's cost more than he reckoned. I have sent your letter and enclosure to General Pope with an endorsement to be governed by it."—ALS, *ibid.*, RG 108, Letters Received. On Feb. 6, Bvt. Maj. Gen. Frank Wheaton, Omaha, endorsed Bowers's letter stating that Col. and Bvt. Brig. Gen. Herman H. Heath, 7th Iowa Cav., had "acted under detailed instructions from me in the operation refered to, and I acted under the Orders of Maj Genl G M Dodge Copies of which are herewith enclosed, my written instruction from the Department Commander requiring me to obey such Orders. I sincereily hope this explanation may be laid before the Lieutenant General Commanding the Armies of the United States at an early date, . . ."—ES, *ibid.*, RG 393, Military Div. of the Mo., Letters Received. On Jan. 20, Sherman had forwarded to USG's hd. qrs. a letter of Jan. 16 from Maj. Gen. John Pope, St. Louis, to Sherman disclaiming knowledge of Heath's activities.—AES and LS, *ibid.*, RG 108, Letters Received. Also on Jan. 16, Pope wrote to Sherman enclosing papers concerning operations against Indians endorsed on Jan. 20 by Sherman. "Respectfully forwarded to the Lt Genl Comdg the armies of the U. S. in further explanation of the subject referred by him to me—No movemt against Indians will be made further than on mere marauders, without due deliberation."—LS and AES, *ibid.* On Jan. 20, Sherman wrote to Brig. Gen. John A. Rawlins. "I enclose herewith a letter of Jan 16. from Maj Genl Pope Comdg Dept of Mo. not so much for any facts it embraces, but for the spirit he displays, in endeavoring to carry out the well known wishes of the Lt Genl Comdg the Armies of the U. S. We did endeavor to reach before winter all the Volunteers in service, but the Regulars assigned to me, came so late that it was physically impossible to push them further than Laramie and Fort Wyse. Even then many were frostbitten and damaged by the intense cold on the Plains, and many of the volunteers relieved only reached Fort Leavenworth for Muster Out, after winter had closed the Missouri River, and made travelling dangerous & expensive. As soon as Spring comes, General Pope will renew his efforts and replace all volunteers in the remote North West—in Utah and NewMexico. You need not notice so much of Gen Popes letter as refers to Capt Sokalski, for the Genl fell into the error of supposing Capt Sokalskis letter to have come from your HeadQuarters, where as it came from me. I have given him all instructions necessary on that point, and as soon as the preliminary inquiries can be made Gen Heath will be discharged. Genl Heath has a good reputation in Nebraska, but like most volunteer officers likes to make as much political capital as he can out of his military service, but the Lt Genl Commdg may rest easy, that ~~he~~ Genl Heath will not be permitted to involve us in any serious complications with the Indian Tribes."—ALS, *ibid.*

On June 22, USG favorably endorsed a letter of April 26 from Wheaton to the AGO recommending Heath for promotion to bvt. maj. gen. and nine other officers for bvt. promotion.—ES and LS, *ibid.*, RG 94, ACP, 497W CB 1866. On July 11, Heath wrote to Secretary of War Edwin M. Stanton. ". . . My unlawful and highly improper muster out by direction from the Hed Quarters of the Army, so promptly & so justly revoked by you, has, notwithstanding the revocation, been of great detriment to me personally in Nebraska, the new home of my adoption; and something more than the mere revocation of the Order seems necessary, to assure public sentiment that I am honorably held by the War Department. The brevet promotion to which I am recommended by Gen. Wheaton, my late immediate commander, would at this, and in all future time be a certain and efficient source of appeal, whenever unjustly aspersed upon the ground of the dishonorable discharge to which I was subjected in May. . . ."—ALS, *ibid.*, H635 CB 1866. On July 21, USG endorsed this letter. "Gen. Wheaton's recommendation for Gen Heath was approved June 22. 66."—ES, *ibid.* Heath was honorably discharged as of July 1.

1866, JAN. 8. To Col. Henry K. Craig. "I desire to invite your special attention to the application now before you, of J. W. Walsh, late Colonel of the 3rd Pennsylvania Cavalry. He served in the regular army for many years before the breaking out of the late war, served in the Volunteer force *with credit*, during the rebellion, and is very anxious to again enter the regular army."—Copies, DLC-USG, V, 47, 109; DNA, RG 108, Letters Sent.

1866, JAN. 9. To Secretary of War Edwin M. Stanton. "I have the honor to recommend that Hamilton P. Bee, late a Brigadier General in the rebel service, and now in Havanna, be allowed to return to the United States on parole."—LS, DNA, RG 94, Letters Received, 964A 1866. Hamilton P. Bee did not return to the U.S. until 1876.

1866, JAN. 9. To Bvt. Maj. Gen. Edward D. Townsend. "please order Bvt. Brig Gen. D. Butterfield to report to Maj. Gen. Hooker, for duty with his Bvt. rank to take the place made vacant by the resegnation of Gen. Burnham"—Copies, DLC-USG, V, 47, 109; DNA, RG 108, Letters Sent.

1866, JAN. 11. To Secretary of War Edwin M. Stanton. "I would respectfully recommend that Bvt. Brig. Gen. Geo. Crook be advanced to the rank of Maj. Gn. by Brevet. I would also recommend Bvt. Col. H. Wallen for the grade of Bvt. Brig. General."—ALS, DNA, RG 94, ACP, G6 CB 1866. On Jan. 2, 4:00 P.M., Bvt. Maj. Gen. Edward D. Townsend had telegraphed to Maj. Gen. Henry W. Halleck. "What are the charges against Colonel Wallen? General Grant would like them dismissed if not too serious—"—ALS (telegram sent), *ibid.*, RG 107, Telegrams Collected (Bound).

1866, JAN. 11. USG endorsement. "Michael Dunn has been employed for several years at my Head Quarters, and has always proven himself an industrious and most efficient man in charge of Army transportation. I take pleasure in commending him to the concideration of whomsoever he may engage in business with."—AES, DNA, RG 94, ACP, D69 CB 1866. Written on an unaddressed letter of Jan. 10 from Bvt. Col. Theodore S. Bowers. "I have personally known the bearer Mr Michael Dunn, for four years past, and cheerfully certify his good character. He enlisted in the 8th Regiment Missouri Infantry Volunteers in the beginning of the war, and was distinguished for gallantry in that famous Regiment. At Vicksburg Miss., in the summer of 1863 he was detailed for special duty at Gen. Grant's Headquarters and placed in charge of the camp and trains; was with Gen. Grant at Chattanooga, and throughout the campaign in Virginia terminating with the surrender of Lee's army at Appomattox, C. H.—always discharging his duties faithfully and rendering entire satisfaction. Mr. Dunn is possessed of great business energy, and is strictly reliable and trustworthy. I take great pleasure in commending him as a deserving man to the favorable consideration of any one to whom this letter is presented"—ALS, *ibid.* On March 3, USG wrote to Secretary of War Edwin M. Stanton. "Mr M. Dunn is an applicant for the position of Sutler at Fort Leavenworth I have known him for some time, he has served through the War faithfully, I consider him a proper person for the appointment"—LS, *ibid.* On April 30, 10:00 A.M., USG telegraphed to Bvt. Maj. Gen. William Hoffman. "You may suspend the change of Sutlership at Leavenworth to give present encumbent reasonable time to dispose of his stock and buildings without too great a sacrifice"—Telegram sent, *ibid.*, RG 107, Telegrams Collected (Bound); copies, *ibid.*, RG 108, Letters Sent; DLC-USG, V, 47, 109. On May 8, Michael L. Dunn, Fort Leavenworth, twice telegraphed to USG. "I am amply prepared to meet all demands and carry on the business at once but parties here are endeavoring to prevent me from taking possession I require more assistance from the commanding officer here" "I offered to buy this building & goods & pay him one third (⅓) cash & the balance with good security also to purchase for Cash nine thousand (9000) dollars which he rejected Gen Thayer trying to dispossess me I have my goods here & incurring expenses daily. Can you assist me"—Telegrams received (both at 3:35 P.M.), DNA, RG 107, Telegrams Collected (Bound); *ibid.*, RG 108, Telegrams Received; copies, DLC-USG, V, 54. On the same day, Dunn wrote to USG. "I feel in duty bound, to explain fully the telegrams sent to you—this day—I could see no other way—and I trust General—you will excuse me—if I am trespassing too much—on your so valuable time—I arrived here on the 23d ult—On the morning of the 24th, I presented myself to the Comd'g-Officer—Bvt. Major Genl: Hoffman, who—after reading the proper papers—received me most courteously. The late Sutler was absent, at this time, and in order to give him an opportunity to settle his business, I consented to wait till the 5th of May—All this was done with the knowledge and approval of the Comd'g: Officer.—But now—General—instead of a ready settlement on the part of the late sutler—he still insists upon a further postponement—he declines to accept my securities or proposals of any kind—and further—declares about the town, 'that my appointment will be revoked—and all he wants—is time.' Of Course, I take all this for what it is worth, but I am sorry to say, that although I have used my utmost endeavors, to commence business—being recognized officially as the Sutler, and have offered to prove and show to the Comd'g: Officer, that the means at my Command are all that can be required—*I am still denied the possession of the store*—There is no doubt in my mind but that underhanded means are used, in order to prevent my taking possession of it—and I respectfully solicit your further kind assistance. In conclusion, I deem it proper to state, that since my arrival—I have been under heavy expenses—for merchandize and people in my employ—"—ALS, DNA, RG 108, Letters Received. On May 9, 12:10 P.M., Bvt. Col. Ely S. Parker telegraphed to Hoffman. "You will please put Sutler M L Dunn in possession of all the rights and privaleges appertaining to the post sutlery at Fort Leavenworth, to which he has been appointed, that he may enter upon the duties and enjoyment thereof without further delay"—ALS (telegram sent), *ibid.*, RG 107, Telegrams Collected (Bound); copies, *ibid.*, RG 108, Letters Sent; DLC-USG, V, 47, 109. On May 10, USG wrote to Hoffman. "Conflicting dispatches having been received here as to the disposition of Dunn, the newly appointed Sutler of Fort Leavenworth, to buy out the former sutlers, and feeling a desire to see the former sutlers have a fair opportunity to sell or remove their goods without too great a sacrifice, I now authorize you to adjust the matter between Dunn and Haas as you deem equitable. You can give Haas reasonable time, say thirty days, in which to sell or remove their goods, or if they are unreasonable in their demands you may give such directions as you deem proper."—Copies, *ibid.* On May 14, Dunn telegraphed to USG. "I am in possession of the store—many thanks for your kindness"—Telegram received (at 12:50 P.M.), DNA, RG 108, Telegrams Received; copy, DLC-USG, V, 54. On May 16, Hoffman wrote to USG. "I have the honor to acknowledge the receipt of your letter of the 10th inst. in relation to the change of Sutlers at this post, and beg leave to submit the following report of the case for your information. Mr. Haas the late sutler was absent when Mr. Dunn arrived and did not return until about two weeks after. Then, after consulting the parties and hearing their propositions, I proposed as a compromise, that Mr. Dunn should pay $3000 in cash for the store houses,—the price at which they were offered,—take all the saleable goods at wholesale prices to be determined by disinterested parties, paying therefore $5000. in cash and the balance by monthly notes running eight months, with interest, to be secured by a mortgage on the store and goods. Mr. Haas was not satisfied with the security, nor would he accept as endorser a gentlemen of Leavenworth City offered by Mr. Dunn, who is a contractor said by some to be a responsible man, and he declined the proposition. Under the instructions contained in your telegram of the 30th ult. and a subsequent one from the Adjt. Genl. I then authorized Mr. Haas to occupy his store and continue to trade as Sutler for thirty days, credit sales to soldiers to cease on the 31 inst. when Mr. Dunn would be permitted to take possession of one room of the store buildings for the sale of goods. At the expiration of the thirty days Mr. Haas was to turn over the store houses with all their fixtures to Mr. Dunn for $3000 in cash. Both parties accepted these terms and the arrangement was about to be carried out when I received your instructions of the 9th inst. through Col. Parker, directing me to place Mr. Dunn in possession of all the rights and privileges of sutler of this post without farther delay, and accordingly on the following day, the store was vacated by Mr.

Haas and Mr. Dunn put in possession, he paying $3000. in cash for it. Today, pursuant to your instructions of the 10th inst. I have authorized Mr. Haas to remain in his dwelling house and offer there for sale, the goods he he has on hand for thirty days from this date. At the end of that time I shall expect him, unless there is good reason for further delay, to make a satisfactory sale of the house to Mr. Dunn as the sutler for whose use it was permitted to be erected There has been much feeling between the parties, each making charges against the other, but to me both have professed a desire to do whatever was fair and reasonable."—ALS, DNA, RG 108, Letters Received.

1866, JAN. 12, 10:20 A.M. To Maj. Gen. Philip H. Sheridan. "If you can dispense with the 34th [In]diana regiment muster it out of service."—ALS (telegram sent), DNA, RG 107, Telegrams Collected (Bound); telegram sent, *ibid.*; copies, *ibid.*, RG 108, Letters Sent; DLC-USG, V, 47, 109. On Jan. 13, Sheridan telegraphed to USG. "The thirty fourth 34 Indiana Regt has been ordered mustered out in accordance with your request of Jany twelfth 12 by telegraph"—Telegram received (at 5:30 P.M.), DNA, RG 108, Telegrams Received; copies, *ibid.*, RG 393, Dept. of the Gulf, Telegrams Sent; DLC-USG, V, 54; DLC-Philip H. Sheridan.

1866, JAN. 12. USG endorsement. "Respectfully forwarded. I have known Mr. Johnson for a number of years and can endorse him as an honest truthful and reliable man. If appointments are to be made in the Pay Dept. from others than those who have served as such during the War then I would earnestly recommend him"—AES, DNA, RG 94, ACP, J21 CB 1866. Written on a letter of Jan. 6, 186[*6*], from Henry Johnson, medical storekeeper, to Secretary of War Edwin M. Stanton asking an appointment as paymaster.—ALS (misdated 1865), *ibid.* See *PUSG*, 9, 582–83.

1866, JAN. 12. Henry C. Burnett, Washington, D. C., to USG. "While I was South, and in the State of Virginia, I purchased of Epperson twenty four Boxes of manufactured Tobacco, for which I paid him and received the Tobacco and left it in the custody of B. F. Dyer Esq of Henry cty Va—Some time after I left Va, Mr Epperson went to the town of Danville, and upon his exparte statement, that the consideration which I paid him had become by reason of the South having failed in the war worthless, the Provost Marshal, sent up to Henry cty, a body of Soldiers, with this man Epperson who demanded of Mr Dyer who was the custodian of the Tobacco its delivery, he refused to give it up and the soldiers then took forcible possession of it and carried it to Danville and the provost Marshal delivered the same to Epperson—I Submit, that the military authorities had no jurisdiction of the rights of citizens arising upon contracts between them; and the Courts being open in the State of Virginia, Mr Epperson had his remedy against me, and if he had been wronged, his rights could be fully adjudicated—I made this representation to the to the provost Marshal through

B. F. Gravely Esq of Va. and the provost Marshal, agreed that his decision had been wrong and that the Tobacco should be delivered to me; he thereupon Sent a Guard and had Mr Epperson arrested and assured my agent that he might rest assured the Tobacco should be delivered Mr Gravely went on to Baltimore informed me what had been done and thatt the provost Marshal would make Epperson Surrender the Tobacco—when Mr G returned from Baltimore, he called upon the provost Marshal, who told him he had changed his mind and left the Tobacco in the possession of—Epperson—Upon the receipt of this information from Mr Gravely I came on here, and now ask you for an Order directing the provost Marshal at Danville, ~~directing him~~ to have this Tobacco redelivered to me or to require Epperson to pay the market value of the same—In a word I ask that I may be put in Statu quo in regard to my property as it was at the time the military authorities took it out of my possession."—ALS, DNA, RG 109, Union Provost Marshals' File of Papers Relating to Two or More Civilians. Burnett, expelled as U.S. representative from Ky. in Dec., 1861, later served as C.S.A. senator from Ky. On April 6, 1865, Burnett sold four slaves to W. S. Epperson for twenty-four boxes of tobacco; Epperson later claimed that since slavery had been abolished already by the lawful (loyal) government of Va., the sale was invalid.—*Ibid.*

1866, JAN. 13. USG endorsement. "I heartily recommend Amnesty to R. F. Hoke, late a General in the Southern Army. The wording of the within application~~s~~ in my opinion gives a good guarantee for the future, coming from an officer of the standing of Genl Hoke."—AES, DNA, RG 94, Amnesty Papers, N. C. Written on a letter of Jan. 8 from Robert F. Hoke, Lincolnton, N. C., to President Andrew Johnson.—LS, *ibid.* Docketing indicates that Hoke was pardoned on June 14, 1867.

1866, JAN. 13. USG endorsement. "I would most respectfully recommend Reuben R. Frazier for the appointment of Cadet at West Point for next June as a reward for his services in the rebellion and for what has been done by his family."—AES, DNA, RG 94, Cadet Applications. Written on a letter of Dec. 22, 1865, from Stephen R. Frazier, Brooklyn, to USG. "At the breaking out of the Rebellion I with my family was living in the town of Belle Plain, Marshall Co State of Illinois. At the first call for three years Men by President Lincoln in 1861 My oldest Son Franklin B. Frazier enlisted in Co "I" 11th Regt Ills Vol Inftry and Served with his Regt in all its various Marches and Skirmishes up to the battle of 'Fort Donaldson', where he received three wounds, of which he was laid up for about Seventy days, when he rejoined his Regt & remained with it up to the time of his death; which was the result of a wound received June 14th, before Vicksburgh: his death occured June 19th. At the 'Call' of 1862, Myself and Second Son enlisted in Co "K" 107th Regt Ills Vol Inftry, with which we served untill Mustered out of the Service in June 1865. While Genl

Sherman's Army was lying encamped on the banks of the Etowah river, I made application to Majr Genl J. M. Schofield, to have My Secd Son R. R. Frazier, appointed as a Cadet in the Military Academy at West Point, which was sent up approved by all the Officers in charge of the 2nd Division 23rd A. C at the time, Genl Schofield had a conversation with the Young Man, and promised him to use his influence to have him appointed. After we were mustered out, and had come on to to New York, My Son called upon Genl Schofield who expressed himself very much Surprized that he was not at West Point; and told him to See the Hon Moses F. Odell of this City and that he would endorse any recommendation he would give him to President Johnson; this recommendation and endorsement he has, also the recommendation of Several influential Gentlemaen of this City. The Young Man is Still anxious to get an appointment to the Military School at West Point and I thought, a Simple Statement of facts in regard to what we as a family had tried to do in an humble way for our Country might interest you in his behalf, in obtaining Such an appointment for the Comeing Season"—ALS, *ibid.*

1866, JAN. 15. To Secretary of War Edwin M. Stanton. "I have the honor to make requisition for Five Thousand Dollars ($5000) of the appropriation for 'Expenses of Commanding General's Office' and request that the warrant may be drawn in favor of Major Geo. K. Leet, Asst. Adjt. Gen., of my Staff."—Copies, DLC-USG, V, 47, 109; DNA, RG 108, Letters Sent.

1866, JAN. 15. To Thomas Stewardson, corresponding secretary, Academy of Natural Sciences. "I have the honor to acknowledge the receipt of a diploma of member ship in the Academy of Natural Sciences of Philadelphia and of your letter announcing my election as Life Member of the same institution. I beg you to convey my thanks to the Academy for the compliment thus paid me, and to receive yourself my acknowledgments for the very Kind language in which it is communicated."—LS, Academy of Natural Sciences, Philadelphia, Pa. On Jan. 13, Stewardson, Philadelphia, had written to USG. "I have the honor of transmitting to you this day by mail your diploma of membership in the Acad. of Natural Sciences of Philad.—I have also the pleasure to inform you that at a meeting subsequent to that of your election, you were created a 'Life member' of the institution; the Acad. by this action desiring to give you the fullest expression of the exalted estimate which they place upon your services in the cause of our common country."—ALS, USG 3.

1866, JAN. 16. To Secretary of War Edwin M. Stanton. "I would respectfully recommend that the Qr. Mr. Gen. be directed to continue to pay rent for the Douglas House until it is restored to its former condition, agreeable to contract, and delivered to the owner."—ALS, DNA, RG 107, Letters Received from Bureaus.

1866, JAN. 16. USG endorsement. "Gen Chamberlain having been disabled by wounds recieved in the service from prosecuting his duties in civil life, his muster out with the first batch of General Officer was contrary to the rule then established. I would now respectfully recommend that the order in his case be revoked and the muster-out be made to take effect from 15th Jany 1866. I understand General Chamberlain has yet to undergo a severe surgical operation before he can possibly recover from the wounds recieved in 1864."—Copy (undated), DLC-USG, V, 58; typescript (dated Jan. 16), Atwood Collection, InU; DLC-Joshua L. Chamberlain. Written on a letter of Dec. 20, 1865, from U.S. Senator Lot M. Morrill of Maine *et al.* to President Andrew Johnson requesting that Brig. Gen. Joshua L. Chamberlain be retained as brig. gen. of vols.—Typescript, *ibid.* Chamberlain was mustered out as of Jan. 15, 1866.

1866, JAN. 16. USG endorsement. "S. B. Maxey resigned from the Regular Army in 1849 and afterwards settled in Texas. I knew him well as a Cadet at West Point and afterwards as a Lieut. in the Mexican war. I believe him to be well worthy of Executive clemency and heartily recommend it."—AES, DNA, RG 94, Amnesty Papers, Tex. Written on a letter of Jan. 8 from Governor Thomas E. Bramlette of Ky. to President Andrew Johnson requesting a pardon for Samuel B. Maxey, former C.S.A. maj. gen.—ALS, *ibid.* On March 23, 1867, Maxey, Paris, Tex., wrote to USG. "*Unofficial.* . . . In January 186~~5~~6, I solicited in person your kind offices on my behalf in the matter of my 'pardon' which were cheerfully rendered by you, and gratefully received by me. Many of my friends did likewise. Amongst others, Gov. Bramlette of Ky, and Senator Guthrie,—the latter visiting the President in company with me. The President granted me authority to resume the practice of the law; from which I had been suspended (along with others in the same condition) by a proclamation of A. J. Hamilton, then acting as Govr of this State. He declined to endorse my application for the sole (assigned) reason that I was a graduate of West Point. It never occurred to me until recently that the delay may have been occasioned by the fact that my application was not endorsed by the Govr of my State—and the delay was otherwise unaccountable, as I was led to believe by what the President said to Mr Guthrie, Mr Grider from my old Ky. District and myself, that I might expect my pardon shortly after the interview, (the day after I saw you) For this reason, and knowing Govr Throckmorton well, I wrote to him not long since, and herewith enclose his letter to the President. I have no one that I can call on so well as yourself, at Washington, to bear this letter, and I again ask your kind offices, and that you will speak personally to the President on my behalf—In view of recent political action, I would feel far better satisfied relieved of this incubus."—ALS, *ibid.* On March 14, Governor James W. Throckmorton of Tex. had written to Johnson on Maxey's behalf.—LS, *ibid.* On April 13, USG endorsed this letter. "Respectfully submitted to His Excellency the President of the U S." —ES, *ibid.* Docketing indicates that Maxey was pardoned on July 22.

1866, JAN. 17, 10:55 A.M. To Bvt. Maj. Gen. John G. Barnard. "You are authorized to visit Washington, D. C., to attend the coming meeting of the Academy of Science."—LS (telegram sent), DNA, RG 107, Telegrams Collected (Bound); telegram sent, *ibid.*; copies, *ibid.*, RG 108, Letters Sent; DLC-USG, V, 47, 109.

1866, JAN. 17. To Bvt. Col. Adam Badeau. "I am going to the Senate Chamber to hear the speaches on reconstruc[tion] this afternoon and will not be back to the office agai[n.] Please tell the orderly that brings my horse to return with him as I wil[l] go home in the Cars."—ALS, Munson-Williams-Proctor Institute, Utica, N. Y.

1866, JAN. 18. Maj. Gen. Philip H. Sheridan, New Orleans, to USG. "I send you to day a map showing the operations of the Cavalry under my command in Virginia from May 4th 1864 to April 9th 1865; also the march from Petersburg to North Carolina, which terminated after crossing the Dan river at South Boston, in consequence of the surrender of the army in front of Sherman. To you and to no one else am I indebted for the handsome record which the Cavalry made in this short period. I had two ideas about Cavalry during this period. The first was when I was in Eastern Virginia; that the cavalry should fight the enemy's Cavalry, and our Infantry fight the enemy's Infantry. You enabled me to carry this out, and the result was the destruction of the esprit and almost annihilation of the Rebel cavalry. The second idea was when I arrived in the Shenandoah Valley; that I would fight both arms of the service together, and this I adhered to. The character of the country suggested it, and it was a success, and it was you who enabled me to accomplish this. May I respectfully then in the name of the Cavalry thank you for giving a standard to the Cavalry of which it is proud; but which does not yet fully illustrate the great power in this arm of the service, in offensive warfare. . . . Note. The Cross-Sabres on the map represent battles only: the skirmishes were innumerable"—LS, DNA, RG 108, Letters Received. See *O.R. Atlas*, Plate LXXIV, no. 1.

1866, JAN. 18. Governor Reuben E. Fenton of N. Y. to USG. "The Seventh Regiment of New York is very desirous that you should attend a reception to be given to its members, who have served in the Regular and Volunteer Army of the United States during the late war on the 31st of this month This organization has acquired a reputation almost National, by its precision of drill and fine military bearing, and would highly appreciate your acceptance of their invitation I hope you may find it consistent with your duties to be present on the occasion"—LS, USG 3.

1866, JAN. 18. Anonymous officer, 6th U.S. Vols., Dakota Territory, to USG. "Allow me to call your attention to the fact that the Sixth Regt of U. S. Vols. is of no account whatever on these plains and is demoralized to such an extent that it is a disgrace to the service, one company has lost fifty eight men by desertion since last Spring (when it was organized) and I do not suppose there is over one or two companies that have lost many less than that number—I should have mentioned before that the Regt was enlisted and made up of prisoners of war and is of entirely the wrong material for U. S. Soldiers they enlisted for the purpose of getting out of prison and nothing else, as I have heard many of them say, and they will all desert sooner or later. there is a rumor that they will be ordered to Salt Lake in the Spring if that is the case there will be scarcely a man left by the time the command is ready to move after receiving the order. You may think Genl. that some lunatic wrote this letter, but I can assure you that it is a fact every word I have written, the Officers are disgusted with the command but can not resign for *that* reason, for fear they would be 'dismissed for resigning for insufficient cause.' I could and would come out over my own signature and make a grand expose of the whole thing but of course I would lay my self liable to the disagreeable (but quite posible) position of proving my statement when I am out of the service I will give you my name and satisfy you that what I have said is true. I would willingly give it you now but I would only get a 'rap over the knuckles' for my pains, there fore I prefer to write anonymously. I presume as the Regt is so much scattered that no Regt Returns get to the War Dept untill they are due two or three months. but just look over the last ones that *have* been recd and see if you think a Regt. that is loosing men as fast as it is. is of any account. or if there can be any discipline in it. Hoping that you will interest your self in this matter I remain Genl. your humble servant. . . . If you wish to learn who I am, for reasons not detrimental to me, means will readily occur to you to find me out. I send this to be mailed by a friend at some place east of here, for my own preservation. P. S. Col Potter is on duty near Salt Lake City Lt. Col. Smith at Fort Bridger U T. and Maj. Norton at Laramie D. T. all comdg. Posts, they do not want to be mustered out not *they* nor are they any of them going to call attention to Genl. Orders No 86 nor 182 A. G. O. 1863 Oh no! but a poor *line* officer that must serve with their compy. and be called 'galvanized' by other officers (though not before their faces) *they* want to get away from the disgracefull organization.—I know Genl. that anonomous writers are generaly supposed to be slanderers but just look into this thing a *little* and see if this is not an *exception*"—AL, DNA, RG 108, Letters Received. On Feb. 14, Bvt. Col. Theodore S. Bowers endorsed this letter. "Respectfully referred to Major General Sherman, Comdg. Military Div. of the Mississippi."—ES, *ibid.* On April 2, Maj. Gen. William T. Sherman endorsed this letter. "Respectfully returned to the Genl. in Chief and attention invited to report of Bvt. Mg. Genl. Wheaton." —ES, *ibid.* The report of Bvt. Maj. Gen. Frank Wheaton is *ibid.*

1866, JAN. 19. Maj. Gen. William T. Sherman to Brig. Gen. John A. Rawlins. "The foregoing was called for by me to enable me to obey the 4th Par of Gen Order No 168. Instead of making specific recommendations I beg to submit the above in confidence that it may not prejudice Officers in actual service. I have no personal or official knowledge of Generals Conner, Wheaton, or Carleton but I do know Generals Corse & Upton to be young, brave & endowed to command. We may need such men, and I should be sorry to lose them. Of General Sully I only know from old association at WestPoint and in the Regular Army. I recommend that no further changes be made, till the Law forces us to make up the New army, out of the materials left on our hands. I will submit the lists of the Generals in the Depts of the Ohio & Arkansas, as soon as I hear from Generals Ord & Reynolds." —ANS (misdated 1865), DNA, RG 108, Letters Received. Written on a letter of Jan. 17 from Maj. Gen. John Pope to Sherman evaluating gen. officers under his command.—LS, *ibid.*

1866, JAN. 22, 10:40 A.M. To Maj. Gen. Philip H. Sheridan. "By all means musterout the three regiments of Cavalry you suggest."—ALS (telegram sent), DNA, RG 107, Telegrams Collected (Bound); telegram sent, *ibid.*; copies, *ibid.*, RG 94, Vol. Service Div., Letters Received, A82 (VS) 1866; *ibid.*, RG 108, Letters Sent; DLC-USG, V, 47, 109. On Jan. 20, Sheridan had telegraphed to USG. "I would like to have permission to muster out three (3) of the volunteer Regts of Cavy in Texas They are very expensive, A good deal dissatisfied and I Could give good Horses to the fourth and Sixth Cavy:"—Telegram received (on Jan. 22, 9:30 A.M.), DNA, RG 108, Telegrams Received; *ibid.*, RG 94, Vol. Service Div., Letters Received, A82 (VS) 1866; copies (one sent by mail), *ibid.*, RG 108, Letters Received; *ibid.*, RG 393, Military Div. of the Southwest and Dept. of the Gulf; DLC-USG, V, 54.

1866, JAN. 22. USG endorsement. "I freely and heartily endorse the application of Mrs. Baldwin for the appointment of her son to West point. I know that Mrs. Baldwin herself has been most patriotic and if she had had a son old enough to enter the Army, during the War, she would not have permitted him to have remained out. Of nine brothers Mrs. B. had at the begining of the War the whole nine, and their father entered the service. I respectfully ask that such endorsement be made on this as will secure the appointment when the Cadet appointments come to be given."—AES, DNA, RG 94, Cadet Applications. Written on a letter of Jan. 18 from Mary I. Baldwin to President Andrew Johnson requesting a USMA appointment for her son William McCook Garard.—ALS, *ibid.*

1866, JAN. 23. USG endorsement. "Respectfully forwarded to the Secretary of War, approved and recommended."—ES, DNA, RG 94, Letters Received, 48W 1866. Written on a letter of the same day from Bvt. Maj. Gen. James H. Wilson to Brig. Gen. John A. Rawlins. "I have the honor to apply for a leave of absence for one year, to enable me to attend to private business."—LS, *ibid.* On Dec. 7, 1865, USG, Augusta, Ga., telegraphed to Secretary of War Edwin M. Stanton. "Please withdraw the muster out of Wilson—Steedman leaves the Department, and I would like

Wilson retained in his absence—"—Telegram received (on Dec. 11, 9:00 A.M.), *ibid.*, RG 107, Telegrams Collected (Bound); copies, *ibid.*, RG 94, ACP, 130 1871; *ibid.*, RG 108, Letters Sent; DLC-USG, V, 46, 109. On Dec. 11, 3:45 P.M., USG, Washington, D. C., telegraphed to Wilson. "The order to muster you out has been revoked. You will remain at Augusta as I wished you to"—Telegrams sent (2), DNA, RG 107, Telegrams Collected (Bound); telegram received, DLC-James Harrison Wilson. On Jan. 8, 1866, Bvt. Maj. Gen. Edward D. Townsend issued Special Orders No. 9 mustering out Wilson as maj. gen. of vols.—Copy, Wy-Ar. Wilson added a note to this order. "*This* was not at my request—nor at Gen'l Grants, The order of Decr 6th *was* at my request—revoked at *request* of Gen. Grant in order that I might take Comd of Dept of Ga. which Comd I assumed—afterwards went on leave of Absence & while in N. Y. received this order—before leave expired. What I want to know is if there were any private orders from A. J. or any body else covering the issuance of this order; I want to know it for my own personal gratification & nothing else. The president told me (that is Gen Gran[t)] that he knew nothing whatever of the presidents (A. J's) cause of action"—AN, *ibid.*

1866, JAN. 23. USG endorsement. "The muster out of Generals Getty, Ayres, ~~Robinson~~, Ames and Turner recommended."—ES, DNA, RG 94, ACP, M54 CB 1866. USG added an undated second endorsement. "Gn. Robinson having lost a leg I recommend his retention for the present."—AES, *ibid.* Written on a letter of Jan. 19 from Maj. Gen. George G. Meade to AGO recommending the muster out of Bvt. Maj. Gens. George W. Getty, Romeyn B. Ayres, John C. Robinson, Adelbert Ames, and John W. Turner.—LS, *ibid.*

1866, JAN. 24. To Secretary of War Edwin M. Stanton. "Maj. Gen. W. T. Sherman, has forwarded a complete Historical Map, showing all the campaigns and marches made by the troops under his command in the Southern States. I respectfully recommend that the Chief Engineer be ordered to have organized Three Thousand Copies of it and when this is done that the original be returned to Gen. Sherman. Gen. Sherman makes the request that he be allowed to retain the original when the engraving is done."—Copies, DLC-USG, V, 47, 109; DNA, RG 108, Letters Sent. See *O.R. Atlas*, Plate CXVII.

1866, JAN. 24. USG endorsement. "Respectfully forwarded to the Secretary of War, and commended to his favorable consideration"—ES, DNA, RG 94, ACP, B93 CB 1866. Written on a letter of the same day from Samuel W. Beall, former lt. col., 18th Wis., and maj., 1st Veteran, to Secretary of War Edwin M. Stanton requesting appointment as sutler at a western post.—LS, *ibid.* On Jan. 30, Bvt. Maj. Gen. Edward D. Townsend endorsed this letter. "Appoint Col. Beall for Fort Kearny—"—AES, *ibid.* On Sept. 12, 1865, Charles S. Hamilton, former maj. gen., had written to

Brig. Gen. John A. Rawlins. "*Confidential* . . . I saw Gen Grant in Milwaukee, and called his attention to the case of Maj. S. W Beall of Vet Res Corps. You will remember Beall as the Lt Col of 18th Wis Vols. He stood by Grant in his dark days after Shiloh. He has long been in public life,—was at one time Lt Gov of this State. He desires to be retained in the service, on the consolidation of the V. ~~C~~ R. C. He has lost almost his entire property during the war, is really very poor, and his youngest son was crippled for life ~~at~~ at the assault on Petersburg, is mustered out, and is a charge for life, on the feeble means of the major. Beall has been a most gallant & faithful officer—bears in his body a shiloh bullet—has been twice wounded, & if he can be retained in service, it will gratify all friends of the Union in this State, and be only justice to the gallant old man. I left with Grant, a letter of Bealls to me, which I wish you would read & return to me."—ALS, *ibid.*, RG 108, Letters Received.

1866, JAN. 25. USG endorsement. "Respectfully forwarded to the Atty. Gen. I know Mr. Beall well and have known him for many years. He is a man whose statements can be relied on and who will keep any obligation. I am satisfied that he never dreamed of such a thing as taking up arms against the Govt. but like many others supposed secession would be peaceable and it was left for him to select which Government he would live under. This is his own statement. I recommend that Amnesty be granted in this case."—AES, DNA, RG 94, Amnesty Papers, D. C. Written on a letter of July 12, 1865, from Lloyd J. Beall, Georgetown, to President Andrew Johnson requesting a pardon.—ALS, *ibid.* On March 11, 1866, Beall, San Antonio, Tex., wrote to USG. "I have to request, that I may be permitted to engage in a business for the support of myself & family, without molestation from the military authorities, unless by your order— . . . P. S. Please address reply, care of W. D. Beall Esq Georgetown D C."—ALS, *ibid.*, RG 108, Letters Received. On March 29, Maj. George K. Leet granted this request. —Copies, DLC-USG, V, 47, 109; DNA, RG 108, Letters Sent.

1866, JAN. 25. USG endorsement. "This applicant is a student at the same College with my two sons and bears the reputation of being among the aptest if not the very aptest student at the Institution. If appointed to ~~w~~West Point I am satisfied he will gaduate with a Star affixed to his name. His father is an old graduate of the Military Academy and has served through the present rebellion with distinction; ~~having~~ has once been wounded in battle and I think eminently entitled to favorable concideration."—AES, DNA, RG 94, Cadet Applications. Written on a letter of Jan. 23 from U.S. Representative Nathaniel P. Banks of Mass. to President Andrew Johnson recommending Francis V. Greene for appointment to USMA.—ALS, *ibid.*

1866, JAN. 25. USG endorsement. "I heartily concur with Gn. Thomas in his estimate and classification of the services of Gn. Stanley and earnestly recommend him for as high rank as can be given him in the re-organization of the Army which must necessarily take place."—AES, DNA, RG 94, ACP, 6571 1880. Written on a letter of Sept. 14, 1865, from Maj. Gen. George H. Thomas to Secretary of War Edwin M. Stanton requesting promotion for Maj. Gen. David S. Stanley (maj., 5th Cav.).—LS, *ibid.*

1866, JAN. 25. USG endorsement. "Respectfully forwarded with the recommendation that this young man receive a commission in the Regular Army. Besides having served through the war and ~~hav~~ receiving this decision he has recommendations from the very best citizens of Phila which indicates high Moral qualifications"—AES, DNA, RG 94, ACP, M67 CB 1866. Written on a report of a board of examiners recommending Alfred C. Markley, former 1st lt., 127th Colored, for a commission.—DS, *ibid.*

1866, JAN. 26. USG endorsement. "The statements in the enclosed papers place the loyalty & good faith of Mr. Coan beyond a doubt. Had his claim been presented to these Head Quarters before the termination of the rebellion, or while the state of Miss. was still in arms against the Government, the District Commander would have been directed to seize property from the disloyal citizens in the vicinity sufficient to make full indemnification for the loss sustained in accordance with the order of Gen Slocum, but now, the war has closed, such seizures would be impracticable, and there seems to be no means of indemnification under the above order. Were any of the property seized in possession of the U S Governmt it would be restored at once"—Copy, DLC-USG, V, 58. Written on papers of John A. Coan concerning damages to his Miss. plantation.

1866, JAN. 27. USG endorsement. "I am not aware of any law that requires foreign powers to surrender deserters from our army, or under the provisions of which we can demand of them to do so. All deserters that are voluntarily surrendered to us should be received and forwarded to the nearest military officer in command of United States troops, who will cause their trial and punishment for desertion."—ES, DNA, RG 94, Letters Received, 95S 1866. Written on a letter of Jan. 5 from Act. Secretary of State William Hunter to Secretary of War Edwin M. Stanton. "I have the honor to enclose herewith a copy of a Dispatch from the U. S. Consul at Vera-Cruz, in regard to some persons arrested by the French Commandant at Bagdad, Supposed to be deserters from the 21st Regiment Indiana Volunteers; and would be pleased to be furnished with your views in regard to recieving Such deserters from the French Authorities."—LS, *ibid.*

1866, JAN. 27. Jean C. Washington, Mount Ida, Va., to USG. "I see by the Baltimore Sun of Jan 23d 1866, that you have in your possession a book, formerly belonging to Genl Washington, from the description of which, I cannot doubt its being one amongst many valuable books taken from my Father's library, while his house was occupied by Federal troops.

My late Father was Mr John A. Washington, formerly of Mount Vernon. The above mentioned book was taken from his home in Fauquier County, Virginia, where he removed after leaving Mount Vernon. I perfectly remember when reading Irvings life of Washington the book was shown me as being the one referred to by him. I also remember Mr Irving's examining it on a visit he made to Mount Vernon for the purpose of collecting materials for his work. My Father was then residing there Fully appreciating the honourable motive which makes you desirous of returning it to its proper owners, I write to claim the book. Should you not feel yourself authorized to deliver it up to me, I can communicate with the executor of my Father's estate. His being at a distance and in a part of the country where the mails are irregularly delivered, and my being in this neighbourhood, made me decide to write myself."—ALS, USG 3. On Jan. 29, Bvt. Col. Adam Badeau noted on the docket. "answered declining until ownership is established"—AN, *ibid.*

1866, JAN. 28, 10:00 A.M. To Maj. and Bvt. Brig. Gen. Alfred Pleasonton. "You have permission to visit Washington City"—Telegram sent, DNA, RG 107, Telegrams Collected (Bound); copies, *ibid.*, RG 108, Letters Sent; DLC-USG, V, 47, 109. On Jan. 27, Pleasonton, Milwaukee, had telegraphed to USG. "Please Grant me permission to visit Washington City for one week on private business"—Telegram received, DNA, RG 108, Letters Received.

1866, JAN. 29. USG endorsement. "At Oxford as I understood the speculators entered into an agreement not to pay more than 25 cents per pound for cotton, and in some instances failed to pay even that after getting possession of it. Hence my order to Captain Eddy of date January 26th 1863, together with copy of extract from letter to Gen. Hamilton, of date Feby 6. 1863, a copy of which is herewith enclosed. But as by my order trade had been opened to Oxford, Miss., and vicinity, and as these parties had proper license to purchase cotton, if they actually bought and paid for the cotton claimed, it would seem to be but just to refund to them the amount for which it sold after deducting all proper charges for its transportation and sale." —Copies, DNA, RG 107, Letters Received, L30 1867; DLC-USG, V, 58. Written on papers concerning the claim of W. W. Cones, purchaser of 252 bales of cotton in Miss. on Dec. 18, 1862. This cotton was seized the following day, turned over to Capt. Asher R. Eddy, and USG ordered its sale. —Copy, DNA, RG 107, Letters Received, L30 1867; *ibid.*, M2108 1865. See *PUSG*, 7, 292–93. On Dec. 15, Capt. Theodore S. Bowers had issued a pass for Cones permitting him to travel from Holly Springs to Oxford, Miss.—Copy, DNA, RG 107, Letters Received, M2108 1865. On Feb. 6, 1867, U.S. Representative John A. Logan of Ill. wrote to Secretary of War Edwin M. Stanton. "I herewith send the claim of W. W. Cones for payment to him of money received by the Quartermasters Department on sale of his cotton, seized without authority of law. I hope the matter may be at once investigated and decided. Please refer this claim to the commission appointed by yourself for the purpose of investigating claims."—Copy, *ibid.*, L30 1867. On Dec. 18 or 19, USG, secretary of war *ad interim*, endorsed this letter. "An examination of the claim of W. W. Cones for cotton taken by U. S. authority shows that Mr Cones had purchased the cotton under existing regulations at the time, and that the proceeds of said cotton went to the benefit of the Government; but believing that under existing laws I have no authority to grant the relief sought, (that is to say, to order the payment of the same) I therefore respectfully refer the claim to Congress, the Court of Claims, or such authority as may have the power to grant the relief sought."—Copies (dated Dec. 18), *ibid.*; (dated Dec. 19) *ibid.*, Orders and Endorsements Sent.

1866, JAN. 29. U.S. Delegate Walter A. Burleigh of Dakota Territory to USG. "I have taken the liberty to send you a Copy of the Resolution offered by me and adopted by the House Relative to the Removal and location of certain Indian tribes—Will you favor me by reading the same—and also, let me know as nearly as practicable—what the cost now is, of keeping up the the military force in the Territories of Dakota, Nebraska, Colorado & Montana—including the troops employed in protecting, the overland routes through those Territories—"—ALS, USG 3. On Jan. 30, Bvt. Col. Adam Badeau wrote to Burleigh. "Lieut. Gen. Grant directs me to state in reply to your inquiries of Jany 29th, that thi~~se~~ Quartermasters Dept. has recently reported the cost of each enlisted man in the Territories you mention, to be $50 per month, in addition to the original cost of clothing and rations, at the East; this is also exclusive of pay. Gen. Grant's attention has only recently been called to this fact, and he has issued orders for the reduction of the average cost. The number of troops employed in that district is greater than it would have been, had it been possible to reduce the force later in the season owing to the difficulties of transportation, but it will in the spring be reduced to the minimum consistent with the public safety in that region. I am also directed to return you the memorial herewith enclosed, and to acknowledge the receipt of a copy of the resolution offered by you in the House, relative to the removal of certain Indian tribes."—Copies, DLC-USG, V, 47, 109; DNA, RG 108, Letters Sent.

[1866], JAN. 29. Benjamin F. Butler to USG. "General Butler has the honor to decline the ~~card of~~ invitation of Lieut. General Grant—General Butler has now no desire for ~~the~~ further acquaintance"—AN, DLC-Benjamin F. Butler. See *New York Tribune*, Feb. 9, 1866.

1866, JAN. 30. USG endorsement. "If the steamboat mentioned is still in the possession of the Q. M. Dept. I would recommend that it be restored at once to Mr Poitevent. As it does not appear that the rest of his property is now in the possession of that Dept. his claim for indemnification will have to go through the usual process for the recovery of seized property"—Copy,

DLC-USG, V, 58. Written on papers concerning the claim of William J. Poitevent, Gainesville, Miss., against the government for seizure of the steamboat *A. J. Brown* and other property.—*Ibid.* See *HRC*, 49-2-3530; *ibid.*, 52-1-1652.

1866, JAN. 30. USG signature (heading many others) on a petition to Congress. "We, whose names are hereto written, come and represent to your Honorable Body, that, for want of constitutional provision so to do, many of the volunteer nurses, who, for one, two and more years, labored in the Many hospitals of our Country, have never received any compensation. —The husbands and sons of many of these mothers and wives have fallen by the ravages of disease or an Enemy's bullet; while others are returned to them with ruined Constitutions & maimed for life. Large numbers of these women are absolutly destitute and suffering for common comforts—They ask for no special remuneration. They simply ask and pray for compensation for actual, absolute and indispensable labors performed under the advisce &, in many instances, by the pressing request of ~~the~~ Surgeon General Hammond of the United States—We, your petitioners, & citizens of the United States, do earnestly recommend that Congress do pass such a law as will secure to all such persons a fair compensation for their Services—and thus we will ever pray."—DS, DNA, RG 233, 39th Congress, Committee on Military Affairs.

1866, JAN. 31. Petition of "Many Colord Citizens," Apalachicola, Fla., to "General." "as things appear to be going on Wrong in this Part of the Country, and as We have Writen to the Secretary of State, the Hon Wm. H. Seward, Stating Some of our Greavances here, We have thought it our Duty, as Well as our Privilage, to Petition you in behalf of the Colord People in this County, and Perticular in and about apalachicola, and also, Seeing an order from the Agt Genls office Dated 12th inst Concerning in Part We think of Maters of Which We Write. the Civil authoritys here are taking from the Colord People all the fire arms that they find in their Persesion, including Dubble barrel Shot Guns, Pistols of any kind, Now We Wish to ask if this is Lawful, or is it not, is it the intention of our Goverment for this to be Done. if not, Do thay allow it to go on. We understand from your order of the 12th, that Militery Commanders Must not allow any Law to be im~~pos~~posed upon us, that is not imposed upon the Whites, With the verry Same Decree. Now Sir, if the Commander of this Department, Gen. foster has taken any Steps in this Direction, Surely the officer Commanding at this Post has not. the officer here is Leiut young 82 U. S. C T. the Civil authoritys has orderd that ~~if~~ No Colord Person Would be allowd to have keep, or Carry a Gun or a Piston, unless thay Got a White Man to Write a Certificate, and have it Signed by the Judge of Probate. a few Days ago, the City Marshal Went into a Shop Where thare Was Some Pistons and Guns for Repars, that belongd to Some of the Colord People and taken them out. thay have Went to houses and taken them, Some of the Parties Went to the Commander of the Post, and he Sent them off to abide by the Laws of the City, Saying that it Was Right to take them a Way, that he Would Do it himself if he Saw one, thease are the Satisfactions that We Get. When We Complain of our Greavences, We are tole that this is one of the Laws that the Legislature of this State Made to Govern us. a few nights ago, two Colord Men Were Shot, one in the Street and one in his own house Sitting by the fire, and the third one Was beaten awfully With a Club by Some of the Vagabons that thay have for Police, and We have heard nothing from it Since. the Men that Done it, Still on Duty. this is the Protection that the Southern States is giving the Freedmen We hope Sir, that the united States Will give us Protection, and Not allow us to be Stript of Every Defence in the World, if We are Not allowd to have ~~to~~ Something to Defend ourselves under Cirtain Circumstancies, We are Werst than When We Were Slaves, yes, ten to one. thease Proceedings Will Cirtainly Sooner or Later Cause Conflicks between White and blacks. their obgects is to take our arms from us, for fear that We Might Resent Some of their impositions, but the best Plan is for them to treat us kindly. the Colord People is anxos to Live Peacefull With the Whites if thay Can, but if We Cannot Do this, Without being Made Slaves off, We had better Leave this Country, and We fear We Will have to Do it yet. We are imposed upon in Every Posible Way, and it Seems that the Militery, if thay Would, Cannot Defend us. We Donnot Expect Protection When We have Done Wrong, but We Expect it When We are Striving to Do Right, and Keep the Laws of the Land, those that Does Wrong, Should be Punished, but Not the ~~En~~ Enocent for the ungust, another thing Genl, Which We Wish to Call your attention too, Some houses Which the Fredmans Beaurou had in their Possesions ~~as~~ as Soon as thay Returnd to their former owners thay Proceeded at once, to Collect all Back Rent, including Some Which had been Recpted for by the Beaurou. Now, Sir, We hope that you Will Not only order a Diferent State of things, but See that our Property Which has been Stolen from us, be Returnd to its Lawful owners, including, Guns, Pistols & Back Rent on houses, the Complaints Which we here make, are not imaginary but Real. We are Sorry, but must Say, that our only Real Protection is ~~through~~ in the united Government. if Congress Donot Stand Squarly up for us, and Make Laws that Will Protect us, over the heads of the States, We are Nothing More than Searfs, that neather have the Protection of an owner, or any Body. We are fully Convinced of this fact. thease are the Proceedings of the Presidents Liberal Policy With the Southern States. We humbly hope, Sir, that We Shall See, and feel the Effects of Some order which you may Isue at an Early Day, on thease import Subjects, having full Confidence in our Govt also, having the Same in you, We Will Patienly await your action"—AD, DNA, RG 108, Letters Received. On Feb. 13, Bvt. Col. Theodore S. Bowers forwarded this letter to Maj. Gen. John G. Foster.—ES, *ibid.* On March 21, Foster, Tallahassee, endorsed this letter. "Respectfully returned with the report that the law authorizing the taking arms from the negroes, has been declared unconstitutional by the Attorney General of the state, and is now null and void—The commanding officers of posts are, however, sometimes obliged to take arms from vagabonds who live by poaching. Some irregularities have occurred at Appalachicola in which it appears the negroes have been as guilty as the whites. I have been forced to increase the garrison of the town and to detail a new commanding officer."—AES, *ibid.* On Feb. 18, Charles H. Van Wyck, former brig. gen., Jacksonville, wrote an unaddressed letter concerning an order "in the Department of Florida prohibiting colored soldiers from purchasing their Arms. . . ."—ALS, *ibid.* On Feb. 28, Bowers endorsed this letter. "Respectfully referred to Maj. Gen. J. G Foster, Commanding Department Florida, for report. In the application of General Orders Nos. 101 and 114, War Department, series 1865, no distinction will be made between white and colored troops."—AES, *ibid.* On March 12, Foster endorsed this letter. "Respectfully forwarded to Hd. Qrs of the Army with the enclosed copy of letter from Maj. Gen'l Sheridan, by which authority the sale of arms to the 34th regt U. S. C. T. (now mustered out) was prohibited That regiment is the only one upon which the order has operated in this Department."—AES, *ibid.* On Oct. 24, 1865, 12:30 A.M., Maj. Gen. Philip H. Sheridan, New Orleans, had telegraphed to Brig. Gen. John A. Rawlins. "In discharging Colored troops by expiration of time of service or otherwise will they be permitted to avail themselves of permission given white troops to purchase their arms? The purchase will create some uneasiness in this section of country—Please reply speedily." —Telegram received (at 12:50 P.M.), *ibid.*, RG 107, Telegrams Collected (Bound); *ibid.*, RG 108, Telegrams Received; copies, DLC-USG, V, 54; DLC-Philip H. Sheridan. On Oct. 26, 12:25 P.M., Rawlins telegraphed to Sheridan. "For the present you will not permit Colored Troops to purchase their Arms."—LS (telegram sent), DNA, RG 107, Telegrams Collected (Bound). See letter to Edwin M. Stanton, May 29, 1865.

1866, FEB. 1. USG endorsement. "General Emory's record entitles him to the Bvt. rank of Maj. Gn. I therefore recommend him for that rank for the battle of Cedar Creek. Respectfully submitted."—AES, DNA, RG 94, ACP, 2577 1875. Written on a letter of Dec. 19, 1864, from Maj. Gen. Philip H. Sheridan to Secretary of War Edwin M. Stanton recommending Brig. Gen. William H. Emory, col., 5th Cav., for promotion to maj. gen.—Copy, *ibid.* On April 4, 9, and 24, USG forwarded additional papers to Stanton recommending Emory for bvt. promotion.—ES, *ibid.* On Nov. 8, 1872, William P. Kellogg and two others, New Orleans, wrote to USG. "We have just learned with profound regret of the death of Maj. Genl George G. Meade. We may seem to be acting with unseemly haste, but, in justice to a soldier whom we believe is entitled to consideration, we respectfully request that the vacancy created by the decease of Genl Meade, or that the vacancy caused by the promotion to his place, be given to Maj. Genl W. H. Emory, now in command of this Department and who has discharg̃ed the onerous duties of his position with faithfulness and fidelity and to the satisfaction of the entire community."—LS, *ibid.* On June 18, 1873, Secretary of the Navy George M. Robeson wrote to USG. "I have held the within personal letter from General Emory for some time with the expectation of seeing the Secretary of War personally, but fearing that in his absence some action might possibly be taken closing out the General's case, I take the liberty of enclosing it directly to you. I do so that you may see what the General has to say in his own behalf, and to say that I have a very strong feeling of friendship and regard for him and his family, and shall be exceedingly glad if the interests of the service, and your own views, will permit his promotion in regular course should there be a vacancy by the retirement of Cooke. I think the General behaved remarkably well during the Johnson troubles in Washington, and that the fact that he is now at New Orleans occupying a General's command under the most difficult and trying circumstances, is evidence that the Department considers him still efficient and fit for the position to which he aspires. I don't believe anybody could have done better than he has at New Orleans. Certainly nobody could have behaved with a more frank determination to carry out the wishes of the Government, and at the same time with discretion and judgment. Besides if he should be thought to be too old for the position within a short time his age and service would entitle him to retirement, and he could thus—after having fulfilled his own hopes—retire to make way for some younger and more active man. But you, of course, understand his case much better than I do, and I have written this letter to you only to express my personal friendship for General Emory, and I hope that his promotion may prove to be consistent with the interests of the service when a vacancy occurs."—ALS, *ibid.* The enclosure is *ibid.* On July 19, Emory, New Orleans, wrote to USG. "Reports come to me from sources I cannot disregard, that a vacancy or vacancies among the Brig Generals of the Army, by the operation of the retiring laws, are about to occur. I know nothing, as a general rule, can be in worse taste, than for an officer to apply personally for an appointment to so high a position, but situated as I am, the oldest Colonel in the Army, & in command of a Department, to be passed over in a case of this kind would be equivalent to an overslaugh. I will not go into the details of my Military History, of that I am sure you must be fully informed, but I will say that in all the high positions I have filled, and the critical positions in which I have been placed, my command has never suffered defeat, and there have been occasions where it turned defeat into Victory I am now in command of the Department where I was assigned by yourself, and I am proud to know that I have discharged the difficult and often delicate duties arising from the complications of political affairs, to the satisfaction of your officers, and I trust to yours, and with a single eye to the preservation & honour of the Country I represent. I have felt it due to myself my family and my friends to write this letter, and I trust you will find yourself able to allow me to end my long military career with a star on my shoulder, to represent the two, which I won in the face of the enemy."—ALS, *ibid.* On Oct. 13, John R. Kenly, Baltimore, wrote to USG. "A friendship founded upon intercourse in the army twenty five years ago, and a present personal regard for Colonel William H Emory, U S Army, induce me to urge his promotion, which I am given to understand is now pending before the Department. I think I know the character of Colonel Emory, and can say with truth, he is a very trusty officer, and a very reliable man. His military experience, has been varied and extensive: his military services, are within your knowledge. He has been identified with the army of the United States for many years, and has helped to build up the reputation which that army enjoys among mankind. Such ability and such knowledge as he has acquired through years of service, are valuable to our country, for the simple reason, if for none other, that death is rapidly diminishing the number of experienced soldiers in the regular army. It is only to such civilians as retain an affectionate regard for those with whom they once served, that the Annual Army Register gives utterance to this painful truth. Colonel Emory is emphatically an army man, with the solidity which that manner of life gives, and I think it would be as well to retain and encourage such officers, in order to give steadiness and countenance to younger soldiers. I believe that the promotion of Colonel Emory would give pleasure and be acceptable to, your friends in Maryland, among whom, I beg you to consider me sincerely and respectfully, . . ." —ALS, *ibid.* An undated petition (three signatures) to USG supporting Emory's promotion is *ibid.* Emory was retired with the rank of brig. gen. as of July 1, 1876.

1866, FEB. 2. USG endorsement. "Respectfully submitted to the Secretary of War, with the recommendation: 1st That Jeffersonville. Ind., be made a principal depot for the storage of Government property, and that all Quartermasters property that requires storage in Ohio, Kentucky, along the line of the Chattanooga Railroad, and such other points as may be practicable, be stored in the Government buildings at Jeffersonville. 2nd That the following buildings at Louisville be disposed of they being no longer necessessary: Barracks, No. 1, Louisville, Ky. Taylor Barracks, Refuge Home, Ware-houses at L. & N.—Railroad Depot 3d. That as soon as the property now stored at Oakland Cavalry Depot can be moved to Jeffersonville, or sold, the Oakland Depot be broken up and the buildings sold. 4th That Jo Holt Hospital at Jeffersonvill Ind. be sold. 5th That the offices of Depot Quartermaster and Chief Quartermaster be united and the duties be performed by one officer."—ES (signature forged, probably by Bvt. Col. Theodore S. Bowers), DNA, RG 92, Consolidated Correspondence, Taylor Barracks; copy (dated Feb. 5), DLC-USG, V, 58. Written on papers concerning Taylor Barracks, Louisville, Ky.—*Ibid.*

1866, FEB. 2. To commanding officer, Fort Leavenworth. "Give military protection to Mapes and Williams Saw Mill on line of Pacific Rail Road against threatened destruction by squatters Leave the law to decide ownership"—Telegram sent, DNA, RG 107, Telegrams Collected (Bound); copies, *ibid.*, RG 108, Letters Sent; DLC-USG, V, 47, 109.

1866, Feb. 2. USG parole. "Jno. S. Mosby, lately of the Southern Army, will, hereafter, be exempt from Arrest by Military Authorities, except for violation of his paroles unless directed by the President of the United States, Sec of War or from these Hd Qrs. His parole will authorize him to travel freely within the State of Virginia, and as no obsticle has been thrown in the way of paroled Officers and men from pursuing their Civil pursuits, or traveling out of their states, the same privileges [will be] extended to J. S. Mosby unless otherwise directed by competant authority."—ADS (facsimile), California Historical Society, San Francisco, Calif. See Charles Wells Russell, ed., *The Memoirs of Colonel John S. Mosby* (Boston, 1917), pp. 390–91.

1866, Feb. 2 or 3. Maj. Gen. William T. Sherman, Washington, D. C., endorsement. "Respectfully referred to the Lt Genl Comdg. the Armies of the U. S.—I am satisfied with the present force in the Dept of Mo. and if the increase is made as in the Bill revised, I will have my full proportion." —AES (undated), DNA, RG 108, Telegrams Received. Written on a telegram of Feb. 2 from Maj. Gen. John Pope, St. Louis, to Sherman. "The time is rapidly approaching when the season will permit us to replace all Vols by regular troops in this Dep[t.] It is necessary as soon as practicable to make preparations for years supply of troops permanently assigned to this Dept & I ought to know as soon as possible what troops the Genl in Chief intends to place in the Dept that I may know how to distribute & supply them—If no other routes over the Plains are to be opened & protected, no more military posts to be established & no extraordinary demands for military force upon this Dept I think we can get along with thirteen or fourteen thousand men—I will however do the best I can with any force the Gen'l in Chief decides on—For reasons stated however I think it essential that I should know as soon as possible what is the force designated for this Dept"—Telegram received (at 6:20 p.m.), *ibid.*; copy, DLC-USG, V, 54.

1866, Feb. 3. To Secretary of War Edwin M. Stanton. "I would respectfully recommend the promotion, by Brevet, of 1st Lieut. and Bvt. Capt. Wm. Burn, Veteran Reserve Corps, who is now on duty in the War Department, to the rank of Major."—ALS (facsimile), Delbert S. Wenzlick, St. Louis County, Mo. On Dec. 1, 1865, Bvt. Col. Theodore A. Dodge, Veteran Reserve Corps, had written to Stanton recommending 1st Lt. William Burns, 14th Veteran, for bvt. promotion.—ALS, DNA, RG 94, ACP, R371 CB 1870. On Jan. 11, 1866, USG endorsed this letter. "Approved for one brevet, for gallantry in the battle where he lost his arm."—ES, *ibid.* On May 8, 1867, Dodge, capt., 44th Inf., wrote to Bvt. Maj. Gen. Edward D. Townsend asking bvt. appointments for Burns, 1st lt., 44th Inf., and two others; on May 23, USG endorsed this letter. "Respectfully forwarded to the Secretary of War. Lt. Burns is recommended for brevet Captaincy for gallant and meritorious services at battle of White Oak Swamp; Lt. Hoppy for brevet 1st Ltcy for gallant and meritorious services at 1st battle of Bull

Run; Lt Northrop for brevet 1st Ltcy for gallant and meritorious services at battle of Malvern Hill.—All to date 2d M'ch 1867"—ES, *ibid.*, D239 CB 1867.

1866, FEB. 3. John Thompson, Philadelphia, to USG. "I called on You in Oct in regard to a small claim I have. You turned me & the papers over to Col. Comstock. after their examination, the Col. reported to You, & returned with an answer from You that if I would make proof that the property in question was mine, You would give me an endorsement that would be of Service to me. I called again at Your Quarters 22nd Ult, & reported my business to Your Secty, who after Seeing You replied that nothing could be done Until after the return of Genl. Comstock. this was to me a Sore disappointment, having only left with my wife $7. for Market Money & only enough Money in my possession to pay my expenses to, at & from Washington. I however turned away believing that the government through You would be true to me, as I had been & am to it. the claim I am Now Urging is $1595. for articles Used by the Army & I have been able to procure the required proof—when the Union army was at our place as stated by Col. Richmond, I there had all my property which was of my own hard earnings, worth at the out break of the War between forty & fifty Thousand dollars out of the whole of that I was able to leave with my Son $2.000 Two Thousand Dollars In Sept last to Commence farming operations, and after having been in business for myself twenty five Years, I have to take a position as Salesman to enable me to Support a large and entirely dependent family, wife & 9 children, all dependents but my Son in Tennessee, whom I kept out of the rebel army by a determined will, having made two Unsuccessfull attempts to Join them on one occasion I followed him to Newhall in Oct 1861, at which place I fortunately overtook him on his way to Join Said Army at Columbus Ky, and I again took him from there in Oct 1862, and before Your Army took possession of our Country I was taken out of my bed in the Mid hour of the Night by 30 Armed rebels & passing to rebel head quarters all to deter me from giving Utterances in favour of the Union; If the Government will now pay me the Amt I think it ought to, it will greatly facilitate me Just at this moment, more than at any other time. The $2.000 I gave my Son is Exausted, & we are now needing money to keep him agoing & I am much in want of money for my own family expenses. Genl. A J Smith's Command destroyed my Tannery for which You gave me a Safeguard on 27th July 1864 I had removed everything from it when Genl. Sherman withdrew his troops in Jany 1864.—I refer you to enclosed Copy's originals of which I have in my possession—I have not the Money to spare to make another trip to Washington, unless I felt Sure of Succeeding in my object. Therefore will You be Kind enough to advise me when to come . . . it was through my aid that Richmond got a Cannon to Davis Mill in time that enabled Lieut. Col. Morgan to make so gallant a defence, turn the rebels back, Killed 30 or 40 of them, & Saved that long tresstle—"—ALS, DNA, RG 108, Letters Received. On Feb. 8, Bvt. Col.

Horace Porter wrote to Thompson. "In reply to your letter of the 5th inst. I am directed by Gen. Grant to say that Gen. Comstock is now absent and will not return for three of four weeks. If at the end of that time, you will forward to this office the original certificates in your possession, the merits of your claims will be examined into, and an endorsement made upon your application in accordance with the result of the examination."—Copy, *ibid.*

1866, Feb. 5. To Secretary of War Edwin M. Stanton. "I have the honor to recommend that all buildings owned by Government, for military purposes that are not absolutely necessary for present use, be sold. I am advised that there are large numbers of such buildings at most of the Depots, Camps and Rendezvous still unsold, that require troops to guard them and that are not needed."—LS, DNA, RG 107, Letters Received from Bureaus. On the same day, Stanton wrote to USG. "I have the honor to acknowledge the receipt of your letter of this date recommending 'that all buildings owned by Goverment for military purposes, that are not absolutely necessary for present use be sold.' Orders having been issued for the disposal of all such public buildings as are referred to in your communication except some hospitals retained in anticipation of the coming of Cholera, I ~~desire you to specify~~ would be glad to have any specific information that may be in your office as to the places at which there are any remaining unsold, so that enquiry may be made as to the cause for a noncompliance with the orders."—Df, *ibid.*

On Jan. 4, Bvt. Col. Theodore S. Bowers had written to Bvt. Col. Orville E. Babcock. "You Will proceed to the Military posts in the States of Ohio, Indiana, Illinois and Wisconsin and such other points as may hereafter be designated and inspect the military establishment of those states, with a view to its further reduction in accordance with the verbal instructions given you by the Lieutenant General. You will report from time to time by mail and telegraph, and upon the execution of these orders you will rejoin these Hdqrs."—Copies, DLC-USG, V, 47, 109; DNA, RG 108, Letters Sent. On Jan. 19, Babcock, Madison, Wis., telegraphed to USG. "Only two here and Milwaukie Public buildings and public property nearly all sold, Hospitals not sold are quartermaster and Commissary. Do you wish me to go to St Louis or will Gen Sherman make the required reduction there? Jones and party will start about the twenty fourth Answer me at Cairo—"—Telegram received (on Jan. 20, 9:30 p.m.), *ibid.*, RG 107, Telegrams Collected (Bound); *ibid.*, RG 108, Telegrams Received; copy, DLC-USG, V, 54. On Jan. 22, 10:40 a.m., USG telegraphed to Babcock. "You had better go to St. Louis before returning."—ALS (telegram sent), DNA, RG 107, Telegrams Collected (Bound); telegram sent, *ibid.*; copies, *ibid.*, RG 108, Letters Sent; DLC-USG, V, 47, 109.

On Jan. 6, Bowers had written to Bvt. Col. Horace Porter ordering him to inspect the Dept. of the East.—Copies, *ibid.* On Jan. 25, Porter, Washington, D. C., wrote a lengthy report to Bowers.—Copies, DNA, RG 108, Letters Received; (incomplete) *ibid.*, RG 192, Letters Received by Referral.

On Jan. 26, USG endorsed this report. "Respy. forwarded to the Sec of War, with the the recommendation that orders be issued to carry into immediate effect the within recommendatns of the Inspecting officer, except so far as they relate to Fort Niagara. I am in favor of continuing that Post"—Copy, DLC-USG, V, 58.

On Jan. 10 (misdated 1865), Babcock, Chicago, had written to Brig. Gen. John A. Rawlins concerning the Q. M. Dept. at Columbus, Ohio.—ALS, DNA, RG 108, Letters Received. On Jan. 26, Bvt. Maj. Gen. Montgomery C. Meigs endorsed this report. "Respectfully returned to Lieutenant General U S Grant, Comd'g Armies of the U S. The Depot at Columbus Ohio was inspected by an Inspector of the Q M Dept on the day of Col Babcocks visit—The inspection was made with a view to reducing the establishment to the lowest possible limits by the discharge of all unnecessary employees, the sale of all unserviceable property, and the shipment of serviceable to other depots; and the necessary instructions will be given as soon as the lists are prepared. Col Burr who has been stationed there since July 1862 is efficient, faithful and thoroughly posted in all the business of the post and it is considered by the Quartermaster General as the best economy to retain him there until the whole business is settled and the post broken up. Relative to reductions recommended by Col Babcock, the Quartermaster General would state that all serviceable stores now at Columbus have been ordered to be stored at Jeffersonville Ind with the least possible delay. By Special Order No 30 A. G. O Jany 24/66 the rendezvous at Camp Chase Columbus is discontinued and the buildings are directed to be disposed of in accordance with General Orders No 113 A. G. O. June 13th 1865. This will be promptly done. The sale of buildings at Camp Dennison Ohio was suspended by telegram from the Secretary of War to that effect and now await further orders from the War Department."—ES, *ibid.*

On Jan. 12, Meigs wrote to USG. "I respectfully state that Colonel M. D. Wickersham, Chief Quarter-Master of the Department of Alabama, under date of the 31st ultimo, reports that all employés of the Quarter-Masters' Department, except Clerks, in the Military Department of Alabama, were ordered discharged on that date."—LS, *ibid.*

On Jan. 19, Meigs wrote to USG. "I have examined the Report of Brevet Colonel O. E. Babcock. A. D. C. relative to the affairs of the Quartermaster's Department at Chicago Ill's, and Detroit Mich, and respectfully return the same herewith. I am fully of the opinion that the Changes recommended by Colonel Babcock, relative to Department or Depot Quartermasters, cannot yet be carried out, with economy and benefit to the service. The principal duty at this time, of Chief Department Quartermasters is to enforce reductions and report for sale, public property at the posts in order to their discontinuance. This requires much detail of inspection and work, and I think it is economical to retain them until the pr[o]perty is got r[id] of, or collected at principal depots. I think that General Hoyt's pay and his office establishment is more th[an] paid for in this way. The time will come when the posts are reduced to those needed in the peace establishment, when his Office can also be properly broken up. I do not think that time has yet arrived. Colonel Pierce at Chicago and Colo[ne]l Lee at Detroit are needed to settle up Rail-Road indebtedness and they also should perform the duties of Post Quartermaster. I have duly requested that no other Quartermasters than Colonel Lee and General Hoyt be allowed at Detroit. The attempt has been made to reduce Colonel Lee and substitute another officer of less experience in his place. I directed that the latter officer be relieved instead. The case of the officer at Detroit was brought by General Ord, to the attention of the Secretary of War, and report made thereon by this Office."—LS, *ibid.*, RG 92, Miscellaneous Letters Sent (Press).

On Jan. 7, Bowers ordered Bvt. Col. Ely S. Parker on an inspection tour of Ky., Tenn., and Miss.—Copies, DLC-USG, V, 47, 109; DNA, RG 108, Letters Sent. On Jan. 20, Parker, Nashville, telegraphed to USG. "Will finish here today. Will then go to Memphis Will send report by mail. Any telegraphic order will reach me at Memphis."—Telegram received (at 11:20 A.M.), *ibid.*, Telegrams Received; copy, DLC-USG, V, 54.

On Jan. 22, Bowers ordered Bvt. Brig. Gen. Cyrus B. Comstock to inspect the Depts. of La. and Tex.—Copies, *ibid.*, V, 47, 109; DNA, RG 108, Letters Sent. On Feb. 1, 3:00 P.M., Comstock, New Orleans, telegraphed to USG. "There are now sixty vessels for water transportation in employ of the United States here, and many of them owned by the United States. That number could be at once reduced to about six, and the transportation be done by contract, or Special Charter. The Victoria and Lavaco Railroad, now in hands of Government, should be turned over to the owners.—I think the thousand Cavalry horses you ordered to be retained here, should be sold—as the muster out of ~~the~~ Cavalry regiments gives plenty of horses.—The above Changes will largely reduce Expenses here, but nothing can be done without authority from Washington—I am told some of the steamers have been laid up for months and would have brought better prices if sold some time ago."—Telegram received (at 3:00 P.M.), *ibid.*, RG 107, Telegrams Collected (Bound); copy, *ibid.*, RG 92, Supplies and Purchases, Public Animals, Letters Sent. On Feb. 2, USG twice endorsed this telegram. "Respectfully forwarded to the Secretary of War with the recommendation that the Quartermaster Genl be directed to dispose of all the Govt vessels at New Orleans except six, that number being deemed sufficient for the necessities of the service,"—Copies, *ibid.*, Consolidated Correspondence, Disposal; *ibid.*, RG 108, Register of Letters Received. "Respy. referred to Maj. Gen. M. C. Miegs Q. M Gen. There is no longer a necessity for Keeping the One thousand horses within referred to at N. Orleans and they should be desposed of without delay."—Copy, *ibid.* On Feb. 5, Meigs wrote to USG. "In reply to telegram of Brevet Brig Gen'l C. B. Comstock. A. D. C, dated February 1st 1866, relative to the steamers laid up at New Orleans, I have the honor to inform you, That authority having been obtained from the Secretary of War, to dispose of these steamers, instructions have been sent to the Chief Quartermaster at New Orleans, to sell them at auction to the highest bidder, after due advertisement in the Northern, and Southern newspapers, An exception to this has been made relative to what have been known as the Morgan Steamers, the 'Crescent,' Clinton,' and 'St Mary's,' which are not to be sold for less than their appraised valuation. All chartered vessels are ordered to be discharged, as soon as the exigencies of the service will admit."—LS, *ibid.*, Letters Received. On Feb. 21, Maj. Gen. Philip H. Sheridan wrote to Comstock. "I find that the Quartermaster Genl. has disapproved of the proposed contract which his own inspector made with Mr Morgan for carrying public freight across the Gulf to Texas, and at the same time authorized the sale of the 'Clinton' 'St Mary' and 'Crescent' but giving me the power of withdrawing them from the sale This disapproval of the proposed contract made with Morgan was equivalent to the withdrawal of these steamers, but I suppose he now thinks it best for me to manage the matter as we have had no offers from any parties for a better one. I will therefore withdraw or secure these boats, and fix this affair up myself. The Quartermaster General after going to the end of his string ends where he began, after a considerable lapse of time and a large amount of financial suffering Parties may come down from New York for the purchase of these boats, and it is possible I can make a contract. Morgan has put down the price of freight and passengers to Texas so as to deter others from bidding for these steamers to their full value in case they should be sold."—LS, *ibid.*

On Feb. 3, Comstock wrote to Rawlins recommending measures to reduce expenses.—ALS, *ibid.* On Feb. 23, Sheridan forwarded papers, received at USG's hd. qrs., concerning Sedgwick Hospital, recommending that the land under the hospital be purchased by the U.S.—*Ibid.*, Register of Letters Received. On March 10, USG endorsed these papers. "Respy. forwarded to the Sec of War, Genl Sheridans recommendation approved"—Copy, *ibid.* On March 5, Sheridan wrote to Rawlins recommending that the land under Greenville stables be purchased by the U.S.—LS, *ibid.*, RG 107, Letters Received, I-J121 1868. On March 15, USG endorsed this letter. "Respectfully forwarded to the Hon. Secretary of War. In view of the small number of cavalry needed at New Orleans it is not deemed advisable to purchase the ground in question and it is recommended that the stables &c be sold as soon as they are no longer needed."—ES, *ibid.* On May 4, Sheridan wrote to Rawlins concerning Sedgwick Hospital.—LS, *ibid.* On May 10, USG endorsed this letter. "Respectfully forwarded to the Hon. Secretary of War, with the recommendation that Gen. Sheridan be authorized to rent the grounds upon which Sedgwicks hospital [s]tands, in conformity to the views expressed hereon by the Surgeon General."—ES, *ibid.* Additional papers are *ibid.*

1866, FEB. 5. U.S. Senator Lafayette S. Foster of Conn. and U.S. Representative Schuyler Colfax of Ind. to USG. "In accordance with a Concurrent Resolution adopted by the Senate and House of Representatives, we have the honor to invite your attendance at the Hall of the House on

Monday, February 12th, at noon, on the occasion of the exercises in honor of the Memory of the late President of the United States, Abraham Lincoln." —LS (printed), USG 3.

1866, FEB. 7. USG endorsement. "Respectfully returned. The creation of New Mexico into a Military Department is disapproved. It is recommended however that orders be given to purchase within the Territory everything it can supply for the troops if expenses can be saved thereby The suggestion made by Genl Sherman that for economy it maybe worthy of consideration whether a contract could not be made with the Territorial authorities to relieve the U. S. altogether of all charge of guarding New Mexico' is not approved."—Copy, DLC-USG, V, 42. Written on documents submitted by Secretary William F. M. Arny, New Mexico Territory, requesting that New Mexico be made a dept.—*Ibid.*

1866, FEB. 9. To Secretary of War Edwin M. Stanton recommending an officer for promotion.—B. Altman & Co. advertisement, *New York Times*, Feb. 10, 1980.

1866, FEB. 9. USG endorsement. "Application for Arms for Military school near Baltimore approved. Now that Government has such a supply of Arms on hand I would recommend the loan of sufficient of them for the use of all Military schools within districts represented in our National Congress. In this case I will state that the head of the school, and all the Cadets except two, subscribed to a stringent oath prescribed by Gn. L. Wallace during the continuance of hostilities. The two delinquents were promptly arrested and imprisoned and held until paroled by authority of the Government."—AES, DNA, RG 107, Letters Received from Bureaus. Written on a letter of Feb. 7 from Thomas P. Chiffelle to USG. "Having called this morning to see you and finding you out, I have requested a friend to hand you, the accompaning note from the Honl R Johnson, Senator from Md Who recommends to your favorable consideration, the application, I had the honor of making to you personally yesterday, for the loan from the U. S. Govt of *150* Springfield Muskets, and *4* pieces of Artillery, with their several appendages, for the use of the Cadets of the Maryland, Military Institute—This school is modeled after West Point (of which I am a graduate) with the same regulations and uniforms, and as far as practicable, the same course of studies—I am induced to make this application from the fact, that a somewhat similar request has been granted to the Principal of St Timothy's school, located in my neighborhood—and also from the fact, that the Arms for which I now make application, can only be procured from the Government—As I am informed that it is the intention of the Government, as it is certainly their true policy, to encourage Institutions like unto mine I would most respectfully request that my application be granted"—ALS, *ibid.* On Feb. 6, U.S. Senator Reverdy Johnson of Md. wrote to USG. "Capt. Chiffelle the head of an admirable school near Baltimore, desires, in order to train the pupils to the use of arms, that the Govt should loan him for the purpose, One hundred & fifty muskets, & 4 pieces of artillery. I respectfully recommend his application to your favour, & that of the Govt, being persuaded that it will contribute to ~~the~~ public good—" —ALS, *ibid.*

1866, FEB. 10. Bvt. Col. Theodore S. Bowers endorsement. "Respectfully returned. The statements submitted in this case go to show that unavoidable accidents, and not want of energy, or neglect of duty, prevented Mess'rs Irwin, Burns and McLean from fulfilling their contract. It is therefore ordered, that under the Provision of Gen Order, No. 16, Mil. Div of West Mississippi of Febry 6, 1865—the amount paid by them for the permits be refunded. The amount should be sent to the Adjutant General at Washington, for delivery to the claimants."—Copies, DLC-USG, V, 58; DNA, RG 107, Letters Received, I52 1866. Written on a letter of June 29, 1865, from George W. Burns, New Orleans, to Maj. Enos B. Parsons, adjt. for Maj. Gen. Philip H. Sheridan.—ALS, *ibid.*, RG 108, Letters Received. Burns and his partners were requesting the return of $7,000 paid for a permit to collect cotton along the Red River which they had been unable to exercise.—*Ibid.*, RG 107, Letters Received, I52 1866. On March 10, 1866, 3:25 P.M., USG telegraphed to Maj. Gen. Edward R. S. Canby. "Please report without delay what has been done in the case of Burns Irwin and McLearn under the orders from these Hdqrs of February 10th 1866"—Telegram sent, *ibid.*, Telegrams Collected (Bound); copies, *ibid.*, RG 108, Letters Sent; *ibid.*, RG 393, Dept. of the Gulf, Two or More Citizens File; DLC-USG, V, 47, 109. On March 11, Canby, New Orleans, telegraphed to USG. "Your telegram of yesterday has just been recd The instructions of Feby 10th were received from Divn. Head Qrs on the twenty third 23. of that month and returned with report on the twenty seventh 27. The fund upon which reclaim was made was expended before I came into the command of this Dept. but an estimate to meet the amount of the award was made upon the Quarter Master's Dept. from funds heretofore advanced to that Dept. from the Provost marshal funds. In my judgment the claim is fraudulent."—Telegram received (on March 12, 2:40 P.M.), DNA, RG 107, Telegrams Collected (Bound); *ibid.*, RG 108, Telegrams Received; copies, *ibid.*, RG 393, Dept. of the Gulf and La., Letters Sent; DLC-USG, V, 54. On March 12, Sheridan, New Orleans, telegraphed to USG. "Papers in connection with the case of Irwin Brown & McLean with an estimate for funds for compliance with directions of Gen Grant were sent by Gen Canby to the Adjt Genl through my Headquarters and forwarded from there to the Adjt General March first (1st)"—Telegram received (on March 13, 4:40 P.M.), DNA, RG 107, Telegrams Collected (Bound); *ibid.*, RG 108, Telegrams Received; copies (one sent by mail), *ibid.*, Letters Received; DLC-USG, V, 54; DLC-Philip H. Sheridan. On March 16, Sheridan wrote a communication received at USG's hd. qrs. forwarding papers in the case and stating that Canby believed that the money should not be refunded.—DNA, RG 108, Register of Letters Received. A notation indicates that on March 31, Secretary of War Edwin M. Stanton directed Bvt. Maj. Gen. Montgomery C. Meigs to refund the money.—*Ibid.*

1866, FEB. 14. To President Andrew Johnson. "I would respectfully submit for your information the accompanying reports of the officers of my Staff of inspections made by them in States lately in rebellion"—Copies, DLC-USG, V, 47, 109; DNA, RG 108, Letters Sent. USG enclosed a letter of Jan. 27 from Bvt. Col. Ely S. Parker, Vicksburg, to Bvt. Col. Theodore S. Bowers. ". . . I think I have now referred to everything that may be considered as within the scope of my instructions. It may not however be amiss to mention in this connection the main cause of the retention of so many troops in these states which is simply to regulate the social and political character of the South. In the three States to which my duties have been confined, slavery no longer exists, and the black race have become as it were the wards of the Government. The management of the relations of the Government with the black people and their new social relations with their former masters is carried on through the agency of the Freedmens Bureau. How long this Bureau will exist, I presume depends altogether upon the political and legal privileges that may be given by the late slaveholding states to its black population. And the idea has become very prevalent that the Southern States will never be thoroughly reconstructed until they have placed the negro in all respects upon an equality with the white man. Whatever the result of these political and social questions may be it seems at present, an act of humanity to retain troops in the late slaveholding states in order to protect the negro in his life, person and the few rights he has acquired by becoming a freedman. Of the three States I have visited I find Kentucky apparently the most disloyal to the policy of the Government. Her citizens are bitter and outspoken in their hostility to the Government and profess the greatest sympathy for the late secession movement of the South. She is hostile to the presence of negro troops within her borders, and so far as I could learn and judge a great many obstacles are intentionally thrown in the way of the successful operation of the Freedmen's Bureau. The same remarks will apply to Tenn, though she is evidently not so hostile as Kentucky. The civil authorities of Miss. pretend much anxiety to work in accord with the General Government in its reconstruction policy and in its efforts to amiliorate the unhappy condition of the negro. In most parts of the State the people are too much occupied in providing the ways and means for their immediate wants to pay any or very little attention to the political condition of the country. Hence to a casual observer of the condition of things here there seems an apparent acquiescence among the people in the results of the war. Their old code of the black laws have however not been repealed but are still enforced against the blacks in all cases where the same can be done with safety from interference by the Freedmen's Bureau or the military authorities. The negroes also are beginning to realize and appreciate the value of their changed condition, and the continued enforcement against them of the black laws in existence before the war, renders them uneasy and unsettled in their newly acquired rights. To guard against an unjust oppression of the negro, to prevent personal conflicts between the two races and to see that equal and just laws are enacted and executed seems to be the combined duty of the Freedmen's Bureau and the military in the South, and until these things are accomplished it seems pretty clear that both of these institutions must be maintained in the South. The honor of the Government will demand that the work left unfinished at the close of the war be thoroughly completed ere military protection and the strong arm of the Government is withdrawn from the protection of the emancipated race. Nor can any further reductions of troops, besides those suggested be made with safety at the present time. If economy is desired it is easy to recommend that the black troops be removed from the Southern districts and one half or less number of white troops sent to replace them, who will do the duty as efficiently and more satisfactorily to the resident population than the black troops can. Whether however this should be conceded to the refractory and rebellious element of the South is a question that I cannot pretend to determine I simply submit that under the present status of things in the states I have visited, and while the Freedmen's Bureau exists and the Black laws are unrepealed and until just and equitable laws are enacted and put into execution by those states for the protection of Freedmen, and until the entire South itself has become completly and thoroughly reconstructed in its subordination to the authority of the General Government, no further reduction of troops is warrantable. The transition of the negro from the condition of a slave to that of a freedman has been so sudden that the white man can hardly yet realize the change, and hence does not seem to see the necessity of any modification in the local statutes regulating his former condition of slave, and therefore continues to enforce them. Time alone will change the long settled convictions of the Southerner into the necessity of granting to the negro all the rights demanded for him by the General Government, and I fear that until that event takes place the presence of troops in the South will be an absolute necessity."—Copy (incomplete), DLC-Andrew Johnson. USG also enclosed a letter of Feb. 1 from Bvt. Brig. Gen. Cyrus B. Comstock, New Orleans, to Brig. Gen. John A. Rawlins. "I reached here day before yesterday and have been busily at work looking at the Qr. Mr's establishment, but have not yet got the figures on which to make definite statements and recommendations for the reduction of expenses. They are already being reduced, and except in the matter of water transportation do not compare with those at Nashville on Jan. 1. I telegraphed today to the general recommending that of 60 or more steamers and sailing vessels now in the U. S. service here—a majority of them owned by the U S.—all be sold or discharged except about six and water transportation be obtained by contract or special charter. If Sheridan had power to act this would have been done ere this, but authority for sales has to come from Washington. I also recommended that the general should rescind the order to retain 1000 cavalry horses at this place, as the cavalry regiments being mustered out give an ample supply, and Sheridan thinks he can still dispense with one or two regiments more of cavalry I think the two items just mentioned will reduce expenses by nearly $100,000 per month. As soon as I can get the detailed statements I will write fully so that official action can be taken on my letters. In coming down the river and while here I have talked freely with officers and citizens as to affairs in general. Opinions of course differ a good deal, but on one point among Union people there is entire unanimity—namely that troops and *martial law* must be retained here until the labor system and northern men who have come here become firmly established, and looked on by the southern people as a permanent part of their condition. Mr. Cochran, a leading business man and presid't of the 2d national bank, told me that in his opinion, save in the large cities, northern men could not remain after the withdrawal of military power, and that the negroes would be far worse off than before the war, as they would no longer be property to be protected. He also said that in case of foreign war the sympathy of the people here would be with the enemy; and that their sympathy would become active assistance if there was any possibility of thus obtaining what they have heretofore sought. —Canby's opinion is just about the same.—Sheridan is more hopeful but says if martial law were revoked; through the courts; thro' insults in the street, it would become exceedingly unpleasant for officers to remain here. A good deal of northern capital is coming here, but I have met and heard of several cases in which, despite the enormous profits offered and the great desire of the planters for it, it has returned in apprehension that it might not be safe here. Sheridan says this part of the country is rapidly becoming northernized, that the railroads and business are passing into the hands of northern people—that the labor question is settling itself—that every thing is going on as well as could be expected, and all that is necessary is to let things be as they are—that the presence of troops, in no large numbers, but with the Knowledge that they will interfere whenever necessary, is all that is needed—that the natural laws will settle the questions of labor and of business—but that this presence of troops and power of control will be long needed—till the present bitter feeling has partly died away, and the new state of things become permanent. Every one who has spoken of the feeling here says it was very submissive at the close of the war—that it became very bad when the large number of pardons seemed to promise general amnesty—but again became better when the flow of pardons was checked, with out however becoming what it was at first. I should except Humphreys —he found the feeling along the Mississippi river very good—entirely without bitterness. But he saw planters, whose very subsistence depended on what he might do to the levees—as they visited him, they would not be apt to show bitterness even if they felt it, and his estimate would necessarily be a favorable one. It seems to me that Sheridan's idea of retaining the power of control till the new state of things becomes permanent, is entirely right—that with it these difficult questions will settle them selves—that without it a state of things here might arise that would make the Union one only in name."—Copy, *ibid.* Incomplete in *HED*, 40-2-57, pp. 57–58. Reports of Feb. 3 and 7 from Comstock to Rawlins are *ibid.*, pp. 58–60. See *Calendar*, Feb. 5, 1866.

1866, FEB. 15. USG endorsement. "Respectfully forwarded to the Hon. Secretary of War, for the information of the President."—ES, DLC-Andrew Johnson. Written on a letter of Jan. 17 from Governor Andrew J. Hamilton of Tex., Austin, to Maj. Gen. Philip H. Sheridan requesting that a large military force be maintained in Tex. to protect Unionists and Negroes.—ALS, *ibid.* On Feb. 5, Sheridan, New Orleans, endorsed this letter. "Respectfully referred to the Lieut General Comdg the Armies of the U. S. for his information. With reference to the state of Louisiana I have for some time believed that the influence of Northern Capital and Northern people, would soon fix a good status for the state, but this will not hold good for Texas, as the people of Texas increased in wealth by the Rebellion while those in Louisiana became very poor Therefore Texas by its wealth and the hostility of its people to northern influence will oblige us to govern them for a long period by a Military force I very much fear that Gov Hamilton has not in the least exaggerated in this letter"—ES, *ibid.*

1866, FEB. 15. USG endorsement. "While the Army was lying near Lake Providence previous to the Vicksburg Campaign Gen McPherson Authorized Messr.s Wagley & Co to pick Cotton upon the abandoned lands in the vicinity, upon Condition that they would provide all the labor, implements &c and turn over to Goverment a Certain portion of the Crop—If Mr Cutler Can Show that he has obtained his Cotton upon Similar Conditions and that the required portion had been duly turned over to the Goverment, he is entitled to indemnification for the amount seized—If not the Govt Cannot be held responsible for the Cotton as its destruction, was a Military necessity and its loss to the owner a misfortune to which all persons owning property upon the theatre of war are liable"—Copies, DLC-USG, V, 58; DNA, RG 107, Letters Received, C443 1866; *ibid.*, C375 1869. Written on a communication of Feb. 12 from John A. Logan received at USG's hd. qrs. "Submits case of Captain O. N. Cutler of the city of Hannibal, Mo., who by his affidavit, says he had in April 1863, 268 bales of Cotton in good condition on west bank of Misspi. river, near Lake Providence, Louisiana; and that same was siezed by Capt B. F. Reno, A Q. M on the Order of Genl Grant for Government purposes—and that to this day he has not recieved from the U. S. Government anything in compensation for his loss of the Cotton."—*Ibid.*, RG 108, Register of Letters Received. On May 29, Bvt. Maj. Gen. Montgomery C. Meigs wrote to U.S. Senator John B. Henderson of Mo. that he had no authority to pay the claim of Otis N. Cutler of Hannibal, Mo.—Copies, *ibid.*, RG 107, Letters Received, C443 1866; *ibid.*, C375 1869. Cutler had requested $62,645 in damages for cotton seized to fortify the *Tigress*, a steamboat sunk during the night of April 22, 1863, attempting to run past Vicksburg's batteries. See *PUSG*, 9, 162–63. On June 25, 1866, Cutler, New York, wrote to USG. "I beg leave to submit the following supplemental Statement of my claim against the Government for cotton taken by your order in April 1863. The cotton claimed by me is the cotton obtained under the Wagley contract, to which you refer in your endorsement. The said Wagley, prior to that time having assigned his interest in said contract to me. The affidavits of Wagley, Reno, and Graham, all persons well known to you, and to which affidavits I respectfully call your attention, are herewith filed. The Quartermaster General has decided the case against me, but in his written opinion, herewith filed, he seems to have ignored your endorsement, as he makes no argument on the case stated by you, viz: that if this was cotton obtained by me through contract with the Government that I should receive indemnification for the amount seized. The evidence herewith filed shows conclusively that I obtained this cotton upon the conditions named in your endorsement of February 15. 1866; that I had duly turned over to the government the portion required by the Contract, and therefore I claim that I am entitled, in accordance with your decision to indemnification for the amount seized and used by the Government. I would therefore ask that you would make such order in the premises, or such further recommendation as may, secure an adjustment of my claim in conformity with your former decision."—Copies, DNA, RG 107, Letters Received, C443 1866; *ibid.*, C375 1869. On June 27, USG endorsed these letters. "Respectfully forwarded to the Secretary of War. The decision of the Quartermaster General does not seem pertinent to this case. I can but repeat my endorsement of February 15th 1866, on enclosed affidavit of Mr. O. N. Cutler."—Copies, *ibid.* Additional papers are *ibid.* Cutler eventually received $50,000. See *SRC*, 40-2-155; *HED*, 44-1-189, p. 11.

1866, Feb. 16. To Brig. Gen. Henry Prince. "On arriving at home I find that a previous engagement prevents me complying with my engagement to dine with you this evening. Please do not let this interupt your arrangements in entertaining the other guests. If I can get arount by 10 p. m. I will do so."—ALS, Connecticut Historical Society, Hartford, Conn.

1866, Feb. 16. USG endorsement. "It is respectfully recommended that in as much as the order for the restoration of the 'Sothoron' estate to Mrs. Sothoron has received the sanction of the President the order be now made positive on the Agt. of the Freedmen's Bureau occupying it that it be restored on the 10th of March, the date at which the report of Gen Fullerton thinks it can be restored."—AES, DNA, RG 105, Land Div., Letters Received. Written on a letter of Feb. 15 from Barnes Compton to President Andrew Johnson concerning the restoration of the property of John H. Sothoron, St. Marys County, Md.—ALS, *ibid.* On Feb. 19, Johnson favorably endorsed this letter.—ES, *ibid.* See *ibid.*, RG 109, Union Provost

Marshals' File of Papers Relating to Individual Civilians; *HED*, 43-1-281; *HRC*, 43-2-47.

1866, FEB. 17. Benjamin F. Butler, Washington, D. C., to USG. "I have the honor to enclose to you copy of a note written by direction of the Secretary of War which will explain itself. As the confidential nature of the letter spoken of can be waived by you I take leave to request a Copy of the letter called for from the writer."—LS, DNA, RG 108, Letters Received; ADf, DLC-Benjamin F. Butler. On Feb. 16, Bvt. Maj. Gen. Edward D. Townsend had written to Butler. "I am directed by the Secretary of War to inform you that your application for a copy of the letter of Lieutenant General Grant requesting you to be relieved from command of the Department of Virginia and North Carolina, has been considered, and that in his opinion it is not consistent with the interests of the service, or the practice of the Department to furnish a copy. Such letters are regarded as confidential communications."—ALS, *ibid.*

1866, FEB. 19. USG endorsement. "Respectfully referred to the President of the United States. I would be pleased to be authorized to write to Genl Hardee, advising him to go on with his private affairs, without fear of molestation from the Government, so long as his course is not inimical to the Govt. An early answer is respectfully asked."—Copies, DNA, RG 94, Letters Received, 871H 1866; *ibid.*, RG 107, Letters Received from Bureaus. Written on a letter of Feb. 9 from William J. Hardee, former C.S.A. lt. gen., Demopolis, Ala., to USG. "The generosity and magnanimity extended by you to the vanquished, leads me to solicit your good offices in procuring me a pardon. On the 7th inst the Stockholders of the Selma & Meridian Rail Road held a meeting, and I was elected President of the Road, without opposition. My usefulness would be promoted by a pardon; but if you cannot procure me that boon, an assurance from the President that I will not be molested would benefit me. If my word is worth anything, you can answer for me as a good and loyal citizen. Your early attention to this matter will greatly oblige."—Copies, *ibid.* On Feb. 19, President Andrew Johnson endorsed this letter. "Respectfully returned to Lieut Gen Grant, who is authorized to state to W. J. Hardee that he will not be molested in his private affairs."—Copies, *ibid.* Additional papers are *ibid.* See also *ibid.*, RG 94, Amnesty Papers, Ala.

1866, FEB. 20. USG endorsement. "Respectfully refered to the President of the United States. The father of this applicant died in the service and like most soldiers left a comparitively destitute family.—I would feel glad to aid this applicant."—AES, DNA, RG 94, Cadet Applications. Written on a letter of Feb. 16 from Alexander D. B. Smead, Carlisle, Pa., to USG. "By the advice of Gen. Stanley I enclose to you my application for an appointment to West Point. As chief of the Army, you would seem to be the natural friend of officers' children. My father was a graduate of West Point, and is still remembered by the older officers of the Army as a brave soldier and patriot. My oldest brother was killed during the Rebellion leaving my mother but one son, besides myself, in feeble health. It has always been my chief desire to receive a military education when I became old enough, and now I ask your assistance in obtaining this appointment. Apart from my taste for the profession, the circumstances of the family render it very desirable. If I do not obtain it I shall be obliged to give up my present studies for some employment. I do not object to work, but wish very much for an education. I am aware that boys who have been in the Army themselves have been, and I think very justly, given the preference by government; but when the war broke out I was scarcely thirteen years of age. I, however, long before its close felt it to be my duty to enlist, and would have done so but for the opposition of my mother. This may seem a poor excuse, but I do not think I could possibly have a better. Last year I applied for an appointment, and obtained letters from Gens. Scott, Anderson and others, as also from the President of Dickinson College in this town. I presume these are still on file and could be seen. If you can procure for me an appointment, you will receive the sincere thanks of my mother and myself." —ALS, *ibid.* On Feb. 18, Maj. and Bvt. Maj. Gen. David S. Stanley, 5th Cav., Wooster, Ohio, wrote to USG. "I have the honor to address you, in behalf, of Franklin Bache Smead, begging that you will bring his case, to the notice of His Excellency the President, with a view of getting the youth, an appointment as a Cadet 'at large' if possible—Young Smead is about 17 years of age,—His Father was a Captain of Artillery, and died soon after the close of the Mexican war, of disease Contracted in that war, His brother John Smead, also a captain of Artillery was Killed, Commanding his battery, in the 2nd Battle of Bull Run—By these Calamities Mrs Smead is left very poor, Her little pittance of a pension being her only dependance, excepting the assistance of her Devoted daughters, who have assisted thier mother by teaching—Notwithstanding her difficulties, Mrs Smead has managed, to give her children a good education, and the youngest, (Bache) is well qualified to enter the Military Academy—He is moreover represented to me, to be a very bright and promising student—I hope you will lay the case of this young man before the President, and I beleive, a more deserving case, of the kind usually filled, by appointments at large, will not be presented to His Excellency"—ALS, *ibid.* Smead was not appointed; however, he was appointed 2nd lt., 3rd Cav., as of Feb. 21, 1868.

1866, FEB. 20. USG endorsement. "Respectfully returned to the Secretary of War.—I see no reason for complying with Gen. Schofield's request. His name is placed at the foot of the list of Major Generals of Volunteers, as he was the last confirmed of those appearing on the register."—ES, DNA, RG 94, ACP, 2556 1883. Written on a letter of Oct. 28, 1865, from Maj. Gen. John M. Schofield to Bvt. Col. Samuel F. Chalfin, AGO, requesting that his position in the U.S. Army register be altered.—ALS, *ibid.* On Nov. 12, 1866, Schofield, Richmond, wrote to USG. "*Private* . . . The enclosed paper is the one I refered to in our conversation at your house the other day, giving your decision of a question of rank in direct opposition to what I understood to be your views on that question. I did not raise the question as one of any *special* interest to me, for it was then no longer a practical one, but to test the correctness of the rule then recently adopted in the Adjutant Generals Office in place of the one prescribed in the Army Regulations, and, I believe, invariably followed until the time arrived for its application to my case. And I now send you this, not on my own account, but because the new rule which appears to have your sanction will, unless reversed, regulate the relative rank of a large number of officers in the new regiments, in spite of differences in previous dates of Commission or even of former grades." —ALS, *ibid.*, RG 108, Letters Received. Schofield enclosed a letter of Feb. 26 from Col. John C. Kelton, AGO, to Schofield incorporating USG's Feb. 20 endorsement.—LS, *ibid.*

1866, FEB. 20. To James W. Webb. "Yours of this date, enclosing a note from your son asking for a five months extension of leave, is just rec'd. I take great pleasure in directing that what he asks shall be granted." —ALS, CtY.

1866, FEB. 20. Francis E. Whitfield, Corinth, Miss., to USG. "Knowing the immense amount of important business, that must ocupy almost everry moment of one filling the high position you do; tis with great reluctance I ask a few minutes consideration of the following statement; But believing you to be as just and honourable as you, have made yourself famous and exalted, I most respectfully ask your perusal and consideration of this communication. I am, and have always been a private Citizen; have led the quiet retired life of a Farmer; have never held or sought office, either Civil or Military; never belonged to, or fully agreed, with any political party; never tried to influence a man's vote; but considered it my duty to inform myself, and vote at elections. Was opposed to the repeal of the Missouri compromise, and to Squatter Sovereighnty; voted for John Bell in 1859, as I thought him the only candidate for the Presidency, who was not a Sectional Man, and who would preserve the Union if elected—Believed in State Sovereighnty, and consequently considered my allegience as due to this state after secession. I lived quietly on my farm, two miles from here, untill about six weeks after the evacuation of this place by Gen Beauregard in the summer of 1862; I had no disposition to go south, was advised by my friends, and distinguished Southern Officers to remain at home, and attend to my business as usual, endeavered to do so, and was congratulated by more than one U S General, the first day they ocupied this place, for so doing. On or about the 8th July 1862 I was arrested by a U. S. Officer, for what, I was never informed never knew, and never heard, except the vague charge of 'attempting to subvert the Government.' I had done nothing that I knew of, or now, know of, to cause my arrest. I had never before, nor have I since, served the Confederacy, or any one of the Southern States in a civil or

Military capacity or in any other way or character whatsoever; never loaned or gave them money, never owned or held any of their bonds, other than what was, here termed money—the paper currency, or circulating medium at that time. I never corresponded ~~with~~ or communicated with any Officer or Soldier of the Confederate or Southern Army, or received any letters from them, or any one else, out side of the Federal lines, from the ocupation of this place by the U S Army, till I left here; except a note sent to a Lady, on business, which was shown to and appoved by a U. S. officer ~~a~~ commanding ~~officer of~~ the outpost guards, and if I correctly remember, named Maj McDermot, and a letter, received, directed to me, but intended for an old woman, living in my field and on my charity—said letter was on private business—my name was not mentioned in it, nor was I alluded to in anyway—I kept it no secret, but voluntarily told of it after my arrest—The contents of the above named two letters, I distinctly recollect, and, which you will find in exhibet A, hereunto appended,—I never, during that time, before nor since, communicated any information to the Southern Army or any one connected therewith, the knowledge of which would be detrimental to the Federal Army or the United States. A day or two after my arrest, I gave my friend Rev. L. B. Gaston, authority to take possession of my property, which authority was approved by Gens Ord and Todd, and Mr Gaston proceeded to act, did take and for several days held possession of all my effects, both personal and real, in this county—and continued so to do, (taking care of the same), untill dispossessed by Officers under your Authority—When my premises became quarters for yourself and Staff. In the exhibet marked B, (which is a copy of the original in my possession) you will perceive I respectfully asked your permission to renew the authority to Mr Gaston—and in the exhibit marked C (which is also a copy of the original in my possession) you will find, that altho you could not grant my request—yet you were kind enough to promise that 'Your (my) property should not be destroyed or carried off, except for the benefit of the U S Government, in the latter case, an acurate account will be kept, so that should you (I) prove entitled to it, you (I) will have recourse upon the Government which you (I) are charged with attempting to subvert.' After my premises were thus occupied by the Military authorities as above named, they were used for several Military purposes, to wit, awhile as your personal quarters, then as a Military Hospital and finally all the improvements were torn down and as I learn, removed to Camp Davis and used as material for constructing U S army quarters All my furneture and other appurtenances to the premises, as well as valuable notes, bonds, deeds, recipts and papers, and memoranda, were also removed, (the latter, at the time of my arrest) my fences stock &c destroyed, in fine, nothing save the naked land was left—In as much therefore, General, as I am ~~G~~guilty of no act of disloyalty to the U S Government, as I have suffered heavily in my person and property—as my property was used for the benefit of the U. S. Government, and in as much as I hold your implied assurance of compensation for this loss, when my loyalty is established, therefore I would respectfully ask that you make some acknowledgemt of the conversion of my property to Military uses by Military authority, without subsequent compensation, and the circumstances thereof, and such other information and assistance as far as convenintly in your power lies, as will aid me in the 'recourse upon the Govt' to which you referr'd in your above mentioned indorsement—"—ALS, DNA, RG 108, Letters Received. Whitfield enclosed a copy of his letter of July 18, 1862, to USG. "Having been informed by L. B. Gaston, that you have taken possession of my premises for Head Quarters and suspended the exercise of authority over the same which I had, with the sanction of Major Genl Ord and Brig Genl Tod, granted to him, I would hereby respectfully ask your permission to renew to Mr Gaston that grant of authority and power of disposal over my property to whatever extent it may be lawful or agreeable to you to allow him to exercise it and I wish the grant of power to embrace not only the matters and things specified in the former grant through Generals Ord & Todd, but also my houses and lands, servants and live-stock, carriages furniture provender and whatever else may demand his attention on my behalf. You will, Sir, please understand me as not expressing the slightest dissatisfaction with your procedure affecting my concerns or soliciting any favor incompatible with my present position but simply divising measures for the protection of whatever interests and rights I may be allowed to retain in the premises"—Copy, *ibid.* On the same day, USG endorsed this letter. "Your property will not be destroyed or carried off except for the benefit of the United States government, In the latter case, an accurate account will be kept so that should you prove entitled to it, you will have recourse upon the goverment which you are charged with attempting to subvert, Knowing my own duties I can allow no interferance on the part of persons who cannot give evidence of loyalty."—Copy, *ibid.* See *PUSG*, 5, 218–20. Whitfield also supplied an undated letter from L. B. Gaston to USG. "Your Applicant, L B Gaston of Corinth Miss, would respectfully State that he was the owner and proprietor of the Female College building situate at that place, with the furnature & belonging to the boarding department of the same, and continued to conduct said School until the occupation of Corinth by the Rebel Army under command of Gen Johnson and others in the winter and Spring of 1862, when he was ordered to leave the premises, so that the same with the furnature &c could be used for Hospital purposes, which was according done, until the occupation of Corinth by the Army of the United States 1st June 1862, When the buildings ~~and~~ furnature &c ~~when~~ were taken possession of by order of the Commanding General and was ~~returned~~ retained and used for Hospital purposes up to the evacuation of Corinth by the U S Army 24 January 1864, during which time all the buildings and other improvements belonging to the premises ~~were taken~~ except the main building were taken down and removed, and used as building material for putting up quarters for Officers and Soldiers, and the furnature was used for Hospital and other purposes by the army, so that the same has been fully lost to your applicant, Your applicant further states that in ~~186~~ February 1865 a Detachment of the U S army visited Corinth, when Some stragling soldiers supposed to be without orders fired the building when it was consumed. Your applicant further states that he has taken no part in the late rebellion but has conducted himself quietly as a private citizen that if by the regulations of the army he is entitled to compensation for the use and occupation of said building, furnature &c, and for the materials &c, so taken and used, he very much needs the same, having by the result of the war been deprived of all his means, If it is within your power to make any order in aid of your applicants claim, he will feel under great obligations for the same."—Copy, *ibid.*

1866, FEB. 23. Maj. Gen. William T. Sherman, St. Louis, to USG. "Genl Barry asks me to write you on the subject of his Brevet. I hate to do so, and believe you will give me credit for not pushing such matters before you, and only do so now that I may write Barry in truth that I have done so. He is now Colonel of the 5th Artillery, is a Brevet Brig Genl of the Regular army, and intimates that others who have done less service than he are Brevet Maj Generals I dont know the fact and deem it enough to simply repeat his wish, to put him so that he will not be prejudiced in his future Rank. He goes to California April 1st next. Barry joined me at Nashville, was made Chief of Artillery and served near me till the close of the War. He relieved me well of the care of that arm of service, and no doubt filled his office well, being an enthusiast as to Artillery. He also cheerfully and without hesitation reduced the number of Guns to suit my wishes and plans. I do not wish him to be prejudiced in rank, by any Brevet Commissions and if other Artillery Colonels or Lt Colonels have the Brevet of Maj Genl, will recommend that the same be conferred on Genl Barry to date from Sept 1, 1864, the date of the Capture of Atlanta."—ALS, DNA, RG 108, Letters Received.

1866, [FEB. 24?]. G. Denton Williams, petition, to USG. "Your petitioner begs leave respectfully to represent that upwards of two weeks ago a negro man formerly a slave, was very insolent to your petitioner, and attempted an assault on him, that your petitioner to avoid a collision, retreated and was pressed upon until he thought 'forbearance had ceased to be a virtue' before he dealt a blow—that somedays thereafter your petitioner was summoned by Lieut Chase agent for the Freedmen & Provost Marshall at Culpeper C Ho Va to answer the charge of an assault on the negro, that your petitioner appeared at the time and place indicated by the summons, expecting to be tried according to the forms of law civil or martial and armed with testimony to justify his course, but Lieut Chase refused to hear his witnesses, and upon the admission of your petitioner that he struck the negro, but refusing to allow him to state the circumstances under which he did it—Lieut Chase as Provost Marshall fined your petitioner Fifteen dollars and costs. Your petitioner thinks as there is a Freedmens Court here, *it* and *not the military* was the proper tribunal for the trial of this class of cases. When Lieut Chase imposed this fine, your petitioner asked him if a negro struck a white man, if the white man had the right to repel force by force, he answered no; Well; Your petitioner asked, what if a negro should spit in my face? Chase replied you must not strike, but report to me for investigation Now your petitioner when recollecting your high and delicate sense of justice and ~~honour~~ known and acknowledged love of Constitutional rights and liberty, cannot for one moment believe that any such rule for the government of men, as that laid down by Lieut Chase can have your approval. Your petitioner further represents that he is a minor of tender years, without property and has no means of paying the fine in question, but if given a fair trial and found guilty by a competent tribunal—he believes his Father would cheerfully pay any fine that might be imposed Praying and believing that your excellency will give the needful redress in this case he subscribes himself with great respect"—ADS (undated), DNA, RG 105, Letters Received. On March 22, Lt. Col. Garrick Mallery, Veteran Reserve Corps, wrote to Col. Orlando Brown, 24th Colored, asst. commissioner, Bureau of Refugees, Freedmen, and Abandoned Lands, reporting that on Feb. 10 Williams had provoked and then assaulted Wesley Abbott, a former U.S. soldier.—Copy, *ibid.*

1866, FEB. 28. USG endorsement. "Gen. Thornton, the father of this applicant for a Cadets Appointment is an old Army officer and has therefore no other means of getting his son to West Point except 'At large.' I therefore recommend him for the favorable concideration of the President." —AES, DNA, RG 94, Cadet Applications. Written on a letter of Feb. 20 from John A. Dix, Union Pacific Rail Road Co., New York City, to President Andrew Johnson recommending Howard Thornton for an appointment to USMA.—ALS, *ibid.* No appointment followed.

1866, MARCH 3. To Robert Bonner. ". . . I think a wagon of 140 lbs to 160 lbs will answer. As I shall always use it myself, and drive carefully over rough places, such a wagon will probably stand . . . I shall be perfectly satisfied with your judgment in this matter."—Carnegie Book Shop, Catalogue 318, no. 163. See letter to Elihu B. Washburne, Nov. 9, 1865.

1866, MARCH 8. J. Forsyth, Buffalo, N. Y., to USG. "Permit me to trespass on your valuable time a few moments, by directing your attention to an Invention recently perfected here,—by a gentleman of this City,—applicable to Fire arms. I take the liberty of addressing you in order to obtain the expression of an opinion of one. eminently qualified to decide its adaptibility to our National Weapons.—It is a simple & effective mode of rendering the accidental discharge of a musquet or rifle impossible. It is a spring-Latch, self adjustable, which prevents the hammer from being lifted, only at volition; So that on the march through ground, or woods, or climbing over fences, it is utterly impossible to remove the hammer from its locked position; at the same time resting ⅛ of an inch above the cap, there can be no possible discharge by any accidental, or sudden Concussion on the hammer.

It is operated by a moderate pressure of the left hand, as the piece is held when brought into position preparatory to firing, & does not necessarily involve any new movement, or change in the 'manual', other than to make use of this pressure, It Certainly very effectually accomplishes the end designed, & should you approve of *the idea*, & will give the matter your able Consideration, with your permission, I will send you the model; which is a section of a U. S. musquet—"—ALS, USG 3.

1866, March 9, 2:00 p.m. To Maj. Gen. William T. Sherman. "The following is an extract from War Dept S. O. March 6th/66. . . . '7. Leave of absence for thirty days with permission to visit the Island of Cuba is hereby granted Brevet Brig General Thomas Sword Asst Q Mr Genl USA By order of the Secretary of War (signed.) E D Townsend Asst Adjt Gen" —Telegram sent, DNA, RG 107, Telegrams Collected (Bound); copies, *ibid.*, RG 108, Letters Sent; *ibid.*, RG 393, Military Div. of the Miss., Telegrams Received; DLC-USG, V, 47, 109.

1866, March 9. USG endorsement. "Respectfully forwarded and the appointment recommended. This applicant was too young to participate in the war but his family have been enthusiastic supporters of the Govt. in the great conflict just closed. His two uncles and brother-in-law have all participated taking distinguished parts, the latter loosing a leg in the service."—AES, DNA, RG 94, Cadet Applications. Written on a letter of Feb. 28 from Richard T. Yeatman to President Andrew Johnson requesting an appointment to USMA.—ALS, *ibid.* Yeatman graduated from USMA in 1872.

1866, March 9. USG endorsement. "I respectfully recommend that the order dismissing Lt. E. L. Appleton 1st U. S. Artillery be revoked in accordance with the within application, that is that he resign from the date of said order."—AES, Menninger Foundation, Topeka, Kan. Written on a letter of Feb. 14 from H. C. Ingersoll to President Andrew Johnson. "I request that in consideration of the honorable record which Lt E L Appleton possessed up to the time of his sickness while on recruiting service at Poughkeepsie New York, and for the reason that his misdemeanors were caused by *mental aberration at the time*, that his sentence of dishonorable dismissal from the service be revoked, and that he be reinstated with permission to resign, his resignation to take effect from date of dismissal."—ALS, *ibid.* On March 12, USG wrote an identical endorsement on a letter of March 7 from U.S. Senator Lot M. Morrill of Maine making a similar request.—Copies, DNA, RG 94, ACP, A100 CB 1866; *ibid.*, RG 108, Register of Letters Received. On April 22, 1865, the AGO had prepared a lengthy memorandum for USG concerning the case of 1st Lt. Edward L. Appleton, 1st Art.—AD, *ibid.* On May 5, Brig. Gen. John A. Rawlins endorsed this memorandum. "The dismissal of Lt. Appleton, as within recommended approved."—ES, *ibid.* On May 9, John Appleton, Bangor, Maine, wrote to USG. "Accompanying this you will receive a letter from Mrs Appleton in relation to her son Lt Edward L Appleton. It would afford great gratification to the public here, if you can accede to the wishes of Mrs Appleton as expressed in her letter to you. Mrs Appleton is a lady who commands the respect & confidence of all who know her & upon whose statements the greatest reliance may be placed. I have known Lt Appleton from his infancy. His family is of the highest respectability. He too, has heretofore sustained a good reputation for integrity & honorable conduct. He entered the service in the first regiment which left this state and early received promotion for good conduct. Trusting you may be enabled to grant the request of a mother, whose *every effort* has been to *sustain the government* in all respects, . . ."—ALS, *ibid.* Appleton resigned as of May 10.

1866, MARCH 10. To Secretary of War Edwin M. Stanton. "I would respectfully ask that the sentence of the General Court Martial promulgated in General Orders, No. 8, Hd. Qrs. Dept of Georgia, February 9th 1866, in the case of Private Charles Treadwell Co. "A" 9th Battn. N. Y. Vols. be remitted."—Copies, DLC-USG, V, 47, 109; DNA, RG 108, Letters Sent.

1866, MARCH 10. USG endorsement. "Respectfully forwarded to the Hon: Secretary of War with the recommendation that, if existing laws do not authorize a pension, this communication be approved and referred to Congress for special relief in this case—"—Copies, DNA, RG 107, Letters Received, I58 1866; *ibid.*, RG 108, Register of Letters Received; DLC-Philip H. Sheridan. Written on a letter of Feb. 23 from Maj. Gen. Philip H. Sheridan to USG. "I take the liberty of calling your attention to the case of the widow of Doctor Ohlenschlager—The Doctor was a Contract Surgeon and Acting Medical Inspector on my Staff at the time I was in command of the Middle Military Division, and was murdered by guerillas whilst enroute from Martinsburg to Cedar Creek in November 1864 in the discharge of his duty—He was one of my most faithful and efficient officers, and it is but justice to his widow and orphan that some action be taken by Congress, to make the same provision for them as is made for those of officers commissioned, and I request that your influence be used to secure this end—"—Copy, DNA, RG 107, Letters Received, I58 1866. Additional papers are *ibid.* See *PUSG*, 12, 313*n*; *O.R.*, I, xliii, part 2, 351.

1866, MARCH 12. William P. Dockray, clerk, U.S. District Court of Northern Fla., St. Augustine, to USG. "I have this day mailed you a copy of a Newspaper called the Florida Union and have marked therein an article of the Editors, most Scurriously attacking a good honest and just Officer of the United States Government. This same Officer I rescued from an open boat in the night with his daughter, in the St Johns River whither they had been driven on account of their loyalty—at the time our vessels took Jacksonville The Title of the above paper referred to 'Union' is but a garb, under which its seeks its attack upon Loyal Citizens, if the same are beyond the control, or, influence of its meshes—Its Editors were and are Secesh and I make the bold assertion, that it is impossible for Loyal Citizens, in this State to obtain any shadow of justice in the State Courts. I do hope your Order in regard to suppressing such papers as are endeavouring to obstruct the Laws of the United States, may be visited upon the sheet above referred to, and any others that may take that course—To substantiate my assertions, with regard to Law and Justice in the State Courts I will Cite this one Instance, among many At a sale of the Direct Tax Commissioners Major John Hay, purchased, some property in the outskirts of this city belonging to Judge Putnam of the Circuit Court of this State—Judge P. failed to redeem according to Law. The purchaser was put in possession by the Commissioners—After Major Hay had gone to Paris Putnam goes and takes forcible possession of this property, Breaks open the House, drives the Negroes off, of it, which Major Hays agent had at work improving it, and still holds possession of it—and refuses to surrender it—The post commander was called upon to dispossess Putnam—He asked my opinion. I thought he had not the authority, as it was not now U. S. property—Would it not, meet the exegencies of such cases until the proper legislation can be had by Congress, for the Lieut Genl to issue a special order to the Commanders of the different departments, to protect all such persons in their property and rights, if need be, at the point of the Bayonet. I only make this suggestion on account of the boasts made by the former propertyholders, that they are the masters of the Yankees—in Law and will show them—"—ALS, DNA, RG 108, Letters Received. The clipping is *ibid.*

1866, March 13. USG endorsement. "Respectfully returned to the Hon. Secretary of War, with the information that the small number of troops at the disposal of Gen Sherman renders it wholly impracticable to comply with Mr. Sawyers request for an escort &c. Every effort will be made to so dispose of the troops along the main routes of travel as to give the greatest possible protection to travellers and emigrants. But until Congress authorizes an increase of the Army and the men are obtained escorts cannot be furnished" —ES, DNA, RG 107, Letters Received from Bureaus. Written on a letter of March 10 from Secretary of the Interior James Harlan to Secretary of War Edwin M. Stanton enclosing a letter of Jan. 22 from James A. Sawyers to Stanton requesting military protection while constructing a wagon road from Niobrara, Nebraska Territory, to Virginia City, Montana Territory. —LS and ALS, *ibid.* On March 31, U.S. Representative Asahel W. Hubbard of Iowa wrote to USG. "It is the intention of Col. James A. Sawyers Superintendent of the wagon road from Niobrara to Virginia City in Montana to commence work upon the Same early in May, and to pass over the entire route during the Season. His party will consist of about Sixty men and as a large portion of the route passes through an Indian country, it is important that they should be well armed. Under these circumstancies cannot the Col obtain a supply of arms and amunition from the war Department? Permit me to make such a request."—ALS, *ibid.*, RG 156, Letters

Received. On April 2, USG endorsed this letter. "Respectfully forwarded to the Hon Secry of War—approved."—ES, *ibid.* On May 21, USG favorably endorsed to Stanton a letter of May 17 from Hubbard to Bvt. Maj. Gen. Alexander B. Dyer, chief of ordnance, requesting two howitzers for Sawyers's use.—ES and ALS, *ibid.* See *HED*, 39-1-105.

1866, MARCH 13. USG endorsement. "Respectfully returned to the Hon. Secretary of War, with a letter from Gen. Sherman explaining the utter impossibility of complying with the request of the acting Governor of Montana."—ES, DNA, RG 107, Letters Received from Bureaus. Written on a letter of Oct. 20, 1865, from Act. Governor Thomas F. Meagher of Montana Territory to Bvt. Maj. Gen. Frank Wheaton requesting cav. to protect the territory from Indians and highway robbers.—Copy, *ibid.* On March 7, Maj. Gen. William T. Sherman, St. Louis, wrote to Brig. Gen. John A. Rawlins. "I have this day received the letter of Hon Wm. H. Seward sec of state covering a communication of T. Francis Meagher, secretary of the Territory of Montana asking for 500 cavalry to be sent to that Territory to maintain order. This paper is similar in character to many others received from the same source, all of which have been answered to the effect that I cannot spare the troops. They are not in existence. We have but one Cavalry Regimnt the 2nd Regulars in all the Dept of Missouri, embracing the territories of Montana, Dahcotah, Nebraska Utah, Colorado and New-Mexico, all clamorous for similar troops. It will require every soldier at my disposal to afford approximate protection to the routes of travel, and these Territories must of necessity protect themselves, and emigrants in transitu will also be forced to move in such strength and order as to protect their trains. All we can attempt is to make a few points of security along the routes of travel. I return these papers that they may be laid before the Military Committees of Congress, to hurry them up in providing an army adequate to the wants of the growing interests in our Remote territories"—ALS, *ibid.*

1866, MARCH 13. James R. Kelley, speaker, Pa. House of Representatives, Harrisburg, to USG. "The House of Representatives of Pennsylvania by resolution have instructed me to invite you to be present at the meeting of the schools for the orphans of our Soldiers and Sailors in the Hall of the House at Harrisburg on Friday March 16th at 12 oclock "M" It will be exceedingly gratifying to our people and their Representatives if you can consistently with your public duties be present on that interesting occasion" —ALS, USG 3.

1866, MARCH 15. To Secretary of War Edwin M. Stanton. "I would respectfully recommend that Lt. Col. & Bvt. Col. Frank J. White, 2nd U. S. Colored Cavalry, be Breveted a Brigadier General of Volunteers to take rank from the 9th of March 1865."—ALS, DNA, RG 94, ACP, W526 CB 1863. On Jan. 31, Bvt. Maj. Gen. William T. Clark, Brazos Santiago,

Tex., wrote to Stanton recommending Lt. Col. Frank J. White, 2nd Colored Cav., for appointment as bvt. brig. gen.—LS, *ibid.* On Feb. 21, USG endorsed this letter. "One brevet recommended."—ES, *ibid.*

1866, MARCH 15, 2:50 P.M. To Maj. Gen. William T. Sherman. "Give four months leave to Bvt Major Wells eighteenth Infantry"—Telegram sent, DNA, RG 107, Telegrams Collected (Bound); copies, *ibid.*, RG 108, Letters Sent; *ibid.*, RG 393, Military Div. of the Miss., Telegrams Received; DLC-USG, V, 47, 109.

1866, MARCH 15. Capt. and Bvt. Col. Samuel S. Carroll, Baltimore, to USG. "I have the honor to enclose herewith an application for Appointment as a Colonel of Infy. in the reorganisation of the Army of the U. S. forwarding therewith letters of recommendation from my former Division, Corps and Army Commanders, I respectfully request that you put such endorsement upon my application as you deem proper, . . ."—ALS, DNA, RG 94, ACP, 1639 1875. There is no endorsement. On March 23, Adam Gurowski, Washington, D. C., wrote to USG. "Again I dare to importunate you in favor of that brave, cripled & *unprotected* Bre: Maj: Gl Sprig Carroll. Before the military Bill ~~will~~ passes the Congress & before you will reorganize the army, Carroll's leave of absence will expire & he will be obliged to rejoin his regiment wherein he is only a Captain. For heavens sake be Kind & good as you allways are, & for the time between now & the organisation put Carroll on some board here or in Baltimore. Create one if there is none & save your faithful officer & my friend, save him from humiliation. If by chance you may throw your eye on the third Volu of my Diary just published, *forgive the accusation of to much magnanimity showed by you towards Meade*; who is—but never mind. Yours, my dear General: not of to day, not since the capture of Lee, but since the first ray of glory at fort Donaldson"—ALS, RPB.

1866, MARCH 19. USG endorsement. "Respectfully submitted to the Hon. Secretary of State."—ES, DNA, RG 59, Applications and Recommendations, Lincoln and Johnson. Written on a letter of Feb. 10 from Governor William Pickering of Washington Territory, Olympia, to Bvt. Col. Theodore S. Bowers requesting USG's assistance in securing reappointment as territorial governor, as promised by President Abraham Lincoln.—ALS, *ibid.* On Feb. 14, Pickering wrote three letters to Bowers on the same subject.—ALS, *ibid.*, RG 108, Letters Received. On March 22, Secretary of State William H. Seward wrote to USG. "I have to acknowledge the receipt of the papers relative to the appointment of William Pickering, Esqr as Governor of the Territory of Washington, referred by you to this Department, and to inform you in reply that Mr. Pickering was reappointed to that office on the 9th of January, last, and his Commission has been duly forwarded."—LS, *ibid.*

1866, MARCH 19. To Secretary of War Edwin M. Stanton. "I would respectfully recommend the appointment of Brig. Gen. John M. Thayer to be Maj. Gn. by Brevet, to rank from the 13th of March 1865, for gallant and meritorious services during the War."—ALS, DNA, RG 94, ACP, T334 CB 1863.

1866, MARCH 19. USG endorsement. "Not approved"—ES, DNA, RG 94, ACP, T465 CB 1863. Written on a letter of March 6 from Lewis Wallace, Washington, D. C., to USG. "I have the honor to recommend Brig. Gen. E. B. Tyler to be Brevt Maj. Gen. U. S. Vol. Not to speak of good service performed by Gen. Tyler in West Virginia as Colonel and Commandant of Brigade, I would recall his very gallant conduct as Brig. Gen.l commanding a brigade at the battle of Monocacy, which was mentioned in full in my official report of that action. The honor I am sure was well merited by him on that occasion."—ALS, *ibid.*

1866, MARCH 19. Professor Albert E. Church, USMA, to USG. "I have this day forwarded to Gen T. M. Vincent Asst Adjt Gen, an application of my son in law, Major M. M. Blunt 7th U. S. Infantry, for advancement on the re-organization of the Army, and other papers including a statement of his military services during the rebellion . . ."—ALS, DNA, RG 94, ACP, B1155 CB 1865. On Jan. 28, 1867, Church wrote to USG. "I last winter made an earnest effort to obtain an appointment as 'Cadet at large' for my nephew William S. Church and failed. I have this winter renewed the application and am deeply interested in its success. . . ."—ALS, *ibid.*, Correspondence, USMA. On Feb. 2, USG endorsed this letter. "Respectfully forwarded to the Sec. of War with the request that this be placed on file as the application of Wm S. Church for Cadet appointment, 'at large.' I would also add my recommendation and say that it would afford me special pleasure to be the means of obtaining this for an old and esteemed Professor whose life has been devoted to the public interest."—AES, *ibid.* No appointment followed. On Feb. 14, 1876, Church wrote to USG. "I wish to make application for an appointment of Cadet at large for June 1877—for my grandson *Albert Church Blunt* son of Col. M. M. Blunt 25th U. S. Infantry. . . ."—ALS, *ibid.* Albert C. Blunt graduated from USMA in 1881.

1866, MARCH 20. USG endorsement. "Respectfully forwarded to the Hon. Secretary of War—approved."—ES, DNA, RG 94, ACP, P145 CB 1866. Written on a letter of March 3 from James Pike, Hillsboro, Ohio, to Maj. Gen. George H. Thomas requesting assistance in securing an appointment in the U.S. Army.—ALS, *ibid.* On Dec. 4, 1863, Brig. Gen. George Crook had recommended Corporal Pike, 4th Ohio Cav., for appointment in the U.S. Army.—*Ohio State Journal*, Sept. 30, 1865. On March 16, 1864, USG endorsed this letter. "The recommendation of General Thomas is cordially concurred in by me. Corporal Pike has proved himself brave and energetic, and I believe would make an efficient commissioned officer"—*Ibid.* See *PUSG*, 9, 316*n.* Pike was appointed 2nd lt., 1st Cav., as of March 31, 1866. On June 22, Pike, Carlisle Barracks, Pa., wrote to USG. "Having known for certain that the wild Comanches, Kiowas and Apaches as well as some smaller tribes in the South-West have a considerable number of White captives as well as many Mexicans, which are reduced to the most abject slavery, I sometime ago made a proposition to the President to release them, and restore them to civilation, at least if not able to find their proper families. His Excellency has perhaps has forgotten me as he has to deal with so many men, and as I wrote without any voucher except my own name my communication has not been answered. Since that time however I have been commissioned as as a second Lieutenant in the 1st U. S. Cavalry, This brings me under your command again. Therefore I deem it proper to submit my plan to you for your consideration. I need not speak to you of the importance of the work. You will understand that better than any one else. I fully understand the dangers and hardships to which it will subject me and the cost of a failure or capture. I am well acquainted with the country I would have to traverse; as I have had to traverse it frequently when I was serving with the Texas Rangers. And I believe I could liberate the last captive held by these tribes in about three Years. The plan I would propose would be to go out to the frontier, with instructions from you, so that when I had found a band of these Indians who held captives I could repair to the nearest one of the frontier Posts and call for a sufficient number of men to effect their release or to punish the Indians if they refused to comply with my demands. I would first travel among them as a hunter and trapper until I got them properly located. Then make for the nearest fort and get men enough for the work. By this way I would be sure never to attack the wrong tribe. As I was a Scout in the Army of the Cumberland all through the Rebellion I would have no hesitancy in undertaking the work. Many of these prisoners were taken before the war, and many others since the war. From recent information I learn that the Comanches alone have about three hundred. The Apaches Cheyennes and Kiowas as many more, besides the Mexicans which they drag away in their anual incursions into that country. I assisted in recapturing a white woman in 1861 who said they had a great many others. But that they seldom allowed a prisoner above nine years old to live. She was afterwards identified as a neice of Capt Parker's an old settler in Texas We also killed another White woman by mistake. The prisoner was rejoiced to be restored to her people although she had raised a family of children among the Indians. A few weeks ago I saw a young man named Joseph Black who was taken from the Wabash in 1837 by the Pottowatomies and in course of time after being sold several times fell into the hands of the Comanches. He says they have many prisoners. I only cite these cases to support what I myself say. If you want me to undertake the work I will do so as soon as I receive the proper detail and instructions. By my plan the Government will be involved in no extra expense that I can see. No extra expense being needed as all troops on the frontier are perhaps properly equiped for traversing the great American desert the staked plane, and the different mountain ranges infested by these tribes, who roam through Texas, New Mexico, Colorado, Arizonia, and the Northern states of Mexico. If, General you consider this proposition worthy of consideration, I hope to hear from you at your earliest convenience as I expect shortly to be sent to my regiment in California. The only drawback in the matter would be that I would be kept away from my regiment a considerable time, and that I might lose my scalp before I got through with it. In order to satisfy you of my *identity* I send you a word from General Sherman which please return to me at all events as I would not part with it for a Colonels Commission. . . . P. S. I had thought to submit this matter to a member of Congress but they would quarrel over it too long and the prisoners would not be released in time. I am afraid of Politicians. They wont do to depend on."—ALS, DNA, RG 393, Military Div. of the Miss., Letters Received. On June 26, Maj. George K. Leet forwarded this letter to Maj. Gen. William T. Sherman.—AES, *ibid.* On June 30, Sherman, St. Louis, wrote to Leet. "I think I understand Pike, he is very restless and adventurous. I enclose a private note for him which I think will quiet him for a few months. . . ."—Stan. V. Henkels, Catalogue No. 1194, June 8, 1917, p. 92.

1866, March 22. USG endorsement. "Respy. referred to the Hon. Secty of State with recommendation that Genl. Wilcox be permitted to return to the U. States. I would say that it would be better to have all ex-rebels any place else than in Mexico."—Copy, DNA, RG 108, Register of Letters Received. Written on a letter of Feb. 22 from Cadmus M. Wilcox, Mexico City, to USG requesting permission to return to the U.S.—*Ibid.*

1866, March 23, 3:25 p.m. To Ind. AG William H. H. Terrell. "Your enquiry cannot be definitely answered but the regiment will be mustered out soon as its services can be spared"—Telegram sent, DNA, RG 107, Telegrams Collected (Bound); copies, *ibid.*, RG 108, Letters Sent; DLC-USG, V, 47, 109. On March 22, Terrell, Indianapolis, had telegraphed to USG. "Is it probable that the one hundred twenty eighth Indiana Infantry now stationed in N Carolina will be mustered out before Expiration of its term of service if so about when may its muster out be expected the Regt is the only one now in service from this state & the solicitude is great on the part of Relatives & friends for its early discharg[e]"—Telegram received, DNA, RG 108, Telegrams Received; copy, DLC-USG, V, 54. On March 24, 1:50 p.m., USG telegraphed to Bvt. Maj. Gen. Thomas H. Ruger. "Can you not muster out the 128th Ia Vols. by their being replaced with six Companies of Regulars? Answer—"—Telegram sent, DNA, RG 107, Telegrams Collected (Bound); copies, *ibid.*, RG 108, Letters Sent; *ibid.*, RG 393, Dept. of N. C. and Army of the Ohio, Telegrams Received; DLC-USG, V, 47, 109. On the same day, Ruger, Raleigh, telegraphed to USG.

"In reply to telegram of this date I have the honor I to say I can muster out the One hundred & twenty eighth Ind Vols if it be replaced by six Cos of regulars"—Telegram received (at 9:15 P.M.), DNA, RG 107, Telegrams Collected (Bound); *ibid.*, RG 108, Telegrams Received; copies, *ibid.*, RG 393, Dept. of N. C. and Army of the Ohio, Telegrams Sent; DLC-USG, V, 54. On April 25, 1:10 P.M., USG telegraphed to Ruger. "Release and send home all Officers and soldiers of the 128th Ia Vols now detained in your Department"—Telegram sent, DNA, RG 107, Telegrams Collected (Bound); copies, *ibid.*, RG 108, Letters Sent; (misdated April 26) *ibid.*, RG 393, Dept. of N. C. and Army of the Ohio, Telegrams Received; DLC-USG, V, 47, 109. On April 30, Ruger wrote to Maj. George K. Leet. "I have the honor to state that in accordance with telegram of date April 26th 1866, directing me to relieve all Officers and Soldiers of the 128th Indiana Infantry Volunteers detained in this Department, I have caused all Enlisted men (three in number) of that command to be relieved and sent home. At the time of the muster out of the Regiment, I directed that all Enlisted men be sent home with the Regiment except two detained for trial on charges for arson and for malicious shooting and wounding of a Citizen. One man however undergoing sentence of General Court Martial at Fort Macon had not been released at date of reception of order of Lieutenant General Grant Commanding Armies. Three Officers of that Regiment are members of the Commission for the trial of the Rebel prison commander Gee. The muster out of such Officers until the conclusion of the trial was suspended by Order of the Secretary of War by telegram from Adjutant Generals Office dated April 7th 1866. I have not construed the telegram of the Lieutenant General as applying to these three Officers, so as to require their muster-out prior to the conclusion of the trial."—LS, DNA, RG 108, Letters Received.

1866, MARCH 23. Maj. Gen. John Pope, St. Louis, to USG. "I have the honor to request that hereafter when officers of the quartemaster or Subsistance Dept'sartments are Ordered to duty in this military Dept. they be instructed to report, for assignment to stations, to the General Commanding the Department, or to the Chief's of their respective Corps at these Head Quarters. Of necessity the qualifications of officers of these Dept's for the particular service required at each of the military Posts in this Dept. as also the character of the service to be thus performed and its relative importance must be known to the Comd'g Genl. of this Dept. and his Chief's of Staff corps, than to the quartermaster or Commissary General—In addition to this it does not seem easy to maintain proper subordination and decipline among officers whose stations are designated by orders emianating from other authority and who cannot be changed except by the same authority. It frequently happens that changes of stations of Officers of the Supply Depts., are necessary by constantly changeing circumstances and necessities of service and under the present system of assigning such officers, these changes cannot be made without much inconvenient delay. It would seem but reasonable that a Dept. commander responsible for the administration of his Dept. should have the power to assign officers to stations, with same view to their qualifications and his knowledge of the peculiar requirements of the case. An officer may be eminently fitted for duty at one post and not at all fitted for duty at an other. of these things the commander of the Dept. must under ordinary circumstances be the best judge, and I hope that this request will secure the favorable consideration of the Genl in chief as I believe from my own experience, that the interests of the service in this Dept. will be much promoted thereby."—Copy, DNA, RG 393, Dept. of the Mo., Letters Sent.

1866, MARCH 23. L. Edwin Dudley, Washington, D. C., to USG. "I have the honor to lay before you for consideration the enclosed bill to equalize the bounties of soldiers—It is the belief of most persons who have expressed an opinion that this bill is the most feasable plan for effecting this ~~I~~ object—The soldiers of the country feel that your endorsement of this measure would greatly aid its passage, and knowing the kind interest you have always manifested in their welfare they have confidence that you will approve this measure of justice to the men who were the first to bear the burdens of war. Should you deem yourself justified in endorsing this measure I should be pleased to receive a note from you"—ALS, USG 3. Docketing indicates that on March 26 Bvt. Col. Adam Badeau wrote to Dudley declining the request. —AN, *ibid.*

1866, MARCH 24. To Secretary of War Edwin M. Stanton. "I would respectfully recommend that orders be made for the Muster out [o]f all Volunteer Bands still remaining in the service. I supposed such orders had been given long since but having before me at this time an application for the discharge of a man from a Band has called my attention to the subject." —ALS, DNA, RG 94, Vol. Service Div., Letters Received, A190 (VS) 1866.

1866, MARCH 24. To Secretary of War Edwin M. Stanton. "I would respectfully recommend that the Qr. Mrs. Dept. be directed to sell all the public buildings in the grounds near Albany N. Y, remove the public property and return the grounds to the owners. There can be no use retaining troops at Albany except to guard public property and that can, without detriment to the service, be removed"—Copies, DLC-USG, V, 47, 109; DNA, RG 108, Letters Sent.

1866, MARCH 24. Maj. Gen. John Pope, St. Louis, to USG. "It trust the interior Department is making proper arrangement for feeding the mumous bands of Indians assembling at Fort Laramie & on the upper Missouri to meet peace Commissioners appointed by the Interior Dept. The military authorities have not the means to meet such extrad demand out side of their legtimate providence if the Indians are under the charge of the Interior Dept That dept should take care of such matters & not depend on the Military I telegh you in order that ~~you~~ it may be understood before hand that we are not prepared to supply these Indians & cannot be without sending supplies from thems missouri River as these supplies are sent by Contract the Interior Dept has the same means as the war Dept to send them I would like to be notified at once so that I may not be called on unexpectedly"—Telegram received (on March 25, 11:50 A.M.), DNA, RG 107, Telegrams Collected (Bound); *ibid.*, RG 108, Telegrams Received; copies, *ibid.*, Letters Received; DLC-USG, V, 54. On March 25, Secretary of War Edwin M. Stanton wrote to USG. "An application was made to me some weeks ago by the Secretary of the Interior to furnish supplies for Indian councils, about to be held by that Department. On reports from the Subsistence & Quarter Masters Departments it appeared that such supplies would exceed the cost of $100 000 and I notified the Secretary of the Interior, at a Cabinet meeting, that they *could not be furnished by the War Department* He replied that then the Interior Department would have to make provision from their own resources. Since that time I have heard no more on the subject. I will call on the Secretary of the Interior today and ascertain what he has done in the matter. But I am apprehensive that trouble will arise from the collection of these bands of Indians and think that measures of precaution should be taken by the Military Commanders where the assemblages are to be held, & would suggest that you give such instruction as you deem expedient for the case."—ALS, DNA, RG 108, Letters Received. On the same day, Maj. George K. Leet endorsed copies of these communications. "Respectfully referred to Maj. Gen. W. T. Sherman, Comdg. Mil. Div. of the Miss., who will, in accordance with the views of the Secretary of War, take precautionary measures to have such supplies furnished as may be necessary to prevent suffering among the Indians assembling at Ft Laramie &c., unless in the meantime he should receive other instructions."—AES and copies, *ibid.*, RG 393, Military Div. of the Miss., Letters Received. Maj. Gen. William T. Sherman endorsed these communications. "These points illustrate the absurdity of the Interior Dept trying to manage Indians without the means or Machinery—If invited to Council they must be supplied, & the Stores replaced *after* at the Cost of the Indian Dept —but if stores be scarce at Laramie the Indian agent must be told emphatically to feed his own people"—AES (undated), *ibid.* For correspondence of March 25 on this matter between Stanton and Secretary of the Interior James Harlan, see *ibid.*, RG 107, Letters Received from Bureaus.

1866, MARCH 24. Isaac N. Arnold to USG. "You may recollect that I mentioned to you some time ago, that I was engaged in preparing a history of Mr. Lincoln's Administration, and the overthrow of slavery in the United States. I commenced this work while Mr. Lincoln was living, and with his approval. I have reached the period at which he issued the Proclamation of Emancipation. I have reason to believe that the note you addressed to Mr. Washburne from Vicksburgh, dated August 30 18623, was brought to his

Knowledge at that time, and most carefully considered by him, in making up his mind to issue that proclamation. In the President's letter to J. C. Conkling Esq., under date of August 26 1863, he alludes to the fact, that '*some of the commanders in the field who had given us our most important victories*' believed that the Emancipation proclamation and the employment of negro troops, constituted the heaviest blows yet dealt the rebellion. On several other occasions, he refers to the opinions of prominent and successful officers, as being favorable to the military advantages of this policy. I always understood the President to allude to you as one of those to whom he referred. If you have copies of any letters addressed to Mr. Lincoln on this subject, or if you could give me the substance of what you said to him, I should regard it as a very important contribution to the history of this most interesting period; and I should feel very greatly obliged for your courtesy. Perhaps I ought to add, that on mentioning the subject to my friend and former colleague, Mr Washburne, he suggested that I should address you on the subject."—LS, USG 3. Bvt. Col. Adam Badeau noted on the docket: "Answered March 24/66 no copy of such letter in existence, and Gen Grant has no recollection of one"—AN, *ibid.* See letter to Elihu B. Washburne, Aug. 30, 1863.

1866, MARCH 25. To Secretary of War Edwin M. Stanton. "I would respectfully recommend that the name of Brig. Gn. John Newton, U. S. Vols be sent to the Senate for confirmation as Brevet Major General of Volunteers. Gen. Newton was appointed a full Major General but I believe his name was never sent to the Senate, as such, for confirmation. In view of this fact and his services during the War I think he is justly entitled to confirmation in the brevet grade."—ALS, Atwood Collection, InU.

1866, MARCH 25, 2:10 P.M. To Daniel Williams, care of Governor Samuel Cony of Maine, Augusta. "Many friends and brother graduates with your son feel desirous of attending his funeral and of having him buried at West Point. If this meets your approval please notify me and officers will at once leave here to accompany the remains to place of burial. Accept my condolance in your deep affliction, and our countrys loss"—Telegram sent, DNA, RG 107, Telegrams Collected (Bound); copies, *ibid.*, RG 108, Letters Sent; DLC-USG, V, 47, 109. On April 2, Maj. George K. Leet wrote to the AG. "I am directed by the Lieutenant General to inform you that Lieutenant Colonel Seth Williams, Assistant Adjutant General and Brevet Brigadier General USA., died on the night of the 23d March at Boston, Mass., of inflammation of the brain."—LS, DNA, RG 94, ACP, G108 CB 1866.

1866, MARCH 26. Bvt. Maj. Gen. Montgomery C. Meigs to USG. "I have received, referred to me by your order, a letter from Colonel Chandler with an endorsement by General Sheridan, who, at the request of Colonel Chandler on his being relieved from duty with several other officers at New Orleans, certifies to the merit and ability of Colonel Chandler as an officer of the Quartermaster's Department. I deem it due to this Department to say, that reports of Inspecting officers lately sent to New Orleans and the Coast of Texas by this office, allege a state of affairs in the transport service, controlled by officers of the Qur Mrs Dept who ~~are~~ were stationed at New Orleans, which is very unsatisfactory. An inspecting officer detailed by Head Quarters of the Army, also, recommended a sale, of nearly all the vessels then employed in this service, on the ground that there were unnecessary expenditures, and orders have been given and sales effected as far as possible. The whole current of Inspection Reports convinced me that there ought to be a change of officers and I requested the issue of Special Order No 103, Adjutant General's Office, March 7, 1866, to effect this, and I hope that a better system will be established under new officers. Several officers will be mustered out and several others, Colonel Chandler among the number, who have had a long service in that Southern Climate and have disbursed large sums of money, will have an opportunity to settle their accounts. I do not wish to trouble your office with the details of these Reports from the Departments of Louisiana & Texas but they are on file in this office and an inspection of them would satisfy you of the propriety of some sweeping change such as has been effected. After Colonel Chandler's accounts are settled, I hope to be able to employ him upon appropriate duty. Permission to go to his home was given him in order not to compel him to await orders at any expensive station while settling up his accounts. I did not ask that he be ordered to his home as that would have, I thought, been less acceptable to him."—LS, DNA, RG 108, Letters Received. On March 17, Maj. Gen. Philip H. Sheridan had favorably endorsed a letter received at USG's hd. qrs. of Lt. Col. John G. Chandler, q. m., apparently protesting his reassignment.—*Ibid.*, Register of Letters Received.

1866, MARCH 27. To Bvt. Maj. Gen. Edward D. Townsend. "Please order Maj. Geo. W. Wallace, 6th U. S. Infantry, on duty with the 12th Infantry, the regiment which his promotion now due will bring him to."—ALS, DNA, RG 94, Letters Received, 241A 1866.

1866, MARCH 28. To Bvt. Maj. Gen. Edward D. Townsend. "Give Col. L. H. Carpenter 5 U. S. Col. Cavalry, now about being musteredout of the Volunteer service, three months to join his regiment, the 6th U. S. Cav.y:"—ALS, DNA, RG 94, Letters Received, 240A 1866.

1866, MARCH 28. Maj. Gen. John Pope, St. Louis, to USG. "I have the honor to request that the three companies of the 5th U. S. Infantry now serving in Arizona and Texas, be relieved as soon as practicable by troops belonging properly to the Department of California and Texas and returned to their regiment in New-Mexico. I need not suggest that it is desirable that all the companies of a regiment for proper administration and control, should serve in the same Military Department. As it is believed that the necessity of keeping the companies of the 5th U. S. Infantry in three sepearate Departments, no longer exists it is hoped that this application will be granted." —Copy, DNA, RG 393, Dept. of the Mo., Letters Sent.

1866, MARCH 30. USG endorsement. "Respy. forwarded to the Hon. Sec. of War, with the recommendation that Dr. Gwin be transferred to one of the Northern forts."—Copy, DNA, RG 108, Register of Letters Received. Written on a petition of March 21 from six New Orleans physicians to Maj. Gen. Philip H. Sheridan seeking the release of William M. Gwin from prison.—Copy, DLC-Philip H. Sheridan. On March 23, Sheridan endorsed this petition. "Respectfully forwarded for the information and instructions of the Lieut. General, accompanied by the report of Asst Surg Asch U. S. A. of an examination made under my instructions and forwarded March 15 1866. for the information of the Lieut Genl."—Copy, *ibid.* The enclosure is in DNA, RG 94, Letters Received, 576A 1866. See *PUSG*, 13, 250–52; *O.R.*, II, viii, 755, 760, 845, 870, 897, 898, 900, 902, 905.

1866, MARCH 30. Thomas Ewing, Lancaster, Ohio, to USG. "My son Charles Ewing Captain in the 13th Regulars—Col. by brevet—is now in Cincinnati on recruiting service—It is apprehended he will be ordered soon to a frontier post, and I write to ask as a personal favor, if the condition of the service will permit, that you retain him in his present position another year—He entered the service in May 1861 a captain in the 13th Regulars—Was stationed and kept a weary year at Alton a kind of jailor guarding the rebel prisoners until at last on earnest importunity & remonstrance he was allowed to join your command in Missisippi—He was with Genl Sherman in his first attack on Vicksburg and afterwards in all his campaigns and battles, down to the Grand review in Washington—He was too far down in rank to be personally known to you but brother officers of his rank and a little way above speak higly of him—He was brevetted a Col in the regular service & commissioned Brigadier General of Volunteers—After the review he was ordered to Memphis where he reported but found nothing to do, and the condition of the service there was so equivocal, the army & its officers being in some sort subordinate to the comissioners & agents of the Freedmans Bureau, that he chose to resign his commission in the Volunteer service—and in order to avoid the dull & stupifying routine of camp life in time of peace—of which he had more than enough at Alton—and to bring himself once more within the influences of social life, he asked to be appointed on the recruiting service at Cincinnati—this was done & he has now been there about six months—When about two weeks in that service he was ordered to Ft Union by an officer, I do not remember his name, who evidently thought that service in the field was an offense which ought to be expiated by some vigorous punishment, such as cutting the culprit off at once from all communion with his family & friends—but on representation at the Department the order was revoked, & and officer who had displayed his energies & earned promotion by bravely dancing at all the evening parties in Washington for the then last five years, or during the war, was sent to Ft Union in his place—I have had three sons & two sons in Law in active service whenever & wherever they were needed during the war except my son-in Law Lieut Col Steele who was disabled by a wound at Charleston harbor—Among my sons Charles has perhaps more uncalculating chivalry than any other but is of a sanguine & somewhat nervous temperament—a year or two in camp remote from social life would crush out & smother his very soul—He had more than his due share of this at Alton—In his five years service he has had in all but ninety days leave, and it would be harsh now to compel him to go to the frontier, drag out a wearisome life for a year or more, and forego all prospect of permanent settlement in life, or to resign & begin the world anew much less qualified than five years ago when he entered the army—I wish him to remain if he may without ruin to his future prospects—The proprieties of my situation forbid me to ask any thing of Genl Sherman and should he interfere, it would bring censure upon him which I would by all means avoid—I therefore appeal to you and ask—that he be suffered to retain his present position for the usual term a year and a half or two years in consideration of past constant & unremitting service in the camp & field & this if it may be without injury to his promotion" —ALS, DLC-Thomas Ewing; ADfS, *ibid.* On April 17, Ewing wrote to USG. "My son Capt Charles Ewing has been in the service since May 1861 all the time in the field, or on more burdensome duties, until a few months ago he was appointed to the recruiting service in Cincinnati—I understand he is now about to be ordered to the frontier—I ask as a favor that he be allowed to remain the usual time a year or two within the pale of civilization & in communication with his family and friends and that you allow some one who danced, during the war to try for a while, in his place the realities of service"—ALS, DNA, RG 108, Letters Received. USG endorsed this letter. "Give the A. Gn. directions not to remove Col. Ewing from where he now is on recruiting service for the present. This paper is not to be sent out of the Office."—AES (undated), *ibid.*

1866, March 31, 2:00 p.m. To Maj. Gen. Winfield S. Hancock. "Gen Dyer reports that you have ordered one company of Infantry to Frankford Arsenal and says there is no necessity there for such troops and no quarters for them Answer—"—Telegram sent, DNA, RG 107, Telegrams Collected (Bound); telegram received, *ibid.*, RG 393, Middle Military Div., Telegrams Received. On the same day, Hancock, Baltimore, telegraphed to USG. "A Company of the 8th U S Infy has been ordered to Schuylkill Arsenal as a guard to the public property where there are quarters for them no troops will be sent to Frankford Arsenal"—Telegram sent, *ibid.*, Middle

Dept. and 8th Army Corps, Telegrams Sent (Press); telegram received (at 10:00 P.M.), *ibid.*, RG 107, Telegrams Collected (Bound); *ibid.*, RG 108, Telegrams Received.

1866, April 5. To Secretary of War Edwin M. Stanton. "I would respectfully recommend that the grade of Lieutenant Colonel of Vols. by brevet be conferred upon Brevet Major J. Warren Miller, Assistant Adjutant General, for gallant and meritorious services in the field during the war."—LS, DNA, RG 94, ACP, 303M CB 1866. On the same day, Brig. Gen. John A. Rawlins wrote to Bvt. Maj. J. Warren Miller informing him of USG's action.—ALS, IHi. On Oct. 15, 1865, Miller, Vicksburg, had written to Bvt. Col. Adam Badeau. "I have sent, sometime ago, to General Rawlins a recommendation (copy.) for my promotion by brevet, believing that he would attend to it for me, unless there should be some strong reason to prevent. I have been recently informed that he is in very poor health, and that he is probably not now in Washington Will it be too much to ask that you will see that my case receives early attention? General Slocum recommended, first, my assignment to duty as A. A. G. of his Department with rank of Lt Colonel. That application not being granted, he asked for *brevet-Lt Colonelcy* for me. It was about the 1st of September when that application was made; and I have yet heard nothing from it. I have, at this date, been two years A. A. G. with rank of Captain, and out of all sorts of kind intentions towards me by the Generals with whom I have served, nothing has resulted to me in the way of promotion. I am sure it is a very modest little promotion that I have asked Gen. Rawlins for; but probably he could not have attended to it. Will you not inform me what the difficulties are in my case, if there are any? In the liberal distribution of brevets I think it very strange that my own recommendations are entirely overlooked"—ALS, USG 3.

1866, April 7. To Bvt. Maj. Gen. Edward D. Townsend. "At the request of Gen. Howard, and ift fully meeting my views, I would like it if the Sec. of War would authorize an order appointing Maj. Gn. T. J. Wood Agt. of the Freedman's Bureau for the State of Miss. in addition to his duties ast Dept. Commander. Also to have Col. Sam.l Thomas, present Agt. for the State, ordered to report to Gen. Howard here."—ALS, DNA, RG 94, Letters Received, 268A 1866.

1866, April 7, noon. To Maj. Gen. Philip H. Sheridan. "I think it will be advisable to muster out the 48th Ohio without trial"—Telegram sent, DNA, RG 107, Telegrams Collected (Bound); copies (dated April 10), *ibid.*, RG 108, Letters Sent; (dated April 9) *ibid.*, RG 393, Military Div. of the Southwest and Dept. of the Gulf, Register of Telegrams Received; DLC-USG, V, 47, 109. On April 10, Sheridan, New Orleans, telegraphed to USG. "I have ordered the muster out of forty eighth Ohio"—Telegram received, DNA, RG 108, Telegrams Received; copies, *ibid.*, RG 393, Military Div. of the Southwest and Dept. of the Gulf, Telegrams Sent; DLC-USG, V, 54; DLC-Philip H. Sheridan.

1866, April 7. Maj. Gen. Benjamin H. Grierson, Washington, D. C., to USG. "I sent to you and Mrs Grant yesterday by the person who delivered the picture, a note enclosing a few card photographs, which I have since understood he lost. Be pleased to accept these herewith enclosed, and oblige, . . ."—ALS, IHi.

1866, April 9. To Secretary of War Edwin M. Stanton. "I would respectfully recommend that one of the boards of engineer officers now in session be directed to inquire into and report whether any of the canvas pontoons used by the armies during the rebellion are an infringement of Brevet Major General R C Buchanans patent of March 13th 1857. The board to be authorized to send for such persons and papers as may be necessary to this examination. I would suggest that the testimony of General E. O. C. Ord, Gen A J Smith, Gen. C. C. Augur and Surgeon C. H. Crane, be taken by the board."—LS, DNA, RG 94, Letters Received, 966A 1866; copies (dated April 10), *ibid.*, RG 108, Letters Sent; DLC-USG, V, 47, 109. On March 3, Col. and Bvt. Maj. Gen. Robert C. Buchanan, 1st Inf., had written a letter received at USG's hd. qrs. concerning his patent on canvas pontoons.—*Ibid.*, V, 51. On Sept. 20, USG endorsed papers concerning Buchanan's case. "The enclosed is a copy of a recommendatn made by me April 10. 1866 Since that—the Board of Eng officers referred to, have been disolved. I would now recommend that a Board composed of Eng officers stationed in this city be convened to examine & report upon the questions suggested within"—Copy, *ibid.*, V, 58.

1866, April 10. To Postmaster Gen. William Dennison. "I would respectfully recommend that in the case of Mr Parker formerly postmaster at City Point, who lost three hundred dollars by the failure of a Soldier, to whom it was entrusted, to deposit it at Washington (the soldier running away with it) the ammount lost be allowed to Mr Parker after his accounts shall be settled."—Copies, DLC-USG, V, 47, 109; DNA, RG 108, Letters Sent.

1866, April 10. Bvt. Maj. Gen. Montgomery C. Meigs to USG. "The attention of this Department having been called to the fact, (as published in the newspapers, see extract herewith enclosed, marked "B") that a Joint Resolution was introduced into the U. S. Senate on the 4th inst, requiring the Secretary of War to take immediate steps to preserve from desecration the graves of Union Soldiers; and, it having come to my knowledge, from the reports on Cemeteries which are being received from officers stationed in various parts of the South, that there is great danger of the marks at such graves and of the graves themselves being obliterated and otherwise defaced by careless and evil-disposed persons, by plowing over them and otherwise; I have the honor to submit for your consideration, the enclosed draft of a General Order (marked "A.") designed to meet the case, with the request that, if it seems to you proper, you will issue the Same. Although the Officers and Agents of the Quartermaster's Department are busily engaged in the work of ~~concentrating~~ collecting the remains of Union Soldiers into appropriate Cemeteries, and of fencing them and marking the graves, yet the field is so large that it cannot all be gone over in this way, in time to prevent the desecration apprehended. The information called for by the Second paragraph of the order, is desired for the same object, viz: that of taking measures to prevent desecration, and to preserve graves or remove the bodies; and it is hoped by this order to reach a large class of officers not directly under the orders of this Department."—LS, DNA, RG 94, Letters Received, 124Q 1866. The enclosures are *ibid.*

1866, April 11, noon. To Bvt. Maj. Gen. Daniel Butterfield. "Come to Washington as early as you can"—Telegram sent, DNA, RG 107, Telegrams Collected (Bound); copies, *ibid.*, RG 108, Letters Sent; DLC-USG, V, 47, 109.

1866, April 12. USG endorsement. "The within statement, so far as I have the means of knowing, is substantially correct. Information was sent to Gen. Burnside at Knoxville to the effect that troops would be dispatched to his relief and to hold out until they reached him, and I have no doubt but that sergeant Rowe was one of the men who conveyed it. Respecting the matter of compensation I would state that a few days since I recommended that the widow of another courier, who was also sent through to Knoxville, was captured and died in a rebel prison, be paid $300, that being the amount of her claim."—ES, DNA, RG 94, Letters Received, 223R 1866. Written on an affidavit of March 20 by William B. Rowe, former sgt., 9th Mich. Cav., requesting compensation for delivering a message from USG to Maj. Gen. Ambrose E. Burnside in Nov., 1863.—DS, *ibid.* On March 16, Mrs. Elizabeth Hodges had written a letter received at USG's hd. qrs. "Transmits for approval, the account of her husband, private Moses J Hodges 5th Ind Cav. showing sum of $300. due him as reward for carrying despatches from Cumbeland Gap to Knoxville during siege of the latter place"—*Ibid.*, RG 108, Register of Letters Received. On March 26, USG endorsed this letter. "Approved and respectfully forwarded to the Hon Secty of War, with the recommendation that this claim be ordered paid."—Copy, *ibid.* See *PUSG*, 9, 423–24.

1866, April 12. William O. Ludlow, Chicago, to USG. "My attention having been drawn to Notice in the 'Chicago Daily Times' of Apl 6th 1866, which please find enclosed, does some-what draw forth a few words from one of your former Writing Clerks who was in your office during the 'Battle of Pittsburg-Landing' & 'Shilo.' I beleive I know the enclosed in refference to tardiness is true. He was tardy and well do I remember the words of our lamented and Brave Maj Genl *C. F. Smith* to Buell beseeching him to go to your assistance instead remaining at HdQrs in conversation with Genl Smith. Again when his troops arrived at Savanah, although the night was exceedingly stormy, and after the troops was embarked on the Steamer' they wanted to remain untill ~~mid~~ day-light. The Captain of the steamer 'Minnehaha' said it was safe & he would risk the chances in finding the way & would lead the way. I went back to office and communicated the facts to our Brave lamented Genl *C. F. Smith* & he immediately ordered me to write an General Order for the Captain of the Several steamers loaded with troops to embark & report to you at Pittsburg-Landing which I did, and the steamers started. The trouble was he Buell wanted to see you get whip & thus bring a Disgrace on you & the 'Army of Tennessee.' I dont think Buell is personally entitled to one praise the honor belongs to Genl Thomas & Nelson' Divisions if to any one, in rendering assistance. Pardon me of interfering in this matter, but I cannot set still to see you slandered. As I Know considerable in this matter of his actions during the morning of the 1st Day engagement, remaining at HdQrs at Savanah very disagreeable I tell you to Genl Smith, I wish to Know if you will allow me to reply to said slanderous notice which I take pains to send you. I should like to Know what Buell has done to gain a name among the Brave—Wild goose chase in Kentucky is not forgotten. I am in the 'Merchants Saving Loan & Trust Co Bank having been here ever since Mustered out of service. Any Communication Directed here will reach me. I sympathize—in the sudden Death of Col *T. A. Bowers* & when I saw it, I read it with tears in my eyes. God' blessing be with you."—ALS, OClWHi.

1866, April 13. USG endorsement. "I cordially endorse Gn. Meade's estimate of Col. Locke's services in the late rebellion. Besides serving with distinction through the War he shew a zeal not often equaled by returning to his duties, in the face of the enemy, whilst laboring under the effects of an unhealed wound which would have justified his remaining at his home. I most heartily wish him success in business and bespeak for him the confidence of all with whom he may become associated."—AES (facsimile), Paul C. Richards, Catalogue No. 164 [1982], p. 18. Written on a letter of March 28 from Maj. Gen. George G. Meade to Frederick T. Locke commending Locke's wartime services as lt. col. and adjt.—Copy, DNA, RG 94, ACP, L361 CB 1864.

1866, April 14. To Secretary of War Edwin M. Stanton. "I would respectfully recommend that the Q. M. Department be directed to furnish to discharged soldiers of the 1st Army Corps who desire to go to other points than those where they were enrolled transportation to such points, but in no case to furnish it in excess of the cost to place of enrolment"—LS, DNA, RG 94, Letters Received, 300A 1866.

1866, APRIL 16. U.S. Representative Schuyler Colfax of Ind. to USG. "The enclosed letter was sent me to lay before Congress; but, as it relates to frontier protection, I thought it better to send it to you."—ALS, DNA, RG 108, Letters Received. Colfax enclosed a letter of March 19 from William Long, Weatherford, Parker County, Tex., to President Andrew Johnson *et al.* concerning depredations of Comanche and Kiowa Indians.—ALS, *ibid.* On May 1, Maj. Gen. Horatio G. Wright endorsed these letters. "Respectfully returned to Hd Qrs Mily Divn Gulf. Two companies have recently been sent to Sherman—one to Weatherford and one to Jacksboro—This is all the force that can be spared for that section of the state so long as the present policy of keeping up garrisons in the interior is maintained, unless additional troops are furnished."—AES, *ibid.* On April 26, Maj. Gen. Philip H. Sheridan wrote to Brig. Gen. John A. Rawlins. "I have the honor to acknowledge the receipt of the resolutions of the Convention of the State of Texas in reference to frontier defence. I know of no depredations having been committed except by the Kickapoo Indians who live in Mexico, near San Fernando. They come iover in bands of four or five and occasionally drive off stock, it is very hard to control these small bands I sent word to their chief last fall that we would go after him if he did not control his people better. The chiefs of the tribe are well disposed towards our people and it should be remembered that it was this tribe that the disloyal Texians attacked under a white flag when they were emigrating from the borders of Western Missouri to get away from Rebellion. They made an agreement with the so-called Imperial Government of Mexico to protect the frontier against hostile Indians since which time the Imperial Government has been unable to fulfil its agreement and the tribe has been left in a destitute condition. I sent to enquire of them some time ago what they wanted and if they disired to again return but no reply has been sent me."—LS, *ibid.* On May 21, USG endorsed this letter. "Respectfully forwarded to Secretary of War for his information."—ES, *ibid.*

1866, APRIL 19. To Secretary of War Edwin M. Stanton. "I would respectfully recommend the dismanteling and disbanding of Fort Ellsworth, Va. There is now at Fort Ellsworth four pieces of Artillery which belonged to Duncan's Battery during the Mexican War. I would recommend sending them to West Point for preservation."—ALS, DNA, RG 94, Letters Received, 299A 1866.

1866, APRIL 20. USG endorsement. "Respectfully returned to the Hon. Secretary of War. I am in favor generally of encouraging and assisting the opening of roads through the Indian Country. They enhance the value of U. S. lands in their vicinity and render military transportation easier. Of the road in question I have not sufficient knowledge to justify an expression of opinion on the propriety of the land grant asked for."—ES, DNA, RG 107, Letters Received, P114 1866. Written on a letter of April 13 from

U.S. Representative Donald C. McRuer of Calif. to Secretary of War Edwin M. Stanton concerning the construction of a military road from The Dalles, Ore., to Fort Boise, Idaho Territory.—ALS, *ibid.*

1866, April 20. USG endorsement. "The construction of a railroad by the proposed route would be of very great advantage to the Govt. pecuniarily, by saving in the cost of transportation to supply troops whose presence in the Country thro' which it is proposed to pass, is made necessary by the great amount of emigration to the gold bearing regions of the Rocky Mountains. In my opinion, too, the United States would recieve an additional pecuniary benefit by the construction of this road, by the settlement it would induce along the line of the road, and consequently the less number of troops necessay to secure order and safety. How far these benefits should be compensated by the General Government beyond the grant of land already ~~gr~~awarded by Congress, I would not pretend to say. I would merely give it as my opinion that the enterprise of constructing the Northern Pacific Railroad, is one well worth fostering by the General Government; and that such aid could well be afforded as would insure the early prosecution of the work—"—Copies, Minnesota Historical Society; DLC-USG, V, 58. Written on a letter of April 18 from Bvt. Maj. Gen. Montgomery C. Meigs to George Gibbs supporting the construction of the Northern Pacific Railroad. —*Ibid.* See *SMD*, 40-2-9.

1866, April 21. USG endorsement. "Respectfully forwarded to the Hon. Secretary of War with the recommendation that these men be released on their parole unless they are charged with having committed some act in violation of the laws of war; and in that case that they be tried by a U S Court and not by a State Court."—ES, DNA, RG 94, Letters Received, 976A 1866. Written on a letter of April 16 from W. C. Kain, Reuben Roddie, and J. R. McCann, Knoxville, to USG. "Reffering to your endorsement of application for release, in forwarding the parpers to the Hon Secretary of War on the 10th ultimo, and returning you our thanks for your prompt and favorable action, the undersigned beg to say that by the refusal of the Governor to comply with the request of the Hon Secretary of war we are still held in prison and like felons, for legitimate acts of war done as you properly say, 'when civil law was subverted and in our capacity as soldiers.' We can but regard the action of the executive as a persistent determination, on the part of the civil authorities wholly to disregard and render of no avail the 'paroles and promises of protection made to us upon our surrender, by the National Military Authorities, and likewise to nullify' and trample upon the promises made to us in the President's Amnesty proclamation, for most assuredly if the act for which we are prosecuted, (the holding of a Military Court) be not a belligerent act then the parole of no Cofederate Officer or soldier affords him the slightest protection; and if said act was not included in the Executive pardon 'for all acts done directly or indirectly in aid of the rebellion' it would be difficut to find one that was. We therefore appeal to you and through you to the President and invoke the Exercise of the Power which must reside in you as the head of the Armies to whom we surrendered and from whom we received our paroles and promises of protection, to enforce an observance of the promises made to us and to secure us the indemnity guaranteed to us in the accepted terms of surrender of the Southern armies; and to the President as the political head of the general government in which alone under our system is lodged the power to make peace and to declare war, to enforce the observance of the very terms proposed by himself, as the great and efficient means of securing peace, viz the Amnesty—which according to Hamilton is in and of itself of higher authority than a treaty of peace between independent nations, being the generous offers of the Victor to the vanquished. If we can be held and confined in this prison for acts which were those of legitimate warfare, then so can every Confederate officer and soldier who ever within the limits of Tennessee drew his sword or fired a musket during the late deplored conflict. The application of the principle to the thousands, who might be subjected to the same treatment we have been, shows how unjust and abhorent it is; but we nevertheless suffer as much as individuals, as we could do were the promises of the United States authorities both civil and military, allowed to be violated by pretended State authority in every instance where they have been given to or accepted by our late companions in arms. The Military and the Political Power of the Genl Government must be and is ~~and is~~ amply sufficient to enable them to keep their plighted faith with the surrendered soldiers of the Confederacy—against the wishes of all who desire under the pretense of State authority to violate these pledges. The power to make peace is not vested in the thirty-six states of the Union, but in the general government, and no state can rightfully nullify or disregard the means adopted to bring about the peace. We therefore ask that you will at once order an officer and a sufficient force, say one company, to take us from the custody of the Sheriff of this County, and place us where we were before, in the custody of the military; and as we shrink from no investigation of our acts as soldiers that you will direct our trial for any alleged violation of the laws and usages of war that can be brought against us. But a short time since in the adjoining county of Jefferson the military released from jail two federal soldiers who in defiance of their acquital by a military court at Chattanooga, were arrested and imprisoned for the same offence by the civil authority who charged them with murder."—ALS, *ibid.* On Dec. 14, 1865, the prisoners wrote to Secretary of War Edwin M. Stanton concerning their confinement.—*Ibid.*, RG 108, Register of Letters Received. On March 10, 1866, USG endorsed this letter. "Respy. forwarded to the sec of war with recommendation that the prisoners J. R. McCann, W. C. Kain and Reuben Rodie be unconditionally released. The acts for which they were arrested and confined having been committed when civil law was subverted & in their capacity as soldiers. If they are not released, I would respectfully urge that instruction be given for their immidiate trial by Military Commission"—Copy, DLC-USG, V, 58. See telegram of the prisoners to

President Andrew Johnson, June 20, 1866, DLC-Andrew Johnson; *New York Times*, April 15, 1866; E. Merton Coulter, *William G. Brownlow* (Chapel Hill, 1937), pp. 275–76.

1866, April 22. Maj. Gen. John Pope, St. Louis, to USG. "I have the honor to invite your attention to the claims, and services of two Officers of the Adjutant Genl Department now serving on my Staff, with a view to their appointment into one of the new Regiments provided for by the Army Bill, now before Congress, and ask earnestly that you give their application a favorable endorsement as propriety warrants. The Officers are Major. D. G. Swaim and Captn J. McC. Bell, Asst Adjt. Genls of Volunteers. Both of these Officers have served with ability, and distinction in the Field, and both have been on duty with me for the past year. They are both educated gentleman of high personal and Official characters, and would be an ornament to the service. Both on public and personal grounds, I am exceedingly axinious that they should be retained in that service, and for this purpose, I desire to use all the Official and personal influence at my command to procure for them proper appointments in one of the new Regiments. Major Swaim would be glad, and is well qualified, for a commission as Major, in one of the Infantry or Cavalry Regiments. Captn Bells former services were in the Artillery Arm, As a Major either of Cavalry or Arttillery he would be an invaluable Officer. May I request General, that you will give this Application a favorable endorsement, and interest yourself in advancing the interests of these two Officers. I will be myself responsible that any recommendation you give them, shall be fully, justified by their merits."—Copies, DNA, RG 94, ACP, P612 CB 1866; *ibid.*, RG 393, Dept. of Mo., Letters Sent. On Feb. 17, 1867, U.S. Representative James A. Garfield of Ohio wrote to USG. "I respectfully recommend Brevet Col D. G. Swaim to an appointment in the army—Col. Swaim Served one year in the Infantry and three years on the Staff as A. A. G. He was for two years on my staff—and when mustered out of Service three months ago—he was Maj. and A A. G. with the Brevet rank of Col—He is one of the best staff officers I knew in the army & is worthy of a good place—I shall be greatly obliged if he can receive an appointed"—ALS, *ibid.*, RG 94, ACP, S108 CB 1867. On Feb. 18, USG endorsed this letter. "Bvt. Col. D. G. Swaim is respectfully recommended for a Capt. of Inf.y, should there be such a vacancy. If not he is recommended for a 1st Lt. of Inf.y."—AES, *ibid.* Bvt. Col. David G. Swaim was appointed 2nd lt., 34th Inf., as of July 28, 1866; Bvt. Lt. Col. Joseph M. Bell, adjt. for Pope, was mustered out as of Sept. 9.

1866, April 24. To Bvt. Brig. Gen. Cyrus B. Comstock from Richmond, Va. "Will reach Washington to morrow evening Via Orange & Alexandria Road."—Telegram received (at 10:45 p.m.), DNA, RG 108, Telegrams Received; copy, DLC-USG, V, 54. On April 21, USG, accompanied by Julia Dent Grant, his father-in-law, and Bvt. Col. Adam Badeau, traveled to Richmond to visit Dr. and Mrs. Alexander Sharp, returning to Washington, D. C., on April 25. See *New York Times*, April 22, 25, 1866; *PUSG*, 14, 422–23, 423*n*. On April 21, S. B. Duffield, New Richmond Theatre, wrote to USG. "I have the pleasure of placing at your disposal a Private Box in my theatre, during your stay in the city—I should be much pleased if you will honor me at any time with your presence—"—ALS, USG 3. On April 23, Briscoe G. Baldwin, Richmond, wrote to Badeau. "The Bearer Mr Vannerson, one of our most successful and respectable Photographists is anxious to obtain a setting from Genl Grant and yourself. It would be gratifying to many of the friends and admirers of the General in this city, to have an original likeness of himself, and such members of his staff as we can catch. Hoping that you may before long again visit our city and afford me an opportunity to present you to some Rebels, not often seen in public or noticed in the papers, . . ."—ALS, *ibid.* On April 24, Williams C. Wickham, Virginia Central Railroad, Richmond, wrote to USG. "Hearing that you propose returning to Washington by way of the Va Central Rail Road I called to tender you the use of our trains for yourself and staff—I have the honor also to enclose you a ticket for yourself & family at any time that you might desire to visit the mountains of our State"—ALS, *ibid.*

1866, April 24. John Kirkwood (formerly 42nd N. Y.) and forty-nine others, 5th U.S. Vols., Fort Reno, Dakota Territory, to USG. "We the undersigned your humble petitioners Beg Leave most respectfully to represent, that the facts Sett forth in the following Statements are true. That we have no possible Means of Knowing what Disposition has been Made of Us, by our old companies and Regiments, in which at the earliest period of this wicked Rebellion, we enlisted and gave our Strength and influence, Wholly & Souly to the cause of the United States Government. The humble prayer of this petition is that We, Each and Severally may recieve an 'honorable Discharge' from our old Companies, Whereby we can be allowed to recieve all our 'Back pay and Bounty' in the Same. That we may also recieve pay and Bounty in and from Said organizations up to the time of our Enlistment in our present organization. That this prayer is Just and Rightous, That we have been true and faithful Soldiers to the United States Service, That we have never wished or hoped but for the cause of the 'Union' and the Success of the United States Government. We beg most respectfully to Refer you to the following Statements personally appeared before me The following Named Non Commissioned Officers and privates of Companies C and D of the 5th Regiment United States Infantry, Now Stationed at Fort Reno D. T. Who are personally Known by Me to be Such, who being Duly Sworn, Depose and Say that the following Statements are true That they Each and Severally Joined the United States Service at the times, places, and in the Different organizations Sett opposite our Respective Names That we were captured at the time & places Stated thereunto also, In the following Scedule. To-Wit— . . . They further State that they were Each and Severally confined in Rebel prisons at Different Stations from the above date of capture until the 20th Day of November 1864. That During the whole of this period they were forced to undergo the Most Rigorous denials of every Kind. That they constantly Suffered from the Want of a Sufficient and Wholesome Diet. That for Days at a time we were only allowed enough Subsistence to Sustain Life without the Least regard for Health or comfort That in Every Instance at the commencement of our confinement our Clothes were taken from us. Such only were Left us as were unfit for their own use. That Very Soon after imprisonment Most of us were almost intirely destitute of clothing enough to hide our Nakedness That owing to these wants Many of us were Sick and Many of our Comrads were being taken each moring from amongst us who had Died from Want and proper care During the preeceeding Twenty-four hours. That Setting aside intirely the Want of clothing and Diet, The filth and Vermin of these prison pens were Sufficient to consume the Vital parts of mankind in a Very Short time. That many of us were daily contracting Diseases which we were certain must put to an End our exhistence in a Very Short Space of time. That During the whole of this period We were daily being requested to take the oath of allegiance to the Rebel cause. That by So Doing we would be allowed our Liberty and a chance to regain & protect our health. The Rebel authorities finding us Still Disposed to firmly resist their overtures finaly reduced Still more our Rations & gave us the most positive assurance that at the expiration of Sixty Days unless we Voluntairly took the oath, We Should all be conscripted. We yet Refused Hoping agains hope, until the 20th Day of November 1864 When with the firm conviction that we could no Longer Stand our present Difficulties and being also convinced that the oath being taken under scircumstances like these could not be Morally binding upon us, We were impelled through the neccesity of Saving our Lives to take the oath this We Done on the Last named Date, With the firm and premeditated determination in each Breast to, Break from the Servitude of the Rebel authorities at our earliest opportunity and give ourselves up once More to the Moving U. States Army, feeling assured that Should we be Successful we Should at once be Sent to our old commands in the Union Army. We neither of us ever enlisted nor were we ever Mustered into the Rebel Service. It was our firm Determination not to do So nor to ever Lift an arm against the United States Government. We were Sent South and upon one occasion We were presented with arms by the authorities and ordered to Stand Guard over Some conscripts, but Instead of obeying these orders we abandoned our posts & Destroyed all the arms we had been presented with. We received no More arms until we arrived at Mobile Alabama Where we were informed that we must recieve arms and be Sent back to Corinth Mississippi This was on the 25th Day of December 1864. When We arrived at Egypt Station we Learned that General Griereson with the U S Forces was at this point. A favorable opportunity offering itself at this time we broke in a Body from the Rebel Ranks, and together with our Rebel arms gave ourselves up to General Griereson. This occured on the 28th Day of December 1864. Thereby having Rebel Arms in our possesion Less than three

Days and this we were forced to Do under a Strong Guard Upon Reporting to General Griereson we informed Him Who and what we were & how we came there That it was for the purpose of being again returned to our old commands in the United States Service The General informed us that we Should be fowarded there as Soon as possible. We were Most of us allowed to retain the arms we brought with us. Contrary to his promises to us, Instead of being fowarded to our commands, we were Sent to Alton and there confined and treated in every respect as Rebel prisoners of war. This Last confinement commenced on the 9th Day of January 1865 From this Date foward we Done Every thing we could to gain a transfer to our own Regiments. We all Joined in applying by Mail and otherwise to Make our wishes Known, but without any Success and we are convinced that our communications were never forwarded by those in authority over us, but on the contrary were Destroyed before Leaving Alton. Here again we were beset by Officers desiering that we Should Enlist in New organizations Which they informed us had been ordered to be Raised by the War Department. Conspicuous among these officers were Captains Moore, & Hallack Who informed, Us that They had these orders and that by these orders we were Stigmatized as Rebel prisoners & also that We could never hereafter be returned to our Regiments. We Demanded to See these orders, but they could not be produced. We Still refused wishing to Show to the authorities that we were Union, Men by being reinstated to our old companies as this had been our only desire Since we were first captured by the Rebels. We were Most positively assured that we could never regain our own Regiments & that unles we Enlisted in the present organization We would be Sent as Exchanged prisoners of war to the South. We Made every effort in our power to Learn Why we could not be transfered to our old companies & why We were expected to Enlist in our present organization but with out any Sucess We Refused to Join the present organization until every hope of gaining our old Ranks was Given up. We were informed that by Enlisting in this we Should Most faithfully recieve all our Back pay and Bounty in the old organization up to the Date of our Inlistment in the present one. We were also informed that in this Regiment We Should be treated & recieve pay in every Respect the Same as all other Volunteer orginizations in the United States Service. Since our Enlistment in the 5th Regiment U S Volunteers We have Served the U S. Goverment in every Respect as honestly and faithfully as We have ever endeavoured to Do heretofore. Since our Enlistment in this Regiment We have ascertained that we are Recognized as Rebel Soldiers, that we are to Recieve no bounty and the usual Emoluments of Volunteers in the Service We have heretofore from this point fowared petitions to the 'Sec of War,' Making the Same request that We now Most humbly pray you to Grant. We are firmly convinced that these petitions have been Destroyed at the Head quarters of this Sub Dist or otherwise & never been fowarded. That These Simple facts May Lead you to Look a Little into our present necessities That the prayer of our petition May not

Seem offensive . . ."—DS (tabular material omitted), DNA, RG 108, Letters Received.

1866, April 25. To Secretary of War Edwin M. Stanton. "Major General Augur reports that one regiment of colored troops can now be spared from his Department. I would respectfully recommend that orders be given for this reduction."—Copies, DLC-USG, V, 47, 109; DNA, RG 108, Letters Sent.

1866, April 27. USG endorsement. "Respy. submitted to the Postmaster General. Col Murphys conduct at Holly Springs was such, that if it does not disqualify him from holding office under the Government, it at least does not entitle him to recieve any of its favors"—Copy, DNA, RG 108, Register of Letters Received. Written on a letter of the same day from George M. Rodgers, former 2nd lt., 6th N. Y. Cav. "Solicits position of 3d class clerkship in the Post office Dept now held by R. C. Murphy who was Colonel of 8th Wisconsin Cav. and surrendered Holly Springs to the enemy—for which act he was dismissed the service."—*Ibid.* See *PUSG*, 7, 104, 106*n*–7*n*.

1866, April 27. To Secretary of War Edwin M. Stanton. "I would respectfully recommend that all volunteer officers of Staff Departments, Asst. Quartermasters, Commissaries, Asst. Adj. Generals, Add.l Aides, Inspectors &c. still remaining in service be Mustered out of service to take effect on the 31st day of May 18676."—ALS, DNA, RG 94, ACP, Q40 CB 1866.

1866, April 27. USG endorsement. "Respectfully returned to the Secretary of War, reference being made to the enclosed copy of Gen. Sherman's letter of instructions to Maj. Gen. Reynolds, and to my endorsement of Feb. 20 1866, relating to the same subject, which was approved by the Secretary of War. The instructions already given are deemed ample and sufficient to meet the requirements of the letter of the Secretary of the Interior. I would however recommend that copies of the letters of Indian Comr Cooley and the Sec. of the Interior be sent to Gen. Sherman for his guidance with respect to these particular Indians."—ES, DNA, RG 94, Letters Received, 33I 1866. Written on a letter of April 18 from Secretary of the Interior James Harlan to Secretary of War Edwin M. Stanton enclosing a letter of April 16 from Commissioner of Indian Affairs Dennis N. Cooley to Stand Watie *et al.*, Cherokee delegates, concerning affairs in the Indian Territory.—LS and copy, *ibid.* On Feb. 13, Harlan had written to Stanton concerning Bvt. Maj. Gen. John B. Sanborn's assignment to regulate treatment of freedmen by their former masters in the Indian Territory.—ALS, *ibid.*, RG 393, Dept. of Ark., Letters Received. On Feb. 20, USG endorsed this letter. "I think that for the present the Indian Country should be considered and treated as under military control, for the purpose of protecting the Freedmen. If the Hon. Secretary of War approves this view Gen. Sherman will be directed to afford all the military aid he can for the purpose of keeping peace and order in the Indian Territory, and to send troops there early in the spring."—ES, *ibid.* Sanborn's report and other papers are *ibid.*, RG 108, Letters Received. On March 12, Bvt. Col. Ely S. Parker endorsed this letter. "Respectfully referred to maj. Gen. W. T. Sherman, Comdg. Military Div. Mississippi, who will give the necessary directions to put into execution the views of the Lt Gen'l, as expressed in his endorsement hereon."—AES, *ibid.*, RG 393, Dept. of Ark., Letters Received. On March 17, Maj. Gen. William T. Sherman, St. Louis, wrote to Brig. Gen. John A. Rawlins. "I have received the papers touching the State of Affairs as connected with the Freedmen of the Indian Country west of Arkansas, and will send them to Genl Reynolds with instructions to have the matter critically enquired into and General Grants instructions put in force so far as it is possible. Gen Sanborn's picture of the condition and conflicts between the Indians and their former slaves, varies so much from Reports I have from Fort Smith that I must venture the belief that General Sanborn may be in error. General Henry J. Hunt who commands on that frontier at Fort Smith under date of Feb 21, says, 'The district is very quiet. The Rebs give no trouble. If the Union men would cause as little we would get on admirably, and they dont make much trouble' Gen Reynolds was positive in his purpose not to reestablishe~~d~~ the old burnt Posts in the Indian Country, but to keep a respectable force at Forts Smith and Gibson and send patrols occasionally among the Indians. I now have my Inspector General in that very Country, and will soon have from him reliable Reports, when I will be better prepared to give positive opinions: but my present impressions are that most of the negros late slaves will fraternize with the Indians, and such as will not, could be moved to some cheap country and there maintained at half the cost of rebuilding half a dozen small Posts in that Country. ~~By~~ By My recent orders for the 3rd Cavalry and one Regmt of Colored troops to march for New Mexico; and the order received yesterday to reduce the number of Black Regimts in this Division to four—Gen Reynolds will have in his Department only the 19th Inf. and two Black Regiments. These are ample provided Agents of Freedmen do not create trouble. I wish Gen Sprague's Authority in the matter of freedmen were coextensive with that of Genl Reynolds, or that Gen Sanborn were made subordinate to Sprague, when we would have unity of counsel and action."—ALS, *ibid.*, RG 108, Letters Received. On March 26, USG endorsed this letter. "Respectfully forwarded to the Hon. Secretary of War, with the recommendation that Gen. Sanborn be made subordinate to Gen. Sprague, in accordance with the wish of General Sherman expressed herein, and that he be instructed to cease all interference with military authorities"—ES, *ibid.*, RG 94, Letters Received, 256A 1866. On March 21, Bvt. Col. Orville E. Babcock had written to Sherman. "The Lieut. Gen'l directs me to inform you that Gen'l Sanborn receives his orders from and reports directly to the Secretary of the Interior —and that he has no authority to interfere with military authorities—any more than any other Indian Agent or Treasury Agent."—Copies, DLC-USG, V, 47, 109; DNA, RG 108, Letters Sent; (misdated March 2) *ibid.*, RG 393, Dept. of Ark., Letters Received.

1866, April 27. USG endorsement. "Respectfully forwarded to the Hon. Secretary of War, with recommendation that Mrs. Randolph be allowed to retain the Government buildings upon her lot, when they are no longer required for military purposes."—ES, DNA, RG 94, Letters Received, 75R 1866. Written on a letter of April 20 from Mrs. Elizabeth S. Eggleston, Vicksburg, to USG. "Influenced by the kindness you displayed towards me after the surrender of this City to the Union Army, I am emboldened to make an appeal to you on behalf of a connection, and dear friend of mine, Mrs Amy B. Randolph. Mrs Randolph is a widow; a strong 'Union woman' and native of Connecticut; many years ago she inherited a house and lot on the outskirts of this place, the rent of which formed her sole income. When the war broke out, Mrs Randolph went to Connecticut, and only returned South when your occupation of the City made it practicable for her to live under the Government of the U. S. About this time the inner line of works was built, and running as they did, directly through her lot, her tenant was ejected, and the house pulled down to make way for the breastworks; she receiving no compensation therefor. Last winter some buildings were put up on the lot, for Officers quarters, and are still occupied as such: Mrs Randolph now asks, that when the Military no longer need her lot, or these buildings, that they may be given to her, as recompense for the house which was pulled down, and the rents which have been lost to her for nearly three years. Mrs Randolph took the oath of allegiance before coming South to see after her property I am aware that it may be impossible for you to recall me to your mind, among the very many to whom you extended your kindness while here; but Mrs Grant will perhaps remember me; and I assure you Sir that I shall ever entertain a vivid and grateful recollection of your courtesy to me. Hoping that you will use your influence to secure the fulfilment of Mrs Randolph's request . . ."—ALS, *ibid.* Docketing indicates that the request was granted.—*Ibid.*

1866, April 27, 2:25 p.m. To Bvt. Maj. Gen. John W. Turner, Richmond. "Cause an investigation to be made of the cause and progress of the Norfolk riots, and send the report here. Send also all the evidence taken in the matter"—Telegram sent, DNA, RG 107, Telegrams Collected (Bound); telegram received, *ibid.*, RG 393, Dept. of Va. and N. C., 1st Military District, Telegrams Received; copies (misaddressed to Maj. Gen. George H. Thomas), *ibid.*, RG 108, Letters Sent; DLC-USG, V, 47, (addressed to Turner) 109. On April 20, Turner had written a communication received at USG's hd. qrs. forwarding reports of mistreatment of Negroes in the District of Norfolk.—DNA, RG 108, Register of Letters Received. On May 1, USG endorsed these papers. "Respy. forwarded to the Hon. Secy of War for his information."—Copy, *ibid.* On May 21, Maj. Gen. Alfred H.

Terry, Richmond, wrote to Maj. George K. Leet. "I have the honor to forward herewith the report of the Board of Officers convened in pursuance of instructions from the Hd Qrs, Armies of the U S, to investigate the circumstances attending the recent riots at Norfolk, Va. I also enclose copies of the orders convening the Board."—LS, *ibid.*, RG 94, Letters Received, 154V 1866. On May 31, USG endorsed this letter. "Respectfully forwarded to Secretary of War."—ES, *ibid.* The report is *ibid.* See *HED*, 39-2-72.

1866, APRIL 28. To Bvt. Maj. Gen. Edward D. Townsend. "Will you please have Capt. Wm McK. Dunn, Jr. A. A. G. mustered out of the volunteer service to take effect from the 30th instant?"—ALS, DNA, RG 94, ACP, 2187 1871. On the same day, Maj. George K. Leet wrote to the AGO. "The Adjutant General will issue an order granting leave of absence for six months, from May 1st, to 1st Lieutenant Wm. M. Dunn, Jr., 10th U. S. Infantry."—ALS, *ibid.*, Letters Received, 331A 1866. On April 19, 1867, Brig. Gen. John A. Rawlins wrote to USG. "The following is a brief record of the military services of Captain Wm McKee Dunn Jr., 21st U S Infantry, as a volunteer prior to his appointment in the Army; and which is respectfully submitted with a view to securing your recommendation for his brevet promotion. Capt. Dunn enlisted in the 6th Regt Indiana Infantry Volunteers in April 1861, and served out the term of his enlistment—three mos. He again entered the service, enlisting in the 67th Reg't Indiana Infantry Volunteers, and as a noncommissioned officer served with this regiment until November 1862, when he was commissioned a 2d Lieutenant in the 83d Regiment Indiana Infantry Volunteers; and served with his Company in the movement against Pemberton on the Tallahatchie and in Sherman's attack on Vicksburg December 1862 and in the battle of Arkansas Post in the January following; and continued on duty with his Company until March 6th 1863, when he was detached from it for staff duty with Brigadier General J. C. Sullivan, and continued with him during the siege, performing the duties of staff officer during the month of June, and until after the fall of Vicksburg at Headquarters Army of the Tennessee. In September 1863 he was promoted to a 1st Lieutenantcy in his regiment, and on the 4th of October following was assigned to duty on your staff and was with you in the campaign and battles of Chattanooga and from Culpeper C. H. to the surrender of the Army of Northern Virginia at Appomattox C. H. He was appointed April 21st 1865 Assistant Adjutant General of Volunteers with rank of Captain, to rank as such from April 9th 1865, and served in that capacity on your staff until his muster-out—May 3d 1866. He was appointed 1st Lieutenant 10th U S. Infantry to rank from Nov. 29 1865, and in the reorganization of the Army, under the Act of July 28 1866 was appointed Captain in the 21st U S. Infantry to rank from July 28th 1866"—LS, *ibid.*, ACP, 2187 1871. On the same day, USG endorsed this letter. "Respectfully forwarded to the Secretary of War, with the recommendation that Capt Wm McKee Dunn, Jr., 21st U S Infantry, be appointed a Major by brevet in the U S Army for gallant and meritorious services in the campaigns and battles of Vicksburg, Chattanooga and Richmond and Petersburg, to date from March 2d 1867."—ES, *ibid.*

1866, April 28. To H. A. Brown. "I have the pleasure of acknowledging the receipt of a set of the 'Cartoons of Raphael' which [you] have done me the honor to forward. They seem to me to be very fine and a desirable collection, for those who can not possess the originals, to have. Please accept my thanks for this token of rememberence and also for the very kind expressions in your letter accompanying."—ALS, John F. Reed, King of Prussia, Pa.

1866, April 30. USG endorsement. "Respectfully referred to the Secy. of War with recommendation that the within contract be approved. By raising sunken vessels in Charleston Harbor a considerable amount of money may be realized and by this contract what the government receives will be without expense. Under other form of contract, or if government attempts to save this property, past experience goes to show that the cost would amount to more than would be realized"—Copies, DLC-USG, V, 58; (undated) DNA, RG 56, Div. of Captured and Abandoned Property, Letters Received. Written on a contract of April 17 between Bvt. Lt. Col. Charles W. Thomas, chief q. m., Dept. of S. C., and Nathaniel A. Haven, New York City, in which Haven agreed to pay the U.S. one-half of the net proceeds from the sale of scrap iron collected in and around Charleston.—DS, *ibid.* On May 2, Secretary of War Edwin M. Stanton endorsed the contract. "The within contract is disapproved. Under the act of Congress & the rules of the Department the Quartermaster's Bureau have no power to make such a contract. It is therefore null & void"—Copy, *ibid.*

1866, April 30. To Maj. Gen. Alfred H. Terry. "If there is another officer present for duty with the company to which Bvt. Capt. I. B. Wright, 11th Infantry, belongs, give him leave of absence for Ninety days."—Copies, DLC-USG, V, 47, 109; DNA, RG 108, Letters Sent.

1866, [April 30?]. USG endorsement to Bvt. Maj. Gen. John W. Turner. "Examine into the case of E. Gordon who is now confined in jail in Petersburg and if possible obtain his release. He is a young boy of good family and from the statements made has not been guilty of any great offence."—AES (undated), DNA, RG 107, Letters Received from Bureaus. Written on a telegram of April 29, Sunday, from Bvt. Brig. Gen. Orlando Brown, col., 24th Colored, to Maj. Gen. Oliver O. Howard, Bureau of Refugees, Freedmen, and Abandoned Lands. "I doubt if the military can get possession of Gordon until Gen Terry returns on tuesday—Will send by mail tomorrow"—Telegram received (at 9:40 p.m.), *ibid.* On April 24, U.S. Representative Thomas D. Eliot of Mass. and William G. Eliot (see *PUSG*, 10, 76*n*) of St. Louis had written to Howard seeking the release of Eliot Gordon, New Bedford, Mass., who had been arrested for stealing a horse. The writers believed that Gordon had not intended to commit a crime and offered to pay damages in behalf of the boy's father.—ALS, *ibid.* On May 5, Brown wrote to Howard. "I visited Petersburg, yesterday, to ascertain whether any thing could be done with the civil authorities to secure Gordon's release. I found it impossible to have the case dismissed; if the civil authorities are allowed to retain custody of him they will try him; if they try him, they will in my opinion convict him. I see no way to reach the case unless the Commissioner should order me to have it tried before the Bureau Court, in that case, the military would not be compromised at all, as arrangements could be mad[e] to get the custody of the prisoner without callin[g] for military aid. The objection to this plans is, th[e] offence with which the lad is charged: was not committed against a colored man but against the Commonwealth. If the Bureau Court should find the boy guilty the case could go before the Commissioner on an appeal." —ALS, *ibid.* Probably on May 7, Howard endorsed this letter. "Respectfully referred to Lieut. Gen. Grant, the offence with which this lad is charged is Capital—I do not know that anything further can be done—What would you think of the suggestion of Gen. Browne within?"—AES (undated, received on May 7), *ibid.* On May 8, USG endorsed this letter. "Respectfully forwarded to the Secretary of War, for instructions."—ES, *ibid.* On the same day, Maj. Gen. George G. Meade forwarded additional papers in the case to USG's hd. qrs.—ES, *ibid.* On May 9, USG endorsed these papers. "Respectfully forwarded to the Secretary of War, in connection with papers submitted the 8th inst. in this case."—ES, *ibid.* Documents in the file indicate that Gordon had run away from home and had attempted to sell a horse and buggy that he had rented under an assumed name. —*Ibid.*

1866, [*April*]. USG note. "Authorize Dr. Gaenslen to proceed to Texas to be placed on the same footing with other paroled Officers on his taking the same parole they did before the proper officer in New Orleans."—AN, DNA, RG 108, Letters Received. Written on a letter of April 17 from John J. Gaenslen, New York City, to William D. Beall requesting permission to go to Tex. to practice medicine.—ALS, *ibid.* Gaenslen resigned as asst. surgeon, U.S. Army, as of Aug. 17, 1861, served in a similar capacity in the C.S. Army during the Civil War, and fled to Cuba in 1865. See *ibid.*, RG 94, Amnesty Papers, Va.

[*1866, April?*]. Charles M. Clarke to USG. "Confidential . . . In compliance to your desire to have me furnish such information as I may possess relative to a B Estvān an Agent in, the United States to the Emperor Maximilian of Mexico, I have the honor to state, that according to the said Estvans own statement he is engaged as a private Secretary to the said Emperor Maximilian, but has no power to act in any diplomatic capacity, his purpose for being here if I have understood him right is to influence the Newspaper press as well as individuals through pecuniary compensations in favor of Maximilian, and probably to report to him such events as may transpire in the American Congress. He has however taken it upon himself to critizise the Actions of the Senate and House of Representatives, and to pretend that with his influence he can rule both these Legislative bodies, stating at the same time that the American Congress which consists of nothing but Political Demagogue's are easily influenced by pecuniare temptations, and that anything can be accomplished in Congress through the free disposal of money among its members—Thus he leads the Imperial Government of Mexico to believe that through his manouvres the Head of the United States Government as well as the leading men of the people have an earnest desire to see the establishment of an Empire in Mexico. His so called Despatches declare that as soon as the Southern States are admitted for representation in Congress the recognition of Maximilian as Emperor of Mexico will no longer be questioned. These Despatches are generally so lenghty that it would be impossible for me to repeat them in detail, they however are all full of praise over the progress he makes for the benefit of the Emperor and pretends that he has established a political party in this City with which he is able to control the leading members of Congress—He has an Office in New York, No 21 Clinton Place, and one at No 203 Pennsylvania Avenue in this City, he has engaged several persons in this City as Correspondents of Newspapers and to report to him in advance such proceedings in Congress as may lead to Mexican interest, but how far the contracts from either side of these parties have been fulfilled I am not now able to state. The expences of Estváns bureau for the first six months from February 1866, has been estimated by the Maximilian Government at $50,000, in this estimate however there appear to be no money appropriated for bribes to individuals, but Estván in his despatches invariably indicate that Members of Congress are open to pecuniare influenses, and have asserted to me that he will have to his disposal a Million of Dollars, and that for the half of that sum he will be able to procure the recognition of the Mexican Empire from the United States Government. Extensive promises of Imperial rewards are being made to those who assist in the noble work Estván proposes to carry out, his expences however, so far as he accounts to his Government will not be covered by $50,000 for 6 months, as they amounted to about $17000 @ 18000 from the end of February when he commenced operations till the beginning of April. I will transmit herewith a copy of a statement made by Maximilians handsecretary which to the best of my memory is an exact copy, also a Memorandum of Newspapers which according to Estváns books have been engaged and paid, for aiding the Imperial cause sinc February last—also a list showing what papers were to be engaged at the time he was to be reembursed, which was expected during May last—I have learned that Estván received a remittance from Mexico some two weeks ago and that his efforts for Maximilian thereby stimulated will be immediately renewed with much Vigor. Maximilian has also in the United States a Military Agent. a Major Graham who resides I think in New York at the present time—

his mission here I am not familiar with, only know through Estvấn that he is Maximilians Military Agent here. Estvấn, with concent, has introduced to the Imperial Government as an Active Aider for its cause—a would be prominent Gentleman, (Geo Francis Train) who in this Country pretends to be one of the leading men for the establishment of an Irish republic— This gentleman pretends to control a million of Votes in this Country, and as he expect to be in the U. S. Senate soon—would be a desirable acquisition to the Maximilian Government and a Valuable oposer of the Mexican Republic—what arrangements for compensating this gentleman have been made between him and Estvan is unknown to me, but I have seen a Train of praise in his favor despatched to the Mexican Emperor. Among bills which according to Estvấns statement has been and will be introduced to Congress by him, through its most influential members, is to be one proposing to the United States the grant of a loan of $200.000.000. to the Maximilian government—this loan he proposes to procure with success, and to do so Assistance from prominent Members of Congress would of course be required. He pretends being the cause of the delay in Congress in granting the $50,000,000 loan to the Mexican Republic, I do not remember him having made mention of any Congressmens name in this connection, except the Chairman of the Committee on Foreign relations of the House of Representatives who I well remember having been mentioned in his despatches as entertaining friendly feelings towards the Empire, and thereby oposing the loan. I am warranted in saying that Estvấn is the only Agent Maximilian has in the United States for the purpose of distributing money among Newspapers and individuals for aiding in the Imperial cause, and have reason to believe that the sooner his Career is ended the sooner will Maximilian come to a true understanding of the feelings of the American people towards his Government."—ALS (undated), USG 3. The accompanying statement, listing newspapers and newspaper reporters allegedly receiving money to report favorably on Maximilian in Mexico, is *ibid.* A letter in the same hand of April 18 from "B. E." to "My dear Wells" concerning disharmony among individuals promoting support in the U.S. for Maximilian is *ibid.* Someone noted on this letter: "(This letter was sent as a trap for Count Risiguier)"—AN, *ibid.*

1866, May 2. To Secretary of War Edwin M. Stanton. "I have the honor to request that Lieutenant Colonel P. T. Hudson, Captain and A D C. U S Vols., be relieved from duty in his rank of Lieut Colonel on my staff, and that Major F. T. Dent, 4th U S Infantry be announced as Aide de Camp with the rank of Lieutenant Colonel in his stead. I wish Col. Hudson to be continued on my staff with his rank of Captain, as announced in General Orders No. 155 series 1864, A G O., until orders mustering out officers of the volunteer staff take effect."—LS, DNA, RG 94, ACP, G171 CB 1866. On May 3, USG wrote to Stanton. "I have the honor to respectfully recommend that Lieut. Col. P. T. Hudson, Brevet Major and Captain and A. D. C., U. S. Vols. be appointed a Colonel of Volunteers by brevet for gallant conduct in the field, to date from the surrender of Gen. Lee, April 9th 1865. Col. Hudson was constantly on duty with me in the field from the fall of Vicksburg to the surrender of Lee, and always discharged his duties bravely and efficiently and to my entire satisfaction."—LS, *ibid.*, G190 CB 1866.

1866, May 2. To Secretary of War Edwin M. Stanton. "I would respectfully recommend that the enclosed order to Lt. Davis, 1st Cavalry, be changed so as to leave him on duty as Act. Insp[r] in Arazona for the present. Lt. Davis was, I believe, sent to Arazona, by yourself for the benefit of his health which had become impaired whilst in the Volunteer service."—ALS, DNA, RG 94, ACP, D167 CB 1870. Capt. Murray Davis, 8th Cav., resigned as of May 23, 1870. On Sept. 23, 1873, Associate Justice Noah H. Swayne, U.S. Supreme Court, wrote to USG. "Capt. Murray Davis. of San Francisco desires the place of a Paymaster in the army. I have known him many years. He is a gentleman of the highest worth and character. I know no one more deserving. It gives me pleasure Earnestly to Commend him to your favourable Consideration for the place in question." —ALS, *ibid.*, Applications for Positions in the War Dept. On Oct. 14, Maj. Gen. Irvin McDowell, Louisville, wrote to USG. "Major Murray Davis of San Francisco Cal. (late Asst. Adjt. Genl. of Volunteers with the rank of Major and subsequently Captain of Cavalry till he resigned) desires the appointment of Paymaster in the Army and asks my endorsement of his application! Major Davis served under me in California—part of the time on my staff—and I am able, therefore, to speak knowingly of his high character, his integrity, his intelligent and more than usually liberal education. He was highly thought of by the War Department whilst in service, and with cause, for I ever found him a devoted and exemplary officer, and as having been such I beg to commend him to your favorable consideration!" —ALS, *ibid.* No appointment followed.

1866, May 2, 2:30 p.m. To Maj. Gen. Henry W. Halleck. "You are authorized to change Head quarters Dept of the Columbia to Portland Oregon"—Telegram sent, DNA, RG 107, Telegrams Collected (Bound); copies, *ibid.*, RG 108, Letters Sent; DLC-USG, V, 47, 109. On May 7, Halleck, San Francisco, telegraphed to USG. "Gen Steele prefers to remain with his H'd Q'rs at Ft VanCouvers—"—Telegram received (on May 10, 12:10 p.m.), DNA, RG 108, Telegrams Received; copies (one sent by mail), *ibid.*, Letters Received; DLC-USG, V, 54. On May 26, Maj. Gen. Frederick Steele, Fort Vancouver, Washington Territory, telegraphed to USG. "My A. D. C. of the Signal corps Lieut Strong is mustered and appointed in the Seventh (7th) Infantry I wish authority to retain him Please reply by telegraph"—Telegram received (on May 28, 5:50 p.m.), DNA, RG 107, Telegrams Collected (Bound); *ibid.*, RG 108, Telegrams Received; copies, *ibid.*, RG 393, Dept. of Columbia, Letters Sent; (dated May 28) DLC-USG, V, 54. On May 29, 10:45 a.m., USG telegraphed to Steele. "You are authorized to retain Lieut Strong."—Telegram sent, DNA, RG 107, Telegrams Collected (Bound); telegram received, *ibid.*, RG 393, Dept. of Columbia, Letters Received.

1866, MAY 3. To Edward H. Knight. "I have examined your 'UNION WAR CHART' with great pleasure. It supplies readily an amount of information which can otherwise be obtained only by reading over volumes of reports not readily obtained. As a matter of reference, too, it will be found valuable in every library, giving, as it does, at a glance, the date, place, etc., of every important event of the War."—Copy (printed), DNA, RG 48, Appointments Div., Letters Received. Knight, born in London in 1824, emigrated to Cincinnati in 1845, and trained as a lawyer, specializing in patent law. A copy of "The Union War Chart" is in CSmH. On May 21, 1870, U.S. Representative William Lawrence of Ohio wrote to USG. "I respectfully recommend Edward H Knight Esq for Assistant Commissioner of Patents & hope he may be appointed—He was for several years Editor of the Patent Office Reports & is now engaged in preparing an 'American Mechanical Dictionery' I take pleasure in saying I esteem him a gentleman of high character, of great Scientific attainments, of large experience in the Patent Office & with all the qualifications to make him a most eminent & useful officer. I very earnestly commend him to your consideration & urge his appointmt."—ALS, DNA, RG 48, Appointments Div., Letters Received.

1866, MAY 3. George W. Dent, Galveston, Tex., to USG. "To aid an old. an esteemed friend, whom I have known for the past thirty years, I take the liberty of enclosing to your address his application for pardon—endorsing every thing he sets forth therein, and vouching, as I would for my own father all his promises—Major Price is a good man, and deserving of this clemency and I trust you will commend his petition to the President."—ALS, DNA, RG 94, Amnesty Papers, Tex. Dent enclosed a letter of the same day from Robert P. Price, Galveston, to President Andrew Johnson requesting a pardon.—LS, *ibid.* On May 21, Francis P. Blair, Jr., and James S. Rollins, Columbia, Mo., wrote to USG. "Without troubling you with lengthy reasons for asking it, we join Geo. W. Dent, Esqr. in requesting you to present the enclosed petition of R. P. Price to the President for pardon. We hope you will do this in person and request his immediate attention to it, as it is important to him, in view of his removal to Texas, that he receive it at once. It may not be out of place to say that Gov. Fletcher of Missouri, where Mr. Price has resided for thirty years, endorsed a similar application now in the hands of the Attorney General."—LS, *ibid.* On the same day, Price, Columbia, wrote to USG. "Have the Kindness to present these papers without delay, and if the pardon be granted in time to reach me *here* within three weeks have it forwarded here; if not, to me at Galveston, Texas."—LS, *ibid.* On May 26, USG endorsed these papers. "Respectfully submitted to His Excellency the President of the United States."—ES, *ibid.* Docketing indicates that Price was pardoned as of May 28.—*Ibid.*

1866, MAY 4. To Secretary of War Edwin M. Stanton. "I would respectfully recommend that Col. Wm Sackett, 9th N. Y. Cavalry, who fell mortally wounded whilst gallantly leading his regiment in the battle of Trevilien Station, Va, June 11th 1864, be promoted a full Brigadier Gen. of Volunteers from that date. Col. Sackett died in the hands of the enemy about the 13th of June 1864. If this promotion cannot be made I would then respectfully recommend the promotion by Brevet."—ALS, DNA, RG 94, ACP, S650 CB 1866.

1866, MAY 4. To Sue Murphy. "I have caused to be examined the papers which you filed for damages done to your property in Decatur Alabama by United States troops—Loyalty is clearly proven and the claim seems to be entirely a just one, if any such claim is allowed—It is a matter left entirely with Congress and I can only say if any claim for damages done by the Army in states that were in rebellion against the government is allowed I would recommend yours."—Copies, USG 3; DNA, RG 107, Letters Received, W31 1867. Additional papers are *ibid.* See *SRC*, 39-1-128.

1866, MAY 5. To Maj. Gen. Philip H. Sheridan. "Give Capt. W. S. Stockton, 4th U. S. Cavalry a leave of absence for four months if there is another officer besides himself for duty with his company. Should there be no other officer with his company give the leave as soon as one can be assigned"—Copies, DLC-USG, V, 47, 109; DNA, RG 108, Letters Sent.

1866, MAY 7. Addressee unknown. "It will be perfectly convenient for me to appear before your commission to-morrow at the hour named in your note, 10.30 a. m."—ALS, University of Illinois, Urbana, Ill.

1866, MAY 8. Maj. Gen. John Pope, St. Louis, to USG. "I shall leave Ft Leavenworth on the 1st of June for an extended inspection of the Military posts in this Dept and shall be absent about four months—It is my purpose to inspect all the Posts on the Platte, go to Salt Lake & thence down into New Mexico—During this tour all Volunteers will have been mustered out & the posts which are retained garrisoned by the regular troops assigned me—This force is insufficient for the necessities of the Dept but I will do the best I can with them—By the time I return every thing in the Dept will be reduced to such system that I think there will be little trouble in administering it. I think the removal of Dept Head Qrs. to F Leavenworth not entirely judicious but perhaps I am mistaken in this opinion—The records of forty years are here in St Louis & the bulk of them has been so increased since /61 that it is not practicable to move them to Leavenworth without putting up a building expressly for them They contain the papers covering the entire organization, muster out, discharge, & other certificates of nearly the whole great Army at various times during the war called into service in the west—In addition the Records of the Provost Marshal Bureau, containing all papers relating to seizure of property, assessments, arrest & confinement of citizens & all matters bearing on the thousands of claims against the Govt—which have arisen during the past five years—A great deal of the office business here consists in answering demands for information from Washington & elsewhere, requiring daily & hourly reference to these records—They are now arranged so that this information can be furnished but to pack up these records & convey them to Leavenworth & there rearrange them will be a laborious & tedious business & will as I said require the erection of a suitable building for them—I shall therefore leave them here in charge of an officer as I feel certain that in a short time the necessities of service & the convenience of the public business will require the retransfer of Dept HdQrs to St Louis—However that may be the object of this letter is simply to let you know that it is my wish, if you do not consider it inconsistent with the public interests, to be ordered to the Command of the Dept of the East on my return from the Plains about October 1st—that Dept is now commanded by my junior in rank & I therefore do not think it inconsistent with propriety to express a wish for this assignment—I make no special application for the assignment but intimate my wishes to you unofficially as I feel sure that you will not be unwilling to know them & to accede to them as far as may be proper. I have served in the West all my life and would be glad to see a year or two of service in the East—If you can do so consistently I will be obliged to you if you can comply with my wishes —If you have any objections to my going to the Plains & being absent so long I trust you will telegraph me by the 15th of this month—"—ALS, DNA, RG 108, Letters Received. See letter to Maj. Gen. William T. Sherman, April 18, 1866. On Sept. 14, Pope, Pomeroy, Ohio, wrote to USG. "I arrived here from the Plains two days ago & shall await here an answer to my letter to you of August 28 from F Larned.—In that letter I stated to you in some detail the reasons which make it very painful if not indeed impossible for me to go to Oregon this winter & requested you to relieve me from the necessity of complying with the order—That you will do all that is proper & considerate I do not doubt & I venture to present to you a few remarks upon the suggestions which I made in relation to going to West Point as Superintendent—I presume that the object of the Law as well as the intention of the Govt, is to place West Point upon a different footing in all respects relating to its Military character—For this purpose I suppose that some officer of high rank in the Army who has seen service in the War will be assigned as Superintendent both to give dignity to the office and to establish such military character for the Institution as has been lacking whilst it was only a school under charge of Engineer officers—An institution which educates & prepares for the military service nearly all the officers of the Army ought to be and is one of the most important Depts in the Army and should be placed on an equality with any Military Dept in the country, so that it would command the highest rank & most thorough qualifications —& would be sought for by our most accomplished General officers—I need not enlarge to you upon the importance of placing West Point upon the best & most respectable footing in all respects—More than ever, the tone

& character of the Army will depend upon the graduates now in service & those who will from time to time graduate from the Academy—I need not tell you either how many things purely military but most essential to a young officer entering the service are omitted in the tuition at West Point, mainly because as a rule, neither Superintendent nor Professors have ever served with the Army or have any ideas of Military service except such as are purely theoretical and of necessity having little practical value—Most of the saddest cases of inefficiency and disgrace which have blurred the generally fair record of West Point officers, have been due to the fact that young men have been graduated at the Academy and thrust without knowledge or preparation into responsible positions, in which they were ruined or disgraced before they really possessed any idea of business or official responsibility—I need not go into such matters with you as you are quite as familiar as I am with the merits & defects of the Military Academy—Without altering the course of study or changing the General management I have no doubt West Point could be greatly improved & the character & qualifications of the young men graduating there, greatly elevated by the assignment of some officer of high rank as Superintendent & making that office so dignified & respectable that it would command the highest rank & best talent of the Army—In that view I wrote you expressing my willingness to accept the position & the more I have considered the matter, the more satisfied I have become that I could do great good to the Academy & through it to the Army, in such a position—At all events I am very willing to try it—I hope you will inform me at as early a date as is convenient what your views are on the subject of the two letters I have written you—My family is here & I shall remain with them until your decision reaches me."—ALS, DNA, RG 108, Letters Received. On Aug. 28, Pope, Fort Dodge, Kan., had written to Secretary of War Edwin M. Stanton protesting his assignment to command the Dept. of Ore.—ALS, *ibid.*, RG 107, Letters Received, P253 1866. On Sept. 17, USG endorsed this letter. "Gen. Pope desires the Superintendency of West Point which of course can not now be given him. I would however recommend that he be allowed to select a Dept. from among those commanded by his juniors except the one commanded [b]y Gn. Hooker which was given to him in conciderations of his health, and this Dept. which was created to keep Gn. Canby here for other special services"—AES, *ibid.* On Sept. 21, Bvt. Col. Adam Badeau wrote to Pope. "General Grant directs me to acknowledge the receipt of your letters of Aug 28th and Sept. 14th, and to say that the assignment to the command of Military Departments were made after consideration, and it is supposed judiciously; that it was believed in making them that the appointment of yourself to the command of the Dept. of Oregon would be acceptable to you. All the officers assigned except yourself having now gone to duty in accordance with the assignment it is not deemed expedient to disturb the arrangements A change cannot be made in the superintendency of the Military Academy, at this time, without detriment to the interests of the service. If however your own private interests require your presence at the East, during the winter, and you will make an application for a six months leave of absence, it will be granted."—Copies, DLC-USG, V, 47, 60; DNA, RG 108, Letters Sent. On Sept. 26, Pope, Pomeroy, wrote to Badeau. "Your letter of the 21st Inst was duly received yesterday—I have important private business which will occupy me until October 16th and which will require my personal presence in Cincinnati three or four times between this & April 15th for a few days at a time & probably once or twice in New York for a day or two—with the exception of the time thus occupied (about ten days altogether) my time is at the service of the Govt and unless I am placed on duty at a great distance I can without interfering with public business attend to the private affairs which require my presence at the places above mentioned—I dislike to apply for a leave of absence as I do not wish to be idle for such a length of time & would prefer therefore to be placed on some sort of duty—Of that however the Genl-in-chief can judge—If it is thought best I hope this letter will be considered an application for leave of absence for six months from October 1st—I am however ready & able to perform any duty whatever which does not put me out of reach of Cincinnati at the times it is necessary I should be there—I regret to learn from your letter that the Genl-in-chief should have thought that my assignment to Oregon would be acceptable to me—Of the Pacific Coast I know nothing whatever—A large part of my service in the Army has been on the Great Plains lying within & east of the most eastern ranges of the Rocky Mts. from the British Line to the Gulf of Mexico—With nearly the whole of that region I am perfectly familiar by actual personal experience & would greatly prefer (if I am to be kept on the extreme frontier) a Dept in the region in question ~~than~~ to one on the Pacific—Of all Depts in the Army that of Oregon is the one I am most reluctant to go to—Whilst neither my personal feelings on the subject nor my unpleasant relations with Genl Halleck furnish any official reasons for relieving me from the command of that Dept, I yet cherish the hope that circumstances may, during the next six months, make it expedient for the Genl-in-Chief to favor my wishes without detriment to the public interests—"—ALS, *ibid.*, Letters Received. On Oct. 1, Maj. George K. Leet wrote to the AGO directing that an order be issued granting a six-month leave to Pope.—ALS, *ibid.*, RG 94, Letters Received, 739A 1866.

1866, May 9. Bvt. Col. Ely S. Parker endorsement. "Respectfully referred to Maj. Gen. G H Thomas. This house should be vacated and turned over to the legal representative of these children, if it can possibly be done without too great detriment to the public service."—AES, DNA, RG 94, Letters Received, 356T 1866. Written on an unaddressed letter of April 27 from J. N. M. Harris, Vicksburg, received at USG's hd. qrs. "You will remember Laura Lane—the once wealthy, brilliant woman, surrounded with all that could make life comfortable. She died last August in utter poverty, leaving three children. Her plantations are involved in debt, and must be either sold, or must remain unavailable until the debts are paid from the rents. In the mean time the children have no means of support or education except the sum of $75 per month paid as rent by the Department Quartermaster, General, Whittlesey, for the use of the residence in Vicksburg by Gen. Wood, at Military Headquarters. This sum, $75, will scarcely feed these children. The point of my request is this, viz The children must have the house or suffer. . . ."—Copy, *ibid.* On May 21, Maj. Gen. Thomas J. Wood, Vicksburg, endorsed these papers stating that it would be inconvenient to vacate the house and suggesting that the rent be raised to $150 per month.—ES, *ibid.* N. V. Lane and N. H. Harris, Vicksburg, wrote an undated letter to USG requesting permission to sell the house.—LS, *ibid.*, RG 108, Letters Received. On Dec. 14, 1867, Lane wrote to USG. "I understood that there hads been an order issued by you in relation to property that had been registered at one time as abandoned property, I have never seen the order and do not know the purport of it, There is a plantation about two miles from Millikens Bend La known as. the Oak. Grove plantation and belongs to the minor children of my deceased brother, Mr H P. Morancey is the administrator of the Estate, and I am guardian of the Children, We have had control of the place for the last two years, If there is any special order necessary to hold the place, Please send me or H. P. Morancy at Millikens Bend the order to that effect. and greatly oblige . . ." —ALS, *ibid.*, RG 105, Land Div., Letters Received.

1866, May 10. To Secretary of War Edwin M. Stanton. "I would respectfully recommend in the case of Lt. T. G. Morrow, 11th Ohio Cavalry, cashiered for drunkeness, that on account of previous good character the sentence of cashiering be revoked and he be honorably mustered out of service, on the same date."—Copies, DLC-USG, V, 47, 109; DNA, RG 108, Letters Sent.

1866, May 10. USG endorsement. "I recommend Bvt. Brig. Gn. G. W. Schofield as an intelligent faithful officer of the Volunteer service, and one who has served faithfully and efficiently during the greater part of the Rebellion, a portion of the time directly under my immediate command. He entered the service late in 1861 as Lt. of Artillery and rose through the various grades to Lt. Col. and Bvt. Brig. Gn. He has commanded during the rebellion from a Company of Artillery up to a Division of troops."—AES, DNA, RG 59, Applications and Recommendations, Lincoln and Johnson. Written on a letter of the same day from George W. Schofield, Washington, D. C., to Secretary of State William H. Seward seeking appointment as U.S. consul, Honolulu.—ALS, *ibid.*

1866, May 11. To Secretary of War Edwin M. Stanton. "I would respectfully recommend the promotion of each of the Major Generals of the Regular Army to the grade of Lieut. Gen. by Brevet, for gallant and meritorious services during the War. I would suggest that Gen. Sherman have his brevet for the fall of Savannah, Ga. and each of the others for the 9th of Apl. 1865."—ALS, DNA, RG 94, ACP, G781 CB 1866.

1866, May 11. To Bvt. Maj. Gen. Edward D. Townsend. "Please have Patrick McEnery enlisted in the General Service, and ordered to report to Surgeon General Barnes for duty"—Copies, DLC-USG, V, 47, 109; DNA, RG 108, Letters Sent.

1866, May 11. Asa D. Smith, president, Dartmouth College, to USG. "I was informed recently, by our excellent Governor Smyth, that there was a possibility of your visiting New Hampshire, the present year, and that he was not without hope of your being able to attend the exercises of our Annual Commencement. That occurs on the 19th of July. I write to say, how greatly your presence on that occasion would gratify not only our Corporation, Faculty & Students, but the whole region round about. Dartmouth College contributed largely of her sons to the Army of the Union, in the Great War lately closed; and you would meet some here, doubtless, who had the honor of serving near your own person. If your plans will allow you to come this way, do not withhold from us, dear Sir, the pleasure and honor of your presence. You will find the air of this hill-country, I am sure, very refreshing to you after those many toils which the millions of your countrymen hold in such grateful remembrance. Governor Smyth will be my guest at Commencement; and I take the liberty to ask, that you, also, will be pleased to accept the simple hospitality of my dwelling."—ALS, USG 3.

1866, May 13. Brig. Gen. Stewart Van Vliet, New York City, to USG. "*Private* . . . I see that Jeff Davis is to be tried at last. This will make the officers of the late Confederate Army feel somewhat uncomfortable as they may imagine that their turn will come next—May I ask your opinion confidentially, if you can consistently give it, whether an officer who is on parole, can be tried—I ask this for you may Know that my brother-in-law Dr S. P. Moore, of the old army, was the Surgeon General of the Confederate Army, & is on parole having surrendered under Shermans arrangement—His wife is exceedingly uneasy & unhappy under the belief that the Dr. will be brought to trial—I have assured her that there is no danger whatever of any such thing occuring—If you feel at all disinclined to say anything on this subject, I shall of course Genl not expect you to do so." —ALS, USG 3. On May 15, Bvt. Col. Adam Badeau wrote to Van Vliet. "In reply to your note of the 13th, Gen Grant directs me to say that he has always held the opinion that the officers and men of the Rebel armies paroled at Appomattox Court House and elsewhere in complicity with Similar stipulations, are exempt from trial or punishment for any acts of warfare against the United States. Gen Grant does not consider that the terms of these surrenders excepts any from the operation of laws of Congress refering to acts other than military acts or from punishment for violation of any of the laws of war; but he has repeatedly expressed to those in authority, both verbally and in writing, his construction of the paroles. He does not think that those who gave those paroles can be tried now or ever for any strictly military acts done during the Rebellion."—ALS, *ibid.*

1866, May 15. To Matías Romero supporting American investors holding a concession to build a railroad across Mexico.—Translated into Spanish in Romero, comp., *Correspondencia de la Legacion Mexicana en Washington durante la Intervencion Extranjera 1860–1868* (Mexico, 1870–92), VII, 527. On the same day, Romero wrote to USG acknowledging his letter.—*Ibid.*, pp. 527–28. See Thomas David Schoonover, *Dollars Over Dominion: The Triumph of Liberalism in Mexican-United States Relations, 1861–1867* (Baton Rouge, 1978), pp. 263–66.

1866, May 18, 12:40 p.m. To Maj. Gen. Henry W. Halleck. "What foundation is there for the stories of a massacre at Fort Goodwin?"—Telegram sent, DNA, RG 107, Telegrams Collected (Bound); copies, *ibid.*, RG 108, Letters Sent; DLC-USG, V, 47, 109. On the same day, Halleck, San Francisco, telegraphed to USG. "There is no foundation for the Fort Goodwin massacre story It was simply a newspaper sensation story gotten up for the benefit of certain contractors."—Telegram received (at 10:45 p.m.), DNA, RG 107, Telegrams Collected (Bound); *ibid.*, RG 108, Telegrams Received; copy, DLC-USG, V, 54. On June 7, Bvt. Brig. Gen. James H. Carleton endorsed an order concerning Fort Goodwin, Arizona Territory. "Respectfully referred to the Adjutant General of the Army. It will be seen by the date of this Order, that Fort Goodwin is still a post. The 'Fort Goodwin Massacre' was doubtless gotten up as many other Indian stories are gotten up. I have seven Cayotero Apaches who came here with a paper signed by Col Pollock, Col Chapins predecessor. It is dated April 26. 1866. They tell me that there was no trouble when they left.—The fellow Mowry who writes to Gen. Grant on the subject of this massacre, seems, therefore to lose the ground of his complaint."—AES, DNA, RG 94, Letters Received, 414C 1866. The enclosed order is *ibid.*

1866, May 18. Governor David S. Walker of Fla. to President Andrew Johnson, Secretary of War Edwin M. Stanton, and USG. "I respectfully request that Maj Genl J. G. Foster commanding Dept of Florida may not be mustered out under the orders issued for the muster out of all volunteers General Officers but that he be allowed to retain his present rank & position."—Telegram received (on May 22, 10:00 a.m.), DLC-Andrew Johnson.

1866, May 19. To Bvt. Maj. Gen. Edward D. Townsend. "Please direct Lt. J. W. Dixon, 3d U. S. Cavy. to report to Gn. Hancock for duty until further orders."—ALS, DNA, RG 94, Letters Received, 400A 1866. On May 22, Maj. Gen. Horatio G. Wright, Galveston, Tex., wrote to USG. "Senator Dixon informs me that his son, who was for a time on my staff as an Actg Aide-de-Camp, has recd an appointment as 2d Lieut in the 3d Cavalry and that you would, on my application, order him to report to me for duty as Aide—I now have two of my old Aides, who are valuable and experienced officers, and they propose to remain with me while I continue in command here—But if it would be permitted for me to have an extra Aide I should be glad to have Lt Dixon, and would ask that he be directed to report to me for that duty—I address myself directly to you, as the subject was between yourself & Senator Dixon."—ALS, *ibid.*, RG 108, Letters Received. On June 8, Wright wrote a letter received at USG's hd. qrs. requesting 2nd Lt. James W. Dixon, 3rd Cav., as an aide.—*Ibid.*, Register of Letters Received. On June 26, Maj. George K. Leet endorsed this letter. "Respy. returned—disapproved."—Copy, *ibid.* On June 27, Dixon, St. Louis, telegraphed to his father, U.S. Senator James Dixon of Conn., that the 3rd Cav. had left Fort Leavenworth before his arrival.—Telegram received, *ibid.*, RG 94, Letters Received, 516A 1866. On June 30, Leet endorsed this telegram. "The Adjutant General will issue such orders in the case of Lt Dixon as will secure him against charges."—AES, *ibid.* On July 2, Senator Dixon, Hartford, telegraphed to USG. "Lieut J W Dixon 3d U. S. Cavalry reported at Ft Leavenworth found Col Sykes had been gone ten (10) days & returned not knowing what to do. Gen Wright informs me he has applied to you for Lieut Dixon. Please order him to report to Gen Wright send order to me."—Telegram received (at 10:50 A.M.), *ibid.*, RG 107, Telegrams Collected (Bound); *ibid.*, RG 108, Telegrams Received; copies, *ibid.*, RG 94, Letters Received, 516A 1866; DLC-USG, V, 54. On the same day, Leet endorsed a copy of this telegram. "Respectfully referred to Gen. E. D. Townsend, Asst. Adjt. Gen., who will issue an order directing Lt. Dixon to report to Gen Wright for staff duty."—AES, DNA, RG 94, Letters Received, 516A 1866. On July 3, noon, USG telegraphed to Senator Dixon. "Despatch received I gave the orders yesterday for the detail of your son to Gen. Wright's staff."—Telegram sent, *ibid.*, RG 107, Telegrams Collected (Bound). On Aug. 17, Senator Dixon telegraphed to USG. "If Genl Wright is ordered [here] I request that Lieut Dixon may come with him before joining his regiment"—Telegram received (at 3:30 P.M.), *ibid.* On Aug. 22, USG wrote to Townsend. "Order Lt. J. W. Dixon, 3d U. S. Cavalry, to report to Maj. Gn. W. S. Hancock for Staff duty until further orders."—ALS, *ibid.*, RG 94, Letters Received, 628A 1866.

1866, May 19. To Bvt. Maj. Gen. Charles R. Woods. "The enclosed letter is referred to you for such action as an investigation of the charges made may warrant."—Copies, DLC-USG, V, 47, 109; DNA, RG 108, Letters Sent. On the same day, D. H. Bingham wrote a letter received at USG's hd. qrs. "States that he has recieved a letter from Surg. Thomas Haughey of Elyton, Alabama, setting forth the murder of two negroes near Elyton, and that Judge Medel refuses to investigate the matter. Encloses military record of Surg. Haughey."—*Ibid.*, Register of Letters Received. On May 21, Maj. George K. Leet endorsed this letter. "Respy. referred to MG. C. R. Wood, comdg. Dept. Alabama in connection with the letter of Doctor Haughey, referred to within, which was enclosed in a communication from

Lt. Genl on 19th inst."—Copies, *ibid.*; *ibid.*, RG 393, Dept. of Ala., Endorsements.

1866, May 21. To commanding officer, board of bvt. appointments. "Enclosed I send you the record of services in the case of officers who have served on my staff during the latter portion of the rebellion for your consideration." —Copies, DLC-USG, V, 47, 109; DNA, RG 108, Letters Sent.

1866, May 22. Bvt. Maj. Gen. Philip St. G. Cooke, Omaha, Nebraska Territory, to USG. "In consequence of information from Montana of the relations between settlers & black feet Indians received through Gen Sherman & of his advice dated May 17th I have ordered first battalion 13th Infantry instead of occupying the cheyenne route to establish a post at Ft Benton The season is the right one. The work is commenced & I think it will be successful"—Telegram received (at 4:35 p.m.), DNA, RG 107, Telegrams Collected (Bound); *ibid.*, RG 108, Telegrams Received; copy, DLC-USG, V, 54.

1866, May 22. H. Latham, Vicksburg, to USG. "I had a Small iron gun, presented to me about ten years Since, by the E Carver gin Stand Co of East Bridgewater Massachusetts which I had loaned to some citizens of this place to fire Salutes and was kept at the court house for that purpose and was there at the time Vicksburg surrendered—It is a Short gun of about five or Six pound caliber and is mounted and has my name in full (H Latham) on the breech cut in the metal by the makers and sent to me as a present for a 4th July gun—It is of no use to the Government and only valuable to me as a gift from worthy friends—Genl McPherson and Genl Smith, each in turn promised to restore the gun but left without doing so—If consistent with the rules of propriety, I would ask of you to send me an order to Majr Genl Th J Wood requesting him to turn over the gun with its mountings to my wife Mrs Lucy A Latham—You will recollect me and my family as the occupants and owners of Magnolia Hall, four miles from Vicksburg—I have no acquaintance with Genl Wood the present commander here and have never spoken to him about the gun—Our beautiful residence has passed into other hands for the payment of debts—Mrs Latham, desires to be remembered with gratitude to you for the kind protection you gave her and family during the terrible seige of Vicksburg—Please direct to me at Vicksburg—"—ALS, DNA, RG 108, Letters Received. On June 5, Maj. Gen. Thomas J. Wood, Vicksburg, endorsed this letter. "Respectfully returned to Head Quarters Armies of the United States—with the information that the statement of Mr Latham in regard to the origin of this gun is doubtless correct and that it was used to fire salutes is equally correct—But its use so far from being confined to firing peaceful salutes for the Union: it was *used to* fire upon and destroy steamboats passing the City supposed to have Government property on Board—I have the authority of the man who fired the gun that this is the first gun fired in favor of the rebellion—I have reported the same to the War Department A. G. O. and have received orders from the Secretary of War to send the gun to the War Department as a relic of the rebellion—"—ES, *ibid.*

1866, MAY 25. To Bvt. Maj. Gen. Edward D. Townsend. "Please publish order dissolving Inf.y Board on Bvt. recommendations and give Gn. King three months to report for orders. I would recommend for the concideration of the Sec. of War that Gn. Robinson be assigned to the Command of the Dist. of N. Carolina and to act also as ~~Agt.~~ ~~of~~ Asst. Com. of Bureau of Freedmen, Refugees &c. Gn. Ruger to be relieved and Mustered out from the 15th of June 1866."—ALS, DNA, RG 94, Letters Received, 415A 1866.

1866, MAY 26. Maj. Gen. John Pope, Fort Leavenworth, to USG. "Whole number of recruits for 5th Infantry in New Mexico has reached here. There can be enough officers belonging to 5th Infy & 3d Cavalry now in the United States furnished to Col Sykes to take out the recruits. It is not necessary that officers of the 5th Infantry should be brought all the way from New Mexico merely to go back again with these recruits. I request that the order for officers of the 5th Infantry to come in here be revoked and that I be authorized to send the recruits under Col Sykes at once. Until they reach New Mexico some Volunteers must be kept there"—Telegram received (at 6:30 P.M.), DNA, RG 107, Telegrams Collected (Bound); *ibid.*, RG 108, Telegrams Received; copy, DLC-USG, V, 54. On May 28, Brig. Gen. John A. Rawlins endorsed this telegram. "Genl Townsend will revoke so much of S. O. No 203 as directs the offices of 5th Infantry in District of New Mexico and Fort Bliss, Texas, to report in person to Col. Sykes at Fort Leavenworth, Kansas, and authorize Genl Pope to send the recruits for the 5th Infantry under Col Sykes to Dist of New Mexico, and, also, authorize him to retain a regiment of N. M. Volunteers until they reach there."—Copy, DNA, RG 108, Register of Letters Received.

1866, MAY 27. To Bvt. Maj. Gen. Edward D. Townsend. "Please send order to 2d Lt R. K, Roberts authorizing him to take thirty days from time of leaving his Volunteer duties before reporting for duty with his Company." —ALS, DNA, RG 94, Letters Received, 434A 1866.

1866, MAY 27. Lewis Wallace, Washington, D. C., to USG. "I called to submit a point, and ask your help. It is of the utmost importance to the Mexican enterprise that the Collector of the Port at Brownsville shd be a *friend.* Understanding this I have long had an arrangement with Mr. Charles Worthington, who has heretofore filled that post. In April last, Mr. W'n resigned, ~~tion of the Collectorship was accepted.~~. ~~He was induced to offer it~~ under supposition that my enterprise was abandoned. Better informed, he is now willing to return to Brownsville in the same capacity, if Mr. McCulloch will grant him a few weeks leave of absence to spend with his family. There are several applicants for the vacancy, but as yet there is no appointment. I am sure you are informed of Worthington's fitness: in fact, of his almost indispensibility. I have therefore thought, that on that ground you might not be indisposed to help me again by requesting that Mr. W.'s resignation may be returned ~~to him~~, and a leave granted him. I repeat, general, this is a point of the utmost importance to me and the cause. You can scarcely do us a greater favor than by helping as requested."—ADfS, InHi.

1866, MAY 29. USG endorsement. "Respectfully submitted to the President of the United States. Mr. Callaway was a Captain and after wards Lt Col of the regiment I commanded at the begining of the war. He was a young man of good character, but I know nothing of his present political views or position"—ES, DLC-Andrew Johnson. Written on a letter of May 25 from James E. Calloway, Tuscola, Ill., to USG. "My friends Gov Yates and Hon H. P. H. Bromwell, the M. C. from the 7th Cong. Dist of this State (in which your old Reg't was raised) have made application to the President for my appointment as one of the Three Commissioners, under a late act of Congress, to investigate the Claim of Missouri for Six Millions vs. U. S. Gov't; but I fear the differences between the President and Congress may render my friends (above named) powerless in my behalf. Another friend of mine (late a Surg of Vols and now a warm friend of Mr Johnson's) upon his return recently from Washington informed me that he thought there would be no difficulty with my appointment and that a note from you to the President in my favor would secure me in the position. Now General, I may be trespassing in asking this favor of you as I do not know that you would *interfere* in any civil appointment, but what I ask is that you will give me whatever endorsement you can *personally* and as one of your old officers is all that I can or do ask. Politically I am understood here to be friendly to the administration and a supporter of its general policy. Since my return from the army last June (after the Surrender of the rebel armies) I have married a wife and have been engaged in the same business I followed prior to the war viz. practicing Law."—ALS, *ibid.* See *PUSG*, 2, 29, 77.

1866, MAY 29. Maj. George K. Leet to Maj. Gen. Henry W. Halleck. "I am directed by the Lieutenant General Commanding to acknowledge the receipt of a communication from Major General Irvin McDowell Commanding Department of California, of date March 23d, in reference to the Indian troubles in Arizona, and bearing your endorsement of date March 25 1866. He directs me to say in reply that General Mason seems to have become involved in a war without any apparent necessity, but if the Indians are really and actively hostile you must be the judge of the means and manner of terminating their hostility."—ALS, DNA, RG 94, ACP, 2232 1871. On Aug. 28, Maj. Gen. Irvin McDowell endorsed this letter. "I have certainly been very unfortunate in my letter within referred to, of March 23d if I have given the impression that General Mason became involved in a war with the Indians in Arizona, without any apparent necessity. The question as to *when* Indian hostilities commenced in Arizona is a matter of fact, and not one of opinion, and, as to this, I beg to say, that they broke out long before I came to this country; that they were in full activity when Arizona was placed under my command and before General Mason went there. It is due to Genl Mason that this fact be properly represented at Army Head Quarters. In my letter of March 23d. there is a paragraph which certainly must have been overlooked. I there state as follows; 'The Territory was reduced to so low a point for want of "troops" *at the time of its being transferred to my command*, that it was fast being abandoned. "Tubac" was entirely deserted; all the farms in the Upper "Santa Cruz" and in the vicinity of "Tucson", in the "Senoita" and the "San Pedro" were abandoned. Valuable mines were given up, as no one could, without Military guard, remain in the country. No person, or no two persons could venture to go into the Valley to either cultivate the land or herd the stock, so that the country produced no food!' This was the condition of the country when General Mason was sent to it . . . in existence—the Indians really and actively hostile—In fact he was sent there on that very account and directed to adopt such measures to terminate these hostilities as after an examination of the subject, on the spot, he should judge expedient and practicable. I can only add to my letter of the 23d that the active measures taken, with a view to terminating the hostilities in Arizona, have given a temporary quiet to the inhabitants, which, I doubt not, would be permanent, if he could continue to have the services of the natives, who, only, seem to have had any success.—" —AES, *ibid.* On May 31, Secretary of the Interior James Harlan wrote to Secretary of War Edwin M. Stanton enclosing two communications concerning Indian hostilities in Arizona Territory.—LS and copies, *ibid.*, RG 107, Letters Received from Bureaus. On July 9, USG endorsed these papers. "Respectfully returned to the Hon. Secretary of War, with the information that Gen. Halleck on the 29th May 1866 was fully empowered to exercise his discretion as to the mode and manner of preventing Indian hostilities, and keeping proper order in the Territory of Arizona—Copies of the within papers have been transmitted to him."—ES, *ibid.*

On Jan. 14, 1868, Thomas A. McGrew, Springfield, Ohio, wrote to USG. "I herewith forward letters from: Gov. J D. Cox, of Ohio, the Hon. S Shellabarger M. C., and Genl. J Warren Keifer member of the Ohio Senate [r]ecommending the transfer of Brevt Brig. Genl. Jno S Mason, now on duty in Texas to the Inspecter Genls Department. Hopeing this application will receive your favorable consideration . . ."—ALS, *ibid.*, RG 94, ACP, 2232 1871. The enclosed letters are *ibid.*

1866, MAY 30. To Secretary of War Edwin M. Stanton. "I would respectfully recommend the appointment of Russel H. Day, as 2nd Lieut. in the Regular Infantry. Mr. Day served in the Volunteer force for the period of twenty two months, when he was honorably discharged by reason of his regiment being mustered out of service. He has been raised in the army, his father Col. H. Day, now being a retired officer."—Copies, DLC-USG, V, 47, 109; DNA, RG 108, Letters Sent. Russell H. Day was appointed 2nd lt., 6th Inf., as of the same day. On April 27, Bvt. Brig. Gen. Hannibal Day, col. (retired), 6th Inf., Fort Hamilton, New York Harbor, had written to USG. "I find that at, present prices, I cannot live on Retired pay and would ask as a personal favor that you put me on duty at Hd. Qrs: Dept: East, available for any light duty such as Court Martial Service &c. There are other 'old fogies' like me now in that position and I flatter myself they have no better claim than I have. By the bye, my impression is of the Army bill now before Congress that it makes no provision whatever for retaining Officers now on the 'Retired List.' How do you view it? If you can steal a moment from more important matters, I should be glad to hear from you." —ALS, *ibid.*, RG 94, Letters Received, 340A 1866. On May 1, Maj. George K. Leet endorsed this letter. "Respectfully referred to the Adjutant General, who will grant the within request if it can be done without detriment to the service."—AES, *ibid.* On Dec. 2, 1867, Gen. Day wrote to USG, secretary of war *ad interim*. "I have the honor to enclose the application of Sylvester Henry Day for a Commission in the Army. He has been a faithful clerk in the Qr. Master's Dept. since the Autumn of 1861. He was a member of an organization, as Volunteers, of Employèes in said Dept. in the Dist. of Columbia for a long period during the rebellion and for the last six years an applicant for such appointment. He being now in Oregon with Capt. I. Gillis A. Qr. M. he would prefer, if appointed, one of the Cavalry Regiments now in the Pacific Division. Said applicant is twenty six years of age and was born in the State of Pennsylvania. . . . If favorably considered, be pleased to enclose to my address."—ALS, *ibid.*, ACP, D629 CB 1867. No appointment followed.

1866, May 30. To Secretary of War Edwin M. Stanton. "I would respectfully recommend that the states of Ky. and Tennessee be constituted one Dept. Maj. Gn. Stoneman to command, and that Gn. Fisk be assigned to the District of Tenn. and Gn. J. C. Davis to the command of the Dist. of Ky. each to perform the duties of Agt. of the Bureau of Refugees & Freedmen in addition to their duties as Military commanders."—ALS, DNA, RG 94, Letters Received, 447A 1866.

1866, May 30, 11:15 a.m. To Maj. Gen. John Pope. "Orders will be given to loan arms to Engineer Pacific Rail Road"—Telegram sent, DNA, RG 107, Telegrams Collected (Bound); telegram received, *ibid.*, RG 393, Dept. of the Mo., Telegrams Received. On May 28, Pope, Leavenworth, Kan., had telegraphed to USG. "The Engineer of the Pacific railroad asks that small arms be loaned or issued to parties of Surveyors for the railroad. I recommend that an issue be made"—Telegram received (on May 29, 4:50 p.m.), *ibid.*, RG 94, Letters Received, 779M 1866; *ibid.*, RG 107, Telegrams Collected (Bound); *ibid.*, RG 108, Telegrams Received;

copy, DLC-USG, V, 54. On May 30, USG endorsed this telegram. "Respectfully forwarded to the Secretary of War with recommendation that arms be loaned on receipt of the Chief Engineer of Pacific railroad."—ES, DNA, RG 94, Letters Received, 779M 1866.

1866, JUNE 9. Wilkinson Call, Washington, D. C., to USG. "Permit me in behalf of the people of Florida to bring to your notice a hardship under which they are suffering which it is in your power to remedy without in any manner contravening the policy of the Govemt. I am advised that the Military Authorities of Florida consider themselves obliged to all civil process from the State Courts and to require that all judicial process shall be submitted to them for their approval before it is executed. I would respectfully submit and in this I am sustained by Judge Usher, Dist. Atty. of the U. S. for the Northern District of Florida—that inasmuch as all cases in which the laws of the U. S. are in any way involved—may under the law be transferred to the U. S. Courts on the application of either of the parties to the suit.—The order in question of it has been issued—creates an unnecessary difficulty to the recovery of their of their rights by parties litigant & respectfully ask that the subject may receive your consideration and if it should receive your approval the order may be so modified as to withdraw from the military the authority to interfere with the ordinary course of the law."—Copy, DLC-U.S. Army: Civil War Miscellaneous. On June 19, Maj. Gen. John G. Foster, Tallahassee, Fla., wrote to USG's adjt. "I have the honor to acknowledge the receipt of the letter of the Hon. Wilkinson Call, Senator elect from Florida, which you referred to me, and to make the following report thereon, for the information of the Lieutenant General. It is not my intention to interfere with the State Courts at all, as long as they deal out impartial justice to all parties, and I have made known such intention in General Orders No 28, a copy of which I enclose.—There have, however, occurred several cases, some at Fernandina in connection with the tax sales, and some of a criminal nature in other parts of the State, where justice was not administered by the State authorities; in which cases action has been taken only for the purpose of having the questions at issue transferred to, and decided by, U. S. tribunals.—No cases of a civil nature, or those in which a Citizen is a party, are now tried by military courts in this Department, or have been thus tried since the letter of instructions of the War Department, dated April 9th, 1866, was received. In general I let all cases go to the proper State Courts, causing all Officers on duty in the State, to watch the proceedings to see that justice is done.—In case it is not, they are directed to take an appeal to the next higher Court, so as to give time to have the case transferred to the U. S. Distr. Court, under the process prescribed in the Habeas Corpus act.—In cases involving the higher crimes, where proper action is not taken by the State authorities to arrest the criminals, I cause the arrests to be made at once, and the prisoners held for trial by the U S. Court alone; it being presumable, that, if there is not public justice sufficient to make arrests, there is not to secure a fair trial.—Genl

Orders No 34 just issued will illustrate my recent action in such cases.—The only drawback to the prompt administration of justice in this Dept, is the absence of the U. S. Distr. Judge, and the consequent closing of his Court, ~~and~~ but this hiatus of the U. S. Court, it is hoped, will be terminated soon, as I have written to Atty Genl Speed upon the subject.—In general every care is taken to secure to the Citizens of the State a fair & impartial administration of justice, and it is to this end alone that I ever interfere militarily, and never to any further extent, than to transfer cases from State or municipal to U. S. Courts.—"—LS, DNA, RG 108, Letters Received. See letter to Elihu B. Washburne, Nov. 9, 1865.

1866, June 23. To Secretary of War Edwin M. Stanton. "I would respectfully recommend the appointment by Brevet of Brig. Gen. Jas R. Slack, U. S. Vols., to be Maj. General. General Slack served during the entire war and all, or nearly all, of the time in the field"—Copies, DLC-USG, V, 47, 109; DNA, RG 108, Letters Sent. See *PUSG*, 5, 149*n*.

1866, June 23. To Secretary of War Edwin M. Stanton. "I have the honor to make requisition for Five Thousand Dollars ($5000) of the appropriation for 'Expenses of Commanding General's Office' and request that it be drawn in favor of Maj. Geo. K. Leet, A. A. G. of my Staff"—Copies, DLC-USG, V, 47, 109; DNA, RG 108, Letters Sent.

1866, June 23. USG endorsement. "Refered respectfully to the sec. of War."—AES, DNA, RG 94, Cadet Applications. Written on a letter of May 8 from Maj. Gen. Frederick Steele, Fort Vancouver, Washington Territory, to USG. "Robt. A. Lovell son of Col. C. S. Lovell 14. U. S. Inf. wishes to get an appointment as Cadet at West Point. He is a promising young man and I have no doubt would be successful at the academy. You know all about his father's services, and I presume were acquainted with him during the war with Mexico. Lovell has a large family to educate, and it is thought that with your recommendation, Bob could get the appointment."—ALS, *ibid.* No appointment followed.

1866, June 25. Helen L. Dent, Charlottesville, Va., to USG. "I will be in Washington this P. M. Will someone meet me?"—Telegram received (at 10:15 A.M.), DNA, RG 107, Telegrams Collected (Bound).

1866, June 26. USG endorsement. "Respectfully submitted to Hon. Wm H Seward, Secretary of State."—ES (undated), DNA, RG 59, Applications and Recommendations, Lincoln and Johnson; copy (dated June 26), *ibid.*, RG 108, Register of Letters Received. Written on a letter of June 9 from John C. Cox, former lt. col. and commissary, Quincy, Ill., to USG. "From the invariable kindness and many instances of confidence you have honored me with in the days down the river, when I was a soldier, I am emboldened to ask you for yet another favor I have applied for the position of Minister to the Hague in the event of a vacancy Your aid would be most potent in securing my appointment and I would ask for the memory of old times, a letter from you giving a brief statement of my general character and services, while on duty near you I am aware General this request smacks of boldness but you taught the old army of the Mississippi that quality & I was one of them As I may not again have an opportunity I wish to mention to you the reason why I left the service at the time I did before the close of the campaign on Atlanta When Genl McPherson assumed command of the Department of the Tennessee, he assured me voluntarily of his intention to continue me in the same position on the Staff of the Department command that I held on that of the Corps but directed me to remain with the Corps until I heard from him—this of course I did and was perfectly satisfied—Before the Corps moved from Cairo I had reason to perceive that in my department there existed a difference in opinion amongst the senior officers of the Department, which seemed to me as likely to lead to petty partizanship, in which I determined not to participate, and as my health had again given way I procured a Surgeons certificate with a view to resignation, which I determined to offer at the close of the campaign This I did after advising frankly with Genl Crocker—I went under orders in advance of the Corps to Huntsville where I had a conversation with Col McFeely, who has invariably been a cordial friend of mine, and for whose honesty and sincerity of character I have the highest regard, during which he stated that there was an intenti[on] to humiliate him and that my arrival at Head Quarters would probably be the occasion I assured him as I was in honor bound to, that under no circumstances would I consent that I should be promoted by what might seem to be a humiliation of himself and we parted on the most cordial terms of friendship, which I hope yet continue to exist between us—I marched with the Corps to Ackworth and had not been there an hour when Col Clark, the Adjt Genl met me with an order relieving McFeely—I asked him to withold it, for the present but he replied, we have been waiting some days for you and you will find the order at your quarters when you return—I replied, in that case I offer my resignation, having the Surgeons advice to leave soon or I should have to be carried home—In a short time I met Genl McPherson, with whom as you are aware my relations were almost fraternal, who met me with his usual heartiness and said 'Col you will find an order for you at Head Quarters.' I then related to him what had transpired affecting myself and told him I had no alternative but to resign—He said nothing for a few minutes & then replied 'You are right—go home & get well again and I will send for you to fill a different position' This was our last interview—he died soon after most gloriously in the blaze of his fam[e] without fear for he never knew it—without reproach, for truer man never died—Excuse this long explanation but it is the only instance I have ever alluded to a subject, which in justice to myself I desired to communicate to you—I should have been glad to have received my brevet and honestly think I earned it, but that is no great matter With sincere wishes for your continued health which is all that is required to enable you to achieve a splendid future . . ."—ALS, *ibid.*, RG 59, Applications and Recommendations, Lincoln and Johnson.

1866, June 26. USG endorsement. "Respectfully forwarded and recommendation of QuarterMasterGeneral approved."—ES, DNA, RG 94, Letters Received, 200Q 1866. Written on a letter of June 16 from Bvt. Maj. Gen. Montgomery C. Meigs to USG. "I have the honor to furnish below an extract from a communication of Col. J. D. Bingham, Inspector, Quartermaster's Department, dated Saint Paul, Minn., June 1. 1866, relative to the retention, &c., of the Military Reservation at Fort Snelling near Saint Paul, Minn. . . . The reservation at Fort Snelling was sold by Floyd when he was Secretary of War to Frank Steele for $100,000, Thirty thousand dollars of that amount was paid about 8 years ago and no payments have been made since. I think the Post should be retained by the Government. The reserve is now composed of 3 square miles. . . . One square mile will be sufficient for Government purposes as there is no timber of any consequence on the reserve. In addition to the Post buildings a Draft Rendezvous has been built since the war and they are all within the square mile recommended to be retained. They are the best buildings of the Kind I have ever seen. These I would fill with such surplus stores as we now have in buildings at St. Louis and Cincinnatti for which we are paying rent. In this way we can store such surplus property as we want to Keep for future use, at no expense for rents, as the buildings and the grounds on which they stand already belong to the Government. This will be a good point to store them, as the Posts of Ripley, Ridgely, Abercrombie and Wadsworth will probably be Kept up for some years yet and this is the proper place to supply them from. . . . The views expressed by Col. Bingham are concurred in by me, and it is respectfully recommended that they be carried into effect."—LS, *ibid.* Printed as addressed to Secretary of War Edwin M. Stanton in *HED*, 40-3-9, p. 6. See letter to Maj. Gen. William T. Sherman, April 18, 1866.

1866, June 27. To Secretary of the Treasury Hugh McCulloch. "Respectfully refered to the Hon. Sec. of the Treasury. Gen. Smith's services during the Rebellion are so well known that comment on that subject is unnecessary. I have known the General for more than Twenty years. He has always maintained a high reputation. I know him to be strictly reliable and believe him to be entirely competant for the position he seeks.—The present encumbent of the office sought has no claims for his place with the present administration."—AES, OFH. Written on a letter of June 1 from Lt. Col. and Bvt. Maj. Gen. Andrew J. Smith, 5th Cav., Washington, D. C., to McCulloch seeking appointment as collector of internal revenue at St. Louis. —ALS, *ibid.* No appointment followed.

1866, June 27. To Secretary of War Edwin M. Stanton. "I have the honor to recommend that the unexecuted portion of the sentence of General Court Martial in the case of Chas. E. Walters, recruit temporarily assigned to Co. H. 4th Regt. Veteran Reserve Corps promulgated in General Orders No. 18. of date May 8th 1865. Hdqrs. Department of the Northwest (copy herewith enclosed) be remitted and the prisoner released from confinement" —Copies, DLC-USG, V, 47, 109; DNA, RG 108, Letters Sent.

1866, JUNE 27. To J. Russell Jones, Chicago. "Washburne is not dangerously sick though he has suffered very much."—ALS (telegram sent), DNA, RG 107, Telegrams Collected (Bound).

1866, JUNE 27. Capt. and Bvt. Brig. Gen. Horatio G. Gibson, 2nd Art., St. Louis, to USG. "Genl Sherman informed me today he had given orders to remove all citizens from Jefferson Barracks Reserve by force—As this includes Capt Kennerly what must I do if called upon?"—Telegram received (at 9:30 P.M.), DNA, RG 107, Telegrams Collected (Bound).

1866, JUNE 28, 10:40 A.M. To Isaac N. Morris. "Your dispatch received and refered to Paymaster General with request."—ALS (telegram sent), DNA, RG 107, Telegrams Collected (Bound). On June 27, Morris, Quincy, Ill., had telegraphed to USG. "Please have all action concerning Edward Prince pending before Paymaster General suspended until next week Other parties interested for whom I will then appear—Answer—" —Telegram received (at 8:30 P.M.), *ibid.* On June 28, USG endorsed this telegram. "Respy. referred to Paymaster General with request that the action be suspended for time asked."—Copy, *ibid.*, RG 108, Register of Letters Received.

1866, JUNE 30. USG endorsement. "Cap't Hickenlooper proved himself during the rebellion one of the ablest and most energetic Volunteer Officers. No one had the confidence of his superiors in a higher degree than Capt Hickenlooper"—Copy, Cincinnati Historical Society, Cincinnati, Ohio. Written on a letter of June 14 from Maj. Gen. Oliver O. Howard, Bureau of Refugees, Freedmen, and Abandoned Lands, to President Andrew Johnson recommending Andrew Hickenlooper, former bvt. brig. gen., for appointment as U.S. marshal for Ohio.—Copy, *ibid.* Hickenlooper was confirmed on July 25.

1866, JUNE 30. USG endorsement. "General Stolbrand proved himself during the rebellion one of the bravest and most efficient Officers.—General McPherson and General Sherman, under whom most of his services were rendered had the greatest confidence in his skill, courage and ability."—Copy, DNA, RG 60, Records Relating to the Appointment of Federal Judges, Marshals, and Attorneys.

1866, JUNE 30. Maj. Gen. Joseph Hooker, New York City, to USG. "I percieve by the report of the Correspondent of the New York Herald of this mornings issue that I am to be relieved of my present Command by

Gen Pope. As this deeply concerns my future I beg you will inform me if there is any foundation to the report—"—Telegram received (at 11:00 A.M.), DNA, RG 107, Telegrams Collected (Bound); (at 10:50 A.M.) *ibid.*, RG 108, Telegrams Received; copy, DLC-USG, V, 54.

1866, July 5. To Bvt. Maj. Gen. Edward D. Townsend. "Please have the order mustering out of Maj. & Bvt. Brig. Gn. W. R. Price, Cav.y Inspector, suspended until July 31st 1866."—ALS, DNA, RG 94, ACP, G286 CB 1866. On July 9, Lt. Col. John C. Kelton, AGO, noted on this letter. "Submitted to the Sec of War July 9. and not approved."—AN, *ibid.*

1866, July 6. Bvt. Maj. Gen. Montgomery C. Meigs to USG. "It is stated to be in contemplation to build barracks at Fort Wayne for the troops in garrison at or near Detroit. During a year's residence, about Sixteen years since at Fort Wayne, my family and myself suffered from severe malarial fevers. The marshes of the River Rouge near the Fort, can not have improved by sixteen years accretion, and as I had spent several years living in Detroit with perfect health, visiting the Fort every day during its construction, I infer that exposure to the night air is very unhealthy. If the troops are moved to this place they cannot expect to escape better than my family, of which eight out of ten were ill,—some of us, dangerously ill. I think that it will be in the interest of health and therefore of efficiency and economy to keep the principal part of the garrison at the Detroit Barracks, and to station at the Fort only a small guard. A heavy sick report is likely to follow the proposed change."—LS, DNA, RG 393, Military Div. of the Miss., Letters Received. On July 10, Maj. George K. Leet endorsed this letter. "Respectfully referred to Maj. Gen. W. T. Sherman, Comdg. Mil. Div. Miss., for remark."—AES, *ibid.*

1866, July 6. Nick W. Casey, Caseyville, Ky., to USG. "Enclosed I send you a communication from my brother in law L McLaws late Major Genl C. S. A. he was elected to a clerkship in Georgia, but the Military have in accordance with orders from the Secy of War directed him to vacate the same; Can you do any thing in his case, he appears to think so, and if you can I assure you it will be appreciated, by McLaws and myself." —ALS, DNA, RG 108, Letters Received. The enclosed letter of June 21 from Lafayette McLaws, former C.S.A. maj. gen., Augusta, Ga., to Casey concerns McLaws's removal as county clerk, Richmond County, Ga., by military authorities because he had not been pardoned.—ALS, *ibid.* On Sept. 7, Mrs. Margaret L. Taylor, Frankfort, Ky., wrote to Mr. Barrett concerning her brother-in-law, McLaws, stating: ". . . When he heard it rumoured, that the ~~military~~ military talked of removing him he wrote Mr Nick Casey, to write Gen Grant about it, as he and Mr Casey were intimate friends, Gen McLaws said it was nothing but justice, he should retain his office, & a mere statement to Gen Grant would be sufficient. Mr Casey saw General Grant in Louisville when he was last there and he told him, to write Gen McLaws to hold on to his office & he would sustain him. Since then, two months ago, they did remove him, but before Gen Grant could have interfered, my sister wrote they hoped to get it back, through Gen Grant. . . ."—ALS, *ibid.*, RG 94, Amnesty Papers, Ga. Additional papers are *ibid.* Docketing indicates that McLaws was pardoned as of Oct. 18. —*Ibid.*

1866, JULY 7, 2:00 P.M. To Maj. Gen. Irvin McDowell. "Massacres are reported in Paradise Valley Nevada and troops withdrawn Send Cavalry if you can"—Telegram sent, DNA, RG 107, Telegrams Collected (Bound); copies, *ibid.*, RG 108, Letters Sent; DLC-USG, V, 47, 60. On the same day, U.S. Senator James W. Nye of Nev. had written to USG. "I have this moment received the within Genl Thomas told me to send it to you I hope you will give it immediate attention as my constituents are greatly afflicted"—ANS, DNA, RG 108, Letters Received. Nye wrote his note on the reverse side of a telegram of July 6 from Judge Edmund F. Dunne, Star City, Nev., to Nye. "For Gods sake send troops masacres every where paradise Valley in flames inhabit fleeing soldiers removed nearer Idaho savage rule four cavalry companys Sufficient Salt Lake might spare them"—Telegram received, *ibid.* On July 7, McDowell, San Francisco, telegraphed to USG. "Your telegram recd. Have but one Co in the direction of Paradise Valley—This is stationed at Camp McDermot northwest of the valley on road to Idaho—Many ~~on~~ of the men absent escorting trains to Owyhee and but one officer present. Gen'l Halleck has just passed through & directed a detachment of this Co to be kept at Paradise Valley—The other Co cavalry in northern Nevada is on the Clino & Susanville road to Idaho about One hundred miles west of Pariadise Valley. It may be able to spare twenty men which with the detachment of eleven at Fort Churchill which will be sent is all that are available—The troops withdrawn were the Vols [— — — — —] of service & were retained to the last moment possible"—Telegram received (on July 9, 12:30 P.M.), *ibid.*, Telegrams Received; copy, DLC-USG, V, 54. On July 12, Capt. and Bvt. Lt. Col. John P. Baker, Fort McDermit, Nev., wrote to Lt. Col. Richard C. Drum, adjt. for McDowell, reporting no hostile Indians in Paradise Valley and observing that ". . . These stampeding reports are gotten up by men in that Valley and below to get another Company stationed there, Knowing that the more troops the get in this country the more money in their pockets in selling their crops. . . ."—LS, DNA, RG 94, Letters Received, 417P 1866. On Aug. 22, USG endorsed this report. "Respectfully forwarded to the Secretary of War for his information."—ES, *ibid.*

1866, JULY 9. USG endorsement. "I know nothing in the case of H. Gilmore which should make it an exceptional one, and as he is threatened with prossecution in the state courts, a danger not generally shard in in by paroled Officers, I would recommend his pardon. My notion is that all paroled officers should be exempt from trial for all acts of civilized warfare, so long as they observe their parole, in the same degree that all persons acting under the Authority of the Govt. during the rebellion should be exempt from trial for alleged wrongs against Southern people and property."—AES, DNA, RG 94, Amnesty Papers, Md. Written on a letter of the same day from Harry W. Gilmor, former C.S.A. maj., to President Andrew Johnson requesting a pardon.—ALS, *ibid.* Docketing indicates that Gilmor was pardoned as of Nov. 12.—*Ibid.* On Feb. 28, Gilmor, New York Hotel, had written to USG. "While you were in this city I called at your Hotel to see you, hoping to obtain from you permission to go to my home in Md, where I have not been for a very long time. I am aware that my parole allows me to *take the risk* of going there, but since my release from prison in July, my friends have all persuaded me not to go to Baltimore unless I had some kind of protection from you. Enclosed you will please find my parole and a letter from my friend Maj Genl Palmer which I had hoped to have recd in time to present to you while you were in N Y. I will not further encroach upon your time, but hope sir you will act favorably upon my request and return my parole with permission to go to Md to See my family—"—ALS, Maryland Historical Society, Baltimore, Md. On July 21, Gilmor, Leesburg, Va., wrote to USG. "I write to thank you in the kindest manner for your endorsement on my application for pardon, as I did not have an opportunity of doing so before I left Washington I am only sorry to add that the President considered it insufficient to cover up the multitudê of my sins, and required the name of a *radical senator* before granting my pardon. Therefore I am still prevented from visiting my home. I hope you will pardon the liberty I take in thus addressing you, but I could not help expressing my thanks to you for the part you took in my affair."—ALS, USG 3.

1866, July 10. USG endorsement. "Approved and respectfully forwarded to the Secretary of War with the recommendation that each of the within named officers be appointed brigadier generals of volunteers by brevet, for gallant and meritorious services."—ES, DNA, RG 94, ACP, R398 CB 1866. Written on a letter of July 9 from Brig. Gen. John A. Rawlins to USG. "I have the honor to submit the names of the following officers, late of your staff, for brevet promotion in the volunteer service. Col. Clark B. Lagow Addl Aide deCamp rank of *Col* Col. Wm S. Hillyer Addl Aide deCamp rank of *Col* Col. John Riggin Addl Aide deCamp rank of *Col* Lt Col. Wm R Rowley. Aide-deCamp by assignment. maj A. D C by commissi[on] Col. Lagow entered the service in June 1861 as 1st Lt. in the 21st Regt. Ills. Infantry Vols., and in August of the same year was assigned to duty on your staff; was in the battles of Belmont, Ft Donelson and Shiloh, the siege of Corinth and operations against Price at Iuka, and Pemberton on the Tallahatchee; was assigned in orders and had charge of the transports that ran the rebel batteries at Vicksburg on the night of the

21st of April, and participated in the battles and siege that resulted in the fall of that place, July 4th 1863. He was also in the battles of Chattanooga. Col. Hillyer joined you as a staff officer in August 1861; was in the battles of Belmont, Fort Donelson and Shiloh, the siege of Corinth, the operations against Price at Iuka and against Pemberton on the Tallahatchie, and the campaign and siege of Vicksburg. Col. John Riggin joined you as ADC. (volunteer) at Cairo in December 1861; was in the battle of Fort Donelson and in the operations ag'st Price at Iuka and against Pemberton on the Tallahatchie, and in the campaign and siege of Vicksburg. Lt Col. W. R. Rowley entered the service in September 1861 as 1st Lt. in the 45th Regt. Ills. Infy Vols., with which he participated in the battle of Fort Donelson, when he was appointed ADC on your staff. He was in the battle of Shiloh, siege of Corinth, and the operations against Price at Iuka and against Pemberton on the Tallahatchie On account of sickness from exposures in the field he was assigned to duty as ProvostMarshal at. Columbus, Ky., consequently he did not participate in the campaign and siege of Vicksburg. He was in the battles of Chattanooga, and in the campaign and battles from Culpeper C. H., Va., to the front of Richmond and Petersburg in 1864."—LS, *ibid.* On Aug. 27, Rawlins wrote to USG. "I have the honor to call your attention to the military record of Lt. Col. Wm L. Duff, 2d Regiment Illinois Light Artillery Volunteers, which was inadvertently omitted by me in the submission of the record of such service of members of your staff during the recent session of Congress with a view to their recommendation for brevet promotion. Col. Duff entered the service at the commencement of hostilities in 1861, as a three-months volunteer, and owing to his knowledge of ordnance, was retained on duty at Springfield, Ills., by Governor Yates. Early in 1862 he was appointed Lieut. Col. of the 2d Regt. Illinois Light Artillery Volunteers, and commanded for some time after its fall the post of Columbus, to the satisfaction of Gen. Quimby, his District Commander. In October 1862 immediately after your army was designated the 13th Army Corps, he was assigned to duty at your HeadQuarters as Chief of Artillery; and as such participated in the campaign against Pemberton on the Tallahatchie, and in the campaign, battles and siege of Vicksburg. Upon your appointment to the command of the military division of the Mississippi, he was assigned Chief of Artillery of your new command, and in that capacity participated in the military operations and battle of Chattanooga. When you assumed command of the Armies of the United States, on your recommendation he was assigned in orders Assistant Inspector General on your staff, and was with you in all your battles from Culpeper C. H., Va., to the front of Petersburg and Richmond; and continued on duty with you until the expiration of his term of service, in January 1865, when he was honorably mustered out. Col. Duff's services as a commissioned officer have always been in the field."—LS, *ibid.*, D790 CB 1866. On the same day, USG endorsed this letter. "Respectfully forwarded to the Secretary of War, with the recommendation that Lt. Col. Wm L. Duff, late of the 2d Regt. Ills.

Light Artillery Volunteers and of my staff, be appointed a Brigadier Gen'l of Volunteers by brevet, for gallant and meritorious services during the war, to rank from the 13th of March 1865."—ES, *ibid.*

1866, July 14. Maj. George K. Leet endorsement. "Respectfully referred to Maj. Gen. W. T. Sherman, Comdg Mil. Div. Mississippi"—AES, DNA, RG 109, Union Provost Marshals' File of Papers Relating to Individual Civilians. Written on a letter of July 12 from John V. S. Adriance, Buffalo, N. Y., to USG. "Through a Stranger to you I take the liberty of calling your Attention to the seeming uprising of the Indians on the Plains. reports lately from the Mountains, say 3000 Hostile Indians are within 15 Miles from Fort Benton & later reports are, that there is 10,000 Indians on the Smokey Hill, or in that vicinity. My reasons for thus Addressing you on this subject, is the Interest that a Father takes in a dear Son, that has fought Three Years for his Country & ~~now~~ is now travelling Acrost the Plains to Montana, with a small Band of Emigrants to meet probably a Savage foe. My son C. B. Adriance was first Lieut in 100th Regt N. Y. S. V Col D. B. Dandy, left Fort Abercrombie about July 1st in Capt Jas L. Fisks Montana Expedition, were promised military protection & where they expected to have a train 2000 Strong I learn they are only about 300 Strong. they go by way of Fort Berthold & Fort Union to Fort Benton. From Letters recieved from them, they want me to see if Government wont watch over them & if danger threatens Fly to their succour. the Boats are running from St Louis to Fort Benton & they could be easily reached. Now my Dear General if you will give this your careful attention & not let this little Band (many of them tried Soldiers) be devoured by savages I shall be truly grateful to you & this Band of Emigrants will forever Bless you. Hoping you will give this due consideration, . . ."—ALS, *ibid.*

1866, July 17. To Secretary of War Edwin M. Stanton. "Enclosed I send my recommendation on the subject of Cadet demerit, in the shape of a Special Order, for your concideration."—ALS, DNA, RG 94, Letters Received, 549A 1866. USG enclosed unnumbered Special Orders: "I Demerit shall not count in arranging the general standing of cadets at the Military Academy in the 2d, 3d or 4th classes. II After the completion of the 4th class studies each cadet shall have a credit of 16.67 for each month during which he shall receive no demerit, to be deducted from the demerit he may have received in previous years of his cadetship. III On final graduation conduct will, after deduction in accordance with par. 2 of this order, count the same in arranging class standing as under existing regulations." —ADf, *ibid.* Docketing indicates that these orders were issued on July 20 as Special Orders No. 350.—*Ibid.*

1866, July 19. To Commodore William Radford.—*ABPC*, 1943–1944, 605.

1866, July 20. To Bvt. Maj. Gen. Amos B. Eaton, commissary gen. "If Col. G. W. Campbell, C. S. is not already mustered out of service I would respectfully recommend that he be given to the 31st of August to complete his papers."—ALS, DNA, RG 192, Letters Received, Special File, G92. On July 21, Eaton wrote to USG. "I have the honor to acknowledge the receipt of your note of this date recommending that Col. G. W. Campbell, C. S. Vols. have until the 31st of August to complete his papers. An application from Col. Campbell of the 14th inst. for a leave of absence for thirty days was yesterday referred to this office by the Adjutant General, and was returned recommending that the leave asked for be granted."—Copy, *ibid.*, Letters Sent.

1866, July 21. To Bvt. Maj. Gen. Edward D. Townsend. "Please extend the leave of Bvt. Brig. Gn. J. S. Brisbin thirty days. His present address is Boalsburg, Center Co. Pa"—ALS, DNA, RG 94, Letters Received, 553A 1866.

1866, July 24. To Secretary of the Treasury Hugh McCulloch. "This will introduce to your acquaintance Col. L. F. McCrellis of Ill. an officer who served under me whilst I commanded in the West and who I introduce with confidence. The Col. has settled in Memphis and by his intercourse with the Citizens has become acquainted with the manner in which frauds have been committed against the Government. His object in seeking an interview will be better explained by himself."—ALS, DNA, RG 56, Div. of Captured and Abandoned Property, Letters Received, 263.

1866, July 24. To Secretary of War Edwin M. Stanton. "I would respectfully request that Special Orders No. 232, War Department, A. G. O., dated May 16 1866, granting Brevet Colonel A. Ames, 5th U S Artillery, leave of absence for one year, to date from August 1st 1866, with permission to go beyond the limits of the United States, be amended so as to give him nine months leave from the 1st of August 1866, and after expiration of that time permission to delay joining his command for three months. I make this recommendation for the reason that Col. Ames has never had the three months leave of absence allowed cadets graduating at the Military Academy."—LS, DNA, RG 94, Letters Received, 560A 1866.

1866, July 24. USG endorsement. "Respectfully returned to Secretary of War.—I know of no law under which this regiment could be raised, and Special legislation would be necessary to provide for its equipment, subsistence and payment."—ES, DNA, RG 108, Letters Received. Written on a letter of June 1 from Governor Richard C. McCormick of Arizona Territory, Prescott, to Secretary of War Edwin M. Stanton.—LS, *ibid.* On June 5, McCormick wrote to USG. "I enclose to you copy of a letter lately addressed to the Honorable Secretary of War."—ALS, *ibid.* The printed enclosure is *ibid.* McCormick pointed out the success of two cos. of the 1st Ariz. composed of Mexican vols. in fighting Apache Indians, and he requested that the War Dept. add eight cos. to the regt. for a two-year period. On May 1, Lt. Col. Clarence E. Bennett, 1st Calif. Cav., Fort McDowell, Arizona Territory, had written to Capt. John Green, 2nd Cav., adjt., District of Ariz., requesting authority to raise a regt. of Mexican vols. in Arizona Territory to fight Apaches because of the prior success of the Mexicans.—ALS, *ibid.* On July 7, Maj. Thomas M. Vincent, AGO, endorsed this letter. "Respectfully submitted to Lt. Gen. U. S. Grant Comd'g Armies of the United States. There is no law under which the regiment could be received into the service, and, therefore, should it be decided to organize it, special legislation will be necessary for its subsistence, equipment, and payment."—AES, *ibid.* Docketing indicates that USG disapproved the proposal.

1866, JULY 28. USG endorsement. "Respectfully submitted to His Excellency the President; pardon recommended."—ES, DNA, RG 94, Amnesty Papers, Tex. Written on a letter of July 15 from Matthew D. Ector, former C.S.A. brig. gen., Henderson, Rusk County, Tex., to USG. "(Private) . . . I was a Brig. Gen. in the Confederate Army and had the misfortune to lose a leg at Atlanta. I would refer you to those under whom I served as to my standing both as an officer & a man. I have a family entirely dependent upon me for support. I have been elected Judge of this District. It was with reluctance that I consented to run for any office; nothing but a sense of duty to my family & myself influenced me. It is important that I should receive a *pardon.* A number of promient men have used their influence with the President for me. I estimate fully the difficulties surrounding him, and on this account felt a greater delicacy in placing myself in a position in which it might become necessary to press my application upon him. After mature reflection I have concluded to appeal to you as a *Soldier* and try to interest you in my behalf. You have seen enough of life to appreciate my condition & feelings. Senator Trumbull of Ill. once knew me, & if he can consistently I believe will serve me. Pardon me for trespassing so long on your valuable time."—ALS, *ibid.* Docketing indicates that Ector was pardoned as of Aug. 8.—*Ibid.* On Oct. 10, 1867, Ector wrote to USG. "Soon after I was elected Judge of 6th District of Texas I wrote you a letter in reference to my application for special pardon. I had been a Brig General in the Confederate Army. My application had been approved by Gov. Hamilton and was strongly urged by several of the most promient Union Men in the State. I told you my true condition, appealed to you as a soldier, and gave my promise if you could consistantly aid me and would do so, I would appreciate it. For your prompt reply and valuable services in that matter you have my lasting gratitude. On the 11th of September, 1867, Gen Griffin the Commanding ~~Genera~~ Officer of the 5th Military District issued an order remove~~d~~ing me from

Office and assigning as a reason 'Known hostility to the General Government. A Copy of this order is herewith enclosed. Gen Griffin must have been deceived by some designing persons in reference to my Course. I positively assert that since I have been upon the bench I have taken ~~I have taken~~ no part in politics and have had as little to say about such matters as ~~any man~~ possible. If any evidence can be found in the official papers of Gen Griffin representing me in any other light I am prepared to prove that there is no truth in it. Enclosed I send you two Editorial Articles: one taken from the Henderson Times, published in the town where I live, and the other from the Texas Republican at Marshall in this District. I offer these to show in what light I am held by those who have the best opportunity of knowing me. In addition to these if I deemed it necessary I could offer abundant testimony from the most promient Union men in the District both of my uniform loyalty to the General Government and of the impartiality with which I have discharged the duties of my office. I have done or said nothing to abuse your confidence or forfeit your good opinion. Trusting that it will not be trespassing too much on your valuable time to read this letter and accompanying papers, . . . P. S. I will forward the President of the United States, and the Comdg officer of the 5th Military Dist, a copy of this letter."—ALS, *ibid.*, Letters Received, 1896M 1867. On Oct. 25, Col. Adam Badeau wrote to Bvt. Maj. Gen. Joseph A. Mower. "General Grant directs me to forward you the enclosed letter and news paper extracts for your information; not with a view to the replacement of Judge Ector. If however you should deem his restoration advisable, this letter is not intended to preclude your reporting that fact to the General of the Army" —ALS, *ibid.* Additional papers are *ibid.*

1866, July 28, 1:15 p.m. To Maj. Gen. George H. Thomas. "If Col H. M Ashley arrested at Knoxville July 26th is a paroled Confederate officer and the arrest was by military authority, you will cause his release. If he was arrested by the civil authorities do not interfere"—Telegram sent, DNA, RG 107, Telegrams Collected (Bound); copies, *ibid.*, RG 108, Letters Sent; *ibid.*, RG 393, Dept. of the Cumberland, Telegrams Received; DLC-USG, V, 47, 60. On the same day, Thomas, Nashville, telegraphed to USG. "Col H. M. Ashby, as I am in[f]ormed, was arrested by the civil authorities. I have not interfered"—Telegram received (at 11:10 p.m.), DNA, RG 107, Telegrams Collected (Bound); *ibid.*, RG 108, Telegrams Received; copies, *ibid.*, RG 393, Dept. of the Cumberland, Telegrams Sent; DLC-USG, V, 54. On July 26, George E. Church, former col., 11th R. I., Loudon, Tenn., had telegraphed to USG. "Col H. M. Ashby Confederate was arrested at Knoxville from the cars this afternoon. I fear mob law. The arrest was violent—Can you save him"—Telegram received (at 6:00 p.m.), DNA, RG 108, Telegrams Received; copy, DLC-USG, V, 54. On July 27, 11:00 a.m., Brig. Gen. John A. Rawlins telegraphed to Thomas, transmitting Church's telegram.—Telegram sent,

DNA, RG 107, Telegrams Collected (Bound); copies, *ibid.*, RG 108, Letters Sent; *ibid.*, RG 393, Dept. of the Cumberland, Telegrams Received; DLC-USG, V, 47, 60.

1866, July 30. To Secretary of War Edwin M. Stanton. "I would respectfully recommend that the Chief Engineer be directed to detail Capt. & Bvt. Maj. Gen. J. H. Wilson, U. S. Engineers to survey Rock River Ill. & Wis. in accordance with a recent Act of Congress. Gen. Wilson is eminently qualified for the duty and he is now available. There are two officers of the Engineer Corps on duty at Fort Delaware, Stewart & Wilson, where one is abundently sufficient."—ALS, DNA, RG 94, Letters Received, 570A 1866. On Oct. 24, U.S. Representative Elihu B. Washburne, Galena, wrote to USG. "With the promotion of Genl James H. Wilson it is greatly to be feared that he may be taken away from his present work on the Mississippi Rapids. I hope it may be deemed compatible with the public interest to have Genl Wilson retained. We have everything to hope from his scientific attainments, his great practical sense and his indomitable energy. Every congressman in the Mississippi Valley will join in an earnest recommendation to have Genl W. placed in full charge of that great work, so vastly important to our interests. I beg leave to submit this matter to your consideration and to express the hope that it will receive favorable action." —ALS, Alcorn Collection, WyU. On Oct. 30, Maj. George K. Leet wrote to the AGO suspending the transfer of Lt. Col. and Bvt. Maj. Gen. James H. Wilson, 35th Inf.—ALS, DNA, RG 94, Letters Received, 810A 1866. On Oct. 31, Wilson, Wilmington, Del., wrote a letter of thanks to Washburne.—ALS, DLC-Elihu B. Washburne.

1866, July 30. USG endorsement. "Respectfully forwarded to the Hon. Secretary of War. It is recommended that officers and agents of the Freedmen's Bureau be directed to furnish copies of their official reports to the Chief of the Bureau, upon such subjects as are within referred to, to the C. O. of the Dept. in which they are on duty, without requiring such commanding officers to furnish clerical force to make them out. I would also call attention to that part of Gen. Meade's letter referring to the writ of habeas corpus issued by Judge Byron of South Carolina."—ES, DNA, RG 108, Letters Received. Written on a letter of July 17 from Maj. Gen. George G. Meade, Philadelphia, to Brig. Gen. John A. Rawlins. "On the 21st August 1865, I received a letter of instructions from the Honl. Secy. of War requiring me to personally visit the Southern portion of my command, . . . My object in recapitulating the foregoing is to explain the manner in which Dept Comdrs were called on to report in relation to the Freedmen's Bureau and to call attention to the accompanying report of Maj Genl Sickles Comd Dept of the Carolinas—who states that the Agents of the Bureau, under instructions of the Commissioner decline to furnish the information necessary to enable him to comply with my orders.—I desire also to call to the special attention of the Lt. Genl Comdg & the War Dept, that portion of Maj. Genl. Sickles report referring to the writ of Habeas Corpus issued by Judge Bryan of So Ca and the action of the court on Genl. Sickles return to the writ.—This question of course involves, the question whether Martial Law, does or does not now prevail in the States lately in rebellion and it is to be hoped advantage will be taken of this case, to have some decided & clear ruling by competent authority on this point—relieving officers from the very embarrassing position in which Maj. Genl Sickles now finds himself.—"—ALS, *ibid.*

1866, JULY 31. To Secretary of War Edwin M. Stanton. "I have the honor to recommend Robert D. Miller, son of Hon Stephen Miller, late Governor of Wisconsin for a 2d Lieutenantcy in the 10th U. S. Infantry." —LS, DNA, RG 94, ACP, G657 CB 1866. No appointment followed for Robert D. Miller, son of former governor Stephen Miller of Minn. Accompanying papers indicate that the appointment had been sent to Wis. and not returned until July, 1867.—*Ibid.*

1866, AUG. 2. To George Bancroft. "Your kind invitation for Mrs. Grant and myself to visit Newport, as the guests of Mrs. Bancroft and yourself, is received. It has been my intention to visit Newport this summer, but the passage of the Army bill at such a late day as it did leaves me with work to do that will take all Summer. I thank Mrs. Bancroft and your all the same however and if it is possible to get to Newport for a few days before warm weather is over I will do so. Mrs. Grant joins me in desiring to be remembered to Mrs. Bancroft and yourself."—ALS, NRU. On Aug. 10, Governor Ambrose E. Burnside of R. I., Providence, telegraphed to USG. "When are you coming to Newport? Will you give me a day in Providence?"—Telegram received (at noon), DNA, RG 107, Telegrams Collected (Bound). On the same day, USG telegraphed to Burnside. "I do not know that I will be able to visit Newport. Will spend a day with you if I go."—Telegram sent, *ibid.*

1866, AUG. 3. To Brig. Gen. Joseph K. Barnes, surgeon gen. "I would prefer keepin[g] Asst. Surgeon Brenneman on duty at Hd Qrs. for the present summer and Fall at least, and until relieved. If the order has been made for his transfe[r] to duty elswhere will you please have the order revoked, and oblige, . . ."—ALS, DNA, RG 94, Letters Received, 754S 1866. USG noted his approval on a note from Barnes that another officer would be detailed.—AN, *ibid.* On July 28, Maj. George K. Leet had written to Barnes. "In reference to your application to have Bvt. Maj. E. de. W Brenneman, Asst Surg. U. S. A. ordered to report to the Medical Director Headquarters Dept of the East, for temporary duty. Gen. Grant directs me to say that upon inquiry he finds that Dr Brennemans services cannot well be dispensed with at these Headquarters and further that he is at present suffering with chronic diarrhaea & it is thought that to order him to N. Y.

where the Cholera prevails would be exceedingly imp~~ortant~~rudent."—Copies, DLC-USG, V, 47, 60; DNA, RG 108, Letters Sent.

1866, AUG. 4. USG endorsement. "Respectfully referred to the Paymaster General. The writer of this is one of the best citizens of Mo."—Typescript, USG 3. Written on a letter of Jan. 11 from John Hess to USG. "Lieut. Col. Johnson of the Pay Master Department has made an application to be appointed to the regular Army, he has the recommendations from most of his superior officers, Sherman, Dodge, etc., and wishes me to say a few words in his favor to you. I do so with pleasure. He is my townsman and an acquaintance of over *fifteen* years—warrant me in saying that he is worthy and I have shown my confidence in him by becoming his surety. If you can aid him it would be a great favor to him and yours."—Typescript, *ibid.* Bvt. Col. Chauncey P. E. Johnson, appointed maj. and paymaster as of June 1, 1861, was mustered out as of Oct. 26, 1866.

1866, AUG. 4. Jesse Root Grant, Covington, Ky., to USG. "Mr Stephen D. Thoburn—a young man twenty three years of age, late a Lt in a reg of Ohio Volunteers, who has served about four & a half years in the Union Army, and promoted from the ranks—a man of good personal appearance, respecable address & good English education, has called on me & shown me his application, & accompanying recommendations, for a second Lieutenancy in the Regelar Army—I know nothing of Mr Thoburn personally, but what I have seen in two short interviews. He has been brough up within two miles of this place, & is well endorsed by many who know him, as being every way worthy, qualified &c Mr Thoburns application is goten up by himself, & would do credit to any Gen in the Union Army—Some of his friends have requested me to make this statement to you, & to ask you if consistent to aid him to get the appointment, which tast & habit so well qualify him to fill"—ALS, DNA, RG 94, ACP, 2029 1871. William S. Rankin, assessor of internal revenue, 6th district of Ky., endorsed this letter. "I have read & fully concur in the above letter & reccommendation of J R Grant"—AES (undated), *ibid.* On Aug. 8, Stephen B. Thoburn, Columbus, Ohio, wrote to USG. "I have the honor to forward to you and through you to the Adjutant General of the Army an application for a Commission as 2nd Lieut in the Infantry Arm of the U S Service accompanied with a letter of reccommendation from Mr J R Grant. My military history is embodied in the enclosed application and I hope the endorsements thereon is satisfactory as regards my character and qualifications. Hoping that you will give this your personal attention . . ."—ALS, *ibid.* On Aug. 13, 1867, Thoburn, Newport, Ky., wrote to USG. "I have the honor to ask for information on the following subject. On or about the 8th day of Aug 1866 I forwarded to you an application for a Commission in the U S Army accompanied with a letter from Mr J R Grant to you of which the enclosed are copies Will you please inform me if such Papers was ever received. an early reply will oblige . . ."—ALS, *ibid.* Thoburn was appointed 2nd lt., 23rd Inf., as of Oct. 4.

1866, Aug. 5. William B. Allison and R. S. Harris, Dubuque, Iowa, to USG. "Mr David has gone to Washington to secure your influence to reinstate him in the Dubuque Post Office—Capt Williams recently appointed is a Soldier, served during the war—We respectfully request that you will not use your influence for David"—Telegram received (on Aug. 6, 10:20 A.M.), DNA, RG 107, Telegrams Collected (Bound).

1866, Aug. 6. F. N. Colwell, Pruntytown, West Va., to USG. "Some days ago I forwarded copies Mittimus & other papers, of Confederate Soldiers now prisioners in the Jail of this County under my charge. Will you please return the copies of detail & other original papers as they will be needed at their trials the 1st September next"—ALS, DNA, RG 108, Letters Received. On July 10, Colwell had written a letter received at USG's hd. qrs. concerning former C.S.A. soldiers held for murdering three West Va. home guards on April 24, 1865.—*Ibid.*, Register of Letters Received. On July 17, 1866, Judge Advocate Gen. Joseph Holt recommended that no action be taken in the case.—*Ibid.* On Aug. 9, Maj. George K. Leet endorsed these papers. "Respy. returned to F. N. Colwell, inviting his attention to the enclosed communication of the Judge Adv. Genl."—Copy, *ibid.*

1866, Aug. 7. To Secretary of War Edwin M. Stanton. "I would respectfully recommend that orders be issued directing Gen. Halleck, Comd.g Mil. Div. of the Pacific, to recruit one regiment of regular Cavalry, new regiment, on the Pacific Coast. He can take such officers from his own command to recruit, and command detachments of Cavalry recruits as he may choose until appointments are made and officers ordered to report to him."—ALS, DNA, RG 94, Letters Received, 593A 1866. On Oct. 1, USG wrote to Stanton. "About three Company officers will be able to command all the Cavalry recruits that we are likely to get in California so that I do not think the appointments recommended by the Governor, Gens Halleck & McDowell ought to be made on the grounds they claim. I would recommend however that California be given from the list submitted by them the number of appointments the state is entitled to by law. I will ~~make~~ keep a copy of their dispatch and make recommendations from it."—ALS, DLC-Edwin M. Stanton.

1866, Aug. 7. To Maj. Gen. George H. Thomas, Nashville. "Give Maj Wainwright the necessary escort to make his work of exhuming and reburying Union dead secure"—Telegram sent, DNA, RG 107, Telegrams Collected (Bound); copies, *ibid.*, RG 108, Letters Sent; *ibid.*, RG 393, Dept. of the Cumberland, Telegrams Received; DLC-USG, V, 47, 60. On July 26, Capt. and Bvt. Maj. William A. Wainwright, q. m., Chattanooga, had written to Col. and Bvt. Maj. Gen. James L. Donaldson concerning harassment of work parties exhuming bodies for reburial in military cemeteries.—Copy, DNA, RG 108, Letters Received. On Aug. 3, Thomas endorsed this letter. "Respectfully forwarded to the Asst. Adjutant General Hd. Qrs. Army of the United States for the information of the General in Chief. The people of the States lately in rebellion are each day growing more and more insolent and threatening in their demeanor, as they find themselves relieved from punishment by the military authorities. Similar reports come in from all sections of the Country. No troops will be furnished unless some overt act be committed, when the parties committing it will be arrested and held for trial under General Orders No 44 C. S. from Hd. Qrs. of the Army."—ES, *ibid.* On Aug. 7, USG endorsed this letter. "Respectfully refered to the Sec. of War for information. Gen. Thomas has been instructed to give Maj. Wainwright an escort to make his work secure without waiting for murders to occur."—AES (undated), *ibid.*; copy (dated Aug. 7), *ibid.*, Register of Letters Received. Additional papers are *ibid.*

1866, Aug. 7. B. W. Hunter, Alexandria, Va., to USG. "I take the liberty of addressing you by letter, to request a company of U. S. forces to be stationed at Warrenton or Warrenton Junction, Fauquier Co., Va. White soldiers would probably not have such a tendancy to produce irritation as colored ones, or augment the feeling now existing in that community. My reasons for so doing are as multifarious as the catalogue of crimes committed by our vicious natures when abandoned by God, and left to work out our own damnation since ante-deluvian days. I will merely cite one instance to justify my apparent presumption, and enclose a letter that you may know from whom it comes. I will also, qualify before a magistrate and get several witness to substantiate my statement, if desirable. Yesterday, while on my way to the Junction and but a mile off, I was accosted by a man claiming to be a Virginian, who desired to know what business any damned yankee had up in that country, remarking that I was outside the protection of the damned theaving sons of bitches now, and he would give me hell. I placed my hand involuntarily on my pistol and walked on, and he, following my example, walked after me, in such close juxtaposition as to render his company anything but agreeable—cursing and damning me at every step. When I arrived at the Junction, among the Confederate soldiers was a man who represented himself as a colonel in the Confederate army. The man Weaver who accosted me on the highway called for pistols when he had one already, and got up the cry of yankee, and that I had drawn a pistol on him. The Confederate Col. said he would whip me, and they, with others, some Mosby's men rushed in the telegraph office after me. I tried to be as bold and indifferent as possible, and picked up a pencil and wrote a telegraphic dispatch while they were crowding around to devour me. Some saw what a delicate fragile creature I was and I suppose, regarded me as an object of pity. I finished my dispatch by saying 'Grant is better today,' and the operator refused to send it because it had that terrible word, 'Grant,' in it. I then turned to the crowd about me and denied the statements of the first man, and got upon the train and went to Warrenton. When I returned it was the same thing over again, and my nerves were still unsteady. Some *ladies* interfered or blood would have been shed. About a year ago I sold some land to a northern man, and he went there to reside upon it. I have frequently, in passing his house enquired of neighbors why his doors and windows seemed always barracated? They told me they did not know, but I found the other day a solution to my enquiry. They said no yankee should live there, and every time his family were seen outside the house were chased into it with pistols and knives and sometimes forcibly entered to the consternation of women and children. This poor, persecuted man, bought a few days ago, a horse, and it was forcibly taken from him by a presentation of firre arms, only a few hours afterwards. A Union man told him to get a warrant issued for the arrest of the one who took the horse. He applied to the magistrate, and without a great deal of difficulty, succeeded in getting the warrant issued, but the constable said he was a yankee and the other a southern man, and he would only arrest him on terms that he pay thirty dollars to him, the constable for so doing. I trust I have said enough, but the half I could never tell."—ALS, DNA, RG 108, Letters Received. U.S. District Judge John C. Underwood and two others endorsed this letter. "Mr Hunters statement may be implicitly relied upon."—ES (undated), *ibid.* On Aug. 24, Maj. Gen. John M. Schofield returned this letter to USG's hd. qrs. with a report recommending that no troops be sent because Hunter's problems resulted in part from a family dispute.—ES and ALS, *ibid.*

1866, AUG. 8. Maj. and Bvt. Col. William Winthrop, judge advocate, Washington, D. C., to USG. "I have the honor to submit as follows, in answer to your endorsement of reference of the 27th. June last, upon the communication of Thos W. Roche to Major General Terry. In this communication, dated at Richmond on May 29th. last, Mr. Roche addresses Gen. Terry as department commander and represents as follows:—1. That in June, 1864, a U. S. soldier who had been detained—his horse giving out—in the rear of the march of a body of our troops, under Major General Wilson, in Charlotte county Virginia, was—after having been thrown off his guard—shot and killed by one Robert Redman a citizen farmer of that county, who thereupon proceeded to appropriate the horse, equipments, and other property of the soldier, which he still retains. It is added that Redman boasts publicly of the perpetration of this crime. 2. That another soldier of the same command was, under similar circumstances, killed by a farmer of Halifax county, Va., named Tom. Watkins, who also appropriated the horse & equipments of his victim. Mr. Roche states that neither of the parties named were 'connected with the confederate army.' It would seem to be clear that the acts charged were murders in violation of the laws of war. Maj. General Terry forwards the communication of Roche 'with request for instructions, as to whether it is desired to have such cases as are mentioned within investigated, and the accused, if guilty, brought to trial.' The question proposed, therefore, is whether these cases are proper for investigation and trial by military authority and by a military court. Although the peace *status* was restored in Virginia by the Presidents proclamation of April 2d., yet in the official letter of the Adjutant General to Brig Gen. Tillson, of April 17, in explanation of the proclamation, it is announced that the same does '*not remove martial law*'; and it is declared that—'it is not expedient to resort to military tribunals in any case where justice can be attained through the medium of civil authority.' Still further —in General Order of the War Department, (A. G. O.,) No. 26, of May 1st. last; issued for the purpose of removing the 'doubts' by which—as it is expressed—'some military commanders were embarassed as to the operation of the proclamation upon trials by military courts, and military offenses'; —it is laid down that—'hereafter, whenever offenses committed by civilians are to be tried where civil tribunals are in existence which can try them, their cases are not authorized to be, and will not be, brought before military courts-martial or commissions, but will be committed to the proper civil authorities.' Construing these several orders together, and in connection with the proclamation, it is conceived to be a proper conclusion, that in any locality of the states recently in rebellion where it shall appear—either that there is no organized civil court, which—by reason of want of jurisdiction, defect of machinery, or otherwise—can duly try a party charged with a military offense, (as an offense against an officer or soldier; or one affecting the military service of the United States,)—or, generally, that 'justice cannot be attained through the medium of the civil authority,'—a military tribunal may still—martial law not being removed—be resorted to for the trial and punishment of the offender. In the present instance, it is shown by the statements of Rochë, (whose communication, forwarded as it is by Gen. Terry for official action, would seem to be regarded by him as reliable,) that the commission of the crimes charged has been a matter of general notoriety, and that one at least of the alleged murderers has openly proclaimed his guilt; and it is to be inferred that no attempt has yet been made to bring to civil trial either of these conspicuous offenders. Under these circumstances it is suggested that these cases be submitted to the Executive, for his determination as to whether this apparent indifference on the part of the civil authorities is not evidence that 'justice can not be attained' herein through the medium of their action; and whether, therefore, the cases are not such as may properly be referred to Maj. Genl. Terry with directions to investigate the same, and—if the facts shall be found to warrant it—to bring the parties to their trial before a military commission, for murder and robbery in violation of the laws of war."—LS, DNA, RG 108, Letters Received. Additional papers are *ibid.*

1866, Aug. 10. USG endorsement. "Respectfully refered to the Sec. of War. Gen. Campbell was undoubte[dly] a very gallant soldier but his habits were rather against him. If the Majorities in the Invalid Corps are not filled up I would recommend Gen. Campbell for that position. If they are all filled I would then recommend him for a Captaincy, Senior Capt. in the Corps."—AES, DNA, RG 94, ACP, C1416 CB 1866. Written on a telegram of the same day from Governor Andrew G. Curtin of Pa., Harrisburg, to USG. "I beg to present to you very earnestly the claims of Gen'l C. T. Campbell for a colonelcy of one of the regiments of the Veteran Reserve Corps. His military record is on file & clean. wounded five times. He is disabled & poor"—Telegram received (at 11:40 A.M.), *ibid.*; *ibid.*, RG 107, Telegrams Collected (Bound). No appointment followed.

1866, Aug. 10. Bvt. Maj. Gen. Montgomery C. Meigs to USG. "I have the honor to inform you that an application of the Commissioner of the Bureau of Refugees, Freedmen &c for the temporary transfer of the Government buildings at the 'Soldier's Rest' in this city to that Bureau, has been referred to this Office from the War Department for report. Before reporting thereon, I respectfully submit the case, for the advice of the General of the Army. These buildings at the 'Soldier's Rest' are now vacant, that establishment having been broken up by orders from the Head Quarters of the Army, as an economical measure. The Commissioner of the Bureau of Refugees, Freedmen &c asks their transfer, as 'the most convenient method of caring for the discharged colored soldiers, collecting claims or settling accounts.' If the transfer is made as desired, for the use of one class of soldiers in place of another, the economical object of discontinuing the 'Soldier's Rest' will be defeated."—LS, DNA, RG 92, Miscellaneous Letters Sent (Press). On Aug. 15, Maj. George K. Leet endorsed this letter. "The Gen-in-chief cannot approve the application of the Commissioner of F. B and A. L. if the buildings at the soldiers rest are to be used for the benefit of one class of discharged soldiers to the exclusion of others; but if white and black soldiers are to be cared for alike—there is no objection to the transfer."—Copy, *ibid.*, RG 108, Register of Letters Received.

1866, Aug. 11. To Bvt. Maj. Gen. Edward D. Townsend. "Please send leave of absence to Capt. Prime, of the Eng. Corps, for six months with permission to leave the United States. Capt. Prime has made no application but he is sick and a physician told me that he would never recover without going away but that he could not be induced to make application. I have spoken to the Sec. of War in this matter and he concurs in it."—ALS, DNA, RG 94, Letters Received, 607A 1866.

1866, Aug. 14. Maj. Gen. Daniel E. Sickles, Charleston, S. C., to USG. "Unofficial . . . The Sec. of War has recently most Kindly tendered me a Colonelcy in the Veteran Reserve Corps.—Frankly, after reflection I do not like that position. It is very near the 'retired list.' I believe I am as Capable as Ever of performing any duty usually devolving on a General Officer. If deemed qualified, I shall be indeed very much gratified to remain in the Army as a General Officer, with Brevet rank Corresponding to my present grade in the Volunteer Service.—The Journals this morning mention the resignation of Gen'l Rosecrans and intimate a probability of my appointment to the Vacancy. Without intending to Solicit unmerited Consideration, or favor, and wishing to avoid being the occasion of the least Embarrassment anywhere, I beg only to assure you that I should appreciate the appointment if Conferred upon me, as the most valued & acceptable compliment that could be bestowed by my Government and Commanding General for my humble Service in the Army.—In the hope that I may be so fortunate as to have your support in this—and without it the position not be desirable— . . ."—ALS, USG 3. On Aug. 28, Sickles wrote to USG. "I am very much obliged to you for your favor of the 20th inst.—I am too well aware of the demands made by official business upon your time to expect you can often reply to private letters upon mere personal matters. Your Kindness is therefore all the more appreciated. The disinclination I feel in regard to the offered Colonelcy is on account of the Corps—It seems to me next door to the 'retired list'—and carries with it an 'unserviceable' association not much to my liking—I will do as you have advised me, however & take the best Colonelcy I can get—my sincere desire is *to Keep out of politics for the present, at least*—and unless I remain in the Army that will be almost impossible—in the Army it will be easy:—Permit me to Express the Earnest hope that Clitz may have a Regiment—I have written a strong letter to the Adjutant General recommending the promotion—He has in my humble judgment, great merit as an officer and as a Man—I believe that a Regiment in his hands would be an honor to any Army—I had occasion to observe his aptitude & tact in this particular in the reorganization of the 6th Infantry when you gave me the recruits last Winter.—*Clitz*—Roy ~~&~~ *Williams* & *Clous* (adjt) and *Smith*, *Hawkins* & Saunders (Captain) are, all of them, officers of high merit. South Carolina does not Endorse Gov. Orrs speeches & votes at Philadelphia—Wade Hampton has denounced the Platform in a recent speech in Gov. Orrs town (Anderson) *at a meeting of rebel soldiers*—Matters in general go on in the Department quite as well as any one could reasonably Expect. There is occasionally some irritation and impatience shewn in quarters where more Equanimity might be looked for, but the more substantial people understand that our presence is Essential to the preservation of tranquility and order; and to these Ends our attention is in the main directed. In the western portions of South Carolina, I regret to say 'bushwhackers and outlaws are too numerous and are more or less tolerated—Even Countenanced—by people of whom better things were anticipated;—the Civil authorities denounce the outrages Committed but do not make arrests or punish often.—I Send to-day to the A. G. O. some recent Correspondence with the Governor in regard to the Civil rights of the Negroes & the opening of the State Courts for them, which I trust may be satisfactory to you—I am going up to Columbia next week by arrangement with the Governor, to help him a little with his Crotchety Legislature—I have sent up the Band of the 6th Infantry—~~to put them~~ in a good humor—

By the way this is *the best* Band I have heard in the Army—Excepting only that at West Point and the one at Governors Island. I hope it may be retained among the fifteen and that you will leave it in my Department, if practicable.—I am somewhat puzzled in deciding whether the revocation of your order about *Newspapers* is intended to remove further *surveillance* over them or whether the object is to remand them subject to the action of Department Commanders.—There are two journals in the Dept.—The 'South Carolinian' (Columbia) and the 'Despatch' (Wilmington) that are disposed to assume they can now go as far as they Choose in seditious appeals. If left to the Exercise of my discretion I would notify them Courteously to be less offensive in their publications and if this were not heeded I would try the Effect of a *plump fine* imposed by a prudent Mil. Commission for the benefit of the Soldiers assylum.—This by the way, would be relished by the best people in both States. These violent journals are mostly in the hands of mere adventurers—and from the North too—who hope to gain Southern patronage by their Extreme tone."—ALS, *ibid.* Sickles was appointed col., 42nd Inf., as of July 28. On Dec. 6, Sickles, Brevoort House, New York City, wrote to USG. "Having passed my Examination before the Board, and in view of the probability that at the proper time you may recommend my brevet promotion to the rank Corresponding with my grade in the Volunteer Service, I beg to Express to you my Earnest desire that these brevets may be Conferred for Conduct in battles, Especially Chancellorsville & Gettysburg—If it be deemed preferable to drop Chancellorsville for any reason,—although, so far as one may judge for himself, I was more useful there than in any other battle,—the part I took in the Engagements of McClellans Campaigns was sufficiently prominent to justify recognition, as it was for these and Fredericksburg that I received my promotions in the Volunteer Service.—If it is desired that I should remain in Command of the Dep't of the South, my relative rank to Gen'l Robinson must be preserved, inasmuch as he is on duty by assignment of the President, according to his Brevet rank of Major General U. S. A.—I do not Know the date of his Brevets—Permit me to add that until Congress restores the old law allowing pay to officers on duty according to Brevet rank, which I hope may be done this Session, it would be at least in a financial point of view, very gratifying to retain the rank and Emoluments of my grade in the Volunteer Service. I Shall have the pleasure to pay you a visit in Washington next week, . . . I beg to be Kindly remembered to Mrs. Grant and the ladies & gentlemen of your family to whom I had the honor to be presented by yourself on my recent visit."—ALS, *ibid.* Docketing indicates that Col. Adam Badeau answered Sickles on Dec. 7. —*Ibid.*

1866, AUG. 15. Supreme Court Justice Henry T. Backus, Tucson, Arizona Territory, to USG. "The people of this Territory feel and believe, that much of the want of success in overturning the Indian power here and obtaining security to life and property is to no inconsiderable extent attributable to the frequent changes of commanders of the District. Colonel H D. Wallen, the present Commander of the District has by his activity and fidelity eminently fitted himself for usefulness and by his soldierly bearing has acquired the fullest confidence of our people. Report now says, he is to be relieved by Colonel Lovell. Without in any way desparaging Col Lovell, I have no hesitation in saying such a change our people here would most deeply deplore, on both public and personal grounds. If such action could be had, as would place Colonel Wallen in command of Arizona with some little permanency, it would be gratefully received by our people and speedily secure the object both of the Government and our people. A petition to the above effect has been, as I understand, forwarded to you."—LS, DNA, RG 108, Letters Received. On the same day, Backus, Charles D. Poston, and forty-seven others petitioned USG to retain Lt. Col. Henry D. Wallen. —DS, *ibid.* On Nov. 21, Bvt. Maj. Gen. Irvin McDowell, San Francisco, endorsed this petition unfavorably, explaining sentiment for Wallen in terms of rivalry for the territorial capital.—ES, *ibid.* On Aug. 31, Attorney Gen. Coles Bashford, Tucson, wrote to Postmaster Gen. Alexander W. Randall seeking Wallen for command of Arizona Territory.—ALS, *ibid.* Randall endorsed this letter to USG. "Mr Bashford who signs this letter was formerly Gov. of Wisconsin and has just been elected Delegate to Congress from the Territory of Arizona. He is a very reliable man. I respectfully refer his letter to you—"—AES (undated), *ibid.*

1866, AUG. 16. To Bvt. Maj. Gen. Edward D. Townsend. "I enclose a draft of order which I advise the immediate publication of."—ALS, DNA, RG 94, Letters Received, 624A 1866. USG enclosed a draft issued as General Orders No. 67. "The following project for fort artillery instruction at posts where not less than one company of artillery is present is adopted and will at once be carried into effect. . . ."—Df, *ibid.*

1866, AUG. 18. USG endorsement. "I would recommend that Gn. Granger be assigned to duty according to his Bvt. rank and placed in command of the Dept. of the Potomac during the absence of Gn. Schofield. His station is now at Dept. Hd Qrs. and he is much better qualified for a Dept. Command than Gn. Miles would be."—AES, DNA, RG 108, Letters Received. Written on a letter of Aug. 16 from Maj. Gen. John M. Schofield, Richmond, to Secretary of War Edwin M. Stanton.—LS, *ibid.* On the same day, Schofield had written to USG. "I enclose herewith a letter to the Secritary of War, written by his direction, relative to my proposed temporary absence from Richmond for the purpose of performing a special duty for which the Secretary informed me I had been detailed. Will you please forward the letter with any endorsement you may desire to make."—ALS, *ibid.*

1866, AUG. 18. To AGO. "Detail for duty with Gen. Terry the following officers of the regular Army, Capt. E. W. Smith, 15th Inf.y A. A. A.

Gn. Lt. C. H. Graves, 14th Inf.y A. D. C."—ALS, DNA, RG 94, Letters Received, 620A 1866.

1866, Aug. 18, 10:30 a.m. To Maj. Gen. Edward O. C. Ord. "I think it will be advisable for you to go to Arkansas as soon as possible"—Telegram sent, DNA, RG 107, Telegrams Collected (Bound); copies, *ibid.*, RG 108, Letters Sent; DLC-USG, V, 47, 60. On the same day (Saturday), Ord, Detroit, telegraphed to USG. "Telegram rec'd. I leave on tuesday next"—Telegram received (at 5:35 p.m.), DNA, RG 107, Telegrams Collected (Bound); *ibid.*, RG 108, Telegrams Received; copy, DLC-USG, V, 54. On Aug. 17, Ord had twice telegraphed to USG. "I saw Genls Sherman and Reynolds Sunday at St Louis. Latter reports good order prevailing in Arkansas [and] received permission to return to Lafayette Ind till relieved. Genl Hooker relieves me next week, after which can I remain here four weeks May Gibbon as Colonel go to Arkansas" "Perhaps I had better go [to the southwest] now and return [with family on] the first."—Telegrams received (the first at 12:30 p.m., the second at 3:20 p.m.), DNA, RG 107, Telegrams Collected (Bound). On Sept. 1, Saturday, Ord, Little Rock, telegraphed to USG. "Arrived here on Wednesday Leave on monday to inspect Department Want an Assistant Adjutant Genl. The absence of an experienced one has been felt here."—Telegram received (at 7:05 p.m.), *ibid.*; *ibid.*, RG 108, Telegrams Received; copy, DLC-USG, V, 54.

1866, Aug. 18, 3:00 p.m. To Maj. Gen. John M. Schofield. "When you send a battalion of the 12th to Washington, send the 1st battalion"—Telegram sent, DNA, RG 107, Telegrams Collected (Bound); copies, *ibid.*, RG 108, Letters Sent; DLC-USG, V, 47, 60. On the same day, Schofield, Richmond, telegraphed to USG. "Your dispatch is recd. I have ordered the 2d battalion to Washington because I supposed the Secy of War wanted Gen'l Augur to come here but will change the order—The battlalion has not yet moved"—Telegram received (at 6:45 p.m.), DNA, RG 107, Telegrams Collected (Bound); *ibid.*, RG 108, Telegrams Received; copy, DLC-USG, V, 54.

1866, Aug. 18. Maj. Robert Morrow, adjt. for President Andrew Johnson, to USG. "The President presents his compliments to you and requests the pleasure of your presence at the reception at the Executive Mansion of the committee from the recent convention at Philadelphia, which will take place to-day at one (1) o'clock p. m."—Adam Badeau, *Grant in Peace* (Hartford, Conn., 1887), p. 38. For Grant's attendance, see *ibid.*, pp. 37–38; *National Intelligencer*, Aug. 20, 1866; Howard K. Beale, ed., *Diary of Gideon Welles* (New York, 1960), II, 581–82. Later asked by a reporter if he had attended on his own, USG responded: "Of course not. That being a purely political gathering, it was none of my business. I was there at the request of the President, and all attempts to attach a political significance to my presence are unwarranted and impertinent."—*Chicago*

Tribune, Sept. 14, 1866. On Aug. 13, Brig. Gen. John A. Rawlins had telegraphed to William S. Hillyer, Philadelphia. "*Private* and *Confidential* . . . I cannot, consistently with my convictions of the duty of Army Officers to abstain from active participancy in politics, accept the honor tendered me"—Telegram sent, DNA, RG 107, Telegrams Collected (Bound). On Aug. 17, H. H. Chadwick, Philadelphia, telegraphed to USG. "A preliminary meeting of [the] officers engaged on both sides [of] the late rebellion will be held [in] Washington this P. M. to arrange for holding a convention. Try [and have] it held in Washington"—Telegram received (at 2:30 P.M.), *ibid.*

On Sept. 1[0], Douglas Taylor *et al.*, New York City, wrote to USG. "The delegates from this city to the late National Union Convention held at Philadelphia (Augst 14–16) have devised, and an extensive committee of arrangements, equally constituted of members of the Conservative Republican and Democratic parties and representing the strength and wealth, the intelligence and integrity, the labor and loyalty of the Metropolitan heart of the Union have taken in hand the car[r]ying out of a great Public Meeting to ratify and endorse the action taken and the declaration of principles promulgated at the said Convention. The action of the Philadelphia National Union Convention was inspired and guided by the Rights Conferred and the blessings heretofore so widely disseminated under the Constitution, as well as faith in the Presidents policy for the restoration of both: hence it has been wisely agreed, that ~~the~~ our great city should set its seal of popular approval on the acts of the administration and convention on the anniversary of the day upon wh[ich] the Constitution was adopted. The Committee earnestly hope you may find it convenient to be present at the Ratification Meeting of the 17 inst."—LS, USG 3. On Sept. 16, Col. Adam Badeau wrote to Taylor. "General Grant directs me to acknowledge the receipt of your invitation to be present at a public meeting in NewYork on the 17th inst to endorse the proceedings of the late political convention held at Philadelphia (August 4th–10th); ~~and~~ He instructs me to say that it is contrary to his habit and to his Convictions of duty to attend the ~~political~~ meetings of any political party whatever, and that he sees with regret the action of any officer of the army ~~tending~~ taking a conspicuous part in the, political discussions of the day"—ADf, *ibid.*

1866, AUG. 21. USG endorsement. "In my opinion the same grade, by Brevet, in the regular Army, should be confered on Gn. Donaldson as is held by Generals Allen, Rucker & Ingalls. They have been Breveted to the rank of Major General and I supposed Gn. Donaldson had also received the same promotion. I now respectfully recommend it."—AES, DNA, RG 94, ACP, 1470 1873. Written on a letter of Aug. 14 from Col. and Bvt. Maj. Gen. (of vols.) James L. Donaldson, Nashville, to Maj. Gen. George H. Thomas concerning his appointment as bvt. maj. gen., U.S. Army.—ALS, *ibid.* On July 26, 1864, USG had favorably endorsed a petition of q. m.

officers recommending Donaldson for promotion to brig. gen.—AES and D (printed), *ibid.* See *PUSG*, 11, 453.

1866, AUG. 25. To Capt. A. McLane.—Stan. V. Henkels, Catalogue No. 1405, June 24, 1927, p. 4.

1866, AUG. 25, 5:50 P.M. To Governor Green Clay Smith of Montana Territory, St. Louis. "See Gen'l Sherman's Adjt. Genl about escort &c."—Telegram sent, DNA, RG 107, Telegrams Collected (Bound); copies, *ibid.*, RG 108, Letters Sent; DLC-USG, V, 47, 60. On Aug. 7, Maj. George K. Leet had written to Smith, Georgetown, Ky. "I am directed by Gen. Grant to acknowledge the receipt, by referance from the War Dept, of your communication of 19th ulto. asking information as to what protection you might hope for, for yourself & family, in crossing the plains to Montana Territory, and to say in reply that by communicating with Lt Gen. Sherman you can arrange to accompany one of the detachments of troops going across the plains from time to time which would afford ample protection against the hostile Indians."—Copies, *ibid.*

1866, AUG. 27. To Secretary of War Edwin M. Stanton. "I have the honor to recommend that 1st Lt. F. E. Crosman 17 U. S. Infy wounded on the 17th 18th & 19th of August 1864 in the battles of the Weldon R. R. and since dead from wounds, receive three brevets for gallant conduct on those three days."—LS, DNA, RG 94, ACP, C886 CB 1867.

1866, AUG. 27, 1:20 P.M. To Maj. Gen. John M. Schofield. "You have authority to absent yourself from the Department as requested in your despatch of this date"—Telegram sent, DNA, RG 107, Telegrams Collected (Bound); copies, *ibid.*, RG 108, Letters Sent; DLC-USG, V, 47, 60; DLC-John M. Schofield. On the same day, Schofield, Richmond, had telegraphed to USG. "I respectfully request permission to be absent from my Dept for a few days to attend to private business"—Telegram received (at noon), DNA, RG 107, Telegrams Collected (Bound); *ibid.*, RG 108, Telegrams Received; copies, *ibid.*, RG 393, Dept. of Va. and N. C., 1st Military District, Telegrams Sent.

1866, AUG. 27. Col. Albert J. Myer, chief, U.S. Signal Corps, to USG. "I have the honor to send you herewith the first issued copy of my Book. I cannot ask you to read it all, but I would like to have you glance over 'Field Telegraphs' Pg. 317. 'The General Service of the Signal Corps' Pg. 328. and 'Opening Communication without preconcert' Pg 165. I think I am right in the belief that this has never been before accomplished in any service of any nation. With the hope that the 'Manual' may aid in the instruction of others to serve you in future victories, if the occasion comes; and with a sense of my personal obligations to yourself—"—ALS, U.S. Signal Center, Fort Monmouth, N. J.

1866, AUG. 28. Michael K. Lawler, Baton Rouge, La., to USG. "Should you think proper to recommend me, for Colonel, of one of the new Regiments to be raised, I will accept. Many worthy men will apply. I shall not enter into the scramble. Should you think others more fitting, be assured I shall not esteem you less."—ALS, DNA, RG 94, ACP, L455 CB 1866. On Aug. 10, 1867, Lawler, San Antonio, Tex., wrote to Brig. Gen. John A. Rawlins. "I have changed my location from 'Egypt' to this place and intend to reside here. If there is a vacancy of Military Store Keeper in the Q Mr Dept, or when it should occur, I would be pleased to have the appointment and be *assigned to duty here.* It would aid me materially while waiting for my stock of horses to become remunerative. Will you be kind enough to give my compliments to the General in Chief and say that I would be grateful to have his help in this matter. I am in good health Thank God and do not feel more than 33 years old"—ALS, *ibid.*, L516 CB 1863. On Nov. 5, USG endorsed this letter. "Respectfully forwarded to the Sec. of War, recommended."—ES, *ibid.* On Nov. 7, Bvt. Brig. Gen. Frederick T. Dent endorsed this letter as aide to USG, secretary of war *ad interim.* "Let the appointment be made to fill the first vacancy"—AES, *ibid.*

1866, SEPT. 3. To Bvt. Maj. Gen. Edward D. Townsend from Niagara Falls. "Extend Genl Watkins time for reporting for duty until Sept 30th"—Telegram received (at 3:30 P.M.), DNA, RG 94, Letters Received, 658A 1866. On Aug. 27, U.S. Representative Lovell H. Rousseau of Ky. had written to USG. "General Watkins, who will be mustered out of service as Brig. Gen'l of Vols., on the 1st September, will apply for a leave of absence till towards the last ~~and~~ of that month. He has already been indulged very greatly by you for which I am grateful and yet I cannot refrain from asking a favorable consideration of this request for leave. His wife, quite a delicate woman, will be confined about the the middle of September, and of course will greatly need the presence of her husband. If the public interests should not require his presence elsewhere, I hope he may be allowed to remain at Portsmouth, N. H., till the end of Sept."—LS, *ibid.*, RG 108, Letters Received.

1866, SEPT. 8. To Bvt. Maj. Gen. Edward D. Townsend from Springfield, Ill. "Please issue an order authorizing Col Jno H King ninth U. S. Infy to delay reporting to his regiment under special order two hundred fifty three adj Genls office current series until the first day of nov. next also Grant Major Genl Jos Hooker a leave of absence for twenty days"—Telegram received (at 10:25 A.M.), DNA, RG 94, Letters Received, 670A 1866; *ibid.*, RG 107, Telegrams Collected (Bound).

1866, SEPT. 17. To Secretary of War Edwin M. Stanton. "I have the honor to recommend for promotion to the grade of Surgeon in the regular army Asst. Surgeon D. L. Huntington This officer served under my immediate notice at Vicksburg and Chattanooga, and has since been constantly in the field I know of no officer of his grade who in my opinion is more deserving of promotion"—Copies, DLC-USG, V, 47, 60; DNA, RG 108, Letters Sent.

1866, SEPT. 17. USG endorsement. "I would approve the recommendation herein on the ground of Mr. Covington's fitness for the position and knowing the difficulty of getting men of the same character and ability on the Pacific Coast for the compensation allowe[d] by Government."—AES, DNA, RG 77, Explorations and Surveys, Letters Received. Written on a letter of Sept. 10 from U.S. Senator James W. Nesmith of Ore., College Hill, Ohio, to Secretary of War Edwin M. Stanton recommending Richard Covington, clerk, U.S. Engineers, Washington, D. C., for the appointment provided for by Congress to improve the navigation of the Columbia and Willamette rivers.—ALS, *ibid.* On March 19, 1869, Bvt. Maj. Gen. James A. Hardie, Washington, D. C., wrote to USG. "Will you permit me to enclose to you the petition of Richard Covington to be made Consul at Honolulu. You know Mr. Covington well from having met him at Vancouver, and how many of the officers serving in that region were indebted to him and his excellent wife for courtesy and kindness. Will you be pleased to take his application into consideration with others for the same place?"—LS, *ibid.*, RG 59, Letters of Application and Recommendation. On March 20, Covington wrote to USG. "I beg leave most respectfully to apply for the position of United States Consul to Honolulu, Sandwich Islands. I am an American citizen of twenty years standing. My former residence at those Islands and my general knowledge of affairs on the Pacific Coast may, if you deem my ability sufficient for the position, induce you to give the application a favorable consideration."—ALS, *ibid.* No appointment followed.

1866, SEPT. 18. Col. Adam Badeau to L. Edwin Dudley, chairman, Soldiers and Sailors Union. "General Grant directs me to acknowledge the receipt of your invitation to be present at a ~~public meeting~~ 'nati[onal] con[ve]ntion of Soldiers & Sailors to be held at Pittsburg Penna, Sept 25th, 1866,' for political purposes. He instructs me to say that it is contrary to his habit and to his convictions of duty to attend political meetings of any character whatsoever, and that he sees with regret the action of any officer of the army taking a conspicuous part in the political dissensions of the day."—ADfS, USG 3. On Sept. 17, Dudley, Washington, D. C., had written to USG. "The Nat. Executive Committee of the Soldiers and Sailors Union, have assigned me the pleasant duty of inviting you to be present at a National Convention of Soldiers and Sailors to be held at Pittsburgh Penna. Sept. 25th/66—I enclose a copy of our call for the convention Hoping that you will find it convienient to accept our invitation . . ."—ALS, *ibid.* On Oct. 27, 1865, Dudley had written to USG. "I have the ~~to~~ honor to address you upon the subject of the great disappointment felt by the members of the 'Soldiers and Sailors National Union League' at not having the pleasure of meeting you at their Hall on Friday evening last, the 20th inst. I should have addressed you sooner but understanding that you were absent from the city I have delayed Our organization is composed entirely of men who have served honorably, either as Soldiers or Seamen, in the Service of the United States, and many of our members have served under your immediate command—We all honor and revere you as the man who made the mighty plans and combinations which made our efforts effective, and which have resulted so gloriously in favor of freedom and the Union. The League meets at Union League Hall 481—9th St on every Friday evening, and we shall feel highly honored if you will kindly consent to pay us a ~~pr~~ visit at an early date. We shall be happy to send a conveyance and a committee for you on any evening you may designate—A note addressed to me at this office will be most gratefully received . . ."—ALS, *ibid.*

1866, SEPT. 19. USG endorsement. "The recommendation for promotion of Gen. Webb to the brevet rank of Major General is approved."—ES, DNA, RG 94, ACP, W283 CB 1870. Written on a letter of Aug. 27 from Maj. and Bvt. Maj. Gen. Gouverneur K. Warren, U.S. Engineers, St. Paul, Minn., to the AGO recommending Capt. and Bvt. Maj. Gen. (of vols.) Alexander S. Webb, 11th Inf., for promotion to bvt. maj. gen., U.S. Army. —ALS, *ibid.* On Aug. 31, Webb, West Point, N. Y., wrote to Maj. Gen. George G. Meade protesting that officers of lesser merit had been appointed bvt. maj. gen.—ALS, *ibid.* On Oct. 2, Meade, Philadelphia, endorsed this letter. "Respectfully forwarded to the General Comdg U. S. Army.—The Genl Comdg is aware that the recent list of Brevets of General officers in the Regular Army was not made on any action on my part.—As a member of the St. Louis Board & in view of the principles & standard sought to be established by that board—I was in favor of the Brevet of Brig Genl being conferred on Genl. Webb; but since the action of that Board was set aside, and the standard modified I am clearly of the opinion that Genl. Webb is entitled from his services to the grade of Bvt Maj. Genl—he having commanded with distinction *a Division* in several battles, and having rendered valuable service as Chief of Staff in the last campaign of the A. P. In view of these circumstances & under the impression that his name was accidental[ly] omitted, I forward this communication recommending the Brevet of Maj. Genl. be conferred."—AES, *ibid.* On Oct. 3, USG endorsed this letter. "Respectfully forwarded to the Secretary of War, in connection with recommendation for promotion of Gen. Webb, forwarded Sept. 19th 1866." —ES, *ibid.* On the same day, USG wrote to Webb. "Your recommendation for Lt. Colonelcy, (White Troops) has been sent in and will no doubt be approved."—ALS, CtY. USG first put quotation marks around "White Troops" and later cancelled them with parentheses. On Oct. 10, USG wrote to Secretary of War Edwin M. Stanton. "I have the honor to recommend Maj. & Bvt. Brig. Gn. A. P. Howe for apt. as Lt. Col. of Inf.y vice Pleasonton declined, and Capt. & Bvt. Maj. Gn. A. Webbe for Lt. Col.

V. R. C. vice Fessenden declined."—ALS, DNA, RG 94, ACP, G462 CB 1866. Webb was appointed lt. col., 44th Inf., as of July 28.

1866, SEPT. 20. To Secretary of the Navy Gideon Welles recommending Henry M. Judah, Jr., orphan son of Brig. Gen. Henry M. Judah, Sr., for appointment to the U.S. Naval Academy.—Samuel T. Freeman Auction, May 6–7, 1969, no. 500.

1866, SEPT. 20. T. E. Roessle and four others, Albany, N. Y., to USG. "The undersigned respectfully reccommend for an appointment in the New Vetera[n] Reserve Regiments, Lieutenant Fielding Neale of th[e] 21st Veteran Reserves, now acting as Deputy Commissioner of Freedman &c at Memphis. Lieut Neale entered the service early in the war as Captain of Engineers (Serrells) After two years service. was taking down with Typhoid Fever, and resigned—After being restored to Health. Entered the 96th N. Y. V. as captain. Fought in all the Battles of his Regt. to Cold Harbor, where he was Shot throug[h] the Head, loosing his right Eye. Was then (after his recovery) made Major of 14th Heavy-Artillery, in command of Seige Trai[n.] At expiration of his service was made Lieut of Veteran Reserves, Neale is an Engineer by Profession and Thoroughly Educated. We reccommend him to you knowing his worth and Services."—LS, DNA, RG 94, ACP, N176 CB 1866. Fielding Neale was appointed 2nd lt., 45th Inf., as of July 28, and died on Nov. 18.

1866, SEPT. 22, 3:15 P.M. To John W. Garrett, president, Baltimore and Ohio Railroad, Baltimore. "Myself family and a few members of the staff go to New York Monday evening. Can you accommodate us with a special car, & oblige?"—Telegram sent, DNA, RG 107, Telegrams Collected (Bound). USG arrived in New York City on Tuesday, Sept. 25, to attend the American Jockey Club races at Jerome Park. He also visited West Point, returning to New York City on Sept. 28, and departed for Washington, D. C., Saturday evening, Sept. 29. See *New York Times*, Sept. 26, 1866; *New York Tribune*, Sept. 27, 29, Oct. 1, 1866.

1866, SEPT. [*23?*]. J. W. Perit Huntington, superintendent of Indian Affairs in Ore., Washington, D. C., to USG. "After presenting the letter herewith enclosed (from Senator Nesmith to Secretary Stanton) to the Secretary of War, and being referred by him to you, I designed calling upon you in person immediately, but have since been confined to my room by sickness. I therefore send it, that you may consider the matter, and I will endeavor to call upon you in the early part of next week to confer upon the matter."—ALS (dated Sept. 13), DNA, RG 108, Letters Received. Huntington enclosed a letter of Sept. 18 from U.S. Senator James W. Nesmith of Ore., College Hill, Ohio, to Secretary of War Edwin M. Stanton concerning the need for small U.S. Army garrisons in Ore. to protect whites from Indians and to protect Indians from ". . . depraved *whites* who always cluster around an Indian Agency, and seek to make a furtive living by ministering to the depraved and vicious desires of the semi-civilized Indians. . . ."—LS, *ibid.*

1866, Oct. 1. To AGO. "Please issue an order directing the Quartermaster's Dept. to give transportation to forage officers, when ordered from one post to another for duty, for the horses & servants they may have, not exceeding in number the law allow~~i~~ance. When the ~~distance~~ ~~is~~ ~~great~~ expence of transportation is great the Qr. Mr. may have the option of purchasing the horses for public use."—ALS, DNA, RG 94, Letters Received, 736A 1866.

1866, Oct. 1. USG endorsement. "I respectfully recommend Robt. C. Scott for appointment to West Point Mil—Academy in the Class of 1867." —AES, DNA, RG 94, Correspondence, USMA. Written on an undated letter from Clara G. Scott, Washington, D. C., to President Andrew Johnson requesting the appointment to USMA of her orphan nephew Robert C. Scott.—ALS, *ibid.*

1866, Oct. 1. Col. Adam Badeau to Fitz John Porter. "General Grant directs me to acknowledge the receipt of your letter of Sept. 22d and also that of Sept. 24th with its enclosure all relating to your restoration to the Army. He instructs me to say that in all cases where application has been made for his interference based on the supposition that some previous action of the Government has been incorrect and such previous action occurred prior to his taking command of the army, he has considered it his duty to decline the interference. In your case the reasons are still stronger, as no change has occurred in the Office of Secretary of War since the action of which you complain, and the Secretary is the authority that General Grant would assume to judge if he should attempt a compliance with your request. He therefore considers himself bound to abide by the rule already laid down—to interfere with the action of no administration occurring prior to his command of the army."—Copies, DLC-USG, V, 47, 60; DNA, RG 108, Letters Sent. On Sept. 22, Porter, New York City, had written to USG. "Flattering myself that the result of my trial by Court Martial in 1863, was not passed unnoticed by you, and believing that you would take pleasure in being instrumental in discovering any erroneous finding and in remedying any wrong resulting from it, I take the liberty of asking ~~you~~ the favor to aid by a letter to the President of the United States, or in whatever manner you may deem best, in effecting by his authority a re-examination of the proceedings of my Court Martial, and if agreeable to you, making known your action to the Hon. Reverdy Johnson, for use at such time as he may deem most proper. Though conscious of innocence of any criminality such as alleged against me & of all intentional wrong doing and knowing of erroneous finding I cannot expect or ask others to be convinced without an examination of the evidence or a presentation by unprejudiced authority—

but having to a certain date, an unblemished record of no ordinary services well and faithfully performed, ~~to which reference can be made with just pride~~ to my country it might be presumed, that, ever careful of my honor, I could not have been reckless of my fame, upon which hang all the hopes of wife & children ~~and friends~~ relatives, and connected as it may be with the history & destiny of my country—and I trust such a record and inference may have weight in causing a reconsideration of the proceedings with a view of ascertaining any wrong resulting from erroneous finding & remedying it if any be found. In the hope my appeal may meet with a favorable response."—ADfS (dated Sept. 8), DLC-Fitz John Porter; copies (both dated Sept. 22—one printed), DNA, RG 46, War Reports. On Sept. 24, Porter wrote to USG. "In the hope that amid your manifold duties, ~~you will be able~~ time can be spared to read the accompanying article from the World of this city, I take the liberty of sending it, as bearing upon the object of my letter of the 22d Inst. This article was written ~~by~~ (as I am informed) by one of the editors of Harper's-Monthly Magzine, without my solicitation or knowledge; and, as far as it goes, is a fair presentatn of facts embraced in my trial—."—ADfS, DLC-Fitz John Porter; copies (2—one printed), DNA, RG 46, War Reports.

1866, OCT. 3, 11:30 A.M. To Maj. Gen. Philip H. Sheridan. "There is no intention of retiring Genl Heintzelman unless he applies for it. If you can spare Genl Getty give him the three months extended to officers mustered out of volunteer service"—Telegram sent, DNA, RG 107, Telegrams Collected (Bound); copies, *ibid.*, RG 108, Letters Sent; DLC-USG, V, 47, 60. On Oct. 2, 1:30 P.M., Sheridan had telegraphed to Brig. Gen. John A. Rawlins. "Gen Getty wants to go north—His health suffered some little while on the Rio Grande—Can you inform me if Gen Heintzleman is to be retired—I have heard rumors to this effect and it is of some importance for me to know and the information will be strictly confidential"—Telegram received (at 6:00 P.M.), DNA, RG 107, Telegrams Collected (Bound); *ibid.*, RG 108, Telegrams Received; copies (one sent by mail), *ibid.*, Letters Received; DLC-USG, V, 54; DLC-Philip H. Sheridan.

1866, OCT. 3. To Mrs. Chapman (Ann Mary Butler) Coleman and daughters. "Your favor accompanying 'Frederick the Great, and his Court,' translated by yourselves, was duly received. I feel many obligations to you for this mark of remberance and esteem and will place the volume in my libray with the acknowledgement written on the title papge of the donors." —ALS, Duke University, Durham, N. C. On Sept. 27, Coleman and three daughters, Baltimore, had written to USG. "Since the close of the war, I have visited Washington several times, with my daughters, for the purpose of seeing you; obtaining the release of prisoners, in whome we were interested; & transportion, for the poor southern soldiers, who were lying about, in the streets of Baltimore. On every occasion, we were kindly received & our petitions promptly acceeded to. We were & are very grateful, Gen'

Grant,!! The book, which we now send, has been translated by us, since that time Will you accept this copy as a tribute of gratitude & heartfelt admiration"—ALS, USG 3. Coleman, daughter of John J. Crittenden, born in Ky. in 1813, married Chapman Coleman in 1830. Upon his death in Louisville in 1850, she took her seven children to Germany to be educated. Along with three of her daughters, she translated historical novels written by L. Mühlbach (the pen name of Klara Mundt) and also wrote a biography of her father.

1866, OCT. 8. To Secretary of War Edwin M. Stanton. "I have the honor to recommend the appointment of 1st Lieut & Bvt. Capt. R. W. Tyler V. R. C. to be 1st Lieut. V. R."—LS, DNA, RG 94, ACP, T411 CB 1866. On Feb. 16, USG had favorably endorsed a letter of Dec. 2, 1865, from Col. and Bvt. Brig. Gen. Samuel D. Oliphant, 14th Veteran, recommending 2nd Lt. Richard W. Tyler for promotion to 1st lt. and bvt. capt.—ES and copy, *ibid.* Tyler was appointed 1st lt., 44th Inf., as of July 28, 1866.

1866, OCT. 9. To President Andrew Johnson. "I would respectfully recommend the appointment of G. N. Whistler to a Cadetship at West Point in the class of 1867. He is the son of an officer of the Army, of long standing, and can only hope for such appointment at large. Representatives in Congress generally prefer giving the one appointment which they are entitled to to the son of a Citizen of their district, thus leaving the sons of Army & Navy Officers no chance for Cadet appointments except at large."—ALS, DNA, RG 94, Correspondence, USMA. Garland N. Whistler was appointed 2nd lt., 5th Art., as of Oct. 9, 1867.

1866, OCT. 9. USG endorsement. "Respectfully submitted to His Excellency, the President of the U. S., approved."—ES, DNA, RG 94, Correspondence, USMA. Written on a letter of Aug. 9 from Michael J. Cramer, Covington, Ky., to USG. "I take great pleasure in introducing to you, my young friend, Mr. *Charles Morrison* of Cincinnati, O. He is very anxious of obtaining a Cadetship at the U. S. Military Academy at West Point. Being personally acquainted with him, I can testify to his unexceptionable moral character, his gentlemanly deportment, and his *Superior intellectual abilities.* For the last three years he has attended the Woodward High School of Cincinnati, and has testimonials from his teachers, that *he is one of their best pupils.* Master Morrison has, with an energy and determination rarely exhibited by one of his years, made the most strenuous efforts *for two years* to obtain a cadetship at West Point. By dint of hard labor, after his school-hours, he earned enough money to take him to Washington in February 1864, and he obtained from Mr. Lincoln the promise of an appointment as Cadet at West Point. But Mr. Lincoln's death put an end to the fulfillment of that promise. Yet with commendable zeal, perseverance and energy he renewed his application. He has the strongest possible recommendations to the President filed at the War Department (copies of which I have read) from the following distinguished gentlemen: viz. Senators *John Sherman* and *Benj. Wade*; W. Dennison, late P. M. General Congressmen Benj. Eggleston and Hays; Lt. Gen. Sherman and Maj. Gen. Rosecrans, Judge B. Storer, Prof. Harper of Woodward High School; A. E. Chamberlain, Esq, late Pres. of the Cinc. branch U. S. C. C., Peter R. Neff, Esq., W. Clifford Neff, Esq., Merchants of Cinc.; and from many other prominent gentlemen. Now, my Dear General, I would *respectfully and Earnestly* request you to interest yourself in behalf of young Mr. Morrison; and go with him to President Johnson, and ask him to appoint him Cadet to West Point. A young man of such superior abilities and of such energy and perseverance ought surely be rewarded with the desire of his heart. He will no doubt make a *faithful* and *efficient officer*. By using your personal influence in his behalf, or *by speaking one word* to the President, his appointment might be secured. You would thereby gratify many of your personal friends. Gov. W. Dennison is especially interested in his appointment. In case there should be no vacancy at West Point, would you not be so kind and secure him an appointment at the Naval School at Annapolis? That would be his next choice.—Sincerely hoping for a favorable answer . . . P. S. Perhaps you remember Mr. Morrison from the fact that John P. Tweed, Esq. introduced and recommended him to you, when you was here on a visit."—ALS, *ibid.* On Aug. 17, Mayor L. A. Harris of Cincinnati endorsed this letter. "The father of this young gentleman is a personal friend of mine & the applicant himself is a worthy and deserving young man whose abilities are of no common order Any aid you can give in securing his appointment will be esteemed an act of personal friendship by me"—AES, *ibid.* On Aug. 12, Charles C. Morrison, Cincinnati, wrote to USG. "Enclosed please find a letter of introduction from Mr. Cramer, which lack of means only has prevented me from presenting in person. The letter will explain my wants, I was advised some weeks since, through your private secretary, that all the appointments at large were filled, but since then I have learned that the President has, by the new Army Bill, forty additional appointments. I hope now to obtain the object of my endeavors—one of these appointments—through that influence which you stated your willingness to lend, when I was presented to you at the Burnett House of this City, by Capt. Tweed. Apologizing for the trouble I have been compelled to give you, but which I have endeavored to lessen by making this note as brief as possible . . ."—ALS, *ibid.* He enclosed a copy of Cramer's letter of Aug. 9 without the postscript or the endorsement.—*Ibid.* See *PUSG*, 14, 457–58.

1866, Oct. 9. To Bvt. Maj. Gen. Edward D. Townsend. "I think it advisable that Department Commanders should have the Authority to assign Field Officers serving under them wherever they deem their services most required, provided the assignment is with troops of their own regiment, without application to Head Qrs. of the Army. I would advise the publication of a Circular extending this Authority."—ALS, DNA, RG 94, Letters Received, 770A 1866. On Sept. 28, Maj. and Bvt. Maj. Gen. John M.

Brannan, 1st Art., Staten Island, N. Y., had written to the adjt., Dept. of the East, concerning his assignment to duty.—ALS, *ibid.*, RG 108, Letters Received. On Oct. 1, Maj. Gen. George G. Meade, Philadelphia, endorsed this letter. "Respectfully forwarded to the General Commanding for his action, attention being invited to a communication from these Head Quarters, forwarded August 17th 1866, in which the removal of the garrison of Fort Wadsworth, was recommended. This communication of Major Brannan is forwarded in consequence of the recent orders from the A. G. O., Washington, assigning officers to posts in this Department, (see Special Orders, No 466, par. 7 & 8—) and the occasion is taken advantage of, to call the attention of the General Commanding, to the military necessity and propriety of the Department Commander having the authority to assign the officers and troops to the posts within his command."—ES, *ibid.*

1866, Oct. 9. To AGO. "Please extend Gn. Wheaton's leave until the end of this month."—ANS, DNA, RG 94, Letters Received, 752A 1866.

1866, Oct. 9. U.S. Senator Alexander G. Cattell of N. J., Union League, Philadelphia, to USG. "Geary elected by over 20.000 majority ~~pro~~ Gain one Congressman, probably two."—Telegram received (on Oct. 10, 8:45 A.M.), DNA, RG 107, Telegrams Collected (Bound).

1866, Oct. 11. To Bvt. Maj. Gen. Edward D. Townsend. "Let Lt. H. M. Bragg, recently transfered to 3d Cav.y, have one month time before starting to join his regiment in New Mexico. You may extend the time for Gen. Oaks ~~to~~ joining his regiment to the 1st of December. . . . Lt. Braggs authority will have to be telegraphed to him."—ALS, DNA, RG 94, Letters Received, 755A 1866.

1866, Oct. 13. To Secretary of War Edwin M. Stanton. "I have the honor to recommend that Lt. Col. Luther Stephenson Jr 32d Mass Vols be breveted Brig Gen. Vols for gallant & meritorious services in the campaign against Richmond."—LS, DNA, RG 94, ACP, S1159 CB 1866.

1866, Oct. 15. Maj. George K. Leet endorsement. "Respectfully referred to Major General D. E. Sickles Comdg. Dept South."—AES, DNA, RG 109, Union Provost Marshals' File of Papers Relating to Two or More Civilians. Written on a letter of Oct. 8 from William A. Smith, Boon Hill, Johnston County, N. C., to USG. "Sometime in may 1865. I was appointed Captain of a local Police company of this county, organized by the commander of the United States forces of this State, for the Purpose of Keepping the Peace, Putting down Marauing Plundering & Bushwacking, &c, in that capacity I gave great offence to certain Rebels of the county. bacause I protected the Colored People in their rights as far as posible, An ex. Rebel Captain by the name of Barney Lane of this county, who had duing the war on various occasions attacked me and threattened to kill me, doged me and abassed me in every conceivable manner because I was opposed to the war —and belonged to the Peace Party, or Holden Party as it was at that time derisively called—after I was appointed Captain of the Local Police of this county, he Barney Lane deliberately Shot at me with a double barrel Gun. but mised me I ordered his arrest. he again attemped to Shoot me with the other barrel, but was prevented by the Sherriff of the county, from shooting me, by this time Several other Rebels came advanceing on me. a man named Barber in front—I caught a Gun out of the hands of a man in the crowd which was emty—I warned Barber off but he continued to advance, I knocked him down, by that time Lane was in Striking distance I hit him—Several Rushed upon me pretending to part us—but in fact to give Lane a chance to kill me. H. B. Watson a notorious Rebel of the county Stood by and cried out to them to kill me, I got away from the Line and ordered the arrest of Lane & others—who had attemped my life, but no white man Save one would obey me, I then called on a lot of negroes to assist me. they immediately obeyed me by this time Capt Lane I understood was at Dr Becwith's I went there. he was not there—I then went to the Sherriffs house and got him for the purpose of assisting me in arresting Lane. he the Sherriff went with me. we found Lane the Sherriff reported him badly wounded—I would not have haim arrested but left the Place where Lane was, to start home Some ten miles distance, a colered man informed me that he heard the Rebels Say they entended to kill me before I left town. when that was told the Colered Boys agained volunteered to gard me out of Town. they went with me about one mile. I there discharged them. I assure you upon my Honer Gen, as a Gentleman that is is a true Statement of the case, Yet Sir—I am indited by the Rebel Attoryney Gen in Three diferent cases, one for Striking Barber. one for Striking Lane, and me & the colered men who went to assist me in Arresting Lane are all indited for a Misdemeanor, and Capt Lane has Sued me for ten Thousand dollars damage, I respetfully ask Gen that this case be investigated by the commander of this State to the end that we may be protected by the United States Authority, as I was acting in a Military capacity—while Marshall Law was declared, and while I am indited and Sued in every case posible others who tried to kill me are not indited at all, and the Attoryny Gen. refused to Send a witness before the Grand Jury to indite Watson. who stood by & told them to kill me, Lane who shot at me is only indited for an assault on me, I acted a prominent Part in the county durg the war for Peace & Submission to the Gen Government, the object in this Persacution is to brake me up root & Branch & drive me from the country, this is a Small matter to you General, but my all is at Stake and nothing but the aid of the authority of the United Stats Govmt will Save me & mine, I appeal to you for Protection"—ALS, *ibid.* Additional papers substantiating Smith's letter are *ibid.*

1866, Oct. 16. To Secretary of War Edwin M. Stanton. "I have the honor to recommend that Captain E. G. Abbott, 2d Massachusetts Vols., be brevetted Major for the battle of Cedar Mountain in which he was killed; and that Major H. L. Abbott, 20th Massachusetts Vols., be brevetted Colonel for the battle of the Wilderness, in which he was killed."—LS, DNA, RG 94, ACP, A560 CB 1865. On Oct. 28, 1865, Fitz John Porter, New York City, wrote to USG. "The Government by Brevet promotions lately published has been pleased to express appreciation of services rendered by worthy officers killed in action during the late war. Many deserving of like reward will doubtless be unnoticed unless the attention of those who can appreciate, and will reward meritorious acts, be called to their record. Believing the case of the late Major Henry Livermore Abbott, of the 20th Mass. Volunteers, one of this class, I presume here to call you attention to it, confident if satisfied, on examination, you will use your influence to cause his memory to be perpetuated and his example commemorated by such Brevets as his services may be found to merit. The father of Maj. Abbott, is the Hon. J. G. Abbott, of Boston, a distinguished lawyer, and a supporter of the war both by voice and means as well as by services in the persons of his three sons. For information of the Military and private character of Maj Abbott, reference can be made to Maj. Genls Hancock & Webb, and I believe to Genl Meade. His particular friend was Maj. Genl Sedgwick, whose influence would have been exerted for promotion to high rank, had it pleased Providence to spare his life. From respect to Maj. Abbott—and to his bereaved parents, to whom an acknowledgment by government of the services of their son would be most gratifying—I make this appeal. It is made without their knowledge or suspicion—and that it shall be unknown to any one I send it under cover to Mrs Grant, and respectfully request it be regarded as confidential. . . . If the memorial be of no use, please have it returned to me."—ALS, USG 3. On Jan. 25, 1867, Maj. Gen. Winfield S. Hancock, Fort Leavenworth, wrote to USG. "It is the desire of many friends of the late Major Henry L. Abbott, 20th Massachussetts Volunteers, who fell while leading his Regiment at the battle of the Wilderness, to have the rank of General associated with his memory. This Officer was one of a class of educated young gentlemen who entered the Army at the Sound of the first hostile gun. (His Regiment was I believe, at one time Officered entirely or nearly So, by graduates of Harvard University). There was great pride and spirit among the Officers of the Regiment: Major Abbott was a fair exponent of it. The Officers always refused staff duty or detached Service—(Major Abbott declining an important position tendered to him on my staff just previous to the battle of the Wilderness—for the reasons just Stated). The 20th was a model Regiment—'Every one at his post', was the watchword. (The General in chief witnessed a drill of this Regiment on the day of the Review of the Second corps, just before the battle of the Wilderness.) Major Abbott was a gentleman of high character and an Officer of great promise. His gallantry, ability, and devotion to duty were conspicuous, and had he lived a great name and a Successful career might have been predicted for him. I trust it may be expedient to add to his Brevet of Colonel, that of Brigadier General."—ALS, DNA, RG 94,

ACP, A48 CB 1867. On Feb. 7, USG endorsed this letter. "Recommendation of Major General Hancock approved."—ES, *ibid.*

1866, OCT. 17. To Secretary of War Edwin M. Stanton. "I have the honor to make special recommendation of Frank W. Paul, who served about Four years in the war against rebellion, most of the time as Lieut. and Captain, for appointment of 1st Lieut. of Infantry. He is from the state of Penna I would be gratified if this appointment could be given soon and sent to me to deliver."—ALS, DNA, RG 94, ACP, P94 CB 1868. On April 18, 1868, USG favorably endorsed a letter of March 25 from 1st Lt. and Bvt. Capt. Frank W. Paul, 24th Inf., Philadelphia, to the AGO tendering his resignation.—ES and ALS, *ibid.*

1866, OCT. 18. USG endorsement. "Respectfully forwarded to the Secretary of War."—ES, DNA, RG 94, Letters Received, 782W 1866. Written on a letter of Oct. 14 from Lt. Col. and Bvt. Maj. Gen. James H. Wilson, 35th Inf., Keokuk, to the AGO. "having made all the orders and directed the movement and dispositions of the troops which resulted in the Capture of Jefferson Davis and other members of the so-called Confederate Government, I have the honor to protest against the decision and recommendation of the late commission in regard to the division of the reward offered by the government for the Capture of Davis, Clay, and their Confederates This protest is based upon the ground that my recommendations in the case were neglected or not fully considered, & that the award which was recommended is unjust to all the parties concerned. In justice to my command, I have therefore to request that a new commission may be appointed—or the old one, reconvened and that I may be ordered to present myself before it for the purpose of making a proper statement of the matters involved."—ALS, *ibid.* Also on Oct. 14, Wilson wrote to the AGO. "I have the honor to request that Copies of all reports, endorsements & other papers which may be on file in the War Department, relating to the pursuit and Capture of Jefferson Davis and other members of the Confederate government may be furnished me, in order that a detailed report may be made of the facts and circumstances connected therewith. The records of 'the Cavalry Corps Military Division of the Mississippi' having been forwarded to the Bureau, I have no other means of getting the documents required. The reports of Lt. Col. Henry Harnden 1st Wisconsin Cavalry, Lt. Col. B. D. Pritchard, 4th Michn Cavalry, Bvt Brig. Genl. R. H. G. Minty, & the other officers who may have reported directly to the Secretary of war are specially wanted. Much valuable information is now in my possession, and without that which has already been transmitted to the War Department no truthful and just account of the incidents alluded to above Can be prepared."—ALS, *ibid.*, 783W 1866. On Oct. 19, USG endorsed this letter. "Respectfully refered to the Sec. of War."—AES, *ibid.* On Nov. 3, Bvt. Maj. Gen. Edward D. Townsend noted on both documents that Secretary of War Edwin M. Stanton disapproved these requests.—ANS, *ibid.*, 782W 1866;

ibid., 783W 1866. On Jan. 17, 1867, Wilson wrote to Brig. Gen. John A. Rawlins at length concerning the role of his command in the capture of Jefferson Davis.—*HMD*, 39-2-82, pp. 4–13. On Jan. 27, Wilson wrote to the Committee on Claims, U.S. House of Representatives, seeking a portion of the reward offered for Davis's capture and basing his claim on the letter of Jan. 17.—*Ibid.*, p. 1. See *ibid.*, 39-1-90; *ibid.*, 40-2-115; *SED*, 39-2-13. Wilson eventually received $3,000. See *U.S. Statutes at Large*, XV, 400–2.

1866, OCT. 19. USG endorsement. "Respectfully returned. It is believed that the line of stages or ambulancs, between Julesburg and Laramie is necessary for the transportation of mails and Government employés. Couriers could not perform this service. Citizens who are not Gov't. employes should pay for transportation and the funds so collected should be turned over to the Qr. Mr. Dept. and duly accounted for. Genl. Babcock of my staff, reports, that in all the Territories large numbers of animals, bearing the U. S. brand, are in the hands of citizens and that it has been the custom to sell Gov't. animals without branding or bills of sale, except where the latter were given when the animals were sold in lots. A great many were sold in this manner at the time Camp Floyd was broken up, and then resold, singly or in numbers to suit farmers, and to deprive them of property acquired by purchase in this way would be extremely unjust, but where the property is known or can be proven to belong to the U. S. it should be taken. In view of these facts, I would recommend that the brand now used by the Qr. Mr Dept. be changed, the public animals now on hand be re-branded and those hereafter purchased to be branded with the new brand."—Copy, DLC-USG, V, 42. On Oct. 31, Bvt. Maj. Gen. Montgomery C. Meigs wrote to USG. "I have reac'd your endorsement of the 29th October 1866. on extract from Inspection Report of Brevet. Brig General James. F. Rusling, Inspector, Quartermaster's Department relative to the affairs of the Quartermaster's Department on the Plains and forwarded to you, with my recommendation, on the 2nd October 1866. I enclose herewith a copy of General Order No 76. Current Series, of the 17th September from this Office. which orders a new brand to be used in this Department. These brands are now being made. They are of Cast-iron, all cast from one pattern and identical. and will be at once distributed to the various Posts and Depots throughout the country. Thus carrying out the measure suggested by you."—LS, DNA, RG 108, Letters Received. The enclosure is *ibid.* On Dec. 6, Meigs wrote to USG. "I have the honor to inform you that brands cast from a new pattern, and all identical, have been forwarded to the Chief Quartermasters of the Military Divisions of the Missouri and the Pacific, and of the Departments of the Lakes, the East, the Tennessee, and the Gulf, with orders to allow none others to be used in branding public animals of the Quartermaster's Department. This is in accordance with your recommendation of the 19th of October last."—LS, *ibid.*

1866, OCT. 19. To Spiner & Thirson (?). "Enclosed pleased find check for $121.50 the amount of bill for clothing just rec'd. . . . two white vests . . . did not come. I will now get them in this City . . . I return by express Gen. Butterfield's clothing. Gen. Butterfield is on duty in New York . . ."—Harris Auction Galleries, Inc., April 26, 1974, no. 166; Joseph Rubinfine, List 51 [*1976*], item 91.

1866, OCT. 21, 8:45 A.M. To Maj. and Bvt. Maj. Gen. William D. Whipple, adjt. for Maj. Gen. George H. Thomas. "Has General Thomas arrived at Head Quarters? Answer"—Telegram sent, DNA, RG 107, Telegrams Collected (Bound); copies, *ibid.*, RG 108, Letters Sent; (misdated Oct. 22) *ibid.*, RG 393, Dept. of the Cumberland, Telegrams Received; DLC-USG, V, 47, 60. On Oct. 22, Whipple, Nashville, telegraphed to USG. "Gen Thomas Arrivded at HdQrs Nashville on the seventeenth inst" —Telegram received (at 7:00 P.M.), DNA, RG 107, Telegrams Collected (Bound); *ibid.*, RG 108, Telegrams Received; copies, *ibid.*, RG 393, Dept. of the Cumberland, Telegrams Sent; DLC-USG, V, 54.

1866, OCT. 23. USG endorsement. "[Respectfully forwarded] to the Secretary of War. I donot see how brevets can be given to an officer appointed to the regular army since the close of the war, for services rendered as a volunteer officer during its existence. If the brevets are conferred in this instance all volunteer officers appointed in the regular army since the war ended, should be brevetted to the highest rank by ordinary commission held by them in the volunteer service."—ES, DNA, RG 94, ACP, 1295 1871. Written on a letter of Oct. 11 from Col. Joseph J. Reynolds, 26th Inf., Lafayette, Ind., to Secretary of War Edwin M. Stanton requesting appointments as bvt. brig. gen. and maj. gen. of vols. because other less deserving officers had received these appointments.—ALS, *ibid.*

On May 20, 1865, Ind. AG William H. H. Terrell, Indianapolis, had written to USG. "By direction of Governor Morton, I have the honor to inclose herewith copy of a letter addressed by him a few days since to the President of the United States in behalf of Maj. Gen. Jos. J. Reynolds, U. S. Vols, to which your favorable attention is invited."—ALS, *ibid.* On June 5, Reynolds (as maj. gen.), Little Rock, Ark., wrote to USG. "I might say a great many things in this letter, but propose to say very few—I desire to be retained in the Army, but do not know how the selections will be made—If you can give me any information in the premises, consistent with your views of propriety and the rules that you may have found it necessary to establish for yourself in such matters, I will be much obliged to you—I forward today to the Adjt Genl a list of General Officers in this Dept. with my recommendations—Also my own formal application to be retained—"—ALS, *ibid.* On Feb. 24, 1866, John Love, USMA 1841, Washington, D. C., wrote to USG. "Our friend, Gen'l J. J. Reynolds would I think, be glad to be retained in service. Knowing the pecuniary sacrifice he made by entering the service at the time he did; and knowing his patriotic motives; and knowing his fitness for the position; I have secured the unanimous endorsement of the Congressional delegation from my state. Without hesitation I can truly say that the appointment of Gen'l Reynolds would be gratifying to the people of Indiana, without distinction of party. The enclosed is a condensed summary of the services of Gen'l Reynolds, which I respectfully submit to you, with the hope that at the proper time it will be laid before the President; and I trust with your favorable endorsement."—ALS, *ibid.* On Aug. 14, Reynolds, Indianapolis, telegraphed to USG. "I want the Rosecrans vacancy and solicit your cooperation Additional recommendations have gone before the President—I am at Lafayette" —Telegram received (at 4:20 P.M.), *ibid.*, RG 107, Telegrams Collected (Bound).

1866, Oct. 23. Maj. Gen. Philip H. Sheridan, New Orleans, to USG. "I have the honor to forward for your information a copy of a letter from Mr King Cutler of this City and the Inspection report on same. I forward this letter and report for the reason that duplicates of Mr Cutlers letter may have been sent North, and if it should reach you, you could be able to estimate its value."—LS, DNA, RG 108, Letters Received. Sheridan enclosed a letter of Oct. 17 from R. King Cutler, New Orleans, to Sheridan warning that conservative elements were planning an uprising in the city on Nov. 1. —Copy, *ibid.* Sheridan also enclosed a letter of Oct. 18 from Maj. and Bvt. Brig. Gen. James W. Forsyth, inspector gen., to Sheridan. ". . . I found Mr Cutler at his Office and had an interview with him lasting some (2) two hours. I have the honor to state that Mr Cutler failed to sustain the Statement made in his letter by any positive facts or evidence, All the information that he could give, was based upon Street and corner rumor and the chattering of disloyal females. For instance 'he said that he was a member of the Convention that resulted in the riot of July last, since that time that his friends had warned him that his life was and would be in danger if he remained here.' 'That Secessionists relatives of his wife had insulted her when she visited them, had abused her husband, said that he ought to have been killed at the Riot.' All this Stuff has been eagerly believed by Mr Cutler; as he seems to have made up his mind to flee the City and become a Martyr. . . . My own opinion arrived at after carefully listening to *all* that Mr Cutler had to say, is that the fears &c. &c. expressed in his letter are absurd and unsubstantiated by him in any way shape or manner and not worthy of credence"—LS, *ibid.*

1866, Oct. 25. To Governor Thomas E. Bramlette of Ky. "Thirty days delay will be authorized for Colonel Crittenden"—Telegram sent, DNA, RG 107, Telegrams Collected (Bound); copies, *ibid.*, RG 108, Letters Sent; DLC-USG, V, 47, 60. On Oct. 24, Bramlette, Frankfort, had telegraphed to USG. "Extend Col. L L Crittenden thirty second (32) regiment one 1 month leave to enable him to close up his settlement as State Treasurer &

obtain 'Quietus', The time is necessary. Answer"—Telegram received (at 3:30 P.M.), DNA, RG 94, Letters Received, 732C 1866. On Oct. 25, USG endorsed this telegram. "The Adj. Gn. will please extend the time for Col. Crittenden to report thirty days."—AES, *ibid.*

1866, Oct. 26. Col. Ely S. Parker endorsement. "Respectfully returned. No objection is known to the enlistment of J. Davis Howell in the Canadian Volunt'rs."—AES, DNA, RG 94, Letters Received, 686H 1866. Written on a letter of Oct. 2 from Jefferson Davis Howell, Montreal, to Secretary of War Edwin M. Stanton requesting either a release from his parole or a speedy trial so that he could enlist in the Canadian vols.—ALS, *ibid.* On Nov. 3, Bvt. Maj. Gen. Edward D. Townsend noted on the docket. "Submitted to the Secretary of War and Mr. Howell's request not approved by him."—ANS, *ibid.* See *O.R.*, II, viii, 648. On Aug. 16, 1867, Howell wrote to USG, secretary of war *ad interim.* "I was captured with Hon Jefferson Davis, and confined in Fort McHenry when released from that place, I was compelled to take a parole to report weekly my whereabouts by letter and in person when called upon, since that time I have been twice arrested, the last time I was confined in Fort Warren for two months and a half nearly, and I never received the *slightest* satisfaction not even the *slightest* reason assigned I have applied repeatedly for a release to the Hon Secty Stanton, and was always refused, I am not aware of ever having done any thing but my duty as a soldier in the service which I was in, consequently Genl ~~if~~ I very Respectfully apply for a release from the parole, if there are any charges against me, I Respectfully beg a speedy hearing that I may refute them hoping for a speedy reply . . ."—ALS, DNA, RG 107, Letters Received, H313 1867.

1866, Oct. 27. Col. Ely S. Parker endorsement. "The Adjutant General will at once relieve, by telegraph, Col. J. K. Dawson, and order him before the Retiring Board."—AES, DNA, RG 94, Letters Received, 201R 1866. Written on a telegram of Oct. 26 from Bvt. Maj. Gen. Edward O. C. Ord, Little Rock, Ark., to USG. "I cannot trust Col J K. Dawson in Command of troops of this Dept all Composed of his old Regt because he is believed by them to be deranged Can he not be ordered elsewhere by telegraph He is here"—Telegram received (at 7:30 P.M.), *ibid.*; *ibid.*, RG 107, Telegrams Collected (Bound); copy, *ibid.*, RG 393, Dept. of Ark., Telegrams Sent. On the same day, Ord wrote to USG. "I have inspected several Posts in my Department, and at every one of them the officers expressed to me a fear that Colonel Dawson, should be sent to Command their Post, or regiment, ~~for~~ He has made himself so obnoxious, and his excentricities are of such a serious, and unmilitary nature, that I am afraid to trust him in any Command—He reported here to day, and was disposed to insist upon selecting his own station, regardless of whether any part of his regiment occupied it or not, and I find him entirely unqualified for Commanding troops on frontier duty, principally because, (whether true or not,) ~~that~~ he is believed to be deranged, and no one is desposed to obey his orders—I am apprehensive that, if left in command of the Department while I go for my family, he will from ignorance of the wants of the Department, and his having so many feuds with officers of the old 19th the regiment, from which all the garrisons in the Department were taken, disorganize the Command—I learn from Medical Director Smith, that he, when last before the retiring board, was allowed to remain in service at his own request, until he could be promoted Colonel; I therefore recommend that he be brought before the retiring board, or ordered on some duty where he may not have to Command ~~of~~ troops—of his old regiment—"—ALS, *ibid.*, RG 94, Letters Received, 844A 1866.

1866, OCT. 29. To President Andrew Johnson. "I have the honor to recommend Thos Corbin Davenport, aged Seventeen years in Apl. 1867, for appointment to the Military Academy, West Point N. Y. Young Davenport is the son of an Officer of the Navy who is therefore unable to procure a Cadet appointment for his son in any other way than 'at large.' "—ALS, DNA, RG 94, Correspondence, USMA. Thomas C. Davenport graduated from USMA in 1872.

1866, OCT. 29. Mayor Samuel Booth, Brooklyn, N. Y., to USG. "In behalf of the City of Brooklyn, I have the honor of forwarding to you a Gold Medal, an exact counterpart of one in Bronze, presented upon the 25th inst., to the veteran soldiers and sailors who so nobly represinted Kings County in the late War. In our attempt to honor these men, we could not fail to remember the great General who so successfully led our Armies to final and complete victory. Assuring you of the deep respect and gratitude which are felt for you by all classes of our citizens, . . ."—ALS, USG 3. See William H. Allen, *The Civil War Book and Grant Album* (Boston and New York, 1894), p. [43].

1866, OCT. "Tewandah, the scout," to USG. "I feel it to be my duty to warn You to be on Your guard against—*Assassination* also to be Very careful of what You *Eat*, and *where* You eat—for the next 60 days—I believe that the *Knights* have spotted, You, Sheridan, and Sherman, I have written them, to be Careful—my warning may not reach them—If You can warn them—do so—"—AL (facsimile), Adam Badeau, *Grant in Peace* (Hartford, Conn., 1887), p. [56].

[*1866, Oct.–Nov.?*]. Anonymous to USG. "From information in my possession, I am induced to believe that unless the Government of the United States interposes ~~with a strong hand~~, a collision between the white people and negroes in the City of Baltimore is inevitable, which in my opinion will result in the massacre of a ~~great~~ number of the latter race. For some time past, political causes have been operating to bring about this state of things, but more recently, the antagonism ~~between the two races~~ of parties seems to be assuming more ~~a~~ the appearance of a conflict of races, and altho' ~~strange as it may appear~~ hard to believe, I think it is beyond a doubt that there are active persons in each political party who believe~~s~~ ~~it~~ their party is to be benefitted by the conflict and ~~is~~ are to that ~~degree~~ extent anxious to precipitate [it.] One party believes that by ~~commencing~~ the collision ~~in Baltimore~~ in Baltimore, the negro race which can be ~~driven out~~ easily crushed in that City if unassisted ~~will share the same fate through all the Southern States~~ will forever be put out of the pale of competition with the white man in Maryland both in the field of labor & in politics. The other party believes that even should the result be disastrous to the negro population in Baltimore, it will have the effect to arouse the North to come to the rescue, & ~~reinstate~~ recover Maryland ~~in possession of the~~ from the government of its present rulers. I In fact, there is every indication that unless some step is taken, we are likely to have the occurrence of riots similar to those which took place last Summer in New Orleans. I think ~~it my duty~~ therefore, it is now time respectfully to ~~suggest~~ recommend that at least two full Regiments of Infantry, and a battery of light Artillery, shall be at once ordered to take post in the vicinity of Baltimore ~~at a~~ to keep the peace. If they cannot be spared from the Regular Army, I recommend that two ~~of the militia~~ volunteer Regiments of ~~Maryland~~, to be selected by the Government of the U. S be mustered into services. I think it proper in this connection to state my belief that there is at present no disposition on the part of either side to place themselves in ~~antagonism~~ conflict with the Authority of the United States."—ADf, USG 3.

1866, Nov. 1. Mary J. Judah, Washington, D. C., depot, to USG. "Important business—Can I see you at twelve 12 friday? Answer to . . ."—Telegram received (at 4:00 P.M.), DNA, RG 107, Telegrams Collected (Bound).

1866, Nov. 3. USG endorsement. "Respectfully recommended for class of 1867."—AES, DNA, RG 94, Cadet Applications. Written on a letter of Oct. 30 from Harry Sedgwick, Cornwall Hollow, Conn., to USG. "I the undersigned am the Nephew of the late Maj Genl John Sedgwick U. S. A. and do solicit on his account an appointment to the United States Mil~~l~~itery Academy at West Point and knowing no other way to apply write to you to interest yourself in my behalf. I am eighteen years old and have received an education qualifying myself for an Examination to that place. I am General Sedgwick's nearest male rel~~i~~ative (as he was a Bachelor) and my application is based on his merits. Further recomendations will be furnished if desired. Hoping General that you will do something, as I am extreemly anxious."—ALS, *ibid.*

1866, Nov. [5]. Matías Romero, Mexican minister, Washington, D. C., to USG. "I enclose you copy of a despatch I have just received from Vera Cruz, with very important news."—ALS, USG 3.

1866, Nov. 8. To Abiel A. Low *et al.*, New York City. "Your kind invitation to me to meet Mr. C. W. Field at dinner on the 15th inst. [to] exchange congratulations on the success of the great enterprise which has engaged so much of his time for some years is received. It would afford me great pleasure to be able to accept but I fear other engagements will prevent. Allow me however to express my appreciation of the enterprise which Mr. Field has been engaged in and to congratulate him upon the success which finally was attained through his perseverence."—ALS (facsimile), Paul C. Richards, Catalogue 201 [1985], no. 141.

1866, Nov. 9. USG endorsement. "Respy. referred to the President of United States. I became acquainted with the writer of this letter at the beginning of the rebellion. He was an active loyalist in the neighborhood where it was by no means safe to be so. He is a man of intelligence and character."—Copy, DNA, RG 108, Register of Letters Received. Written on a letter of Nov. 4 from James Lindsay, Ironton, Mo., received at USG's hd. qrs. "Was appointed Register of Land Office by President Lincoln—but has been superceded by President Johnson, who has appointed Jno. A. Miller who is not and never was a loyalist. Asks the General in Chief to see President Johnson and have him (L) reinstated."—*Ibid.* John A. Miller was rejected by the U.S. Senate; Lindsay, however, was not reinstated. On March 15, 1869, USG nominated Lindsay as pension agent at St. Louis.

1866, Nov. 9. Elizabeth and Sarah S. Hare, Philadelphia, to USG. "Our nephew, Philetus A. Stevens, having recently arrived in the City and being naturally of an aspiring disposition, he is desirous of obtaining a commission in the Marine Corps or Regular Army, that will lead him to eminence. He is at present a Sergeant in the Marine Corps on his second enlistment and on duty at the Philadelphia Navy Yard. As he has held positions much higher than his present one we feel that he is perfectly competent to fill any position in the line of advancement you might possibly obtain for him. Before the Rebellion he enlisted, together with his brother, in the Marine Corps, at Philadelphia; he advanced rapidly and obtained the highest position possible—that of an Orderly Sergeant—after serving out his time (four years) as a marine and receiving an honorable discharge and after a few months of private life, he again enlisted as a private in the 84th New York Militia for one hundred days—returing home he raised a Company and joined the 25th regiment of New Jersey volunteers for the war, receiving his Commission as Captain. His wife being taken very ill, and he being sent for, returned home from the field, and finding his wife very low, was compelled to resign (after seven months service)—his wife has since deceased—prefering the Navy to the Army, he again enlisted in the Marine Corps, where he rapidly advanced to the position in which we now find him. He was one of the first to reinforce Fort Pickens, under command of Col Harvey C. Brown—was in the battle at Fredericksburg under General Burnside—was in the battle on the Blackwater above Suffolk Va and has been in several other engagements both by land and sea. It would give us much pleasure, if you could place him in a position where his services could be appreciated."—LS, DNA, RG 108, Letters Received. For the Hare cousins of USG, see *PUSG*, 1, 246.

1866, Nov. 13. To Secretary of War Edwin M. Stanton. "I have the honor to recommend that the dismissal of Capt E. L. Hartz, A. Q. M., of July 29 1864, be revoked, and his resignation accepted as of that date. I would then renew the recommendation made in my list for promotions to Captaincies from the Regular Army, that he be appointed Captain of Infantry (White.)"—LS, DNA, RG 94, ACP, Q62 CB 1868. Edward L. Hartz was appointed capt., 27th Inf., as of July 28. On March 12, April 2, and Aug. 1, USG had favorably endorsed to Stanton papers recommending Hartz for reappointment in the U.S. Army.—ES and AES (2), *ibid.* On Oct. 12, 1867, USG unfavorably endorsed papers recommending Hartz for bvt. promotion.—ES, *ibid.*

1866, Nov. 14 (Wednesday), 7:40 P.M. To Judge Hugh L. Bond, Baltimore. "I will probably be in Baltimore Friday. Have written to Mr Albert." —Telegram sent, DNA, RG 107, Telegrams Collected (Bound); copies, *ibid.*, RG 108, Letters Sent; DLC-USG, V, 47, 60. On Nov. 15, 10:35 A.M., USG telegraphed to William J. Albert. "I will be unable to go to Baltimore before Saturday."—Telegram sent, DNA, RG 107, Telegrams Collected (Bound); copies, *ibid.*, RG 108, Letters Sent; DLC-USG, V, 47, 60.

1866, Nov. 15. To Secretary of War Edwin M. Stanton. "I have the honor to recommend that John R. Brooks, late Brig. & Bvt. Maj. Gen. of Volunteers, appointed Lt. Col. 347th Inf.y be appointed Col. 34th Inf.y, vice J. F. Hartranft declined, and that Chas. T. Campbelle or E. M. Gregory, both late Brig. Generals, be appointed Lt. Col. 37th Inf.y vice Brooke apptd Col. 34th Inf[y.]"—ALS, DNA, RG 94, ACP, G588 CB 1866. On Nov. 19, USG wrote to Stanton. "In my letter of Nov. 15th I recommended Gen. Campbell or Gen. Gregory, to fill the place that would be left by Lt. Col. J. R. Brooke's promotion to a Colonelcy. I would now recommend Gen. Pennypacker for the vacancy so created, in preference to either of the others. I enclose a letter from Gov. Curtin in the case."—Copies, DLC-USG, V, 47, 60; DNA, RG 108, Letters Sent. John R. Brooke was appointed lt. col., 37th Inf., as of July 28; Galusha Pennypacker was appointed col., 34th Inf., as of July 28.

1866, Nov. 16. USG endorsement. "Respectfully forwarded."—ES, DNA, RG 94, ACP, 1990 1875. Written on a letter of Nov. 8 from Lt. Col. and Bvt. Maj. Gen. James H. Wilson, 35th Inf., Wilmington, Del., to USG. "*Personal:* . . . I venture to ask a recommendation from you, for Col Wickliffe Cooper late 4th Ky. Cavalry. I *know* the man—and hope he may not be disappointed. *Croxton* & *Winslow*, will both decline their captaincies I think, as neither cares to go into the Army—Cooper might be put into either place, if there are no other vacancies. The following extracts from his letter will show something of the condition of affairs in Ky: 'We who perilled every thing for the Government are now decidedly small potatoes. By the unwise action of our State Legislature, and the equally unwise encouragement of the Administration, the rebels have changed from the "*Couchant*" to the "rampant." In plain terms federal officers and soldiers have no chance to live by their own exertion in this part of our state: And as I have some little notoriety by a skirmish in this place (Lexington) with John Morgan, I am peculiarly obnoxious to the traitors. This is natural for I gave him a genteel thrashing with one sixth his numbers. I want an appointment in the Regular army, though really I have not much hope, for I was in Earnest in the war, and tried to do my duty. Men who acted as I did *then* and think as I do *now*, are not meeting with much encouragement in this State.' This will give you an idea of the man; Hoping something may be done for him . . ."—ALS, *ibid.* Wickliffe Cooper was appointed maj., 7th Cav., as of July 28.

1866, Nov. 22. To Secretary of War Edwin M. Stanton. "The application of John H. Coal. for Military Storekeeper in the regular Army has been called to my attention. Col. Coal was Chief Comy. of Subsistence of the 9th A. C. at Vicksburg and in East Tennessee and from the Wilderness to Petersburg. As A. C. S. he performed his duties to the entire satisfaction of his Superior Officers. I believe he would make a good military storekeeper"—Copies, DLC-USG, V, 47, 60; DNA, RG 108, Letters Sent. On Sept. 19, 1867, John H. Coale, Washington, D. C., wrote a letter received at USG's hd. qrs. requesting an appointment in the U.S. Army.—*Ibid.*, Register of Letters Received. On Sept. 27, USG endorsed this letter. "Approved for appointment of 2d Lt. in Infantry."—Copy, *ibid.* Coale was appointed 2nd lt., 27th Inf., as of Oct. 2.

1866, Nov. 24. To Secretary of War Edwin M. Stanton. "I have the honor to recommend Capt. Walter B. Pease, 17th U. S. Infantry for promotion to Lieut. Col. by brevet for gallant & meritorious services in the Battle of the Wilderness in 1864, and subsequent battles of the Army of the Potomac."—ALS, DNA, RG 94, ACP, P393 CB 1870. On Dec. 21, Capt. Walter B. Pease, 17th Inf., Galveston, Tex., wrote to Brig. Gen. Lorenzo Thomas. ". . . It would give me great pleasure to accept the honor thus conferred, but as I was not present in the engagement specially named in the letter of appointment, I cannot conscientiosly do so—If it is possible to substitute for the 'Wilderness' the name of another engagement I would be glad to accept—and in that case would respectfully suggest 'Bethesda Church or 'Cold Harbor', or for one of the grades, the campaign of Antietam or of Mine Run."—ALS, *ibid.* On Jan. 9, 1867, USG endorsed this letter. "Application for substitution of 'Bethesda Church,' for 'Wilderness' in brevet commission is approved."—ES, *ibid.* Pease received a bvt. of maj. for the battle of Bethesda Church, Va.; the wording for Pease's bvt. of lt. col. remained as USG had first requested.

1866, Nov. 24. Maj. George K. Leet endorsement. "Respy. returned to the Q. M. Genl. Prior to the date of Lieut. Barlows reciept for the 74 bales cotton in question, orders had been given by Genl Grant for the siezure of cotton to be used as a protection to transports running the Vicksburg batteries. It is not known whether this cotton was used for that purpose.—If not it should have been sent to the Q. M. Dept. at Memphis, Tenn., to be sold—orders having been given to dispose of all surplus cotton in that way. It is suggested that Colonel J. D. Bingham than Ch. Q. M. Tenn. Dept., or Capt. Reno, A. Q. M., then on duty at Millikens Bend, La., may be able to give full information as to what disposition was made of this cotton."—Copy, DNA, RG 108, Register of Letters Received. Written on papers submitted to USG's hd. qrs. on Nov. 16 by Bvt. Maj. Gen. Montgomery C. Meigs. "Asks for information relative to claim of Benjamin Roach for 74 bales cotton and reciept for that amount of Lieut. W. H. Barlow, Q. M. 31st. Mo. Vols., 'shipped to Genl Grant, at Youngs Point, La.', siezed by order of Maj Gen Steele."—*Ibid.* In late 1863 or early 1864, USG had written that Benjamin Roach's claim should be paid "in the shortest possible time, and with the least trouble and expense."—*HRC*, 38-1-73. In 1875, Margaret Roach received $8,911.83 to settle this claim.—*HED*, 44-1-189, p. 33.

1866, Nov. 26. To Secretary of War Edwin M. Stanton. "I have the honor to recommend that Maj. L. Jones, retired, be breveted to the rank of Colonel"—Copies, DLC-USG, V, 47, 60; DNA, RG 94, ACP, G591 CB 1866; *ibid.*, RG 108, Letters Sent.

1866, Nov. 26. USG endorsement. "Respectfully forwarded to the Secretary of War with the recommendation that this officer be appointed Captain in the 10th Cavalry, instead of Capt. J. W. Blunt, 2d N. Y. Cav recommended by me in my list of Nov. 15th '66."—ES, DNA, RG 94, ACP, A455 CB 1865. Written on General Orders No. 20, Dept. of the Platte, Nov. 12, commending 2nd Lt. George A. Armes, 2nd Cav., for bravery in action against Sioux Indians.—*Ibid.* Armes was appointed capt., 10th Cav., as of July 28. See *PUSG*, 11, 444. On July 20, 1870, Armes, Washington, D. C., wrote to USG. "I have the honor most respectfully to request that the Judge Advocate Genl. reopen my case, on the ground that I have received injustice from the court, which tried me, & who furnished an incomplete record, leaving out any *quantity* of evidence which was in my favor."—ALS, DNA, RG 94, ACP, A455 CB 1865. Possibly on the same day, U.S. Representative Luke P. Poland of Vt. *et al.* wrote to USG. "Capt. George A. Armes of the Army of the United States, has recently been tried by Court Martial, and sentenced to be dismissed from the service—The substance of the charge upon which he was found guilty, was sending an obscene picture to a notorious prostitute. The evidence was vague and contradictory upon which he was convicted and can hardly be said to warrant a finding of guilty of the allegation.—But we are satisfied that the whole matter has its origin in malice, and has no foundation in truth. Maj. Armes is a most gallant officer and has shown his bravery on many occasions, We respectfully ask that the sentence may be disapproved, and Maj. Armes restored to his position"—LS (undated), *ibid.* On Sept. 20, John M. Chivington, National Central Committee of the Soldiers and Sailors Convention, wrote to USG. "I take great pleasure in saying that from a personal Knowledge of an acquaintance with Capt George A Arms U. S. A. I believe him to be one of the most efficient Officers that has been on duty on the *plains*, and that he is in evry way worthy, To be more particular, I was at Forts Laramie, Mitchel, and Sedgewick during the winter of 1866–7 and Know from personal observation that the service that Capt Arms performed in the pursuit of and punsishment of the Indians and recapuring citizens stock and Genl Cooks complimentary order to Capt Arms for his ~~success he~~ services so well performed in mid winter caused much envy and Jealousy towards Capt Arms and I state that I heared many officers speak disparagingly of Capt Arms owing as I believe to his great activity and persistence in his Indian campaigns. Capt Arms bears the name and has the reputation of being a *strictly sober* and other wise moral man, and in this respect far above the average of his fellow Officers. I can but think the charge on which he was tried as the merest pretext, I will say that in common with ten thousand (and more) other citizens of Kansas, Nebraska Colorado, Wyomg, and Montana, I earnestly trust your Excellency will restore Capt Armes to his rank & place in the army to date from the time of his dismissal, so that he may continue to serve or be at liberty to honorably resign the place he has so successfully filled If your Ex requires it in order to his restoration I would enguage to get such a number of signers to a petition as will show how Capt Arms is appreciated in the West where he has served for four years or nearly so"—ALS, *ibid.* Numerous letters from Armes and others to USG are *ibid.* On June 1, 1874, Henry T. Crosby, chief clerk, War Dept., wrote to USG. "I have the honor to return herewith the Act (Senate 249.) providing for the honorable discharge, with a years pay and allowances of George A. Armes, late Captain 10th Cavalry. George A. Armes was dismissed as Captain 10th Cavalry, by sentence of Court Martial, 7 June. 1870. Numerous applications to the President and Secretary of War for the re-opening of the case have been declined, but in December, 1870, the President directed the reappointment of Capt Armes on condition of his tendering his immediate and unconditional resignation. He was accordingly nominated December 21. 1870. (having previously placed his resignation in the hands of the Secretary of War.) but was not confirmed by the Senate prior to its adjournment. The many papers presented to the Department by Capt. Armes since that date have been placed on file without action. This Act provides that Captain Armes shall 'be paid the same pay and allowances *as if he had been discharged under the provisions of the third section of "the Act" of July 15. 1870.* He could not have been discharged under that Act June 7. '70, nor prior to the date it became a law—July 15. 1870—as it was not retroactive in its operation. The Official circumstances of his case are entirely against the favorable action as provided for in the Act, and the relief granted thereby is viewed as establishing a very bad precedent. The foregoing are viewed as objections and reasons why the Act should not receive the approval of the President. The Secretary of War before leaving for West Point directed the preparation of this letter as expressive of his views in reference to the case of Mr. Armes."—LS, *ibid.* On June 9, 1874, Congress, without USG's approval, granted Armes an honorable discharge as of June 7, 1870.—*U.S. Statutes at Large*, XVIII, part 3, 564. See *HRC*, 42-3-19; *SRC*, 43-1-125; *SED*, 43-2-21. Armes was restored as capt., 10th Cav., on May 11, 1878, to rank from July 28, 1866.

1866, Nov. 26. USG endorsement. "Respectfully returned to the Secretary of War. I concur in the views of the Judge Advocate General, and do not therefore recommend the restoration of Mr. Pike."—ES, DNA, RG 94, ACP, P740 CB 1867. Written on a letter of Nov. 12 from Judge Advocate Gen. Joseph Holt to Secretary of War Edwin M. Stanton recommending against the reinstatement of Horace L. Pike, former 1st lt., 1st Art., who had been dismissed for desertion as of Oct. 14, 1864.—LS, *ibid.* On Nov. 30, 1866, USG wrote to Stanton. "After hearing more of the case of Lieut. R. S. P. Pike, 1st U. S Artillery, who was dismissed the service in 1864, I would respectfully ask to change my endorsement, concurring with the Judge Advocate General, to a recommendation that the order dismissing him be revoked, and that he be retired from the date of dismissal. I am induced to make this change in consideration of the youth of Lt. Pike and the further fact that he lost a leg in the service and whilst in the direct line of his duty."—LS, *ibid.* On Dec. 7, 1867, Pike, Salisbury, N. C., wrote to USG, secretary of war *ad interim.* "The undersigned begs respectfully to represent, that on the 11th day of October A D 1864, he was dropped from the List of the Army for Absence without Leave—he holding at that time the commission of 1st Lieutenant of the First Regiment of Artillery—that subsequently, under date of Jany 26, A D. 1867, the order of dismissal was revoked, on the recommendation of Gen. Grant, for the purpose of enabling him to be retired as of the date of dismissal: and that he was accordingly retired by an Examining Board sitting in Philadelphia, said retirement being promulgated on the 21st day of Feby A D 1867, and dating as from the date of the dismissal. He further represents that he has recived no pay of any kind for the period included between the date of his dismissal and the date of issuing the order of restoration:—and being restored on the retired list by reason of disability resulting from the loss of a leg in the battle of Williamsburg—and said retirement being ordered specifically to date back to the date of dismissal, he prays that he may be allowed his retired pay for that period. He is well aware that he could have no claim for full pay, inasmuch as full pay can only follow the actual discharge of duty:—but retired pay is in the light of an honorary pension, and expressly excludes the idea of performing of duty—excludes it not only directly, but indirectly, by the fact that a retired officer is at once allowed full pay when ordered to the performance of any active duty. All which is most respectfully submitted"—ALS, *ibid.* On March 28, 1868, USG unfavorably endorsed a letter of Dec. 24, 1867, from Pike, Morganton, N. C., to USG requesting bvt. promotion.—ES and ALS, *ibid.*, W38 CB 1867. On March 15, 1870, U.S. Senator Joseph C. Abbott of N. C. and others, Washington, D. C., wrote to USG. "We, the members of the North Carolina delegation to the Congress of the United States, do most earnestly request that you will appoint Col. Horace L. Pike to be United States Consul at Honolulu. Col Pike has done good service in the ~~in~~ field, and is now suffering frm a severe wound received during the rebellion. He is a firm supporter of the goverment and has done much to aid in placing North Carolina in the list of states whose adherence to the goverment cannot be questioned. Owing to these facts we think that his services fully warrant us in urging that he may have the appointment herein mentioned."—LS, *ibid.*, RG 59, Letters of Application and Recommendation. Pike was confirmed as consul gen., Tampico, Mexico, on April 28.

1866, Nov. 28. To Secretary of War Edwin M. Stanton. "I have the honor to recommend Clayton S. Burbank, son of Gen. Sidney Burbank of the Army, for appointment of 2d Lieut. in one of the old Infantry regiments of the Army, the 2d if a vacancy exists there."—ALS, DNA, RG 94, ACP, 2699 1875. On July 31, Col. and Bvt. Brig. Gen. Sidney Burbank, 2nd Inf., Louisville, had written to Col. and Bvt. Brig. Gen. Frederick T. Dent requesting the appointment of his son Clayton S. Burbank to the U.S. Army.—ALS, *ibid.*, B1169 CB 1866. On Jan. 21, 1867, Burbank wrote to Dent requesting the appointment of young Burbank to the 2nd Inf.—ALS, ICarbS. Burbank was appointed 2nd lt., 10th Cav., as of March 7.

1866, Nov. 28. U.S. Representative Elihu B. Washburne, New York City, to USG. "I expect to reach Washington tomorrow thursday night at six (6) oclock"—Telegram received (at 10:40 A.M.), DNA, RG 108, Telegrams Received; copy, DLC-USG, V, 54.

1866, [Nov.?]. USG signature on petition to President Andrew Johnson. "We the undersigned officers and Ex-officers of the Regular and Volunteer Service, who have served under the flag of the United States during the late Rebellion, do hereby respectfully and most earnestly unite in recommending to your Excellency the pardon of George H. Stuart, late Brigadier General in the Confederate service. We make this recommendation with a full knowledge of all the facts in the case, and satisfied that such a pardon as we solicit will be for the public interest."—DS, DNA, RG 94, Amnesty

Papers, Md. Docketing indicates that George H. Steuart was pardoned as of Nov. 26.—*Ibid.*

1866, DEC. 1, 1:20 P.M. To Maj. Gen. Henry W. Halleck, San Francisco. "Give Col. Blake of the Cavalry six months leave. He is wanted home without delay."—ALS (telegram sent), DNA, RG 107, Telegrams Collected (Bound).

1866, DEC. 1. USG endorsement. "This man served in my company as 1st Sergeant, and was a good and faithful soldier. I recommend him for appointment of Ordnance Sergeant if there are any vacancies."—ES, DNA, RG 94, ACP, 2470 1874. Written on a letter of Nov. 21 from Corporal Edward Davis, Newport Barracks, Ky., to USG. "This is my writing & so is Col J T Curtus. Vouchers & ord returns of 64 at Depts at Washington D. C. . . . The undersigned having had the honor of serving under your Command in former years viz as 1st Sergt of your Compy "F" 4th U. S. Inf Stationed at Fort Humboldt Humboldt Bay Cal at the time of the date of my discharge viz the 4th Day February *1854*, on that occation you Honl Sir gave me a Writen recommendation to Ryan Duff &c co at Eureka Humboldt Bay. Your reason for dooing so being in justice to me for my services under your Command on the Isthumus of Panama in 1852 as Sergt of the rear Guard on the Chagress River at Gorgona, & Crusses in bringing sick soldiers to Panama, then you were Q M, Lt Whithers A. A. Q. M. Dr Tripler Medical director, &c for the Pacific Dept., and Whilst at Fort Humboldt I allwise endeavoured to do my duty in a obedient & soldier like maner hence your good will & testimonal to Ryan Duff & Co for Employment Col R. C. Buchanan did not do me justice after serving 4 yrs & 7 mo. as Non Comssd off out of my five years enlistment, by his action on my discharge I lost all Back half pay for Ord Services from 16 Aug /52 till the date of my discharge—Please find enclosed a true copy of said recommendation to Ryan Duff & *co* 2nd enlistment I served in "M" Co 3rd Artillery Capt E. D. Keyes, Comdg Co Served with Co "M" all through the Oregon War /55 & 1856. though Major Genl E. D. Keyes. has resigned from the U. S. army during the later part of the War Therefore I can not well refer to him for my Services in Oregon But I respectfully refer to Major Maurice Malony, formerly Capt of Co "A" 4th Inf who was Commander of many expeditions against hostile Indians on Puget Sound during said opperations in the fall & winter of 1855 & sumer of 1856, I was then Sergt of artillery and a General Favorate with my superior officers in all their scouts & in fitting out parties of artilliry with mountain Howtzers &c Major Malony Can not avoid Commending me for services under him at the Battle of White River & elswhere in Constructing Millitary Roads & Cordroying Swamps &c during the said Indian Campaign as Sergt. John Davis of M Co 3d arty—being still in California at the breaking out of the late War I enlisted in Co "B" 4th Cal Infy. Capt J Ives Fitch Comdg Compy The said Reg. was raised and organized by H M Judah, for the purpose of

Coming home East, but unfortunately it was sent to Garrison Posts in the Southern District of California it was employed in supressing Copperhead movements & Political aggitations I joined the said Co "B" by the Name of Edward Davis, thinking that the flaw in my first enlistment Could not be brought against me as a Preventive in the line of Promotions then so Common in the ranks of the Cal Vollunteers Co "B" was stationed at Fort Mojave Colorado River from April /63 till Dec /63, then recalled to Hd Qrs. at Drum for the purpose mustering out of the old Members of said Co, I was appointed act Ord Sergt at Drum Bks Col James F Curtus Comdg post. Reg Hd Qrs Dist of Southern Callifornia. I had to Class all the accumulated Ord & ord stores at the said post there being no previous returns of Ordnance ever made out at the Post oweing to uncompentcy of the Vollunteer Officers no Blanks &c at the post for proof please see Col Curtus returns from April 64 till Dec /64 and Vouchers at the pay department & office of Chief of Ordnance at Washington. My time having expired on the 1st Day of February 1866—in Co "C" 4th Cal Infy after Consolidation "B" to other Companies at Hd Qrts of Reg at Drum &c Bks. Cal, I was honorably discharged as Duty Sergt of Said Co. at San Francisco Cal on Feb 1st/66 By Brigr Gen *Sewell* U. S. A. Mustering Officer left San Francisco Cal Feb 10th/66 for New York enroute to Saint Paul Minnesota, where I have an only Brother Wm Davis owner of a Steam Saw Mill &c being a good Mechanic Myself I Confined Myself strictly to my Business as a Sawyer Worked for Mayer John S Prince of the City of Saint Paul during this Sumer By referance to that Gentleman and others at Saint Paul it will be found I am a good American Citizen as well as tried Union Soldier on the 24th Day of Oct the notion took me to enlist in the rank of the U S A at Recruiting Rendevouse at Saint Paul, was sent down to this Post in Charge of a Detmt of recruites for the regular army—& at present I am dooing duty as Corpl Edward Davis *Co "C" Select, Recruites*, Brigdr Genl Potter comdg Dept & post Hon Sir, if by changing my name from John—to Edward Davis, that I have to loose all my former Services I am sorry as I intend to respectfully request from you sir, an appointment as ordnance sergt of *Fort Ridgely Min*, or any other Billet which you Hon Sir might please Procure me by your Illustrous influence I sincerly hope that these few lines will find my old Captain enjoying good health and every felicity in life— . . . P S I crave your pardon for this methot of Writing please give a promt & decisive answer to my humble request"—ALS, *ibid.* Davis enclosed a copy of a letter of Feb. 4, 1854, from USG, Fort Humboldt, Calif., "To Whom it May Concern." "Know that the bearer John Davis a 1st Sergt of Co "F" 4th Inf is honorably discharged by reson of expiration of term of service. I have Known him in his Capacity as a soldier and beleive him to be a strictly sober man, to be relied on and Capable of fullfilling any Place of employment that he would make applications for"—Copy, *ibid.* On Oct. 11, 1871, Davis (sgt., 20th Inf.), Fort Ripley, Minn., wrote to USG renewing his request, and on Oct. 20, 1872, did so again.—

ALS, *ibid.* On Aug. 14, 1876, Davis, ordnance sgt., Fort McKavett, Tex., wrote to USG requesting a transfer.—ALS, *ibid.*

1866, Dec. 4. USG endorsement. "Respectfully forwarded to the Secretary of War, for instructions"—ES, DNA, RG 94, Letters Received, 823T 1866. Written on a letter of Nov. 16 from Maj. Gen. George H. Thomas, Louisville, to USG. "I have the honor to herewith transmit the following papers: application of Job Powell f~~rom~~or relief from persecution by the Civil Authorities, with report on the case by Bvt. Maj. Gen'l. R W Johnson Acting Judge Advocate: letter from J. J. Noah, ~~a~~Attorney, relating to the case of I. T. Wilder: letter from J. J. Noah, Attorney, asking for an order enforcing War Department Orders No. 3. C. S., in the case of Samuel Hayes: copy of a letter from J. J. Noah Attorney, with copy of affidavit in the case of Felix G. Young: and copy of a petition of fifty-six (56) citizens of Bradley and Polk Counties Tenn., for relief for J. C Duff and John Long. These papers relate to grievances that are constantly being complained of, and applications for relief are accumulating at these Head Quarters. I forward these recently recieved, as instances, showing the *animus* of the people, for your information. The States of Tennessee and Kentucky being represented in Congress, the Civil Authorities of these states especially, repudiate all military interference with them; and Union citizens, knowing from experience, that justice cannot be obtained in the Civil Courts, appeal to the Military, as an only hope against persecution by their rebel neighbors. Military interference with the Civil Authorities having on a previous occasion been deprecated by the President, and the suffering condition of these people requiring attention, I respectfully request general instructions, to cover not only these, but all cases of like character, that will enable me to act promptly for their relief, or to let it be known that they cannot expect any from the Military"—LS, *ibid.* On Nov. 26, Governor Charles J. Jenkins of Ga., Milledgeville, wrote to Thomas concerning the arrest of J. C. Duff and John Long, former Union soldiers.—ALS, *ibid.* On Dec. 3, Thomas endorsed this letter. "Respectfully referred to Gen'l. U. S. Grant, General-in-Chief armies of the U. S. for his information, the complaint of citizens in this case having previously been referred to him. The petitioners in the case were good citizens, and no doubt believed their statements, and I am gratified that their fears appear to be groundless."—ES, *ibid.* On Dec. 24, USG endorsed these papers. "Respectfully forwarded to Secretary of War for his information, in connection with papers forwarded Dec. 4. '66." —ES, *ibid.* Additional papers are *ibid.* On June 3, Job Powell, Hiltons, Tenn., had written to USG. "I wish to State to you that I am now under arrest by the Cival authorities for the alledged Murder of John Thornhill which was in Obediance to Orders from a superior Officer tryed before a Military Court convened at Chattanooga sumtime in July or August. 1865 and was honorably discharged by the Same I have bin twice arrested by the civil Law and as often have bin released by the Military, but it appears that they intend to harrass and imprisin me which I believe is through the Course that is to be persued by the Rebels of the Rebellious States and if the Goverment intends to have her Soldiers imprisoned for Obediance of Orders I cannot look for any aid from her but having seen an order of yours, I deemed it prudent to notafy you of the fact, hoping that you will take such action as the emergency of the case in your Jujment demands as I believe my Own life is indangered I believe ~~was arrested~~ there are many such cases in this county being arrested for ~~an~~ offence which your order covered in my Jujment, (indeed I Know So) that one one was arrested and in carrying him to prison along with me and he attemted to make his escape he was [s]hot and probably will die I have filed a petition for a writ of Habeas Corpus in this case I am near 40 miles from the Circuit Judge and I am doutful whether or not the sheriff will carry me before him on before [bring]ing me to prison. I was a Vetnarian Sergent of 9th Tennessee Cavalry. My references for conduct is Coln Parsons my own Commander Liut Colnel Pate Rutherford. and Major Honsbey of the Same the Capt of the Company which I hale from is Rufus McSpatton. General Gillam Comd. Colon Wm Palmer Should he not recollect me Say to him I am the man that acted as Pilet for him in the Carter Station Battle also pilet for him through Virginia to prestonsburg K. Y. to delever a dispatch to Gen Burbridge for the purpus of arranging the Stonman Raid through Our portion of Cuntry you can also inquire of president Johnson who knows me well &c I hope the goverment will take Some action in relation to this cuntry and Stop things that are passing. General Granger passed through this portion of cuntry and I living 20 miles from the Rail road did not get to see him until he had left the cuntry again . . . Address Capt Greshan Jonesboro Tennessee to be fowd to me"—ALS, *ibid.*, 401T 1866. On June 11, Thomas endorsed this letter. "Respectfully returned to the Head Quarters of the Armies of the United States inviting attention to enclosed copy of Gen. Ct. Martial order in the case of Col. Jo Parsons who was of the same party as Powell. Powell's statement is in all respects true. I believe and the case clearly comes within the meaning of General Orders No. 3. Hd-Qrs A. U. S. but the proclamation of the President of April 2nd virtually forbids the enforcement of that order by the Military, and the Act of Congress Amendatory of the Habeas Corpus act indicates the course to be pursued. It makes no difference how often I may relieve prisoners held by the Civil Authorities (as in the case of Job Powell) the moment the Military leave the place they will be arrested again, and unless some means are provided for punishing such violations of orders, it will only bring contempt upon the Military to attempt the enforcement of orders protecting Union soldiers from the prosecution of rebels. The Attorney of Job Powell has himself written to me in behalf of his client and I have sent him a copy of the Act of Congress amending the Habeas Corpus ~~a~~Act."—ES, *ibid.*

1866, DEC. 5. To Miss Henry, daughter of Joseph Henry. "Through Gen. Porter of my Staff you have called on me to perform the most difficult task, that of writing a letter without a subject. I know you will excuse me from attempting what I could not perform."—ALS, Blumhaven Library & Gallery, Philadelphia, Pa.

1866, DEC. 7. USG endorsement. "Respectfully forwarded to the Secretary of War, with recommendation that the Secretary of the Interior be requested to furnish the desired information."—ES, DNA, RG 94, Letters Received, 89I 1866. Written on a letter of Nov. 9 from Maj. Gen. George H. Thomas, Louisville, to USG. "I have the honor to enclose herewith a letter of inquiry to the Honorable Secretary of the Interior, and request that you endorse it favorably, that I may obtain the desired information. The occupation of private property by troops of the United States, in the states lately in rebellion, is a cause of frequent complaint, and I desire, if possible, to remove that cause; at the same time it is necessary to keep troops in certain districts where there is no public property to guard, but to preserve order and aid in the enforcement of the laws."—LS, *ibid.* The enclosure and additional papers are *ibid.*

1866, DEC. 7. C. W. Coffin, Walnut Grove Gold Mining Co., Prescott, Arizona Territory, to USG. "I am perfectly aware that should address you through Official channels in the matter I am about to lay before you, but I fear if I should do so, it would not meet your own eye, and I therefore write to you personally—I wish to make known to you the condition of affairs, in regard to our Indian troubles, and to ask from you some relief—At the present time, the whole country is over-run with them, and it is exceedingly dangerous for even three, or four men to travel in any direction; several lives have already been lost, and much valuable property destroyed, and stolen; three men were killed in escorting some of our machinery from the vicinity of Prescott to the mine; Mr Leihy the Indian Agent, and his clerk Mr. Everett were both murdered within a short distance of us; the mail was attacked at Fort Rock, within fifty miles of Prescott, and three persons badly wounded; my own Ranche was attacked, and all the stock driven off, and killed, and many other acts of a like character, have occurred within a radius of fifty miles around Prescott, which it would be useless for me to enumerate—I do not know the exact number of troops stationed, in the vicinity of Prescott, but I am quite confident, the number within fifty miles of it, does not exceed seventy five men; you will at once perceive that with that number, it is impossible for the Officers in command, to furnish any men to pursue the Indians, or to do escort duty; I applied at Fort Whipple for an escort, a short time ago, but could not obtain it, because there not more than 12, or 15 men for duty, and they were absolutely necessary, to protect Government property; in consequence of not obtaining it, the three men before referred to were killed. I would respectfully ask, that a larger force be sent to this portion of the Territory; I should say, if they can be spared, that a full Regiment could be profitably employed—In my opinion, it has come to this, the Government must send more troops here, or we must give up the country to the Indians—The Citizens have raised a company of thirty men, for three months, and may be able to find enough money in the country, to pay them, but I doubt it somewhat, although we have one of the richest mineral regions in the U-States, it is comparatively undeveloped, owing in a great measure, to the Indian difficulties—I understand Governor McCormick, has reported to the Secty of War, that there are, but one thousand Apaches in the Territory; all sensible men, with whom I have conversed, place the number at from 8 to 10,000; the truth of the matter is, no one knows anything about it; it is all guess work; we do know that they travel in bands of, from 100 to 150 warriors, and are exceedingly dangerous, and troublesome—Besides the Apaches, we have to contend with the Hualapais, Yarapais, and some of the river Indians. I would ask, that if more troops are sent to the Territory, that a detachment of 25 to 30 men, and an Officer be stationed in the vicinity of our mill; we are in the most exposed part of the District, and have no protection except what is afforded by my own men; the main Indi[an] trails pass close to us, and we are in constant danger of losing property, and lives—If my request should be complied with, I will afford all assistance in my power, in building quarters &c. I trust you will excuse me for occupying your valuable time, but I know it is the only way to obtain immediate relief—You may remember me, by having furnished me, with a letter of introduction to the Military Authorities of this Territory, at request of my brother Mr Wm Coffin, of Phila—The letter has been of considerable service to me, and I feel under many obligations for it"—ALS, DNA, RG 108, Letters Received.

1866, Dec. 7. U.S. Delegate John N. Goodwin of Arizona Territory to USG. "I would earnestly call your attention to the request of Messrs. Bradley & Barlow for protection of the mail route between Messilla, New-Mexico, and Tucson Arizona. It is the only communication between Arizona & New Mexico, and the most convenient route between New Mexico and Cala. I am well acquainted with the route, and know that without protection it is impracticable. Part of the Route is in the Department of California and part in the Department of New-Mexico—Application was made to the Department Commanders for military protection but it was not furnished—I am informed that Gen. Carleton suggested that an application should be made for a General Order—If an order is made, I would ask to be furnished with a copy—"—ALS, DNA, RG 108, Letters Received. The enclosure is *ibid.* On Dec. 10, Maj. George K. Leet endorsed copies of these papers. "Respectfully referred to Major General W. S. Hancock, Comdg. Dept. of the Missouri, who will furnish all the protection to this mail-route that the means at his command will permit."—AES, *ibid.*, RG 393, Dept. of the Mo., Letters Received.

1866, Dec. 8, 2:20 p.m. To Bvt. Maj. Gen. Philip St. George Cooke. "Is it practicable for an Officer to reach Fort Philip Kearney with baggage this winter?"—Telegram sent, DNA, RG 107, Telegrams Collected

(Bound); copies, *ibid.*, RG 108, Letters Sent; *ibid.*, RG 393, Dept. of the Platte, Telegrams Received; DLC-USG, V, 47, 60. On Dec. 9, Cooke, Omaha, Nebraska Territory, telegraphed to USG. "It is practicable but very hard Captain Hartz started for Reno yesterday but severe weather Set in last night"—Telegram received (at 3:00 P.M.), DNA, RG 108, Telegrams Received; copy, DLC-USG, V, 54.

1866, DEC. 10. USG endorsement. "Respectfully forwarded to the Secretary of War."—ES, DNA, RG 94, Letters Received, 376E 1866. Written on a letter of Nov. 23 from J. Walter Elliott, former capt., 44th Colored, and seven others, Guntersville, Ala., to USG. "We the undersigned disch'd Fed. Soldiers citizens of this County—have the honor report to you the case of one W. T. Beard of this place who was a noted bush-whacker, prowler, high-way robber—belonging to no com'd in the Con. Fed Gov. He, with 'Pete' Whitecotton in Dec'r 1864 murdered Wm Burgess a union man whom Whitecotton band had captured at his home just across the Tenn. river from this place. Whitecotton was afterward killed. The courts have taken no cognizance of Beard's crime, but instead he has been apt'd County Solicitor—in which position he persecuted each and every man who was known to have been loyal to the U. S. Government, arresting, prosecuting and imprisoning them on all kinds of imaginary pleas. One case will suffice as a sample of the many. On the 13th day of Oct, 1866, this W. T Beard made complaint obtained a warrant and ordered the arrest ~~of~~ and confinement in the county jail—no bail being allowed—of Capt Elliott for kidnapping one idiot negro. On the 16th of same month the trial was continued for want of witnesses for the State. None had been ordered. Just so it remains to this date. Beard meanwhile swearing that he will put every yan[k]ee thro'. We most earnestly but humbly beg action in the case that will protect all good loyal men from further persecution by this man W. T. Beard, County Solicitor"—LS, *ibid.*

1866, DEC. 10. USG endorsement. "Respectfully forwarded to Secretary War, recommended for 2d Lieut of Infantry"—ES, DNA, RG 94, ACP, M53 CB 1867. Written on a letter of Nov. 27 from Maj. Gen. Daniel E. Sickles, New York City, to USG. "I beg your Kind aid & recommendation for the appointment of Br. Col. Alexander Moore for several year A. D. C. on my Staff to a Captaincy in the Cavalry—He is truly a most Competent and meritorious officer and worthy gentlemen and I shall ever feel under personal obligation to you for any service you will Kindly render him. His testimonials from Kearney, Meade, Hooker, Torbert & others are of the most flatter[in]g tenor."—ALS, *ibid.* Alexander Moore was appointed capt., 38th Inf., as of Jan. 22, 1867. On Oct. 9, 1876, John J. Jenkins, Cheyenne, Wyoming Territory, wrote to USG. "I have the honor of addressing you with reference to Gen—Reynolds & Maj. Moore 3rd U. S. Cav—and would respectfully ask your Excellency to take some steps whereby the charges prefered against them by Gen. Crook may in some way be disposed of—

They are both gallant officers & true men, and are in an exceedingly embarassing condition—charged as they have been through the press & by Gen. Crooks friends with cowardice & inefficiency upon the battle field—as friends of theirs we here would like some action taken—Several months have elapsed since charges were prefered against them—& now that Gen. Crooks command is so near here—it seems that some action ought to be taken—They do not fear investigation—but do want to be vindicated—It is but a little while ago that—one of Gen—Crook's officer friends published the statement—that he was happy to state that Reynolds & Moore whose inefficient & cowardly conduct—caused Crooks expedition to be a failure were now to be court-martialed & punished as they so richly deserved—& these officers have to move daily among the people who read the Statement—with no chance to disprove the charge—The charges were not only prefered by Gen. Crook at a time when he knew they could not be investigated—but to still further injure them they were placed in arrest—The Government can not afford to be unjust even to an individual—& as their good-name fame & character is involved this case ought to receive attention—as soon as the service will permit—It will be more satisfactory to have this matter disposed of while you are President—Gen. Crooks claims that he has great influence with Gen—Hays & that if he is elected—He, Crook can have any thing he wants—I heard a prominent man of good character say that Crook told him—he Crook could be Secretary of War if he wanted it—Hence I am anxious to have the matter moved as soon as possible—in justice to these officers—Both served their country long & faithfully—& Gen. Reynolds is an old man—proud of his record—who cant stay many years longer—& who will have no opportunity to vindicate himself by further service—I would therefore respectfully ask that a court martial be convened—to try these officer upon the charges prefered—or if no reasons exist therefor—that an order be published—reciting that the charges are unfounded—"—ALS, *ibid.* See J. W. Vaughn, *The Reynolds Campaign on Powder River* (Norman, Okla., 1961), pp. 183–85.

1866, DEC. 11. USG endorsement. "Respectfully returned to the Secretary of War. The experiments upon one of our old works need cost but little, if any, more than properly built targets. The target, to be equal in resistance to an old work, must be built *large*, and left to settle and harden. This will take at least one year. The firing into the old work will demonstrate such changes in plan, elevation and cross section as the increase of calibre and penetration of projectiles renders necessary. The experiments should be extended so as to show the most expeditious and surest way to protect the forts, with iron, earth or other material. On the whole, though there are objections to making these experiments now, I would recommend that they be authorized, before there is further expenditure on fortifications."—ES, DNA, RG 107, Letters Received from Bureaus. Written on papers concerning the need to test experimental art. against existing fortifications.—*Ibid.*

1866, DEC. 15. Natt Head to USG. "In behalf of the Committee of Arrangement of the Second Annual Levee and Re-union given by the surviving officers of the late New Hampshire Regiments, I have the honor to state that the volunteered hospitality of Hon. Onslow Stearns, our leading citizen of this city and one who has been most conspicuous for his substantial sympathies in behalf of our late volunteers, has been gratefully accepted, which hospitality constitutes the entertainment of yourself and such members of your family and Staff as may accompany you during your visit to this city. If this proceeding meets with your approval, I have the honor to respectfully request that you will inform me of same and advise me of the time of your probable departure from New York City, that proper arrangement for transportation may be made."—ALS (press), William F. Head & Sons Collection, New Hampshire Historical Society, Concord, N. H.

1866, DEC. 31. USG endorsement. "Respectfully returned to the Secretary of War. It is believed that if more troops are needed in New Mexico, they can be supplied from the regular army. Local organizations are believed to be the most expensive and for the number of troops employed the least efficient means of affording protection against Indians."—ES, DNA, RG 108, Letters Received. Written on a memorial addressed to President Andrew Johnson, Secretary of War Edwin M. Stanton, and USG. "The undersigned citizens of the Territory of New Mexico would most respectfully represent, that our Territory embraces an area of more than two hundred thousand square miles, and is as great in extent as all the New England States and New York combined, and that we are infested on all sides by hostile and discontented Indians—that the Comanches, Navajos, Apaches and Utahs are constantly committing murders and roberies which we are convinced will never cease till they are effectually punished and placed on reservations with military posts, garrisoned with troops sufficient to keep them away from the settlements, and an Indian Agent stationed on each reservation, which we are satisfied is the only true policy for the Indians of New Mexico. Your memorialists, would further represent, that this vast Territory is traversed throughout its entire area with numerous mountain ranges, in which are vast deposits of gold, silver and other valuable minerals which are not developed in consequence of their being in possession of the savages, who are living on the flocks and herds of our people coming within a few miles of our capital to commit their depredations, and retreating with their booty into the mountains, which offer at all times convenient and accessible hiding places for these marauding bands of Indians, requiring the most thorough knowledge of the country and of the habits of the Indians, as well as habits of endurance on the part of those who are required to hunt them out and punish them. And in as much as these qualities are to be met in so high a degree in no people as the inhabitants of this Territory, and in as much as no other portion of the inhabitants of the United States, are so much and so directly interested in the subjugation of the Indians, and as the native troops can be obtained here at less expense, than their transportation from the States. We would most respectfully request that an order be issued to authorize His Excellency the Governor of New Mexico, to reorganize the two regiments of New Mexican Volunteers, and to recruit volunteers enough to fill them up to be retained in the service for two years at least. These with the regulars and other troops promised will subjugate the Indians, place them on reservations, protect our citizens and open and develope this rich country."—D (printed in both English and Spanish, and undated), *ibid.* On Nov. 27, Act. Governor William F. M. Arny of New Mexico Territory, Santa Fé, had written to USG. "I have the honor herewith to send to you a copy of a memorial which has been sent to Hon I. F Chaves our Delegate in Congress to be presented by him. We hope you will consider the condition of our people and furnish sufficient troops to whip the Indians and protect our people,"—ALS, *ibid.* Arny enclosed the memorial and additional papers.—*Ibid.* On Dec. 18, Arny wrote to USG. "In compliance with the resolution of the Hon Council of the Legislative Assembly of this Territory I have the honor to transmit to you the enclosed Preamble resolutions and memorial adopted *unanimously* and to ask your favorable consideration and action thereon and please acknowledge its receipt."—ALS, *ibid.* The enclosures are *ibid.* On Jan. 10, 1867, Lt. Gen. William T. Sherman, St. Louis, wrote to Maj. George K. Leet. "I have the honor to acknowledge receipt of the Memorial from NewMexico, transmitted by Hon W. F. M Arny acting Governor under date of Novr 27, 1866, and referred to me by your endorsement of Jan 3, inst. You have in Washington full records of the vast outlays of men and money employed during the past twenty years to protect the People of NewMexico against the Indians, and all seem to have failed either to subjugate the Indian or to extract a feeling of gratitude from the People of that Territory. From the tone and spirit of this memorial, with the manifold proclamations, Joint resolutions and newspaper comments that are enclosed and made part of it I despair in the future of giving them even approximate satisfaction. We have had in the past, and still have employed in that Quarter soldiers and officers whose courage, industry and honesty have been tested in other fields and if the good people of NewMexico have failed to appreciate the fact, and if their wishes are to be consulted we had better abandon the effort, and leave Governor Arny who alone seems to command their confidence to work out the Problem. Every officer & soldier of the U. S. Army sent to NewMexico goes to a worse than Siberian banishment, and if I can relieve my troops from such a fate I will gladly do so. The vast territory is a desert waste, and only inhabited by the remnants of old Spanish & Indian settlements left there centuries ago by a bolder & more hardy race in search of Gold & Silver that exists in the Desert mountains, and a few white People who have gone there since its conquest by us in 1846, to profit by the civil offices created by Law, or the necessary expenses of the troops banished there. Our Regular army is now established by Law, and the New-Mexicans, are free to enlist like our other citizens, but if they will not do that, I recommend that the Regular army be withdrawn except from Lines of travel, and the Territorial Governmt be entrusted with their own defense as against the hostile Indians, Congress giving them the money annually expended hitherto, or better still that we remove the Inhabitants from their misirable homes to a land where they can by reasonable industry join in the General prosperity of our Country, and give the Territory back to the Indians that are being pressed from all other parts of our Country. As this memorial is addressed to Congress, I will state for their information that the very best we propose to do this year is to keep in NewMexico the 5th Infantry now there and a Regimt of Black Infantry now forming, with one Regimt of Cavalry the 3rd. These are all good troops, the very best, and well commanded, and it is criminal on the Part of the Territorial legislature to question their fidelity to the Governmt of the United States. But these troops cannot fill the Territory, or protect its scattered settlements, nor can I expect them to reconcile all the Conflicting questions that are raised in that Country. General Hancock commands the Departmt embracing New-Mexico and proposes to give command out there to two of the best officers in any army, viz Generals A. J. Smith and Getty. If these arrangements be not satisfactory to the memorialists I see no alternative for them but to relieve us altogether and undertake to protect themselves, and like other Territories bear a full share of the expense, and blame for failure. Judging from the usual lists of names appended to NewMexican Petitions especially when we attempt to remove our troops from the towns to the Frontiers I do not know but they have men enough in the Territory if organized to protect themselves, better than we can do by troops such as we have to use. I beg you will submit all these papers to Congress that they may devise a remedy, for I confess it surpasses my power, or ability."—ALS, *ibid.*

In July, 1866, Governor Robert B. Mitchell of New Mexico Territory, Santa Fé, had written to USG. "I am most desirous of calling your attention to the deplorable condition in which I find this country, consequent upon the want of protection from Indian raids upon the settlements—The number of troops stationed in this country since the commencement of the late rebellion has been totally inadequate for the protection of the lives and property of its inhabitants—The almost daily raids made upon the settlements by hostile Indians have reduced the people to penury and in some cases to the verge of starvation, and it is universally beleived here that the muster out of the New Mexican Regt's whose time of enlistment has nearly expired will increase the danger and misery already existing These troops understand Indian warfare and are familiar with the country and can endure more hardships and privations than any men that I have seen: And in addition they naturally feel a deeper interest in the welfare of the people than can be expected from strange troops—It is a fact conceded by the military as well as the civil authorities here, that much more can be accomplished in this country by New Mexican troops than by any others—I therefore respectfully urge in behalf of an unfortunate people, the reorganization of the two remaining New Mexican Regt's, to serve at least until the troops now arriving here become familiarized with the country and Indian warfare—Gen'l Carleton does the very best that he can with the means furnished him, but he has not an adequate number of troops to protect this people—Gen. Pope is now here and will I am satisfied reccomend this policy, as will all officers serving in this district It is a fact humiliating to every American citizen that there is not to day one half the wealth in this country that there was at the time of its annexation to the United States, and this is due entirely to the failure of the Government to give that protection that it then guaranteed—I am satisfied that when the Indians are repressed and the resources of this country can be developed, that it will furnish more mineral wealth than any equal area of the national domain . . . P. S I have written the President a similar letter asking his aid in the protection of this people"—LS, NNP. On Sept. 20, Maj. Thomas M. Vincent, AGO, wrote to Maj. Gen. Winfield S. Hancock. "I have the honor to inform you that General Field Orders No. 4, from your Head Quarters, dated Santa Fe, New Mexico, July 26th 1866, authorizing the Commanding General of the District of New Mexico to retain four companies (one battalion) from the two regiments of New Mexico Volunteers, now in service, 'until the difficulties with the Ute Indians are settled, or until the original term of service of the regiments from which the men are transferred shall expire,' has been approved by the General-in-Chief."—LS, DNA, RG 108, Letters Received. Additional papers are *ibid.* On Dec. 13, Leet endorsed papers concerning New Mexico Territory. "Respectfully referred to Major General W. S Hancock, Commanding Department of the Missouri who will suspend the orders for breaking up the Posts of Santa Fe and Albuquerque until an inspection is made in the Spring, and until further instructions from Lieut General Sherman after such inspection."—Copy, *ibid.*, RG 393, Military Div. of the Mo., Letters Received. On Dec. 17, Hancock, Fort Leavenworth, wrote to Brig. Gen. John A. Rawlins. "Your endorsement of September 13th upon petition of Citizens of New Mexico, asking that the posts of Sante Fe, and Alburquerque N. M, be not broken up, and directing that my order in the case be suspended, until an inspection is made in the spring, and until further instructions from Lieutenant General Sherman after such inspection, has been recieved. I have already suspended that order, upon a representation of General Carleton, Commanding the District (copy of the order, and of General Carleton's communication, enclosed) I will further modify the order as you direct. I will state that the order in question, was based upon General Sherman's views, after he had made a visit to that country. I expect to make a tour of inspection, passing the points referred to, next spring, and until that time, I am not prepared to give a valuable opinion in the matter; but I am now inclined to think that there are good reasons for keeping the Headquarters and a detachment of Cavalry at Sante Fe, and that there is no great necessity for troops at Albuqueque, as I think the Troops can better be used elsewhere."—LS, *ibid.*, RG 108, Letters Received.

1866, DEC. 31, 1:10 P.M. To Maj. Gen. John M. Schofield. "Can you not spare two regiments of Infantry from your command If so name the two you would have go."—Telegram sent, DNA, RG 107, Telegrams Collected (Bound); copies, *ibid.*, RG 108, Letters Sent; DLC-USG, V, 47, 60; DLC-John M. Schofield. On the same day, Schofield, Richmond, telegraphed to USG. "There is now very little apparent necessity for troops in Virginia yet I think it would be prudent not to send away more than one regiment for the present unless the necessity is great—The eleventh and twentieth except one 1 company are at Richmond and can be moved most readily by rail—The twenty ninth can readily be concentrated at Ft Monroe—I have no choice as to regiments"—Telegram received (at 3:45 P.M.), DNA, RG 108, Telegrams Received; copies, *ibid.*, RG 393, Dept. of Va. and N. C., 1st Military District, Telegrams Sent; DLC-USG, V, 54. On Jan. 2, 1867, 10:30 A.M., USG telegraphed to Maj. Gen. Philip H. Sheridan. "I have ordered from here a full regiment of Infantry to, report to you: Muster out all the colored troops you can on their arrival. Where will you have these troops sent to"—Telegram sent, DNA, RG 107, Telegrams Collected (Bound); telegram received (at 6:00 P.M.), *ibid.*, RG 393, Dept. of the Gulf, Telegrams Received. On Jan. 3, Sheridan, New Orleans, telegraphed to USG. "Your telegram of Second (2nd) received. Order the Regiment to report to me at New Orleans"—Telegram received (on Jan. 4, 6:00 P.M.), *ibid.*, RG 107, Telegrams Collected (Bound); *ibid.*, RG 108, Telegrams Received; copies, DLC-USG, V, 55; DLC-Philip H. Sheridan.

1866. To Julia Dent Grant. "The train leaves at 4 instead of ½ past 4. Dinner had better be ready ¼ before 3."—ALS (dated "12th, *1866*"), DLC-USG.

1866. USG signature on a testimonial, dated April. "To Whom it may concern: The undersigned Members of the Senate and House of Representatives of the Congress of the United States, and and other persons, some of us being personally acquainted with Miss Vinnie Ream, take great pleasure in recommending her for public patronage, as a most worthy and accomplished young lady, possessing fine genius in the beautiful art of sculpture. She has executed a bust of President Lincoln, a statuette of General Grant, . . ."—DS, DLC-Vinnie Ream Hoxie; printed (with signatures rearranged) in R. L. Hoxie, ed., *Vinnie Ream* (Washington, D. C., 1908), pp. 1–3.

Index

All letters written by USG of which the text was available for use in this volume are indexed under the names of the recipients. The dates of these letters are included in the index as an indication of the existence of text. Abbreviations used in the index are explained on pp. xvi–xx. Individual regts. are indexed under the names of the states in which they originated.